CIVIL RIGHTS 1960-66

CIVIL RIGHTS 1960-66

Edited by Lester A. Sobel

FACTS ON FILE, INC.   NEW YORK

CONTENTS

nessee Desegregation Action (50); North Carolina Indians
Demonstrate (50)

1961

Rights Campaign Intensified, Rioting Follows (179); Truce Suspends Demonstrations (182); Agreement to Limited Desegregation (183); Bombings Interrupt Truce (184); President Orders Troops to Birmingham (184); 1,081 Negro Pupils Ousted From School (186); 4 Girls Killed in Bombing (187); President Sends Mediators (188)

1964

INTRODUCTION

THE CIVIL RIGHTS MOVEMENT in the U.S. has been growing explosively in these middle years of the 20th century. Its beginnings, however, could probably be traced back at least 300 years to the early foes of slavery in the British colonies.

Negro slaves were reported to have been brought to the New World as early as 1502, when several were shipped to Haiti. In the following years the Spanish and Portuguese colonies imported large numbers of Negroes to slave in mines and on plantations. Slavery began in British America in 1619, when 20 Negroes arrived in Jamestown as part of a cargo brought from the coast of Guinea by a Dutch vessel. The first Negroes sold to British colonists appear to have been considered indentured servants, but the status of those who followed quickly degenerated to that of chattel slaves. As the colonies began to find a need for cheap field labor, a lucrative slave trade grew to fill the demand. The importation of Negro slaves continued as long as the colonies remained under British control and did not end until 1807, when the U.S. Congress voted to outlaw the trade.

Opponents of slavery had begun to make their voices heard in the British colonies not long after the first Negro slaves landed on American shores. The Quakers in Pennsylvania spoke out against slavery at least as early as 1696. In 1774 they barred from membership anybody involved in the slave trade. 2 years later they excluded any slave owner who would not free his slaves. And like action was taken by Quakers in the other colonies. A society for the abolition of slavery was founded in Pennsylvania in 1774 by James Pemberton and Dr. Benjamin Rush, and similar organizations sprang up elsewhere in the U.S.

George Washington opposed slavery, provided in his will for the emancipation of his own slaves and asserted that a law to abolish slavery was "among his first wishes." Others among the founders of the nation shared Washington's aversion to the ownership of one human being by another. But slavery remained legal in the new nation as the price exacted by South Carolina and Georgia for joining the Union.

Piecemeal abolition of slavery began in 1777, when Vermont outlawed the practice, and ultimately the ownership of slaves was illegal in all Northern states. Illegal means of freeing slaves were also available. Thousands of slaves just ran away. In the early 1800s Quakers and other abolitionists began encouraging and aiding runaway slaves by means of an Underground Railroad—a network of refuges along which runaways were hustled from the slave South to the free North and Canada. Several unsuccessful slave insurrections were also attempted, among them the uprisings led by the slaves Gabriel Prosser in Richmond, Va. in 1800, Denmark Vesey in Charleston, S.C. in 1822 and Nat Turner in Southhampton County, Va. in 1831. The charismatic John Brown dreamed of freeing the slaves by invading the South. He attacked the federal arsenal in Harpers Ferry in 1859 to get weapons, but he was captured, convicted of treason and hanged. Prominent among abolitionists was William Lloyd Garrison, who began his emancipation campaign in Boston in 1831, when the New England Anti-Slavery Society was founded. The American Anti-Slavery Society was organized in Philadelphia in 1833, and the long, bitter struggle against slavery ended only with the Civil War. In 1863, as a wartime measure, Pres. Abraham Lincoln issued an Emancipation Proclamation freeing all slaves in states then in rebellion against the Union. Slavery was not prohibited throughout the U.S., however, until Dec. 6, 1865, when the 13th Amendment to the Constitution was ratified.

The first civil rights law was enacted by Congress over Pres. Andrew Johnson's veto in 1866. It declared the free slaves to be U.S. citizens with the same rights as all other citizens. The law was adopted during the 2d of the dozen years of the Reconstruction Era, a troubled period of continued tensions between North and South during which the Southern states won their way back to full membership in the Union. The civil rights act was reinforced by the 14th Amendment, ratified July 9, 1868. It gave constitutional guarantees of citizenship to the freed slaves, barred states from abridging the "privileges or immunities" of citizens and guaranteed to all citizens "the equal protection of the laws." The 15th Amendment, ratified Feb. 3, 1870, barred states from denying or abridging the right to vote because of race. And a ·civil rights bill passed in 1875 guaranteed to Negroes the same rights as whites in public places.

Some states had always permitted free Negroes to vote, and in only 4 of the original 13 states were there statutes barring otherwise-qualified Negroes from voting. Reconstruction brought the vote—but only temporarily—to millions of illiterate Negroes and opened important positions to Negroes. Negroes served as lieutenant governor in Louisiana, Mississippi and South Carolina. 2 Negroes, Hiram R. Revels and Blanche Kelso Bruce, served as U.S. Senators from Mississippi.

But by various means, lawful or otherwise, Negro rights and privileges were eroded in the South in the decades after the close of the Reconstruction period. The civil rights law of 1875 was ruled unconstitutional by the Supreme Court in 1883. The court held that federal law gave Negroes protection only against discrimination by states but not against unequal treatment by hotel or theater owners or by common carriers. Separation of the races was enforced by state statute in schools and public places, and the Supreme Court held in 1896 that such segregation was legal wherever "separate but equal facilities" were provided. In almost all cases, however, facilities for Negroes were far inferior to those for whites. Poll taxes, unfair literacy tests and other devices were adopted throughout the South to keep Negroes from voting.

The erosion of Negro rights was fought consistently by people of both races. The outstanding Negro leader of the late 1800s and early 1900s was Booker T. Washington, who founded Tuskegee Institute for Negroes in Tuskegee, Ala. in 1881. Washington favored working with sympathetic whites and stressed education and economic betterment for Negroes as the best method of assuring eventual victory for Negro rights. His gradualist views were opposed by such militants as William Edward Burghardt Du Bois, the first Negro to win a Harvard PhD degree (in 1895). In 1905 Du Bois led a small group of like-minded Negroes in the founding of the Niagara Movement, which called for direct protest as a weapon to win full citizenship rights for Negroes. Du Bois and his Niagara Movement joined Negroes and whites of similar views in 1909 in creating the NAACP—the National Association for the Advancement of Colored People. The NAACP used propaganda, mass pressure, lobbying techniques and litigation in its campaign on behalf of America's Negroes. The National Urban League was founded a year later, and its first goal was to secure jobs and economic opportunities for Negroes who were streaming in ever-greater numbers from the rural South to Northern cities.

World War II appeared to mark a new beginning in the efforts to win for Negroes their fair share of all American rights and privileges. Negroes found growing acceptance in war industries and the armed forces. After the war, Negroes and white opponents of discrimination engaged in wide civil rights activity.

The "separate but equal" doctrine was abolished May 17, 1954, when the Supreme Court overturned its 1896 decision and ruled, in the case of *Brown v. Board of Education of Topeka, Kan.*, that "separate educational facilities are inherently unequal." This decision served as the wedge that opened opportunities for unsegregated education to Negro children in community after community.

This book describes the important events in the civil rights movement during the explosive years from 1960 to 1966. It tells the story of a war for equality being fought on many battlegrounds. The history of this struggle illustrates the depth of the change in the relationship between the 2 major U.S. races. The book details the story of Negro efforts to win equal educational opportunities, equal employment opportunities, equal housing opportunities, equal political rights, in sum, equal rights to all things taken for granted by white Americans.

Much of the material in this book appeared earlier in one form or another in various Facts on File publications, including the Interim History book *Civil Rights 1960-63*. All of this material has been revised, expanded and brought up to date in *Civil Rights 1960-66*.

4

1960

An off-shoot of the civil rights movement mush-roomed throughout the South during 1960 when Negro students joined in widespread sit-in demonstrations against segregated lunch counters. A compromise Civil Rights Act of 1960, aimed at guaranteeing Negro voting rights, was adopted by Congress after Southern Senators opposed the measure with a filibuster of unprecedented length. Federal officials invoked the new law on behalf of Negroes who claimed that their right to vote had been denied. The federal courts insisted throughout 1960 that Southern public schools desegregate, but more than 90% of the South's Negro children continued to attend all-Negro classes. Political platforms with strong civil rights planks were adopted by both parties.

THE SIT-IN MOVEMENT

Sit-Ins Start in North Carolina

4 Negro students from North Carolina Agricultural & Technical College quietly took lunch-counter seats in the Woolworth variety store in Greensboro, N.C. Feb. 1 in what became the first of a series of widespread but peaceful sit-in protests against the "local custom" of refusing counter service to seated (but not standing) Negroes. The seated Negroes were asked to leave. When they refused to do so, they were arrested. Negro students then extended the sit-in campaign to the local Kress store. The 2 stores were closed Feb. as a result of a false bomb threat and heckling.

The sit-in movement spread Feb. 8-9 to Charlotte, Durham and Winston-Salem. 8 department and drug store managers in these communities closed their lunch counters, and the Greensboro counters remained closed even after North Carolina A & T and Bennett College students had agreed Feb. 8 to a 2-week cooling-off period. Joseph Charles Jones, graduate ministerial student reportedly leading the Charlotte protest, said the sit-ins were "interrelated" but "not part of a plan and were undertaken independently." He said there was no organization behind the movement.

The sit-ins spread to 15 Southern cities in 5 states by Feb. 16, and it became clear that a new technique had been adopted by American civil rights activists.

Chief targets of the sit-ins were F. W. Woolworth and S. H. Kress stores. Other variety and drug stores also were involved, and many were closed for varying periods as a result of the disturbances. Cities affected included: Concord, Elizabeth City, Fayetteville, High Point and Raleigh, N.C.; Rock Hill, S.C.; Hampton, Newport News and Portsmouth, Va.; Deland, Fla.; Nashville, Tenn. In New York, nearly 100 persons picketed 3 Kress and Woolworth stores in Harlem Feb. 13 and urged shoppers not to patronize "a chain store that makes money from minority groups in the North while refusing them service in the South." Gordon R. Carey, field secretary of CORE (the Congress of Racial Equality), said in Raleigh Feb. 10 that his organization was negotiating with the stores' New York headquarters on the students' behalf. Kress and Woolworth spokesmen said in Raleigh Feb. 10 that company policy was to let local managers decide whom to serve and to avoid interfering with "local customs."

In Richmond, Va. Feb. 22, police arrested 38 Negro students when they refused to leave department store dining areas. In Hampton, Va., Negro demonstrators obtained service at a white lunch counter Feb. 22 but were charged $1 per cup of coffee, $1.45 per hot dog and $1.50 per barbecue bun. The movement reached Alabama Feb. 25 when 35 Alabama State College students conducted a sit-in in the county courthouse snack shop in Montgomery.

3 anti-trespassing bills were rushed through the Virginia Legislature and signed by Gov. J. Lindsay Almond Jr. Feb. 25 in a move to outlaw sit-in demonstrations.

The Southern Regional Council in Atlanta Feb. 27 issued a report asserting that the sit-in demonstrations "show that segregation cannot be maintained in the South, short of continuous coercion and the intolerable social order which would result." It said the South's 3 choices were: (1) to maintain segregation, which would invite a test of strength and accompanying violence; (2) to eliminate lunch counters or whatever else was attacked as discriminatory, which eventually could destroy the community, and (3) to give equal treatment to all.

As a direct result of the sit-in movement, major cracks in Southern lunch-counter segregation began to appear by mid-March.

White & Northern Support

Some white students joined the sit-in movement, and it was endorsed by the interracial North Carolina Council on Human Relations and the all-white Unitarian Fellowship for Social Justice Feb. 16. Harold C. Fleming, director of the interracial Southern Regional Council, said: "The lunch-counter sit-in demonstrates . . . the mounting determination of Negroes to be rid of all segregated barriers. . . . We may expect more . . . protests of this kind against enforced segregation in public facilities and services of all types."

The *N.Y. Times* reported Mar. 20 that informal organizations to support Southern Negro students in their protests against lunch-counter segregation had appeared in these 21 non-Southern colleges and universities: Harvard, Yale,

Princeton, Brown, CCNY, the Universities of Chicago, Indiana, Wisconsin, Colorado and California (in Berkeley), Oberlin, Antioch College and Wilberforce University in Ohio, Lehigh University and Chatham and LaFayette colleges in Pennsylvania, Harpur College in Vestal, N.Y., Rutgers, and Vassar, Smith and Bennington colleges.

The National Student Association and the National Student Christian Federation (NSCF) served as clearing houses for Northern students' actions. NSCF Secy. Herluf M. Jensen said Mar. 20 that Northern students probably were responding to 10,000 NSCF letters sent to individuals in "an effort to undergird the whole demonstration movement with intellectual and theological substance." The NSCF said Mar. 14 that demonstrations would put "pressure on the national chain store system that may be helpful in procuring a change of policy."

About 300 Yale Divinity School students marched in New Haven, Conn. Mar. 23 to urge support for sit-ins and efforts to solve racial problems.

About 400 persons, mostly white students from Harvard, Boston University, Brandeis and MIT, picketed 12 Woolworth stores Mar. 26 in relays in Greater Boston. Hundreds of local NAACP members Mar. 26 picketed Connecticut branches of national variety stores that maintained lunch-counter-segregation in the South.

1,380 students of all-Negro Hampton Institute in Hampton and Newport News, Va. staged a day-long peaceful demonstration in Hampton Mar. 26. They appealed to 108 student groups throughout the U.S. and to CORE and the NAACP (National Association for the Advancement of Colored People) to join and aid "Operation 26," the student name for the nationwide protest movement.

Violence Begins

Negro sit-in demonstrators leaving an F. W. Woolworth lunch counter in High Point, N.C. Feb. 15 were embroiled in a brief fist fight when they were met outside by a group of whites. Police quickly dispersed the mixed crowd of about 75 and made no arrests.

The first serious outbreak of violence in the sit-ins occurred Feb. 16 in Portsmouth, Va., where 250 white and Negro high school boys fought in the Rose Department Store parking lot after unsuccessful Negro attempts to get lunch-counter service inside. Police arrested 3 Negro pupils.

Rioting broke out in Chattanooga, Tenn. Feb. 23 when Negroes and whites, mostly students, fought each other during a sit-in demonstration as the management tried to close an S. H. Kress store. Police arrested 11 whites and one Negro. 11 Negroes and 9 whites were arrested there Feb. 24 during demonstrations marked by rock and bottle throwing and attacks on cars. Mayor P. R. Olgiati ordered fire hoses used to disperse the mob.

Nashville, Tenn. police arrested about 100 Negro and white students Feb. 27 after fights had broken out in 2 of 5 stores where Negroes had staged nonviolent lunch-counter sit-ins. During a 4-hour demonstration, white persons angered by passive resistance to their taunts attacked Negro demonstrators and a white youth seated beside a Negro girl at a lunch counter. One white student was fined $50 and 2 Negroes $100 and $10, respectively, Feb. 29. 76 of those arrested later went to jail rather than pay fines or maintain $50 bond each pending trial. Their lawyers said payment of fines, for which sympathizers had made money available, "would be contributing to and supporting the injustice and immoral practices that have been performed in the arrest and conviction of the defendants." Those who chose jail were mostly Negroes. The first 3 to refuse to pay $50 fines were given 33-1/3-day sentences Mar. 1. Police arrested at least 57 Negroes in Nashville Mar. 2 when they refused to leave Greyhound and Trailways bus stations in the face of a bomb threat after lunch counters were closed. No bomb was found.

The home of Z. Alexander Looby, 62, Nashville Negro city councilman and NAACP lawyer, was destroyed by a dynamite bomb Apr. 19, but Looby and his wife escaped injury. The bomb damaged several other homes in the middle-class Negro neighborhood and blew out 147 windows at predominantly-Negro Meharry Medical College. Several dormitory students were cut by flying glass. Looby had been chief counsel for 153 students arrested in sit-ins. More than 2,000 Negroes (mostly students) marched on Nashville's city hall Apr. 19 to protest police failure to halt racial violence. The Rev. C. T. Vivian, pastor of the First Community Church, charged that Mayor Ben West had "encouraged violence by permitting the police to use their authority with partiality."

West denied the charge. He said he favored ending lunch-counter segregation, but added: "I can't tell a man how to run his business. He has got rights too."

Movement Reaches Alabama

Students from Alabama State College staged the first "deep South" sit-in Feb. 25 in the Montgomery County court-house. Sheriff Mac Sim Butler arrived carrying a club and lined up the 35 demonstrators single file against a wall. Armed deputies patrolled the halls until the passive demonstrators left, 45 minutes after the lunchroom had closed. A group of white men carrying small baseball bats lined a main thoroughfare in Montgomery, Ala. Feb. 27 and formed groups outside 2 variety stores operating lunch counters. One of the club-carriers struck a Negro woman on the head and injured her in a pushing incident. No arrests were made. Gov. John Patterson warned Feb. 29 that there were "not enough police officers" in the U.S. "to prevent riots and protect everybody" if Negroes "continue to provoke whites."

The Rev. Dr. Martin Luther King Jr., president of the integrationist Southern Christian Leadership Conference, spoke at a mass student rally in Montgomery Feb. 29. Nearly 1,000 students in his audience pledged to quit the college en masse if any were expelled for the Feb. 25 sit-in and planned further demonstrations. They marched Mar. 1 to the first capitol building of the Confederacy, where they prayed and sang the national anthem during a peaceful 25-minute demonstration against segregation. The State Board of Education Mar. 2 expelled 9 students for participating in demonstrations.

About 500 state, county and local armed police Mar. 6 halted a march of about 800 Negroes to the Alabama state capitol in Montgomery for a protest meeting after a church rally one block from the old capitol building. Police pushed the marchers back to the church and separated them from a large mob of jeering whites. There were a few scattered fist fights, but mounted deputies and fire trucks prevented further violence.

Montgomery police broke up a Negro protest demonstration on the Alabama State College campus Mar. 8 and arrested 35 students, a teacher and her husband. All but 2 students were convicted Mar. 11 in municipal court of disorderly conduct and were fined $200 each and costs.

Eisenhower Expresses Sympathy

Pres. Dwight D. Eisenhower said at his press conference Mar. 16 that he could give no "sweeping" opinion on sit-in strikes of Negroes protesting lunch-counter segregation. But he said: "I am deeply sympathetic with the efforts of any group to enjoy the rights of equality . . . guaranteed by the Constitution." Mr. Eisenhower said that if "every city and every community of the South" held biracial conferences to help settle racial problems, this "would be much better than" a national White House conference on civil rights because "there is too much interference in our private affairs . . . and personal lives already."

(At the National Urban League Conference in New York, Gov. Nelson A. Rockefeller Sept. 8 called sit-ins an "inspiring example" to the nation. Rockefeller said civil rights problems could be solved by "the moral force and the appeal to human conscience personified [by] the young men and women who sit at the segregated lunch counters. . . .")

Demonstrations Spread through South

As the demonstrations continued and spread throughout the South, Negro leaders made increasing efforts to give greater meaning and direction to the movement. Much of the rights activity, however, seemed almost aimless, and repercussions of varied nature were reported.

About 100 Negro students from Texas Southern University staged orderly sit-ins in Houston, Tex. Mar. 4. 3 days later 4 masked white youths kidnaped Felton Turner, 27, a Negro, from a lonely Houston street Mar. 7. Felton said later that the youths had forced him into a car at gunpoint and had driven him to a field, where 3 of them beat him with a tire chain, carved the letters KKK (for Ku Klux Klan) on his chest and stomach and left him loosely trussed up in the branches of an oak tree, from which he finally freed himself. He said one of his abductors told him: "We were just hired to do a job because of the publicity Texas Southern University Negro students received over sit-ins at a lunch counter at Houston in the past few days."

50 Negroes carrying clubs demonstrated Mar. 5 in a Columbia, S.C. drive-in restaurant and pounded on several cars. A white woman was cut by flying glass. 15 Negro stu-

dents from Allen University and Benedict College were convicted of the attacks in recorder's court Mar. 18. The 9 admitted leaders were fined $100 each, the others $50.50 each.

6 white students and 29 Negroes were arrested in Tallahassee, Fla. Mar. 12 during a sit-in demonstration that had
begun in a Woolworth store and that police broke up with tear
gas. Students at Florida Agricultural & Mechanical University
later called off further demonstrations. 11 of the Negro students were convicted in city court Mar. 18 of disturbing the
peace and were sentenced to pay $300 fines each or serve 60
days. 8 chose the jail terms.

388 Negro students were arrested in Orangeburg, S.C.
Mar. 15 on breach-of-peace charges after fire hoses and tear
gas had been used to disperse about 1,000 Negroes demonstrating against lunch-counter segregation. Those arrested
were released in $10 bail each. 15 of them were sentenced in
magistrate's court Mar. 19 to pay fines of $50 each or serve
30 days for disturbing the peace. All were freed on $100 ap-
peal bonds.

Police arrested and later released on bond 70 students as
they picketed the Rock Hill, S.C. city hall Mar. 15. 10 more
were arrested the same day in Columbia, S.C. when they
attempted lunch-counter sit-ins.

At least 76 Negroes were arrested Mar. 15 in the first
mass sit-in demonstrations in Atlanta. 200 students participated at 10 downtown eating places. Of those arrested, 17
were held Mar. 16 for trial on criminal charges under new
state "anti-sit-in" laws.

11 Negroes were convicted Mar. 14 of trespassing Mar. 7
at the Petersburg, Va. public library in the first legal test
of a new city anti-trespass ordinance. While hundreds of Negroes sang hymns outside the courthouse, the court fined 2
ministers $100 each and costs and sentenced them to 30 days
in jail. The others arrested were fined $50 and costs each, and
one student was sentenced to 10 days in jail. All were freed
on appeal bond. 15 Negroes were arrested during a lunch-
counter sit-in at a Trailways bus station in Petersburg July
30. 10 of these were re-arrested and 17 other persons were
arrested in the same bus station and in a W. T. Grant store
in Petersburg Aug. 1.

36 Negro students, arrested Mar. 19 during sit-ins at 2
Memphis public libraries, were fined $25 each in city court
Mar. 21 for disorderly conduct. L. F. Palmer Jr., editor of

the Negro weekly *Tri-State Defender*, arrested with them, was fined $50. Judge Beverly Boushe said the fines were for violation of a city ordinance and had nothing to do with civil rights.

District Judge Sam B. Hall in Marshall, Tex. Apr. 4 ordered a probe of "possible outside influences" in the first Negro demonstrations in Marshall since Reconstruction days. He said he felt that the racial disturbances were "not a child of local citizens." Marshall had a population of about 15,000 Negroes, 15,000 whites. Demonstrations had begun there Mar. 30 as Negro students tried for a 3d time within a week to be served seated at lunch counters. Police arrested 20 immediately, took 18 to jail later and then arrested more than 250 as at least 700 singing Negroes thronged the courthouse square, reformed the crowd faster than its members could be arrested and surged onto the courthouse steps. Finally, firemen drove 2 trucks into the crowd and forced it to retreat. The police then began freeing those taken into custody, and the firemen dispersed the crowd with high-pressure hoses.

Trespass charges against 43 Negro students, arrested Feb. 12-13 during anti-segregation demonstrations on the sidewalks of the privately-owned Cameron Village shopping center, were dismissed in Superior Court in Raleigh, N.C. Apr. 22. Their demonstration had been directed against a Woolworth store. The dismissal was based on a 1946 Supreme Court ruling that had reversed a trespass conviction in a similar case on grounds that property "ownership does not always mean absolute dominion." Defense and prosecution attorneys agreed that "the more an owner, for his advantage, opens up property for use by the public in general, the more do his rights become circumscribed by the statutory and constitutional rights of those who use it."

Gov. Buford Ellington of Tennessee charged in Nashville Mar. 26 that sit-ins in the state capitol Mar. 25 had been "staged for the convenience of the Columbia Broadcasting System." He ordered an investigation of a CBS-TV camera crew whose members said they were in Nashville to film background material for a documentary on "the training methods by which Negroes are coached in how to conduct themselves in sit-in demonstrations." Negro leaders, who previously had halted sit-ins pending talks with city officials, said Mar. 26 that CBS had nothing to do with a decision to resume demonstrations. CBS Pres. Frank Stanton telegraphed Ellington Mar. 26 that there was "not the slightest foundation in fact for your serious allegation. . . ."

Public Service Commissioner Ralph A. Smith of Alabama charged Apr. 25 that an NBC-TV camera crew had "staged and directed" anti-segregation demonstrations by Alabama State College students in Montgomery between Feb. 27 and Mar. 7. Smith said, in a letter to the FCC, that a state investigation had revealed "positive proof" of his charges. NBC denied the charges.

Students & Faculty Members Rebel

18 students at Southern University in Baton Rouge, La., the U.S.' largest all-Negro school, were suspended Mar. 30. The suspensions followed (a) Mar. 28-29 lunch-counter sit-ins in which 16 were arrested and later released in $1,500 bail each, and (b) an orderly anti-segregation rally by an estimated 2,000-5,000 students on the state capitol steps 10 miles from the campus. The suspension of the 16 arrested students and the 2 leaders of the capitol rally touched off a student rebellion at the university Mar. 31. A majority of the student body of 5,400 boycotted classes and requested withdrawal forms in protest. The rebellion waned Apr. 1 when the heart-attack death of Prof. J. Warren Lee, 50, was attributed to the students' demonstration against school authorities, but class boycotts and withdrawals continued. Officials said that about 270 students had quit by Apr. 4. The Louisiana State Board of Education, an all-white elective body that administered Southern University, had warned Mar. 1 that any student participating in "sit-in" demonstrations faced "stern disciplinary action."

10 faculty members of the Vanderbilt University Divinity School in Nashville, Tenn., including the school's dean, the Rev. Dr. J. Robert Nelson, resigned May 30 in protest against the university's refusal to re-admit the Rev. James Morris Lawson Jr., 31, a Negro divinity student who had been expelled Mar. 3 for leading sit-ins. (Lawson, projects director for the National Christian Leadership Council, had urged Mar. 1 a sustained policy of non-violence and Christian forbearance to end racial discrimination.) The university board's executive committee accepted Nelson's resignation June 3 and offered his post to Dr. Walter J. Harrelson, dean of the

University of Chicago Divinity School. Harrelson rejected the offer June 7 and also declined a post he previously had accepted as a professor of Old Testament at Vanderbilt. Vanderbilt accepted the resignation of 11 other divinity school faculty members June 7. Vanderbilt Chancellor Harvie S. Branscomb June 13 announced a settlement of the Lawson dispute. He said Lawson would be permitted to obtain his degree at Vanderbilt, either by written examination without re-enrollment or by transfer of credits from Boston University (where Lawson was studying).

Student Nonviolent Committee Formed

A Student Nonviolent Coordinating Committee (SNCC, later referred to as "Snick"), to guide anti-segregation activities, was set up by Southern Negro student leaders at the close of an Apr. 15-17 meeting sponsored by the Southern Christian Leadership Conference in Raleigh, N.C. on the Shaw University campus. The meeting was attended by 132 Negro and 10 white students from 11 states and the District of Columbia. They represented 37 communities involved in lunch-counter sit-in demonstrations. Marion S. Barry Jr. of Fisk University served as chairman.

The Rev. Dr. Martin Luther King Jr., head of the conference, and the Rev. James M. Lawson Jr. were named advisors to the committee. Lawson had been expelled from Vanderbilt University Divinity School for leading sit-ins. He attacked the NAACP (National Association for the Advancement of Colored People) as too conservative in approaching segregation problems by legal means. But Ella J. Baker, executive director of the conference, denied any conflict between the 2 groups.

King recommended Apr. 15 a national "selective-buying" campaign against businesses that practiced segregation. He urged the training of an elite group of volunteers who would go to jail rather than pay fines for protest activities.

Dr. Robert C. Weaver, chairman of the NAACP board of directors, told 918 people from 40 states at the annual NAACP convention, held June 21-26 in St. Paul, Minn., that the sit-ins contributed to "functioning democracy." Weaver, speaking at the opening session, said NAACP objectives were "the objectives of many whites as well as most Negroes" and that "by working together we can accelerate the achievement of our goals." Thurgood Marshall, NAACP special counsel, told the convention June 21 that the NAACP had "deliberately stayed out of the planning for [more sit-in demonstrations]." A resolution adopted June 25 backed the sit-in demonstrations and pledged "moral, financial, legal, consultant and participatory" support.

Lunch-Counter Desegregation Begins

The first integration of lunch counters in a large Southern city had occurred Mar. 16 in San Antonio, Tex. as 4 Negroes and a large group of whites ate side-by-side in a 5-&-10¢ store. San Antonio store officials had agreed Mar. 15 to open drug and variety store lunch counters to Negroes. Negroes had planned a sit-in for Mar. 16. (San Antonio had integrated schools, buses, parks and swimming pools without violence.)

2 students from Fisk (Negro) University were served coffee Mar. 16 at a previously segregated bus station restaurant in Nashville, and lunch counters of 4 national variety and 2 local department stores were desegregated peacefully in Nashville May 10 after 4 weeks of negotiation by merchant and Negro leaders. Negro students in small groups of 2 or 3, by pre-arrangement with negotiators, sought and received lunch-counter service at Woolworth, Kress, McClellan and Harvey variety stores and at Harvey's and Cain-Sloan's department stores. A Negro boycott was believed to have been a major factor leading to the settlement, which followed sit-in demonstrations, some violence and the arrests of 150 Negroes from February through April.

Chrmn. Paul L. Troast of S. H. Kress & Co. said at the company's annual meeting in New York May 17 that the desegregation of chain variety store lunch counters in the South would come "community by community." He spoke as pickets representing CORE (the Congress of Racial Equality) marched outside with signs urging Kress to open its lunch counters to all. James Peck, editor of CORE's magazine, *Corelator*, and owner of a single share of Kress stock, warned other stockholders of a nationwide Negro boycott against Kress stores unless its lunch counters were desegregated. He issued a similar warning May 18 at the annual stockholders' meeting of the F. W. Woolworth Co. in Watertown, N.Y., where he was joined by Barbara Bruxton, 18, a Florida A. & M. University student who had served a 48-day jail sentence for a sit-in at a Woolworth store in Tallahassee. Miss Bruxton, armed with stockholders' proxies, said Negro students would continue lunch-counter sit-ins. Woolworth Pres. Robert C. Kirkwood called the demonstrations "unjustified." He said 86% of Woolworth lunch counters throughout the U.S. were integrated.

The first Virginia desegregation of a national chain restaurant (Hot Shoppes) was reported June 23 in Arlington. Leading drug, variety and department stores had announced June 2 that they would serve Negroes at their lunch counters in Arlington. (The Woolworth store in Shirlington previously had become the first Virginia chain store to desegregate without insisting that others nearby also desegregate.)

The Friendly Relations Committee of Charlotte, N.C. announced July 9 that segregated lunch-counter service was being discontinued at 7 downtown stores after 5 months of Negro efforts to end bias at formerly all-white counters. Resumption of demonstrations after a 2-month truce hastened the decision to desegregate.

Lunch counters in Greensboro, N.C., where the 1960 sit-in movement had started, were desegregated July 25, and lunch-counter segregation was ended in several stores in Durham, N.C. and Miami, Fla. Aug. 1.

Officials of variety chains informed Atty. Gen. William P. Rogers Aug. 10 that lunch counters had been desegregated in their stores in 69 Southern communities. In more than 70% of the communities, integration took place without sit-ins. Rogers said he had invited representatives of Woolworth, Kress, W. T. Grant Co. and other major store chains to discuss informally June 1 how Southern communities could desegregate eating facilities voluntarily. They had agreed, he said, to work community by community with the aid of interested local groups and merchants. He indicated that the results showed that "where responsible local citizens take the first steps . . . desegregation of eating facilities in stores can be accomplished without disruptions and loss of business."

Officers of 4 national chain stores announced Oct. 17 that their lunch counters in about 150 stores in 112 cities in North Carolina, Virginia, West Virginia, Kentucky, Texas, Tennessee, Missouri, Maryland, Florida and Oklahoma had been integrated. Officials of the stores—Woolworth, Kress, Grant and the McCrory-McLellan Stores Corp.—had met with leaders of the National Student Association in New York Oct. 13 to discuss integration.

Curfew Imposed in Greenville

A 9-p.m.-to-6-a.m. curfew on all persons 20 years of age or younger was imposed in Greenville, S.C. July 26 after a series of clashes July 18-25 between whites and Negroes engaged in lunch-counter sit-ins. The clashes began July 18 after the postponement of a trial of 8 Negroes involved in a July 16 sit-in at the Greenville Public Library. 75 Negroes who had been spectators at the proceeding left the court and demonstrated at several variety stores. They were led by Charles J. Helms, 24, a white Atlantan who described himself as a student at Union Theological Seminary in New York. Helms charged that he had been "roughed up" by a group of white men. New clashes occurred in Greenville during sit-ins July 21, 24 and 25.

Strife in Jacksonville

Clashes between Negroes and whites broke out in Jacksonville, Fla. Aug. 27 after 10 days of sit-ins at 2 downtown stores. A hair-pulling tussle between a white woman and a Negro woman Aug. 26 apparently triggered the eruption. Bands of white men armed with clubs gathered the next morning and fought with a handful of Negroes. Isolated fights started throughout the town. 50 persons were reported injured. Patrolmen armed with shotguns dispersed a crowd of 3,000. Mayor Haydon Burns said Aug. 28 that "more than 100 troublemakers of both races" had been arrested. He ordered "drastic law enforcement action" and announced that any group of more than 4 persons found loitering would be subject to arrest.

Negro youth gangs started roaming the streets Aug. 27 ready for reprisal "rumbles" against whites but were prevailed on by NAACP youth workers Aug. 30 to declare a truce.

Municipal Court Judge John Santora Aug. 29 imposed short jail terms or fines ($10-$250) on 26 white and 57 Negro participants in the disorders. The stiffest sentence—90 days in the road gang—was meted out to Richard Frank Parker, 25, a white Florida State University student and NAACP member who had been a leader in the sit-ins. Parker had lost several teeth and suffered a broken jaw earlier Aug. 29 in a jail scuffle with a segregationist prisoner.

About 1,400 Negroes met Aug. 28 and voted to ask Pres.

Eisenhower and the Justice Department to investigate the situation. Sit-ins were cancelled by Negroes Aug. 28, but Rodney Hurst, 16, president of the local NAACP youth council, urged Negroes "to refrain from any and all downtown purchases."

King Gets Jail Sentence

The Rev. Dr. Martin Luther King Jr., one of 80 persons arrested during Atlanta sit-ins Oct. 19-22, was sentenced to 4 months in jail in Decatur, Ga. Oct. 25 by Judge J. Oscar Mitchell for violating a probated traffic sentence. King's 12-month sentence from Mitchell Sept. 23 for driving without a Georgia driver's license had been suspended after King had pleaded guilty and paid a $25 fine.

King had been arrested Oct. 19 under a 1960 Georgia law that made it a crime to refuse to leave an establishment when asked to do so by the owner or his representative. Refusing to post $500 bond, King had been jailed to await trial. Charges against King by the Rich's, Inc. department store, the biggest in the South, reportedly were dropped the day he was removed from the Atlanta jail to Decatur.

King was released from Georgia State Prison at Reidsville Oct. 27 on $2,000 bond. Judge Mitchell stayed King's 4-month sentence pending an appeal of King's September traffic sentence. Mitchell said pressure to free King had included a telephone call from Robert F. Kennedy, Sen. John F. Kennedy's brother. Sen. Kennedy, then campaigning as Democratic nominee for President, telephoned Mrs. King in Atlanta Oct. 26 and was reported to have told her he "would do all he could to help."

Truce & Some Desegregation in Atlanta

Atlanta sit-ins were halted Oct. 22 under a 30-day truce between the Atlanta Committee on Appeal for Human Rights (the Negro college student group behind the demonstrations) and Atlanta Mayor William Hartsfield. Negroes had injected into the truce an agreement that the mayor would seek "fair employment practices" and integrated rest rooms at the stores.

The Rev. Otis Moss Jr., leader of the Negro committee, said Oct. 22 that the truce was contingent on efforts to release jailed demonstrators. Hartsfield agreed Oct. 22 to order the immediate release of 22 Negroes and one white in city jail on disorderly conduct charges and of 39 Negroes in county jail (including the Rev. Dr. King) on state trespass charges. He also said he would seek an "ultimate solution" to the problems, including employment, with merchants.

Renewed Atlanta sit-ins Nov. 25-30, ending the Oct. 22 truce, were met by lunch-counter closings whenever demonstrators appeared. No arrests were made, and there was no violence although about 100 white-robed Ku Klux Klansmen picketed Rich's department store Nov. 26 in support of the store's segregation policy.

The first desegregation of a public cafeteria in Atlanta since the sit-ins began occurred Nov. 30 when 5 Negroes were served without incident among white diners at the YWCA.

RIGHTS LEGISLATION

Civil Rights Act of 1960

The compromise Civil Rights Act of 1960 was passed in April after a record Senate filibuster and Pres. Eisenhower's personal intervention to pry the measure out of the House Rules Committee.

Congressional action on the measure had started Jan. 18 when the Senate Rules & Administration Committee opened hearings on legislation to assure Negroes' rights to vote. Jurisdiction over the issue had been shifted from the Southern-dominated Senate Judiciary Committee, which had blocked all rights legislation during the 1959 session. Dr. Robert G. Storey of Texas, vice chairman of the federal Civil Rights Commission (CRC), told the Senate committee Jan. 18 that he was certain of the constitutionality of a CRC proposal that Congress authorize the President to appoint federal voting registrars for Southern areas where state officials refused to register Negroes. Pres. Eisenhower, at his Jan. 13 press conference, had expressed doubt that such legislation would be constitutional.

Civil rights legislation meanwhile was blocked in the Southern-controlled House Rules Committee, and by Jan. 21 a discharge petition to force it to the floor had gained only 176 of the 219 signatures needed. Democrats pointed out that there were only 30 GOP signatures on the petition. Some Republican leaders said they backed the legislation but did not want to circumvent House rules by signing the petition. Representatives of the Leadership Council on Civil Rights had met separately with Congressional leaders Jan. 14 to urge them to try to break the deadlock on rights legislation. House GOP leader Charles A. Halleck (Ind.) told them he would not "persuade or dissuade" Republicans on signing the discharge petition but would approach Republican members of the Rules Committee to suggest they vote for sending the bill to the floor.

Atty. Gen. William P. Rogers outlined to newsmen Jan. 26 an Administration bill the Justice Department had drafted to protect Negro voting rights in federal and state elections. The Administration plan would amend and supplement the Civil Rights Act of 1957. It was offered as a substitute for a Civil Rights Commission proposal to appoint federal voting registrars. The Administration bill would have: (1) authorized federal courts to appoint "voting referees" to certify qualified voting applicants who had been denied registration because of color, race or religion, (2) empowered referees to watch elections to make sure Negroes were permitted to vote and that their votes were counted, (3) authorized judges (without juries) to jail on contempt charges persons who interfered with qualified voters' rights to vote, (4) given referees powers equal to those of masters in federal courts, (5) authorized the federal government to sue states in which illegal voting deprivations occurred.

Chrmn. Emanuel Celler (D., N.Y.) of the House Judiciary Committee, a frequent critic of the Administration's alleged failures in the civil rights field, promptly indorsed the Administration plan. Sen. Philip A. Hart (D., Mich.) of the Senate Judiciary Committee criticized the plan on the ground that the administration of voting was an executive and legislative duty and should not be turned over to the judiciary.

Rogers, testifying before the Senate Rules Committee Feb. 5 on behalf of the Administration plan, urged civil rights advocates to abandon rival bills (S 2684, S 2719, S 2783 and S 2814) for the appointment of federal voting registrars with "no real enforcement machinery." The Administration proposal, he said, could be enforced by court injunction. The rival plan "just won't work," he asserted. "It won't permit the Negroes to vote." He pointed out that the registrar proposals were limited to federal elections whereas "the 15th Amendment is not so limited; nor is the Administration proposal."

The Administration's full civil rights legislation "package" was introduced Feb. 8 by Senate GOP leader Everett M. Dirksen

(Ill.) and 23 other Republican Senators. The bill would have: (a) authorized the appointment of federal voting referees, (b) established criminal penalties for the use of force or threats to obstruct federal court orders to desegregate schools, (c) authorized aid to communities in integrating schools, (d) authorized federal officers to help hunt for suspects in bombing cases.

Senate Democratic leader Lyndon B. Johnson (Tex.) Feb. 15 redeemed his Sept. 1959 pledge to bring civil rights legislation to the Senate floor by about Feb. 15. With normal procedure blocked by Southern Democrats, who kept rights legislation bottled up in the Senate Rules Committee, Johnson bypassed the committee by a maneuver that caught rights-bill opponents unprepared. Johnson Feb. 15 obtained unanimous consent to bring up a House-passed bill, HR8315, unconnected with civil rights. (HR8315 was drafted to give the Stella, Mo. public school system free use of an Army barracks as a temporary school for 2 years to replace a burned-downed school.) Johnson then said civil rights legislation would be introduced as amendments to HR8315. He said the Senate would "do what is right . . . even though we do not satisfy the extremists on either side."

Sen. Richard B. Russell (D., Ga.) led the Southern attack Feb. 15 on what he called "lynching of orderly procedure in the Senate." He charged that "feeling against the South has gotten to be almost a national disease," that Northern Senators "expect one standard from us, whereas those who harass the South can bring in amendments as they will." A Russell motion to delay rights debate for a week was defeated by 61-28 Senate vote Feb. 16. One of the few non-Southern votes for delay was cast by Sen. Wayne Morse (D., Ore.), who favored rights legislation but opposed "wash[ing] out the [Senate's] whole committee procedure." Morse was defeated by a 68-4 vote Feb. 16 when he proposed that the Senate discharge its Rules Committee from further consideration of a civil rights bill if it failed to report it out by Feb. 25. Morse held that the discharge petition was the proper procedure for bringing committee-blocked bills to the floor.

The Administration bill was offered by Senate GOP leader Dirksen Feb. 15 as an amendment to House-passed HR8315, but Dirksen, in a move to avert possible parliamentary attack on the amendment, resubmitted it Feb. 24 as a substitute for the House bill.

Southern Democrats Set Filibuster Record

18 Southern Democratic Senators Feb. 29 began a filibuster by which they hoped either to keep the Senate from voting on civil rights legislation or to persuade the Senate to accept a mild bill. In preparation for the filibuster, 40 cots had been moved into Senate offices and committee rooms for the use of Senators unable to go home to sleep for days at a stretch. To counter earlier delaying tactics used against civil rights legislation, Johnson had announced Feb. 23 that he would call around-the-clock sessions starting Feb. 29 to wear down the delayers and make sure the Senate was given a chance to vote on the rights proposals. The Southerners, who had never lost a civil rights filibuster but who had far too few votes to defeat a rights bill, said they would use every parliamentary device at their disposal to keep the Senate from transacting any business—no matter how pressing—as long as the bipartisan majority insisted on bringing the civil rights bill to a vote.

Russell acted as overall leader of the filibuster effort. The filibusterers were divided into 3 teams—one each under Sens. Russell, Lister Hill (D., Ala.) and John C. Stennis (D., Miss.). The 6-member teams had been set up to take turns in keeping the Senate floor for periods of 24 hours each for as long as the filibuster lasted. This meant each filibusterer would have to speak for an average of only 4 hours every 3 days.

As the filibuster droned on through the very early morning hours of Mar. 1, the filibusterers began harassing the rights forces by calls for a quorum. The rights forces then had to get enough sleeping Senators off the cots and on to the Senate floor to bring the number on the floor up to at least 51. Failure to muster a quorum would have given the filibusterers the right to adjourn the Senate. Senators to fill the quorum, therefore, had to be supplied by the rights forces, which wanted the non-stop session to continue in order to exhaust the filibusterers. The filibusterers, however, who were quite ready to take whatever respite they could get provided no harm was done to their cause, ignored quorum calls and thereby got more continuous rest than many non-filibusterers.

Before the start of the filibuster, Southern Democrats had attacked Johnson's call for 24-hour sessions as an act of cruelty to aging Senators. Johnson, asserting Feb. 26 that he did "not want to have blood on my hands" or to be accused of making "an individual decision" against the Senate's "majority wishes," moved to have the Feb. 29 session adjourn at 5 p.m. but announced simultaneously that he would vote against his own motion. The Senate Feb. 26 then rejected the motion by a 67-10 vote. Many Southern Senators voted against the motion in an effort to make the test valueless.

The non-stop session was interrupted after 43 hours and 13 minutes for a 15-minute clean-up of the Senate chamber between 7:13 and 7:28 a.m. Mar. 2. The Senate then set a record for a continuous session by sitting for 82 hours and 3 minutes until, at 5:31 p.m. Mar. 5, Senate majority leader Johnson recessed it until noon Mar. 7. With the exception of the Mar. 2 break, the Senate had been in continuous session for 125 hours and 31 minutes; this was a record for sessions with only short interruptions.

Round-the-clock sessions were called off by Johnson Mar. 8 after a motion to break the filibuster by imposing cloture (limitation of debate) was presented by 23 Democratic and 8 Republican sponsors. The move, opposed by the leadership of both parties as premature, was defeated Mar. 10 by a 53-42 vote (33 D. and 20 R. vs. 30 D. and 12 R.). It was the 9th time cloture had been rejected in a Senate civil rights filibuster.

House Acts on Rights Bill

In the meantime, the House Rules Committee, which since mid-1959 had kept from the floor an omnibus civil rights bill approved by the House Judiciary Committee, agreed Feb. 17 to permit the House to debate the measure. The committee cleared the bill by a 7-4 vote Feb. 18 but postponed floor debate until Mar. 10. Rowland Evans reported in the *N.Y. Herald Tribune* Feb. 19 that Pres. Eisenhower, at his Feb. 16 conference with GOP Congressional leaders, had applied pressure personally to get the 4 Republicans on the House Rules Committee to line up with the committee's 4 Northern Democrats against its 4 Southern Democrats and vote to clear the House bill.

It was reported that Democratic Congressional leaders had decided on strategy under which the House bill, with a voting-referee amendment added, would be adopted by the House and then offered to the Senate to replace the stronger Senate bill. Such a bill (HR8601) was passed by 311-109 House vote (179 D. and 132 R. vs. 94 D. and 15 R.) Mar. 24 and sent to the Senate.

The bill, sponsored by Reps. Emanuel Celler (D., N.Y.) and William M. McCulloch (R., O.), would have: (a) empowered federal judges to appoint referees to register qualified Negroes to vote in all elections (federal, state and local) in areas where they had been denied such rights; (b) required local authorities to preserve federal registration and voting records for 2 years and to let Justice Department officials inspect them; (c) made it a federal crime (punishable by 60 days' imprisonment and $1,000 fines) to obstruct court orders for school integration or to interfere with them by force or threats; (d) made it a federal crime punishable by up to 5 years' imprisonment and $5,000 fines to flee across state lines to avoid prosecution for bombings or to avoid testifying in bomb cases and made it a crime punishable by a year in jail and $1,000 fines to cross state lines to avoid prosecution for bomb threats; (e) provided federal aid to educate servicemen's and federal workers' children where integration disputes closed local schools.

The bill would have authorized federal judges to appoint voting referees only on Justice Department request and only after determining that discrimination against Negro voters existed in the area. Negroes seeking to register through referees would have had to show that local officials had denied them their rights. Local officials would have had the right to contest referees' decisions but would have been prevented from using the appeal right as a delaying tactic to keep Negroes from voting. This key voting right amendment had been approved by the House Mar. 23 by 295-124 vote (172 D. and 123 R. vs. 100 D. and 24 R.)

Less than 2 hours after receiving the House-passed bill, the Senate Mar. 24, by 86-5 vote, referred the measure to its Judiciary Committee, which had never sent a civil rights bill to the Senate floor. The Senate referral, however, was on a motion by Senate Democratic leader Lyndon Johnson that instructed the committee to return the bill to the Senate "not later than" Mar. 29. The committee's chairman, Sen. James O. Eastland (D., Miss.), pledged to maintain the committee's record. He asked the Senate to give his unit the bill without instructions, but the Senate rejected his motion by a 72-19 vote. The Senate committee cleared the bill without recommendation Mar. 29 with Sen. Milton R. Young (N.D.) providing the only Republican vote in support of Eastland.

Senate Version Enacted

A modified version of the House's Civil Rights Act of 1960 was approved by 71-18 Senate vote Apr. 8 and returned to the House. It was the first time a Senate filibuster had failed to block the passage of a civil rights bill. 42 Democrats and 29 Republicans voted to approve the measure. 18 Southern Democrats voted against it.

Summary of the 6 titles of the Senate version of the bill:

(1) The use of "threats or force" to obstruct federal court orders would be a federal crime punishable by jail terms of up to a year and/or fines of up to $1,000.

(2) Crossing a state line or fleeing abroad to avoid prosecution for burning or bombing a building or vehicle or to avoid testifying in such a case would be federal crime punishable by imprisonment for up to 5 years and/or fines of up to $5,000. Transporting explosives in interstate commerce for the purpose of damaging a building or other property would be a federal crime punishable by (a) imprisonment for up to a year and/or fines of up to $1,000, (b) imprisonment for up to 10 years and/or fines of up to $10,000 if the bombing injured anybody, and (c) the death sentence or life imprisonment if anybody was killed. Use of the mails, phone or telegraph to threaten or give false warning of a bombing would be a federal crime punishable by a year's imprisonment and/or a $1,000 fine.

(3) State election officials would be required to retain all registration and voting records in federal election for 22 months and to let the Justice Department inspect and copy them. Destruction or theft of such records would be a federal crime punishable by imprisonment for up to a year and/or fines of up to $1,000.

(4) Civil Rights Commission members would have clear authority to take sworn testimony.

(5) The Health, Education & Welfare Department would be authorized to provide for the education of servicemen's children in areas where public schools were closed.

(6) Federal courts would be authorized to appoint "voting referees" who would be empowered to enroll Negroes in areas where racial discrimination against voters had been proven. Referees could be appointed only after (a) the Justice Department sued under the Civil Rights Act of 1957 to obtain a federal court order requiring the registration of one or more persons unjustly disqualified by local registrars on racial grounds, (b)

the Justice Department won the suit and then asked the judge to find that a "pattern or practice" of discrimination had blocked the Negroes from voting. Referees appointed under this procedure would be authorized to enroll not only those involved in the case but others in the area who proved that they were qualified under state law, had tried to enroll after the judge had issued his discrimination finding and had been rejected.

The original House bill had been altered by 16 amendments before it achieved Senate passage. Democratic leader Johnson was given credit for the success of the bill despite massive Southern opposition. He was supported by Senate GOP leader Everett Dirksen.

Sen. John L. McClellan (D., Ark.) asserted as the debate drew to a close Apr. 8 that the Southern fight had resulted in the defeat of "the far more odious and obnoxious proposals." "We have repelled . . . vicious assaults on the rights and liberties of our people," he said. Sen. Joseph S. Clark (D., Pa.) of the civil rights bloc said that his side had "suffered a crushing defeat" and that the bill was "only a pale ghost of our hopes."

The Senate version of the Civil Rights Act of 1960 was approved by 288-95 House vote (165 D. and 123 R. vs. 83 D. and 12 R.) Apr. 21, and it became law May 6 when Pres. Eisenhower signed it.

Republican Bill Fails

Senate GOP leader Everett M. Dirksen Aug. 9 introduced a bill to enact 2 civil rights proposals made by Pres. Eisenhower in a message Aug. 8 on the reconvening of Congress after the 2 national political conventions. The bill was killed Aug. 9 by a 54-28 vote (on almost straight party lines) to table it.

The Dirksen bill called for (1) federal grants to help school districts desegregate and (2) permanent status for the Committee on Government Contracts. Sen. Richard Russell, leading the opposition to the bill, said that Dirksen had voted against both proposals during the 8-week Senate fight over the 1960 Civil Rights Act and that Mr. Eisenhower had made no strong plea for the 2 proposals then.

Sens. John F. Kennedy (Mass.) and Lyndon B. Johnson (Tex.), who had just won the Democratic nominations for

President and Vice President, respectively, objected Aug. 8-9 to early consideration of rights legislation. They argued that bringing up the issue would cause lengthy debate and probably kill the chances of other important bills. Democratic backers of rights legislation joined them in charging that Republicans were bringing up rights during the pre-election session to make political capital among minority groups and to block minimum-wage, Social Security, housing and other Democratic bills.

Kennedy told the Senate Aug. 8 that the 2 Administration rights proposals could have been passed with the rest of the 1960 Civil Rights Act if there had been "vigorous administrative leadership." He said that when the 1960 act was being passed, 20 Democrats and only 10 Republicans had voted to provide federal aid for school desegregation, and 27 Democrats and only 11 Republicans had voted for "the Administration's own proposal for a statutory government contracts committee." Kennedy added that some rights actions required only "the stroke of a Presidential pen." As an example, he cited the 11-month-old unanimous proposal of the Civil Rights Commission "that the President issue an executive order on equal opportunity in housing." "The President has not acted. . . . He could and should act now," Kennedy said. "A new Democratic Administration will carry it [the proposal] out," Kennedy pledged, "but there is no need to wait another 6 months."

Senate Approves Poll Tax Ban

The Senate Feb. 2 approved by 70-18 vote and sent to the House a proposed amendment to the U.S. Constitution that would: (1) ban payment of poll tax as a requirement for voting in federal elections; (2) let state governors fill U.S. House vacancies by appointment should more than 50% of House members be killed in a disaster such as a nuclear attack; (3) let District of Columbia residents vote in Presidential elections and elect non-voting delegates to Congress. The House took no action on the proposal.

The measure was subject to 2/3 majority vote for passage by the House. Should the House have adopted the amendment, each part then would have been subject to ratification separately, within 7 years, by 3/4 of the state legislatures.

The omnibus amendment, when introduced originally by Sen. Estes Kefauver (D., Tenn.), contained only the provision for reconstituting the House in event of a disaster. This was approved by 72-16 vote. Sen. Spessard L. Holland (D., Fla.) then moved to attach the poll-tax ban as a proposed constitutional amendment. This was opposed by Sen. Jacob K. Javits (R., N. Y.), author of a pending bill to outlaw the poll tax by federal statute. Javits moved to substitute his statutory measure for Holland's amendment but was defeated.

Southerners generally felt obliged to vote against any anti-poll-tax measure although it was conceded that (1) the poll tax no longer was a major weapon against Southern Negro voting and (2) segregationists preferred the slower process of constitutional amendment to enactment of a statute in racial legislation. Southern Senators were united against Javits' proposal, but Sens. Russell B. Long (D., La.) and B. Everett Jordan (D., N.C.) voted with Holland for the Floridian's constitutional amendment after Javits' alternative was defeated. Lyndon Johnson voted against the Javits proposal but voted for final approval of the omnibus amendment. John F. Kennedy, absent, was paired for the omnibus amendment.

The 3d part of the omnibus amendment, dealing with District of Columbia voting, was proposed by Sen. Kenneth B. Keating (R., N.Y.) and approved, 63-25, on a preliminary vote.

Platforms Outline Party Proposals

The legislative programs of both political parties were outlined in the platforms adopted in July at the 2 national conventions. As is frequently the case with such declarations, both parties had deep internal disagreements over various proposals that formed their platforms, and neither platform could be taken as representing a firm commitment of purpose. This was especially true of the 1960 civil rights planks.

The Democratic National Convention July 12 approved a platform that made the toughest civil rights pledges in party history. The rights plank was repudiated in advance by delegates of 10 Southern states, but none even threatened a walkout. Southern members of the platform committee charged in a bitter minority report that the plank was part of "a calculated effort . . . by the radicals of both parties to drive . . . the South from the Democratic Party." The rights plank pledged action to guarantee Negroes' voting rights, to win compliance with the school desegregation decisions, to prevent employment discrimination and to enlarge the Justice Department's power to fight racial bias.

The plank also implied support for peaceful Southern "sit-in" demonstrations against segregation.

The Republican platform was adopted by voice vote of the National Convention July 27 over the disappointed objections of Southern delegates who opposed a strengthened civil rights plank.

Summary of the Democratic civil rights plank:

"We shall also seek to create an affirmative new atmosphere in which to deal with racial divisions and inequalities which threaten both the integrity of our democratic faith and the proposition on which our nation was founded—that all men are created equal. It is our faith in human dignity that distinguishes our open free society from the closed totalitarian society of the Communists.

"The Constitution . . . rejects the notion that the rights of man means the rights of some men only. We reject it too.

"The right to vote is the first principle of self-government. The Constitution also guarantees to all Americans the equal protection of the laws. It is the duty of the Congress to enact the laws necessary and proper to protect and promote these constitutional rights. The Supreme Court has the power to interpret these rights and the laws thus enacted. It is the duty of the President to see that these rights are respected and the Constitution and laws as interpreted by the Supreme Court are faithfully executed.

"What is now required is effective moral and political leadership by the whole Executive Branch of our government to make equal opportunity a living reality for all Americans. As the party of Jefferson, we shall provide that leadership.

"In every city and state in greater or lesser degree there is discrimination based on color, race, religion or national origin. If discrimination in voting, education, the administration of justice or segregated lunch counters are the issues in one area, discrimination in housing and employment may be pressing questions elsewhere.

"The peaceful demonstrations for first-class citizenship which have recently taken place in many parts of this country are a signal to all of us to make good at long last the guarantees of our Constitution. The time has come to assure equal access for all Americans to all areas of community life, including voting booths, schoolrooms, jobs, housing and public facilities.

"The Democratic Administration . . . will therefore use the full powers provided in the Civil Rights Act of 1957 and 1960 to secure for all Americans the right to vote. If these powers, vigorously invoked by a new Attorney General and backed by a strong and imaginative Democratic President, prove inadequate, further powers will be sought.

"We will support whatever action is necessary to eliminate literacy tests and the payment of poll taxes as requirements for voting.

"A new Democratic Administration will also use its full powers—legal and moral—to insure the beginning of good faith compliance with the constitutional requirement that racial discrimination be ended in public education. We believe that every school district affected by the Supreme Court's school desegregation decision should submit a plan providing for at least first-step compliance by 1963, the 100th anniversary of the Emancipation Proclamation. To facilitate compliance, technical and financial assistance should be given to school districts facing special problems of transition.

"For this and for the protection of all other constitutional rights of Americans, the Attorney General should be empowered and directed to file civil injunction suits in federal courts to prevent the denial of any civil rights on grounds of race, creed or color.

"The new Democratic Administration will support federal legislation establishing a fair employment practices commission effectively to secure for everyone the right to equal opportunity for employment.

"In 1949 the President's Committee on Civil Rights recommended a permanent commission on civil rights. A new Democratic Administration will broaden the scope and strengthen the powers of the present commission and make it permanent. Its functions will be to provide assistance to communities, industries, or individuals in the implementation of constitutional rights in education, housing, employment, transportation and the administration of justice.

"In addition, the Democratic Administration will use its full executive powers to assure equal employment opportunities and to terminate racial segregation throughout federal services and institutions and on all government contracts. . . . Similarly the new Democratic Administration will take action to end discrimination in federal housing programs, including federally assisted housing.

"To accomplish these goals will require Executive Orders, legal actions brought by the Attorney General, legislation and improved Congressional procedures to safeguard majority rule. Above all, it will require the strong, active, persuasive and inventive leadership of the President. . . .

"The Democratic President who takes office next January will face unprecedented challenges. His Administration will present a new face to the world. . . . It will draw new strength from the universal truths which the founder of our party asserted in the Declaration of Independence to be 'self-evident'. . . .

"As the party of hope it is our responsibility and opportunity to call forth the greatness of the American people. In this spirit, we hereby rededicate ourselves to the continuing service of the rights of man—everywhere in America and everywhere else on God's earth."

Summary of the Republican civil rights plank:

"This nation was created to give expression, validity and purpose to our spiritual heritage—the supreme worth of the individual. In such a nation—a nation dedicated to the proposition that all men are created equal—racial discrimination has no place. . . . It is immoral and unjust. As to those matters within reach of political action and leadership, we pledge ourselves unreservedly to its eradication.

"Equality under law promises more than equal right to vote and transcends mere relief from discrimination by government. It becomes a reality only when all persons have equal opportunity . . . to acquire the essentials of life—housing, education and employment. . . .

"We recognize that discrimination is not a problem localized in one area of the country, but rather a problem that must be faced by North and South alike. Nor is discrimination confined to the discrimination against Negroes. Discrimination in many, if not all, areas of the country on the basis of creed or national origin is equally insidious. . . . "

(1) *Voting*—"We pledge: continued vigorous enforcement of the civil rights laws to guarantee the right to vote to all citizens in all areas of the country; and legislation to provide that the completion of 6 primary grades in a state-accredited school is conclusive evidence of literacy for voting purposes."

(2) *Public schools*—"We pledge: The Department of Justice will continue its vigorous support of court orders for school

desegregation. . . . We will propose legislation to authorize the Attorney General to bring actions for school desegregation in the name of the United States in appropriate cases, as when economic coercion or threat of physical harm is used to deter persons from going to court to establish their rights. . . . Our continuing support of the President's proposal to extend federal aid and technical assistance to schools which in good faith attempt to desegregate. We oppose the pretense of fixing a target date 3 years from now for the mere submission of plans for school desegregation. . . . "

(3) *Employment*—"We pledge: Continued support for legislation to establish a commission on equal job opportunity. . . . Use of the full-scale review of existing state laws, and of prior proposals for federal legislation to eliminate discrimination in employment now being conducted by the Civil Rights Commission, for guidance in our objective of developing a federal-state program in the employment area; and special consideration of training programs aimed at developing the skills of those now working in marginal agricultural employment so that they can obtain employment in industry, notably in the new industries moving into the South."

(4) *Housing*—"We pledge: Action to [ban bias in housing built] . . . with the aid of federal subsidies."

(5) *Public facilities and services*—"We pledge: Removal of any vestige of discrimination in the operation of federal facilities or procedures . . .; opposition to the use of federal funds for the construction of segregated community facilities; action to ensure that public transportation and other government authorized services shall be free from segregation."

(6) *Legislative procedure*—"We pledge: Our best effort to change present Rule 22 of the Senate [which curbs the breaking of filibusters] and other appropriate Congressional procedures that often make unattainable proper legislative implementation of Constitutional guarantees.

"We reaffirm the Constitutional right to peaceable assembly to protest discrimination in private business establishments. We applaud the action of the businessmen who have abandoned discriminatory practices in retail establishments, and we urge others to follow their example.

"Finally we recognize that civil rights is a responsibility not only of states and localities; it is a national problem and a national responsibility. The federal government should take the initiative in promoting inter-group conferences among those who, in their communities, are earnestly seeking solutions of the complex problems of desegregation—to the end that closed channels of communication may be opened, tensions eased, and a cooperative solution of local problems may be sought.

"In summary, we pledge the full use of the power, resources and leadership of the federal government to eliminate discrimination based on race, color, religion or national origin and to encourage understanding and good-will among all races and creeds."

VOTING BIAS FOUGHT

Government Invokes New Law

Atty. Gen. William P. Rogers invoked the 1960 Civil Rights Act May 9 by demanding voting registration records of 4 "deep South" counties that had large Negro populations but no registered Negro voters. FBI agents handed the county registration boards letters in which Rogers said he had "information . . . tending to show that distinctions on the basis of race or color have been made with respect to registration and voting within your jurisdiction." Rogers' letter went to these "cipher" counties (counties with no Negroes registered to vote): Wilcox, Ala.; Webster, Ga.; East Carroll (Parish), La.; McCormick, S.C.

The Justice Department asked election officials in Clarendon and Hampton Counties, S.C., Sumter County, Ala. and Fayette County, Ga. June 6 to let the FBI inspect their voting records to determine whether Negroes had been denied voting rights. The request brought to 12 the number of counties asked for such information under the 1960 Civil Rights Act. McCormick County, S.C. and Early and Webster Counties, Ga. had already complied with earlier requests, but Macon County, Ala. and several other counties had challenged the act's constitutionality.

Immediately after the attorney general's June 6 request, Alabama Circuit Judge Walter B. Jones in Montgomery issued a temporary injunction blocking such voting-record examination in any Alabama county. The injunction had been requested by the office of State Atty. Gen. MacDonald Gallion. It was granted after Chrmn. Early Godfrey of the Sumter County Board of Registrars had given 2 FBI agents permission to see the voting records.

U.S. Judge Frank M. Johnson Jr. ruled in Montgomery Aug.

11 that Montgomery County's board of registrars must surrender voter registration records within 15 days to the scrutiny
of the Justice Department. Johnson dismissed Jones' injunction
on the ground that Jones had no authority to control federal
agents acting under the 1960 Civil Rights Act. Johnson denied
Alabama Atty. Gen. Gallion's contention that the act was unconstitutional. (He simultaneously refused to order Alabama
officials to give the NAACP a charter as an out-of-state corporation. A state court injunction barring the NAACP from
doing business in Alabama had been in effect since June 1956.)

Judge Johnson Nov. 17 ordered the Macon County (Ala.)
Board of Registrars to open to federal inspection voter registration records dating back as far as Jan. 1951. But he rejected
Gallion's request to examine federal documents on which
charges of discrimination were based. Johnson Nov. 17 upheld
the constitutionality of the 1957 and 1960 federal civil rights
acts.

Gallion refused Oct. 31, Nov. 11 and Dec. 1 to comply with
U.S. Atty. Gen. Rogers' request that he open Sumter County
voter registration records to federal inspection. Gallion said
Dec. 1 that he was acting in obedience to an Oct. 11 order of
Alabama Circuit Judge Emmet F. Hildreth, who, according to
Gallion, had put the records "in my constructive custody and
directed that I reveal them to no one other than members of
the [Sumter] Board of Registrars." Gallion Nov. 11 denounced
"Rogers and the rest of the civil rights mob in Washington" for
refusing to "recognize the right of a state court to rule concerning purely state records."

The U.S. Supreme Court had ruled unanimously May 16 that
the 1960 Civil Rights Act could be applied to make Alabama a
defendant in a Justice Department suit to enforce Negro voting
rights even though the suit had been instituted before the act
was passed. The Justice Department had appealed lower court
decisions that the 1957 Civil Rights Act did not provide for suits
against states.

The Justice Department filed suit in U.S. District Court in
Shreveport, La. June 7 to order the names of 560 Negroes
restored to Bienville Parish voting rolls and to appoint a voting
referee to register other Negroes. This was the first such suit
to be filed under the 1960 Civil Rights Act. The suit charged
that all but 26 of 595 Negro voters had been removed from
parish registration rolls between Sept. 26 and Oct. 9, 1956
(before permanent registration became effective Dec. 31) as a

result of "racially discriminatory challenges filed by the Citizens Council of Arcadia, Inc., and the Citizens Council of Gibsland, Inc." The suit named Bienville Parish Registrar Pauline A. Culpepper and 16 individual members of each council as defendants. It asserted that the removal of Negro voters from the rolls was part of a "pattern of discrimination" that made appointment of a voting referee necessary. The complaint said that "as of March 31, 1960, there were 5,143 white persons but only 26 Negroes registered to vote in Bienville Parish, whereas . . . there were approximately 6,120 white persons and 4,475 Negroes of voting age in the parish."

Negro Voting Rights Upheld

U.S. District Judge J. Skelly Wright in New Orleans Jan. 11 ordered a Washington Parish, La. voting registrar to restore the names of 1,377 Negroes to the voting rolls. Their names had been removed because of technical challenges by 4 Citizens Council members. Wright simultaneously enjoined the council and its members from filing further challenges for purposes of racial discrimination. Wright's order was stayed Jan. 21 by the U.S. 5th Circuit Court of Appeals pending its decision on an appeal. The Justice Department, which had filed the original anti-bias suit, asked the Supreme Court Jan. 22 to set aside the circuit court's stay, and the stay was voided Feb. 29.

The Supreme Court Feb. 29 also unanimously upheld the right of Negroes to register and vote in Terrell County, Ga. The high court reversed U.S. District Judge T. Hoyt Davis' decision that the Civil Rights Act of 1957 was unconstitutional, in part at least, because it could be construed as permitting the Justice Department to bring civil suits against voting registrars as individuals. Justice William J. Brennan Jr., author of the Supreme Court opinion, said that federal courts had a duty to limit themselves to cases at hand and that "the delicate power of pronouncing an act of Congress unconstitutional is not to be exercised with reference to hypothetical cases." Brennan also denied that Congress had no power to authorize government suits to insure private citizens' voting rights.

U.S. District Judge William A. Bootle in Macon, Ga. Sept. 13 issued an order forbidding further discrimination by Terrell County voter registrars. Bootle, however, refused to appoint a voter referee, as requested by the Justice Department. He ordered the registrars to notify him within 10 days that they had put 4 Negro complainants on the voting rolls. The registrars Sept. 23 filed a compliance report that stated that the 4 Negroes had been added to the list of qualified voters. This case was the first filed under the 1957 Civil Rights Act and the first in which the Justice Department had asked for appointment of a voting referee under the 1960 Civil Rights Act.

A consent judgment was entered in federal court in Memphis Apr. 25 to end restrictions against Negro voting in Fayette County, Tenn. This was the first voting case under the 1957 Civil Rights Act to be settled by negotiation but was the 4th brought under the act. The judgment ordered an end to the ban on Negro voting in the county's Democratic primary elections, which, the Justice Department said, were "the only meaningful elections."

Court Backs CRC's Inquiry Powers

The U.S. Supreme Court ruled 7 to 2 June 20 that the federal Civil Rights Commission (CRC) could subpoena voting registrars and compel them to testify without giving them the names of persons charging voting irregularities. The high court ruling opened the way for the resumption of CRC hearings, suspended since 1959, on complaints of voting discrimination against Negroes.

The decision overturned 2 lower federal court injunctions, issued for western Louisiana in 1959, which held that the CRC could not deny voting registrars or citizens involved in voting complaints the right to confront and cross-examine their accusers without specific Congressional authorization. The CRC had refused to identify complainants for fear of reprisals against them. Chief Justice Earl Warren, speaking for the majority, held that Congress had explicitly authorized commission hearings without full disclosure to witnesses. Justices Tom C. Clark, John Marshall Harlan, William J. Brennan Jr., Charles E. Whittaker, Potter Stewart and Felix Frankfurter concurred. Justices William O. Douglas and Hugo L. Black dissented; they contended that those subpenaed by the CRC would be denied due process of law provided for in the 5th Amendment unless complainants were identified. Douglas termed the majority's concept of due process "chameleon-like," reflecting personal judicial preference, "not reason."

35 Negroes appeared as witnesses before the CRC in New Orleans Sept. 27-28. The commission had received more than

150 complaints from Negroes in 17 Louisiana parishes. (28%
of eligible Negro voters were registered in Louisiana, compared
with 82% of eligible whites.) James Sharp, a Monroe lawyer,
testified Sept. 27 that Sheriff C. E. Hester had threatened to
"take me for a ride" for trying to have Negroes registered in
Madison Parish. Frederic Lewis, 55, a farmer, testified Sept.
27 that he had been trying to register in Claiborne Parish since
1935 without success. 4 witnesses testified Sept. 28 that segregated voting machines were used in St. Helena Parish.

Economic Pressures Charged in Tennessee

The Justice Department sued in U.S. District Court in
Memphis Sept. 13 for an injunction to restrain 27 persons and
2 banks—the First State Bank of Brownsville and the Peoples
Bank of Stanton—from using economic pressure to dissuade
Haywood County Negroes from voting. This was the first such
use of the Civil Rights Act of 1957. (Of 7,921 voting-age Negroes
in the county, less than 300 were registered to vote whereas
nearly all 6,500 eligible whites were registered.)

The Justice Department charged that the discriminatory
Haywood County sanctions began immediately after a Civic &
Welfare League was organized by Negroes in 1959 to encourage
registration and voting. The suit said "coercive acts and
practices" were applied against Negroes who were registered
and who were active in getting Negroes to vote. The defendants
were charged with circulating lists of these Negroes "among
the white business community" and with applying pressure
against Negroes on the lists by: (a) asking wholesalers not to
deal with listed Negro merchants, (b) refusing to sell food and
other goods and services, even for cash, to those on the lists,
(c) refusing to deal with white merchants suspected of selling
to listed Negroes, (d) dismissing employed Negroes and ending
agreements with Negro sharecroppers and tenant farmers and
(e) denying them credit or loans.

The Justice Department filed suit in U.S. District Court in
Memphis Dec. 14 for a permanent injunction to restrain 82
defendants, including 45 landowners, 24 merchants and a bank,
from allegedly using similar economic pressures to keep
Fayette County Negroes from voting. The suit was the 3d use
of the 1957 Civil Rights Act in Tennessee.

The 2 suits also sought temporary injunctions to block 700
eviction notices (effective Jan. 1) that had been served on Negro

tenant farmers in Haywood and Fayette Counties since about 1,400 Fayette County Negroes had registered to vote in a Negro registration drive started in May.

U.S. District Judge Marion S. Boyd in Memphis refused Dec. 22 to enjoin the evictions. On Justice Department appeal, the U.S. 6th Circuit Court of Appeals in Cincinnati Dec. 30 ordered maintenance of the *status quo* in the Haywood County case until a Feb. 6, 1961 hearing. After the circuit court's order, Boyd issued an injunction Dec. 30 to forbid the eviction of about 400 Fayette County Negroes. He set Jan. 5, 1961 as the date for a hearing. (About 75 Negro tenant farmers subject to eviction had left the farms already and were living near Somerville, Tenn. in a tent city on farmland owned by Shepherd Towles, a Negro.)

Tuskegee (Ala.) Boundary Change Attacked

The Supreme Court ruled unanimously Nov. 14 that a 1957 Alabama law resetting the city boundaries of Tuskegee was unconstitutional if Negro voters had been effectively eliminated by the change. The ruling overthrew lower court decisions and sent the original suit back for trial. Justice Felix Frankfurter, author of the court's opinion, wrote that the impairment of voting rights "cloaked in the garb of the realignment of political subdivisions" was a violation of the 15th Amendment. Solicitor Gen. J. Lee Rankin had asserted in a memo filed with the Supreme Court Mar. 1 that the Alabama law had changed Tuskegee city lines to exclude nearly all Negroes as residents and voters. His memo had urged Supreme Court review of the 1957 law.

Lower federal courts had upheld the statute, and a suit filed by disfranchised voters on grounds of racial discrimination had been dismissed without trial. The U.S. 5th Circuit Court of Appeals had affirmed the dismissal on grounds that the states had full authority over city boundaries and were not subject to federal court review in exercising this control. Rankin's memo disputed the ruling. It said the state law violated (a) the 15th Amendment by depriving Negroes of voting rights and (b) the 14th Amendment by taking away their benefits as municipal citizens.

Students at Tuskegee Institute Mar. 1 began a full-scale boycott of all white merchants in Tuskegee in protest against the state law.

Negroes Try Voter 'Stand-Ins'

Negroes staged sparsely-attended "stand-in" demonstrations in several cities Oct. 3 in protest against barriers to Negro voter registration. Dr. Martin Luther King Jr., whose Southern Christian Leadership Conference originated the "stand-in" movement, said in Atlanta that the demonstrations were "an experiment . . . to see how effective it can be." 50 Negroes sought to register in Atlanta but were told by the Fulton County registrars that they were too late for 1960 registration; the registrars reported registering about 12 for 1961's elections. About 20 Leon County Negroes registered without difficulty in Tallahassee, Fla. Negro voter applicants also appeared in Clarksdale, Miss., and in Birmingham and Tuskegee, Ala.

SCHOOL INTEGRATION

94% of Negro Pupils Segregated in South

Despite the 1954 Supreme Court decision against segregation in public schools, 94% of the South's Negro students still attended segregated classes, a *Southern School News* survey revealed Apr. 9. Of 3,039,133 Negroes and 9,901,310 whites (enrolled in the 17 Southern states and the District of Columbia) affected by the decision, 524,425 Negroes were in integrated school districts, but only 182,104 were being taught with whites.

The report said Alabama, Georgia, Louisiana, Mississippi and South Carolina had rejected any steps toward desegregation. Elsewhere, pupil assignment plans and the reluctance of some Negroes to transfer to formerly white schools had slowed integration. The report noted that even in states with complete integration policies, many Negroes still attended schools that had no whites. All of West Virginia's 24,010 Negro students were in integrated districts, but only about 12,000 were in mixed classes. Delaware, Kentucky, Maryland, Missouri, Oklahoma and Texas, which had substantial integration, had 584,512 Negro pupils but only 94,946 of them in desegregated classrooms. 16,121 of the District of Columbia's 90,403 Negro students studied in 21 all-Negro schools.

States with token integration: Arkansas, with 98 of 104,205 Negroes in mixed classes; Florida, with 512 of 192,093 Negroes in integrated classes; North Carolina, with 34 of 302,060

integrated; Tennessee, with 169 of 146,700 integrated, and
Virginia, with 103 of 203,229 integrated.

Supreme Court Bars Integration Delays

The U. S. Supreme Court Sept. 1 unanimously denied appeals to delay school integration in Houston, New Orleans and
Delaware. It upheld lower court decisions in all 3 areas. The
court also denied an NAACP plea that integration begin in New
Orleans Sept. 7, the first day of the school year, instead of
Nov. 14 (at the start of the 2d school quarter), as the lower court
had ruled. *Details of the 3 cases:*

Houston—In this, the largest segregated school district in
the U.S., Federal District Judge Ben Connally had ordered Aug.
14 that integration was to begin in the first grade Sept. 7 and
was to go up a grade a year. The school board then requested a
Supreme Court stay until their appeal could be taken before the
5th U.S. Circuit Court of Appeals. The board said it did not
have enough time to solve the problems involved. It also said
it might lose $6 million a year (approximately 1/9 of the city's
$54 million school budget) under a state law forbidding school
integration unless voters approved. State Atty. Gen. Will Wilson
held Sept. 6, however, that the state could not withhold aid if
the integration were forced by federal courts and the school
board had to act involuntarily.

The 5th U.S. Circuit Court of Appeals refused in New
Orleans Sept. 6 to rule on the request for a delay on the ground
that the matter was rightly within the province of the U.S.
district court.

The school board ordered Schools Supt. John McFarland
Sept. 6 to receive all applications for admission to formerly
white schools regardless of race. But the board directed that
children of the "opposite race" who were accepted at white
schools should not be notified until Sept. 9—2 days after the
start of school. Relatively few Negroes applied. A 6-year-old
boy Sept. 8 became the first Negro to attend a non-segregated
school in Houston under Connally's integration plan. By Sept.
12 there were 12 Negro students attending non-segregated
classes. No incidents were reported.

New Orleans—Faced with U.S. District Judge J. Skelly
Wright's May 16 order that integration start in the first grade
Sept. 7, Gov. Jimmie H. Davis had announced Aug. 17 that he
had taken over administration of the school system under 1960

State Act No. 496. Davis said he would go to jail if necessary to keep the schools segregated. Wright had ordered grade-a-year integration after the Orleans Parish school board refused to offer an integration plan.

The NAACP and a citizens group of 31 white parents asked a special 3-judge federal court in New Orleans Aug. 26 to prohibit state interference with the proposed integration plan. During this session Louisiana Atty. Gen. Jack P. F. Gremillion angrily walked out after telling the judges, "I am not going to stay in this den of iniquity." Presided over by Chief Judge Richard T. Rives of the 5th U.S. Circuit Court of Appeals, the court Aug. 27 issued an injunction forbidding Louisiana state officials to interfere with the integration and declaring 7 state segregation laws (including Act. No. 496) unconstitutional. Gremillion was cited for contempt.

The school board petitioned Wright Aug. 29 to delay the scheduled integration. It said Davis' seizure of the schools had made it impossible to implement plans in accordance with the court's previous ruling. Wright, "impressed with the sincerity and good faith of the board," agreed Aug. 30 to extend the date to Nov. 14.

New Orleans had 95,000 students in 118 public schools and 47,378 in 86 parochial schools. Both school systems were segregated, but Archbishop Joseph Rummel, in a letter read in all New Orleans' Roman Catholic churches Aug. 21, had ordered a day of prayer for integration and had said: "In principle, we are committed to the racial integration of our Catholic schools." Rummel had pledged in 1959 that the parochial schools would be integrated "not later than the public schools."

Delaware—The U.S. 3d Circuit Court of Appeals in Philadelphia Aug. 29 had denied Delaware a review of its July 19 ruling that all grades be integrated fully within one year and that 20 Negro children be admitted to white schools in the current fall term. (The appeals court ruling was made on an appeal filed for the 20 Negroes.) The appeals court asked the State Board of Education and the state superintendent of public instruction to submit by Dec. 31, "for the approval of the district dourt, a modified plan of integration." The court directed that the plan must allow "for the integration at all grades . . . at the fall term 1961 and at all subsequent school terms."

A plan to provide complete desegregation of Delaware's

public schools by 1970 was filed in U.S. District Court in Wilmington Dec. 29 by the State Education Board in compliance with the court's order. Delaware agreed under the plan: (1) to eliminate distinctions between Negro and white school districts; (2) to have school boards establish attendance areas "without regard to race or color"; (3) to allow Negro pupils to transfer to white schools in Sept. 1961.

Delaware had 77,000 public school pupils. Nearly 36,000 (46%) attended integrated schools, largely in the Wilmington area. More than 7,000 Negroes were in segregated classes.

Louisiana Desegregation Turmoil

28 laws to block public school integration were passed by the Louisiana House Nov. 6 and received final approval of the Senate Nov. 8. The state Legislature had been called into a special 12-day session beginning Nov. 4 by Gov. Jimmie H. Davis to pass the anti-integration program.

The main bill adopted was an interposition measure that authorized Louisiana to disregard any federal order the state considered unconstitutional. Other approved bills, all designed to block integration, authorized the state to close schools, deny accreditation and free textbooks to schools, deny promotion and credits to pupils, suspend school boards and revoke teaching certificates. Another adopted bill replaced the Orleans Parish (county) School Board with an 8-man legislative committee. (The legislative committee took control of New Orleans public schools Nov. 10.) All New Orleans senators voted against most of the anti-integration program.

U.S. Judge J. Skelly Wright prohibited implementation of Louisiana's anti-school-integration laws by issuing 2 temporary restraining orders Nov. 10 against state officials (the controller, director of public safety, adjutant general and superintendent of public education), New Orleans Schools Supt. James F. Redmond and an 8-member legislative committee that had been created to supercede the New Orleans school board. The restraining orders, issued at the request of white parents and served by federal deputy marshals, nullified the new state anti-integration laws and the legislative committee's Nov. 10 take-over of New Orleans schools. The New Orleans school board Nov. 10 then approved plans to admit 5 Negroes to 2 all-white schools, as proposed by Redmond.

U.S. Atty. Gen. William P. Rogers warned Gov. Davis by

telegram Nov. 12 that the "full powers of my office" would be used to support the scheduled integration. Rogers also pledged New Orleans Mayor deLesseps S. Morrison his full cooperation to preserve order.

A 2d special session of the Legislature convened Nov. 13 on a call from Davis although the first special session was still meeting. The 2d session Nov. 13: (1) took control of the New Orleans schools, (2) ordered schools to be closed Nov. 14 for a holiday and (3) discharged Redmond. The Legislature Nov. 14 also dismissed 4 New Orleans school board members (who held office by election). Morrison had sent a letter to the Legislature Nov. 13 asking that no steps be taken to disturb the peace or close the schools.

Wright Nov. 13 signed another restraining order prohibiting state interference with the schools.

The first actual Louisiana school integration was achieved in New Orleans Nov. 14 when U.S. marshals and parents accompanied 3 Negro girls into McDonogh No. 19 School and one Negro first-grader into William Frantz School. (One Negro student scheduled to attend an all-white school remained at home.) Deputized state police Nov. 14 served orders directing the closing of New Orleans' 48 elementary schools, but the closing orders were rejected by school officials. Angry white crowds milling outside the 2 integrated schools booed as the 4 Negro children entered, and some white parents escorted their children from the schools. Only 50 of 575 pupils remained in the Frantz School Nov. 14, and few more than 30 of 460 remained at McDonogh.

11 whites were arrested in disturbances Nov. 15, and that night about 5,000 attended a Louisiana Citizens Council, Inc. rally where segregationists called for a march on the school board. About 2,000 whites, largely teen-agers later joined by older hoodlums, demonstrated Nov. 16 at city hall and chanted for Morrison. Mounted police and firemen used fire hoses to break up a rush on school board offices. 4 Negroes, attacked by whites, were hospitalized, and at least 50 persons were arrested. Many cars, windows and neon signs were damaged.

The worst rioting since the schools were integrated occurred Nov. 17. 194 persons were arrested for loitering, 29 for carrying concealed weapons and 27 for vandalism. John H. Cockerham, 17, was charged with attempted murder after Negroes fired at 2 whites Nov. 17. Incidents involved stabbings and gas bombings, and there was a clash between more than

200 white and Negro longshoremen at a shape-up.

Mobs of angry white women Nov. 29-Nov. 30 reviled and in one instance scuffled with Mrs. James Gabrielle, a white mother accompanying her daughter, Yolanda, 6, from the Frantz School. A mob shoved and taunted the Rev. Lloyd A. Foreman, a white Methodist pastor accompanying his daughter Pamela Lynn, 5, to the Frantz School Nov. 29. The crowd jeered Foreman and Mrs. Gabrielle outside their homes Nov. 30. Vandals damaged Foreman's house Dec. 5 and stoned the Gabrielle home Dec. 7. Foreman had been jeered outside 2 churches in which he had officiated Dec. 4. Gabrielle said Dec. 6 that he had resigned his city job because of the enmity of his fellow workers. A 24-hour police guard was placed on the Foreman home Dec. 6 and on the Gabrielle home Dec. 7. The Gabrielles announced Dec. 8 that they were moving from New Orleans.

23 white pupils attended Frantz School Dec. 6. Most were driven to school by members of Save Our Schools (SOS), a white citizens' back-to-school group. No whites attended McDonogh No. 19. Police formed a barricade a block away from Frantz School to restrain jeering pickets, who had thrown eggs and stones at cars taking the pupils home from school Dec. 5.

100 New Orleans business and professional leaders appealed in a *Times-Picayune* ad Dec. 14 for an end to the street demonstrations. They asked citizens to back the school board and restore dignity "to our community." The Junior Chamber of Commerce, League of Women Voters and Committee for Public Education came out in support of the school board Dec. 8. Taunting women segregationists failed to appear before the integrated schools for the first time Dec. 13.

Davis' secretary, Christian Faser Jr., and 4 Louisiana legislators flew to Palm Beach, Fla. Nov. 20 to ask Pres.-elect John F. Kennedy for his opinion on the federal orders prohibiting state interference with the court-enforced school integration in New Orleans. Kennedy designated Clark M. Clifford to meet with the group. Clifford told them that it was "highly inappropriate" for a President-elect to comment on matters pending before a federal court.

Redmond announced Nov. 22 that there were no funds to pay 4,500 school employes because the Legislature had stopped state aid to New Orleans schools. The school board, with a $2,300,000 monthly payroll, had applied for bank loans, but the banks had attached 14 conditions to school loans. One of the conditions was that the Legislature reverse itself and release the state funds to the school board. The state had moved to take away all state business from a New Orleans bank that had made $45,000 of school deposits available to the school board Nov. 18.

The Louisiana Teachers Association voted at its annual convention in Baton Rouge Nov. 23 to fight federal court orders to integrate New Orleans.

The Louisiana House of Representatives Nov. 23 unanimously passed a resolution accusing Pres. Eisenhower and the federal courts of "making common cause with the Communist conspiracy." The Senate, modifying the accusation to "some" of the federal judiciary and "some of the members of the Executive Branch," also passed the resolution. The Legislature Nov. 29 contributed a day's pay ($50 for each legislator) to parents of white children boycotting integrated schools.

A 3-judge federal court in New Orleans Nov. 30 reaffirmed the school desegregation plan. It also (1) voided new state laws, including the Interposition Act, designed to thwart integration, and (2) enjoined 700 officials, including Davis and the members of the Legislature, from any "purport to act as administrators of the local schools."

In a 3d state attempt to replace the New Orleans school board, legislation was approved by the Legislature and signed by Davis Dec. 3 but was blocked by a temporary restraining order issued by a 3-judge federal court Dec. 5. The Justice Department had intervened as a friend of the court Dec. 3 to oppose a Legislature-chosen school board.

The Supreme Court Dec. 12 upheld the federal court ruling that Louisiana's interposition and other new anti-integration laws were unconstitutional. The unanimous ruling was given in an unsigned denial of Louisiana's Dec. 7 application for a stay, pending appeals, of the Nov. 30 federal court order reaffirming New Orleans' school desegregation plan.

A 3-judge federal court in New Orleans Dec. 21, acting on a suit brought by the Justice Department Dec. 20, ordered contempt citations against Lt. Gov. C. C. Aycock, House Speaker Thomas Jewel and State Education Supt. Shelby M. Jackson for refusing to pay the salaries of teachers in the 2 integrated schools. The court also (1) ordered 4 New Orleans banks to release school funds, (2) voided the Legislature's 5th attempt Dec. 15 to abolish the New Orleans school board.

The Louisiana Legislature Dec. 21 rejected a proposal to raise the 2% sales tax to 3%. The proposal was intended to provide $28 million for grants-in-aid to white pupils who wanted to transfer from integrated to segregated schools. It failed by 3 votes to receive the necessary 2/3 majority.

Georgia Schools Threatened

Gov. S. Ernest Vandiver told the Georgia Legislature at its opening session Jan. 11 that he would deny state funds to any school that desegregated. He called on Negroes and the NAACP to end legal actions to gain admission to white Georgia schools to avert a "head-on collision between federal and state sovereignty" and the probable closing of schools. "But if they [Negroes] persist," Vandiver continued, "we are going to resist . . . again and again. We are going to exhaust every legal means and remedy available to us."

The United Churchwomen of Georgia, representing all faiths, adopted in Atlanta Jan. 15 a resolution asking political leaders to keep the schools open, "making whatever changes necessary in the laws of Georgia."

James S. Peters, State Board of Education chairman, said in a letter published in the *Atlanta Journal-Constitution* Jan. 17 that "some form of integration is inevitable, and the only question . . . is whether integration will be under the control of the friends of segregation or the proponents of integration." He suggested that segregation leaders meet and seek a solution or face "defeat and the loss of our power and influence" in Georgia's state government. Peters warned fellow supporters of Sen. Herman Talmadge that unless they compromised on segregation, Talmadge might be defeated for reelection and the state's next governor might be ex-Gov. Ellis Arnal, who had said that if the schools were closed, he would campaign for governor on a pledge to reopen them.

Desegregation of public education in Georgia had made a tentative start Jan. 10 with the peaceful enrollment of 2 Negro students, Charlayne Alberta Hunter and Hamilton E. Holmes, at Georgia University in Athens.

Atlanta Integration Ordered

The Atlanta Board of Education amended its public school integration plan Jan. 4 to conform with criteria U.S. District Judge Frank A. Hooper had set forth when he gave qualified approval to the program Dec. 30, 1959. The plan, submitted

Nov. 29, 1959, provided for gradual integration of the races despite Georgia laws (a) denying state funds to "mixed" schools and (b) requiring the governor to close any public school that had been ordered desegregated. The Jan. 4 changes prohibited the barring of a pupil from a school to forestall possible "economic retaliation" and provided for speedier handling of applications for transfers. Hooper, who had ordered that the amendments be adopted by Jan. 6, had upheld the use of "psychological factors" as a basis for placing pupils in schools but had ruled that there must be no "reference to race or color" and that officials using this basis "must specifically designate the facts upon which the findings are made."

Hooper ordered the board May 9 to begin public school desegregation in Sept. 1961. He granted the year's delay to give the state Legislature "just one more chance" to avert conflict between Georgia laws forbidding school integration and his earlier court order to end segregation. Hooper's order directed the school board to make the court-approved pupil placement plan effective regardless of whether the 1961 session of the Legislature voted permissive legislation. The 1960 session had refused to change laws under which any school faced with a desegregation order was to be closed.

Hooper suggested that the Legislature could obtain a "solution without chaos" by: (a) adopting a pupil-placement act along lines suggested by the Atlanta Board of Education in its court-ordered desegregation proposal, or (b) passing a measure to give Atlantans the right to vote on a choice between desegregation and abolition of public education.

Local option had been recommended by the General Assembly Committee on Schools. Its report (scheduled for delivery to the 1961 Legislature) was cited by Hooper in his order. The commission had found in statewide hearings that a 3-2 majority opposed changing school desegregation laws.

Some Virginia Schools Comply

A 6th Virginia public school locality complied peacefully with federal court desegregation orders Jan. 25 when 13 Negroes entered Floyd County's 2 formerly all-white high schools in Floyd and Check.

The Virginia Pupil Placement Board Aug. 15 voluntarily assigned 11 Negro students to previously segregated all-white schools in Richmond and Roanoke. The board simultaneously assigned 13 Negroes to white or predominantly white schools in Alexandria and Richmond, both of which previously had been integrated. The assignments raised to 10 the number of Virginia counties and cities with at least some integration. A previous Pupil Placement Board had assigned Negroes to all-white schools only once in 4 years (in Norfolk, to avoid a federal court contempt citation). This original board had resigned, effective June 1, and Gov. J. Lindsay Almond Jr. had appointed a new board July 21.

The Galax (Va.) High School closed its doors to 285 white Grayson County pupils Sept. 9 rather than admit 8 Grayson County Negroes who had been assigned to it Sept. 9 by U.S. District Judge John Paul in Roanoke. Galax High School previously had accepted white students from the county. Faced with public agitation over the school closing and a petition reportedly signed by 590 of 598 Galax High pupils, the Galax school board Sept. 12 agreed to admit the Grayson County pupils. The agreement was reached at a hearing before Chief Judge Simon E. Sobeloff of the U.S. 4th Circuit Court of Appeals. 7 Negro pupils enrolled quietly Sept. 13.

21 public schools for 3,200 Prince Edward County children remained closed for the 2d school year to avoid integration, but the private Prince Edward School Foundation, charging tuition ($240-$265), enrolled about 1,400 white children by mid-September. The enrolled children were each eligible for state grants of $125-$150 and county grants of $100. 50 of the county's 1,600 Negro pupils were placed in out-of-state schools with the aid of the American Friends Service Committee, and several other Negro pupils also were sent to out-of-state schools. But most Negro children remained out of school.

Dallas (Tex.) Integration Method Revised

U.S. District Judge T. Whitfield Davidson in Dallas June 4 ordered the city school board to start in Sept. 1961 a voluntary "salt-and-pepper" integration plan designating certain schools for integration. Under the plan, white and Negro pupils could go to these schools voluntarily but would not be forced to attend them. Davidson said he thought the plan avoided any possible conflict with state law, which banned integration unless approved by a majority vote of the school district.

The U.S. 5th Circuit Court of Appeals in New Orleans Nov. 30 approved a "stair-step" integration plan for Dallas public schools and reversed Whitefield's approval of the "salt-and-pepper" plan. The "stair-step" plan called for integrating the first grade in Sept. 1961 and an additional grade each year.

Tennessee Desegregation Action

U.S. District Judge Robert L. Taylor in Knoxville, Tenn. Aug. 19 approved the Knoxville school board's grade-a-year desegregation plan but ordered the board to present within reasonable time a plan to permit Negroes to take the technical courses offered at Fulton High School. The plan, which lawyers representing 17 Negro pupils had asked Taylor to disapprove, was similar to Nashville's 3-year-old integration plan. 28 Negro first graders enrolled in 8 previously all-white Knoxville schools Aug. 31. No incidents were reported, but 2 Negro boys were denied admission to technical courses at Fulton High.

Knoxville County schools (as distinguished from Knoxville city schools) desegregated Aug. 30 and became the first in Tennessee to do so without a lawsuit. They authorized Negro first graders to attend previously all-white schools but withheld announcement of the change until the morning of registration—Aug. 30; as a result, there were no Negro applicants. 12 Negroes, however, were denied entrance to higher grades in Knoxville County's all-white schools. (Negroes comprised a little more than 1% of the Knoxville County school population.)

U.S. District Judge William E. Miller in Nashville Oct. 27 ordered Davidson County (Tenn.) schools to desegregate their first 4 grades in Jan. 1961 and thereafter to desegregate an additional grade each year.

Chattanooga's School Board Dec. 20 filed a proposal to desegregate the first 3 grades of selected Chattanooga schools for the 1962 school year. The plan, submitted to meet U.S. District Judge Leslie R. Darr's deadline, called for desegregating an additional grade annually after 1962.

North Carolina Indians Demonstrate

7 Indian children and 5 Indian adults were arrested Sept. 1 for staging "sit-ins" Aug. 31 and Sept. 1 in an effort to gain admittance for the children to all-white Dunn (N.C.) High School in Harnett County. They were accused of violating an order, signed in Lillington, N.C. Sept. 1 by Superior Court Judge W. H. S. Burgwyn, that restrained picketing or "sit-in" activi-

ties at Dunn High School.

As a hearing opened before Burgwyn in Lillington Sept. 2, charges against the Indians were dismissed and an agreement was reached wherein the Indians promised to forego "sit-ins" at Dunn High and the Harnett County Board of Education promised to provide a separate high school for the Indians. 2 Indian teen-agers defied the court order Sept. 5 by attending Dunn High School classes.

Some North Carolina districts provided separate schools for Negroes, whites and Indians, but Harnett County's Indian community—numbering about 75 rural Croatan, Cherokee and Lumbee families—was considered too small by the school board to warrant the separate school the Indians had asked for 6 years previously. Harnett County Indians had been directed to attend East Carolina Indian School 35 miles away in Sampson County.

(7 Negroes were enrolled in 2 formerly all-white Yancey County, N.C. high schools Oct. 17. This was the first North Carolina integration by federal court order.)

SOCIAL-ECONOMIC DEVELOPMENTS

Negro Population Shifts to North & West

Census statistics confirmed that a major movement of the U.S. Negro population had taken place during the first 6 decades of the 20th century. The shift was from the South to the Northern industrial areas—largely to the cities—and to the West. More than 5 million Negroes took part in this migration. Whereas perhaps 90% of American Negroes had lived in the 11 former Confederate states of the Old South in 1900, the proportion declined to about 65% by 1960 [see map]. During this period, the U.S. Negro population was increasing at a greater rate than the general population. In 1900 the country's 8,833,994 Negroes comprised 8½% of the total population of 75,995,575. By 1960 there were 18,871,831 Negroes forming 9½% of the U.S. population of 179,323,175.

Despite this increase of the proportion of Negroes in the total population, the percentage of Negroes in the Southern population declined in the 60-year period as a result of the Northward migration. In South Carolina, for instance, the proportion of Negroes in the population declined from 58.4% in

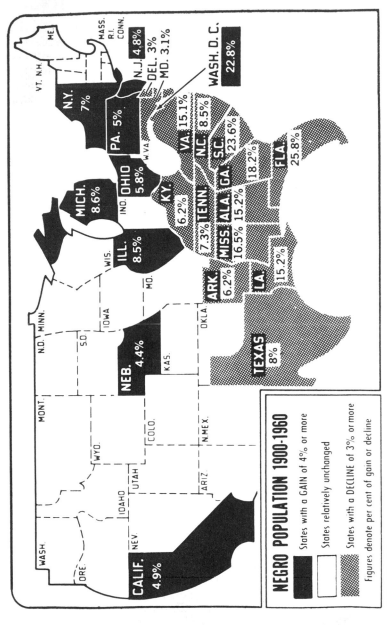

NEGRO POPULATION 1900-1960

States with a GAIN of 4% or more
States relatively unchanged
States with a DECLINE of 3% or more

Figures denote per cent of gain or decline

Wide World map

1900 to 34.8% in 1960. Georgia's drop was from 1900's 46.7% to 1960's 28½%. The biggest percentage gain in Negro population took place in the District of Columbia, where the proportion rose from 31.1% in 1900 to 53.9% in 1960. And New York (where the 1,417,511 Negroes in 1960 accounted for 8.4% of the state population) became the state with the largest number of Negro citizens. 1,087,931 of them were clustered in N.Y. City, where they made up 14% of the population and constituted the most populous urban Negro community in the U.S.

Social Gains Reported

The Labor Department said in a report released by the White House Nov. 2 that in recent years there had been "steady improvement in the social and economic status of Negroes." The report said: (a) Non-white population had risen 25½% since 1950 (the white population gain was 16.2%); (b) non-white males' average earnings rose between 1939 and 1958 from 41% to 58% of comparable white earnings; (c) the number of non-whites living in their own homes rose from 24% in 1940 to 36% in 1958 (comparable figures for whites were 46% in 1940 and 63% in 1958); (d) there was an 11½% non-white unemployment rate in 1959 (the white rate was 4.6%) because "Negro skill rates [had] remaine[d] disproportionately low" (in 1960 unemployment rates averaged 8.7% for non-whites, 4.7% for whites); (e) 1/3 of non-whites lived in northern and western states, 1/3 in southern cities, 1/3 in southern rural areas.

Council Fights Union Bias

1,000 Negro labor unionists met in Detroit May 27-29 and founded the Negro American Labor Council (NALC) to fight all forms of discrimination practiced by unions. The 3-day convention was also dedicated to work for fuller representation on union staffs for the U.S.' estimated 1,250,000 Negro union members.

A. Philip Randolph, sole AFL-CIO Negro vice president and president of its Brotherhood of Sleeping Car Porters, became temporary chairman of the new group at its founding meeting May 27 and was elected NALC president May 29. Delegates from 18 states applauded Randolph's call May 28 for a "civil rights revolution in labor," although he emphasized that the NALC's aim was not to war on the AFL-CIO but to strengthen AFL-CIO prestige among Negroes. Randolph said the new union group would be non-partisan, non-segregated, anti-Communist and "not a black federation of labor."

The formation of the NALC reportedly was opposed by the AFL-CIO leadership, which contended that the AFL-CIO's Civil Rights Committee was capable of dealing with union discrimination. Of 4 AFL-CIO leaders invited to the NALC meeting—Pres. George Meany, Director Boris Shishkin of the federation's Civil Rights Department, Pres. George M. Harrison of the Brotherhood of Railway Clerks and UAW Pres. Walter P. Reuther—only Reuther attended.

At its convention in Cleveland Jan. 19, the Brotherhood of Railroad Trainmen had eliminated race requirements for membership from the union constitution.

Thomas Watkins of Haverstraw, N.Y. became the first Negro president of an integrated lodge in the Brotherhood of Railway Clerks. He defeated his white opponent Jan. 20 by a 2-1 margin to head Lodge 173, a local for N.Y. Central workers in the N.Y. City area. Lodge 173's election in 1958 of a Negro business agent had been challenged and set aside by the national union on the ground that the Negro agent, William R. Scott of Spring Valley, N.Y., had not worked continuously for a year—a union eligibility requirement for elective office.

A conference to explore the needs of Puerto Ricans in the U.S., the first meeting of its kind on a national scale, was held in New York Jan. 15 by the AFL-CIO Community Services with Leo Perlis presiding. Delegates of 90 groups fighting worker exploitation heard AFL-CIO Secy.-Treasurer William F. Schnitzler promise that merged labor would aid them with money and manpower. Regarding discrimination and segregation because of color, he said that "N. Y. City, Newark, Chicago, Cleveland and other northern cities" with many Puerto Ricans "are in no position to point the finger of scorn at the South for its treatment of Negroes."

Housing Discrimination Charged

A Fund for the Republic report, issued Oct. 31 and entitled "Residence and Race," charged that "27 million Americans still suffer[ed] to some extent from housing discrimination because of their race." The report, based upon 3 years' research, was written by University of California Prof. Davis McEntire. It said the groups discriminated against included Negroes, Japanese, Chinese, Filipinos, Mexican-Americans, Puerto Ricans and Jews.

The report said: (a) Discrimination could be attacked best through economic, legal or public opinion pressure aimed at "decision-makers—builders, mortgage lenders, real estate brokers, government agencies . . . "; (b) citizen groups should be mobilized "to effect changes in law and conduct"; (c) minority members should be encouraged to participate in community affairs, and different racial groups should be encouraged to work on common community problems; (d) the supply of low-priced housing should be expanded.

Airport & Bus Terminal Bias Banned

U.S. District Judge Boyd Sloan in Atlanta Jan. 6 issued an injunction ordering the Dobbs Houses, Inc. restaurant at Atlanta's municipal airport to stop discriminating against Negroes. Sloan held that such bias was unconstitutional. The ruling was in a suit brought by Birmingham Negro insurance executive H.D. Coke, who said the management had not let him eat in the regular dining room but had offered him a "table for Negroes" behind a screen.

The Supreme Court, in a 7-2 decision Dec. 5, held that discrimination in bus terminal restaurants operated primarily for the service of interstate passengers was a violation of the Interstate Commerce Act. The majority opinion, written by Justice Hugo L. Black, upheld an appeal argued by the NAACP on behalf of Bruce Boynton, a Negro. Boynton had been fined $10 in 1958 after being denied service and refusing to leave the Trailways Bus Terminal in Richmond, Va. on his Trailways bus trip from Washington to Selma, Ala. Dissenting Justices Charles E. Whittaker and Tom C. Clark held it improper for the court to apply the Commerce Act (introduced by the Justice Department as a friend of the court) because no evidence had been presented that the Trailways Co. owned or controlled either the terminal or the restaurant. Black said "an interstate passenger need not inquire into . . . title . . . in order to determine whether he has a right to be served. . . . "

Restaurant Bias Upheld

The U.S. 4th Circuit Court of Appeals in Richmond, Va. Dec. 27 upheld the right of restaurant operators to select customers

on the basis of color. The ruling upheld a decision of U.S.
District Judge Roszel C. Thomsen, who had ruled in Baltimore
Feb. 16 that an Atlantic White Tower restaurant had violated
no law when it had refused service to Sara Slack, a Negro
reporter for New York's *Amsterdam News*, in June 1957.
Thomsen held that the restaurant's action was a private, not
public matter.

The Delaware Supreme Court had ruled Jan. 11 that
privately owned restaurants in Delaware were not legally
required to serve Negroes. The decision reversed a chancery
court ruling that Wilmington City Councilm. n William H.
Burton, a Negro had been denied service illegally at a private
Wilmington restaurant in a state garage.

Biloxi (Miss.) Riots End Beach Demonstration

The worst race riots in Mississippi history erupted in
Biloxi Apr. 24 when 40 or 50 Negroes sought to swim in the Gulf
of Mexico. The city's entire 26-mile beach was open only to
whites. A crowd of whites attacked the Negroes with sticks,
chains and blackjacks and wounded 4 before being dispersed by
police. Later, 2 white men and 8 Negroes suffered gunshot
wounds in street clashes, and 7 white airmen from nearby
Keesler Air Force Base were attacked by whites.

Police arrested 4 Negroes in an automobile Apr. 24 on the
ground that one had carried a shotgun. One of those arrested
was Dr. Gilbert R. Mason, 31, a leader of the beach demonstrators, who had been in trouble with police before for using
the beach. A justice of the peace found him guilty of disturbing
the peace and obstructing traffic. He fined him $50.

Mayor Laz Quave ordered a curfew, and Keesler officials
told base personnel to keep out of the city unless they had to
visit it on urgent business. Police armed with riot guns
patrolled Biloxi Apr. 24-25. Biloxi Negroes began to boycott
stores whose policies were considered anti-Negro.

The Mississippi Legislature Apr. 27 enacted an anti-riot
law that authorized prison terms of up to 10 years for anybody
convicted of inciting riots in which there was death or injury.

The Justice Department filed suit in U.S. court in Biloxi
May 17 to compel Biloxi city and Harrison County officials to
open a government-reconstructed Gulf of Mexico beach to
Negroes. The suit charged that the officials had violated a
federal contract and the U.S. Constitution by "discriminating

among members of the public on the basis of race or color."
The Justice Department said $1,133,000 of federal aid had been
used in 1951-1953 to repair a seawall and to rebuild and
repair the beach.

A plan to protest racial discrimination at tax-supported
beaches had been announced in Atlanta May 7 at a 10-state
NAACP meeting. Roy Wilkins, NAACP executive secretary,
said the "wade-in" campaign would extend from Cape May,
N.J. to Brownsville, Tex. "this summer." Wilkins said plans
were made at the meeting to boost Negro voter registration
and NAACP membership and to speed school desegregation.
He said the NAACP would continue to guide, advise and support students participating in nonviolent sit-in demonstrations
and similar activities.

Arkansas Listing Attempts Invalid

The Supreme Court Feb. 23 unanimously voided the convictions and fines of 2 Arkansas NAACP leaders who had refused
to give names of members and contributors to city officials.
The court ruled that Mrs. Daisy Bates and Mrs. Birdie
Williams, presidents, respectively, of the state NAACP and of
its North Little Rock branch, could not be punished for denying
Little Rock officials information to which they had no constitutional right. The women had been fined $25 each. They said
they had refused to supply the names because of "the anti-
NAACP climate in the state" and fear that release of the
information might cause harassment and even bodily harm to
those named.

The Supreme Court held by 5-4 Dec. 12 that teachers could
not be required to list all organizations to which they had be-
longed in the previous 5 years. Declaring such a requirement an
impairment of teachers' rights of free association, the court
invalidated as unconstitutional a 1958 Arkansas law that
required every public school and college teacher to file annually an affidavit listing all such organizations. Justices John
Marshall Harlan, Tom C. Clark, Charles E. Whittaker and
Felix Frankfurter dissented on the ground that the court should
act against the state only if the law were used for some unconstitutional purpose, such as to punish teachers backing integration. They pointed out that racial discrimination was not
brought up in the case—althought the law had been adopted as
a weapon against desegregation.

Other Events

A special U.S. grand jury in Biloxi, Miss. Jan. 4 opened an inquiry into the Apr. 1959 lynching of Mack Charles Parker but announced Jan. 14 that it had been unable to indict any alleged lynchers "on the basis of the evidence presented" by the Justice Department. The 23-member jury, including one Negro, had examined suspected lynchers and several FBI agents among the 32 witnesses who testified. The Justice Department had charged that 2 Reconstruction Era laws had been violated.

The UPI had reported Jan. 8 that the FBI report on the case had named 23 white men as "known and suspected participants" in the lynching.

The U.S. 5th Circuit Court of Appeals in New Orleans Apr. 18 upheld a lower court decision that a Montgomery, Ala. city ordinance banning the use of city parks by Negroes was unconstitutional. The court pointed out that Montgomery's parks had been closed "to all peoples of all races since Jan. 1, 1959." It termed this situation "a pyrrhic victory . . . depriving all persons in the city of public park and recreation facilities."

Mississippi's State Sovereignty Commission, meeting secretly, voted unanimously to give the state's segregationist Citizens Councils $20,000 for a radio-TV series, the UPI reported July 9. Among the commission's members: Gov. Ross R. Barnett, who also was a Citizens Council member.

Elijah Muhammad, self-proclaimed prophet and leader of a sect called the Black Muslims, demanded at a meeting of about 4,000 followers in New York July 31 that an exclusively Negro state be created either in America or Africa. He urged the crowd to tell whites: "If we're going to live together, there must be a state for you, a state for us."

A charge against Queens College (N.Y.) of discrimination against Roman Catholics in the hiring and promotion of teachers was filed Oct. 4 with N.Y. Supreme Court Justice Henry Epstein by the N.Y. State Commission Against Discrimination. SCAD's 2-year informal probe of bias charges against Queens College had been stayed Sept. 1 when Epstein issued a temporary injunction on the request of the N.Y. Board of Higher Education. The board said SCAD had no jurisdiction over the municipal college faculty. SCAD's charges were denied by the board Oct. 5 and by Queens College Pres. Harold W. Stoke Oct. 6. Stoke accused faculty members of falsely alleging acts of discrimination "to explain their lack of academic success."

1961

Negro and white integrationists began a series of "Freedom Rides" through the South during 1961; these demonstrations led to violence and arrests— but also to some desegregation of Southern travel facilities. The Kennedy Administration urged Southern leaders to help in stopping incidents of bias toward Negro diplomats. Federal courts continued to order desegregation of Southern public schools, but Southern school desegregation since the 1954 Supreme Court decision remained at less than 7%. Action was taken against *de facto* segregation in several Northern schools. Some gains were reported in Negro efforts to win employment equality. In Congress, civil rights legislation lagged, and the Kennedy Administration was criticized by rights backers for inaction.

FREEDOM RIDES

Violence Erupts on First Ride

A new, dramatic—and sometimes violent—phase of the Negro struggle for equality began May 4 when 6 whites and 7 Negroes left Washington by public bus on the first of a series of "Freedom Rides" through the South to test desegregation of facilities at bus terminals. Their intended destination: New Orleans.

The tour was sponsored by CORE (Congress of Racial Equality). Participants, trained in passive resistance techniques, announced that they would try to use eating counters, waiting rooms, restrooms and other facilities designated for "whites only" at the public bus terminals en route. The number of participants fluctuated as individual members joined or left the group, and the party on occasion split into 2 or more groups as its size, bus facilities or other circumstances warranted.

The first trouble encountered took place May 8 when one of the members, Joseph B. Perkins Jr., 27, a Negro and field secretary of the Freedom Riders, was arrested in Charlotte, N.C. for entering a bus terminal barber shop (he was released May 10). Another, John Lewis, also a Negro, was punched when he tried to enter a restroom at the Greyhound bus terminal in Rock Hill, S.C. May 9. 2 participants in the tour—Henry Thomas, 23, a Negro, and James Douglas Peck, a white—were arrested in Winnsboro, S.C. May 10 after Thomas tried to enter a restaurant (they were held 8 hours).

Serious incidents of violence began to erupt May 14 when the Freedom Riders, traveling in 2 mixed groups aboard 2 buses, were attacked by whites in Anniston and Birmingham, Ala.

The first of the attacks took place when one of the groups stopped in Anniston to get sandwiches. According to a member of the group, Dr. Walter Bergman, 61, a former Michigan State University professor, 3 policemen stood nearby while about 10 whites beat and kicked passengers. Peck was injured and later admitted to a hospital in Birmingham, the bus' next stop. There, according to an eyewitness report by Howard K. Smith of the Columbia Broadcasting System, 30-40 white "toughs," who had been waiting all day, "grabbed the passengers into alleys and corridors, pounding them with pipes, with key rings and with fists. . . . Police did not appear until around 10 minutes later, when the hoodlums had got into waiting cars and moved down the street . . . where I watched some of them discussing their achievements. . . . That took place just under Police Commissioner [Eugene] Connor's window."

Alabama state investigator Ell M. Cowling was on the 2d CORE bus when it arrived in Anniston May 14. About 200 whites milled about, and several bus windows were broken. The bus left with the crowd following by car. Several miles outside Anniston a tire went flat. This forced the bus to stop, and Cowling tried to keep the white mob from storming the bus. Then a fire bomb was thrown into the bus, and the bus was destroyed by fire while CORE members fled. 12 were hospitalized briefly for smoke inhalation. 2 patrolmen, summoned from a nearby house, arrived and dispersed the crowd by firing shots into the air.

The Justice Department said May 15 that Atty. Gen. Robert F. Kennedy had telephoned Alabama officials to urge police protection for the Freedom Riders. Gov. John Patterson later released a statement in which he refused "to guarantee their safe passage."

The original Freedom Riders were reinforced in Birmingham by volunteers from the Nashville Non-Violent Movement. This movement included students from Nashville colleges who were veterans of sit-in demonstrations that had won integration of Nashville lunch counters and movies and had helped increase job opportunities for Negroes. Using the tactics of "Christian non-violence," the students had taught or demonstrated elsewhere in the South. The Rev. James Lawson Jr., who had worked under the Rev. Dr. Martin Luther King Jr., principal Negro leader of the non-violent campaign to win integration, had established teaching workshops in such tactics while he was a student at Vanderbilt University in 1958.

15 Negroes and 2 whites were jailed in Birmingham May 17 after trying to take a scheduled bus from the city. The driver refused to drive if the group, which included 8 students from Tennessee, boarded the bus. 10 of the group, including the 2 whites, had arrived in Birmingham on the bus an hour before the arrests. The others had met them at the bus station. 14 of those jailed were held in protective custody. 2 others were charged with failing to obey an officer (they were fined $25 each, but the fines were suspended), and the Rev. Fred L. Shuttlesworth, president of the Alabama Christian Council on Human Relations, was charged with interfering with and refusing to obey an officer.

7 of the Negro college students from Nashville were removed from jail May 19 and taken by police to the Tennessee line. Refusing to go back to Tennessee, they returned to Birmingham and joined 11 other Negroes and 3 whites at the Greyhound bus terminal's "white" waiting room to continue the Freedom Ride. After waiting almost 18 hours, they boarded a bus to Montgomery, Ala.

When the bus from Birmingham arrived in Montgomery May 20, the Freedom Riders were immediately attacked by a mob of about 200 whites. Police Commissioner Lester B. Sullivan, sitting in a car on the side of the station away from the fighting, told a reporter: "We have no intention of standing guard for a bunch of troublemakers coming into our city." Police arrived 10 minutes after the fighting began, but the crowd, swollen to about 1,000, continued to beat Freedom Riders and several newsmen with clubs and fists. An hour and 15 minutes after the violence had started, 11 mounted sheriff's deputies and 10 more police cars arrived. Then, with the aid of tear gas, the authorities halted the rioting.

On learning of the Montgomery incident, Pres. John F. Kennedy May 20 expressed "deepest concern" and ordered the Attorney General "to take all necessary steps." He called on Alabama state and city officials to "meet their responsibilities" and on Alabama citizens and visitors to refrain from provocative actions. Immediately after the President's statement was released, Atty. Gen. Kennedy announced that about 350-400 U. S. marshals were being dispatched to Montgomery He said the marshals were being sent "to assist state and local authorities in the protection of persons and property and vehicles."

A mob of about 1,000 whites formed the evening of May 21 and was held in uneasy check by U.S. marshals across the street from Montgomery's First Baptist Church, where about 1,500 Negroes held a well-publicized mass meeting at which the Rev. Ralph D. Abernathy, 34, pastor of the church and president of the Montgomery Improvement Association, introduced the Freedom Riders. A rock was hurled into the church, and several tear gas bombs thrown at the mob were tossed back at the marshals. Inside the church, the Rev. Dr. Martin Luther King Jr., who had come to Montgomery to advise Negroes in the situation, phoned Atty. Gen. Kennedy to express his concern for the Negroes' safety. Just prior to the call, Kennedy, after a report that the mob was forming, had phoned Pres. Kennedy in Middleburg, Va. to inform him of the situation.

Faced with this threat to peace, Gov. Patterson proclaimed martial law in Montgomery May 21, and National Guardsmen late May 21 took up posts around the church. The Negroes inside were told to remain and were given police and National Guard escorts home early May 22.

The Alabama Congressional delegation asked Atty. Gen. Kennedy May 22 to withdraw the marshals from Montgomery. Kennedy promised in a reply May 23 that the marshals, used with "great reluctance," would not remain "a minute longer than is necessary."

Patterson ended martial law in Montgomery May 29 and praised the National Guard for showing "the world that this state can and will continue to maintain law and order without the aid of federal force."

(The Greyhound Corp. May 24 announced the dismissal of 3 employes of its Montgomery bus terminal who had refused to serve 2 Negroes Apr. 30. One of the Negroes, J. L. LeFore, said he and a Negro companion had been served at the terminal May 15 after they had complained to Greyhound and the Interstate Commerce Commission about the Apr. 30 incident.)

Clergymen Arrested in Montgomery

11 integrationists, including the Rev. William Sloane Coffin Jr., 36, Yale University chaplain, were arrested in Montgomery May 25 when they sought service at a segregated lunch counter at the Trailways bus terminal. 6 of those arrested had accompanied Coffin by bus from Atlanta. 3 were whites, the Rev. Gaylord B. Noyce, 34, a Yale Divinity School associate professor, Dr. John Maguire, 28, and Dr. David Swift, 47, both Wesleyan University (Middletown, Conn.) professors of religion; and 3 were Negroes, Clyde L. Carter and Joseph Charles Jones, both Johnson C. Smith University (Charlotte, N.C.) theological students, and George B. Smith, 24, a Yale law student. The other 4 arrested were Negro integration leaders who had joined Coffin's group in Montgomery: the Rev. Ralph Abernathy, the Rev. Fred L. Shuttlesworth, the Rev. Wyatt Tee Walker, chairman of the Atlanta Southern Christian Leadership Conference, and Atlanta student leader Bernard S. Lee. All were released on bond.

Coffin's bus group had arrived peacefully in Montgomery

May 24. Their Greyhound bus from Atlanta had been escorted from the Georgia-Alabama line by state and city police. 200 National Guardsmen were on duty near the Montgomery station when the bus arrived. Several hundred persons had gathered. The integrationists did not enter the terminal but got into 2 waiting cars, one driven by Abernathy. Shuttlesworth and the Rev. Dr. King also met the group.

Coffin's group had given notice of its intended appearance at the lunch counter (where 2 groups of Freedom Riders had been served without incident May 24) and had been warned that it faced arrest. Coffin said his group had assembled on impulse to exercise "academic freedom" and was not associated directly with other Freedom Riders.

The 11 members of Coffin's group were convicted of breach of the peace and unlawful assembly by County Court Common Pleas Judge Alex Marks in Montgomery Sept. 15. 10 were fined $100 each plus costs and sentenced to 10-90 days in jail. Walker was sentenced to 90 days in jail on an unlawful assembly charge. The convictions were upheld in Montgomery Nov. 20 by Circuit Court Judge Eugene Carter. All were released on appeal.

15 Protestant Episcopal priests were arrested in Jackson, Miss. Sept. 13 after seeking service at the city's segregated Trailways bus terminal restaurant. The group was composed of 3 Negroes and 12 whites, including the Rev. Robert L. Pierson, 35, N.Y. Gov. Nelson A. Rockefeller's son-in-law. They were part of a 27-man group on a Southern "prayer pilgrimage" sponsored by the Episcopal Society for Cultural & Racial Unity. They were convicted Sept. 15, fined $200 each and sentenced to 4 months in jail. All were later freed on bond.

Rides Banned in Alabama

U.S. District Judge Frank M. Johnson Jr. in Montgomery June 2 issued restraining orders to halt interstate travel through Alabama "for the purpose of testing segregation laws." Johnson simultaneously issued a preliminary injunction to bar the Montgomery Police Department from withholding protection from interstate passengers and to prevent the Ku Klux Klan from interfering with interstate travel.

Johnson acted in a suit brought by the Justice Department May 24. He had held hearings May 29-June 1. In his June 2 ruling, Johnson accused the Montgomery police and, specifically, Police Commissioner Lester B. Sullivan and Police Chief Goodwin J. Ruppenthal of "willful and deliberate failure" to protect interstate passengers who arrived in Montgomery May 20.

Johnson conceded that Freedom Rides "may be a legal right," but he said the public's right "to be protected from the evils of their conduct is a greater and more important right." His order applied to "any individual or group" "sponsoring, financing, assisting or encouraging" Freedom Rides and specifically included: CORE, the Southern Christian Leadership Conference; the Student Nonviolent Movement; the Montgomery City Jail Council (established the week before by 11 jailed Freedom Riders); King, Abernathy, Shuttlesworth, Walker and the Rev. Solomon S. Seay Sr.

Johnson's ban on Freedom Riders in Alabama expired June 12 after Johnson postponed a scheduled hearing that day on his earlier ruling. Johnson warned that his original restraining orders might be reinstated "if it becomes necessary." The postponement was ordered because of failure to notify CORE and other defendants formally.

(In Montgomery Nov. 1, Johnson barred authorities from enforcing racial barriers on public buses or at terminals. Johnson's ruling was made in a case brought by 6 Negro Freedom Riders who had been involved in the May riots.)

Riders arrested in Jackson

27 Freedom Riders rode in 2 buses from Montgomery to Jackson, Miss. May 24 and were arrested in Jackson within minutes of their arrival. (But before leaving Montgomery some Freedom Riders were served at the previously segregated lunch counter in the city's Trailways terminal.)

The first bus from Montgomery left at 9:12 a.m. On it were Alabama Adjutant Gen. Henry V. Graham, 11 Negro and one white Freedom Riders, 17 newsmen and 6 armed National Guardsmen. A squad of city motorcycle police preceded the bus to the city limits, where 16 highway patrol cruisers carrying National Guardsmen and state troopers took over. 20 cars with reporters trailed behind, and 3 L-19 reconnaissance planes and 2 helicopters flew overhead. 1,000 National Guardsmen were stationed along U.S. Route 80, the road the bus took.

In Alabama there were no major incidents. Rest stops were made at isolated spots. At Demopolis a hard object struck the bus. At the Mississippi line, Graham and the Alabama Guardsmen were replaced by Lt. Col. Gillespie V. Montgomery (who also was a state senator) and 7 Mississippi National Guardsmen. In Mississippi the bus stopped only once to change drivers.

During the trip the Rev. James M. Lawson, one of the Freedom Rider passengers, told reporters: "We see this ride as one that is attempting to get the nation to make a final decision on segregation." He reiterated a statement made by King, as he saw the group off from Montgomery, that the trip under military escort was not a "valid" test of segregation.

The bus terminal at Jackson was cordoned off by police, who held 3 leashed dogs. About 100 Guardsmen were stationed nearby when the bus arrived at 3:55 p.m. The Freedom Riders disembarked and were arrested minutes later as they tried to enter the terminal's "white" restrooms.

The 2d busload—14 Negroes and one white—arrived in Jackson at 6:47 p.m., and all 15 were arrested 3 minutes later for refusing Police Capt. J. L. Ray's demand they leave the terminal's "white" cafeteria.

Freedom Riders arrested included James L. Farmer, executive director of CORE, and the Rev. C. T. Vivian, 36, of Nashville, Tenn. (Farmer sent from his Jackson jail cell May 25 instructions to extend the Freedom Ride movement to rail and air terminals.)

Freedom Riders continued to flock into Jackson—and into the arms of the police—by bus, train and plane. Many refused to post appeal bonds or pay fines and took the option of remaining in jail to work out their fines at $3 a day. By June 12 the Hinds County jail in Jackson was overcrowded and Freedom Riders convicted of breach of the peace were being transferred to the Mississippi State Penitentiary outside of town. Eventually, more than 300 Freedom Riders were arrested in Jackson.

Among subsequent Freedom Rides reported from Jackson:
▲ A group of 5 whites and 3 Negroes, led by James K. Davis Jr., a South Carolina Negro, arrived aboard a train from New Orleans May 30 and was arrested for refusing to leave the "white" waiting room.
▲ 5 whites and 2 Negroes who arrived by bus from New Orleans June 6 were arrested, fined $200 each and were sentenced to 4 months in jail (2 months of the terms suspended).
▲ 3 Negroes were arrested June 7 when they tried to use dining and restroom facilities at the Municipal Airport after a "Free-

dom Flight" from St. Louis.

▲ Percy Sutton, 40, a Negro and head of the Manhattan (N.Y. City) chapter of the NAACP (National Association for the Advancement of Colored People), and N.Y. Assemblyman Mark Lane, 33, white, were arrested June 8 when they sought to use segregated restroom facilities at the airport after a flight from Montgomery. Both were freed on $500 appeal bonds. (Sutton and Lane had arrived in Montgomery June 7 aboard a Greyhound bus and had been served without incident at the terminal restaurant. Montgomery bus terminal waiting-room signs with the words "colored intrastate passengers" and "white intrastate passengers" had been removed by the Greyhound Corp.)

▲ 5 Negroes and 4 white girls who arrived by train from New Orleans were arrested June 8 when they refused to leave the station's segregated waiting-room.

▲ 14 Freedom Riders, mostly California college students, were arrested at the train terminal after alighting from a passenger train June 20.

▲ 5 Negro and 4 white Freedom Riders were arrested when they entered the "white only" waiting room at the Jackson Trailways bus station June 21. (This group, aboard a Greyhound bus from Atlanta, had arrived June 20 in Montgomery, where about 60 policemen, firemen and other officers surrounded the terminal and a crowd of 400-500 watched. The group, led by the Rev. Wyatt Tee Walker, did not enter the terminal after being told that 2 anonymous bomb threats had been received. No bombs were found.)

▲ 11 Negro and 9 white Freedom Riders (14 from California) were arrested June 25 after refusing to leave the segregated waiting room of the train terminal following a ride from New Orleans.

Supreme Court Justice Hugo L. Black July 26 denied a writ of *habeas corpus* for Elizabeth Porter Wyckoff, 45, a white Freedom Rider who had been convicted in Jackson. The denial, concurred in by Justice Tom C. Clark, was on the ground that it had not been proven that the state had no legal processes available for her appeal. (U.S. District Judge Sidney C. Mize had refused Miss Wyckoff a *habeas corpus* writ on similar grounds. In his written opinion July 3, Mize said that the arrests of Freedom Riders in Mississippi had prevented more racial violence.)

An appeal to federal court by 5 other Freedom Riders con-

victed in Jackson was denied by U.S. Judge Harold Cox
in Jackson Aug. 26. Cox said the riders' "status as interstate passengers is extremely doubtful. Their destination was Jackson but their objective was trouble."

The Supreme Court Dec. 18 refused to stay prosecution of the more than 300 Freedom Riders arrested in Jackson.
The NAACP, with the Justice Department's endorsement,
had sought the stay pending appeal of a Nov. 17 U.S. court
ruling that rejected a request for an injunction against
enforcement of segregation at Mississippi travel terminals.
The latter case had been brought by the NAACP on behalf
of 3 Jackson Negroes, none of whom were involved in the
Freedom Rider arrests. It had been rejected by the lower
court on the ground that all possible state court action had
not yet been exhausted. The NAACP sought Supreme Court
intervention because of the costly court action necessitated
in the Jackson Freedom Rider cases. In all cases brought
thus far to the county court, the convictions, first imposed
by city court, had been upheld. Mississippi officials rebuffed efforts to allow a single test case to be taken through
the entire court process.

Negro Riders Attacked in McComb (Miss.)

Negro Freedom Riders were attacked or menaced by
white mobs at the Greyhound bus terminal in McComb, Miss.
Nov. 29-Dec. 2. The violence erupted after a 3-judge federal
court in Jackson, Miss. Nov. 21 had ordered McComb authorities to comply with an ICC ruling by removing bus and
railroad terminal signs designating separate waiting rooms
for Negro and white intrastate passengers. Judge Sidney
C. Mize, sole dissenter in the Nov. 21 court order, issued
Dec. 2 a temporary injunction barring further Freedom
Rides in McComb. Mize's order, requested by McComb
authorities and the Greyhound terminal managers, was served
Dec. 3 on CORE.

The violence had begun Nov. 29 when 5 young Negroes
from New Orleans sought service at the ticket window and
lunch counter. A white youth struck one of the Negroes.
Other whites then joined in beating all the Negroes. The
Negroes, none severely injured, escaped in a taxi. 5 minutes
later police arrived from city hall, a block away. The 5
Negroes stayed overnight at a Negro hotel and then, escorted

by police to the terminal, boarded a New Orleans bus as a-
gents of the Federal Bureau of Investigation watched. The
riders were led by Jerome Smith, 22, president of CORE's
New Orleans chapter.

Members of a 2d CORE-sponsored Freedom Ride to
McComb escaped attack Dec. 1 although they were threatened by a mob of 500-700 whites, some of whom did beat
or threaten 4 out-of-town newsmen. The 6 Negro riders
arrived aboard a bus from Baton Rouge, La. Protected
by McComb's 15-man police force, they entered the station
but left in a car after a few minutes. The riders later returned to the station. Guarded by police reinforced by 2
sheriffs and 10 deputies from nearby counties, they safely
boarded an outgoing bus. The white mob dispersed after the
bus' departure.

A small group of whites menaced an unheralded 3d Freedom
Ride into and out of McComb Dec. 2. 3 Negroes arrived
aboard a bus from Jackson, spent a few minutes in the
terminal's "white" waiting room, then entered a waiting car
driven by CORE Field Secy. Thomas Gaither, a Negro. 4 whites
attacked the car but were repulsed by police, and nobody was
injured.

John Oliver Emmerich, 61, a white, editor of the *McComb
Enterprise-Journal*, was attacked in McComb Dec. 3 by a
white. Emmerich said the man had complained about out-
of-town newsmen using the *Journal*'s office as headquarters.

Racial unrest had broken out previously in McComb
when students from a Negro high school had held sit-ins
Aug. 27 and Aug. 29 at a variety store and the bus terminal.
5 were arrested, including Brenda Travis, 15, who was released to Juvenile Court. The other 4, convicted of breach
of the peace, were fined $400 each, sentenced to 8 months
in jail, but freed on appeal. When the 5 were refused readmission to school, 116 students walked out of school in
protest Oct. 4 and marched to city hall. All were arrested
including Brenda Travis. Juvenile Court then sentenced her
to serve a year at a state school for juvenile delinquents.
The others under 18 were released. 19, including one white,
Robert Zellner, an SNCC field secretary, were held on charges
of breach of the peace. Zellner's group was convicted by a
city court Oct. 31. 11 were fined $200 each and sentenced
to 4 months in jail; 4 others who had participated in the
sit-ins were fined $500 each and given 6-month terms.

Movement Spreads

Civil rights leaders had taken action to attract sympathizers from every possible part of the country, and the arrests of a growing number of demonstrators from neighboring and Northern states gave evidence of the success of these efforts. The Southern Christian Leadership Conference, the Student Nonviolent Coordinating Committee, the Nashville Christian Leadership Council and CORE had established in Atlanta May 26 a Freedom Ride Coordinating Committee. Edward B. King Jr., 21, named recruiting chief for the committee, said May 26 that members in 16 Southern states and the District of Columbia were being asked to volunteer for Freedom Rides and to picket bus terminals. NAACP Executive Secy. Roy Wilkins in New York May 25 had urged Negro college students to return home at the end of the school year on a "nonsegregated transportation basis," to "sit where you choose" and to use terminal facilities "without discrimination." Wilkins, however, said in Jackson, Miss. June 7 that the NAACP preferred to test laws in court, not by "staying in jail."

Ex-Pres. Harry S. Truman told reporters in New York June 2 that Northerners who took part in Freedom Rides in the South were meddlesome intruders who "stir up trouble." Southerners, however, had a right to test the laws and customs of their own states because this was "their own business," Truman said. Truman had similarly opposed the Negro sit-in movement in 1960.

The Freedom Ride movement spread to Florida and other Southern states during the later half of 1961.

Among the first Freedom Riders arrested in Florida were 7 white and 3 Negro clergymen detained in Tallahassee June 16 for refusing to leave the airport terminal. They had waited 24 hours to enter the closed restaurant there. They posted $500 bond each and were released June 17. (2 Negroes and a white from Tallahassee were also arrested with the 10 Freedom Riders at the airport after refusing to disperse.) The 10 clergymen were convicted by a city court June 22 of unlawful assembly. They were ordered to pay fines of $500 each or to serve 60 days in jail. All posted $1,000 bonds.

The 10 were part of a CORE-trained group of 18 clergymen, including 4 rabbis, who had begun their Freedom Ride on a regularly scheduled bus from Washington. They had arrived in Raleigh, N.C. June 13, spent the night at Shaw University campus, then proceeded to Sumter, S.C., Savannah, Ga. and Jacksonville, Fla. before arriving June 15 in Tallahassee, where they were served without incident at the Greyhound bus terminal. Their only refusal of service prior to Tallahassee had occurred in Lake City, Fla. 8 of the group flew to New York June 15. The 10 who were arrested had stayed to test the airport restaurant's policy.

(U.S. District Judge G. Harold Carswell ordered Tallahassee Oct. 17 to end segregation at its airport facilities.)

7 white and 7 Negro Freedom Riders had been unmolested during a similar CORE-sponsored trip on a regularly scheduled bus from Washington. They had arrived June 13 in Raleigh, S.C. Then 2 of them joined the clergymen and proceeded to Wilmington, where police were on guard and about 150 persons watched their arrival. Splitting into 2 groups and rejoining for overnight stops in Charleston, S.C., Jacksonville and Tampa, the Freedom Riders finally arrived in St. Petersburg June 16. Other unmolested Freedom Riders included 4 Negroes and a white woman who had eaten with the clergymen at the Jacksonville bus terminal June 15 before leaving for Thomasville, Ga. and then riding through Florida.

One white and 2 Negro Freedom Riders were arrested in Ocala, Fla. June 16 after a slight scuffle with 2 white men who blocked them from the bus station's cafeteria. 4 other Freedom Riders obeyed police and returned to the bus. Those arrested—the Rev. Leslie Lee Smith, 35, of Albany, N.Y., Herbert A. Collendar, 27, of Mahwah, N.J., both Negroes, and James O'Conner, 31, Barnard College (N.Y.) economics instructor—pleaded not guilty June 21 to charges of unlawful assembly and failure to obey a police officer. Smith and O'Connor were convicted by a county court in Ocala July 17. Smith's sentence was 30 days in jail plus a $500 fine or 6 months in jail; O'Conner's was a $250 fine or 90 days in jail. Collendar, convicted Aug. 22, was fined $300 and sentenced to 6 months.

4 Freedom Riders were arrested in Little Rock, Ark. July 10 after refusing to leave the bus terminal's "white" waiting room. The group, which had traveled from St. Louis, was led by the Rev. B. Elton Cox, 30, field secretary of CORE's St. Louis branch. They were convicted July 12 by Little Rock Municipal Judge Quinn Glover on breach-of-the-peace charges. Glover ordered them to serve 6 months

in jail and to pay fines of $500 each, but he suspended the sentences July 13 in return for the riders' promise to leave Arkansas without further tests of the state's segregated transportation facilities. The group continued by bus to Shreveport, La. July 14. The terminal was guarded by police, and they did not try to use its segregated facilities. (4 Negroes from Shreveport were arrested at the city's Continental Trailways bus terminal Aug. 4 after trying to use the segregated facilities.)

ICC Bars Discrimination on Interstate Buses

The Interstate Commerce Commission Sept. 22 issued rules requested by Atty. Gen. Kennedy May 29 to prohibit racial discrimination in interstate buses and bus facilities. The ICC ruled unanimously that, effective Nov. 1, interstate buses and terminals must display signs saying that seating there was "without regard to race, color, creed, or national origin." Interstate carriers were also banned, effective Nov. 1, from using terminal facilities where travelers were segregated by race. The anti-bias sign was to be printed on interstate tickets by 1963.

The ICC ruling was obeyed Nov. 1 at the McComb Greyhound station, but McComb police then put signs denoting segregated waiting rooms on the pavement outside the terminal. The 3-judge federal court in Jackson Nov. 21, acting on a suit brought by the Justice Department Nov. 2, barred McComb from interfering with its bus or train terminal desegregation. McComb Mayor C. H. Douglas said Nov. 27 that the city would comply. He said Nov. 30 that the police had not been at the station when Freedom Riders had been attacked because their presence could have been interpreted as an attempt to enforce or coerce segregation.

The Nov. 21 decision simultaneously declared unconstitutional 3 Mississippi segregation laws. The laws provided for the posting of segregation signs at terminals and for the maintenance and enforcement of the use of segregated facilities there. The decision was not unanimous: Appellate Judges Elbert P. Tuttle of Atlanta and Richard T. Rives of Montgomery concurred; Judge Mize dissented.

The ICC ruling was defied Nov. 1 when 3 Negroes were arrested in Jackson, Miss. and 4 were arrested in Atlanta for trespassing on "white" terminal facilities. The 7 Negroes were participating in CORE-sponsored desegregation tests. In Louisiana, a Shreveport bus station manager was arrested Nov. 1 for refusing to remove the ICC's anti-segregation sign, and a Monroe bus station was ordered to replace segregation signs removed under the ICC ruling.

A 3-judge federal court in Greenville, Miss. Nov. 20 barred efforts to enforce segregation at the Greenwood bus terminal. Leflore County Atty. John Fraiser had sought a state court injunction against removal of the terminal's segregation signs. The order said the bus terminal manager was entitled to remove the signs despite state laws calling for such signs.

The Justice Department sued in U.S. district court in Shreveport Dec. 15 for the removal of racial segregation signs in the Ruston, La. Trailways bus terminal. Such signs had been removed but later had been replaced by order of State District Judge J. R. Dawkins at the request of District Atty. Ragan D. Madden.

A suit seeking to ban state or local interference with compliance with the ICC ruling had been filed in U.S. district court in Oxford, Miss. by the Justice Department Oct. 31. The suit also sought an injunction against enforcement of an Oct. 27 state court order to the Greyhound Corp. to maintain segregation signs in its Greenwood, Miss. terminal. In a similar suit filed in New Orleans Sept. 1 the department requested that a Louisiana law requiring segregated bus terminal facilities be declared unconstitutional and that Baton Rouge officials be barred from enforcing it. A suit seeking injunctions against the enforcement of Louisiana segregation laws in Monroe, La. was filed in U.S. district court in Shreveport by the department Nov. 3. A similar suit against Alexandria, La. was filed by the department in Shreveport Nov. 22.

Mass Arrests in Albany (Ga.)

737 Negroes, including the Rev. Dr. Martin Luther King Jr., were arrested in Albany, Ga. Dec. 12-16 as a result of 5 mass marches on city hall. Negro leaders suspended the marches Dec. 18 after agreement with city officials on a plan providing for the temporary release of those arrested and for negotiations on removing racial barriers.

The marches had begun in protest against the trial of Freedom Riders arrested Dec. 10 at the Central of Georgia

Railway station. The riders, 5 Negroes and 4 whites, had arrived from Atlanta and had entered the "white" waiting room, where segregation signs had been removed as required by ICC regulations. The riders complied with Police Chief Laurie Pritchett's order to leave, but they and 2 other Negroes were arrested outside the terminal and charged with disorderly conduct, obstructing traffic, failing to obey the police and disturbing the peace.

When the riders went on trial Dec. 12 about 400 Negro students, singing hymns, marched 3 abreast around city hall. 267, including 61 juveniles, were arrested on charges of disorderly conduct and blocking the sidewalks.

3 mass marches Dec. 13 lead to the arrest of 205 Negroes. During the day 21 Negroes entered the Trailways bus terminal, where some used the "white" waiting room and some were served in the lunchroom. 9 of the latter were arrested but were released shortly afterwards.

The Freedom Rider trial ended Dec. 14. 10 were held for county court on a new state charge of unlawful assembly. 4 of the 10 were released after posting bonds of $750-$1,000 each; 6 remained in jail.

King, the Rev. Ralph D. Abernathy and W. G. Anderson, leader of the Albany Movement (which had sponsored the protests), 262 other Negroes and a white youth were arrested after a march Dec. 16.

The demonstrations had been marked by a conflict over Negro leadership. The groups involved were the Albany Movement, a coalition of Negro groups mainly supported by the Student Nonviolent Coordinating Committee (SNCC), and King's Southern Christian Leadership Conference (SCLC). The SCLC leaders had arrived after the demonstrations had started, and Abernathy of the SCLC was reported to have spoken of the SCLC assuming command.

The peace plan was negotiated Dec. 18 by Mayor Asa D. Kelley, Marion S. Page (secretary of the Albany Movement and a Negro) and Donald L. Holowell (lawyer for the SNCC and a Negro). Under the plan, the Negroes agreed to end, for 60 days, mass protests and a boycott against white merchants; the city agreed to (a) comply with the ICC's terminal desegregation ruling, (b) release any arrested marcher able to get a signature bond, (c) reduce bonds on the Freedom Riders, (d) allow the Negroes to present desegregation demands Jan. 11, 1962.

King at first refused bond after his arrest. He said he would stay in jail during Christmas as a symbol of protest. But after talks with Anderson, who was jailed with him, King agreed to go free on bond.

Some Travel Facilities Desegregated Voluntarily

Atty. Gen. Kennedy announced Oct. 16 that the Illinois Central, the Southern and the Louisville & Nashville railroads had agreed to desegregate their terminal facilities. The agreement had resulted from a month of discussions by Asst. Atty. Gen. Burke Marshall and Southern Railway counsel Francis M. Shea, spokesman for the 3 lines.

The agreement had been disclosed earlier Oct. 16 by Dr. King after a meeting with Pres. Kennedy. (King said he had met with the President to urge the issuance of "a 2d Emancipation Proclamation" and an executive order banning segregation in public housing. He said he had also requested investigation of Negro voting rights in Mississippi.)

The voluntary desegregation of facilities at the Raleigh-Durham, N.C. and Columbus, Ga. airports was also announced by Atty. Gen. Kennedy Oct. 16.

DIPLOMATS MEET BIAS

Incidents in Maryland

Pres. Kennedy urged Maryland civic leaders Sept. 25 to extend "voluntary cooperation for an immediate end to segregation in restaurants and other places of public service." The appeal, in a telegram to 200 Maryland civic leaders meeting in Aberdeen as guests of the White House, fortified a State Department drive to prevent further instances of bias toward African diplomats. (The State Department's chief of protocol, Angier Biddle Duke, had met Sept. 12 with representatives of 30 states to discuss ways to assure that traveling African diplomats would encounter no bias. The governors of Mississippi, Alabama and South Carolina had refused to send representatives to the meeting.)

A public appeal to the Maryland Legislature to pass a bill banning segregation in public facilities was made by the State Department Sept. 13. The appeal said that during a 2-week period 4 African ambassadors "were humiliated by private restaurant owners . . . in Maryland." Gov. J. Millard Tawes publicly apologized for the 4 incidents July 11.

One incident had occurred Mar. 9 when Dr. William Fitzjohn, chief Sierra Leone diplomat in the U.S., had been denied service at a Howard Johnson restaurant in Hagerstown. Apologies were made by the State Department and by Pres. John F. Kennedy, who invited Fitzjohn to a meeting at the White House. Fitzjohn and other Sierra Leone dignitaries later attended in Hagerstown June 23 a banquet in their honor arranged by Duke and Mayor Winslow F. Burhans.

Another incident took place June 26 when Chad's Amb.-to-U.S. Adam Malick Sow, en route to present his credentials to Pres. Kennedy, was denied service at a restaurant.

A Nigerian diplomat, Aliyn Y. Bida, 38, and his family were denied service Oct. 3 at a highway restaurant northeast of Baltimore. They later dined in a 2d restaurant in the area in a section reserved for Negroes.

A scheduled Nov. 11 mass Freedom Ride on U.S. Route 40 in Maryland was canceled Nov. 8 by CORE's executive director, James L. Farmer, after he had been informed that 35 restaurants along the route had agreed to desegregate starting Nov. 22. CORE, concentrating on Route 40 because the incidents involving diplomats had occurred on that road, had announced Nov. 3 that about 1,400 Freedom Riders would test segregation policies there unless a "substantial number" of restaurants were desegregated.

About 500 Freedom Riders staged sit-ins Dec. 16 in about 40 restaurants along Route 40 between Baltimore and New Castle, Del. The riders, whites and Negroes, traveled in about 100 cars. They were served without incident in many restaurants, but at least 8 riders, including James Peck, were arrested on trespassing charges in other restaurants. Farmer had said Dec. 15 that the ride would be undertaken because 13 of the 35 restaurants "went back on their word" to desegregate by Nov. 11.

More than 300 Negro and white students demonstrated at restaurants in Baltimore, Annapolis and Ferndale, Md. Nov. 11, and 33 were under arrest by nightfall. The 22 arrested in Baltimore included the Rev. Logan Kearse, leader of the group. The demonstrators, most of them CORE members, limited their activities to peaceful picketing and sit-ins except at Hooper's restaurant in Baltimore, where entry was forced after the management had tried to block it.

5 Negro NAACP members were arrested on trespassing charges in a sit-in in a diner near Baltimore Oct. 27. They were convicted and fined $100 each by the Baltimore County Circuit Court in Towson, Md. Dec. 8.

(Other integrationists arrested on similar charges in Maryland included 14 in Annapolis Dec. 2, 6 in Baltimore Dec. 22 and 10 in Crisfield Dec. 24.)

Action Against Discrimination in Washington

State Department representatives conferred with Washington, D.C. real estate men July 6 and July 10 in a successful drive to open apartments to rental by Negro diplomats.

State Department protocol chief Duke confirmed Aug. 8 that he had resigned his 20-year membership in Washington's fashionable Metropolitan Club because of its policy of withholding membership from Negro diplomats. The club traditionally had granted honorary membership to all ambassadors posted to Washington but had discontinued the policy when the emergence of new African nations had resulted in the assignment of Negroes as ambassadors. Atty. Gen. Robert F. Kennedy, also a member, had urged in July that the club stop excluding Negroes. Kennedy resigned Sept. 19. Other Administration officials also resigned from the club following Duke's action.

Guinea Aide Vs. N.Y. Police

N.Y. City policemen were accused of racial bias against a Negro UN delegate after a diplomatic car carrying Michel Collet, 38, Guinea's deputy UN representative, bumped into the back of a taxi in Harlem (N.Y. City) Aug. 26. Following the accident, Collet reportedly pushed the taxi-driver and fought with a patrolman who intervened. Collet then was forcibly taken to the police station, where he identified himself and was released.

Statements of regret, but not apology, were made by the State Department, U.S. Amb.-to-UN Adlai E. Stevenson and N.Y. Mayor Robert F. Wagner.

Guinea's chief UN delegate, Diallo Telli, charged Aug. 28 that Collet had been subjected to police brutality and racial discrimination. But N.Y. Police Commissioner Michael J. Murphy, in an Aug. 28 report on the incident to Wagner, denied the charges and accused Collet of being "belligerent" and "profane." Wagner backed the report. All 12 Negro witnesses to the incident, including the Negro taxi-driver whom Collet allegedly pushed, reportedly agreed with the police version.

The incident was taken up Aug. 30 at a UN meeting of representatives of 25 African nations, who then issued a statement deploring the "recurrent and serious incidents" in the U.S. involving African diplomats. 38 of 46 Asian-African members joined Aug. 31 in a statement expressing "outrage" over the affair and their decision to complain to the UN Secretary General. An indication that the group would not press charges before the UN, however, was revealed Sept. 1 by the group's chairman, Chandra S. Jha of India.

The Guinean delegation confirmed Sept. 6 that Collet had been recalled.

African Students Affected

77% of the African students in American colleges said they had encountered racial bias in the U.S., according to a survey conducted by the Institute of International Education (released Dec. 4). The survey included answers from more than 1,208 of the 1,533 African students at 366 American institutions.

Other survey findings: (a) 75% of the Africans attending Northern institutions reported experiencing bias; 15% reported no bias. (b) 49% found bias in restaurants, 44% in housing, 16% in churches. (c) 38% of the African students throughout the U.S. had no American Negro friends; 20% of those attending Southern institutions (all-Negro schools in all but one case) had no U.S. Negro friends (the common reason given was that U.S. Negroes felt superior to the Africans). (d) Despite reported unhappiness over discrimination, 79% were satisfied with their U.S. education.

Pres. Kennedy, greeting 20 top-ranking foreign students in observance of Foreign Student Day Dec. 5, urged Americans to "show the best side of our country" and to invite foreign students into their homes.

2 Nigerian exchange students who had been refused lodging at a motel near Staunton, Ill. July 11 received an apology from Gov. Otto Kerner and ate lunch with the governor Aug. 1.

SIT-IN MOVEMENT

Widespread Effects Reported

The Southern Regional Council (SRC) reported Sept. 29 that the Negro sit-in movement had affected 20 states and more than 100 cities in Southern and border states during the period Feb. 1960-Sept. 1961. At least 70,000 Negroes and whites participated actively, the report said. It estimated that 3,600 had been arrested and that at least 141 students and 58 faculty members had been dismissed by college authorities for alleged participation.

The SRC said that eating facilities in one or more establishments in 108 Southern border-state cities had been desegregated as a result of sit-ins. The number of cities listed: Arkansas 1, Florida 15, Georgia 3, Illinois 3, Kansas 1, Kentucky 9, Maryland 3, Missouri 5, Nevada 2, North Carolina 17, Ohio 1, Oklahoma 5 (116 restaurants were desegregated in Oklahoma City), Tennessee 7, Texas 10, Virginia 23, West Virginia 3. But no desegregation occurred in Alabama, Louisiana, Mississippi or South Carolina.

Desegregation by Negotiation

Many previously segregated restaurants, lunch counters and other eating facilities in Atlanta were desegregated without incident Sept. 28. This was done under an agreement reached by Atlanta Negro and business leaders. Charles Black, chairman of the Committee on Appeal for Human Rights, said that about 300 Negroes had been served for the first time in about 177 Atlanta restaurants in 77 stores and other establishments. The committee represented college students who had led demonstrations against the stores. The original agreement, announced Mar. 7 by the Atlanta Chamber of Commerce, said the Negro and business leaders had agreed (a) to desegregate lunchrooms and other facilities eventually in "the same patterns" by which Atlanta public schools were desegregated in Sept. 1960, (b) to end immediately the Negro sit-in demonstrations, picketing and boycotts against stores that practiced segregation. The stores would continue current segregation until the patterns of school desegregation were established. 500-600 Negroes who had lost jobs in stores affected by sit-ins were to be rehired wherever practicable.

Prior to the settlement, lunch counters had been closed since Thanksgiving 1960 because of the sit-ins, and many Negroes had boycotted the stores. Stores covered by the agreement: Rich's, Sears-Roebuck, Davison's (a Macy's affiliate), the Woolworth, McCrory, S. S. Kresge, H. L. Green, Newberry and Grant variety stores and Walgreen's, Jacob's and Lane drugstores.

Negroes were served at lunch counters in Jacksonville, Fla. May 16 in an uneventful start of integration that reportedly had been planned at meetings of business and Negro leaders.

159 Negroes dined at 36 previously all-white restaurants and cafeterias in Dallas, Tex. July 26 without incident. The demonstration was part of a local movement to prepare the city for the court-ordered integration of schools in September. It had been arranged by a committee of 7 whites and 7 Negroes in cooperation with the Dallas Citizens Council, an all-white organization of Dallas business leaders headed by C. A. Tatum, president of the Dallas Power & Light Co. Prior to the demonstration, a documentary film designed to promote moderation in civil rights had received wide showing in Dallas. The film had been prepared by the council and filmed in Dallas.

The Columbus (Ga.) Chamber of Commerce announced Dec. 11 that some downtown Columbus lunch counters would be desegregated voluntarily in 1962 under plans devised by a bi-racial community group.

'Jail-In' Movement

A new variation of the sit-in movement developed following the arrest Feb. 6 of 13 sit-in demonstrators in Rock Hill, S.C. and of 6 more, 4 of them whites, in Lynchburg, Va. They refused to pay $100 fines and were given 30-day jail sentences. The arrests had been made under state anti-trespass laws that made it illegal to remain after notification to leave by a store proprietor. 4 of those arrested were student leaders of the Student Nonviolent Coordinating Committee. They became known as the "Rock Hill 4," and their group's headquarters in Atlanta urged a South-wide campaign of "jail, no bail." By Feb. 10 "jail-ins" had resulted in 80 persons being imprisoned in Atlanta on similar charges.

The Negroes arrested in Rock Hill were sent to York

County prison farm and put to work in a road gang. They were placed in solitary confinement for ½ day for refusing to stop singing hymns and later for 3 days for refusing to work. They refused to work because one of their group, John A. Gaines, had disappeared. The Rev. C. A. Ivory, president of the Rock Hill NAACP, said Feb. 19 that he had been transferred to another jail for making a motion toward a prison official. Ivory said the group also was protesting against overwork. The 11 were released Mar. 2, and 9 of them came to New York the next weekend to speak to congregations and on the radio. (Ivory, another Negro and a white were arrested and jailed in Rock Hill Feb. 23 for antisegregation demonstrations in front of a drugstore.)

A drugstore sit-in in Lynchburg Feb. 21 resulted in 60-day jail sentences for 4 Negroes, including 2 ministers, the Rev. Virgil A. Wood, 29, and the Rev. William Walker Roberts, 23. The 6 Negroes jailed in Lynchburg went on a hunger strike from Feb. 28 to Mar. 2 because they were not allowed books.

7 Negro ministers and one white minister were arrested and jailed in Atlanta Feb. 15 for demonstrating in support of the "jail-in" movement. Another Negro minister was arrested in Atlanta Feb. 21 for the same reason.

Supreme Court Frees Students

The Supreme Court, in a unanimous decision Dec. 11, reversed the breach-of-the-peace convictions of 16 Negro college students who had staged sit-ins in Baton Rouge, La. This was the court's first decision on sit-in cases.

The students had been arrested Mar. 28-29, 1960 after seeking service at 3 "white" lunch counters in a drug store, a department store and a bus terminal. They had been denied service and then had refused police orders to leave the lunch counters.

Chief Justice Earl Warren, who wrote the opinion, said a Louisiana law defined disturbing the peace as acting "in such a manner as to unreasonably disturb or alarm the public." He said there was "no evidence to support a finding that petitioners disturbed the peace, either by outwardly boisterous conduct or by passive conduct likely to cause a public disturbance."

Tear Gas & Dogs Used in Baton Rouge

Police used tear gas and 2 leashed dogs to quell 5 mass demonstrations by 1,500 Negroes in Baton Rouge Dec. 15. About 50 demonstrators were arrested on disorderly conduct charges.

Many of the demonstrators were students of Baton Rouge's Southern University, a Negro school administered by the state. (The Louisiana State Education Board Dec. 16 ordered schools under its jurisdiction to expel students who were arrested and to ban unsanctioned student demonstrations.) The demonstration had been called in protest against the arrest Dec. 14 of 23 Negroes who had picketed downtown stores and had staged CORE-sponsored sit-ins at lunch counters.

Following the mass protest, temporary injunctions barring CORE from picketing or unlawful gatherings were obtained by Baton Rouge officials Dec. 15 from federal and state courts. The federal order was issued by U.S. District Judge E. Gordon West.

Among demonstrators arrested were Ronnie Moore, an SU student and CORE's Baton Rouge leader, and the Rev. B. Elton Cox, a CORE field secretary, who had led the demonstrators. Cox, charged with inciting riot and conspiracy to incite riot, was held in $4,000 bond. Moore, 18, was charged with violating an anti-noise ordinance by using a portable loudspeaker. He was released Dec. 15 after posting $1,500 bond, but he was re-arrested as he left the courthouse. He was charged with conspiracy to commit criminal mischief, and his bond was set at $2,000.

A CORE-sponsored demonstration was staged by Negroes in New Orleans Dec. 18 in protest against the Baton Rouge use of tear gas and dogs. The Negroes were starting a march to the State Office Building when 292 were arrested on charges of parading without a permit. Another demonstration in New Orleans Dec. 19, sponsored by the Consumers League of New Orleans, resulted in the arrest of 11 more Negroes.

Jackson (Miss.) Library Sit-In

9 Negro students of Tougaloo Christian College were arrested Mar. 27 and, after refusing to post bond, were jailed for staging a sit-in at the Jackson, Miss. city library. They were fined $100 each and given suspended 30-day jail

sentences Mar. 29. About 200 Negro students held a mass protest meeting at Jackson State College Mar. 28. Police gathered on the campus and later, using clubs, tear gas and 2
German police dogs, halted a march by 50 of the demonstrators
about 10 blocks from the jail. The day of the trial about 100
Negroes gathered outside the crowded, segregated courtroom
and started to clap. The police then moved in with swinging
nightsticks and the 2 leashed dogs, and they quickly dispersed
the crowd.

SCHOOL DESEGREGATION

93.1% in South Still Segregated

6.9% of the 3,088,261 Negro pupils in 17 Southern states
and the District of Columbia attended schools that had desegregated since the 1954 Supreme Court desegregation decision,
Southern School News reported in June.

The report said 213,532 Negroes attended desegregated
schools at the end of the 1960-61 school year. The total was
an increase of 17,907, or .6%, over the figure for 1959-60.
But 17,871 of the 17,907 increase was due to Maryland figures
that included, for the first time, the number of Negroes
attending school with white pupils in formerly all-Negro schools.

The June report said 783 of the area's 6,663 school districts
had desegregated since the 1954 decision. A later *Southern
School News* survey revealed that 29 formerly segregated
school districts in 8 Southern states had started the 1961-62
school year under new policies calling for school desegregation.
2 of these districts, however, remained segregated since no
Negroes had applied for admission to enter white schools.

In previously desegregated districts, Negro attendance at
formerly all-white schools increased slightly and was extended
to more schools. Of the Southern states, only Alabama, Mississippi and South Carolina still maintained completely segregated public school systems. Negro attendance at formerly
all-white schools in various states (1961 spring term figures
given first, 1960 fall figures in parentheses): Florida, about
400 (28); North Carolina, about 200 (90); Tennessee, more
than 550 (376); Texas, about 4,000 (3,500); Virginia, about
530 (200).

Civil Rights Commission Blames Government

A Civil Rights Commission (CRC) report to the President, released Jan. 15, charged that "the federal government bears a heavy responsibility for . . . discrimination against . . . Negroes."

It said: (a) The "federal government has been a silent partner in the creation and perpetuation of separate colleges for Negroes"; (b) no consideration was given "by the federal government to the presence or absence of discrimination by the recipient institution" in federal programs to aid education; (c) federal funds allocated "without regard to the discriminatory policy of the recipient institutes accentuate the disparity of educational opportunity" in 6 "resistant" states—Alabama, Georgia, Mississippi, South Carolina, Florida and Louisiana—where college and pre-college "education for the Negro is indeed separate and unequal"; (d) in Mississippi only 2.6% of Negro high schools (compared with 52.4% of white high schools) were approved by the Southern Association of Colleges & Secondary Schools; (e) such "deprivations" were "self-perpetuating" since graduates of segregated high schools tended "in overwhelming numbers" to go to segregated colleges taught by teachers trained in segregated colleges; (f) in the 1959-60 school year "racial segregation was still maintained in at least 86 public colleges and universities of Southern states."

The report made these recommendations:

▲ Executive or Congressional action should assure that federal aid to higher education was disbursed "only to such publicly controlled institutions of higher education as do not discriminate on grounds of race, color, religion, or national origin." (3 commissioners—Dr. John A. Hannah, chairman, the Rev. Theodore M. Hesburgh and George M. Johnson—recommended that the ban also be applied to private colleges. Vice Chrmn. Robert G. Storey said only Congress had power to act. Doyle E. Carlton said withholding of funds "as a club" was politically and morally "unsound." Commissioner Robert S. Rankin opposed a "punitive" ban that would deprive education of needed funds.)

▲ No individual should be subjected to the current "long, arduous and costly" "delay in securing a judicial determination of his constitutional rights"; instead, Congress might establish 3-judge courts with direct appeal to the Supreme Court.

(Storey and Carlton dissented.)

▲ The federal government should sponsor in the states (a) institutes to improve public school teaching, (b) summer and special academic-year institutes conducted by colleges for talented students "who are handicapped . . . as a result of inferior educational opportunity."

The CRC Sept. 24 urged a 12-point program to speed public school desegregation. The program called for federal action to: (1) Require all school boards that maintained segregated facilities to file a desegregation plan, to start within 6 months after such a law's enactment; (2) reduce, in ratio to the number of segregated schools, federal education aid to any state that continued segregated schools (Rankin dissented); (3) accelerate federal court action; (4) give federal aid to desegregating local school systems; (5) provide loans to school districts deprived of state funds because of desegregation; (6) authorize the CRC to be a clearinghouse for information concerning desegregation problems; create a CRC advisory panel for local communities; (7) protect citizens carrying out desegregation plans from reprisals; (8) install desegregated schools on military bases in districts with segregated schools; (9) help states establish programs to identify and aid talented teachers and students handicapped by unequal opportunity; (10) withhold library-aid funds from states maintaining segregated libraries; (11) withhold aid from segregated public higher-education institutions; (12) take an annual survey of the ethnic classification of all public-school students.

Louisiana School-Closing Law Upset

A 3-judge federal court in New Orleans Aug. 30 overturned as unconstitutional a Louisiana law that permitted the closing— by popular vote—of public schools in school districts under federal court orders to desegregate. The ruling was made on a case brought by Negro citizens of St. Helena Parish, whose electorate had voted under the new law Apr. 22 to close their public schools rather than integrate them. St. Helena Parish had 4,700 Negroes in a total population of 9,000, but only 4 Negroes voted. The vote was 1,147-57.1

(The new state law was one of 8 segregation bills passed by the state Legislature Feb. 8 and signed by Gov. Jimmie H. Davis Feb. 20. The new law made students eligible for state education grants to pay tuition in private schools.)

The ruling, delivered by Court of Appeals Judge John Minor Wisdom and District Judges J. Skelly Wright and Herbert W. Christenberry, said: "This is not the moment in history for a state to experiment with ignorance." The school-closing law was "a transparent artifice designed to deny the plaintiffs their declared constitutional right to attend desegregated public schools. . . . Its application in one parish, while the state provides public schools elsewhere, would unfairly discriminate against the residents of that parish, irrespective of race." Although the law contained no reference to race, "legislative leaders announced without equivocation that the purpose . . . was to keep the state in the business of providing public education on a segregated basis."

(The Virginia Supreme Court Nov. 27 declared uncon-stitutional a 1959 state law permitting the sale of public schools if approved by local referendums. Such a referendum had been sought by a group of white Alleghany County citizens. The court said the state had "the obligation to establish and maintain . . . public free schools throughout the state.")

New Orleans School Boycott

The white students' boycott in effect since Nov. 14, 1960 at McDonogh No. 19, one of New Orleans' 2 integrated public elementary schools (the other: Frantz School), was broken Jan. 27, 30 and 31 by Gregory Thompson, 9, but his family was forced out of New Orleans Feb. 1. Gregory's brother Michael, 8, also attended McDonogh Jan. 31. The boys were accompanied to and from school by federal marshals. A jeering crowd of white women gathered at the school each day.

The boys' father, John N. Thompson, 33, a $70-a-week employe of a New Orleans Walgreen Co. drug store, said Jan. 30 that he had been ordered by his landlady to vacate his apartment. Thompson had said he had been told not to report for work, but Walgreen officials said Jan. 28 that Thompson was being transferred to another store in "a routine normal procedure." The store was picketed Jan. 31.

3 Negro girls were the only other pupils to attend Mc-Donogh No. 19.

Integration was extended to 6 New Orleans public schools Sept. 7 when 12 Negro pupils entered the schools at the beginning of the fall term. The white-pupil boycott was still largely in effect, however. A 360-man police detail stood guard, and 60 U.S. marshals were on hand on orders of the Justice Department. At McDonogh No. 19, one white student attended opening classes with 5 Negro pupils, and 3 white pupils attended in the afternoon. At Frantz, 16 white children and one Negro girl attended classes. Enrollments in the other 4 integrated schools were below normal, but white enrollments increased later.

Georgia Replaces Segregation Laws

4 bills replacing Georgia's laws for "massive resistance" to public school desegregation were passed by the state legislature Jan. 27 and 30 and signed by Gov. S. Ernest Vandiver Jr. Jan. 31.

The bills provided for: (a) repeal of 6 anti-integration laws; (b) grants for pupils who chose to attend private, nonsectarian schools; (c) permission for local boards to set academic, psychological and other standards governing pupil transfers (formerly a state function); (d) local elections on whether to close desegregated schools; (e) a constitutional amendment, to be voted on in 1962, that asserted that "freedom from compulsory association at all levels of public education shall be preserved inviolate." The amendment was to replace a constitutional requirement for "separate schools . . . for white and colored races."

Vandiver had proposed the bills in a statewide TV address before a joint session of the Georgia General Assembly Jan. 18. He said he rejected any hint "of defiance of lawful processes" and opposed school closings. "Defiance, no," he said, "private schools offered as a last resort, yes." He pledged "every legal means" to prevent desegregation.

Georgia University Desegregated

The first desegregation in public education in Georgia was started Jan. 10 when 2 Negro students, Charlayne Alberta Hunter, 18, and Hamilton E. Holmes, 19, enrolled in Georgia University in Athens. The U.S. Supreme Court, shortly after the Negroes' admission, unanimously denied Georgia Atty. Gen. Eugene Cook's plea to stay integration pending an appeal.

U.S. District Judge William A. Bootle in Macon, Ga. Jan. 6 had ordered the university to admit the 2 Negroes. Bootle's ruling barred the university from further discrimination against Negro applicants. But Bootle Jan. 9 granted a stay of his integration order pending Cook's appeal to the U.S. 5th Circuit Court of Appeals. The stay interrupted the registration of the 2 Negro students, but the Negroes' lawyers Jan. 9 requested that the Appeals Court, sitting in Atlanta, set aside the stay. Chief Judge Elbert P. Tuttle complied, and the students completed registration Jan. 10.

Bootle's order barred Gov. Vandiver from cutting off state funds to the university. Vandiver said Jan. 7 that the university was in danger of closing. But Vandiver told the General Assembly at its opening session Jan. 9 that "we cannot abandon public education," and he denied Jan. 10 that he had halted state aid to the university. Bootle Jan. 12 issued a permanent injunction barring Vandiver and other state officials from implementing an anti-integration clause in a state appropriations act that prohibited the payment of state funds to integrated schools.

500 white students had demonstrated in Athens Jan. 6 against integration and had hanged an effigy of Holmes. Police had difficulty controlling more than 1,000 youths in downtown Athens Jan. 9, and demonstrators jeered at Miss Hunter Jan. 10.

A riot Jan. 11 resulted Jan. 12 in the suspension of Holmes and Miss Hunter. But Bootle ordered their reinstatement Jan. 13, and they returned to class without incident Jan. 16. Bootle said the Negroes' rights were not to be sacrificed to violence.

The Jan. 11 riot, by about 600 students and some adults, followed the school's defeat in a basketball game. Rioters threw bricks and firecrackers at the dormitory in which Miss Hunter was staying. A handful of Athens police reportedly watched the beginning of the riot but initially made no serious attempt to restrain it. Fighting broke out later between the students and police, and 16 persons were arrested.

After tear gas had dispersed the rioters, state police arrived. They escorted Miss Hunter from the dormitory, picked up Holmes from the Athens private home in which he had been lodged and drove them to their homes in Atlanta. The state police had not responded to phone calls for help from university officials and Athens Mayor Ralph Snow although a state police barracks was about 5 miles away. But Gov. Vandiver denied Jan. 13 that he had hesitated in dispatching the troopers. The university suspended or expelled

13 students for participating in the riot.

Miss Hunter and Holmes were suspended Jan. 12 by Joseph A. Williams, dean of students, who said he was acting for "their personal safety." 300 of the university's 600 faculty members met later Jan. 12 and adopted a resolution that condemned the riot and insisted that the 2 Negro students "be returned to their classes." The resolution said it regretted that state officials "were unable or unwilling to protect the [students'] rights." Bootle's order to reinstate the 2 Negroes was issued the next day.

State-controlled Georgia Tech in Atlanta desegregated Sept. 18 by admitting 3 Negro students. This was the first voluntary desegregation of a Georgia college. State and Atlanta policemen and school guards patrolled the campus, but there were no incidents.

Atlanta High Schools Desegregate

9 Negroes entered 4 previously white high schools in Atlanta Aug. 30. This was the first public school desegregation in Georgia below college level.

A long and intensive campaign to gain public acceptance of the move had preceded Atlanta's peaceful school desegregation. Spearheaded by 2 civic groups, the OASIS (Organizations Assisting Schools in September) and HOPE (Help Our Public Education), the campaign included sponsorship of discussion groups and a series of one-minute appeals on TV. The 9 Negro students had been introduced to white students weeks prior to school opening.

Prince Edward County (Va.) Loses Funds

U.S. District Judge Oren R. Lewis in Richmond, Va. Aug. 24 barred Prince Edward County (Va.) officials from using public funds to operate segregated private schools while the county's public schools, closed in June 1959, remained shut. (Prince Edward's private white schools reopened for the fall term, but its public schools remained closed.)

The closing of the county's public schools, Lewis said, effectively deprived citizens of "freedom of choice between public and private education. County tax funds have been appropriated [in the guise of tuition grants and tax credits]

to aid segregated schooling. . . . That . . . is circumventing
a constitutionally protected right." He held that these actions
were "designed to preserve separation of the races" in
schools despite the court's Apr. 1960 order to provide education for Negro children in desegregated public schools.
Lewis ordered county officials to prepare a desegregation
plan for the elementary schools and to have it "readily
available when and if" its public schools were reopened.

Lewis said in the ruling: About $132,000 of general
tax funds had been paid to white county residents who sent
1,327 children to segregated schools maintained by the Prince
Edward School Foundation. The state provided tuition grants
of $125 for each elementary pupil and $150 for each high
school pupil in the foundation's schools.   An additional
$56,000 in tax revenue was used for this purpose in the
form of credits. "Like aid" was not available to the colored
residents of the county because there was no private colored
school.   The Prince Edward County Christian Association,
a Negro organization, had conducted centers for children since
1959, but they received no county or state aid. About 2/3 of
the county's Negro school children had received no "schooling
or training of any kind since the closing of the public schools."

Lewis' ruling was made in a case brought by the NAACP
(National Association for the Advancement of Colored People)
on behalf of Prince Edward County Negro children.

Lewis June 14 had denied an Apr. 26 Justice Department
motion to enjoin Virginia state and local officials "from
failing or refusing to maintain in Prince Edward County a
system of free public schools." The motion also sought to
bar state officials from using funds for public schools any-
where in Virginia as long as public schooling was not provided
in Prince Edward.

New Rochelle (N.Y.) Schools Desegregate

The predominantly Negro Lincoln Elementary School in
New Rochelle, N.Y. was desegregated at the beginning of the
fall term Sept. 7. 2/3 of the school's Negro students were
quietly absorbed into 11 other New Rochelle schools. The
order to desegregate had been issued in federal district
court in New York May 31 by Judge Irving R. Kaufman.
Kaufman rejected the school board's desegregation plan,
which was submitted under protest. Kaufman May 15 had

invited the Justice Department to enter the case as a friend of the court, and "guidelines" for the desegregation plan were submitted to Kaufman by the department May 24.

The U. S. 2d Circuit Court of Appeals in New York Aug. 2 upheld Kaufman's order. The Supreme Court, in effect, upheld Kaufman's decision by refusing Dec. 11 to review it.

Kaufman had ruled in New York Jan. 24 that the New Rochelle Board of Education had "intentionally created" and for 11 years had purposefully maintained "Lincoln School as a racially segregated school, and has not . . . acted in good faith to implement desegregation." The ruling was based on testimony during 7 days of hearings in Nov.-Dec. 1960 on a suit filed by parents of 11 Negro children who had been denied the right to register in any New Rochelle school but Lincoln. Kaufman said: "The presence of some 29 white children . . . [did] not afford the 454 Negro children in the [Lincoln] school the educational and social contacts and interaction of desegregation envisioned" by the Supreme Court's 1954 school desegregation decision; "compliance with the Supreme Court's edict was not to be less forthright in the North than in the South; no double standard was to be tolerated"; the Lincoln School had been established "by the gerrymandering of district lines, and by the transfer of white children residing in the district to schools outside the district"; the board had "constantly reiterated its belief in racial equality."

Parochial School Desegregation

The 3 Roman Catholic bishops of Georgia and South Carolina announced in pastoral letters Feb. 19 that Catholic parochial schools in the 2 states would be desegregated no later than the states' public schools. The announcement was signed by Bishops Francis E. Hyland, Thomas McDonough and Paul J. Hallinan.

Similar announcements had been made previously in Virginia, North Carolina and Louisiana. Parochial school desegregation in varying degrees had been reported in Arkansas, Florida, Kentucky, North Carolina, Texas, Tennessee, Virginia and in Rock Hill, S.C.

Catholic parochial schools in Galveston, Tex. desegregated grades 1-7 Sept. 5, one day before the city's public schools opened on an integrated basis.

Other Desegregation Events

Among other school desegregation developments:

Arkansas—The U.S. 8th Circuit Court of Appeals in St. Louis Mar. 2 ordered the Little Rock school board to take "affirmative action" "in more than a token fashion" toward public school desegregation.

5 more Little Rock public schools were desegregated Sept. 5. The number of Negroes attending integrated classes rose from 11 in the spring term to 49 in the fall term.

Delaware—U.S. District Judge Caleb M. Wright in Wilmington June 26 approved the State Education Board's short- and long-range plans to desegregate Delaware's public schools completely by 1970.

Florida—U.S. Judge G. Harrold Carswell in Tallahassee, Fla. Sept. 8 approved the Escambia County (Pensacola) school board's plan for gradual desegregation of its public schools and ordered the desegregation to begin in the fall of 1962.

The Pinellas County (St. Petersburg) school board approved the transfer of 3 Negroes to 2 previously all-white public schools in September. It also admitted 2 white students to 2 previously all-Negro schools.

Volusia County (Daytona Beach) and Broward County (Fort Lauderdale) desegregated public schools voluntarily in the fall term; Daytona Beach admitted 2 Negroes, Fort Lauderdale 23.

Illinois—A suit accusing the Chicago Board of Education of altering school district lines to maintain a segregated pattern was filed in U.S. district court in Chicago Sept. 18 on behalf of parents of 32 Negro school children assigned to 5 elementary schools. About 100 Negro students accompanied by about 70 parents and adults had made an unsuccessful attempt Sept. 6 to enroll in 9 all-white public schools in Chicago.

Michigan—The scheduled reopening of public schools in Highland Park Sept. 6 was prevented because of a suit charging discrimination in an all-Negro school. U.S. District Judge John Feikens dismissed the suit in Detroit Sept. 7 after the school board agreed to place 42 white pupils in the school.

New Jersey—Negro parents in Montclair picketed a predominately Negro school Sept. 7-8 in protest against the school's alleged discriminatory policy and inferior quality.

North Carolina—5 Negroes were admitted voluntarily to previously white schools in Asheville in the fall term. 20 Indian children started attendance at previously white Dunn High School Aug. 31 without incident.

Tennessee—2 undergraduate schools of the University of Tennessee in Knoxville were desegregated Jan. 2 with the registration of 2 Negroes, Theotis Robinson Jr. in the College of Liberal Arts & Sciences and Charles Edgar Blair in the College of Business Administration.

Davidson County schools were desegregated Jan. 25 under federal court orders. About 50 Negro pupils enrolled for integrated classes.

U.S. Judge William E. Miller in Nashville Sept. 11 ordered the Wilson County Board of Education (1) to admit 3 Negroes to a previously white school in Lebanon, near Nashville, (2) to prepare a desegregation plan for other schools.

Kingsport, Johnson City and Knox County public schools desegregated without court orders in the fall term.

13 Negro first graders were admitted without incident to 4 previously white public schools in Memphis Oct. 3. The desegregation was voluntary and carried out without advance publicity. About 25 white students withdrew from the 4 schools after the desegregation.

The U.S. 6th Circuit Court of Appeals in Cincinnati, O. Nov. 13 upheld U.S. District Judge Leslie R. Darr's rejection of Chattanooga's school desegregation plan as too slow. The board's plan, submitted to Darr Jan. 23, called for desegregating the first 3 grades of selected schools in 1962 and for desegregating one grade a year thereafter.

Texas—U.S. District Judge T. Whitfield Davidson in Dallas June 27 ordered Dallas schools to integrate according to a previously approved grade-a-year plan starting with the first grade. Davidson said his order had been "forced" by a U.S. 5th Circuit Court of Appeals order Jan. 20 to put the plan into operation. 18 Negro first-graders entered 8 previously white schools in Dallas Sept. 6 in the first step in the plan. The desegregation was preceded by a community drive to foster peaceful acceptance of it.

Galveston desegregated Sept. 6 as 37 Negro children entered previously white public elementary schools.

Public schools in Judson, Lockney, Andrews and Yorktown counties were desegregated voluntarily in the fall term.

U.S. District Judge Leo Brewster in Fort Worth Nov. 9

ordered the city school board to begin desegregation in the 1962 fall term and to submit a desegregation plan "with all deliberate speed."

Virginia—Newport News, under court order, accepted Negro children in 5 of its 24 white elementary schools Sept. 6. Adjoining Hampton admitted one Negro to its previously white high school. Richmond, Arlington, Norfolk and Fairfax counties desegregated other previously white schools.

VOTING BIAS FOUGHT

Rights Commission Urges Legislation

The Civil Rights Commission Sept. 9 issued a report urging legislation to ban voter qualifications other than age, residence, confinement or conviction for felony. Vice Chrmn. Robert G. Storey and commissioner Robert S. Rankin dissented on the ground that such legislation would disrupt existing federal-state relations.

Other recommendations in the report, all unanimous, backed legislation: (a) to make completion of 6th grade sufficient educational qualification in states that used "literacy" or similar voter-qualification tests; (b) to ban arbitrary action or inaction that deprived persons of the right to vote; (c) to require that voting districts "be substantially equal" in population and to give federal courts jurisdiction to enforce federal law regarding such districts; (d) to initiate a nationwide compilation of registration and voting statistics by race, color and national origin (the report said current "incomplete" statistics indicated that no Negroes were registered to vote in 13 counties where they formed the majority of the population—2 counties in Alabama, 2 in Georgia, 4 in Louisiana and 5 in Mississippi).

Among the report's findings: (1) "Substantial" numbers of Negroes were denied the right to vote on grounds of race or color in about 100 counties in Alabama, Florida, Georgia, Louisiana, Mississippi, North and South Carolina and Tennessee; (2) although provisions of the 1957 and 1960 Civil Rights Acts were "useful," "broader measures" were necessary "if denials" of constitutional voting rights "are to be quickly eliminated"; (3) the right to vote was denied mainly by the discriminatory application of legal qualifications or registration procedures; (4) "the malapportioned condition of state

and Congressional voting districts throughout" the U.S. "dilutes
the right to vote of many citizens," and U.S. courts showed "ex-
treme reluctance" to provide a remedy.

Vote Right Cases in Court

An Alabama state law that virtually disenfranchised Tuskegee Negroes by shifting the Tuskegee city boundaries was ruled
unconstitutional by U.S. District Judge Frank M. Johnson Jr.
in Montgomery, Ala. Feb. 17. Johnson issued an order
prohibiting city and county officials from enforcing the law.
The case had been returned to the district court after the
Supreme Court had ruled in 1960 that the boundary shift was
unconstitutional if its effect was to eliminate Negro voters.

Johnson ruled Mar. 17 that Macon County, Ala. voting
registrars must register 64 Negro complainants as voters.
His ruling, on petition of the Justice Department, also ordered
the registrars to start reducing the backlog of unprocessed
Negro voter applications. The ruling banned: (a) discrimination against prospective Negro voters; (b) any difference in
the administration of qualifying tests to Negroes and whites;
(c) refusal to register Negro voter-applicants whose test
performances were equal to the performance of the "least
qualified white applicant" who was registered.

Johnson ruled Sept. 14 that qualified Negro applicants in
Bullock and Macon counties, Ala. had been denied the right
to vote. Johnson ordered the county registrars to end discrimination, to submit monthly progress reports and to keep vote
records available for federal inspection. He also ordered
the state to appoint an "effective" 3-man board of registrars
for Macon County.

U.S. District Judge Ben C. Dawkins in Shreveport, La.
Aug. 21 ordered the reinstatement of eligible Bienville Parish
Negro voters who had been purged from the voting rolls in
1956. The Justice Department, suing for the reinstatement, said
about 570 Negroes had been removed from the rolls. Dawkins
also enjoined the Bienville Parish Registrar of Voters "against
any further discrimination in conducting the affairs of that
office."

The Justice Department's first voting rights suit under
the Kennedy Administration was filed with U.S. Judge Daniel
H. Thomas in Mobile, Ala. Apr. 13 against the Dallas County
Board of Registrars and Alabama state. The suit also sought

an order for federal inspection of the parish's voter records.

The Justice Department filed in Shreveport, La. Apr. 28 a suit charging that Negroes in East Carrol Parish had been deprived of their vote by illegal registration procedures. The suit sought an end to such practices. Although the number of eligible Negro voters outnumbered eligible white voters by 4,183 to 2,990 in the parish, no Negroes were registered to vote. Negro voter-applicants were blocked, the complaint said, by requirements that they be identified by 2 registered voters from their own precinct, whereas identification of prospective white voters was by "such reasonable means as Selective Service cards, driver licenses or library cards." Since no Negroes were registered and no registered whites had been willing to identify Negro applicants, all Negro applications had been rejected so far.

The Justice Department sued in federal district court in Mississippi July 6 to ban discrimination against prospective Negro voters in Clarke and Forrest counties, Miss. In the Clarke suit, filed in Meridian, the department charged that none of 2,988 Negro residents was registered as a voter while a substantial majority of 6,072 white persons of voting age was registered. Only 25 of 7,495 Forrest County Negroes were registered, the department said, compared to the registration of a majority of the county's 22,431 eligible whites.

A suit to ban discrimination against eligible Negro voters in Ouachita Parish, La. was filed by the Justice Department in U.S. district court in Monroe, La. July 11. The suit accused the parish's Citizens' Council and voting registrar of purging 4,775 of 16,377 eligible Negroes from voter registration rolls since Jan. 1956.

The Justice Department Aug. 3 filed 3 suits demanding federal injunctions to stop discrimination against Negroes seeking to register to vote in Walthall and Jefferson Davis counties in Mississippi and Montgomery County in Alabama. The Montgomery complaint, filed in Montgomery, said that 29,615 of the county's 62,911 eligible whites but only 2,885 of the 33,056 eligible Negroes were registered. Both Mississippi complaints were filed in Jackson, Miss. The Walthall complaint said Negro applicants were rejected arbitrarily. The registrants (out of 3,222 eligibles) had dropped from about 1,200 in 1955 to about 130 in 1960 as a result of a new registration ordered in Feb. 1956 but that a majority of whites was registered.

The Justice Department sued in federal district courts Oct. 16 to ban discrimination against prospective Negro voters in Plaquemines Parish, La. and in Panola County, Miss. A similar suit was filed by the department Oct. 26 against Madison Parish, La. The Plaquemines suit, filed in New Orleans, asserted that only 45 of 2,897 eligible Negroes were registered to vote while the comparable white registration totals were 6,714 of 8,633. In the Panola County suit, filed in Oxford, the Justice Department said that more than 5,000 of 7,639 eligible whites and only 10 of 7,250 eligible Negroes were registered. In the Madison Parish action, filed in Shreveport Oct. 26, the Justice Department sought to prohibit a "voucher" registration system under which Negro applicants had to be identified by 2 registered voters. The suit said no Negroes had been registered to vote there in 36 years, but 81.4% of eligible whites, who were allowed to identify themselves "by reasonable means," had been registered in 1960.

The Justice Department filed suit in federal court in New Orleans Dec. 28 in an effort to invalidate a Louisiana law requiring prospective voters to pass a state constitutional interpretation test. The test, required under a 1921 clause added to the state constitution, had been used to deprive otherwise qualified Negroes of their right to vote, the suit charged. The suit named as defendants Louisiana state and the state Board of Registration's members, Gov. Jimmie H. Davis, Lt. Gov. C. C. Aycock, state House Speaker J. Thomas Jewel and Hugh E. Cutrer Jr., the board's director.

Negro Registration Drive Planned

Plans for a Negro voter registration campaign were made at the 4th annual meeting of the Southern Christian Leadership Conference (SCLC), held in Nashville, Tenn. Sept. 27-29. About 250 delegates from 70 affiliates in 20 states attended. The Rev. Dr. Martin Luther King Jr., SCLC president, said Sept. 29 that "one of the most significant steps a Negro can take is the walk to the ballot box."

King had announced at a news conference in Miami Beach Aug. 16 that a program of Negro "stand-ins" would be instituted soon "at places where they have been denied the right to register." He said the 2-year goal was to double the number of registered Southern Negro voters. There currently were an estimated 1,300,000 such registrants.

The NAACP annual report, issued July 9, said that in 1960 Negro political action had increased in 95% of the 400 cities and counties in which the group had conducted voter registration programs.

EMPLOYMENT ACTION

Pres. Kennedy Orders Equal Rights

Pres. John F. Kennedy Mar. 6 ordered the creation of "vastly strengthened machinery" "to insure that Americans of all colors and beliefs will have equal access to employment" by the government and its contractors. His Executive Order 10925 set up a President's Committee on Equal Employment Opportunity to replace the Committee on Government Employment Policy and the Committee on Government Contracts.

Vice Pres. Lyndon B. Johnson was designated chairman of the committee. Labor Secy. Arthur J. Goldberg was named vice chairman and was directed to supervise the committee's work and to execute and implement its policies. Members of the committee were to include the Secretaries of Commerce, Defense, Army, Navy and Air Force, the Attorney General, the chairmen of the Atomic Energy Commission and the Civil Service Commission and the administrators of the General Services and the National Aeronautics & Space Administrations. (Asst. Labor Secy. Jerry R. Holleman was appointed by the President Mar. 21 as ex-officio executive vice chairman.)

The order forbade discrimination in any phase of employment by any government contractor. In supervising contractor compliance, the committee was empowered to investigate, hold public or private hearings, publish names of non-compliers, terminate or refuse contracts and recommend to the Justice Department that "appropriate proceedings [including enjoining] be brought to enforce" its provisions against non-compliers and that criminal proceedings "be brought for the furnishing of false information."

Committee Wins Job-Equality Agreements

An agreement guaranteeing full racial equality at all Lockheed Aircraft Corp. plants was signed at the White House May 25 by Lockheed Pres. Courtlandt Gross and by Vice Pres.

Johnson as chairman of the President's committee. The agreement was reached in negotiations started by the Johnson committee after Herbert Hill, NAACP labor secretary, had lodged a complaint accusing Lockheed's Marietta, Ga. plant of discrimination.

Agreements pledging equal job opportunities to Negroes were signed by the committee with 8 leading defense contractors July 12 and with 12 defense contractors Nov. 30.

The committee said Oct. 27 that the Charleston (S.C.) Naval Shipyard, named in an NAACP complaint filed July 14, had taken action to end job bias. The committee disclosed Dec. 1 that of 473 complaints of discrimination by federal contractors received so far, 178 had been dismissed and remedial action had been taken on 71 others. The committee had also received more than 700 complaints charging bias in promotion and hiring policies by federal agencies or business organizations.

Johnson Dec. 1 called the status of federal Negro employes "very unsatisfactory." He said the results of a survey conducted by the committee disclosed that 51,881 Negroes among the 478,721 persons employed by 45 federal agencies were mainly in the lowest 1/3 of the salary grades.

Randolph Censure to 'Die'

The AFL-CIO Executive Council Oct. 11 accused its only Negro vice president, A. Philip Randolph, president of the Bro'hood of Sleeping Car Porters, of causing "the gap that has developed between organized labor and the Negro community." In an attempt to heal the rift caused by this council censure vote, it was agreed at the AFL-CIO convention in Bal Harbour, Fla. Dec. 13 that the motion should be referred back to the council and "die."

The censure action, voted during the council's quarterly meeting in New York, came in council approval of a report rejecting Randolph's charges that AFL-CIO Pres. George Meany had been lax in pushing for equal employment rights for Negroes and that several AFL-CIO affiliates had been guilty of bias. The report countercharged that Randolph's union employed only Negro staff members and that he had never tried to get a nondiscrimination clause in his own Pullman contracts.

Meany said Oct. 12 that "we can only get moving on civil rights if he [Randolph] comes over to our side and stops throwing bricks at us."

Nearly 2 months of bitter controversy followed the council's action. Seeking to undo the harm to labor unity, Meany met Dec. 5 with a delegation from Randolph's Negro American Labor Council. (In an address to the Negro group Nov. 11, Randolph had accused the AFL-CIO of "moral paralysis" in its racial policies. He called for a crusade to desegregate the labor movement in the South and for the development of a "bonafide American labor party." The council, which had about 10,000 members, had agreed Nov. 10 to accept non-union members on the ground that many Negroes were excluded from unions by bias.) Reversing a policy of ignoring the Negro labor group, Meany promised Dec. 5 to work with it and to submit its civil rights plan to the AFL-CIO Executive Council.

In his opening address to the AFL-CIO convention in Bal Harbour Dec. 7, Meany affirmed that he understood the impatience of those "who seek to give real meaning to the rights guaranteed by the 14th Amendment." But the feud flared anew Dec. 12 when Randolph described the censure report as "dishonorable, disgraceful, pety and cheap." Under the Dec. 13 agreement, Randolph retracted his description and the censure report was "deposited" with the AFL-CIO Executive Council.

A civil rights resolution approved by the convention Dec. 12 pledged an intensified drive for (a) "equal rights for all Americans in every field" and (b) full union membership benefits for all workers.

At its annual meeting in Miami Beach Feb. 20-28, the AFL-CIO Executive Council had adopted a resolution that urged the elimination of segregated locals, but the council rejected Randolph's demand that it set a 6-month deadline for compliance. Randolph told the council that it had "failed completely" in its efforts to desegregate labor. He said fewer than 1% of apprentices were Negroes.

Employment Gains Reported

Southern Negroes were making small but important gains in achieving equal job opportunity, according to a *Wall Street Journal* article Nov. 24. The article credited the Negroes' increased voting power and the President's committee for much of the progress. The article said: (a) in Dallas, Tex. in recent weeks about 100 Negroes had been upgraded or hired for jobs formerly held by whites; (b) transit firms in Mobile, Memphis, Atlanta, Nashville, Jacksonville, Tallahassee and Tampa had hired Negro drivers, and the New Orleans Public Service Co. had agreed to hire Negro drivers; (c) 152 of 238 jobs found for Negroes by the New Orleans Urban League were formerly held by whites; (d) the South Carolina and Texas employment commissions reported an increasing demand for skilled Negroes.

According to a National Urban League survey made public Mar. 4, however, the unemployment rate of Negroes was 2 to 3 times the total unemployment rate. The survey, which covered 50 cities, revealed that: (a) the Negro unemployment rate was 17.3% in Chicago (where the total rate for Negroes and whites was 5.7%); (b) the Negro unemployment rate was 28% in Philadelphia (where the total rate was 7%); (c) about 81% of persons on welfare in Detroit were Negroes.

Rights Commission Urges Federal Action

The Civil Rights Commission Oct. 13 issued a report urging Congressional and Presidential action to end the "vicious circle of [nationwide] discrimination in employment opportunities." CRC staff director Berl I. Bernhard said: Federal efforts to end job bias "have been limited and sporadic"; since 1946 such efforts had been "confined, in large measure, to actual federal employment including membership in the armed forces, and to employment by government contractors." The report urged Congress to bar unions from segregating, expelling or refusing membership beacuse of race. It praised 3 AFL-CIO unions—the United Packinghouse Workers, the United Automobile Workers and the Textile Workers Union—for taking "forceful steps" against bias. But, it said, "most international unions," and especially those in the construction field, "have failed to exhibit any profound concern over civil rights. . . ."

LEGISLATION

Pres. John F. Kennedy was criticized by civil rights backers for failing to ask Congress to pass rights legislation pledged in the 1960 Democratic platform. When Democratic legislation to fulfill the platform pledges was introduced

May 8, the President said he considered it unecessary. His attitude was attributed to a belief that other Administration legislation had a better chance of being adopted if he did not antagonize Southern Democrats by demanding action on rights bills. The only rights legislation adopted in 1961—a 2-year extension of the life of the Civil Rights Commission—was approved not on its own merits but as a rider to an appropriations bill.

Senators Offer Legislation Packages

Sen. Joseph S. Clark (D., Pa.) and Rep. Emanuel Celler (D., N.Y.) May 8 introduced in the Senate and House 6 bills to fulfill the 1960 Democratic platform pledges on civil rights. But no action was taken on the bills during 1961.

The bills would have (a) barred poll taxes and literacy tests for voting; (b) required school boards in segregated districts to file "first-step compliance" desegregation plans; (c) authorized the Attorney General to file civil suits in rights cases; (d) provided court remedies for job discrimination and banned discriminatory practices in business or unions with 50 or more members; (e) made the Civil Rights Commission permanent.

White House Press Secy. Pierre Salinger said May 9 that the bills were "not Administration-backed." Senate Democratic leader Mike Mansfield (Mont.) explained: We want to get the . . . [President's program] through, and after that we will consider civil rights if necessary." NAACP Executive Secy. Roy Wilkins assailed the Administration May 10 as taking a "mistaken and regrettable" position.

Sens. Jacob K. Javits and Kenneth B. Keating (both R., N.Y.) had introduced in the Senate Jan. 17 a package of 7 civil rights bills—none of them adopted—that would have (a) authorized the Attorney General to bring suits on behalf of individuals in certain civil rights cases; (b) provided aid to school districts seeking to desegregate; (c) made lynching a federal crime; (d) eliminated the poll tax; (e) made completion of 6th grade sufficient proof of literacy for voting purposes. Most co-sponsors of the 7 bills were Republicans, but Senate Democratic whip Hubert H. Humphrey (Minn.) also co-sponsored all 7 bills, and Democratic Sens. Paul H. Douglas (Ill.), Philip A. Hart (Mich.), Frank E. Moss (Utah) and Oren E. Long (Hawaii) co-sponsored several.

Rights Commission's Life Extended

Legislation extending the life of the Civil Rights Commission (CRC) for 2 years—until Nov. 30, 1963—was passed by both houses of Congress Sept. 13 and signed by Pres. Kennedy Sept. 21. The legislation was in the form of an amendment added by the Senate to a House-passed bill appropriating $756,422,550 in fiscal 1962 for the State and Justice Departments, the Judiciary and related agencies. House approval was by 300-106 vote.

The rider method of considering the CRC extension was adopted because of the failure of the Senate Judiciary Committee to report a separate CRC measure. The amendment, offered by Mansfield and Senate GOP leader Everett M. Dirksen, was originally approved by the Senate Aug. 30 by 70-19 vote with 18 Southern Democrats and Sen. Milton R. Young (R., N.D.) voting against it.

Wisconsin Rights Bills Defeated

The Wisconsin legislature, despite pressure from a 12-day sit-in, rejected 3 state civil rights bills Aug. 11. The Assembly, by 53-39 vote, killed a measure that would have permitted prosecution for discrimination in realty dealings. The Senate (1) voted 23-9 against giving the Governor's Commission on Human Rights additional power in investigating housing discrimination and (2) voted 22-10 against moving the state's fair employment division to the commission.

OTHER DEVELOPMENTS

Ban on Housing Bias Urged

The Civil Rights Commission Oct. 5 issued a report urging the President or Congress to prohibit racial discrimination in federally-aided housing. The report also urged that non-bias agreements be required of all financial institutions under federal supervision. The CRC estimated that its report's recommendations, if enacted, would affect about 90% of privately financed home sales. The report, primarily referring to discrimination against Negroes, said federal "resources are utilized to accentuate" bias "at all levels of the housing and home-finance industries."

The Federal Home Loan Bank Board June 1 approved and distributed to its field offices a resolution opposing any racial discrimination in mortgage lending by the 4,700 savings and loan associations it supervised.

3 private housing groups, meeting separately in Washington Sept. 27-Oct. 31, also called for an end to housing bias. The National Committee Against Discrimination in Housing said Sept. 27 that the U.S. government was the "architect and enforcer" of segregated housing; it urged a ban on bias in federally-aided projects. A similar resolution was adopted Oct. 29 by the directors of the National Housing Conference. The National Association of Housing & Redevelopment Officials Oct. 31 adopted a resolution urging equal housing opportunity "for all people."

Police Brutality Charged

Police brutality was "still a serious and continuing problem" in the U.S., the Civil Rights Commission charged Nov. 17 in its final 1961 report. "Although whites are not immune," it said, "Negroes feel the brunt of official brutality, proportionately, more than any other group."

To remedy the situation, the CRC urged Congress to consider: (a) grants-in-aid to state and local governments for development of recruiting programs, police administration schools, training programs in scientific crime detection and in constitutional rights and human relations; (b) amendments to laws to outlaw specifically such acts as physical injury, unnecessary force during arrest or custody, violence or unlawful restraint to get a confession, aid to private violence or refusal to protect from known violence; (c) legislation to make county, city or local (but not state) governments liable to victims of their officers' misconduct; (d) legislation to enable the U.S. government to start civil suits to prevent exclusion from juries because of race.

The report criticized the Justice Department's failure to act on brutality cases in instances where state authorities acted.

In a concluding statement, the CRC scored delay and urged an attack against bias "on all fronts simultaneously." It exhorted the President to use the prestige of his office to explain the "moral issues involved in critical situations when they arise," to reiterate his backing of the Supreme Court's desegregation decision and to stimulate voting interest.

Courts Rule on NAACP

The Supreme Court May 22 unanimously reaffirmed that 2 Louisiana laws could not be used to compel the NAACP (National Association for the Advancement of Colored People) to disclose its members' names or to attest that officers of its affiliates were not connected with subversive organizations. Justice William O. Douglas said the court had found previously that such disclosure of membership resulted in reprisals and hostility to members. 2 state laws the court barred Louisiana from using against the NAACP were (a) a 1924 law requiring the annual filing of membership lists (originally passed to curb Ku Klux Klan activities) and (b) a 1958 anti-Communist law previously found unconstitutional by a special 3-judge U.S. court in New Orleans.

Alabama Circuit Court Judge Walter B. Jones issued in Montgomery Dec. 29 a permament injuction barring the NAACP from intrastate activities in Alabama. The order made permanent a temporary injunction that had been in effect since June 1956. The Supreme Court had ordered the case transferred to federal court unless a state court acted by Jan. 2, 1962. Jones ruled that the NAACP had violated state law by failure to register as an out-of-state corporation.

NAACP Convention

The NAACP's 52d annual convention, held in Philadelphia July 10-16, was highlighted by a 22-car "Freedom Train" trip to Washington July 12 by most of the more than 1,000 convention delegates. About 65 delegates, led by NAACP Executive Secy. Roy Wilkins and Bishop Stephen Gill Spottswood, NAACP chairman, met with Pres. Kennedy. They praised his executive action in the civil rights field but told him they were dismayed at "the absence of a clear call" from him for rights legislation. The President replied that current rights legislation had not been fully utilized.

In an address at the convention July 14, Chrmn. Adam Clayton Powell Jr. (D., N.Y.) of the House Education & Labor Committee pledged to "do everything in my power" to block legislation favorable to labor unions until they "start practicing common equality for black workers."

The NAACP's annual report, released July 9, said NAACP membership had increased to 388,347 and its 1960 income had exceeded $1 million.

(Jack Greenberg, 36, a white New York lawyer, was chosen by the NAACP as its chief counsel Oct. 4. He succeeded Thurgood Marshall, who had been appointed a U.S. judge.)

Other Court Decisions

The Supreme Court ruled 6-3 Apr. 17 that a privately-operated restaurant on space leased from a state agency could not refuse to serve Negroes. The case involved a coffee shop located in a garage owned by a Delaware state agency, the Wilmington Parking Authority, which leased the space. The Supreme Court upheld the complaint of Wilmington City Council member William H. Burton, a Negro, who had sued after being refused service in the coffee shop. The Delaware Supreme Court had ruled against Burton on the grounds that (a) the shop was a "purely private" business, (b) a state law allowed a restaurateur to refuse service to persons "offensive to the major part of his customers."

U.S. District Judge H. Hobart Grooms Oct. 24 ruled unconstitutional a Birmingham, Ala. ordinance requiring segregation of public recreation facilities.

Chicago Disturbances

65 Negroes were arrested in Chicago July 13-15 during an outbreak of racial incidents in which roving gangs of Negro youths beat 21 whites. Police attributed the attacks to reprisals for the fatal shooting July 12 of Matthew Tolbert, 17, a Negro.

200 police were on hand when about 200 Negroes attempted a wade-in at Chicago's Rainbow Beach July 16. The demonstrators, watched by angry groups of whites, dispersed; 12 whites were arrested for refusing to obey police. 12 persons had been arrested on the same charge during a Negro wade-in demonstration at the beach July 9. But 3 Negroes and 3 whites swam together at the beach July 22.

Actors Bar Theater Discrimination

The AFL-CIO Actors' Equity Association announced Oct. 8 that, effective June 1, 1962, its members would refuse to appear in theaters where segregation was in effect either in seating or backstage. The new policy had been agreed on

May 31 by Equity, which represented legitimate stage actors, and the League of New York Theaters.

Henry Lewis, 28, became the first Negro to conduct a major symphony orchestra at its home auditorium during a regular concert season when he led the Los Angeles Philharmonic in Los Angeles Feb. 9. Dean Dixon of New York, who had been the first Negro to conduct a major orchestra in the U.S., had been the conductor of the Goteborg Symphony of Sweden before he received his current conducting position with the Hesse Radio Orchestra in Frankfurt, West Germany.

Negro Population

Washington was the only major U.S. city in which a majority of the population was Negro, a Census Bureau report revealed Mar. 14. It said the Negro population of Washington was 411,737, or 53.9% of the total 763,956 population.

Figures for other major cities with large Negro populations:

	Total Population	Negroes	Negro Percentage
New York	7,781,984	1,087,931	14.0
Chicago	3,550,404	812,637	22.9
Los Angeles	2,479,015	334,916	13.5
Philadelphia	2,002,512	529,240	26.4
Detroit	1,670,144	482,223	28.9
Baltimore	939,024	326,589	34.8
Houston	938,219	215,037	22.9
Cleveland	876,050	250,818	28.6
St. Louis	750,026	214,377	28.6
San Francisco	740,316	74,383	10.0
Boston	697,197	63,165	9.1
Dallas.	679,684	129,242	19.0
New Orleans	627,525	233,514	37.2
Pittsburgh	604,332	100,692	16.7
Buffalo	532,759	70,904	13.3
Cincinnati	502,550	108,754	21.6
Memphis	497,524	184,320	37.0
Atlanta	487,455	186,464	38.3

The Census Bureau reported Dec. 27 that nonwhite emigration from the South had risen from a total of 1,245,000 in the 1940s to a record 1,457,000 in the 1950s. In the 1950s 1,100,000 Southern Negroes moved to the North, 332,000 to the West.

States with the largest nonwhite emigration: Mississippi 323,000; Alabama 224,000; South Carolina 218,000; North Carolina 207,000; Georgia 204,000.

States with the largest nonwhite immigration: California
354,000; New York 282,000; Illinois 189,000; Ohio 133,000;
Michigan 127,000; New Jersey 112,000; Florida 101,000.

Bias Shifts Centennial Meeting

Maj. Gen. Ulysses S. Grant 3d, chairman of the National
Civil War Centennial Commission, announced Mar. 25 that the
meeting place of the commission's 4th national assembly, held
in Charleston, S.C. Apr. 11-12, had been shifted to the
Charleston Naval Station to avoid segregated hotels in Charleston. The change was made after the commission's New Jersey
unit had voted Mar. 9 to boycott the meeting and after Pres.
Kennedy, an ex officio member of the commission, had written
to Grant Mar. 15 to protest.

Mr. Kennedy's Mar. 15 protest had been rejected initially
Mar. 21 when the commission replied that it had no right to
"dictate" to "motel-keepers as to the management of their
property." The President told reporters Mar. 23 that "we
cannot leave the situation as it is." Withdrawals from the
assembly were announced by centennial units of New York,
Illinois and California Mar. 23 and of Massachusetts Mar. 24.
The capitulation was announced Mar. 25 although Rep. William
M. Tuck (D., Va.), chairman of the commission's executive
committee, said Mar. 26 that "I do not acquiesce" in the shift.
The New Jersey unit reversed its withdrawal decision Mar.
28.

1962

Rioting erupted in Mississippi when segregationists fought—unsuccessfully—against federal court orders requiring the University of Mississippi to admit its first Negro student. Despite frequent court action and some voluntary desegregation, Southern schools remained more than 92% segregated during 1962, and more than 30 Northern communities were accused of segregating their schools almost as effectively although by subtlety and subterfuge. 3 Louisiana segregationists were excommunicated by the Roman Catholic Church for fighting the desegregation of Catholic parochial schools. A Senate filibuster killed proposed legislation to bar unfair use of literacy tests to prevent the registration of Negro voters. But congress approved a constitutional amendment to abolish poll taxes as a requirement for voting in federal elections. Discrimination in federal or federally aided housing was forbidden by Presidential order.

MEREDITH & THE UNIVERSITY OF MISSISSIPPI

Riot in Oxford (Miss.)

The university town of Oxford, Miss. became a focal point of international interest when thousands of white students and other segregationists clashed with federal marshals and troops there Sept. 30-Oct. 1 in a futile effort to prevent the registration, under federal court order, of the first Negro knowingly enrolled at the University of Mississippi. The Negro, James H. Meredith, 29, became a member of the student body despite the active opposition of the governor, other high state officials and a violent mob. But the government found it necessary to keep federal troops in Oxford for the rest of the year and on into 1963 to maintain order and protect Meredith.

Meredith's enrollment—halted 3 times previously by Gov. Ross R. Barnett and Lt. Gov. Paul B. Johnson of Mississippi— was accomplished Oct. 1 and marked the first desegregation of a public school in Mississippi. (Harry S. Murphy Jr., 35, a Negro, disclosed in New York Sept. 24 that he had attended the University of Mississippi in the 1945-46 school year under the Navy V-12 program. Murphy, light-complexioned, said the university officials had not known he was a Negro.)

A heavy guard of U.S. marshals had escorted Meredith when he took up residence on the campus Sept. 30. A few hours later— about 8 p.m.—the rioting broke out and continued during a nationally televised plea by Pres. John F. Kennedy (at 10:30 p.m.) urging the students and citizens of Mississippi to comply peacefully with federal law. Rioting on the campus and in downtown Oxford was finally quelled by 3,000 federal troops and federalized National Guardsmen and 400 U.S. marshals at about 11:00 a.m. Oct. 1.

The rioting brought death to Paul Guihard, 30, a correspondent for Agence France-Presse, found with a bullet in his back, and to Walter Ray Gunter, 23, a jukebox repairman from nearby Abbeville, shot in the head. More than 60-70 persons were injured, including 25 U.S. marshals. 150 alleged rioters were arrested, including ex-Maj. Gen. Edwin A. Walker of Texas, who had commanded federal troops in the Little Rock, Ark. school desegregation crisis in 1957 and who had resigned from the Army in 1961 following an official reprimand for directing the rightwing political orientation of

his troops. (12 more persons, none students, were arrested
Oct. 2.)

Barnett's defiance of federal court orders requiring Meredith's registration had begun to evaporate Sept. 30. A few hours
prior to the President's appeal Barnett's resistance was shaken
by a series of federal actions: Mr. Kennedy, in the mounting
tension, had federalized the Mississippi National Guard Sept.
30; the force of deputy U.S. marshals had been increased, and
a staging base had been set up at the Memphis (Tenn.) Naval
Air Station.

Barnett said in a statement issued Sept. 30: "My heart still
says 'never,' but my calm judgement abhors the bloodshed that
will follow"; "we are now completely surrounded by armed
forces, and . . . we are physically overpowered." He urged
Mississippi citizens and officials to try to preserve peace and
avoid violence.

Less than an hour later, Pres. Kennedy, who had spoken 3
times with Barnett by phone Sept. 29, addressed the nation on
TV. Mr. Kennedy said: Meredith was on the campus, and the
orders of the court "are beginning to be carried out"; "our
nation is founded on the principle that observance of the law
is the eternal safeguard of liberty and defiance of the law is
the surest road to tyranny"; "Americans are free . . . to
disagree with the law, but not to disobey it"; "I deeply regret
. . . that any action by the executive branch was necessary in
this case," but "my responsibility as President was . . . in-
escapable." He closed with this appeal to the university students: "Show that you are men of patriotism and integrity" by
upholding the law; "it lies in your courage to accept those laws
with which you disagree as well as those with which you
agree."

The campus had been relatively deserted Sept. 30 when
Meredith arrived. Many students were away for a football
game. Returning students, joined by some adults, began gathering on campus Sept. 30 before the line of about 300 marshals
encircling the administration building, the Lyceum. Tension
mounted, heckling increased, and members of the crowd began
pelting the marshals with rocks, bottles and bricks. At first,
only about 100 students took part in the disorder, but the number eventually swelled to 2,500.

At the height of the riot, 2 charges were made on marshals
and were repulsed by tear gas. The 2d charge allegedly was led
by Gen. Walker at the head of about 1,000 students. Students also

seized a bulldozer from a nearby construction site and a fire engine and tried unsuccessfully to run the unmanned bulldozer into the marshals. The fire engine was run across the campus, which, by this time, was overcast with tear gas and strewn with debris. Then shotgun blasts and rifle fire was begun by hidden snipers. The marshals thereupon retreated inside the Lyceum, and the snipers concentrated their fire on the Lyceum. Groups of students roamed the campus and committed acts of vandalism. A favorite target was cars; 5 autos and a mobile TV unit were burned. Other cars were stoned or overturned and their windows smashed.

The beleaguered marshals were reinforced at about midnight Sept. 30 by the Mississippi National Guard's Troop E, 2d Reconnaissance Squadron, 108th Armored Cavalry, which arrived from Tupelo. Federal combat troops—elements of the 503d Military Police (MP) Battalion—arrived at Oxford airport by helicopters Oct. 1 at 1:20 a.m. after having been prevented from landing on the campus by the dense smoke; they left immediately by bus for the campus, where they were met with flying bricks, stones and Molotov cocktails. The MPs moved in toward the fatigued marshals with fixed bayonets but did not fire. The remainder of the battalion arrived by convoy on the campus at about 4:30 a.m. after being detained by an ambush at a railroad trestle, where it had been pelted with heavy objects. After a final assault by 100 students was turned back at the Lyceum, the troops began rounding up rioters. At about 5:30 a.m. the rioting on the campus had ceased.

Rioting, however, broke out in downtown Oxford at about 9 a.m. Oct. 1 and continued until nearly noon. Soldiers, Negroes and newsmen were beaten and pelted. Cars and homes were damaged. Order finally was restored by troops firing over the heads of the mob. Roadblocks were then set up outside town, and the square was ringed with troops. By this time, about 3,000 troops were in Oxford under the command of Brig. Gen. Charles Billingslea, assistant commander of the 2d Infantry Division.

(Newsman Claude Sitton reported in the *N.Y. Times* Oct. 2 that 200 state troopers "stood by on and around the campus" during the rioting but "made no effort to break up the mob" and "pulled back from the riot scene shortly after 9 o'clock [p.m. Sept. 30], leaving the marshals to defend themselves." Sitton reported that the troopers' withdrawals were authorized by

State Sen. George Yarborough, Barnett's official representative on the campus.)

By Oct. 2, troops in and around Oxford (population: 6,500) numbered about 13,500 and included the National Guard's 108th Armored Cavalry Regiment, federal forces of the First Infantry Regiment and 3,500 paratroopers of the 101st Airborne Division. The paratroopers were withdrawn later Oct. 2 and 3. Withdrawal of some of the regular and National Guard troops began Oct. 8.

Meredith's Early Registration Attempts

Meredith's 3 previous registration attempts had been blocked Sept. 20-26 by Gov. Barnett and Lt. Gov. Johnson.

Meredith, an Air Force veteran, was a native Mississippian, born in Kosciusko. He was married and the father of a son. His reason for enrolling at the university, he said, was that it offered him the best course in his major, political science. He had 3 semesters—a year and a half—to go to complete studies for a degree. He had applied for admission to the university in Jan. 1961. After 2 of his applications had been rejected, he instituted a federal court suit charging racial bias. He was represented by NAACP lawyers Jack Greenberg and Mrs. Constance Baker Motley. The U.S. Justice Department entered the case on his behalf later.

U.S. District Court Judge Sidney C. Mize ruled in Dec. 1961 that the denials had not been solely on racial grounds. The U.S. 5th Circuit Court of Appeals Jan. 12 upheld Mize's ruling but held unconstitutional the university's requirement that applicants submit letters of recommendation from alumni of the all-white institution. Mize reheard the case and refused Feb. 5 to order the university to admit Meredith. Mize's decision was upheld in New Orleans Feb. 12 by a 2-1 decision of a 3-judge panel of the 5th Circuit Court, with Chief Judge Elbert P. Tuttle dissenting. State officials then sought to prosecute Meredith on a charge that he had violated state law in 1960 by listing his residence as Hinds County on his voter registration and Attala County on his university application. Prosecution of this charge was barred June 12 by the U.S. 5th Circuit Court. (Justice of the Peace Homer Edgeworth in Jackson convicted Meredith on the charge *in absentia* Sept. 20, but the conviction was reversed the same day by U.S. District Judges Mize and Harold Cox on Justice Department request.)

An injunction to force Meredith's admission to the school was issued in New Orleans June 25 by a 2-1 decision of a 3-judge panel of the 5th Circuit Court (Judge Dozier De Vane dissenting). The court held that Meredith had been rejected "solely because he was a Negro." U.S. District Judge Ben F. Cameron in Meridian, Miss. issued 4 stays of this order. 3 of the stays were reversed by the 5th Circuit Court by Aug. 4. The 4th, issued Aug. 6, was appealed to the Supreme Court, and Supreme Court Justice Hugo L. Black Sept. 10 nullified Cameron's stays and ordered Meredith's admission to the university.

In a statewide TV-radio address Sept. 13, Gov. Barnett (a) invoked, under a 1956 state resolution, the doctrine of interposition of state sovereignty between the federal government and the people of the state, and (b) proclaimed that all public schools and institutions of higher learning would henceforth be operated under state supervision answerable only to state laws. The governor said every public official should be willing to go to jail for the cause of segregation. The Legislature Sept. 18 indorsed Barnett's Sept. 13 proclamations and adopted legislation Sept. 19 to block Meredith's entrance to the university.

Chancery Court Judge L. B. Porter in Oxford Sept. 19 issued an injunction forbidding Meredith's admission to the university. Porter acted on the request of 47 white citizens of Mississippi, including parents of students at the university. At Justice Department request, the U.S. 5th Circuit Court voided Porter's injunction Sept. 20.

Just prior to the first attempt Sept. 20 to get Meredith admitted, Barnett had the Board of Trustees of Institutions of Higher Learning appoint him as special registrar for Meredith. He flew to Oxford and rejected Meredith's application at a 20-minute meeting in a campus building. Meredith was accompanied by U.S. Atty. St. John Barrett, Chief U.S. Marshal James J. P. McShane and another U.S. marshal. A crowd of 2,000 students jeered Meredith on the campus. About 100 state and local policemen were on hand.

The Justice Department applied to Mize and to the U.S. 5th Circuit Court of Appeals later Sept. 20 for contempt citations against university officials. A 3-judge panel of the Appeals Court in Hattiesburg Sept. 20 issued a show-cause order requiring the university's trustees to answer the charges, but in Meridian Sept. 21 Mize denied an order against the university's 3 top officials on the ground that they were powerless under Barnett's assumption of authority in the matter.

On Justice Department request, the 5th Circuit Court then included the 3 officials in the proceedings against the trustees. At the 5th Circuit Court hearing in New Orleans Sept. 24, with 8 judges in attendance, the trustees and officials agreed to abide by "any order or any act that this court orders them to." The court, presided over by Chief Judge Tuttle, ordered the university to accept Meredith and to rescind its transfer of registration authority to Barnett.

Barnett Sept. 24 ordered the summary arrest and imprisonment of any federal official who sought to arrest or fine any Mississippi official for defying court desegregation orders.

The first court action against Barnett, a proceeding the Justice Department had tried to avoid, took place Sept. 25, on application of Meredith's NAACP lawyers, when a 3-judge panel of the U.S. 5th Circuit Court (a) enjoined Barnett, as well as other state and local officials, from blocking Meredith's entrance and (b) nullified any state injunctions blocking Meredith's entrance.

Meredith, accompanied Sept. 25 by U.S. Atty. John Doar and U.S. Chief Marshal McShane, again attempted to register at the trustees' office in Jackson, but Barnett blocked the doorway and again denied him admission to the university. Barnett refused to accept copies of the 5th Circuit Court's restraining orders or of a summons to appear before the court. Meredith then returned to New Orleans. On Justice Department application, a different 3-judge panel of the 5th Circuit Court issued a contempt citation against Barnett the night of Sept. 25.

Meredith Sept. 26 attempted to enter the university a 3d time, but he and McShane were halted near the main entrance in Oxford by Lt. Gov. Paul B. Johnson, backed by 20 unarmed state troopers and about 15 country sheriffs. Johnson, announcing that he was acting on Barnett's orders, refused to admit Meredith and scuffled several times with McShane as he and the troopers blocked McShane's efforts to push through to the university.

The Justice Department later Sept. 26 obtained a contempt citation against Johnson from the U.S. 5th Circuit Court. The court also issued a 2d contempt citation against Barnett, who had evaded attempts to serve him with notice of the court's first action against him. A U.S. marshal trying to deliver the contempt citation to Barnett's office was blocked by state highway police.

A crowd of 2,500 persons Sept. 27 awaited the scheduled

4th attempt of Meredith to register. 200 police officers equipped with clubs were deployed around the campus by Barnett, who, with Johnson and his top adviser on segregation matters, William J. Simmons, national administrator of the Citizens Councils of America, also waited on the campus. But the Justice Department canceled the attempt Sept. 27 and said that the "force accompanying Mr. Meredith [25 U.S. marshals] might not be sufficient to accomplish its mission without major violence and bloodshed for the citizens of Mississippi."

Meredith, guarded by U.S. marshals, returned to the campus Sept. 30 for his 4th—and successful—attempt to register. His arrival led to the 15 hours of rioting.

Blame for Disorders Disputed

U.S. Atty. Gen. Robert F. Kennedy and Gov. Barnett engaged in a verbal duel Oct. 1 over the responsibility for the violence. Kennedy asserted in a statement that Meredith's entrance to the campus had been "arranged by" Barnett and that Barnett had "assured" the Justice Department that law and order would be maintained by the state police. He charged that the state police had been withdrawn from the campus area shortly after the rioting began, were returned after the first violence had subsided and were withdrawn again when further violence erupted. During this latter period, he said, "approximately 150 of the police were observed sitting in their automobiles within ½ mile of the rioting and shooting." He praised the U.S. marshals' "restraint and judgment."

Barnett, in a TV address taped Oct. 1 and broadcast partially that night, denied Kennedy's charges and asserted that the fatal rioting was caused by "inexperienced, nervous and trigger-happy federal marshals." He said: Mississippians were "enraged, incensed—and rightly so"; "free men do not submit meekly to the kind of treatment Mississippians received." The bloodshed could be ended if Meredith and the troops were removed from the university; he had "begged" federal officials not to place Meredith on the campus until tension had eased. The violence was due to the marshals' firing of tear gas at the backs of unarmed state patrolmen; this had occurred after a pop bottle shattered on the street as the patrolmen were "successfully moving the students," who were "noisy and boisterous, but not violent."

A LaFayette County grand jury Nov. 16 blamed federal officials for the rioting. The jury's findings were presented in a report to a state Circuit Court in Oxford. U.S. Chief Marshal McShane was accused in the report of having "precipitated" the riot. The jury gave the court 2 sealed indictments connected with the disturbances. The jury report, based on testimony from 19 witnesses (none of them federal officials) and reports submitted by state and federal officials, said: (a) Meredith's registration was instituted without "proper notice" to university officials of the time it was to take place; (b) "the encircling of the Lyceum by the marshals when it was definitely known that registration could not occur on Sunday did nothing but inflame the situation . . . [and] was apparently done for the sole purpose of agitating and provoking violence"; (c) McShane's order for marshals to fire tear gas was unwarranted, "illegal," "done for the purpose of inciting a riot" and given "without notice and at a time when the Mississippi Highway Patrol was successfully moving the crowd back"; "until the gas was fired, the actions of the crowd consisted primarily of shouting, name-calling, taunts, the flicking of cigarettes, and the throwing of eggs and small rocks"; (d) several state patrolmen were injured by the firing of the gas-bombs; the use of gas "caused great commotion" among the patrolmen, who were then ordered by their colonel to reorganize and assemble at an entrance to the university's campus; (e) the death of Walter Ray Gunter was caused by a stray bullet, but Paul Guihard "was murdered by a party unknown"; (f) "many cruel and inhuman acts of violence were inflicted by the marshals" on alleged rioters they arrested.

The U.S. Justice Department Nov. 16 rejected the report's findings against McShane and other marshals. Atty. Gen. Kennedy said: The grand jury "could not or did not consider all the evidence available about the riot"; "all federal actions [concerning Meredith's registration] Sept. 30 were made by prearrangement with Gov. Barnett of Mississippi."

State Circuit Court Judge Walter M. O'Barr, to whom the jury's report was presented, had accused the Kennedy Administration Nov. 12 of moving toward a "totalitarian dictatorship" and had ordered the grand jury to bar evidence produced by "unlawful" Army searches. He denounced the U.S. Supreme Court as "diabolical" and "made up of political, greedy old men . . . not qualified to serve as a judge of any court." He told the jury that federal employes, including Pres. Kennedy and "little stupid brother Robert Kennedy," were not immune from prosecution.

The defendant in one of the indictments was revealed Nov. 21, when McShane surrendered in Oxford to Lafayette County Sheriff Joe Ford and was released 3 hours later on a writ of *habeas corpus*. He was scheduled for trial in federal court.

Meredith at School

Meredith attended 2 classes after his enrollment Oct. 1 with no incidents except jeering and shouts of "nigger" from students. Meredith at first was escorted by U.S. Chief Marshal McShane and another marshal, but his guard was increased to 75 marshals before he reached his first class. 4 marshals stood on duty outside his classrooms. He attended classes peacefully Oct. 2 with an escort of marshals and with his car followed by an Army truck carrying 12 armed soldiers.

About 35-50 students demonstrated near Meredith's campus residence early Oct. 3 and burned him in effigy. Armed federal troops quickly dispersed the group. Just after daybreak soldiers removed a 2d effigy hanging from a building adjoining Meredith's.

The football game between the University of Mississippi and the University of Houston, scheduled for Oxford Oct. 6 to coincide with homecoming festivities, was transferred to Jackson after the Defense Department barred the playing of the game in Oxford. The Defense Department acted under Pres. Kennedy's executive order requiring the removal of "all obstructions to justice" in Mississippi.

Meredith's attendance at classes continued despite several incidents. A rock was thrown through a window of the campus cafeteria Oct. 8 while he was eating, and he was escorted by U.S. marshals back to his troop-guarded dormitory. A crowd of about 400 students that gathered during the incident was watched by about 15 troops and dispersed by a university dean, Leston L. Love. Love warned Oct. 12 that students participating in demonstrations would be subject to disciplinary action. During his 2d week of classes Meredith dined in the cafeteria and walked to class unguarded by marshals and had coffee with 3 faculty members.

A charge that Army units in the Oxford area had been "re-segregated" was made by Meredith Oct. 9. Meredith said Negro soldiers had been "purged from their positions in the ranks" and given menial duties such as garbage collection. Meredith simultaneously assailed a statement, reportedly made Oct. 2 by Aaron Henry, chairman of the NAACP's Mississippi chapter, that Meredith had been picked by the NAACP to enter the university. Meredith called the statement "an insult to my dignity."

Army Secy. Cyrus R. Vance later Oct. 9 issued a statement admitting that "during the difficult period when troops were first employed in the Oxford area, Negro soldiers were not used on patrols in order to avoid unnecessary incidents." The Negro troops were ordered returned to "all normal functions" Oct. 6, "when the situation became more stabilized," the statement said.

Henry said Oct. 9 that the NAACP had "not picked" Meredith to enter the university and had gone to his aid "only after he requested it."

Meredith told a reporter Oct. 9 that the NAACP was paying "no part" of his school costs. His schooling was financed by his own U.S. Savings Bonds and under the GI Bill, he said.

Several demonstrations and acts of hooliganism by University of Mississippi students were directed Oct. 24-31 against Meredith and troops guarding him. 2 U.S. marshals quickly escorted Meredith from the campus dining room Oct. 24 after about 30 white students had left the room at Meredith's entrance and gathered outside the door, where they blocked Meredith's exit (one white girl student had remained in the dining room). While Meredith was dining at the cafeteria Oct. 29, about 200 students exploded firecrackers and threw soft drink bottles at soldiers assigned outside. The night of Oct. 30 a bottle was thrown through the window of a car carrying Meredith and 2 marshals. The next night a firecracker thrown from a dormitory window hit a military policeman in the face. Troops with fixed bayonets immediately surrounded the dormitory while MPs searched it. (Meredith was in another dormitory, where the guard was increased.) The search produced an Army M-1 rifle and pistol, both dismantled, several tear gas grenades and fireworks.

Chancellor J. D. Williams addressed a student convocation Nov. 1 and warned that students participating in disorders would be subject to "swift and drastic disciplinary action, including expulsion." 4 students were expelled Nov. 3 on charges based on the discovery of the weapons in the dormitory. Expulsion had been recommended by the Student Judicial

Council.

(A University of Mississippi student, Taylor Robertson, 19, expelled after explosives were found in his dormitory, was ordered reinstated Nov. 30 by Chancery Court Judge J. S. Stennett in Jackson.)

Federal concern over the outbursts was evidenced by the return to Oxford Oct. 30 of Deputy Atty. Gen. Nicholas deB. Katzenbach. Katzenbach, who had said in Oxford Oct. 5 that he could not understand why university officials had taken no disciplinary action against students involved in the rioting, conferred with university officials Oct. 30 and told them that students arrested for disturbances concerning Meredith would be charged with contempt of federal court. The school announced the same day that 8 of the 11 students whose names had been given to the university by the Justice Department for their roles in the rioting had been put on probation for the current semester. (Katzenbach had addressed the university's Law School students Oct. 8 at the invitation of officials. He told them Meredith "is not going to withdraw." State Atty. Gen. Joe T. Patterson, at his own request, spoke in rebuttal to Katzenbach Oct. 16 and said students had "the constitutional right to ignore and ostracize any undesirable student." Law School Dean Robert J. Farley told the students after Patterson's address that "I don't agree with most of what Mr. Patterson said.")

A handbill urging students to "banish" white students who befriended Meredith was circulated on the campus Nov. 7.

The withdrawal from the university of one of 7 students who had dined on campus with Meredith Nov. 15 was reported Nov. 21 by the student's roommate, who said their room had been ransacked later Nov. 15 and Dean Love had advised the 2 to leave the campus for the weekend.

Sidna Brower, 21, editor of the campus daily newspaper, was reprimanded by the school's student senate Dec. 4 for her editorials urging the students to go about their normal business despite Meredith's presence. Petitions urging her impeachment as editor were circulated on the campus.

The Justice Department Dec. 11 estimated its costs of enforcing the court-ordered enrollment of Meredith at $406,508, and the Defense Department Dec. 13 estimated its costs at about $3,850,000 (both estimates were through Oct. 31).

The Army force guarding Meredith on campus was reduced Dec. 19 from 500 men to 300. But there were indications that the Army expected to keep men there for an extended period.

The Army's Corps of Engineers in Mobile Dec. 21 opened competitive bidding for about $75,000 worth of "troop-support facilities" at Oxford.

Court Action Against Gov. Barnett

The U.S. 5th Circuit Court of Appeals in New Orleans Sept. 28 found Gov. Barnett guilty of civil contempt and ordered him to purge himself of the charge by 11 a.m. Sept. 30 or be fined $10,000 a day and be committed to the custody of the U.S. Attorney General. The contempt finding was approved by the 8 judges hearing testimony, but 3 dissented on the imposition of a fine. The court ordered Barnett to purge himself by directing his law enforcement officers and state officials to end resistance to and interference with the court's desegregation orders, to maintain law and order at the University of Mississippi and to cooperate with court and federal agents to attain Meredith's registration and attendance at the university.

Before hearing the case, Chief Judge Elbert P. Tuttle said that "the court has practically exhausted its powers in this matter" and "the burden now falls upon the executive branch of the government."

Barnett did not appear in court.

A 3-judge panel of the court tried Lt. Gov. Johnson *in absentia* Sept. 29 and found him guilty of contempt. It ordered him to purge himself or face a $5,000-a-day fine.

The 8-judge court Oct. 2 declined to dismiss the contempt cases against Barnett and Johnson, but it set another hearing for Oct. 12 with the judgments of arrest and fines to be held in abeyance. Neither defendant was in court, but the court's jurisdiction in the case was recognized by them for the first time by their representation by counsel, headed by Mississippi Atty. Gen. Patterson. The court held Oct. 2 that the university officers and trustees were complying with the court's orders and freed them of civil contempt charges.

The court Oct. 12 postponed its decision on whether Barnett and other Mississippi officials had purged themselves of contempt. Barnett's lawyers said Barnett would not promise compliance with the court's orders. They said Barnett would comply whenever he determined that the orders were not in conflict with the state constitution.

The Justice Department filed with the court Oct. 15 briefs asking the court to fine Barnett $100,000 plus a continuing fine of $10,000 a day until he had purged himself of contempt. The request was made on the grounds that Barnett had not ordered Meredith protected and had not disavowed his defiant actions or statements. The government briefs said the department did not propose imprisonment because Barnett had ended "his affirmative obstruction." NAACP lawyers for Meredith at the same time asked the court to arrest Barnett and Johnson.

Barnett said in a statement Oct. 16 that he had "upheld the law" and was "not in contempt of any court." "I have never taken the position that I have purged myself nor have I authorized anyone to take such a position on my behalf," he said.

The court in Atlanta Oct. 19 again deferred decision on contempt cases against Barnett and Johnson. The court (a) denied state motions to dismiss the cases and (b) ordered Mississippi and its officials not to interfere in any way with Meredith's attendance at the university. (The ban on such interference included a ban on proceeding with the illegal-voter-registration case brought against Meredith by the state; Meredith had been found guilty in the case, had been sentenced to a year in jail and had been fined $300.)

Criminal contempt-of-court charges against Barnett and Johnson were filed by the Justice Department with the court in New Orleans Dec. 21. They were accused of obstructing court orders that Meredith be enrolled. The Justice Department blamed them for the violence that erupted in Oxford. The court had requested the contempt action.

A private attorney, Leon Jaworski, president of the Texas State Bar Association and past president of the American College of Trial Attorneys, was named by Atty. Gen. Kennedy Dec. 22 to prosecute the contempt case.

Gen. Walker Accused

Ex-Maj. Gen. Edwin A. Walker was arrested in Oxford Oct. 1. He was charged under 4 sections of Title 18 of the U.S. Code. The charges: assault or opposing federal officers, preventing a federal officer from discharging his duties, inciting or engaging in an insurrection against the U.S., conspiracy to overthrow or oppose by force the execution of U.S. laws. He was arraigned before U.S. Commissioner Omar D. Craig in Oxford Oct. 1, bail was set at $100,000, and he was taken to the Federal Bureau of Prisons in Springfield, Mo. that night. U.S. District Judge Claude Clayton in Oxford Oct. 2 ordered psychiatric examination of Walker and barred his release on bond until the examinations were completed.

When the Mississippi crisis had arisen Walker had broadcast a radio appeal from Dallas, Tex. Sept. 28 for segregationists "to move" "to a stand" beside Barnett. Walker urged: "10,000 strong from every state in the union! Rally to the cause of freedom! The battle cry of the Republic: Barnett, yes! Castro, no! Bring your flag, your tent, and your skillet. It's now or never!"

Walker was released from the U.S. Medical Center in Springfield, Mo. Oct. 6 on $50,000 bond after Judge Clayton halved the required bond and ordered Walker to undergo psychiatric tests beginning within 5 days of his release.

Clayton ruled Nov. 21 that Walker was mentally competent to stand trial. He acted on the basis of a report by a Dallas psychiatrist, Dr. R. L. Stubblefield. During the 2-day hearing on Walker, Clayton had refused a defense motion to delete from the record a memo by a government psychiatrist, Dr. Charles Smith, that Walker was mentally disturbed and should undergo observation. Smith's opinion had served as the basis of federal action to commit Walker to a mental hospital following his arrest.

(A federal grand jury failed in Jan. 1963 to indict Walker and 6 other alleged instigators of the rioting. U.S. Atty. H. M. Ray therefore requested that the charges against them be dismissed "without prejudice," and Clayton complied Jan. 21, 1963.)

Widespread Reaction

Gov. Barnett's position in the Meredith situation was supported Sept. 26 by Mississippi Democrats James O. Eastland and John Stennis in the U.S. Senate and Thomas G. Abernathy, Jamie L. Whitten, Arthur Winstead, John Bell Williams and William M. Colmer of the U.S. House.

Sens. Kenneth B. Keating (R., N.Y.) and Paul H. Douglas (D., Ill.) urged Congress Sept. 26 to express support of the attempts to enforce the federal court's order.

Ex-Pres. Dwight D. Eisenhower Sept. 27 called Mississippi's refusal to admit Meredith "absolutely unconscionable and indefensible."

2 Southern governors publicly supported Barnett's stand: Gov. John Patterson of Alabama wired Pres. Kennedy Sept. 27

that Barnett was right and the federal government wrong and that if federal force were sent to Mississippi it would be "dictatorship of the foulest sort." Gov. Orval E. Faubus of Arkansas said Oct. 1 that the federal government and not Barnett was responsible for Meredith's safety on the campus.

Gov. S. Ernest Vandiver of Georgia Sept. 30 denounced Barnett's actions and upheld obedience to law. Gov. Bert Combs of Kentucky said Oct. 1 that "Ross [Barnett] is dead wrong" and "should stop playing Custer's last stand."

In Jackson, Miss. Oct. 2, 200 Mississippians prominent in business or the professions met and signed a statement urging "all our mayors and local public officials . . . to advocate . . . the maintenance of law and order."

The university's chapter of the American Association of University Professors Oct. 3 issued a statement deploring the disorders and calling the attempt to blame the marshals for the riot "unfair and reprehensible . . . [and] false."

The Mississippi Legislature Oct. 6 abandoned its investigation of the riot on the ground that the university's standing might be injured. The Southern Association of Secondary Schools & Colleges placed all Mississippi schools on probation Nov. 28 but did not withdraw accreditation from them.

SOUTHERN SCHOOL DESEGREGATION

92.4% of Negro Children Segregated

246,988 (or 7.6%) of the Negro pupils in public schools in 17 Southern and border states and the District of Columbia were attending integrated classes, *Southern School News* (Nashville, Tenn.) reported May 10. The percentage was .7% higher than reported for May 1961. Of 6,368 school districts in the region, 3,047 had both Negroes and whites, and of these 912 were desegregated, according to *Southern School News.* It reported total white enrollment for the region at 10,376,069, Negro enrollment at 3,240,439.

The Southern Education Reporting Service said Dec. 20 that 255,367 Negroes were enrolled with white pupils for the 1962-63 school year in 972 public school districts in Southern and border states.

It was also reported that: (a) The only remaining states with completely segregated schools were Alabama, Mississippi (except for James H. Meredith at the University of Mississippi) and South Carolina. (b) The number of desegregated districts in the region increased from 912 in the previous school year to 972 (while the number of school districts there decreased from 6,368 to 6,229 because of consolidations). (c) 165 of 292 colleges and universities were desegregated in 1962, compared with 152 of 285 in 1961. (d) 150 of 240 all-white or predominantly white colleges admitted Negroes and 15 of 52 all-Negro or predominantly Negro colleges admitted whites. (e) 140 of the 165 desegregated colleges desegregated voluntarily. (f) An estimated 24,000 Negroes attended public colleges with whites; about 7,000 of them were in formerly all-white schools and about 17,000 were in formerly all-Negro schools.

Catholic Conflict in Louisiana

3 Louisiana segregationists were excommunicated Apr. 16 by Roman Catholic Archbishop Joseph Francis Rummel, 85, of New Orleans for continuing their attempts to "provoke . . . disobedience" to his order Mar. 27 that the church's schools in the New Orleans Archdiocese be desegregated. Those excommunicated were Leander H. Perez Sr., 71, Plaquemines Parish Council president; Jackson G. Ricau, 44, executive director of the South Louisiana Citizens Councils; Mrs. E. B. J. (Una) Gaillot Jr., 41, head of Save Our Nation, Inc.

This was the first time Rummel had invoked excommunication and only the 2d time excommunication had been invoked in a racial dispute in Louisiana. Rummel's order said the 3 had shown "flagrant disregard" of a cautioning letter he had sent them Mar. 31. His action was upheld Apr. 16 by a Vatican spokesman, who said Rummel was forced to excommunicate Catholics unwilling to admit the fundamental equality of all human beings.

Perez Apr. 16 characterized the excommunications as an attempt "to impose forced racial integration or communistic regimentation of our children" and to "terrorize the parents of parochial school children." He said: Children must be protected "against the unmoral curse of forced racial integration"; "I am a lifelong Catholic and will continue to be so, regardless of communistic infiltration and the influence of the National Conference of Christians & Jews upon our church leaders." (Perez had urged Louisiana Catholics to "cut off

[Rummel's] water" by not contributing to the church.)

Ricau said Apr. 16: He would "continue to fight integration in Louisiana"; "race mixing is not a religious matter, . . . and to oppose Communist operations in the integration movement . . . should merit warm ecclesiastical approval."

Mrs. Gaillot said Apr. 16: "I do know what God has written in the bible"; "God does demand the segregation of the races and curses all integrators no matter who they are."

Mrs. Gaillot had sought an audience with Rummel ever since she had received his "cautioning" letter. An audience was scheduled for Apr. 16 but was canceled later, the church office said, when Rummel "became convinced" she intended to use the interview to publicize "her personal interpretation of holy scripture." She and several other women had picketed the chancery shortly before the excommunication was announced. Mrs. Gaillot, accompanied by news photographers and reporters, went to see Rummel Apr. 17. Interrupting him while he led women pilgrims in prayer on his lawn, she knelt before him and, according to a report she gave later at a news conference, "I begged him to bless me, but I didn't back down on my stand for segregation." Rummel turned away without replying.

Rummel's Mar. 27 order, requiring an end to segregation in all Roman Catholic schools in the New Orleans Archdiocese, effective in the fall term, covered 116 elementary and 37 high schools with a total enrollment of 75,276.

Roman Catholic parochial school desegregation in Louisiana began Aug. 29 in Buras, where 5 Negro and 44 white children entered school together for the first time. The only incident: a bystander punched a TV cameraman. The Negro children failed to attend classes Aug. 30, and only 25 white pupils appeared. Church officials, reporting threats of violence, closed the school Aug. 31. It was reopened Sept. 4 with the Negroes again absent and white attendance below normal. No pupils attended Sept. 7 as about 50 white parents congregated outside.

Parochial schools in and near New Orleans were desegregated Sept. 4, and about 150 Negro children attended 30 previously white schools. White mothers, including Mrs. Gaillot, picketed 2 of the schools and the archbishop's residence.

In suburban Westwego, there was a brief scuffle in the school when a white father attempted to withdraw his child from the school after a Negro had entered. Later, parents were allowed to take their children from the schools. A crowd of about 200 whites gathered at the school Sept. 5 to jeer Negroes and white parents who allowed their children to remain. Police checked the crowd, but a stone smashed into the windshield of a car bringing a Negro child to school accompanied by her mother. The white crowd continued to keep vigil at the school, but white student attendance increased after opening day.

Public School Desegregation in Louisiana

The New Orleans public schools, opening Sept. 6, began their 3d year of desegregation. A total of 104 Negro children attended 20 formerly all-white schools without major incidents. A white parents' boycott at Semmes, Bradley and Shaw kept attendance low in those schools, and 11 bomb hoaxes caused brief evacuations of several schools, but attendance at the McDonogh 19 and Frantz schools, scenes of turmoil in 1960, was increased over the previous year (it was tripled at Frantz). The overall district attendance continued to increase; by Sept. 10 there were 8,047 students in 20 integrated public schools, compared with 6,876 opening day and 9,454 in Oct. 1961. By Sept. 10 about 300 Negroes were attending 55 desegregated public and parochial schools in New Orleans and surrounding counties.

U.S. District Judge J. Skelly Wright in New Orleans had invalidated Louisiana's pupil-placement law Apr. 3 and ordered the New Orleans public schools to accept Negro students in the first 6 grades beginning with the fall term. Under the pupil-placement law, in operation for 2 years, the school board had first tested students and then assigned them to schools. Wright called the operation of such a law in a segregated school system "discrimination in its rawest form."

Wright's ruling was stayed by U.S. District Judge Frank Ellis in New Orleans May 1 after Wright's elevation to the U.S. Court of Appeals in Washington. Ellis modified Wright's decision May 23 by requiring that only the first grade be integrated in September.

Acting on an appeal from Ellis' decision, the U.S. 5th Circuit Court of Appeals in New Orleans Aug. 6 ordered the New Orleans public schools (a) to remove all racial bars from the first 3 grades in September, (b) to abolish, for the first 2 grades in Sept. 1963 and for the 3d, 4th and 5th grades in

Sept. 1964, the separate-but-equal system of school districts for whites and Negroes, (c) to have desegregation and the abolishing of the dual-school system proceed at the rate of a grade a year from Sept. 1964 onwards.

The Supreme Court Feb. 19 had upheld a ruling that upset as unconstitutional a 1961 Louisiana law permitting the closing of public schools in school districts under federal orders to desegregate.

Prince Edward Case

The Virginia Supreme Court of Appeals ruled Mar. 5 that the Prince Edward County board of supervisors could not be compelled under state law to appropriate funds to support the county's public schools. Prince Edward public schools had been closed in 1959 to prevent racial integration.

U.S. District Judge Oren R. Lewis ruled in Richmond July 26 that the Prince Edward public schools must be re-opened in September "without regard to race or color." Lewis, directing the school board to submit a desegregation plan, held that the county did not have "the sole control" of its schools but that local boards were given responsibility for maintaining the schools along with the state, which came within the scope of the federal constitution and its ban against discrimination.

The county's public schools, however, remained closed for the fall term. White students attended a private school established by white residents, but about 1,500 Negro children had no formal school opportunities.

Atty. Gen. Robert F. Kennedy urged the U.S. 4th Circuit Court of Appeals Dec. 20 to order the reopening of the Prince Edward public schools on a non-segregated basis. He said that for the schools to "remain closed is a disgrace to our educational system and to our country." The statement was made as the Justice Department asked for the court's permission to enter the case as a friend of the court.

Tulane and Clemson Rulings

U.S. District Judge J. Skelly Wright in New Orleans Mar. 28 had barred Tulane University from discriminating against Negro applicants and had ordered the university to admit 2 Negro students, Barbara M. Guillory and Pearlie H. Elloie.

Wright ruled that Tulane was "a public institution" receiving "very substantial state subsidy" and thus subject to the 14th Amendment's ban on bias. U.S. District Judge Frank B. Ellis, reversing Wright's decision after Wright's elevation to the U.S. Court of Appeals in Washington, ruled in New Orleans Dec. 5 that Tulane was a private institution and therefore that (a) it could not be forced by the court to admit Negroes, but (b) it could admit them voluntarily, and the State of Louisiana could not bar such admissions.

U.S. District Judge C. C. Wyche in Spartanburg, S.C. Dec. 21 rejected Harvey Gantt's suit to gain admission to all-white, state-owned Clemson University. Wyche said the rejection was not "because of his [Gantt's] race" (Negro) but because Gantt had failed (a) to comply with Clemson's application regulations and (b) to prove he was being discriminated against. Hearings had been held in Anderson Nov. 19-21, and Gantt was represented by an NAACP attorney, Mrs. Constance Baker Motley. A 3-judge Court of Appeals Oct. 5 had rejected Gantt's request for an order for immediate admittance pending the lower court decision.

Desegregation Gains Reported

Among Southern states in which increases in school desegregation were reported during 1962:

Arkansas—Mansfield Aug. 27 became the 11th state school district to desegregate; 14 Negroes enrolled with 725 whites in 2 previously all-white schools. Negro attendance in integrated public schools in Little Rock was increased by 33 to 78 (9,460 whites) in the fall term. Throughout the state about 225 Negroes attended integrated classes.

Florida—Escambia became the 6th Florida county to desegregate its public schools when 21 Negroes enrolled Aug. 27 in 9 formerly all-white schools. Although under court orders to desegregate only 2 grades in 1963, Negro pupils were accepted in all grades.

Georgia—5 more Atlanta public high schools accepted Negro students for the first time Aug. 29. The Most Rev. Paul J. Hallinan, 51, Roman Catholic archbishop of Atlanta, announced June 10 that students would be admitted on a nonracial basis to the archdiocese's 18 elementary and 5 high schools beginning in September, and Roman Catholic parochial school desegregation began without incident in Atlanta

Sept. 4 when 17 Negroes enrolled in 6 previously all-white schools. But Albany school authorities Sept. 4 refused to admit, on the ground that pupil assignments had already been made, 19 Negro students who applied at 3 white schools. Parents, led by Albany Movement Pres. William G. Anderson, accompanied the children. Police barricades had been set up at the schools; at the high school the words "No Niggers, Please" had been lettered on the window at the entrance.

Maryland—About 45 Negro pupils attended previously all-white schools in Wicomico and Dorchester in the fall term.

Tennessee—Jackson voluntarily desegregated its public schools Jan. 25 when 3 Negroes were admitted to previously all-white Tigrett Junior High School. Chattanooga public schools were desegregated Sept. 5 as 44 Negro children attended classes in 6 previously all-white elementary schools (including schools in Hamilton County, which desegregated voluntarily). The fall term began the 2d year of integrated schooling in Memphis as 36 Negroes enrolled in 7 previously all-white schools.

Texas—Negro attendance with whites increased from 18 the previous year to 28 as Dallas public schools Sept. 5 began the 2d year of a grade-a-year desegregation plan.

Virginia—Court-ordered desegregation of Lynchburg public schools began Jan. 29 when 2 Negro 9th-graders entered the city's previously all-white high school. No incidents were reported. School desegregation involving 16 Negroes in 5 schools began Sept. 4 in Amherst, West Point and Loudon counties. 14 Negro students enrolled Sept. 5 in previously all-white schools in Portsmouth, and 14 others entered 8 Lynchburg schools under the court-approved grade-a-year integration plan. Desegregation of Richmond schools was extended Sept. 6 to 5 more schools. 2 Winchester and 3 Princess Anne County schools were desegregated with the entry of 44 Negroes.

Impacted-Area Schools

Health, Education & Welfare Secy. Abraham A. Ribicoff told a House Education subcommittee Mar. 30 that segregated schools would be considered "unsuitable" for children living on federal bases. If children from the bases were withdrawn from such schools, federal aid to the schools also would be withdrawn, he said. Ribicoff said that about 200 federal installations were in segregated school districts and that about

45,000 school-age children lived on federal property and attended public schools in 11 Southern states. Ribicoff revealed that the U.S. Commissioner of Education was being authorized to build and operate public schools on the bases currently served by segregated schools. Ribicoff said the new policy would not go into effect until Sept. 1963 to permit Congress time to review the situation.

The Justice Department filed in U.S. district court in Richmond, Va. Sept. 17 a suit to bar segregation in Prince George County (Va.) public schools receiving federal aid under the "impacted-areas" program. The schools were attended the previous academic year by 1,818 children (including 117 Negroes) of military or civilian personnel of Fort Lee, an Army base. The suit, the first of its kind brought by the department, charged that the segregation caused "impairment of the service and morale of its military and civilian personnel and the separation of servicemen from their families when Negro servicemen send their children to schools outside the area of Fort Lee."

Unrest at Southern University

Student demonstrations Jan. 16-Feb. 1 disrupted the normal operation of Southern University, an all-Negro college in Baton Rouge, La. The university was closed Jan. 18-28.

Students demonstrated Jan. 16 in protest against the expulsion of 7 students who had participated in an anti-segregation demonstration in Baton Rouge in Dec. 1961. The expelled students were members of the Baton Rouge chapter of CORE, which had sponsored the 1961 protest. The university had suspended an 8th student. (The Rev. B. Elton Cox, a CORE field secretary, was convicted in state district court in Baton Rouge Jan. 31 on charges of disturbing the peace during the Dec. 1961 demonstrations. He was sentenced to one year and 9 months in jail and fined $5,700. U.S. District Judge E. Gordon West in Baton Rouge Feb. 2 made permanent a previous injunction barring CORE from sponsoring demonstrations in Baton Rouge.)

At the beginning of the mid-term vacation Jan. 18 the university's 4,344 students were told the school would be closed until further notice because the campus disturbances had "seriously hampered the academic program." The university announced Jan. 20 that it would resume classes Jan. 29,

2 days later than normally. CORE announced Jan. 23 that it would try to shut the university unless all students were readmitted. It sponsored mass meetings for 2 days during registration in an attempt to start a student boycott. The university, refusing to readmit the 8 students and denying readmission to 40 others, reopened classes Jan. 29 with 5,000 enrollments. About 50 students picketed the campus Jan. 30 and about 200 marched through buildings during classes Jan. 31, but only about 300 students boycotted classes the first day and fewer the 2d day. Unauthorized student demonstrations were barred by the university Feb. 1, and attendance was described as near normal by Feb. 2.

NORTHERN SCHOOLS ACCUSED

Segregation Charged in 32 Communities

The NAACP Feb. 11 and Apr. 20 issued 2 lists of a total of 32 non-Southern communities that it said had some form of segregated schooling. The Feb. 11 list, a preliminary report on questionnaires sent to more than 500 non-Southern branches, accused: Amityville, Hempstead and Manhasset, N.Y.; Englewood, Montclair, Newark, Orange and Plainfield, N.J.; Stamford, Conn.; Chester, Coatsville and Philadelphia, Pa.; Cleveland, O.; Chicago, Danville, East St. Louis, Joliet, Maywood, Mount Vernon and Robbins, Ill.; Detroit and Grand Rapids, Mich.; Pasadena, Calif. The Apr. 20 list accused: San Francisco, Berkeley, Oakland, Los Angeles and San Diego, Calif.; Portland, Ore.; Seattle, Wash.; Phoenix, Ariz.; Salt Lake City, Utah.

Dispute in Englewood (N. J.)

300-350 Negro pupils stayed away from Lincoln School in Englewood, N.J. the first 3 days of the new term Sept. 5-7 in protest against alleged *de facto* segregation there. The 189 pupils who attended on opening day included the school's total white enrollment of 15 students. 139 pupils were absent from near-by Liberty School (60% Negro) in a one-day sympathy boycott Sept. 7. Attendance was normal in both schools Sept. 10.

A petition accusing the Englewood Board of Education of maintaining a separate school without equal educational opportunities for Negro children was filed by the NAACP Sept. 8 with the state Commissioner of Education.

Englewood Major Austin N. Volk announced Sept. 9 that the results of a poll on various plans for desegregating the Lincoln School indicated "that our citizens feel that Englewood is a well-integrated community . . . and they want a cautious approach to any changes in pupil assignment procedures." Volk said: Questionnaires were mailed to 7,800 households, and replies were received from 3,577; the results were 5-1 in favor of preserving the current neighborhood school policy and 20-1 against some plans for correcting racial imbalance.

Gov. Richard J. Hughes urged the Englewood board Sept. 6 to present a plan for "reasonable desegregation" soon. He said: "I am rather sure that the courts would eventually rule that the present racial imbalance in Englewood schools was depriving Negro youngsters there of equality of education."

A suit seeking to bar Englewood from "operating and maintaining" a "racially segregated" elementary school had been filed in U.S. district court in Newark Feb. 5 by Paul B. Zuber, a lawyer, on behalf of 9 Negro children who had been refused admittance to the predominantly-white Donald A. Quarles Elementary School. U.S. District Judge Anthony T. Augelli July 9 dismissed the suit on the ground that all available state remedies had not been sought.

Following a Feb. 1 meeting at which the Englewood Board of Education had re-affirmed its decision not to admit the Negroes to the Quarles school, 7 whites and 4 Negroes supported by CORE staged an all-night City Hall sit-in and were arrested the next morning. Disorderly-persons charges against them were dismissed Feb. 16 for lack of evidence. 4 other integrationists were arrested Feb. 2 at the arraignment of the first 11 for refusing to leave the courtroom in obedience to a magistrate's order that the court be cleared because of applause for the 11. The 4 pleaded guilty Feb. 16 and were fined $25 each. Gov. Hughes Feb. 6 had criticized the Englewood demonstration on the ground that it could lead to "violence."

Negroes Feb. 8 began picketing Englewood stores owned by whites in an attempt to enforce a Negro boycott.

The Englewood Board of Education May 14 announced a plan to establish a "demonstration school" for pupils from kindergarten through the 6th grade. The plan did not gain public support and was abandoned. The board July 12 proposed that all 5th-grade pupils attend a Central Intermediate School in one building and that the plan be expanded the following year to include the 6th grade. This plan was presented by John H.

Perry, the board's only Negro member, who had been elected president that day; it was opposed July 21 by the Save Our Schools Committee, a new group whose expressed policy was to preserve the neighborhood school system but not to oppose integration.

About 500 persons—many of them whites—attended an anti-segregation rally in Englewood Aug. 18. Sponsored by the Englewood Movement, an informal group of about 200 persons opposed to segregation, the rally was organized by Zuber. Zuber, who had predicted an attendance of 3,000 to 4,000, proposed at the rally: (a) a "telephone-in" campaign of 10,000 simultaneous calls that would block all phone service to Gov. Hughes in an effort to call his attention to the situation; (b) a campaign of "selective buying" to force local merchants to support integration proposals. Zuber said that Negroes who patronized merchants during the boycott would be photographed.

Zuber, referring to dissension among Negroes about the campaign for Englewood school integration, asserted at the rally that "the first thing the Negro has got to get through his thick head is that he has to achieve unity before he gets equality." Much of the dissension had been evoked by an invitation Zuber had extended Aug. 4 to Malcolm X, 36, leader of the anti-white Black Muslim movement in New York, to address the rally. The Muslim leader at first had accepted the invitation. But he declined Aug. 7 to attend because of "the narrow-mindedness of some of [Englewood's] . . . Negro ministers," who had condemned the invitation and urged their congregations not to attend a rally that featured Black Muslims.

John Patler, 24, of New York, leader of the anti-Negro American National Party, was arrested near the Aug. 18 rally after he had refused to stop picketing. He had also distributed his party's magazine, *Kill*. Patler was found guilty of disorderly conduct Aug. 22 and sentenced to 10 days in Bergen County jail.

The Rev. Walter S. Taylor, who had boycotted the rally despite Malcolm X's withdrawal, was made temporary chairman of the Englewood Movement Aug. 22 at a reconciliation meeting attended by 26 Negro and white leaders. Taylor said afterwards that "we are going to rally the entire community around our program." However, Taylor and Zuber had a dispute at a "peace" meeting in Taylor's church Aug. 24. Taylor called police to eject Zuber from the meeting, and Zuber left as the police arrived.

Other Desegregation Suits Filed in New Jersey

A suit charging the Newark, N.J. public school system with racial segregation was dismissed by U.S. District Judge Anthony T. Augelli in Newark Mar. 19 on agreement between the school board and Paul B. Zuber, attorney for the Negro parents who had instituted the case. Both sides had worked together to devise a "voluntary-option pupil transfer program" adopted by the board Mar. 16. Under the plan, which went into effect in September, pupils had the right to transfer from predominantly Negro schools to schools in other neighborhoods. The board was not required to furnish transportation.

Augelli July 9 dismissed school-integration suits brought against Orange and Montclair on the ground that all available state remedies had not been sought.

In the Orange case, the NAACP had sued Mar. 5 to bar city and state officials from continuing alleged segregation in Orange public elementary schools. The suit charged that such segregation was a "fact, ... whether with or without design," and that it was maintained by "controlling transfers within the school system" and "by seeking to maintain existing patterns of racial segregation." The suit sought the submission of a desegregation plan and the creation of boundaries to "perpetuate positive racial integration patterns." The NAACP Feb. 14 had rejected as "completely inadequate" the Orange school board's plan, adopted Feb. 13, to transfer pupils to reduce the percentage of Negro enrollment in certain schools.

The Montclair decision was in a case brought by parents of white children. The parents contended that the school board had permitted Negro children the choice of junior high schools while denying this choice to white students, who had to attend the nearest school under a neighborhood policy. In April the board had decided to close a predominantly Negro junior high school and to redistribute the pupils to their choice of 3 other schools.

Assignment on Racial Basis Charged in N.Y. City

A suit accusing the N.Y. City Board of Education of using an unconstitutional "racial quota" in assigning students to high schools was filed in federal district court in New York Jan. 16. The suit was filed by Paul Zuber on behalf of Sheldon Rector, 15, a Negro, and on behalf of "all Negro and Puerto Rican children similarly situated." Rector had refused to attend school after the board had offered him the choice of attending either of 2 schools to which, the suit charged, the majority of Manhattan's Negro male students were assigned. The suit said about 90% of the Negro pupils were assigned to 20% of the city's high schools.

14 Negro students boycotted a Queens (N.Y. City) junior high school Sept. 10-Oct. 25 to back their parents' protest that the city Board of Education had gerrymandered zoning lines for racial reasons to keep their children from attending a school closer to their homes. Queens Family Court Judge Peter M. Horn Oct. 24 convicted the parents of neglect and ordered the children returned to school. The parents had staged a 26-hour sit-in at the board's headquarters Sept. 24-25. The protest also resulted in a suit, filed on behalf of 47 children by Zuber in U.S. district court in Manhattan Sept. 25, accusing the board of operating a segregated school system.

San Francisco School Plan Revised

The San Francisco Board of Education quelled a racial-discrimination conflict by revoking plans to establish a school under conditions that had been attacked by Negro groups as constituting *de facto* segregation. The board's plan for a junior high school (in an old high school building) with a 60% Negro and 40% white enrollment was withdrawn in favor of absorbing the 450 students involved in 4 or 5 other schools. A suit seeking to block the proposed school was dismissed by U.S. District Judge Alfonso J. Zirpoli, who urged those concerned to "approach the problem with even greater desire to understand than to be understood."

VOTE RIGHTS STRUGGLE

Senate Filibuster Kills Literacy Bill

The Kennedy Administration's first civil rights bill, a measure to bar the arbitrary use of literacy tests to block Negroes trying to register to vote in federal elections, was introduced in the Senate Jan. 25 by Senate majority leader Mike Mansfield (D., Mont.). The bill would have made a 6th grade education evidence of anyone's literacy for voting purposes. But after committee action, a 3-week Senate debate (Apr. 24-May 15), a Southern Democratic filibuster and 2 defeated cloture motions, the bill was laid aside.

The Administration bill (S 2750) had received bipartisan backing Jan. 29 when Senate GOP leader Everett McKinley Dirksen (Ill.) joined Mansfield as its co-sponsor.

Vice Pres. Lyndon B. Johnson then ruled Jan. 30 that the bill must be referred to Sen. James O. Eastland's Senate Judiciary Committee, which had never voluntarily sent a civil rights measure to the full Senate in modern times. Sen. Jacob K. Javits (R., N.Y.) protested and moved that it be sent to the Rules & Administration Committee. But Mansfield indicated that he would bring the bill before the full Senate as an amendment to unrelated legislation if the Judiciary Committee did not report the bill by May, and Javits' move was defeated by 61-25 vote (44 D. & 17 R. vs. 13 D. & 12 R.).

The Senate Judiciary Committee's Constitutional Rights Subcommittee held hearings Mar. 27-Apr. 12 on 3 literacy bills: (1) the Administration's S 2750; (2) S 480, introduced Jan. 17 by Javits and co-sponsored by Sen. Clifford P. Case (R., N.J.), to apply S 2750's provisions to state and local elections as well as federal elections; (3) S 2979, introduced Mar. 13 by Sen. Kenneth B. Keating (R., N.Y.), to add to S 2750's provisions a proviso that citizens could vote if they met reasonable age and residence requirements and had not been convicted of a felony. Subcommittee Chrmn. Sam J. Ervin (D., N.C.) charged in an opening statement Mar. 27 that the bills were an unconstitutional attempt to deprive the states of their right to determine voter qualifications. This position was backed by Sens. Herman E. Talmadge (D., Ga.) and Lister Hill (D., Ala.) Mar. 27, by Sen. John J. Sparkman (D., Ala.) Mar. 28 and by Sherwood Wise, Mississippi State Bar Association president, Apr. 6. Opposition to the bills was expressed Apr. 10 by Sen. Barry Goldwater (R., Ariz), who said Arizona Gov. Paul Fannin (R.) agreed with him.

Testimony in favor of S 2750 was given Apr. 10 by Atty. Gen. Robert F. Kennedy, who said the bill would set up an objective standard instead of the "subjective color bar to federal voting." He said protection for Negro voters "cannot be provided by lengthy litigation on a piecemeal, county-by-county basis." He interpreted S 2750 to provide that a state could set educational voting standards other than the 6th grade one as long as they applied equally to all citizens.

NAACP Executive Secy. Roy Wilkins in testimony Apr. 12 backed S 480 but said the bills were "a token offering" of

Congress to supervise enrollment and management of federal elections "instead of continuing to rely upon those state officals who have time and again discriminated against Negro voters." Also testifying in favor of the legislation were Sen. Edward V. Long (D., Mo.) Mar. 27, Erwin N. Griswold of the U.S. Civil Rights Commission Mar. 28, Andrew J. Biemiller of the AFL-CIO Apr. 6, Joseph L. Rauh Jr. of Americans for Democratic Action Apr. 12. Lawrence Speiser of the American Civil Liberties Union supported the legislation in a statement Apr. 12.

The 3-week Senate debate began Apr. 24 when Mansfield announced his intention to offer S2750 as an amendment to a House-passed bill (HR1361) to relieve Texas farmer James M. Norman from refunding excess federal crop insurance payments. S2750 was still before the Senate Constitutional Rights Subcommittee.

The filibuster began immediately after the bill's introduction. It was led by Sen. Richard B. Russell (D., Ga.). About 18 other Southern Democrats participated as members of 3 teams led by Sens. Hill (Ala.), Allen J. Ellender (La.) and John Stennis (Miss.).

Mansfield announced May 1 that he and Dirksen would offer May 7 a petition for cloture—limitation of debate—to cut off the filibuster. He also announced that if the cloture vote failed to pass (an affirmative vote by 2/3 of Senators present was required) but gained a majority vote, he would move to table the literacy bill and then vote against tabling. If the vote were heavily against tabling, he said, he would allow the debate to continue and try for a 2d cloture invocation. This was done. The first cloture motion was rejected May 10 by 53-43 vote (23 R., 23 Southern D. & 7 Northern D. vs. 30 Northern D. & 13 R.). Immediately afterwards the tabling motion was defeated by 64-33 vote (38 D. & 26 R. vs. 23 D. & 10 R.). The 2d cloture motion was rejected May 14 by 52-42 vote (30 D. & 22 R. vs. 31 D. & 11 R.).

A small group of civil rights advocates, including New York Republican Sens. Javits and Keating and Sens. Joseph S. Clark (D., Pa.) and Wayne Morse (D., Ore.), continued the debate until the Senate May 15, by 49-34 vote (30 D. & 19 R. vs. 22 D. & 12 R.), ended.

The cloture votes were the 25th and 26th since the adoption of the cloture rule (Senate Rule 22) in 1917. They were the 9th and 10th on civil rights, on which a cloture vote had never succeeded.

Anti-Poll Tax Amendment Clears Congress

A constitutional amendment (SJ Res. 29) to abolish the poll tax as a requirement for voting in federal elections was approved by 77-16 Senate vote (47 D. & 39 R. vs. 15 D. & 1 R.) Mar. 27 and by 295-86 House vote (163 D. & 39 R. vs. 71 D. & 15 R.) Aug. 27. If approved within 7 years by the legislatures of 3/4 of the states (38), the amendment would become the 24th Amendment to the Constitution. Currently, 5 states— Alabama, Arkansas, Mississippi, Texas, Virginia—levied such poll taxes.

The vote in the Senate had been preceded by a 10-day "friendly filibuster" led by Southern Democrats. Senate majority leader Mike Mansfield, taking advantage of a lull in Senate business Mar. 14, had proposed consideration of SJ Res. 29, which originally was only a proposal to make a former home of Alexander Hamilton in New York a national monument. Then Mansfield announced that if the Senate approved the motion, Sen. Spessard L. Holland (D., Fla.) would substitute for SJ Res. 29's original language a constitutional amendment to abolish poll taxes. Mansfield's announcement was immediately followed by the filibuster, led by Sen. Richard B. Russell (D., Ga.).

The Holland amendment had been opposed not only by Southern Democrats but by civil rights advocates, who held that the amendment approach would set a bad precedent for other civil rights proposals. A proposal by Sen. Jacob K. Javits (R., N.Y.) to outlaw the poll tax by statute instead of by constitutional amendment was defeated by 59-34 vote Mar. 27.

A Mar. 6 letter from Pres. John F. Kennedy supporting the Holland amendment was read to the Senate by Holland Mar. 16.

The filibuster was allowed to run its course, although Mansfield began holding the Senate in session longer than usual Mar. 20 and barred committee hearings. The Senate Mar. 26 approved by 62-15 vote Mansfield's motion to take up SJ Res. 29. Holland then offered his amendment as a substitute, a motion questioning the constitutionality of the procedure was tabled by a 58-34 vote, and the Holland amendment was approved. Senators voting against the Holland amendment: *15 Democrats*—Byrd (Va.), Eastland (Miss.), Ellender (La.), Ervin (N.C.), Fulbright (Ark.), Hickey (Wyo.), Hill (Ala.), Johnston (S.C.), McClellan (Ark.), Robertson (Va.), Russell (Ga.), Sparkman (Ala.), Stennis (Miss.), Talmadge (Ga.), Thurmond (S.C.); *one Republican*— Tower

(Tex.). Young (R., N.D.) was paired against the amendment.

Illinois Nov. 14 and New Jersey Dec. 3 became the first 2 states to ratify the proposed amendment.

Voting Rights Cases Fought in Courts

Negroes and the federal government continued to use the courts during 1962 in the drive to end discrimination against prospective voters. Among the year's court cases:

Alabama—The Justice Department, in its 28th voting-rights case brought under the Civil Rights Acts of 1957 and 1960, sued in federal district court in Mobile June 15 to bar Choctaw County voter-registration officials from discriminating against Negroes.

A suit seeking to halt discrimination in voter registration in Perry County was filed by the Justice Department in U.S. district court in Mobile Aug. 27. The state of Alabama and county vote officials were named as defendants.

The Supreme Court Oct. 22 summarily affirmed a U.S. 5th Circuit Court of Appeals decision upholding U.S. District Judge Frank M. Johnson Jr.'s order that 54 Negroes be registered as qualified voters in Macon County. The decision held that the Civil Rights Act of 1957 gave federal judges the right to order the registration of specific Negroes as voters.

Georgia—U.S. District Judge William A. Bootle in Macon June 1 ordered the desegregation of all Bibb County voting places within one year. Desegregation of 6 of the voting places was ordered by Sept. 12, the date of the Democratic primary, but the deadline for 14 others was extended to a year to prevent confusion. The order was issued against the County Democratic Executive Committee. In filing the case May 16, the Justice Department said this was the first time it had charged discrimination in the physical conduct of elections.

The Justice Department sued in U.S. district court in Columbus Aug. 13 to bar the intimidation of prospective Terrell County Negro voters. It charged that intimidation had occurred July 21 and 25 at Negro meetings called to give instructions on voting and July 30 during an attempt to register a group of Negroes in Dawson. The suit said that Ralph Allen, a white representative of the Student Nonviolent Coordinating Committee, which had begun a registration drive in the county, had been beaten severely at the July 21 meeting. Discrimination against Negro voters and registrants in the county had been barred under a 1960 federal court ruling.

Louisiana—U.S. District Judge Edwin F. Hunter Jr. in Shreveport July 24 certified 26 East Carroll Parish Negroes as voters qualified to participate in the state Democratic primary July 28. They became the first Negroes to cast votes in the parish in at least 40 years. The registration, done by Hunter after the local registrar had resigned, was the first such registration under terms of the 1960 Civil Rights Act. U.S. District Judge Ben C. Dawkins, in a May 30 ruling, had agreed with the Justice Department that voting discrimination existed in the parish and should be halted. A state district court stay of Dawkins' ruling was vacated July 3 by the U.S. 5th Circuit Court of Appeals. Another state court ruling July 19 barred Hunter's voter-application hearings, but U.S. Judge John Minor Wisdom July 23 barred the state courts and state officials from further interference.

Mississippi—The Justice Department filed in federal district court in Jackson Aug. 28 a suit charging that 2 sections of the Mississippi constitution and 6 state laws were unconstitutionally designed to "perpetuate white political supremacy, a racially segregated society and the disenfranchisement of Negroes." The suit asked the court to bar state and local officials from interfering with prospective Negro voters and to find a "pattern or practice" of racial discrimination in voting. Under attack were (1) the state constitution's requirements that voter applicants be able to interpret the constitution and to show "good moral character" and (2) state laws: (a) requiring publication of the names of applicants and perfect completion of applicant forms without help from the registrar, (b) permitting challenge of an applicant by any registered voter and refusal to divulge reasons for rejection.

The Justice Department sued in the U.S. 5th Circuit Court of Appeals in New Orleans Apr. 30 to have Theron C. Lynd, Forrest County voting registrar, held in contempt of court. The department, in its first contempt suit in a voting-rights case, charged that Lynd had refused to register at least 19 Negro applicants, including a National Science Foundation fellow, in violation of the court's Apr. 10 and 16 orders barring him from such discrimination. The orders had been issued pending consideration of the department's appeal on a voting suit brought against Forrest and Clarke Counties in 1961. The department said that U.S. District Judge Harold Cox Mar. 7 had rejected its request under this suit for an injunction barring such discrimination. A temporary injunction barring discrimination in voter registration in Forrest County was issued by the U.S. 5th Circuit Court June 11 and was upheld in effect Nov. 5 by Supreme Court refusal to review it.

A suit charging that Greene County school officials had refused to renew the contract of a Negro school teacher, Mrs. Ernestine Denham Talbert, "in an effort to intimidate her and other Negroes from registering and voting" was filed by the department in U.S. district court in Jackson June 16. Mrs. Talbert had filed an affidavit in support of the department's Apr. 16 suit alleging that George County Negroes were being deprived of their right to vote. (A temporary restraining order against such bias was issued by Cox Apr. 21.) The Greene County officials subsequently failed to renew Mrs. Talbert's contract despite her principal's recommendation that she be rehired.

Voter Registration Drives

27,839 Southern Negroes were registered to vote during registration drives conducted in April-June by the Southern Regional Council in key Southern areas, Wiley Branton reported Dec. 1. Addressing the 16th annual convention of the National Association of Intergroup Relations in Washington, Branton, who headed the drives, said they were held in Atlanta; in Memphis, Chattanooga and Knoxville, Tenn.; in Baton Rouge, La.; in Jackson, Miss., and in Virginia's 4th Congressional district. He said that only about 1½ million of 5 million eligible Negroes were registered to vote in the 11 states of the Old Confederacy.

Southern Negro Churches Burned

2 Negro churches near Sasser, Ga. were destroyed by fires early Sept. 9. One had been used as the site for weekly voter registration rallies. A Leesburg, Ga. church used for voter registration rallies had been razed by fire 3 weeks previously. Pres. Kennedy, denouncing the church burnings, pledged Sept. 13 that "we'll do everything we possibly can do to make sure that . . . protection is assured" those seeking to register Negroes. Speaking at his press conference, Mr. Kennedy added that "if it requires extra legislation and extra force, we shall do that." A 4th Negro church was burned near Dawson, Ga. Sept. 17.

Shooting incidents by unidentified nightriders had been

reported near Leesburg Aug. 31 and in Dawson Sept. 5. No one was injured in the first incident although 4 rural homes of Negroes active in a voter-registration campaign were struck by rifle fire. In the Dawson incident, 3 shotgun blasts were fired into a Negro's home used by voter-registration workers, members of the Student Nonviolent Coordinating Committee. The integrationists reported that 4 hours prior to the attack 4 of them had been chased out of Sasser by policeman D. E. Short, who, they said, had shot at their car.

More Negroes Elected

In the Nov. 6 elections Negroes were elected to 5 seats in the U.S. House of Representatives. This was the greatest number of U.S. House seats won by Negroes in any national election since 1874. 4 of the winners were incumbents—Adam Clayton Powell Jr. in New York, Charles Cole Diggs Jr. in Michigan, William Levi Dawson in Illinois and Robert N. C. Nix in Pennsylvania—and one victor was a newcomer, Augustus F. Hawkins, elected from California's newly-created 21st District. Hawkins was the first Negro elected to Congress from west of the Rocky Mountains. All were Democrats, and all ran against Negroes.

Among Negroes in Nov. 6 contests:

Edward W. Brooke (R.) was elected Massachusetts attorney general and became the first Negro to hold statewide office in Massachusetts.

Gerald Lamb (D.) was elected Connecticut state treasurer (his opponent was also a Negro).

Edward R. Dudley (D.), Manhattan (N. Y. City) borough president and the first Negro ever nominated for statewide office in New York, was defeated for state attorney general by incumbent Louis J. Lefkowitz (R.).

10 Negroes (9 from Philadelphia and one from Pittsburgh) were elected to the Pennsylvania House of Representatives.

Otis M. Smith (D.) was elected to a full term on the Michigan State Supreme Court.

Mrs. Edith Sampson became the first Negro woman elected to a judgeship in Illinois; she won a municipal judgeship in Chicago.

Leroy R. Johnson became the first Negro elected to the Georgia State Senate since Reconstruction days; he defeated another Negro. A 3d Negro candidate for the Georgia Senate, Rod Harris (R.), lost to Oby T. Brewer Sr., a white man.

EMPLOYMENT & UNION PRACTICES

Hearings on Job Equality Bill

A House Special Labor Subcommittee headed by Rep. Adam Clayton Powell Jr. (D., N.Y.) held hearings Jan. 15-24 on an equal employment opportunities bill. The bill, proposed by Powell in 1961, would bar federal aid to apprenticeship programs where racial bias was practiced. The subcommittee Jan. 23 sent its draft of the bill to the parent House Education & Labor Committee, and no further action on the measure was taken during 1962.

(The Labor Department announced Apr. 24 that it had adopted a policy calling for withdrawal of its approval of apprentice training programs that barred Negroes. Acting under the new policy, it withdrew approval of the program at the David Ranken Jr. School of Mechanical Trades in St. Louis.)

Presidential Committee Active

Representatives of 31 leading defense contractors signed agreements with the President's Committee on Equal Employment Opportunity Feb. 7 to eliminate job discrimination. The agreements were under the committee's program of "plans for progress."

The companies included Chrysler Corp., Curtiss-Wright Corp., Ford Motor Co., General Motors Corp., Goodyear Tire & Rubber Co., International Business Machines Corp., International Telephone & Telegraph Corp., Pan American World Airways, Inc., Raytheon Co., Republic Aviation Corp., Socony Mobil Oil Co., Inc., Sperry Rand Corp.

Pres. John F. Kennedy addressed the group and hailed the anti-bias progress made by 21 firms that previously had signed such agreements. Vice Pres. Lyndon B. Johnson, the committee's chairman, had reported Feb. 6 that "measurable benefits" had been achieved by 6 of the earlier signatories—RCA, Lockheed, Boeing, North American Aviation, Douglas and Martin. He said the ratio of non-white hiring in these firms had been doubled since May 15, 1961 (when non-whites held 3.4% of the 377,484 jobs available). The number of non-whites in official-supervisory jobs had been increased 47½%.

But NAACP Labor Secy. Herbert Hill criticized the program Apr. 5 as producing "more publicity than progress," and the

NAACP June 21 filed charges with the committee accusing a plant of one signatory—the Beaumont, Tex. refinery of Socony Mobil—of discriminatory labor practices.

The committee Apr. 17 barred 2 companies—Comet Rice Mills, Inc. and Danly Machine Specialties, Inc.—from getting federal contracts on the ground that they discriminated against minorities in employment. And Johnson reported Apr. 23 that 9 major defense contractors had taken "substantial" "corrective action" toward eliminating racial discrimination in employment practices; bias charges had been filed against all 9 firms, and 4 of them had signed "plans for progress" with the committee.

Representatives of 33 more major U.S. firms signed agreements with the committee at the White House June 22. The new signatories raised to 85 the number of firms participating in the "plans for progress" program. Among the new signatories: The Aluminum Co. of America; American Can Co.; American Cyanamid Co.; American Telephone & Telegraph; Bell Telephone Laboratories; E. I. du Pont de Nemours & Co.; Eastman Kodak Co.; Firestone Tire & Rubber Co.; Monsanto Chemical Co.; Olin Mathieson Chemical Corp.; Union Carbide Corp.; U.S. Rubber Co.; Western Union Telegraph Co.

119 of the AFL-CIO's 131 affiliated national unions signed anti-discrimination pledges with the committee Nov. 15. The unions represented about 90% of AFL-CIO membership. Representatives of 100 of the unions and AFL-CIO Pres. George Meany signed the pledges at a White House ceremony attended by Pres. Kennedy, who asked them "to make sure that in the ranks of labor, labor itself practices what it preaches."

(Johnson said Nov. 19 that federal employment of Negroes in the past year had been increased by 10,270, although an increase of only 3,772 had been anticipated. He said 4,481 Negroes had also been promoted to middle-level federal jobs and 343 to top executive posts. He made the comments at the annual Equal Opportunity Day dinner in New York sponsored by the National Urban League. Awards for contributing to the anti-bias campaign were given by Johnson at the dinner to IBM Chrmn. Thomas J. Watson Jr. and Pres. A. Philip Randolph of the International Bro'hood of Sleeping Car Porters.)

Unions Accused of Bias

The NAACP Oct. 16 filed 3 separate charges of job discrimination as the "beginning" of "a frontal attack on barriers to Negro employment and job promotion." 2 of the charges were filed with the NLRB—one in San Francisco against the Seafarers' International Union of North America (Pacific district) and the 2d in Atlanta against United Steelworkers Local 2401 at the Atlantic Steel Co. The 3d complaint was filed in U.S. district court in St. Louis against the Bro'hood of Railroad Trainmen and the St. Louis-San Francisco Railway Co. (The NAACP charged in a motion filed with the NLRB Oct. 25 that the Independent Metal Workers Union of the Hughes Tool Co. in Houston discriminated against Negroes in employment at the company. The NAACP said the union had 2 locals—Local 1, all of whose members were white, and Local 2, made up entirely of Negroes. The motion requested that the union's certification as bargaining agent there be rescinded.)

NAACP Labor Secy. Herbert Hill said Oct. 16 that a "decade-long attempt to resolve these problems within the labor movement itself" had resulted in "negligible" progress. The drive was aimed at unions because they had to be certified under the Taft-Hartley Act as legal bargaining agents.

AFL-CIO Pres. George Meany Nov. 9 accused Hill of untruths and smears in accusing labor unions of racial bias. The Hill-conducted NAACP drive to seek decertification of unions practicing discrimination had evoked considerable anger against the NAACP within the labor movement. Hill also had been embroiled in controversy in August when he had acted as a consultant to a special House subcommittee investigating the AFL-CIO International Ladies Garment Workers Union (ILGWU) on complaints of bias in job opportunities for Negroes and Puerto Ricans. Charles S. Zimmerman, an ILGWU vice president, resigned as a member of the NAACP Legal Defense & Education Fund because of Hill's involvement in the probe.

The decertification drive and the ILGWU probe were cited by Meany in his attack on Hill, which he made at the opening of the Negro American Labor Council's (NALC) Nov. 9-11 convention in New York. AFL-CIO Vice Pres. Walter Reuther, president of the United Auto Workers, addressed the convention Nov. 10 and said that discrimination within the labor movement was "basically not a lack of goodwill, but a lack of machinery." (Reuther had said Oct. 18 that the UAW had no quarrel with the NAACP but that NAACP "staff people" made "indiscriminate and inaccurate" charges of racial bias.)

A. Philip Randolph, the AFL-CIO's only Negro vice president, was reelected NALC president Nov. 11. He then com-

mended the delegates for rejecting a resolution indorsing
Hill's union-decertification project. He was "unalterably committed to the support of the NAACP," Randolph said. "But
we must carry on our fight within the house of labor."
    Meany announced Nov. 13, after a meeting of the AFL-CIO
Executive Council, that the council had authorized him to write
a letter telling the NAACP that the AFL-CIO wanted to work
with the NAACP but "could not under the circumstances we are
faced with by their labor secretary." In a Nov. 20 letter to
Roy Wilkins, NAACP executive secretary, Meany stressed
that it was of "great importance" to both sides that they
"reestablish the mutual understanding and goodwill with which
we once worked."

Government Curbs Propaganda

    The National Labor Relations Board (NLRB) announced
Aug. 10 that it would void the results of bargaining elections
when inflammatory racial propaganda had been injected into
the campaign. But it said it would tolerate campaign statements
about racial conditions if the statements were "temperate in
tone, germane and correct factually." Such statements, it said,
pertained "to a subject concerning which employes are entitled
to have knowledge—the union's position on racial matters."
    This criterion was applied by the board in the cases of
bargaining rights elections lost July 21, 1961 by 2 unions—the
Amalgamated Clothing Workers of America at the Sewell
Manufacturing Co. plants in Bremen and Temple, Ga. and the
Textile Workers Union of America at the Allen-Morrison Sign
Co., Inc. in Lynchburg, Va. Both unions had appealed the
elections to the NLRB on the ground that the employers had injected race hatred into the campaigns. The board ordered a
new election at Sewell but refused to set aside the election
at Allen-Morrison.

Boycotts Bring Job Gains—& Violence

    400 Negro ministers led a boycott Apr. 15-June 10 against
the *Philadelphia Bulletin* on charges of employment bias. Some
of the ministers had met with the newspaper's management Mar.
16 and had asked the paper to give Negroes equal job opportunities and to start by hiring 28 more Negroes. The ministers
announced from their pulpits Apr. 15 that the *Bulletin* had

rejected their demand. They urged the city's 700,000 Negroes to boycott the paper. The *Bulletin* responded Apr. 16 with an article saying that it employed more than 50 Negroes in supervisory and white-collar jobs and that it could not meet the demand without firing "people of one race to make room for people of another." The boycott remained in force for nearly 2 months before the ministers announced June 10 that the paper had yielded and that the boycott, therefore, was ended.

A state court in Clarksdale, Miss. Jan. 3 had convicted 5 Negroes of conspiracy to harm public trade by participating in a Negro boycott against Clarksdale stores owned by whites. The defendants, fined $500 each and given 6-month jail terms: the Rev. Theodore Trammell, a Congressional candidate; Aaron E. Henry and John C. Melcher, the NAACP's state and local chapter heads; R. L. Drew, president of the Clarksdale Voters League; J. W. Wright. All were released on $1,000 bond.

The Birmingham (Ala.) City Commission, retaliating against a Negro boycott of downtown stores, voted Apr. 3 not to pay the city's $45,000 share of a $100,000 county program supplying surplus food to the needy. More than 9% of the recipients were said to be Negroes. The boycott against stores owned by whites had started Mar. 23. Protests against the city's reprisal, made by NAACP Executive Secy. Roy Wilkins and AFL-CIO Community Service Activities director Leo Perlis, were dismissed Apr. 5 by Mayor Arthur J. Hanes as "typical reaction from New York Socialist radicals." (Birmingham's City Parks & Recreation Board Apr. 11 approved a plan to issue permits for the private and segregated use of city parks. A federal court order to desegregate the parks had gone into effect Mar. 15. The parks had been closed by the city since early 1962.)

Lesley Lee Luttes, 16, a white, was shot and killed in Augusta, Ga. Apr. 19 during racial tension arising from a Negro boycott of 2 supermarkets. The boycott had begun Apr. 16 in a protest against alleged discriminatory hiring practices. Incidents of rock and bottle throwing, mostly involving juveniles, were reported Apr. 17-18, and gangs carrying firearms and bats roamed the city. Luttes was killed as he and 2 other white youths were driving through a Negro section; their car, carrying bricks and an air rifle, was attacked by gunfire from both sides of the street. Another of the youths was seriously wounded and hospitalized. An agreement to end the picketing and discriminatory hiring practices was reached Apr. 21 by Negro leaders and the supermarkets' owners.

HOUSING DISCRIMINATION

President Bans Federal Bias

Pres. John F. Kennedy Nov. 20 issued an executive order barring racial and religious discrimination in federal and federally aided housing. The long-awaited action (Mr. Kennedy had pledged it during his 1960 Presidential campaign) was hailed by many civil rights leaders. Sen. John Stennis (D., Miss.) said Nov. 20, however, that the order was an "audacious usurpation of power."

Mr. Kennedy, asked at his news conference Nov. 20 why he had delayed in issuing the order, replied: "I have said I would issue it at the time when I thought it was in the public interest, and now is the time."

The order, effective immediately, covered housing built or bought with federal aid or financed by private mortgages guaranteed or insured by federal agencies. It did not cover loans from financial institutions having federal insurance on their deposits. The order created a cabinet-level President's Committee on Equal Opportunity in Housing to implement the action. It directed that an attempt to gain voluntary compliance would be made before violators would be subjected to cancellation of their commitment or court action.

An attempt to gain compliance through persuasion was emphasized when rules to implement the order were issued by the Federal Housing Administration (FHA) and Veterans Administration Nov. 30 and by the Urban Renewal Administration, the Public Housing Administration and the Community Facilities Administration Dec. 4. Under the regulations, builders or lenders accused of bias were to be invited by the pertinent federal agency or office to attend at least 2 informal conferences to seek elimination of any discriminatory practices involved. If these failed, offenders could be barred from participation in projects covered by the order. The rules did not cover the sale or rental of one-family or 2-family houses occupied by the owner where a Negro was barred on racial grounds after the owner had approved sale or rental to him.

Robert C. Weaver, administrator of the Housing & Home Finance Agency, stressed Dec. 4 that "conferences, conciliation and persuasion" would be attempted "so far as possible" before "sanctions" would be invoked. Weaver said the Administration might extend the order to "conventional" mortgages (the 3/4 of the U.S.' financing of housing not insured or guaranteed by federal agencies).

Broadening of the order to cover all mortgage lending by federally chartered and insured institutions was urged Dec. 7 by Dale M. Thompson, president of the Mortgage Bankers Association of America. Thompson warned in a letter to Pres. Kennedy that if the order affected only loans insured by the FHA and Veterans Administration, the FHA and VA mortgage systems would be bypassed for systems not covered.

(Urban Renewal Commissioner William L. Slayton had ordered Apr. 7 that federally-aided urban renewal projects must comply "with all state and local laws" barring discrimination "in the sale, lease or occupancy of property." Notification of the new policy was sent to 539 local public agencies dealing with the Urban Renewal Administration.)

Courts Rebuff Anti-Bias Efforts

The Supreme Court Apr. 2 upheld by declining to review a ruling that overturned a Washington State law barring racial discrimination in the sale or rental of publicly aided housing. The decision held that the law violated both the federal and state constitutions. The ruling, by the Washington Supreme Court in Sept. 1961, was in a case in which Coast Guard Cmndr. John O'Meara had refused in 1959 to sell his Seattle home, bought with the aid of an FHA loan, to Robert L. Jones, a Negro. The Washington State Board Against Discrimination had ordered O'Meara to sell to Jones on the ground that he had refused to sell for racial reasons. But the state Supreme Court had reversed the order, and the U.S. Supreme Court refused to review the reversal.

The Illinois Supreme Court Nov. 30 upheld the right of Deerfield, Ill. to condemn appropriate land for needed parks despite the fact that a builder had started an interracial housing project on the tract. The court held that "the power of eminent domain cannot be made to depend upon the peculiar social, racial, religious or political predilections of either the condemning authority or the affected property owner." Deerfield, a Chicago suburb, had an all-white population. Joseph L. Rauh Jr., ex-chairman of Americans for Democratic Action and attorney for the builder, Progress Development Corp., called the ruling "encouragement of the use of the power of eminent domain to keep Negroes out of all-white areas."

CORE Active in Housing Cases

Demonstrations against alleged segregation in off-campus student housing were staged by students against the University of Chicago Jan. 23-Feb. 5. The demonstrations were sponsored by the Congress of Racial Equality (CORE), which charged that the university operated about 100 segregated apartment houses. The university said that only 12 of its 55 apartment houses were segregated and that it was following a policy to create a "stable inter-racial community" by "stages." The main protest was a sit-in maintained in shifts in a corridor outside the office of the university president, George Wells Beadle. The sit-in began Jan. 23 and ended Feb. 5, when the students left after being served with an eviction order under threat of suspension. 41 persons, many of them non-students, were arrested Jan. 24-Feb. 5 after demonstrating at a university-owned real estate office. Charges against 13 of those arrested were dismissed Jan. 24. 10 others were convicted Jan. 31 of trespassing and were fined $10 each (sentences suspended). Beadle attended a protest meeting Feb. 5 and indorsed a suggestion for an inquiry by a committee composed of representatives of the university and of civil rights and other groups.

A 35-day Los Angeles sit-in organized by CORE was staged successfully in suburban Monterey Park. The sit-in was started Mar. 3 after Negro physicist Bobby Liley's attempts to buy a home there had been rebuffed. The sit-in, conducted by Mrs. Liley and several others in the tract office, ended when another developer bought the tract and told Mrs. Liley, who had remained on the sit-in all 35 days, that she could be "my first customer."

CORE members picketed the home of Jersey City (N.J.) Mayor Thomas Gangemi Aug. 11 to protest alleged discrimination against Negroes in the city's low-income housing projects. Protest demonstrations against housing bias were staged by CORE against the Forest Hill Manor apartments in Bloomfield, N.J. Sept. 15 and by 200 Negro residents of Port Chester, N.Y. Sept. 24.

Lag in Negro Housing Reported

A Housing & Home Finance Agency report made public Dec. 30 said that despite a "spectacular rise" in Negroes' incomes in the past decade, Negroes generally lived in "older, less-expensive and lower-quality housing than white families of similiar incomes." The report also said: This "discrepancy is largely unchanged as the non-white family income rises"; "a sizable non-white middle class" had emerged.

OTHER DEVELOPMENTS

Administration's Actions Assessed

Disappointment over the Kennedy Administration's failure to promote new civil rights legislation or to issue "the long-promised" executive order banning bias in federal housing, was expressed Jan. 2 by Roy Wilkins, executive secretary of the NAACP (National Association for the Advancement of Colored People). (The ban on discrimination in federally aided housing was issued by the President Nov. 20.) Wilkins, speaking at the NAACP's annual meeting in New York, admitted, however, that there had been "accelerated progress toward first-class [Negro] citizenship" in 1961. He also praised Pres. Kennedy's "personal role" in civil rights. (During the Jan. 1-2 meeting: Arthur B. Spingarn was reelected NAACP president; membership was reported to have dropped some 15,000 to about 375,000 in 1,494 units; 1961 NAACP income was reported to have been $1,019,000, expenditures $1,150,000.)

The Southern Regional Council issued in Atlanta Mar. 25 a report praising the Kennedy Administration's civil rights actions as "comparable" in importance to the Supreme Court's 1954 school desegregation decision. The report said that 1961 was "a year of establishing a national mood and direction" and that the Administration had "built momentum for civil rights into the structure and the policies of government." Pres. Kennedy, the report said, had used executive power to achieve "a genuine turning point in American racial relations" and had "taken away any uncertainty the people may have earlier acquired as to whether the capital regarded the removal of segregation as a matter of national interest." While praising Atty. Gen. Robert F. Kennedy for his civil rights activities, the report criticized him for congratulating the mayor of Albany, Ga. on the settlement of the city's racial crisis in 1961 after more than 700 Negroes had been arrested. The Council Nov. 14 criticized the Administration for alleged in-activity in the unsuccessful Albany rights campaign.

(Mr. Kennedy had asserted in his State-of-the-Union message Jan. 11 that "this Administration has shown as never before how much could be done through the full use of executive powers." "But there is much more to be done" to win full rights for Negroes, he conceded.)

At the opening session of the 6th annual national convention of his Southern Christian Leadership Conference (SCLC), the Rev. Dr. Martin Luther King Jr. in Birmingham, Ala. Sept. 25 complimented the Kennedy Administration on "its firmest stand to date in enforcing integration" for its action in James Meredith's enrollment in the University of Mississippi. In an interview Aug. 29, however, King had said Negroes "have been disappointed" by the President's "failure to carry out his [civil rights] campaign promises." In other statements urging federal action in civil rights, King, (a) addressing the National Press Club in Washington (the first American Negro to do so), urged July 19 that the Justice Department "utilize the Civil Rights Act of 1960 extensively and seek court-appointed referees in thousands of communities" in a drive to assure Negroes the vote; (b) speaking Sept. 12 at a New York dinner marking the 100th anniversary of the signing of the Emancipation Proclamation, said that "no President can be . . . fit for office if he attempts to accommodate injustice to maintain his political balance."

Dr. Whitney Young Jr. of New York, director of the National Urban League, told the SCLC delegates Sept. 27 that Negroes had made little progress on the "meat, bread and potatoes issues" of integration. He said that the average Negro family income in the U.S. was 54% of the average white family's income and that 85% of Negroes would live in major cities, mostly in the North, by 1985 if current trends continued.

King said in his Sept. 25 address that a "vigorous campaign" would be started to enroll Negro students in the universities of Alabama and Auburn. He was reelected president of the conference Sept. 28. 425 delegates of 75 affiliates from all Southern states except Texas attended the convention. (During the closing session Sept. 28, King was assaulted by Roy James, 24, of Arlington, Va. James, who called himself a member of the American Nazi Party, struck King twice in the face. King did not press charges, but James was convicted a few hours later by Recorders Court Judge C. H. Brown of assault and battery and was sentenced to 30 days in prison. He was also fined $25 and costs.)

Turmoil in Albany (Ga.)

An intensive drive to get city officials to discuss desegregation of city public facilities was undertaken by Negroes in Albany, Ga. following the jailing July 10 of the Rev. Dr. Martin Luther King Jr. The drive was conducted by the Albany Movement, led by a Negro clergyman and osteopath, Dr. William G. Anderson, 34, and by King's Atlanta-based Southern Christian Leadership Conference (SCLC), which established an office in Albany to cooperate with the Albany Movement. Other Negro groups participating were the Student Nonviolent Coordinating Committee (SNCC) and the Congress of Racial Equality (CORE). The Albany Movement had been formed and the desegregation drive conducted along lines proposed to Albany Negro leaders in Sept. 1961 by SNCC field secretary Charles Sherrod.

Opposing the drive were the city commissioners, Mayor Asa D. Kelley Jr. (who said July 16 the city would not "deal with law violators") and Police Chief Laurie S. Pritchett, who, with his city police reinforced by county and state officers, appeared at virtually every mass protest and jailed many of the demonstrators. About 346 arrests were made in July, about 1,100 since the protest movement began in Oct. 1961.

Pres. Kennedy, who had directed the Attorney General July 21 to report on the controversy, said at his news conference Aug. 1 that the refusal of Albany officials to negotiate with Negro leaders was "wholly inexplicable." He said the federal government would "try to provide a satisfactory solution for the protection of the constitutional rights of the people of Albany." Kelley, in reply to the President's remarks, said there was no prospect for negotiation until "outside agitators" (King and other integrationists) left the city. (Other non-residents of Albany who appeared there during the controversy included Robert Shelton of Tuscaloosa, Ala., imperial wizard of the United Klans, Inc., Calvin Craig of Atlanta, the Georgia Klans' grand dragon, and 3 representatives of the American Nazi Party.)

King and 3 other Negroes, including the Rev. Ralph D. Abernathy, SCLC treasurer, had been convicted July 10 of violating a public assembly ordinance by failing to get a permit when they led a Dec. 1961 demonstration in which more than 700 persons were arrested. King and Abernathy were given the choice of paying fines of $178 each or of serving 45-day sentences. They were jailed after refusing to pay the fines. A mass protest meeting was held at the Shiloh Baptist Church July 11, and 32 Negroes led by the Rev. C. K. Steele of Tallahassee, Fla. marched from the church to city hall, where they were arrested. A mass meeting was held at the church that night, and Negroes outside the church threw bricks and bottles at police. Negro leaders at the church then helped Pritchett calm the crowd.

King and Abernathy were released from jail July 12 after an unidentified Negro paid their fines without their knowledge or consent. After this the tension in Albany appeared to have been eased somewhat although small groups of Negroes continued vainly to seek admission to a segregated library, a pool and stores and bus terminals in a series of moves largely led by the Rev. Wyatt Tee Walker, SCLC executive director, and by Joseph Charles Jones, an SNCC field secretary.

Anderson notified the city July 20 that 300-500 Negroes would demonstrate peacefully July 21 in front of city hall despite a federal court order barring the demonstration. 160 Negroes and a white person were arrested July 21 and 39 were arrested July 24 in mass marches on city hall. After the latter arrests a crowd of about 2,000 Negroes jeered police and pelted them with bricks and rocks without police retaliation.

On learning of the crowd's behavior, King declared a day of pennance for the violence and toured the city's Negro district to appeal against further outbreaks. He said neither the demonstrators nor Albany Movement members were involved in the outbreak.

King was arrested again July 27 when Pritchett intercepted 2 prayer pilgrimages to city hall. 26 other Negroes, including Anderson and Abernathy, and one white person were also arrested. 7 kneeling demonstrators were put onto stretchers and carried into jail. King and the other leaders were tried and convicted but freed Aug. 10 after being given suspended sentences of 60 days in jail and being fined $200 each (the fines were also suspended).

The next mass demonstration occurred Aug. 28 when 5 Georgian and 70 Northern and Midwestern Jewish, Protestant and Roman Catholic clergymen were arrested and jailed for holding an anti-segregation prayer demonstration at city hall. The group included 54 whites and 21 Negroes. The clergymen were released in groups as they posted $200 bond each; the last group of 18 was released Sept. 3. 11 had fasted throughout their

6-day jail stay.

U.S. District Judge J. Robert Elliott July 20 had issued, at the request of city officials, an injunction banning further public demonstrations in Albany. The injunction was set aside July 24 by Chief Judge Elbert P. Tuttle of the 5th U.S. Circuit Court of Appeals, who found that Elliott lacked jurisdiction because no federal issues were involved. Elliott held July 30, however, that he had jurisdiction, and he began hearings on the reinstatement of his injunction. He refused Aug. 3 to dismiss a motion for its reinstatement. Mrs. Constance Baker Motley, NAACP Legal & Defense Education Fund lawyer, helped represent the Negro groups in their action against the city's injunction appeal. The U.S. Justice Department Aug. 8 filed a brief also opposing the injunction.

Negro leaders also had filed with the federal district court (1) an omnibus desegregation suit to ban segregated practices in Albany (Elliott Aug. 31 rejected the suit's application for a preliminary injunction against Albany), and (2) a suit to bar the police from interfering with "peaceful demonstrations" by the integrationists.

The Southern Regional Council Nov. 14 criticized the Kennedy Administration's alleged inactivity in the unsuccessful civil rights campaign in Albany. The council said the Justice Department had "hovered" about Albany all throughout the crisis but, "incredibly," had not acted. The council's report was made public by the council's executive director, Leslie W. Dunbar. The report was written by Dr. Howard Zinn of Spelman College, Atlanta. Zinn's report criticized the Administration, Albany officials and police (for running Albany "in the silent, sure manner of an efficient police state"), the FBI (for taking many Negro complaints of injustice but making only one arrest and then because an FBI agent was attacked by a white man) and the Negroes' tactics (which Zinn said had brought no "tangible" results although the protest movement was a year old).

(A Negro bus boycott had been started in Albany in January. The Cities Transport Co., forced to shut down Feb. 1, reopened later with limited runs for whites. An attempt to ease the situation was reported Mar. 2 when the company hired its first Negro driver. But bus service ended Mar. 7 because of financial losses. Albany Movement leaders had attempted to negotiate with the City Commission Jan. 23 for bus desegregation, but the commission later refused, by 6-1 vote, to approve a desegregation pact.)

Court Action on Travel Rights

The Supreme Court said Feb. 26 that its prior decisions had "settled beyond question that no state may require racial segregation of interstate or intrastate transportation facilities." It made this statement in backing a suit that sought an end to enforcement of segregation laws at Mississippi travel terminals. The suit, filed by the NAACP on behalf of 3 Negroes, had been taken to a 3-judge federal court, which had refused to rule on the constitutionality of the laws until decisions on the laws were given by state courts. The Supreme Court asserted that the special court did not have to be convened because the question "is no longer open." It ordered that the case be heard by a federal district court in Mississippi "for expeditious disposition, in the light of this opinion, of the claims of right of unsegregated transportation service."

Acting on the Supreme Court's order, U.S. District Judge Sidney C. Mize ruled in Biloxi May 2 that 9 Mississippi laws requiring separate but equal travel accommodations for whites and Negroes were unconstitutional. Mize said his ruling applied only to the 3 plaintiffs, whose right to unsegregated travel service he upheld. He denied their appeal for an injunction against such discrimination. He also said the ruling was not applicable to Freedom Riders' cases involving breach-of-peace statutes, which were pending in state court.

Louisiana laws requiring segregation at bus and train terminals had been declared unconstitutional by a 3-judge federal court in Alexandria, La. Jan. 5.

A 3-judge federal court in Augusta, Ga. Feb. 13 ruled by a 2-1 decision that state and Augusta city laws providing for segregation on buses were unconstitutional. The case involved 5 Negro students who had been arrested in May 1960 for refusing to move to segregated seats.

Federal Judge W. A. Bootle ruled similarly in Macon, Ga. Mar. 1 that Georgia bus segregation laws were illegal. Bootle also upset a Georgia Public Service Commission rule permitting carriers to provide separate vehicles for white and Negro passengers. He specifically ordered the Bibb Transit Co. of Macon to end segregation practices. Negroes had been boycotting buses in Macon since Feb. 12. A company appeal for white riders to "ride a bus and help break the boycott" evoked enough response to keep buses running. Minor violence erupted

Feb. 16: rocks were thrown at buses and cars; Negro and white youths fought in downtown streets, and one Negro reported being beaten by other Negroes for trying to board a bus. 4 Negro ministers had been arrested Feb. 9 for trying to sit in the "white" section of a bus.

15 white and Negro Episcopalian ministers, including the Rev. Robert L. Pierson, son-in-law of N.Y. Gov. Nelson A. Rockfeller, were freed May 21 of breach-of-the-peace charges resulting from their 1961 arrest in Jackson, Miss. at the bus depot's segregated lunch counter. Hines County Judge Russel Moore, getting the cases on appeal from municipal court convictions, declared the first defendant not guilty and then granted city prosecutor Jack Travis' motion not to prosecute the other cases. Travis had joined with the defense's earlier request to dismiss the charges. (Moore had granted the dismissal Apr. 9, then had reversed his decision Apr. 10 and had ordered the trials.) Similar charges against Mark Lane, New York Assemblyman, and Percy Sutton, a Negro and NAACP official of New York, had been dismissed Mar. 29 when Moore granted Travis' motion for acquittal on the technicality that the 2 had not been "congregating" with other people at the time of their arrest at the Municipal Airport's segregated waiting room.

U.S. District Judge Frank M. Johnson Jr. had ordered Montgomery, Ala. Jan. 3 to desegregate its Dannelly Municipal Airport and to remove segregation signs there by Jan. 5. He acted in a suit brought by the Justice Department. The city's request for a stay of the order pending appeal was denied Jan. 4 by Johnson and Judge Richard T. Rives of the U.S. 5th Circuit Court of Appeals. The signs were removed Jan. 5 and a Negro youth, accompanied by 3 white youths, sat in the airport's formerly "white" waiting room without incident.

The Supreme Court Mar. 26 directed a 3-judge federal district court in Memphis to bar segregation in the restaurant at the Memphis municipal airport. The suit had been brought by Jesse Turner, a Negro who twice in 1959 had been refused service in the restaurant. The restaurant said it was required to segregate under a Tennessee regulation. The Supreme Court held that: (a) the case should not have been heard by a 3-judge court (which had refused to decide it on the ground that it should go first to a Tennessee court); (b) the suit should have been heard by a single federal judge and then on appeal by the U.S. circuit court of appeals; (c) in order to expedite the case, the Supreme Court had taken the case from the appeals court and was returning it to the district court with instructions to order desegregation. "Our [prior] decisions have foreclosed any possible contention" that a state segregation rule could be valid, the Supreme Court said.

The Supreme Court June 4 voided the convictions of 6 Negro Freedom Riders who had been arrested in Shreveport, La. Aug. 4, 1961 on breach-of-the-peace charges for refusing to obey a police order to leave a segregated bus depot. The court, in an unsigned opinion delivered without hearing oral argument, said there was "no evidence of violence" in the depot. It quoted a 1917 Supreme Court decision (upsetting a Louisville, Ky. ordinance for racial zoning), which said that although "race hostility" must be given "a measure of consideration," "its solution cannot be promoted by depriving citizens of their constitutional rights."

The Justice Department had filed in federal court in Shreveport May 31 a suit to bar the city from enforcing racial segregation at its interstate bus terminal. According to the suit, the depot manager had been arrested for removing the signs requiring segregation, and Shreveport police continued to compel segregation there. The department described as "fruitless" its "customary" efforts seeking "voluntary compliance in the case before going to court."

Suits to bar racial segregation in restaurants and other facilities at airports in Birmingham, Ala. and Shreveport were filed by the Justice Department June 19.

Segregationists Sponsor Reverse Freedom Rides

A plan to give 1,000 Negroes from New Orleans free one-way rides to Washington or any Northern city of their choice was put into effect Apr. 20 by George L. Singelmann, director of the segregationist Citizens Council of Greater New Orleans. The plan was denounced by civil rights leaders. The first Negroes to accept the rides were Louis Boyd, 41, who had been unemployed for about a year in New Orleans, his wife and 8 children. They arrived in New York Apr. 21 after a bus trip paid for by the council ($263 for the tickets plus $50 for food). Boyd, counseled by the Urban League, got a job as a $100-a-week handyman in Jersey City, N.J.

Singelmann said Apr. 20 that the council had made a standing offer to finance such trips on an individual or family basis. Handbills advertising such trips by "Freedom Bus" were distributed in New Orleans by the council. They listed addresses and phone numbers of welfare departments, the Urban League and NAACP offices in New York, Chicago, Pittsburgh, Detroit and Washington as "organizations who will help you when you arrive."

The plan to send Negroes North on "reverse freedom rides" spread to white citizens councils in Little Rock, Ark., Shreveport, La. and Montgomery, Ala. Negroes accepting the rides received free one-way transportation to such destinations as New York, California, Chicago, New Hampshire, Boston, Minnesota and Hyannis, Mass., site of Pres. Kennedy's summer home. About 100 Negroes took the trip to Hyannis during 1962, but virtually all left to settle elsewhere.

Desegregation of Lunch Counters

Dining facilities in 29 Memphis stores operated by 10 companies were voluntarily and peacefully desegregated Feb. 6 under arrangements worked out by Negro and business leaders. Key figures in the arrangements were Lewis R. Donelson 3d, a lawyer, the Rev. Dr. Paul Tudor Jones, president of the 100-member Memphis Community Relations Committee, and Jesse H. Turner, the NAACP's Memphis chapter president and executive vice president of the Tri-State Bank.

Desegregation of almost all lunch counters in Pensacola, Fla. department, variety and drug stores was effected without incident Feb. 21 under plans made by the Community Council.

17 Negroes and 2 whites, including Prof. Everett W. McNair of Talladega (Ala.) College, were arrested in Talladega Apr. 9 for a sit-in at drugstore lunch counters. Negro pickets against the drugstores were dispersed Apr. 25 after whites tore up their placards and a tear gas bomb was thrown from a passing car. 12 more Negro pickets and a white youth were arrested Apr. 26.

Desegregation of lunch counters in about 15 New Orleans drug, department and variety stores, including branches of national chain stores, was effected Sept. 11 when about 20 Negroes, in groups of 3 or 4, were served without incident. The action, taken without advance publicity, had been planned by a negotiating team of 6 white merchants (purposely unidentified to avoid reprisals) and 6 Negro leaders. Similar quiet desegregation in Atlanta and Dallas had been studied in January by J. W. Simon Jr., Greater New Orleans Chamber

of Commerce president, who had presented his findings to the
negotiators and then withdrawn from the negotiations.

60 persons, all but a few of them Negroes, were arrested
and charged with trespassing in anti-segregation demonstrations at 2 cafeterias and a theater in Greensboro, N.C. Nov. 22.
Similar demonstrations there the week before by some of the
same persons had resulted in 50 arrests.

21 persons were arrested Nov. 23-24 and 31 Negroes were
arrested Nov. 28 for sit-in demonstrations at Gadsden, Ala.
lunch counters.

Complaints Against Hospitals

U.S. District Judge Edwin M. Stanley in Greensboro, N.C.
Dec. 5 dismissed the NAACP's anti-bias suit against the Moses
H. Cone Memorial and the Wesley Long Community hospitals.
Stanley said the court lacked jurisdiction because the case had
been brought on behalf of individuals (9 Negro doctors) against
other individuals or private corporations. He therefore denied
a request of the Justice Department (which had intervened in
the suit on behalf of the NAACP) for a ruling on the constitutionality of the Hill-Burton Act provision under which the
hospitals had received federal funds for construction. According to Stanley: (a) the hospitals were not "instrumentalities
of government in the constitutional sense" despite federal and
state contract dealings; (b) privately controlled and operated
hospitals were not subject to constitutional civil rights requirements. The NAACP, in filing the suit Feb. 12, had asserted that
the separate-but-equal provisions of the Hill-Burton Act were
unconstitutional. (The Moses H. Cone hospital announced Dec.
19 that it would consider applications from Negro doctors and
dentists for staff privileges.)

The federal district court in Atlanta was asked June 19 to
require the Grady Memorial Hospital of Atlanta to end alleged
segregation in its patient-care and medical training programs
and on its medical staff. The suit was filed by NAACP attorneys
in cooperation with local attorneys on behalf of 8 Negro complainants. The suit said the tax-supported hospital had received
$6 million in public funds in 1960 and had received $1,789,719
under the Hill-Burton Act, whose separate-but-equal provisions it challenged. The suit applied for anti-segregation
injunctions against the Northern District Dental Society, the
Georgia Dental Association, the Fulton County Medical Society

and the Medical Association of Georgia on the grounds that these groups nominated appointees to state boards and to a medical board that had jurisdiction over "controversial medical questions in claims for workmen's compensation." (22 Negroes and a white man had been arrested Feb. 13 for demonstrating at the hospital against segregation. The demonstrators had been part of a larger, earlier demonstration at the state capitol during which 11 Negroes had been arrested.)

A suit to prevent the Orangeburg (S.C.) Regional Hospital from maintaining segregated waiting rooms, wards and other facilities was filed by the NAACP in federal district court in Columbia, S.C. Mar. 24. The suit was brought on behalf of Mrs. Gloria Rackley and her daughter, Jamelle, Negroes, who had been ordered to leave the hospital's "white" waiting room on 2 occasions. Mrs. Rackley was arrested on a trespass charge after the 2d incident.

Action Taken Against Bias in Armed Services

Pres. Kennedy June 23 appointed an Advisory Committee on Equal Opportunity in the Armed Forces to investigate and recommend ways to combat discrimination in the services and the "hardship and embarrassment" suffered by armed forces personnel and their dependents from bias in communities near military installations.

Full and effective racial integration in the Reserve units, including disbanding of all-Negro and all-white units, was ordered Apr. 3 by Deputy Defense Secy. Roswell L. Gilpatric. The directive, implementing a 1948 executive order banning racial segregation in the armed forces, did not apply to the National Guard, which the Defense Department classified as "an organization of volunteers under command of the respective governor." 10 states had segregated Guard units.

Lt. Cmndr. Samuel L. Gravely Jr., 39, had assumed command of the destroyer escort *U.S.S. Falgout* at Pearl Harbor Jan. 31. An announcement from the 14th Naval District said he was the first Negro ever to command a U.S. warship.

Campaign in Cairo (Ill.)

6 Negro youths and a white woman were beaten by whites Aug. 17 during an attempt to integrate a skating rink in Cairo. About 80 integrationists went Aug. 20 to Springfield, where the

group's leaders, including Dr. L. H. Holman, president of the
NAACP's Illinois chapter, met with Gov. Otto Kerner (D.) to
demand protection by National Guard troops or state police
and to protest the denial of civil rights in Cairo. Kerner promised an investigation.

The integration campaign in Cairo had been initiated in June
by Student Nonviolent Coordinating Committee leader Mary Mc-
Collum, 22, of Nashville, Tenn. and 6 volunteer field workers.
The campaign had been successful against a restaurant but was
rebuffed at a swimming pool and the roller rink. The first
demonstration at the pool had been held June 29, and 30 integrationists had been arrested July 13-14 in stand-ins there and at
the rink. 17 of these, all but one of them Negroes, were convicted July 19 of "mob action" at the rink and were fined $100
each. 4 were found guilty July 20 and fined $50 each for the
swimming pool incident. A march was staged through downtown
Cairo July 21 by more than 200 Negroes and whites in protest
against the convictions and fines.

Urban Affairs Plans Killed in Congress

Pres. Kennedy was defeated twice during 1962 in his efforts
to create a Cabinet-level department to handle urban affairs.

Mr. Kennedy's bill to create a Department for Urban Affairs
was killed Jan. 24 by a House Rules Committee vote of 9 to 6
not to clear the measure for House consideration. Voting against
the bill were Chrmn. Howard W. Smith (Va.), 3 other Southern
Democrats and the committee's 5 Republicans. The losing votes
were cast by a Texas Democrat, Homer Thornberry, and 5 non-
Southern Democrats. The House Republican Policy Committee
had announced its opposition to the bill Jan. 20.

Pres. Kennedy said at his news conference Jan. 24 that he
was "astonished at the Republican leadership which opposed
this bill" because he thought they "shared our concern for some
effective management and responsibility of the problems of 2/3
of our population who live in cities." He said he would reintro-
duce his proposal to Congress in the form of a reorganization
plan. He said that if the department were created, he would
appoint Housing Administrator Robert C. Weaver as its secretary (and thus make Weaver the first Negro member of a U.S.
Cabinet). House Republican Policy Committee Chrmn. John
W. Byrnes (Wis.) accused the President Jan. 25 of a "callous
attempt" to exploit the racial issue by announcing his intention

to appoint Weaver. He termed the new department a "fraud" that would solve "not one single urban problem."

A reorganization plan to create a Department of Urban Affairs & Housing was submitted to Congress by Pres. Kennedy Jan. 30. The plan would have gone into effect if not disapproved by a majority vote of either house within 60 days. But the House vetoed the plan Feb. 21. The new department would have (a) had a secretary, an undersecretary, 3 assistant secretaries and a general counsel; (b) absorbed the Housing & Home Finance Agency (HHFA), including the Urban Renewal Administration, the Community Facilities Administration, the Public Housing Administration, the Federal Housing Administration and the Federal National Mortgage Association.

The President and his plan were attacked Jan. 30 by Congressional Republican leaders Everett M. Dirksen (Ill.) and Charles A. Halleck (Ind.). Sen. Dirksen said the President had "endangered the whole civil rights program" by his "unfortunate handling" of the matter. Rep. Halleck accused Mr. Kennedy of trying "to take the Democrats off the spot" by announcing his intention to appoint Weaver.

The plan was reported favorably to the House Feb. 15 by the Government Operations Committee, whose Democratic majority warned that the problems of city dwellers were "serious" already and "will be more serious 10 years from now, and much more difficult of solution thereafter." The committee's 7 GOP members filed a minority report calling the plan "premature" and "unnecessary." During the committee's hearings Feb. 6-8, the plan had been supported by: Budget Bureau Dir. David E. Bell; Govs. Matthew E. Welsh of Indiana and Elbert N. Carvel of Delaware; Mayors Robert F. Wagner Jr. of New York, Richard J. Daley of Chicago, Gordon S. Clinton of Seattle, Richard C. Lee of New Haven, Conn. and John Ridley of Smyrna, Tenn. (on behalf of the American Municipal Association). Witnesses against the plan: Leonard L. Frank, president of the National Association of Home Builders; Stuart Davis on behalf of the U.S. Chamber of Commerce; Henry E. Pogue of the National Association of Real Estate Boards. (The plan was indorsed by the National Housing Conference.)

In an effort to get a Senate vote on the issue before the predicted House veto, Senate Democratic leader Mike Mansfield (Mont.) attempted to discharge the plan from Chrmn. John L. McClellan's Committee on Government Operations before the committee had completed its hearings. The maneuver, attacked solely as a political interference in Senate procedures, was defeated Feb. 20 by a 58-42 vote (32 R. & 26 D. vs. 38 D. & 4 R.). The House veto of the plan Feb. 21 was by 264-150 vote (153 R. & 111 D. vs. 137 D. & 13 R.). During debate the opposition argued that the new department would either be too powerful and encroach on state authority, or be unnecessary because it merely would elevate the HHFA but not include (a) urban programs for juvenile delinquency and air pollution and (b) housing programs currently administered by the Veterans Administration and the Home Loan Bank Board. 93 of 106 Southern Democrats voted against the plan.

The President said at his news conference Feb. 21 that the defeat was not "so much the Administration's loss as it's a loss for the city and the country." Attributing opposition to the bill to "many of those who do not live in urban areas," he warned that if such sectionalism prevailed on other issues "this country would come to a grinding halt."

(N.Y. Gov. Nelson A. Rockefeller said Feb. 14 that he had been "misrepresented" as opposing a Department of Urban Affairs. He said he was against such a department only "in its present form." An urban affairs office should be established in the White House and not be formed as a "Frankenstein" bureau, he said.)

Governors Debate Rights

The 54th annual Governors Conference, held in Hershey, Pa. July 1-4, was highlighted by controversies over the conference's positions on civil rights and on "a medical care plan for the aged." Gov. Wesley Powell (R., N.H.) was conference chairman. Gov. Albert D. Rosellini (D., Wash.) was chosen to be chairman of the 1963 conference.

In the civil rights dispute, Govs. Rockefeller (R., N.Y.) and John B. Swainson (D., Mich.) introduced "liberal" resolutions in place of a moderate resolution approved by a conference committee. Unable to agree on any, the conference adopted Gov. David L. Lawrence's (D., Pa.) suggestion to withdraw all 3 and have each governor sign the one he favored. This dispute was marked by a filibuster by Gov. Ernest F. Hollings (D., S.C.).

Gov. Orval E. Faubus (D., Ark.) was elected chairman of the Southern Governors Conference in Hollywood, Fla. Oct. 4.

In line for the chairmanship since 1960, Faubus reportedly had been sidetracted twice because of his controversial role in the Little Rock integration crisis. The conference Oct. 4 adopted a resolution urging amendment of the U.S. Constitution to strengthen states' rights (as proposed by the National Legislative Conference in Phoenix, Ariz. in September).

Cosmos Club in Washington Attacked

Several prominent members resigned from the private Cosmos Club of Washington Jan. 9-10 in protest against the club's rejection Jan. 8 of a membership application for Deputy Asst. State Secy. Carl T. Rowan, a Negro.

Amb.-to-India John Kenneth Galbraith, who had co-sponsored an application for membership for Pres. Kennedy, resigned from the club Jan. 9. As a result, the President's application was considered withdrawn. Mr. Kennedy said at his news conference Jan. 15 that his application would not be renewed. Mr. Kennedy said that "every individual must make his judgment in the way that he believes to be right, and I have stated mine."

Among those who resigned: U.S. Information Agency director Edward R. Murrow Jan. 9; Asst. State Secy. Harlan Cleveland, historian Bruce Catton and economist James P. Warburg Jan. 10. N.Y. Gov. Nelson A. Rockefeller protested the club's action Jan. 10 but said he would remain a member to try to effect changes in the club's racial policy.

A resolution stating opposition to racial, color or religious discrimination in the admission of new members was adopted by the club Jan. 15, but the rejection of Rowan was not revoked.

John Hope Franklin, 47, chairman of Brooklyn College's History Department, was accepted Dec. 10 as the Cosmos Club's first Negro member.

Riot at Washington School Game

32 white persons and 8 Negroes were injured and 15 persons were arrested when a riot broke out in Washington Nov. 22 following a Thanksgiving Day high-school football game in which St. Johns, a Catholic School with a predominantly white student enrollment, won a 20-7 victory over Eastern High, a public school with 1,951 Negro and 5 white pupils. This was the 4th such incident in 5 years of play-offs for the city

championship. The fighting began after a Negro player, removed from the game for roughness, came back to the field
swinging at white players. Fist fights erupted there and in
the stands, and when the game ended about 1,000 Negro
youngsters charged a section of whites. Fighting continued
for an hour before police stopped it.

Muslims & Police Clash in Los Angeles

A member of the militant Black Muslim sect was killed
and 14 Negroes, including 8 policemen, were wounded in a
riot in front of the local Black Muslim headquarters (Mosque
No. 27) on South Broadway in Los Angeles Apr. 27. About 75
policemen had been called out to quell the riot, which began
when 2 policemen were attacked as they tried to question a man.
One of the officers fired a shot, hitting an attacker. Other
Black Muslim members rushed from their headquarters to
join the fight. A county grand jury later indicted 9 of 16 Black
Muslims involved on charges of assaulting and resisting
officers. Malcolm X, leader of the Negro separatist movement
in New York, accused Los Angeles Police Chief William H.
Parker of "Gestapo" tactics.

1963

The Negro campaign for equality was dramatized during 1963 by a peaceful 'march' that brought more than 200,000 Negro and white integrationists to Washington. In the South, anti-integration violence took several lives: 4 Negro girls were killed in a church bombing in Birmingham, Ala.; Negro leader Medgar Evers was ambushed in Jackson, Miss.; a white 'freedom walker' was slain on an Alabama road as he marched in a lone protest against segregation. Demonstrations against discrimination brought thousands of arrests in the North and South. Pres. John F. Kennedy federalized the National Guard in Alabama twice during 1963 as he forced Gov. George C. Wallace to back down in his efforts to maintain segregation in public schools and the University of Alabama. After Mr. Kennedy's assassination, the new President, Lyndon B. Johnson, vowed to continue the civil rights struggle.

MARCH ON WASHINGTON

More than 200,000 persons gathered in Washington :. throughout the U.S. Aug. 28 for a massive but peaceful demoi stration calling attention to Negro demands for immediate equality in employment and in other areas of civil rights.

Development of the Idea

The "march-on-Washington" idea had been suggested publicly at least as early as Feb. 24. A. Philip Randolph, president of the Bro'hood of Sleeping Car Porters and only Negro vice president of the AFL-CIO, announced at that time that the Negro American Labor Council would plan a mass "pilgrimage" to Washington to dramatize the Negro "employment crisis." As action on civil rights legislation lagged in Congress, other Negro leaders took up the "march-on-Washington" suggestion as a means of protesting filibusters and delays in the passage of rights legislation.

Congressional civil rights supporters cautioned Negro leaders that demonstrations in the capital might harm instead of help their cause. But James Farmer, national director of the Congress of Racial Equality (CORE), asserted June 19 that demonstrations "should help persuade legislators of the urgency of the situation." Roy Wilkins, executive secretary of the National Association for the Advancement of Colored People (NAACP), asserted June 20 that while a demonstration in Washington "may be right" in protesting a filibuster, the "greatest care" should be exercised not to hold demonstrations without specific objectives.

Pres. John F. Kennedy, speaking to civil rights leaders June 22 during a series of White House meetings on rights problems, questioned the wisdom of holding demonstrations in Washington while Congress was in session but did not ask that demonstrations be canceled. The Rev. Dr. Martin Luther King Jr. said after leaving the June 22 White House conference that Negroes would conduct a "non-violent peaceful demonstration in Washington" if there was a Senate filibuster on rights legislation.

The CORE convention, held in Dayton O., authorized CORE's leaders June 29 to cooperate with other rights groups in planning the march on Washington. During the NAACP convention, held in Chicago, the Rev. Dr. James H. Jackson,

ational (Negro) Baptist Convention, was
eaking and threatened with violence at a
se of a June 30 statement in which he had
The NAACP convention approved the march

appeared by July to have changed his mind
At his July 17 press conference he cat-
egorized the march as "in the great tradition" of peaceable
assembly "for a redress of grievances." "I'll look forward to
being here," he said, and "I'm sure members of Congress will
be here." At his Aug. 20 press conference, he confirmed that
he had agreed to meet the leaders during the day. He described
the march as an effort "to bring focus to the strong concern of
a good many citizens." But he cautioned that the problem "concerns all of our people" and "must, in the final analysis, be
settled by the Congress and by the Executive Branch working
with 180 million people."

The AFL-CIO Executive Council, meeting in Unity House,
Pa., refused its formal indorsement to the march but said
Aug. 13 that it backed the march's goals. The council's refusal
to back the march was criticized by several council members,
including A. Philip Randolph, who had become chairman of a
joint committee of rights groups planning the march.

Civil rights advocates' opposition to the march stemmed
primarily from concern (a) that such a mass demonstration
might disintegrate into disorder and bring discredit on the
rights movement, and (b) that an attempt to pressure Congress
into action could backfire into Congressional resistance. To
quiet the first objection, the march was planned carefully and
in great detail. The many Negro goups taking part in the march
cooperated in seminars held throughout the U.S. to school
participants in orderly march behavior. Negro leaders held a
Leadership Conference on Civil Rights in New York July 2
to plan for the march and to coordinate their drive for "racial
desegregation and equal opportunity." They pledged that the
march would include no "civil disobedience."

'Marchers' Rally in Washington

The more than 200,000 participants in the march arrived
in Washington Aug. 28 as scheduled by plane, train, bus and
automobile. The marchers included large delegations from
churches, synagogues and unions. Many Negroes participated

as individuals. And there were several thousand whites who came as representatives of various groups or as individuals.

The "marchers" gathered in the morning at the Washington Monument while 13 of their leaders called on Congressional leaders. Then, led by the organizers of the demonstration, the marchers moved in 2 paths, down Constitution Avenue and down Independence Avenue, to the Lincoln Memorial. The demonstrators eventually filled almost the entire mall between the monument and the memorial. Leaders of the march addressed the crowd, then went to the White House and conferred with Pres. Kennedy.

On checking in at a headquarters tent set up at the Washington Monument, the demonstrators signed a pledge to dedicate themselves to the civil rights struggle. While their numbers grew, members of the crowd broke into song and handclapping, setting a festive tone that continued throughout the day. The march to the Lincoln Memorial began spontaneously about 10 minutes before it was scheduled. The marchers sang as they walked. They carried thousands of placards demanding "An End To Bias," "Integrated Schools," "Decent Housing," "An End To Police Brutality"—almost all of them ending with the word "Now!" After the speeches at the Lincoln Memorial, the demonstrators dispersed quickly and orderly. Law enforcement was handled by 5,000 policemen, National Guardsmen and Army reservists. No marchers were arrested, and no incidents involving marchers were reported.

10 leaders of the march met with Pres. Kennedy in the White House after the demonstration. Mr. Kennedy later issued a statement in which he said that "the cause of 20 million Negroes has been advanced by the program conducted so appropriately before the nation's shrine to the Great Emancipator." The President said he had been "impressed" with "the deep fervor and the quiet dignity" that characterized the marchers. He lauded the demonstration as one of which "this nation can properly be proud."

The rights leaders meeting with the President were: A. Philip Randolph, director of the march; the Rev. Dr. Martin Luther King Jr., president of the Southern Christian Leadership Conference; Roy Wilkins, NAACP executive secretary; Whitney M. Young Jr., executive director of the National Urban League; Walter P. Reuther, president of the AFL-CIO United Automobile Workers; the Rev. Eugene Carson Blake, stated clerk of the United Presbyterian Church in the U.S.A.

and a representative of the National Council of Churches; Rabbi Joachim Prinz, chairman of the American Jewish Congress; John Lewis, chairman of the Student Nonviolent Coordinating Committee; Matthew Ahmann, executive director of the National Catholic Conference for Interracial Justice; Floyd B. McKissick, national chairman of CORE (a replacement for CORE's president, James Farmer, who was in jail in Plaquemine, La. as the result of a civil rights demonstration).

Also participating in the White House meeting were Vice Pres. Lyndon B. Johnson, Labor Secy. W. Willard Wirtz and Burke Marshall, head of the Justice Department's Civil Rights Division.

The rights leaders' calls on Congressional leaders, before their meeting with the President, were described as courteous and restrained. The Congress members visited included Senate Democratic leader Mike Mansfield (Mont.), Senate Republican leader Everett McKinley Dirksen (Ill.), House GOP leader Charles A. Halleck (Ind.), House Speaker John W. McCormack (D., Mass.) and House Democratic leader Carl Albert (Okla.). McCormack was the only Congressional leader to say that the demonstration, if orderly, would be "helpful" in getting the civil rights legislation enacted. Dirksen reported that "there was no pressure . . ., no insistence" from the rights leaders. "They were expressing the hope that we could see the picture as they see the picture," he said.

About 15 Senators and 60 Representatives attended the rally at the Lincoln Memorial, where they were introduced in a group and were met with the chant, "Pass the bill! Pass the bill!" Each of the 10 rights leaders addressed the throng at the Lincoln Memorial.

King, who received the loudest ovation after his introduction, said: "We have . . . come to this hallowed spot to remind America of the fierce urgency of *now*. . . . Now is the time to make real the promises of democracy. Now is the time to rise from the dark and desolate valley of segregation to the sunlit path of racial justice. Now is the time to open the doors of opportunity to all of God's children. . . . There will be neither rest nor tranquility in America until the Negro is granted his citizenship rights. . . . Our white brothers . . . have come to realize that their destiny is tied up with our destiny. . . . Even though we face the difficulties of today and tomorrow, I still have a dream. . . . I have a dream that one day this nation will rise up and live out the true meaning of its creed: 'We hold these truths to be self-evident, that all men are created equal.' I have a dream that one day on the red hills of Georgia the sons of former slaves and the sons of former slave-owners will be able to sit down together at the table of brotherhood. . . . I have a dream that my 4 little children will one day live in a nation where they will not be judged by the color of their skin but by the content of their character. This is our hope. This is the faith that I go back to the South with—with this faith we will be able to hew out of the mountain of despair a stone of hope."

Excerpts from other addresses:

A. Philip Randolph—"The 'march on Washington' is not the climax to our struggle but a new beginning, not only for the Negro but for all Americans, for personal freedoms and a better life. Look for the enemies of Medicare, of higher minimum wages, of Social Security, of federal aid to education, and there you will find the enemy of the Negro, the coalition of Dixiecrats and reactionary Republicans that seek to dominate the Congress."

Roy Wilkins—"It is simply incomprehensive to us here today and to millions of others far from this spot that the United States government, which can regulate the contents of a pill, apparently is powerless to prevent the physical abuse of citizens within its own borders. . . . We expect the passage of an effective civil rights bill."

Whitney M. Young Jr.—"We must support the strong, we must give courage to the timid, we must remind the indifferent, and warn the opposed. Civil rights, which are God-given and constitutionally gauranteed, are not negotiable in 1963."

John Lewis—"We are involved in a serious social revolution. But by and large American politics is dominated by politicians who build their career on immoral compromising and ally themselves with open forums of political, economic and social exploitation."

LEGISLATION BLOCKED

Civil rights legislation was proposed by Pres. John F. Kennedy in 2 special messages to Congress during 1963.

But the year ended with the Kennedy rights bill pigeonholed in the House Rules Committee.

First Kennedy Message

Pres. Kennedy sent to Congress Feb. 28 his first special message on civil rights. In it he presented "a list of priorities" for executive and legislative action.

The message stressed the need to end curtailment of Negroes' right to vote. It recommended as an interim measure that federal voting referees be used to eliminate undue judicial delays in registering Negro voters.

The message said: "Equality before the law has not always meant equal treatment and opportunity. And the harmful, wasteful and wrongful results of racial discrimination and segregation still appear in virtually every aspect of national life, in virtually every part of the nation." The Negro, compared with the white citizen, had about ½ as much chance of completing high school, 1/3 as much chance of becoming a professional man, twice as much chance of becoming unemployed; he had prospects of earning only ½ as much and a life expectancy 7 years less. Race bias "hampers" U.S. economic growth and world leadership and "mars the atmosphere of a united and classless society in which this nation rose to greatness. . . . Above all, it is wrong." "No state or section of this nation can pretend a self-righteous role, for every area has its own civil rights problems."

In calling for new voting-rights legislation, Mr. Kennedy said the Civil Rights Acts of 1957 and 1960 had 2 "major defects: (a) the "long and difficult" delay between the filing of a suit and its conclusion, and (b) "failure to deal specifically with the most common forms of abuse of discretion on the part of local election officials who do not treat all applicants uniformly." He made 4 proposals:

(1) Appointment of "temporary federal voting referees . . . to determine the qualifications of applicants for registration and voting during the pendency of a lawsuit in any county in which fewer than 15% of the eligible number of persons of any race claimed to be discriminated against are registered"; the referees would apply state law, and their decisions would be subject to court review.

(2) "Expedited treatment in the federal courts" of voting suits brought under the federal statutes.

(3) Prohibition of "the application of different tests, standards, practices or procedures for different applicants seeking to register and vote in federal elections."

(4) A guarantee that completion of 6th grade would constitute presumption of literacy for voting in federal elections.

Mr. Kennedy urged "prompt action" by the states in ratifying the proposed constitutional amendment to bar poll taxes as a condition to voting. He also recommended: (a) A program of federal technical and financial assistance to help school districts desegregate. (b) Elimination of the phrase "separate but equal" from the Morrill Land Grant College Act. (c) Extension of the Civil Rights Commission for at least 4 years and its expansion so that it could serve as a "national civil rights clearing house providing information, advice, and technical assistance to any requesting agency, private or public."

Mr. Kennedy said he had directed the Justice Department to participate in NLRB cases involving charges of racial discrimination by unions.

2d Kennedy Message

As pressure built up for more thorough-going action to secure equal rights for Negroes, Pres. Kennedy sent to Congress June 19 a draft Civil Rights Act of 1963. His message proposed ways of eliminating discrimination and assuring that Negroes were not deprived of "every American's right to vote, to go to school, to get a job and to be served in a public place without arbitrary discrimination." The President asked Congress to stay in session in 1963 until the rights act was enacted. He appealed for Congress members "to set aside sectional and political ties . . . to look at this issue from the viewpoint of the nation . . . to look into your hearts—not in search of charity, for the Negro neither wants nor needs condescension—but for . . . a sense of justice."

Mr. Kennedy's draft bill included provisions: (a) "To secure the right of all citizens to the full enjoyment of all facilities which are open to the general public" (hotels, restaurants, places of amusement and retail establishments). (b) To permit federal initiation of public school desegregation suits whenever such intervention was fairly requested by someone otherwise unable to sue. (c) To put an estimated $400 million more into his previously proposed programs of federal aid to education. (d) To extend the anti-bias injunction to federal or federally-aided construction projects and implement it throughout all federal activities. (e) To establish a Community Relations Service to act as a mediator in "tension-torn" communities. (f) To enact a general provision "making it clear that the federal government is not required, under any statute, to furnish any kind of financial assistance . . . to any program or activity in which racial discrimination occurs."

In calling for passage of his public facilities proposal, Mr. Kennedy said that rebuffs to a Negro's requests for normal accommodations were "a daily insult which has no place in a country proud of its heritage." The message asked Congress to make the Committee on Equal Employment Opportunity permanent. The President also renewed his request for enactment of legislation to continue and broaden the role of the Civil Rights Commission, to help school districts meet the costs of desegregation and to eliminate racial bars to voting.

Administration's Legislation Introduced in Congress

Pres. Kennedy's civil rights legislation was introduced in the Senate June 19 in 3 forms: (1) S1731, introduced by Senate Democratic leader Mike Mansfield (Mont.), the entire omnibus bill; (2) S1750, co-sponsored by Mansfield and Senate GOP leader Everett McKinley Dirksen (Ill.), the omnibus bill without the section to guarantee to all persons equal access to public facilities; (3) S1733, co-sponsored by Mansfield and Sen. Warren G. Magnuson (D., Wash.), the public facilities guarantee.

Republican support for the rights legislation was considered essential for a 2/3 vote to break the expected Southern Democratic filibuster in the Senate. Dirksen had said June 17 that he would support all of the Administration's proposals except the public accommodations section. Sen. Barry Goldwater (R., Ariz.), who previously had maintained that no legislative action was needed currently on civil rights, indicated June 20 that he would support some of the President's proposals but not the public facilities provision. Goldwater said he would support the proposal to permit the U.S. to sue for school integration if there were proof instead of merely a complaint of segregation.

In the House, the President's civil rights bill (HR7152) was introduced June 20 by Chrmn. Emanuel Celler (D., N.Y.)

of the Judiciary Committee. A GOP civil rights bill, including
a provision to bar bias in public facilities, had been introduced
in the House June 3.

Compromise Bill Blocked in Committee

A civil rights bill with bipartisan backing was finally
approved Oct. 29 by the House Judiciary Committee. The bill
was a compromise between the Administration's original
measure and stronger legislation that had been reported Oct.
2 by the committee's Subcommittee No. 5. The Administration
had fought (1) to head off the subcommittee plan on the ground
that it did not have a chance of enactment, and (2) to gain
from the Republicans support necessary to offset Southern
Democratic opposition to any rights bill.

Atty. Gen. Robert F. Kennedy, appearing before the full
committee Oct. 15-16, objected particularly (a) to "unclear"
language in the subcommittee bill's proviso to bar segregation
in public facilities, which went beyond the Administration's
plan and included all businesses operating under state or local
license, and (b) to a subcommittee proviso to let the Justice
Department sue for injunctions against local police forces
using brutal methods against racial demonstrators. There was
a "basic danger . . . [in] relying on injunctions to control in
advance the actions of local police," he said.

Kennedy's views were backed by Committee Chrmn. Emanuel
Celler (D., N.Y.) and the committee's ranking Republican,
William M. McCulloch (O.). But the committee's liberal
Republicans and liberal Democrats continued to press for the
subcommittee bill. Celler and McCulloch conferred secretly
at the White House Oct. 23 with Pres. Kennedy and Justice
Department officials. At a 2d White House meeting, held
Oct. 29, the Administration and House GOP leader Charles A.
Halleck (Ind.) agreed to back a compromise bill.

The committee later Oct. 29 rejected the subcommittee
bill by 19-15 vote (7 Southerners, including 2 Republicans,
voted for the subcommittee bill on the assumption that it
would be easier to kill in the final showdown). The bipartisan
measure was then approved by 20-14 vote.

Pres. Kennedy issued a statement hailing the bill as
"comprehensive and fair." The President said it "will provide
the basis for men of goodwill in every city in our land to work
together to resolve their racial problems within a framework

of law and justice."

Negro leaders of the Leadership Conference on Civil Rights said in an Oct. 29 statement that they "deplored" the defeat of the subcommittee plan; they called the bipartisan bill "inadequate to the needs of 1963."

The subcommittee bill would have extended anti-bias voting provisions to state and local elections as well as to federal elections and would have provided for impounding ballots cast under the temporary referee. It would have exempted from the public accommodations section only owner-occupied lodgings with 5 or fewer rooms. It would have permitted the federal government to institute suits not only in school cases but in cases involving parks and playgrounds and in suits in which individuals claimed breach of constitutional liberties. It would have barred bias by employers and unions and, like the President's bill, provided for a Community Relations Service to mediate racial disputes locally.

The compromise would have restricted the voting section to federal elections, dropped the referee plan and allowed 3-judge courts to hear vote suits. It would have exempted retail stores from the public facilities section unless they had eating accommodations and would also have exempted small lodgings. It would have permitted federal suits in school desegregation and public facilities cases but have restricted federal intervention in individual rights cases to those initiated by the individual. It would have provided for a fair employment section, would have made the CRC permanent and would have dropped the Community Relations Service.

As 1963 drew to a close, the bill was still pigeonholed in the House Rules Committee, whose chairman, Rep. Howard W. Smith (D., Va.), opposed rights legislation. Pres. Johnson, after Pres. Kennedy's assassination, renewed Administration pressure for the rights bill, and he won from Smith Dec. 5 a promise that hearings on the bill would be held "reasonably soon in January" 1964. Smith had said Dec. 2 that his committee had planned no hearings on the bill. House Republican leader Halleck announced his support for the rights bill after breakfasting with the President Dec. 5.

Commission's Life Extended

Stop-gap legislation extending the life of the Civil Rights Commission for one year (until Nov. 30, 1964) was passed by

70-15 Senate vote Oct. 1 and by 265-80 House vote (136 D. & 129 R. vs. 71 D. & 9 R.) Oct. 7. Pres. Kennedy signed the measure Oct. 17.

The extension had been brought to the House floor under a suspension of the rules (thus requiring a 2/3 vote) after an attempt to introduce it by unanimous consent Oct. 2 had been blocked by an objection from Rep. John Bell Williams (D., Miss.). The rules-suspension and unanimous-consent maneuvers were invoked to keep the bill from being pigeonholed in the Rules Committee.

The extension was in the form of an amendment to a private bill (HR 3369) for the relief of Mrs. E. G. Mason.

The 15 opposing votes in the Senate were cast by Southern Democrats. Only 4 Southern Senators—Sens. Ralph W. Yarborough (D., Tex.), John G. Tower (R., Tex.), Albert Gore (D., Tenn.) and Herbert S. Walters (D., Tenn.)—voted for the extension.

VIOLENCE IN BIRMINGHAM

The Negro campaign for equality in Birmingham, Ala. led to fresh outbursts of violence during 1963. The city became a center of international attention in September when 4 Negro girls were killed there in the bombing of a Negro church. Pres. Kennedy sent 2 personal representatives to the city to try to help bring peace to the community.

Rights Campaign Intensified, Rioting Follows

An intensified drive was started by Negroes in Birmingham Apr. 2 in an effort to desegregate lunch counters and public facilities and to end discrimination in employment. The campaign led within 2 months to the arrests of more than 3,000 persons, in most cases on charges of trespass, parading without permit and loitering.

Persons arrested during the early days of the campaign included: the Rev. Fred L. Shuttlesworth, president of the Alabama Christian Movement for Human Rights and local director of the campaign, who was arrested Apr. 6, released Apr. 8 and arrested again Apr. 12; the Rev. Dr. Martin Luther King Jr. and the Rev. Dr. Ralph D. Abernathy, who were arrested Apr. 12 with more than 60 others as they led a march of about 1,000 Negroes.

King, head of the Southern Christian Leadership Conference, and Abernathy, conference secretary, remained in jail until Apr. 20, when they were released under $300 bond. King and about 48 other Negroes were charged with violating an Apr. 10 state court injunction, obtained by Birmingham Public Safety Commissioner Eugene (Bull) Connor and Police Chief Jamie Moore, barring further demonstrations. (Pres. Kennedy phoned Apr. 13 to the Justice Department for information about King's arrest, and he made a sympathetic call Apr. 15 to Mrs. King.) King and 10 of the other Negro leaders were convicted by Alabama Circuit Court Judge W. A. Jenkins Jr. Apr. 26. The judge fined them $50 each and permitted them to remain free pending appeal.

In the midst of the desegregation drive, Mayor Albert Boutwell and a new 9-man city council were sworn in Apr. 15. They had been elected in a court-sanctioned election in Nov. 1962, and Birmingham had been scheduled to change over from commissioner-type government Apr. 15. But the commissioners, including Connor, who had been defeated by Boutwell in the election, refused to surrender their offices on the ground that their terms would not expire until Oct. 1965. The new officials filed suit Apr. 16 to oust the commissioners, and the State Supreme Court May 23 unanimously upheld the right of Boutwell and the council to take office immediately. Connor and his fellow commissioners yielded and left office May 23. (Boutwell, an avowed segregationist, was considered a moderate in comparison with the outgoing commissioners, who had spearheaded opposition to the desegregation campaign.)

While the outcome of the struggle between Connor and Boutwell was still in doubt leaders of the desegregation drive applied to both of the city governments for permits to stage peaceful protest marches. Both governments refused the request Apr. 30. The refusal precipitated mass protests.

Hundreds of Negro children demonstrated May 2 in groups of 10 to 50. More than 700 of them were arrested, and they offered no resistance. Instead, they sang and laughed and some even ran to school buses commandeered by police to bring them to jail. The Rev. A. D. William King, brother of Dr. Martin Luther King Jr., was among those arrested but was later released. (The Rev. King had also been arrested Apr. 14.)

The police used high-pressure fire hoses and police dogs May 3 to repulse marchers, mostly high school and college students. Most of them did not resist. But rocks and bottles were thrown at police and firemen from the top of a building, and 2 firemen and a news photographer were injured. 3 students were bitten by the dogs. 250 arrests were made May 3. Dr. King said at a mass meeting that night: "Today was D[emonstration] Day. Tomorrow will be Double-D Day."

Groups of Negro youths in their teens and younger left 2 Negro churches early May 4. When the first group neared city hall, they unfurled a banner reading "Love God and Thy Neighbor." They were immediately arrested. Orders were then issued to arrest the other groups, and the police closed the churches.

Violence erupted in a park May 4 when an unorganized crowd of about 2,000 adult Negroes became the targets of fire hoses and the police were pelted with bottles and rocks. As the disturbance mounted, one of Dr. King's lieutenants, the Rev. James Bevel of Cleveland, Miss., borrowed a police bull horn to plead: "If you're not going to demonstrate in a non-violent way, then leave." More than 200 persons were arrested, including more than 100 juveniles.

The next day, Sunday, several hundred Negroes held a prayer vigil in church, then marched peacefully to nearby Julius Ellsberry Park (named after a Negro who had died at Pearl Harbor) but stopped on the way to pray at a police barricade blocking them from downtown. Only a few arrests, of stragglers, were made.

More mass protests took place May 6, when police arrested about 1,000 persons, including Negro comedian Dick Gregory, who attempted to lead 19 teen-agers on a march.

About 3,000 adult Negroes rioted May 7 in the business district. They threw rocks and bottles at the police but were eventually forced to the Negro district by fire hoses spouting water at pressure so high that it tore the bark off trees. An armored police car was used to herd crowds. An undetermined number of persons were injured, including Shuttlesworth and 6 policemen, the latter having been hit by rocks. 28 persons were arrested (the total number of arrests since May 2 rose to 2,453).

After the rioting, Gov. George Wallace ordered 250 state highway patrolmen to bolster Connor's city force. 575 more troopers armed with tear gas, submachine guns and sawed-off shotguns moved into the city the night of May 7. About 1,200 law officers were in Birmingham by May 8, which, however, was a day of uneasy peace.

182 Civil Rights 1963

Truce Suspends Demonstrations

King and Shuttlesworth announced May 8 that the mass demonstrations in Birmingham would be suspended for 24 hours while Negro and business leaders negotiated. A few hours later Pres. Kennedy opened his news conference by citing "the progress in the efforts by white and Negro citizens to end an ugly situation in Birmingham." He said: "The business community . . . has responded in a constructive and commendable fashion and pledged that substantial steps would begin to meet the justifiable needs of the Negro community."

An hour after Mr. Kennedy spoke the truce was jeopardized by the jailing of King. He had been convicted by City Court Judge C. H. Brown of having paraded on Good Friday without a permit. 26 others, including Abernathy, were also convicted and jailed. Brown imposed the maximum penalty on each: 180 days in jail plus $100 fine. Bond was $2,500 each. Several Negro leaders called for huge demonstrations the next day. But King and Abernathy were released on bond and made conciliatory statements expressing hope for success in the negotiations.

The negotiations had been initiated by Asst. Atty. Gen. Burke Marshall, 40, head of the Justice Department's Civil Rights Division, and Asst. Deputy Atty. Gen. Joseph F. Dolan, who had been dispatched to Birmingham May 4 by Atty. Gen. Robert F. Kennedy. They worked behind scenes in daily maneuvering to have city officials, businessmen and Negro leaders confer. Atty. Gen. Kennedy had said May 3: "Everyone understands that their [the Negroes'] just grievances must be resolved. Continued refusal to grant equal rights and opportunities to Negroes makes increasing turmoil inevitable." He said he regretted the participation of the children and he urged "good faith negotiations" to achieve a settlement in conference and "not in the streets."

At his news conference May 8, the President said Marshall was "representing the Attorney General and myself." He stressed that the effort at settlement was between Negro and white citizens of Birmingham: "In the absence of . . . federal jurisdiction, our efforts have been focused on getting both sides together to settle in a peaceful fashion. . . ."

Gov. Wallace May 8 issued a statement describing as "unjust and unfair" the President's news conference remarks that the people of Birmingham (in Wallace's paraphrase) "had, in effect, a long-time record of abuses inflicted upon Negroes."

Wallace said he would "not be a party to any . . . meeting to compromise on the issues of segregation." In his statement Wallace referred to the Negro leaders as "King and his group of pro-Communists."

Agreement to Limited Desegregation

A limited desegregation plan was worked out May 9 by King, Shuttlesworth and Abernathy in negotiations with a Senior Citizens Committee. The latter group was a committee of white Birmingham businessmen set up by the Chamber of Commerce in 1962 to seek some arrangement with Negro leaders. The committee's chief negotiator was lawyer-real estate operator Sidney W. Smyer Sr., who said his group represented employers of about 80% of Birmingham's working force. The agreement was announced May 10 by Shuttlesworth, who listed its terms as:

(a) The desegregation of lunch counters, rest rooms, sitting rooms and drinking fountains in large downtown department and variety stores within 90 days.

(b) The promotion and hiring of Negroes on a nondiscriminatory basis in stores and industries, the hiring of Negro clerks and salesmen within 60 days by the stores, the appointment of a fair employment committee.

(c) The release of jailed Negro demonstrators on bond or on their personal recognizance (about 800 demonstrators remaining in jail were released May 10 on bonds totaling $240,000 posted by 10 persons).

(d) The creation of a biracial committee within 2 weeks.

The agreement reportedly had been achieved after the Negroes had retreated from their previous demands for (1) immediate steps, not promises, toward desegregation, (2) the dismissal of charges against the thousands arrested during the demonstrations and (3) a pledge that no disciplinary action would be taken against school children involved.

King May 10 called the agreement "the most significant victory for justice that we have seen in the Deep South." "We must now move from protest to reconciliation," he said. Atty. Gen. Kennedy lauded the agreement May 10 as "a great lesson" in "the importance of getting a dialogue going between people in the North and the South." But the agreement was attacked May 11 by Connor, who appealed by radio for whites to boycott stores honoring the agreement.

Bombings Interrupt Truce

A bombing abruptly punctured Birmingham's truce the night of May 11. The target was the $26,000 home of the Rev. A. D. William King, Dr. King's brother. The Rev. King, his wife and his 5 children were in the house when it was bombed but were not injured, although the front half of their house was demolished.

A 2d bombing occurred a few minutes before midnight May 11 at the integrated A. G. Gaston Motel, headquarters for the Negroes' campaign. 4 persons were injured (none seriously), and heavy damages were inflicted on the motel.

The bombings triggered a 3-hour riot early May 12. 2,500 Negroes participated in the riot, and about 50 persons were injured.

Tires on police and fire vehicles were slashed and punctured by Negroes gathering at the King home after the bombing late May 11, and police and firemen arriving at the scene of the motel bombing were met with a hail of bottles and rocks. Fires razed 6 nearby neighborhood stores as firemen were driven away by Negroes throwing bottles and rocks. A white taxi driver was pulled from his cab and stabbed, and the cab was burned. Persons injured included W. J. Haley, chief inspector of the city's police force, who was aided by Negro civil defense workers trying to help police and Negro leaders restore order.

A 28-block area was sealed off eventually by about 250 state troopers and about 100 deputized irregulars under the direction of Col. Albert J. Lingo, state director of public safety.

When Lingo had arrived on the scene with an automatic shotgun (his troopers arrived with carbines), he had been urged by Haley and Birmingham Police Chief Jamie Moore to "please leave." "We don't need any guns down here," Moore said, "you all might get somebody killed." "You're damned right it'll kill somebody," Lingo replied. (The *N.Y. Herald Tribune* reported May 13: After the riot subsided, "the state troopers began clubbing Negroes sitting on their porches." Those clubbed had been "taking no part in the fight.")

President Orders Troops to Birmingham

In Washington May 12, Pres. Kennedy held a 3-hour emergency meeting with Atty. Gen. Kennedy, Defense Secy.

Robert S. McNamara, Army Secy. Cyrus Vance, Army Chief of Staff Earle G. Wheeler and other officials. The President then went before the TV cameras to announce that he had dispatched federal troops to bases near Birmingham and had ordered the "necessary preliminary steps" to federalize the Alabama National Guard. "This government will do whatever must be done to preserve order, to protect the lives of its citizens and to uphold the law of the land," he said. "There must be no repetition of last night's incidents by any groups." He lauded the integration agreement and said "the federal government will not permit it to be sabotaged." He appealed to Birmingham citizens to "make outside intervention unnecessary."

While Mr. Kennedy spoke, federal troops, all from outside Alabama, were on the move. By May 13 about 3,000 troops were in the area, and a headquarters with about 30 Army personnel was established in Birmingham.

Pres. Kennedy's authority to send federal troops into Alabama was questioned by Gov. Wallace May 12. In a telegram to the President, Wallace said there were "sufficient state and local forces" to handle the situation, which he described as "well in hand." He said that neither he nor the legislature had asked for the troops, and he requested their withdrawal. Pres. Kennedy replied by telegram May 13 that he "would be derelict in my duty" if he had not taken steps to "enable this government, if required, to meet its obligations without delay." He said he had acted under Title 10, Section 33, Paragraph 1 of the U.S. Code, which, he said, "entrusts to the President all determinations as to (1) the necessity for action; (2) the means to be employed; and (3) the adequacy or inadequacy of the protection afforded by state authorities to the citizens of that state."

Wallace protested later that the federal government was trying to "enforce a worthless agreement" worked out by "unauthorized, anonymous individuals." The negotiators of the agreement, however, expressed confidence in it. After the rioting May 12, King had said he did not feel the violence had "nullified" it. Smyer held a televised news conference May 13 to confirm the agreement.

Wallace asked the U.S. Supreme Court May 18 to rule that Pres. Kennedy had violated the Constitution by ordering federal troops to Alabama. He asked the court to invalidate, as unconstitutional, (a) the section of the U.S. Code under which

the troops had been dispatched and (b) the 14th Amendment.
The Supreme Court rejected Wallace's request in a unanimous
unsigned order May 27. The court said the suit showed "no
more than that the President has made ready to exercise the
authority conferred upon him by 10 U.S.C. 333" and that "such
purely preparatory measures and their alleged adverse effects
. . . afford no basis for the granting of relief."

1,081 Negro Pupils Ousted From School

The Birmingham school board May 20 expelled or suspended
1,081 Negro public school pupils who had been arrested in the
demonstrations. The board voted to expel all arrested students
16 or more years old and to suspend those under 16. The students involved were to be permitted to make up for the lost
time at summer school (which required fees). The board's
action was denounced May 20 by the city school superintendent,
Dr. Theo R. Wright.

The immediate reaction of Negro leaders May 20 was to
distribute leaflets urging the city's other 31,877 Negro students
to participate in a sympathy boycott of school and to enroll in
a "first class on freedom." The Rev. Dr. Martin Luther King
Jr., however, flew to Birmingham May 20 and appealed against
a boycott or a renewal of demonstrations. He said the board's
action would be fought in the courts. The boycott was canceled
May 21. (King, urging patience, told students "not to throw
away the victory when it's so close at hand.")

A suit to reverse the board's action was filed May 21 in
federal court in Birmingham by Mrs. Constance Baker Motley,
a lawyer for the NAACP Legal Defense & Educational Fund,
Inc., on the grounds that the expulsions violated the 14th
Amendment's due process and equal protection clauses and
that the students had been given no warning, hearings or
chance for appeals. Judge Clarence W. Allgood refused May
22 to issue an injunction against the board. The case was
immediately taken on appeal before Chief Judge Elbert P.
Tuttle of the U.S. 5th Circuit Court of Appeals in Atlanta, and
the Justice Department entered the case as a friend of the
court. Tuttle May 22 reversed Algood's ruling and issued the
injunction. Tuttle held that the Negro pupils would be "irrepa-
rably harmed" unless they were permitted to return to school
to finish the school year. The school year was scheduled
to close May 31.)

4 Girls Killed in Bombing

4 Negro girls were killed by a bomb explosion in Birmingham's Negro 16th Street Baptist Church during Sunday School Sept. 15. The explosion injured 14 other Negroes, blew holes in the church and wrecked or damaged 5 cars in the street.

Negroes rushed to the scene, where they hurled rocks at police and at cars carrying whites. 2 Negro boys were killed during the continuing violence Sept. 15. Johnny Robinson, 16, was slain by a shotgun blast fired by a policeman, who said he had shot low to disperse a group of rock-throwing Negro youths. Virgil Wade, 13, was shot and killed as he rode a bicycle on the outskirts of town.

Mayor Boutwell, tears in his eyes, called the bombing "just sickening." He and Police Chief Jamie Moore appealed to Gov. Wallace for help against further violence. Wallace, who described the bombing as "tragic," sent 300 state troopers to Birmingham that day and offered a $5,000 reward for information leading to the bombers' arrest and conviction. 25 FBI agents and Asst. Atty. Gen. Burke Marshall with Justice Department investigators rushed to Birmingham Sept. 15 to investigate.

The Rev. Dr. King Sept. 15 sent Pres. Kennedy a telegram urging immediate federal action before "the worst racial holocaust the nation has ever seen" erupted in Birmingham and Alabama. King said he would "plead with my people to remain nonviolent in the face of this terrible provocation." King also sent Wallace a telegram saying "the blood of 4 little children and others . . . is on your hands" because of "your irresponsible and misguided actions." King said at a news conference Sept. 16 that the Army "ought to . . . take over this city and run it." The proposal was made in the name of 150 Negro business and professional leaders.

Pres. Kennedy, in a statement Sept. 16, expressed his "deep sense of outrage and grief" over the bombing. He said: "If these cruel and tragic events can only awaken that city and state—if they can only awaken this entire nation—to a realization of the folly of racial injustice and hatred and violence, then it is not too late for all concerned to unite in steps toward peaceful progress before more lives are lost."

About 1,500 persons attended the funeral Sept. 17 of Carol Robertson, 14, one of the 4 girls killed in the bombing. The other 3 victims were buried Sept. 18. About 4,000 persons attended.

(There had been about 50 bombings of Negro property in Birmingham, all unsolved, since World War II. The Sept. 15 bombing was the 21st bombing of Negroes there since 1955.)

Prior to the bombing, white Birmingham residents and students protesting the recent desegregation of 3 schools had engaged in motorcades and rallies. Demonstrations were staged in front of segregated schools to induce participation in a school boycott. The group sponsoring the demonstrations canceled further protests Sept. 15 because of the "present emergency."

President Sends Mediators

Pres. Kennedy Sept. 19 appointed ex-Army Secy. Kenneth C. Royall, 69, and ex-West Point football coach Earl H. Blaik, 66, "to represent me personally" in helping Birmingham try to overcome "the fears and suspicions" arising from its racial problems. Pres. Kennedy Sept. 19 also met with the Rev. Dr. King and 6 other Negro leaders, who told the President that Birmingham's Negroes were "almost on the verge of despair as a result of this reign of terror." King said Mr. Kennedy had expressed "the kind of federal concern needed." The Negroes indicated that, as a result of Mr. Kennedy's actions, they were withdrawing, at least temporarily, their demand that federal troops police Birmingham.

The President met Sept. 23 with Royall, Blaik and 2 Birmingham groups—one representing the city officials and the business community, the other clergymen. Mr. Kennedy said the Birmingham groups and the Negro leaders he had met Sept. 19 had expressed willingness to cooperate with Royall and Blaik and a confidence "that these matters can be settled on a local level." At a news conference later, the civic leaders said "outsiders" attempting to interfere with Birmingham's problem would not be welcome unless specifically invited, as were Royall and Blaik. They indicated that King and Gov. Wallace of Alabama would be considered "outsiders."

Royall and Blaik arrived in Birmingham Sept. 24 and were met by an all-white delegation headed by Boutwell, who told them that he considered their mission to be "advisory" and that "the lines of communication between our local citizens have been hampered largely by professional outsiders who thrive on the fruits of tension and unrest." Royall and Blaik conferred with white and Negro leaders that week. A committee of 16 white and 9 Negro leaders was established Oct. 1 to work toward a solution; the Right Rev. C. C. J. Carpenter, a white Episcopal bishop, served as chairman.

While Royall and Blaik were in the city, a Negro neighborhood of Birmingham was rocked Sept. 25 by 2 bomb explosions, which damaged 8 homes and 4 automobiles. The 2d bomb, which went off about 15 minutes after the first, had been loaded with staples, nails, bolts and other metal bits. Most of the damage was from this shrapnel. Police Inspector W. J. Haley said that "this was a booby trap," that the bomber probably had expected Negroes to rush into the streets after the first explosion and then be mangled by the shrapnel of the 2d bomb. Nobody was injured, however, since most Negroes attracted by the decoy blast had returned to their home before the 2d explosion.

SOUTHERN EQUALITY MOVEMENT

Medgar Evers' Jackson Drive

The Mississippi NAACP announced May 12 its determination to end "all forms of segregation in Jackson," Miss. The NAACP said Negroes sought "good-faith attempts" to negotiate, but it warned that if these efforts failed, a campaign of boycotts, protest marches and sit-ins would begin.

After meeting with 75 business leaders May 13, Mayor Allen Thompson announced the rejection of the Negro demands. "No biracial committee will be appointed," he declared. He asserted that such action could lead only to "compliance with the demands of racial agitators from outside."

The Negroes picked a 14-man committee May 21 to meet with Thompson. Thompson replaced 10 of the 14 committee members with his own nominees, then met with the committee May 27 and read a statement banning demonstrations, upholding school segregation and rejecting the demand for a biracial committee.

Under the direction of Medgar W. Evers, 37, a Negro and the NAACP's field secretary in Mississippi for 9 years, the Negro action campaign began May 28 with a sit-in at a "white-only" F. W. Woolworth lunch counter. The participants were 3 Tougaloo Southern Christian College students—Memphis Norman, 21, and 2 girls, all of them Negroes—Tougaloo Prof. John R. Salter, a white, Walter Williams, a Negro, and several white girls. Norman was knocked from his stool and kicked in the face by a white man, Benny G. Oliver, 26, a former Jackson policeman. (City police, on hand but ordered not to enter private property unless invited, arrested Oliver later. Norman, admitted to the hospital, was charged with disturbing the peace. The charge was dismissed at the city's request May 31. Oliver was sentenced to 30 days in jail and fined $100.) A crowd of about 200 whites gathered and sprinkled the demonstrators with mustard, catsup and sugar from the counter. Salter was struck in the face; Williams was thrown to the floor and beaten; one of the white girls was seized and pushed out of the store by a white youth. All demonstrators continued the sit-in without resisting.

5 other Negroes were arrested in Jackson May 28 after they started picketing a block away. A bomb explosion that night wrecked the home of an integrationist leader.

The campaign was marked by the use of Negro school children in integration parades and by the use of Negro prison trustees to help arrest Negro demonstrators, mainly by carrying them to patrol wagons.

400 Negro school children demonstrated in a Jackson school yard May 30. Police barricaded streets in the area and directed the students back into school. An even larger group of Negro children began a march downtown May 31, and about 600 were arrested by the city police force, which was reinforced with sheriff's deputies, and by state highway patrolmen. The arrested children were loaded into trucks and taken to a temporary jail set up on a fair ground. They were joined June 1 by more than 100 additional Negro children arrested in another march. 300 of the children were soon released. Also arrested June 1 for picketing were Evers and NAACP Executive Secy. Roy Wilkins; both were freed on bond of $1,000 each.

Mayor Thompson and the City Commission agreed June 1 to 3 of the Negroes' demands—to hire Negroes as policemen and school crossing guards, to desegregate city facilities and to upgrade Negro employment in city jobs. The Negroes' key demand, for the establishment of a biracial committee, was rejected.

Evers Slain by Gunman

Evers attended an integration rally at a Jackson church June 11. Returning to his home in Jackson just after midnight,

he was shot in the back and killed from ambush. A caliber
.30-06 rifle with a telescopic sight was found nearby.

Gov. Ross R. Barnett of Mississippi said of the slaying
that "apparently it was a dastardly act," and Mayor Thompson
said Jackson citizens were "dreadfully shocked, humiliated
and sick at heart" over it. The city offered a $5,000 reward
for information leading to the murderer's arrest and conviction.

About 2,800 persons, including UN Undersecy. Ralph Bunche,
attended Evers' funeral services in Jackson June 15 and heard
Roy Wilkins charge in eulogy that "the Southern political system put that man behind the rifle" that killed Evers. Pres. and
Mrs. Kennedy sent Mrs. Evers a letter of condolence. Evers,
who had received 2 Bronze Stars for World War II Army
service, was buried in Arlington National Cemetery June 19.

Jackson Negroes reacted to Evers' murder with mass
demonstrations June 12 that resulted in 158 arrests. 13 of those
arrested were ministers walking to city hall in pairs at widely
spaced intervals. Several hundred Negro teen-age demonstrators were halted by a 100-man police force equipped with riot
guns and automatic rifles.

A riot broke out briefly June 15 following a mourning march.
Officials had granted a parade permit for the march, in which
thousands of Negroes and about 50 whites participated. A
group of young Negroes, breaking from the ranks, stopped at
a line of policemen, who were accompanied by police dogs.
Several Negroes hurled bottles and rocks before the police
moved forward and began making arrests. U.S. Asst. Atty.
Gen. John Doar was credited with keeping the riot from
growing worse by ignoring the missiles, walking toward the
crowd and appealing for calm. Several Negro leaders aided
him. 27 persons, including 2 white integrationists, were arrested.

A 2d march in protest against Evers' slaying resulted
June 15 in the arrest of 82 persons, including Prof. Salter.
37 Negro youths were arrested June 16 (Flag Day) as they
appeared downtown in 2s and 4s carrying small American
flags.

Following a suspension of demonstrations June 17 and
several phone calls from Pres. Kennedy and Atty. Gen.
Kennedy to Mayor Thompson, Thompson met with 5 Negro
leaders June 18 and announced later that the city would
(a) hire 6 Negro policemen and 8 Negro school-crossing
guards and (b) promote 7 Negro sanitation workers to truck

drivers and a Negro truck driver to crew leader, all for Negro districts.

The demonstrations were suspended June 20. More than 1,000 Negroes and whites had been arrested in the final 4 weeks. Byron de la Beckwith, 42, of Greenwood, Miss. was arrested in Greenwood June 22 (June 23 Washington time) and charged in Jackson June 23 with Evers' murder. Beckwith, a fertilizer salesman, was a member of the Citizens Council of Mississippi. Beckwith's arrest by FBI agents was announced in Washington by FBI Director J. Edgar Hoover, who said clues leading to the arrest were the telescopic sight and Beckwith's fingerprint on the rifle found near Evers' home after the slaying. The federal charge against Beckwith: violating the 1957 Civil Rights Act by conspiring to prevent Evers from exercising his civil rights. Federal authorities June 24 turned Beckwith over to the Jackson police and deferred the federal case until the resolution of the state case. A county grand jury in Jackson indicted Beckwith on the murder charge July 2. He pleaded not guilty July 8.

A small group of Negro demonstrators was arrested in a resumption of the campaign Dec. 6. (14 persons, including 9 ministers and some whites, were arrested in attempts Nov. 17 and Dec. 15 to integrate "white-only" Jackson churches.)

Greenwood (Miss.) Turmoil

In Greenwood (Leflore County), violence and arrests accompanied a major Negro voter registration campaign that got under way Mar. 1. Negro comedian Dick Gregory, 30, of Chicago, led several marches. During the drive, several hundred Negroes applied for registration in Leflore County, where 64% of the population of 47,142 were Negroes but where (before the drive) only about 250 of 10,050 registered voters were Negroes.

Violence had erupted as early as Feb. 28, when James Travis, 20, a Negro voter-registration worker, was wounded (not seriously) by gunfire from an auto carrying 3 white men. 4 major civil rights groups—the NAACP, the Southern Christian Leadership Conference, the Congress of Racial Equality (CORE) and the Student Nonviolent Coordinating Committee (SNCC, or "Snick")—announced the following day that they would coordinate the registration drive. After holding mass rallies each night, Negroes marched during the day Mar. 27-Apr. 3 in groups of 35 to 50 to the courthouse in attempts to register. The police, armed and sometimes accompanied by police dogs, attempted to disperse them.

A federal suit against voting discrimination in Leflore County arose out of the arrest of 11 marchers Mar. 27. 8 of those arrested, including Robert P. Moses, 28, an SNCC field secretary and the campaign's leader, and James Forman, SNCC secretary, were sentenced Mar. 29 to 4 months in prison and fined $200 each for disorderly conduct.

The Justice Department sued Mar. 30 for a federal court order banning interference with Negro voter registrations. U.S. District Judge Claude F. Clayton Jr. in Aberdeen, Miss. Apr. 1 refused the federal request for a temporary injunction.

But federal and city officials Apr. 4 came to an agreement easing the situation. They agreed on the simultaneous withdrawal of the petition for a temporary injunction and the staying of sentences of the 8 arrested Mar. 27.

During the campaign, shots were fired at 4 Negro voter-registration workers Mar. 6. The Greenwood voter-registration headquarters was damaged by fire Mar. 25; shotgun blasts were fired Mar. 26 into the home of the father of Dewey Roosevelt Green Jr., who had been unsuccessful in an attempt to enroll in the University of Mississippi, and flaming gasoline bombs were thrown Apr. 12 into the Clarksdale home of Aaron Henry, a Negro and president of the NAACP's Mississippi chapter (2 whites arrested hours after the bombing said they were "just having fun"). No one was injured.

Earlier in 1963 Gregory had organized food shipments to low-income Leflore County Negroes after county officials had cut off the distribution of surplus federal food. Negroes charged that the food distribution had been halted as a means of applying pressure against the registration campaign. County officials resumed the distribution Apr. 1 after Agriculture Secy. Orville L. Freeman threatened to end their authority over the program.

Freedom Walker Slain

William L. Moore, 35, a white postal worker, was found shot to death on a road near Attalla, Ala. Apr. 23. He had been walking, wearing pro-integration signs, on a personal pilgrimage from Chattanooga, Tenn. to Mississippi to protest segregation.

Moore, before starting his journey Apr. 22, had left at the

White House Apr. 19 a letter saying that he was not "making this walk to demonstrate either federal rights or state rights, but individual rights," and that he was doing it "to illustrate that peaceful protest is not altogether extinguished down there." A letter he had planned to deliver to Mississippi Gov. Ross Barnett said: Mississippi had acquired a reputation as "the most backward and most bigoted [state] in the land. Those who truly love Mississippi must work to change this image."

3 attempts were made to complete Moore's pilgrimage, but each ended in the arrest of the participants:

(1) The first group was composed of 8 Negroes, including Mrs. Diane Nash Bevel, wife of the Mississippi field secretary of the Southern Christian Leadership Conference. The 8 Negroes were apprehended by Etowah County sheriff deputies near Attalla May 1 and jailed at Gadsden. The group, unsponsored, carried signs reading "Love Thy Neighbor" and "Equal Rights for All."

(2) Another group of walkers, 5 whites and 5 Negroes, sponsored by CORE and the Student Nonviolent Coordinating Committee (SNCC), took up Moore's integration walk May 1 from Chattanooga, Tenn. The marchers passed through Georgia and were followed into Alabama by about 100 cars carrying whites. As soon as they crossed the state line May 3, they were arrested by Alabama state troopers using electrical prod poles customarily used on cattle. They were jailed on breach-of-the-peace charges. Also arrested were SNCC Executive Secy. James Forman and SNCC Field Secy. Landy McNair, both of whom had accompanied the walkers by car; Forman and McNair were released May 4 on bond of $300 each.

(3) A 3d attempt to resume Moore's "Freedom Walk" was started by 5 whites and 6 Negroes at the site of the slaying. The group, sponsored by CORE, was arrested May 19 by Etowah County sheriff's deputies.

Floyd E. Simpson, 40, a white, operator of a grocery store in Collbran, DeKalb County, was formally charged in Gadsden Apr. 29 with Moore's slaying, but he was freed Sept. 13 when an Etowah County grand jury in Gadsden refused to indict him.

Campaign in Gadsen (Ala.)

Anti-segregation demonstrations were begun in Gadsden, Ala. June 10 in the form of silent marches. Despite a state court injunction barring interference with normal business operations, demonstrators lay down on sidewalks, in store aisles and in front of the courthouse. Police, using electric prod poles, made mass arrests. By June 23, 523 persons had been arrested, including about 180 under 16 years of age. A protest march June 27 was led by mothers whose children were being held by authorities after arrests for demonstrating. 52 of the mothers were then arrested.

Negro negotiators, led by Dr. J. W. Stewart, agreed to a long-term truce July 1 following the desegregation of buses and a promise by a quasi-official group of whites to negotiate other issues.

But demonstrations were renewed Aug. 3 with the largest anti-bias gathering in Gadsden's history—about 1,000 Negroes. About 685 were arrested; they included some 200 juveniles, who were quickly released. 132 Negroes were arrested in demonstrations Sept. 24, and 28 were arrested Sept. 25 for picketing the Dallas County courthouse. Among those arrested Sept. 25 was John Lewis, chairman of the Student Nonviolent Coordinating Committee, sponsor of the Gadsden protests. 2 rights leaders, the Rev. Wilson Brown and Worth W. Long, were fined $300 in county court in Gadsden Sept. 26 and sentenced to 180 days in jail.

4 movie actors—Marlon Brando, Paul Newman, Anthony Franciosa and Virgil Frye—went to Gadsden Aug. 23 but were rebuffed in an attempt to confer about Negro complaints with Mayor Lesley Gilliland.

Baltimore Activity

413 integrationists were arrested in Baltimore Feb. 15-21 for demonstrating against the Northwood movie theater's exclusion of Negro patrons. The picketing ended Feb. 21 when the theater management agreed to "admit all law-abiding persons."

Operators of the Gwynn Oak Amusement Park near Baltimore agreed July 19 to open the park to Negro patrons (starting Aug. 28) following civil rights demonstrations July 4 and 7 in which 383 persons were arrested. Integrationists arrested included the Rev. Dr. Eugene Carson Blake, stated clerk of the United Presbyterian Church in the U.S.A., and many other prominent clergymen. CORE had coordinated the demonstrations. An agreement to open the park to Negroes and to drop charges against the demonstrators was negotiated at meetings attended by the disputants and a Human Relations Commission established

July 8 by the Baltimore County Council.

Strife in Cambridge (Md.)

A campaign of anti-discrimination demonstrations in the cannery town of Cambridge, Md. led to violence and ultimately to the use of the National Guard and the imposition of limited martial law.

The demonstrations started Mar. 30-31 at a movie theater and a skating rink. They were held each weekend through the May 11-12 weekend and then were continued through May. 17.

A truce was arranged by Negro and white leaders May 18. The Negroes pledged to end demonstrations for a week; the white business and professional leaders agreed to (a) the release of more than 50 demonstrators remaining in jail and (b) cooperation to implement Negro demands.

As the truce was reaching its May 31 expiration date, it was imperiled by an incident in which a Negro girl, Dinez White, 15, was arrested with 4 others in an individual demonstration at a recreation center May 30 and was held without bail. Circuit Judge E. McMaster Duer, who had ordered Miss White held, released her on a writ of *habeas corpus* June 3 but sentenced her and a 15-year-old Negro boy June 10 to indeterminate terms in correction schools. (The state Court of Appeals unanimously reversed the sentences Oct. 8.)

Negro leaders denounced the sentencing as a "double cross." 100 Negroes demonstrated June 10, and 20 were arrested. A march June 11 in protest against the new arrests led to rioting and clashes between whites and Negroes, and 2 white men were injured by shotgun blasts. Several hundred counter-demonstrating whites were prevented by police and state troopers June 13 from breaking into the Negro district.

The mayor, City Council and Negro leaders met in Annapolis June 14 with Gov. J. Millard Tawes, who ordered the National Guard late June 14 to maintain order in Cambridge under a "civilian and military government."

400 to 500 National Guardsmen moved into Cambridge June 14 and enforced a ban on demonstrations, a 10 p.m. curfew and prohibition of liquor sales. These and other limited martial law rules remained in effect until noon July 8, when Tawes directed the Guard to leave. Demonstrations resumed the day the Guardsmen departed, and Tawes ordered the Guard back July 11 after the demonstrations had led to

shootings and other violence. Modified martial law was reinstated July 12.

Tawes appealed to all citizens in a statewide TV address July 19 to "appreciate the magnitude of the social revolution now under way." He warned that "we will face not weeks nor months of racial strife, but years" unless "all the citizens of this state" acted to satisfy the legitimate pleas" of Negroes for equality.

National Guardsmen in Cambridge fired tear gas July 20 to disperse Negroes defying orders to move off the streets. Negro leaders who were conferring with the troops' commander, Brig. Gen. George C. Gelston, after being stopped from leading a protest march, helped restore order.

An agreement tentatively settling the dispute was signed July 23 by Negro and white leaders. The agreement was reached in Atty. Gen. Robert F. Kennedy's office after 72 hours of intensive federal mediation. Under the agreement the Negro leaders promised to end demonstrations "for an indefinite period."

The agreement called for:

(a) Desegregation of the first 4 grades of Dorchester County public schools by September and processing of admission applications to any grade regardless of race.

(b) Construction of a low-rent public housing project for Negroes. (The Negro leaders met in Washington with Dr. Robert C. Weaver, federal housing administrator, who assured them the city's application for the project, already filed, "would be expeditiously processed.")

(c) Appointment of a biracial Human Relations Commission.

(d) Hiring of a Negro interviewer for the state Employment Security Department.

(e) Negroes' acceptance of a possible referendum on a city charter amendment desegregating public accommodations.

Much of the controversy centered around demands for the desegregation of public accommodations. Tawes originally had proposed that the City Council adopt an ordinance against such discrimination, but his proposal was rejected by the Cambridge Nonviolent Action Committee. The City Council July 1 then adopted a plan even more objectionable to the Negroes—a city charter amendment prohibiting discrimination in public accommodations.

Negro leaders opposed the amendment plan because, unlike an ordinance, a charter amendment was subject to referendum by petition of 20% (about 750) of the registered voters. A petition for the referendum was filed by segregationists Aug. 8. In the vote, held Oct. 1, the amendment was defeated by a 1,994-1,720 vote. 3,095 of 3,474 registered whites voted but only 619 of 1,535 registered Negroes voted (587 for the amendment). Mrs. Gloria H. Richardson, Negro leader who said she was not for defeat of the amendment but against "voting on our rights," had urged Negroes to boycott the election. Negro clergy and NAACP leaders had called for approval of the amendment, which also had been strongly supported by Mayor Calvin W. Mowbray.

Savannah (Ga.) Demonstrations

About 3,000 Negroes marched into downtown Savannah, Ga. June 11 in an anti-segregation demonstration that ended in the arrest of 49 adult Negroes and many children. All of the children were quickly freed.

Daily marches continued, without police interference, until their suspension June 14. The demonstrations were halted after Negro leaders met with the Chamber of Commerce June 14 and the Chamber then issued a statement calling for desegregation of businesses "soliciting business from the general public." Negro leader Hosea Williams charged, however, that the "white citizens" had failed to back the Chamber's proposal, and demonstrations were resumed June 17.

Following the arrest of 300 demonstrators, violence erupted at a demonstration June 19 despite the presence of state troopers, sent to Savannah June 17 at the request of Mayor Malcolm MacLean. Negroes, protesting the arrests, threw bricks and bottles but were dispersed with tear gas.

The marches were suspended again June 21 on the scheduling of a meeting of Negroes with restaurant and hotel owners.

Williams was arrested July 9, and his arrest led to further demonstrations culminating in a riot the night of July 10-11. Police used tear gas to quell the riot.

Williams was arrested on the complaint of a white woman who said the racial protests made her fear for her life and kept her awake nights. The warrant was obtained under a century-old state law honoring complaints when "the peace of any person is in danger of being injured or disturbed." It required a $2,500 bond. Williams' bond later was raised to $30,000 when more whites filed "peace warrants" against him. 19 Negroes jailed on similar warrants were released Sept. 3 after signing statements promising not to breach the peace.

Williams refused Sept. 5 to sign such a statement, and he was sentenced Sept. 5 to 5 days in county jail for contempt of court on the ground that he had told a Savannah newspaper that the court's actions were a "mockery of justice."

Americus (Ga.) 'Insurrection' Case

Georgia's insurrection and unlawful assembly statutes were held unconstitutional Nov. 1 by a 2-1 decision of a special 3-judge federal court in Americus, Ga. The case stemmed from a Negro voter registration drive in Americus. More than 250 persons had been arrested following the drive's expansion in July to demands for desegregation of a movie theater and public facilities.

3 field workers for the Student Nonviolent Coordinating Committee—John Perdew, 21, of Denver, a white Harvard student, Ralph Allen, 22, of Melrose, Mass., also white, and Donald Harris, 24, of New York, a Negro—were arrested during a demonstration Aug. 8 and charged with insurrection under the 1871 state law, which carried a maximum penalty of death. Zev Aelony, 25, of Minneapolis, a white field representative for CORE, was arrested on the charge Aug. 17. All were held without bail. Also held without bail for participation in an anti-bias protest was Sallie Mae Durham, 14, a Negro. An Americus Negro, Thomas McDaniel, 21, was arrested under the unlawful assembly charge and freed on $12,000 bail.

Morris B. Abram Jr., formerly of Atlanta but currently associated with the New York law firm of Paul, Weiss, Rifkind, Wharton & Garrison, filed suit with U.S. District Judge J. Robert Elliott in Albany Oct. 9 for the release of Aelony and for a court order to halt a "conspiracy" of state and local officials to oppose the Negro campaign by misusing the law.

The 3-judge federal court held hearings and then, in a 2-1 decision, invalidated the 2 Georgia laws Nov. 1 and ordered local officials to set reasonable bail on other state and city charges against the 6 defendants. The court ruled that bail was not to exceed $500 on each misdemeanor charge or $1,000 on each felony charge. Following the ruling, the 6 defendants were freed under bonds totaling $11,150.

(A county jury Dec. 5 convicted Allen of assaulting a police officer with intent to murder. The jury sentenced Allen to 2 years' imprisonment. He was freed under $5,000 bond pending appeal.)

Albany (Ga.) Developments

The Albany, Ga. city commission Mar. 6 rescinded its racial segregation ordinances in order to have "the decisions on integration or segregation rest solely with individual citizens and not with the city of Albany."

The city's formerly all-white public library, closed for 7 months, reopened Mar. 11 on a desegregated basis but with its chairs and tables removed. The library accepted an application for a card from Dr. W. G. Anderson, Negro president of the integrationist Albany Movement; the movement had spearheaded a citywide desegregation drive that resulted in mass arrests in 1962.

Anderson and 8 other members of the movement were indicted by a federal grand jury in Macon Aug. 9 on charges involving retaliation against a juror for his vote in a federal case. Anderson and 2 others were charged with conspiring to picket the Carl Smith Supermarket in Albany because Smith had voted against a Negro plaintiff in his civil damage suit against the sheriff of Baker County (the store was closed as a result of the picketing). The other 6 were accused of perjury before a grand jury in denying participation in either the alleged conspiracy or the picketing.

Nashville Desegregation Agreement Ends Protests

Desegregation demonstrations were started in Nashville, Tenn. May 8, and demonstrating Negro students clashed May 10 and 13 with white youths and police.

Mayor Beverly Briley met May 10 with Negro and business leaders. They worked out an agreement under which a truce was called May 11 and a biracial committee was formed May 16 to consider Negro grievances, which largely were aimed at segregated eating facilities.

The biracial committee announced June 10 that Nashville's leading hotels and restaurants had agreed to desegregate.

Plaquemine Voter Campaign

Anti-bias demonstrations—marches, restaurant sit-ins, church kneel-ins and picketing—were started in Plaquemine,

La. in July and intensified beginning Aug. 19. 330 persons
were arrested by early September. Those arrested included
CORE Executive Secy. James Farmer, 43, who had arrived
Aug. 18 to spark the protests. Plaquemine had been chosen
by CORE as the base of an area-wide drive to enroll Negro
voters.

A major Negro grievance was the charge that a predominantly Negro area had been gerrymandered out of the city
of Plaquemine to deprive Negroes of city services and a
vote in city affairs. Negroes also demanded the formation
of a biracial committee. Later they expanded their demands
to include desegregation of employment, schools and public
facilities.

Farmer, arrested Aug. 19, refused to post $300 bail
until Aug. 29 and spent 10 days in jail. Convicted Sept. 3
of disturbing the peace and obstructing streets and sidewalks,
he was sentenced to 30 days in jail and fined $100 on each
charge. He was freed on bail pending appeal.

Negroes continued demonstrations until Aug. 21, when U.S.
District Judge E. Gordon West in Baton Rouge issued a temporary injunction banning demonstrations. West's order was
voided Aug. 29 by the U.S. 5th Circuit Court of Appeals in New
Orleans, but West Sept. 6 refused to end his ban. State District
Court Judge Daniel Kimbell Oct. 10 also issued a preliminary
injunction barring CORE demonstrations.

A march on city hall by 500-600 Negroes the night of Aug.
31-Sept. 1 was repulsed by law officers, including state policemen on horses, who employed tear gas, high-powered hoses and
electric cattle prods. 69 persons were arrested. Farmer
charged "police brutality." He said: 15 children had been
injured (2 hospitalized); the horses were used "to trample,
kick and hospitalize children"; "it was a night of wild terror, . . . and police acted like a legal lynch mob."

Demonstrations by Negro high school students Oct. 4-10
were broken up by police using tear gas and electric prods.
Nearly all the Iberville Negro High School students demonstrated at the school Oct. 4. The school board suspended 35
pupils Oct. 5 for participating. The students began a boycott
Oct. 7 and marched on the school board office. Tear gas was
used on them then and again Oct. 9 when they tried to assemble
in the Freedom Rock Baptist Church after having been chased
from the streets during an attempted march on the school.
Demonstrations were also broken up by tear gas Oct. 10.

Danville (Va.) Desegregation Drive

Negroes began a campaign for total desegregation in Danville, Va. June 1. The drive led to violence when police used fire hoses June 10 to break up a demonstration by about 150 persons. 47 demonstrators were injured, and 38 arrests were made.

Negro leaders met with Mayor Julian R. Stinson June 14, but the council passed an anti-demonstration ordinance later June 14, and 2 police cars were hit by gunfire after police suppressed a march to city hall. 35 marchers were arrested under the new ordinance June 15.

A truce was called June 17 after Negroes held their first meeting with the mayor's all-white advisory committee, but the truce was broken June 19 by a demonstration resulting in 29 arrests.

Stinson's office had announced earlier June 19 that 10 Negroes had been assigned by the State Pupil Placement Board to 4 previously all-white schools. (7 of the Negro children were enrolled without incident Aug. 26.) This was the first desegregation there.

10 leaders of the desegregation drive were indicted by a Corporation Court grand jury June 21 on a charge of "inciting the colored population to acts of violence and war against the white population." Those indicted included the Rev. L. W. Chase, president of the Danville Christian Progressive Citizens Association, and executive director James Forman of the Student Nonviolent Coordinating Committee. Chase was arrested again July 29 on a charge of contributing to the delinquency of 2 minors by permitting them to demonstrate.

Demonstrations were increased after the Rev. Dr. Martin Luther King Jr. arrived in Danville July 11 and denounced the city police for "vicious and brutal" tactics. Arrests continued until, by Aug. 8, 347 demonstrators were facing trial.

William Kunstler, a lawyer for the Gandhi Society of New York, appealed under a Reconstruction Era statute to have the cases removed from the city court to the federal court. The U.S. Justice Department supported the Kunstler appeal July 2 as a friend of the court, but the request was refused July 11 by U.S. District Judge Thomas J. Michie. Michie, however, voided the city injunction prohibiting demonstrations.

A permanent injunction against demonstrations was issued Aug. 2 by Corporation Court Judge A. M. Aiken. Aiken Aug. 5.

directed that 40 cases be transferred for trial in 5 other localities. Further action in the cases was enjoined by the U.S.
4th Circuit Court of Appeals in Baltimore Aug. 8 pending 2
appeals—one on the injunction against demonstrations, the
other on the farming out of the cases. The court urged the
opposing groups to "establish communications" because "the
basic problems themselves can be resolved only by the people
concerned." The city informed the court Sept. 23 that Aiken
had rescinded his transfer of the cases. Demonstrations were
resumed in Danville Dec. 10-11 with sit-ins in restaurants
and theaters. 16 arrests were made.

North Carolina Activity

Gov. Terry Sanford of North Carolina appealed in a statewide radio-TV address June 18 for Negroes to end their
demonstrations and negotiate their grievances, for which he
indicated sympathy. He said the Negro had "delivered the message that he is not content, that he has a burning desire to
break down the barriers that prevent his normal patronage
in places open to the public." He announced his appointment
of a personal representative to negotiate with Negro leaders.

Sanford met with about 125 Negro leaders June 25 to further
his appeal, but North Carolina CORE leader Floyd McKissick
of Durham later rejected the appeal and said: "We seek nothing
less than complete acceptance of Negroes as full, first-class
citizens of North Carolina."

Sanford pledged July 3 to end racial discrimination in
hiring for state jobs and pleaded for open hiring in industry.
He said at a meeting of about 200 mayors and city leaders
in Greensboro July 5 that "we must remove the indignities
long suffered by Negroes." The mayors voted their unanimous
support.

Among civil rights developments in North Carolina during
1963:

Raleigh—A Negro campaign for desegregated public facilities was initiated in Raleigh May 8. Arrests of demonstrators
totaled 194 by May 14. The Raleigh Merchants Bureau May 13
indorsed the desegregation of theaters, restaurants, hotels and
other businesses. A biracial committee was established, and it
announced June 20 that "a large number of businesses have
started desegregation on a gradual basis."

Greensboro—Mass Negro demonstrations aimed at total

desegregation of public businesses were started in Greensboro May 15. More than 1,000 demonstrators were arrested, and the city began releasing many against their will without bail pending trial on trespass and fire-violation charges. 2 movie theaters and 2 cafeterias were prime targets of the drive. They refused to desegregate even after the Greensboro Merchants Association and the Greensboro Chamber of Commerce, acting separately May 16, adopted resolutions calling for an end to segregation policies in government and businesses.

Mayor David Schenck May 22 announced the creation of a biracial study commission to work toward meeting Negro demands.

Mass demonstrations were resumed June 6 after North Carolina Agricultural & Technical College student leader Jesse Jackson was arrested during a peaceful demonstration the previous night. 280 of about 800 demonstrators were arrested June 6.

Mayor Schenck, saying segregation of customers was "not in keeping with either democratic or Christian philosophy," appealed June 7 for businesses in the city to desegregate at once. About 50 restaurants, hotels, motels and theaters agreed June 13 to desegregate.

Lexington—Several Negroes asked for service June 5 at segregated restaurants, a segregated theater and a "whites-only" bowling alley in Lexington.

A mob of about 2,000 white men gathered the next night, and about 500 of them marched to the Negro section, where they were met by about 100 Negroes. A riot ensued. Rocks and bottles were thrown and several shots fired. Fred Link, 24, a white, was killed by one of the shots. Another shot injured a white news photographer, Art Richardson, 25. Mayor C. V. Sink declared a state of emergency June 7, and 200 state troopers were alerted.

10 whites and 7 Negroes were arrested June 7 for alleged involvement in the riot. 3 of the Negroes, who admitted firing a caliber .22 rifle into the crowd of whites, were sentenced Nov. 13 by Supreme Court Judge John R. McLaughlin: 2 of the Negroes, who pleaded guilty to charges of engaging in a riot, were given 6-month jail terms; the 3d, who offered no plea to a 2d-degree murder charge, was sentenced to 4-7 years in prison.

Durham—Negroes held mass demonstrations for desegregated public facilities May 18-20. More than 1,400 were arrested and released pending trial. The demonstrations were suspended May 21 after Mayor R. Wense Grabarek announced that 7 drive-in restaurants had agreed to desegregate. Grabarek had met with an integration committee May 20, his first day in office.

South Carolina Demonstrations

Negro sit-ins began June 10 at Charleston, S.C. lunch counters and expanded into mass, NAACP-backed demonstrations, spearheaded by the Charleston Movement, for a 6-point desegregation program. A night march July 16 ended in a riot in which 6 policemen and a fireman were injured. The police were reinforced by state highway patrolmen, and National Guard units were alerted. But negotiations between a biracial committee and merchants led July 23 to an agreement by 62 stores to end discriminatory practices. More stores signed the agreement Aug. 1, and picketing against non-complying stores continued. More than 700 Negroes had been arrested prior to the truce.

In Orangeburg, 1,033 Negroes, most of them college students, were arrested in demonstrations Sept. 28-Oct. 1. The demonstrations were suspended Oct. 2 while Negro leaders met with city officials, but they were resumed Oct. 4, and by Oct. 7 the arrest total had risen to 1,448. Negro teachers picketed 7 Negro schools Oct. 8 in protest against the dismissal Oct. 7 of a teacher, Mrs. Gloria Rackley, Negro leader of the local protest movement.

High Court Reverses Convictions

The convictions of 187 Negroes on breach-of-the-peace charges for demonstrating on the State Capitol grounds in Columbia, S.C. Mar. 2, 1961 were reversed by the Supreme Court in an 8-1 decision Feb. 25. The demonstrators, who had been protesting alleged discriminatory laws, had been fined $5-$100 each and sentenced to 5-30 days in jail. The majority opinion was based on the First Amendment, which guarantees freedom of speech, assembly and petition for redress of grievances, and on the 14th Amendment, which "does not permit a state to make criminal the peaceful expression of unpopular views."

The Supreme Court held in 6 decisions May 20 that it

was unconstitutional for a city to prosecute Negroes for seeking service in private stores if the city required segregation either by ordinance or by official statement. The decisions voided the convictions of 28 Negroes and 3 white students for sit-in demonstrations at lunch counters in Alabama, Louisiana and North and South Carolina. Chief Justice Earl Warren wrote the main opinions. 3 of the decisions were unanimous. Justice John Marshall Harlan was the sole dissenter in the other 3 cases (Nos. 2, 3 and 5 below). The Justice Department had entered the cases as a friend of the court. The 6 cases:

(1) 10 Negroes had been convicted of trespassing and had been sentenced to fines of $100 each or 30 days in jail for a sit-in at an S. H. Kress store in Greenville, S. C. Greenville had a segregation ordinance.

(2) 10 Negroes had been convicted of trespassing and had been fined $100 each and sentenced to 30 days at hard labor for lunch-counter sit-ins at 5 Birmingham, Ala. department stores. Birmingham had a segregation ordinance.

(3) The Rev. Fred. L. Shuttlesworth and the Rev. Charles Billups, both Negroes, had been convicted of "aiding and abetting" a violation of Birmingham's trespass law by encouraging the student sit-ins in the above case. Since the sit-in was not illegal, "abetting" it could not be illegal, Warren said.

(4) 5 Negroes and 2 white college students were sentenced to up to 30 days in jail for a sit-in at a Kress store in Durham, N.C. Durham had an ordinance requiring the segregation of restaurants.

(5) 3 Negroes and a white were fined $350 each and sentenced to 60 days in jail for a sit-in at a McCrory store in New Orleans. New Orleans had no restaurant segregation ordinance, but the police chief and mayor had announced that the sit-ins would not "be permitted." Warren said that the convictions, "commanded as they were by the voice of the state directing segregated service at the restaurant, cannot stand."

(6) 6 Negro boys were convicted in Savannah, Ga. of breach of the peace for ignoring police orders to stop playing basketball in a segregated park. Warren held that the police order was based either on a segregation ordinance, which would thus be invalid, or on a park rule so vague that the boys had inadequate notice of it.

Federal Government Files Voting Suits

The Justice Department continued to initiate federal court action to end Southern discrimination in voting registration procedures. Among counties involved in suits filed by the department in 1963:

Alabama—Wilcox County, where no Negroes were registered although 6,085 were eligible, and Elmore County. (The suits were filed July 19.)

Jefferson County, which included Birmingham (suit filed July 31). The suit requested the immediate registration of 2,032 Negroes rejected since 1960. This was the largest voting-discrimination suit filed by the department under the 1957 Civil Rights Act. According to the suit, only about 14,000 of 116,100 eligible Negroes were registered in the county whereas about 120,000 of 256,300 eligible whites were registered.

Sumter and Hale Counties (Dec. 16).

Louisiana—Red River and Webster Parishes (suits filed Feb. 18). Some 3,085 of 3,294 eligible Red River whites were registered compared to only 30 of 2,181 eligible Negroes. In Webster, about 8,448 of 15,713 eligible whites and 113 of 7,045 eligible Negroes were registered.

St. Helena Parish (filed Oct. 22).

West Feliciana Parish (filed Oct. 29).

(The Justice Department sued in Baton Rouge Oct. 8 to bar the use of the Louisiana voter registration application form as a test to discriminate against Negroes. Only 29.3% of Louisiana's eligible Negroes were registered as of Sept. 1962 whereas 73.7% of eligible whites were registered.)

Mississippi—Sunflower County, the home of Chrmn. James O. Eastland of the Senate Judiciary Committee (suit filed Jan. 22). The department said that only 114 of the county's 13,524 eligible Negroes were registered to vote whereas more than half of the 8,785 eligible whites were registered.

Rankin County (filed May 6). The suit charged that Sheriff Jonathan R. Edwards Jr. and 2 other whites had struck 3 Negroes attempting to complete voter-registration forms at the courthouse Feb. 1; it said 43 of 6,944 Rankin County Negroes eligible to vote were registered whereas 6,865 of 13,245 eligible whites were registered.

Hinds County (filed July 13). The suit sought the reopening of voter registration books; it charged that the books had been closed after the Negroes' rights drive had been turned from demonstrations to an intensive vote-registration campaign. Oktibbena and Chickasaw Counties (filed Dec. 16). According to the Justice Department, Chickasaw County Negroes were not permitted to pay the poll tax required for voting. Copiah and Lauderdale Counties (filed Dec. 17). (Theron C. Lynd, Forrest County, Miss. vote registrar, was convicted by the U.S. 5th Circuit Court of Appeals July 15 of civil contempt of court for disobeying a federal court order to end discrimination against Negro voter applicants. To purge himself of the charge, the court ordered him to register 43 Negroes whom he had rejected and to let federal agents check his records.)

Kentucky Bars Business Bias

An executive order barring racial bias in state-licensed businesses was signed by Kentucky Gov. Bert T. Combs June 26. The order covered such businesses as taverns, restaurants, barber shops, beauty parlors, funeral homes and real estate concerns. Combs July 7 issued a clarifying statement saying the order "will be construed to authorize only those steps which have been directed or clearly implied by decisions of the federal courts or Kentucky Court of Appeals." Referring to an ordinance adopted in Louisville May 14, Combs said that "first consideration should be given to the areas covered by the [Louisville] ordinance . . . so as to have uniformity throughout the state." The Louisville ordinance prohibited racial discrimination in public facilities providing food, shelter, recreation or amusement.

NORTHERN PROTESTS

New York Job Action

A series of demonstrations at construction sites in N.Y. City during 1963 resulted in about 800 arrests but ended in agreement by the construction unions that Negroes and Puerto Ricans would be considered for admission to apprenticeship without discrimination. White integrationists participated with Negroes in most of the demonstrations.

In an early protest, pickets at the construction site of an annex for Harlem Hospital clashed briefly with police June 12 and 13. The demonstration was sponsored by the NAACP and a Joint Committee for Equal Employment Opportunity, composed of representatives of CORE, the Negro-American Labor Council, the Worker Defense League, the Urban League of Greater New York and the Association of Catholic Trade Unionists. After the June 12 skirmish, Acting Mayor Paul R. Screvane warned that the city would halt the construction if the unions took no action to end discrimination. After the June 13 skirmish, Screvane called a halt to the work.

The N.Y. City branch of the NAACP warned city officials June 18 that "mass anti-discrimination demonstrations" would be held unless a conference was called to air Negro grievances about housing, jobs and political representation. The national NAACP backed the warning with telegrams to Vice Pres. Lyndon B. Johnson, Gov. Nelson A. Rockefeller and Screvane. The city immediately scheduled a conference with Negro leaders for June 19. At the meeting, city officials heard NAACP Labor Secy. Herbert Hill accuse the city of "collusion" by failure to enforce anti-discrimination codes.

Rockefeller June 23 appointed a special cabinet committee on civil rights. He announced June 27 that he would accelerate $4 billion worth of state construction work to create more jobs. The June 27 announcement was made at a joint news conference with Peter Brennan, president of the AFL-CIO State Building Construction Trades Council, who promised that his group would eliminate "any existing discrimination" in membership practices.

The arrests took place largely in July and August after mass demonstrations were renewed at construction sites July 11. Most arrests were of demonstrators who blocked access to sites by getting in front of trucks or other equipment and refusing to move. The Negroes' demands were reinforced by sit-ins at City Hall July 19-Aug. 22 and at Rockefeller's N.Y. City office July 10-Sept. 16. Arrests were made during both sit-ins.

Rockefeller met with Negro leaders Aug. 6 and pledged (a) to act on enforcing non-discrimination in employment and apprenticeship, (b) to cooperate with civil rights groups in recruiting qualified workers from minority groups for union membership and (c) to bar state funds from construction projects if discrimination was practiced.

Rockefeller Aug. 9 ordered the State Employment Service to help at 2 centers opening Aug. 12 to recruit Negroes for construction unions. The centers, set up by Negro clergymen, processed applications and referred them to a biracial, employer-union committee that Brennan had established.

Brennan's committee announced Dec. 18 that 682 of the Negroes and Puerto Ricans referred to it had qualified for nondiscriminatory consideration as applicants for apprenticeship.

New York Boycott Averted

A threatened boycott of N.Y. City public schools by Negro children was canceled Sept. 5 after the Board of Education agreed to submit by Dec. 1 a specific timetable for further integration. The agreement provided for the board's submission of a final integration plan by Feb. 1964. The agreement was reached at a meeting sponsored by the City Commission on Human Rights, acting as a mediator. It was attended by the Citywide Committee and the Board of Education. The Citywide Committee comprised representatives of the NAACP, CORE, the Urban League of Greater New York, the Harlem Parents Committee and the Parents Workshop for Equality in the N.Y. City Schools.

The boycott had been threatened by the NAACP July 30 and had been set for opening day (Sept. 9) by Negro leaders Aug. 22 following conferences that day and Aug. 19 with Schools Supt. Calvin E. Gross. The major issues in dispute were Negro demands for the board's adoption of a timetable for ending alleged racial discrimination in the system and for involuntary transfer of white and Negro pupils from schools with a "high ethnic percentage." After the Aug. 22 meeting, Gross stated his opposition to any involuntary moving of school children.

62 persons were arrested in attempted sit-ins Dec. 16 and Dec. 30 at the Board of Education office in Brooklyn.

New Jersey Progress & Protests

An agreement to accept qualified journeymen apprentices regardless of color or race on state construction projects was reached in Trenton, N.J. July 9 following a conference attended by the Rev. S. Howard Woodson, president of the NAACP's New Jersey chapter; Vincent J. Murphy, president of the state AFL-CIO executive council; Sal Mazo, president of the New Jersey Building & Construction Trades Council. Earlier July 9,

Gov. Richard J. Hughes had conferred with contractors involved in state projects.

Similar agreements to open apprenticeship and journeyman programs were negotiated with building trades officials for Essex County July 24 and for Paterson July 26.

Violence erupted at the construction site for a new high school in Newark July 3 when anti-bias pickets attempted to block workers from entering.

In Elizabeth, 128 persons protesting discrimination were arrested in construction-site picketing Aug. 5-19.

In Englewood, about 100 Negro pupils from the predominantly Negro Lincoln Elementary School, accompanied by about 100 parents, marched Sept. 4 to 3 predominantly white schools and engaged in sit-ins at 2 of them. They were protesting a delay in a plan to reduce the racial imbalance at Lincoln School. The Englewood Board of Education, under orders from State Education Commissioner Frederick M. Raubinger to rectify the imbalance, had adopted July 29 a plan to establish a city-wide integrated 6th-grade school in an abandoned junior high school and to assign Lincoln pupils of the first through 5th grades to 3 predominantly white schools. The plan was approved by Raubinger Aug. 1 and by the State Board of Education Aug. 23. On opening day about 140 Lincoln pupils were granted transfers to the 3 other schools as part of the board's plan pending the renovation of the abandoned school for the new 6th grade school. The protest Sept. 4 was led by city councilman Vincente K. Tibbs, a Negro, who asserted that the board should have established the 6th-grade school at the Lincoln School pending the renovation of the abandoned school. During the previous school term, Lincoln School had been boycotted from Feb. 26 until graduation June 20. The boycott began with 239 pupils absent Feb. 26, but the number of absentees dropped to 34 by graduation. (38 of the boycotters' parents were convicted Apr. 26 by a municipal magistrate of keeping their children from classes illegally and were fined $5 each.)

Chicago Disturbances

The drive for equality in Chicago during 1963 was aimed mainly at alleged *de facto* segregation in public schools. Trouble also erupted when several Negro families moved into predominantly white neighborhoods on the South Side and met with strong objections from whites. A CORE-sponsored sit-in

at the Board of Education offices started July 10 but was ended
July 18 when police seized 10 of the demonstrators on charges
of unlawful assembly and trespass. 3 demonstrators were
arrested in a clash with police July 17.

The school controversy led Oct. 4 to the resignation of
School Supt. Benjamin C. Willis. The school system, under
attack starting in the summer, had adopted a plan to let a few
gifted students transfer from their neighborhood high schools
to schools with honors courses. Some schools were then
picketed by white parents protesting that the plan would over-
crowd classes. Willis deleted some receiving schools from the
plan, but some of these were reinstated by the Board of Education. Parents of 4 students sued successfully to have the board
readopt the original plan; Willis appealed, but his appeal was
rejected. Willis then resigned from his $48,500-a-year post,
charging that the board had invaded his administrative responsibilities. The board, by 8-2 vote Oct. 7, refused to accept
the resignation. Sit-in demonstrations at the Board of Education building were begun Oct. 11 in protest against Willis' re-
tention. Willis withdrew his resignation Oct. 17.

About 225,000 pupils were absent from school Oct. 22
during a "Freedom Day" boycott, and about 6,000 persons
picketed City Hall and Board of Education offices.

About 1,000 persons had demonstrated Apr. 17 against
a Negro family's moving into a South Side apartment building
in an all-white section. 20 persons were arrested Apr. 17 and
18. Police, accompanied by dogs, cordoned off the area.

The moving of 4 Negro families into the predominantly
white Englewood neighborhood on Chicago's South Side resulted
July 29-Aug. 5 in gatherings of protesting white crowds. Bricks
and bottles were hurled at the apartment building housing one
of the families July 30. 149 arrests were made July 31.

The City Council Sept. 11 passed an ordinance barring
racial discrimination in the sale or rental of real estate
despite a march on city hall that day by more than 4,000 whites
opposing the ordinance.

Pennsylvania Disputes

Mass picketing was begun May 24 at a school construction
site in Philadelphia in protest against alleged discrimination
in hiring on city construction projects. Scuffling May 27, 29
and 31 involved Negro pickets and police guarding workmen

entering the site. 46 persons were injured, including 23 policemen. The picketing ended late May 31 after an agreement was reached on the hiring of 6 Negro artisans for the project (Negro laborers were already employed there).

A Negro couple moved into a previously all-white housing development in Folcroft, 5 miles southwest of Philadelphia, despite violence and demonstrations by white mobs Aug. 29-30. The couple, Horace and Sara Baker, tried to take possession of their home Aug. 29 but were repulsed twice by about 500 jeering demonstrators who smashed windows in their house and car. That night a homemade bomb hurled into the house started a fire, and firemen broke in the front door. The crowd, mostly teenagers, returned Aug. 30 and, despite a force of 50 state policemen, again threw things— at the house and at the policemen. 7 persons were arrested.

California Action Vs. Discrimination

Gov. Edmund Brown July 24 signed a state code of fair practices prohibiting racial or religious discrimination by the California state government and its outside contractors. Under the code, contractors were required to give written notice of their commitment to the code to labor unions with which they had collective bargaining pacts.

In San Francisco, ex-Labor Secy. James P. Mitchell was named Sept. 19 as the city's Human Relations Coordinator. His function: to head the city's drive to solve its minority problems. The appointment was announced by Mayor George C. Christopher after conferences with Negro leaders of the United San Francisco Freedom Movement. The group was headed by Dr. Thomas N. Burbridge, local NAACP leader.

Boston School Boycott

About 3,000 Negro students participated June 18 in a public school boycott to dramatize a protest against "de facto segregation" in Boston.

The students attended workshops at churches and social centers to hear talks by prominent clergymen and others supporting the movement.

Following the boycott, committees to seek solutions in economic and educational fields were established by Mayor John F. Collins and the Boston School Committee.

City Rights Rallies

An estimated 125,000 Negroes and whites participated June 23 in a giant freedom parade and rally in Detroit to demonstrate opposition to discrimination. Mayor Jerome P. Cavanagh had urged participation. Speakers included the Rev. Dr. Martin Luther King Jr. and United Auto Workers Pres. Walter P. Reuther. Other participants included the Very Rev. John Weaver of the Protestant Episcopal Diocese of Michigan, ex-Gov. John B. Swainson and 2 representatives of Gov. George Romney. (Romney did not make public appearances on Sundays because of his Mormon beliefs, but he led about 450 demonstrators on a "freedom march" through the Detroit suburb of Grosse Pointe June 29.)

About 10,000 persons participated in a rights rally in Cincinnati, O. Oct. 27, a day proclaimed "Jobs & Freedom Day" by Mayor Walton Bachrach.

About 4,000 persons took part in a rights march in Trenton, N.J. Oct. 26. The leaders, including CORE Executive Director James Farmer, met with Gov. Richard J. Hughes before the march.

In St. Louis Oct. 28 about 250 Roman Catholics, including many priests and nuns, demonstrated against racial bias. A CORE-sponsored protest at City Hall Dec. 31 resulted in 24 arrests. (Negroes had boycotted St. Louis stores Nov. 14-15.)

SOUTHERN SCHOOL & COLLEGE DESEGREGATION

150 school districts were desegregated in the fall in the 17 Southern and border states. *Southern School News,* reporting the latest desegregation statistics Sept. 11, said that 130 of the districts acted voluntarily, 20 under federal court orders.

Studies of integrated Southern districts indicated that "token" rather than true desegregation had taken place in most cases. A report on such a study was issued jointly July 13 by the Southern Regional Council and the Anti-Defamation League of B'nai B'rith. The report asserted that (a) only .4% of Negroes in the 11 "most recalcitrant" states were attending school with whites in the current term, (b) only 11.8% of their biracial school districts had been opened to nominal desegregation, and (c) nearly 92 of every 100 Negro pupils in the 17 Southern and border states and the District of Columbia were attending segregated classes. "The plans for keeping integration at token

levels," the report said, "have been devised to try to satisfy
the courts. It is quite obvious now that they are not doing so
and that the courts are becoming less and less patient with
the bad faith implicit in them."

As the fall term began, desegregation—token or otherwise—
was effected quietly in many Southern cities. In Alabama, however, Gov. George C. Wallace blocked integration—but only
temporarily—in Tuskegee, Birmingham and Huntsville. (And
protests, sit-ins, arrests, boycotts and marches attended
school openings in Chicago, Malverne, N.Y. and Englewood,
N.J.)

Trouble in Alabama

13 Negro students were scheduled to enter classes at the
all-white Tuskegee high school under a desegregation order
issued by Federal Judge Frank M. Johnson Aug. 22. But Gov.
Wallace issued an executive order Sept. 2 to delay the school
opening one week. 108 state troopers were dispatched to enforce
the order by sealing off the school and preventing teachers and
students from entering.

State troopers arrived Sept. 3 in Birmingham, where public
schools were under federal court orders to begin desegregation
Sept. 4. The Justice Department let it be known Sept. 3 that
federal troops or marshals would be sent to enforce Birmingham's desegregation if necessary. The Birmingham city council
Sept. 3 adopted a resolution asserting that the city had the situation under control. It urged the state not to interfere. 2
Negro students registered in a Birmingham school without
incident Sept. 4. White demonstrators, led by members of the
National States Rights Party, an anti-integrationist and anti-
Semitic group, demonstrated at 2 schools scheduled to accept
Negro students. (A federal grand jury in Birmingham Sept. 23
indicted 8 whites, all associated with the National States Rights
Party, on charges involving violent interference with school
desegregation.)

The home of Arthur D. Shores, a Birmingham Negro lawyer
active in desegregation cases, was bombed the night of Sept. 4,
and Mrs. Shores was injured. (Shores' home also had been
bombed Aug. 20.) A crowd of Negroes gathered, and, when
a detail of police arrived, a 2-hour riot ensued. The police
fired over the heads of the crowd, and a 20-year-old Negro
was shot and killed. Police officials said the victim had burst

from a home firing a gun; but the Rev. Fred L. Shuttlesworth (Negro integration leader who had tried to calm the mob) and 2 members of a TV-camera crew denied that he had a gun. 21 persons, including 4 policemen, were injured.

Birmingham's Board of Education Sept. 5 closed the 3 white schools scheduled to be desegregated that morning. The board said it was acting on Wallace's request. It also cited the bombing and riot as reasons for the closings.

The court-ordered desegregation of Huntsville schools, scheduled for Sept. 3, had been deferred Sept. 2 for 3 days in compliance with a request from Wallace. Wallace used state troopers Sept. 6 to block the delayed opening of 4 white Huntsville schools set to accept one Negro student each.

Mobile's Murphy High School was permitted to open Sept. 6 only after it was ascertained that 2 prospective Negro students would not attend.

Wallace allowed the Tuskegee, Mobile and Birmingham schools to open Sept. 9. But by executive order and the use of state troopers and deputized National Guardsmen, he blocked the entry of Negro students. In Huntsville, however, he took no such action, and the 4 formerly white Huntsville schools opened with the 4 Negroes in attendance; this marked the first desegregation below college level in Alabama.

A restraining order prohibiting the governor and state forces from intervening to block desegregation was issued the night of Sept. 9 by all 5 U.S. district court judges in Alabama at the request of the Justice Department. And a White House statement Sept. 9 accused Wallace of trying to provoke federal intervention "for his own personal and political reasons—so that he may later charge federal interference."

Wallace withdrew the state troopers from the schools and ordered National Guardsmen to replace them. But Pres. Kennedy early Sept. 10 federalized the state's National Guard, prohibited Wallace's interference with federal court orders and directed enforcement by the Defense Department. The Guardsmen posted at the schools by Wallace went back to their barracks. Wallace then held a news conference at which he conceded that further defiance was futile because "I can't fight bayonets with my bare hands."

20 Negroes entered previously white schools in Birmingham, Tuskegee and Mobile later Sept. 10. The only trouble occurred at West End High School, where some white adults joined white students in 2 hours of demonstrations; 12 whites were arrested.

2 Negroes Enter University of Alabama

2 Negro students were enrolled in the University of Alabama in Tuscaloosa June 11 after Pres. Kennedy federalized the Alabama National Guard and forced Gov. George C. Wallace to stop blocking the court-ordered desegregation of the university. The 2 students, Vivian Juanita Malone and James Alexander Hood, both 20, became the 2d and 3d Negroes admitted to the university. (The first, Mrs. Autherine Lucy Foster, admitted under a 1955 court order, had attended for 3 days and then had been expelled for making "defamatory" charges against university officials.)

U.S. District Judge H. Hobart Grooms in Birmingham May 21 had ordered the admission of Miss Malone at the Tuscaloosa campus. He simultaneously ordered the university's extension school at Huntsville to enroll Dave M. McGlathery, 26, a Negro mathematician employed at the George C. Marshall Space Flight Center. (McGlathery was enrolled June 13.)

Wallace's reaction to Grooms' ruling was to pledge: "I will be present to bar the entrance of any Negro who attempts to enroll." Acting on a request of the U.S. Justice Department, Federal Judge Seybourn H. Lynne in Birmingham June 5 specifically prohibited Wallace from "physically interposing his" person to bar the Negroes' entry.

Strict security measures went into effect in Tuscaloosa and on the campus June 8 as 825 state troopers and deputized law enforcement officers sealed off access to the university by unauthorized personnel. 600 Alabama National Guard military police troops began moving into the city June 9.

Wallace, on TV June 9, renewed his pledge to defy the court's desegregation order. He received from Pres. Kennedy June 10 a telegram calling such defiance a "violation of accepted standards of public conduct" and "the only announced threat to orderly compliance with the law."

About 150 state troopers and 150 newsmen appeared at the registration auditorium June 11 to witness the confrontation between Wallace and federal authority, in the person of Deputy Atty. Gen. Nicholas deB. Katzenbach, who carried a Presidential proclamation (signed earlier that day) commanding Wallace "to cease and desist" "unlawful obstruction" of a court order.

Wallace, wearing a microphone, stood at the door behind a lectern. Katzenbach asked him to step aside and permit the entry of the 2 Negro students, who remained in a car during the scene. Wallace refused. Katzenbach told him that "from the outset, governor, all of us have known that the final chapter of this history will be the admission of these students." Katzenbach then left, and the 2 Negro students were taken to their dormitories.

Pres. Kennedy, on being informed of Wallace's defiance, signed an executive order putting the Alabama National Guard into federal service. Federalized National Guard troops arrived on campus several hours later, led by Brig. Gen. Henry V. Graham, who conferred with Katzenbach and confronted Wallace. Graham told Wallace that it was his "sad duty" to request that the governor step aside. Wallace, returning Graham's salute, stepped aside and left. Miss Malone and Hood then entered the auditorium and were registered. (Hood withdrew from the university Aug. 11 "to avoid a complete mental and physical breakdown.")

Pres. Kennedy told the nation in a TV address the evening of June 11 that the use of troops had been required to enforce a federal court order for the admission "of 2 clearly qualified young Alabama residents who happened to have been born Negro." He asked every American to "stop and examine his conscience about this and other related incidents." When Americans "are sent to Vietnam or West Berlin we do not ask for whites only," he said, and "it ought be possible . . . for every American to enjoy the privileges of being American without regard to his race or his color." Mr. Kennedy said the problem of segregation was "not a sectional issue" but existed "in every city, in every state of the Union, producing in many cities a rising tide of discontent that threatens the public safety."

"The fires of frustration and discord are burning in every city, North and South," the President warned, and the crisis "cannot be met by repressive police action. It cannot be left to increased demonstrations in the streets. It cannot be quieted by token moves or talk. It is a time to act in the Congress, in your state and local legislative body, and, above all, in all of our daily lives. . . . A great change is at hand and our task, our obligation is to make that revolution, that change peaceful and constructive for all. Those who do nothing are inviting shame as well as violence. Those who act boldly are recognizing right as well as reality. . . . We have a right to expect that the Negro community will be responsible, will uphold the law. But they have a right to expect the law will be fair. . . ."

Some Southern Cities Integrate Schools

Among Southern cities whose schools were desegregated in September:

Charleston, S.C.—11 Negroes attended previously all-white elementary and high schools in the first public-school desegregation in the state. The integration had been ordered by U.S. District Judge J. Robert Martin Jr. Aug. 22. Roman Catholic elementary schools also desegregated Sept. 3.

Baton Rouge, La.—27 Negro students peacefully entered previously all-white 12th-grade classes. This was the first desegregation of high schools in Louisiana. The desegregation plan called for the progressive desegregation each year of the next lower grade. The plan had been approved July 17 by U.S. District Judge E. Gordon West.

Savannah, Ga.—Under a similar plan desegregating 12th grades and a lower grade each year thereafter, 14 Negroes attended formerly all-white schools. Several parochial schools were also integrated.

Jacksonville, Fla.—Duval County public schools integrated with the acceptance of 13 Negro first-grade students on court order.

Cambridge, Md.—20 Negroes attended formerly all-white schools without major incidents. It was the first time Negroes and whites had gone to school together in Cambridge.

Fort Worth, Tex.—Public schools desegregated Sept. 4 with the uneventful entry of 20 Negroes into first grade.

Prince Edward County Plan Aids Negroes

The formation of a privately financed organization to provide schooling for Negro children of Prince Edward County, Va., which had closed its public schools in 1959 to avoid court-ordered desegregation, was announced by Gov. Albertis S. Harrison Jr. in Richmond Aug. 14. Nearly all of the county's Negro school children had been without schooling since 1959; white children attended privately sponsored schools. The new plan, establishing the Prince Edward Free School Association, would set up schools to be open to white as well as Negro pupils.

Under the new school plan, a biracial board of trustees was to lease for one year the county's public school buildings and recruit a racially mixed faculty to concentrate on remedial training during a 225-day school year. Financing was to be obtained from private sources. The planners stressed that the plan was a temporary one to be abandoned if the county's public schools were reopened.

Colgate W. Darden, ex-Virginia governor and ex-president of the University of Virginia, was named by Harrison to head the association's board of trustees. Dr. Neil V. Sullivan, 48, was named superintendent of the new school system Aug. 31. To accept the post, he took a leave of absence from his regular job as superintendent of the Union Free School in East Williston, N.Y.

The association opened its first school Sept. 16; about 800 Negro and 4 white children attended.

(The Virginia Supreme Court of Appeals ruled by 6-1 Dec. 2 that the state constitution gave localities the option of operating public schools or of not providing them. The ruling upheld the closing of Prince Edward County public schools by county officials as a violation of neither state nor federal law. Chief Justice John W. Eggleston dissented.

(U.S. District Judge John D. Butzner Jr. in Richmond, Va. Jan. 3 had ordered Powhatan County to admit 3 Negro children to its all-white public school. He held that "public schools in a county must remain open while other public schools in the state are operated." County authorities had indicated that they might follow neighboring Prince Edward County's precedent of closing the schools.)

Meredith Wins Mississippi Degree

James H. Meredith graduated from the University of Mississippi Aug. 18. He was the first Negro graduate in the school's 115-year history. He received a BA in political science. An attempt had been made by Gov. Ross R. Barnett to bar Meredith's graduation pending an investigation of charges that statements by him had violated a school order against inflammatory remarks. The attempt failed when the State College Board voted 6-5 Aug. 15 to take no action.

A 2d Negro enrolled at the University of Mississippi in Oxford June 5 without incident. He was Cleve McDowell, 21, of Drew, Miss., an honor graduate of Jackson State College, a Negro school. He registered in the university's law school while 300 federal military policemen and 20 deputy U.S. marshals maintained a security guard. McDowell was arrested by a sheriff in Oxford Sept. 23 on a charge of carrying a concealed pistol. He was expelled from the university Sept. 24, convicted by a justice of the peace Sept. 28 and fined $100.

Negroes Enroll in Other Southern Colleges

5 Negroes registered at Tulane University in New Orleans Jan. 25. They were the first of their race admitted to the school. Tulane's board of administrators had announced Dec. 12, 1962 that the school would not deny admission because of race or color. The board did so after a federal court had ruled that the school could not be forced to admit Negroes but could do so voluntarily. The Negroes were all faculty members of Southern University in Baton Rouge.

Harvey Bernard Gantt, 20, became the first Negro to attend school with whites in South Carolina Jan. 28 when he enrolled without incident at Clemson University as an architectural student. Gantt's enrollment had been ordered Jan. 16 by the U.S. 4th Circuit Court of Appeals in Alexandria, Va. Before Gantt's admission, South Carolina had been the only state never to have taken any action toward public school desegregation. Lucinda Brawley, 17, enrolled Sept. 8 and became the 2d Negro student at Clemson.

3 Negro students registered at the University of South Carolina in Columbia Sept. 11 without incident. The 3—a girl, Henri Monteith, 18, Robert G. Anderson Jr., 20, and James L. Solomon Jr., 33, a graduate student—were accepted under federal court orders and were the first Negroes to enroll at the school since 1877.

Court Bars Integration Delay

The Supreme Court further clarified its 1954 and 1955 public school desegregation decisions by declaring May 27 that it "never contemplated that the concept of 'deliberate speed' would countenance indefinite delay in elimination of racial barriers in schools, let alone other public facilities not involving" as difficult a change-over problem. "It is far from clear," the court said, that the 1955 decision "requiring that desegregation proceed with 'all deliberate speed' would today be fully satisfied by types of plans or programs for desegregation of public educational facilities which 8 years ago might have been deemed sufficient."

The decisions meant, the court said, that delay in school desegregation would not be "tolerated unless it imperatively and compellingly appeared unavoidable." Constitutional rights were "present rights" and "warrants for the here and now, unless there is an overwhelming compelling reason, they are to be promptly fulfilled."

The clarification was expressed by Justice Arthur J. Goldberg in writing the court's unanimous opinion that Memphis, Tenn. must immediately desegregate its parks, playgrounds and all public facilities.

(The Supreme Court June 3 ruled unconstitutional a school desegregation plan permitting pupils to transfer if their race was in the minority in their school or grade. The court unanimously held invalid any plan permitting transfers "solely on racial factors" and leading to "perpetuation of segregation." The suit, brought by the NAACP and entered by the Justice Department as a friend of the court, was based on desegregation plans of Knoxville, Davidson County and Memphis, Tenn.)

OTHER DEVELOPMENTS

Civil Rights Commission's Proposals

The Civil Rights Commission, in its 3d biennial report, recommended Sept. 30 a broad program to eliminate discrimination in voting, education, employment, the administration of justice and health facilities and services and in urban areas and the armed forces. It was the first report unanimously indorsed by all CRC members.

The commission said for the first time that it had detected "an atmosphere of hopefulness" in civil rights. But it warned that in the current struggle whites and Negroes could be driven further apart and "left again with a legacy of fear and mistrust." The "new hopes" must be fulfilled for all Americans, it said, or the nation would have to give up its "best hope for national greatness." The commission particularly stressed the need to eliminate discrimination in voting.

The CRC recommended establishment of uniform voting qualifications, with disqualification limited to age, length of residence, legal confinement, judicially determined mental disability, conviction of a felony or failure to complete 6 grades of education. It would authorize (a) federal investigation wherever 10 or more persons alleged bias and (b) temporary appointment of a federal registrar. If these failed, it said, Congress should reduce House representation proportionately by the number of qualified citizens not allowed to vote.

The report made these recommendations in other areas:

Education—Require school boards maintaining segregated districts to submit desegregation plans within 90 days or be subject to federal court action. Give technical and financial aid to districts seeking help to desegregate. Hold a White House conference of experts on equal schooling opportunity for all children. Remove impediments to local efforts to reduce racial imbalance in schools in renewal areas.

Employment—Require equal rights in employment in enterprises assisted by the federal government or affecting interstate commerce. Require nonsegregation in federally aided vocational programs and in selection of trainees. Provide vocational programs for persons unable to qualify educationally for training. Insure open employment in programs directly or indirectly generated by federal aid.

Justice—Permit federal initiation of civil proceedings to prevent civil rights denials. Provide federal aid to states and localities requesting it to improve police forces. Make local government liable with local officers if the officers violated a citizen's rights. Permit removal to federal court of state court cases in which the defendant "cannot, in state court, secure civil rights."

Health facilities & services—Bar aid under the separate-but-equal provisions of the Hill-Burton (Hospital Survey & Construction) Act of 1946.

Urban areas—Resolve civil rights problems at the local level through Presidential encouragement, "possibly through the form of . . . awards of merit."

Armed forces—Require equality of opportunity in the Navy. Discontinue ROTC programs at colleges not accepting students without regard to race or color. "Insure that in dealings with local communities the policy of the armed forces of equality of treatment prevails." Provide that school aid under the impacted-areas program "be conditioned upon assurances that all children in the district be assigned without regard to race."

The CRC had urged Pres. Kennedy in its first interim report, submitted Apr. 16, to "explore his legal authority" to cut off federal funds from Mississippi until the state "demonstrates its compliance" with the federal constitution and laws. The unanimous report said there had been "open and flagrant violation of constitutional guarantees" in Mississippi since Oct. 1962. The CRC expressed the opinion "that only further steps by the federal government can arrest the subversion of the constitution," and it suggested that Congress "consider seriously whether legislation" was needed to rectify a "situation where, in large measure, the lawless conduct and defiance of the constitution by certain elements in one state are being subsidized by the other states."

Apprenticeships Ordered Open to All

Pres. Kennedy June 4 ordered (1) a review of all federal construction programs for the purpose of ending or preventing discriminatory hiring practices and (2) admittance of young workers to federal apprenticeship programs on a nondiscriminatory basis. Labor Secy. W. Willard Wirtz, who was to carry out both orders, said June 4 that "contracts will be canceled, or they will not be let," wherever he encountered opposition to the President's action in the construction program.

NAACP Labor Secy. Herbert Hill conferred with Wirtz June 4 and then said that in reliance on the President's orders and Wirtz' assurances, the NAACP was canceling planned demonstrations at federal construction sites. The presidents of 18 AFL-CIO building trades unions urged their locals in a statement adopted in Washington June 21 to eliminate bias in apprenticeship, union membership, job assignments and any other labor union areas. (Delegates to the Bro'hood of Locomotive Firemen & Enginemen's convention in St. Louis voted July 11 to remove from their constitution a ban on non-white membership. The union was the last to conform to an AFL-CIO directive for affiliates to open membership to Negroes.)

Pres. Kennedy June 22 issued an executive order authorizing the withdrawal of federal funds from construction projects where racial discrimination was practiced.

The Labor Department's Bureau of Apprenticeship & Training July 26 issued new rules to bar racial discrimination in federally-sponsored apprenticeship programs jointly backed by labor and management. The rules provided for withdrawal of aid from non-conforming programs. An appeal to regional directors to intensify efforts at obtaining applicants from minority groups was also issued.

The rules, applying to 9,000 joint programs with a membership of 150,000 apprentices, were criticized by both labor and management groups in the construction industry. A joint Committee on Equal Employment Opportunity was established July 26 to apply to Labor Secy. Wirtz to suspend them. Wirtz refused the request Aug. 2, but he met with construction industry groups Aug. 9 and agreed to a compromise plan under which (a) committees representing various crafts were to review their apprenticeship programs to insure that an applicant's qualifications were "the sole standard" used in selection, (b) a listing of job-openings was to be sent to school systems, (c) appeal boards were to adjudge applicants' grievances.

The Labor Department issued revised standards Oct. 19: Apprentices were to be selected solely on the basis of qualifications; federal certification was to be withdrawn from programs failing to comply.

NAACP Seeks Stronger Federal Action

The National Association for the Advancement of Colored People held its 54th annual convention in Chicago July 1-6. Describing Pres. Kennedy's rights program as "inadequate to meet the minimum demands of the existing situation," it called July 2 for stronger federal action in virtually every civil rights area.

The convention July 5 voted to extend "the NAACP's direct action policy" by calling on all NAACP units to implement anti-discrimination programs through activities that "shall include picketing, sit-ins, mass action protest [and] selective-buying campaigns."

The convention was marked by incidents in which Chicago Mayor Richard J. Daley and a Negro minister were booed off a speakers' platform and James H. Meredith, the first Negro knowingly enrolled at the University of Mississippi, was publicly rebuked by an NAACP official after he had expressed "moderate" views on the race issue.

Daley had incurred the wrath of some convention participants July 1 when he had denied at the opening of the convention that Chicago had Negro ghettos. At a July 4 Grant Park rally, demonstrators hooted every time Daley tried to speak. He finally retreated after welcoming the convention to Chicago.

NAACP Executive Secy. Roy Wilkins said that "the people who interrupted the meeting were not members of the NAACP and were not part of our rally." Messages of regret for the ill-treatment were sent to Daley July 5 by NAACP officials, and the convention July 6 adopted a resolution praising Daley for helping with convention arrangements.

The Rev. Dr. James H. Jackson was booed from the platform and had to be rescued from belligerents at the July 4 rally. His opponents booed him because of a statement he had made opposing the march on Washington, and about 50 militants chased him with shouts of "Kill him! Kill him!" Ushers finally helped him and an aide to a car. (Executive director Edward Marcniak of the Chicago Commission on Human Relations charged that members of the local SNCC chapter led the attacks on Daley and Jackson.)

Meredith, rumored as due for similar treatment at a meeting July 5, was received with slight applause. He then launched into a speech criticizing "the low quality and ineffectiveness of our Negro youth leaders" and said: "Negro youth has that 'yeah, maybe, but not me' attitude. Bull! Anyone of you burr-heads out there could be the owner or manager of a large department store, president of a corporation or even mayor of the city of Chicago. . . . All things are possible if you only believe."

Meredith was followed to the platform by James Davis, 22, Rutgers University pre-law student and head of the NAACP's college and university division, who evoked approving shouts and a standing ovation by attacking Meredith.

Wilkins said that Meredith "was criticized because he called the audience 'burr-heads'."

CORE Convention

The Congress of Racial Equality held its annual convention in Dayton, O. June 27-30. About 250 Negro and white delegates attended. Floyd B. McKissick, 41, of Durham, N.C. was elected national chairman June 29 (he was the first Negro to serve in the post) following the withdrawal of Charles R. Oldham, chairman for 7 years. Rudolph Lombard, a Negro of Louisiana, was elected first vice president. James Farmer, a Negro, remained national director. A resolution adopted June 30 accused the Kennedy Administration of failing to recognize "the immediacy of the impending retaliation and mass violence on the part of the Negro community . . . as evidenced by the fact that Negroes are increasingly arming themselves for the purpose of self-defense against continued oppression and violence."

Urban League Urges Negro 'Marshall Plan'

A "Marshall Plan" for redressing Negro grievances was promulgated by the National Urban League at its 53d annual convention, held in Los Angeles July 27-Aug. 1. The plan was proposed July 27 by the league's executive director, Whitney M. Young Jr., to provide "indemnification," or services and preferment, to compensate Negroes for past racial discrimination.

League resolutions adopted Aug. 1 as part of its "Marshall Plan" demanded: (a) a Presidential order banning discrimination in public hospitals and health and welfare facilities; (b) establishment of offices by the U.S. Office of Education and state and local public school system to promote racial understanding; (c) elimination of practices and policies restricting adoption based on race; (d) development of a basic-skills program for long-time unemployed Negroes and increased apprenticeship opportunities for young Negroes.

A league proposal for the creation of a national skills bank to offer employers a central listing of available Negro workers was put into effect immediately by means of a $100,000 grant from the Rockefeller Brothers Fund.

Henry Steeger 3d, a white publisher (*Argosy* magazine), was elected unanimously Aug. 1 to a 4th term as National Urban League president.

'Over-All Social Reform' Urged

A change in the approach to the Negro drive for equality was recommended by Bayard Rustin, principal organizer of the August "march on Washington." Rustin made his proposal at the closing session of the 4th annual conference of the Student Nonviolent Coordinating Committee, which was held in Washington Nov. 29-Dec. 1. Rustin said: "Heroism and ability to go to jail should not be substituted for an over-all social reform program"; "we need a political and social reform program that will not only help the Negroes but one that will help all Americans." Rustin warned that the rights drive risked decline into a sectarian movement that would stagnate unless it broadened to include all underprivileged minority groups. He opposed such ideas as preferential treatment for Negroes in employment inasmuch as unemployment affected more whites than Negroes. Full employment should be the Negroes' national goal, he said.

Earnings Gap Grows

A Census Bureau study reported July 31 that in 1962 the average Negro male worker had earned $3,023 or only 51% of the amount earned by the average white male. In 1951 the comparable figures were $2,060 and 62%. The study also reported: (a) 80% of Negroes with only grade school education held unskilled jobs as laborers, porters, etc., compared to 50% of the whites with similar education; (b) 60% of Negro high school graduates were laborers compared to 30% of white graduates.

But improvements in Negro job opportunities were hailed by Pres. Lyndon B. Johnson Dec. 12 at a meeting with 90 representatives of 64 companies participating in "Plans for Progress" programs initiated by the President's Committee on Equal Employment Opportunity. 179 companies had signed Plans for Progress since the program was started in May 1962. The President listed nonwhite gains of 13.8% in total employment, 23½% in salaried posts, 46.3% in management posts, 53.1% in sales positions, 31.6% in technical jobs. He pointed out, however, that "we still have a long way to go" to achieve equality; he said that among salaried employes, the ratio of whites to nonwhites had dropped from 65-1 to only 60-1.

Military Measures

The Defense Department announced June 27 that the armed forces Reserves had been integrated racially. It said "progress had been achieved" in integrating the National Guard in that "practically all of the all-Negro units have now been eliminated" and "the principal problem remaining is with regard to 10 of the Southern states which do not yet have Negroes in their National Guard units" (the 10 states: Alabama, Arkansas, Florida, Georgia, Louisiana, North and South Carolina, Mississippi, Tennessee and Virginia).

Defense Secy. Robert S. McNamara July 26 authorized military commanders to designate as "off limits" to servicemen areas near their bases where "relentless discrimination" was practiced against Negroes. The announcement was assailed by Sen. Strom Thurmond (D., S.C.) July 27 as "economic blackmail" and by Sen. Barry Goldwater (R., Ariz.) July 31 as a "police state" action. Chrmn. Carl Vinson (D., Ga.) of the

House Armed Services Committee introduced Sept. 17 a bill that would make it a court-martial offense for a base commander to carry out the order.

The Defense Department confirmed Sept. 17 that McNamara had banned participation of military units in any events where audiences were segregated or admission denied to Negroes.

Gains Reported by AJC

A survey published by the American Jewish Committee Dec. 15 concluded that, despite certain "shameful events," there had been "a positive gain" in civil rights in the U.S. during 1963, "primarily because of the determination and discipline of the Negro community itself." Among gains listed: the number of Southern public school districts desegregated increased by 161 to a total of 1,141; states with fair employment laws increased by 2 (Indiana, Hawaii) to a total of 22; California became the 11th state to adopt anti-bias housing legislation; Maryland and South Dakota became the 29th and 30th states to bar bias in public accommodations.

Black Muslims

The Black Muslims held their annual convention in Chicago Feb. 26 with about 2,000 delegates present. Malcolm X (originally Malcolm Little), then leader of the movement's New York Mosque, was the main speaker in place of the Muslims' national leader, Elijah Muhammad (originally Elijah Poole), who said he was too ill to attend. In his speech, Malcolm X reiterated a principal theme of the separatist Black Muslim movement by demanding that the government give "the black man" "some states" and "everything we need to start our own independent civilization." "How can you get the white people to move out?" he asked. His answer: "How did they get the Indians out?" He denounced "the white man" as "our open enemy" (Black Muslim leaders customarily assailed whites as "blue-eyed devils") and Negro integrationists as "Uncle Toms." For the first time, however, he appealed for unity in the fight for Negroes' civil rights and for cooperation of the Muslims, the NAACP and CORE.

Malcolm X was disciplined by Elijah Muhammad Dec. 4 for a speech in which he indicated that he was "glad" at Pres. Kennedy's assassination. Muhammad said in a Chicago statement Dec. 4 that Malcolm X's remarks did not reflect Muslim thinking. "We are very shocked at the assassination of our President," Muhammad declared. He said in a phone interview from his winter home in Phoenix, Ariz. Dec. 4 that "Malcolm is still a minister, but he will not be permitted to speak in public."

Malcolm X had been quoted as saying at a rally in New York Dec. 1: Mr. Kennedy had been "twiddling his thumbs" when South Vietnamese Pres. Ngo Dinh Diem and Diem's brother were killed; Pres. Kennedy's own assassination was a case of the "chickens coming home to roost"; "being an old farm boy myself, chickens coming home to roost never did make me sad; they've always made me glad."

Among events involving Black Muslims during 1963:

▲ 11 members of the movement were convicted by an all-white Superior Court jury in Los Angeles June 14 on charges stemming from a 1962 riot in which a Muslim was killed and several others and policemen injured. 3 defendants acquitted included John Henry Morris (known in his sect as John Shabazz), 32, minister of the Black Muslim Temple before which the riot had taken place. Judge David Coleman sentenced 10 of the convicted men July 31 to jail terms ranging from 90 days to 5 years plus terms of probation.

▲ A U.S. Civil Service Commission spokesman confirmed July 16 that a dozen Black Muslim members had been fired from federal jobs on their admissions that their first allegiance was not to the U.S. but to the projected "State of Islam," which their sect proposed forming in the U.S. The admissions were made to commission investigators, and the dismissals then took place on the ground that the Muslims had "mental reservations" when they took the oath of allegiance to the U.S. Constitution. Other Muslims were dropped from federal jobs during their probationary year, usually because of misstatements on their applications, the commission spokesman said.

▲ The U.S. Court of Appeals in Chicago held Nov. 6 that the Black Muslim movement was not a religion and hence not covered by the constitutional guarantee of religious freedom. The ruling was in the case of Thomas Cooper, 32, a prisoner in Joliet state penitentiary, who requested permission to receive religious literature in prison. A ruling that Black Muslims had no constitutional right to special privileges in observing their rites in prison had been issued by the 4th U.S. Circuit Court of Appeals in Richmond, Va. in August.

1964

Under Presidential prodding, Congress in 1964 passed a civil rights act that barred most racial discrimination in places of public accommodation. In the drive to pass the law, a Southern civil rights filibuster was killed by the Senate for the first time in Congressional history. Lyndon B. Johnson was reelected President by an overwhelming vote despite predictions that a 'white blacklash,' inspired by opposition to the Johnson civil rights program, would bring wholesale defections from Mr. Johnson to his Republican opponent, Sen. Barry M. Goldwater. Continuing violent opposition to the rights movement resulted in the murder of 3 young civil rights workers in Philadelphia, Miss. and of a Washington Negro educator in Georgia. Civil rights demonstrations and some race riots took place in most sections of the country—in the North as well as the South. Public school desegregation in the South continued at at minimal level, and agitation continued in the North to end the *de facto* segregation caused by the ghetto system. The country's outstanding civil rights leader, the Rev. Dr. Martin Luther King Jr., won the Nobel Peace Prize.

CIVIL RIGHTS ACT OF 1964

Bias in Public Accommodations Banned

A new, Administration-sponsored civil rights act became law July 2. The measure was passed after an expected Southern filibuster was cut off by a vote of cloture—the first such action ever taken by the Senate to limit time-killing debate on a civil rights measure. The most controversial feature of the new law was its ban on most racial discrimination in hotels, restaurants and other places of public accommodation.

The adoption of the bill was largely the result of strong pressure from the Johnson Administration, backed by civil rights groups who demanded action on rights legislation during the Presidential election year. Pres. Lyndon B. Johnson had said in his State-of-the-Union message Jan. 8 that passage of the 1964 Civil Rights Act was essential to provide "increased opportunity" in employment, education, housing and every other field "to Americans of every color." Mr. Johnson added: "As far as the writ of federal law will run, we must abolish not some but all racial discrimination. . . . All members of the public should have equal access to facilities open to the public . . . should be equally eligible for federal benefits financed by the public . . . [and] should have an equal chance to vote for public officials—and to send their children to good public schools—and to contribute their talents to the public good. . . ."

The House of Representatives had begun debate on the Administration's civil rights bill Jan. 31. It passed it by 290-130 vote Feb. 10. The House version of the bill provided for racial integration of all public accommodations. It carried provisions to close voting-rights loopholes in the 1957 and 1960 Civil Rights Acts by: (a) barring the application of different standards to Negro and white voter-applicants in administering and interpreting literacy tests; (b) barring disqualification of applicants for inconsequential errors in their applications; (c) authorizing the Justice Department to bring cases of voting-rights violations before special 3-judge panels. The House version also included provisions: (a) forbidding the denial of access to, or the denial of use of any public facility owned, operated or managed by a state, because of race or color; (b) authorizing the federal Attorney General to institute school desegregation suits and the Commissioner of Education to give assistance to local communities in planning school desegregation; (c) extending the Civil Rights Commission's life until 1968; (d) permitting but not requiring a cut-off of federal funds from federally-assisted programs if discrimination existed; (e) barring racial discrimination by labor unions or employers in interstate commerce; (f) establishing a Community Relations Service, with a director appointed by the President, to help communities with racial problems.

The Senate began debate on the bill Mar. 30 after more than a month of delaying tactics by Southern Democrats. (During previous debate on the motion to take up the bill, Sen. Richard B. Russell [D., Ga.], a leader of the Southern bloc, had repeated Mar. 16 a proposal for a $1½ billion "racial relocation" program in which Southern Negroes would be moved voluntarily to Northern states and Northern whites moved South until all states had a roughly equal proportion of Negroes and whites.) Majority whip Hubert Humphrey (D., Minn.) opened debate on the bill. He said Mar. 30: "Until racial justice and freedom [are] a reality in this land, our union will remain profoundly imperfect. . . . That is why the bill must become law." In his first major speech in the Senate, Sen. Edward M. Kennedy (D., Mass.) called Apr. 9 for passage of the bill. He said: "My brother was the first President of the United States to state publicly that segregation was morally wrong. His heart and soul are in this bill. If his life and death had a meaning, it was that we should not hate but love one another." Early in the debate, Southern Democrats began to maneuver to keep the Administration bill from coming to a vote. By the end of April the Senate's Democratic and Republican leaders had reached agreement to seek cloture (limitation of debate) should a Southern filibuster threaten the bill or other important Senate business.

The Senate June 10 voted, 71-29, to limit further debate on the civil rights bill to one hour per Senator. This was the first time the Senate had ever invoked cloture in a civil rights debate. A 2/3 vote of Senators present and voting (100) was required. Senate majority leader Mike Mansfield (D., Mont.) had introduced the cloture motion June 8. Sen. Richard B. Russell (D., Ga.), heading the Southern opposition to the bill, insisted just before the vote June 10 that the invoking of cloture "is not and cannot be a moral question" but was "a political question." Senate minority leader Everett M. Dirksen (R., Ill.) maintained, however, that "we are confronted with a moral issue." Pres. Johnson June 10 praised the cloture vote as "a major contribution to meet a national responsibility."

Many suggested amendments to the bill were defeated in subsequent Senate debate. The Senate voted on 115 amendments and registered 106 roll-call votes following the imposition of cloture. Finally, a revised bill worked out by Dirksen and Administration representatives was substituted for the pending bill June 17 by 76-18 vote. Sen. Barry M. Goldwater (R., Ariz.) announced June 18 that he was "unalterably opposed to discrimination of any sort" but would vote against the bill because he believed it unconstitutional.

The Senate passed the substitute bill June 19 by 73-27 vote with Goldwater and 5 other Republicans opposing it. The House voted July 2, by 289-126, to approve the Senate-passed measure. Pres. Johnson signed it into law a few hours later.

The signing ceremony July 2 was televised and attended by Congress leaders, 5 cabinet members and Negro, religious, labor and women's leaders. Pres. Johnson said in a brief speech: "We must not approach the observance end enforcement of this law in a vengeful spirit. Its purpose is not to punish. Its purpose is not to divide, but to end divisions— divisions which have lasted too long. Its purpose is national, not regional. . . . [The act] relies first on voluntary compliance, then on the efforts of states and local communities to secure the rights of citizens. It provides for the national authority to step in only when others cannot or will not do the job. . . . We have come now to a time of testing. We must not fail. Let us close the springs of racial poison." Mr. Johnson announced in his talk the appointment of ex-Gov. LeRoy Collins (D., Fla.), president of the National Association of Broadcasters, as director of the Community Relations Service provided for by the bill. The President also announced that (a) he would appoint a citizens' advisory committee to assist Collins, (b) he would ask for supplemental appropriations to meet the costs of the bill, (c) he had requested at a cabinet meeting that afternoon the implementation of the law by federal agencies, (d) he was asking appropriate officials to confer with representative groups to promote understanding of and compliance with the law. (Ex-disarmament negotiator Arthur H. Dean was named by the President July 3 as chairman of the advisory committee, the National Citizens Committee for Community Relations.)

Major provisions of the act as finally passed:

Title I (Voting Rights)—Barred unequal application of registration procedures, rejections for minor errors; made a 6th-grade education a rebuttable presumption of literacy;

required that literacy tests be administered in writing and that copies of the test and an individual's answers be furnished on request. Allowed the Attorney General or defendant state officials to request trial by a 3-judge federal court.

Title II (Public Accommodations)—Barred discrimination in restaurants, hotels, motels, places of amusement and gasoline stations if the discrimination were "supported" by state laws or "action" or involved interstate commerce; this prohibition covered such establishments as a barber shop within a hotel, a department store with a restaurant in it; it did not specifically cover barber shops, retail stores, bars, small bowling alleys; it specifically exempted owner-occupied lodging houses with 5 or fewer rooms for rent (the "Mrs. Murphy" clause) and private clubs (except if such facilities were offered to patrons of covered establishments). Permitted (a) individuals to bring injunction suits, (b) the court to name an attorney for the complainant and to authorize the suit without payment of costs, (c) the Attorney General to intervene for the complainant at the court's discretion or to file an injunction suit and get a 3-judge court if he found a pattern of resistance. In states (34) having public accommodations laws, prohibited the individual's suit until the state or local authority had had 30 days' notice; in states not having such laws, permitted reference to the Community Relations Service for 60-120 days for voluntary compliance effort.

Title III (Public Facilities)—Permitted the Justice Department, on a written complaint deemed "meritorious" and where the complainant was found financially unable to sustain legal action (or if such action would cause potential economic or other injury), to initiate suits to secure desegregation of state or locally owned, operated or managed public facilities (parks, playgrounds, swimming pools, libraries, etc.).

Title IV (Public Education)—Authorized the Attorney General to file school desegregation suits on written complaint (but did not cover busing of pupils or other such steps to end "racial imbalance"). Called for a U.S. Office of Education survey on desegregation progress and authorized the office to give technical and financial aid, if requested, to local systems undergoing desegregation; such aid could be used for institutes for training school personnel in desegregation problems, for paying stipends for trainees and for grants to school boards for local training and for hiring specialists.

Title V (Civil Rights Commission)—Extended life of Commission through Jan. 31, 1968, authorized it to serve as national clearinghouse on civil rights information and to investigate vote frauds as well as denials of the right to vote, barred it from investigating membership or internal practices of fraternal or religious organizations.

Title VI (Federally Assisted Programs) —Barred discrimination under any federally-assisted activity, ordered federal agencies extending aid to issue rules (to be approved by the President) to carry out the title's provisions. Before enforcement, agencies would be required to seek voluntary compliance, provide public hearings and give Congress 30 days' notice. The aid cutoff action was subject to judicial review. Exemptions included Social Security, veterans' pensions, FHA and VA mortgage insurance, federal insurance of banks and savings-and-loan deposits, farm subsidies. Title was not to be used to enforce equal employment practices unless the primary purpose of the program was to provide employment.

Title VII (Employment) —Barred discrimination by employers or unions with 100 or more employes or members (but the number would be reduced over 4 years to 25 or more employes/members). Provided for an Equal Employment Opportunity Commission to investigate complaints and try voluntary compliance; states (31) having fair employment laws were allowed a 60-day period for action on the complaint before it could be filed with the commission (120 days during the first year of a new state law). Authorized the Attorney General to sue if he found a "pattern or practice" of resistance and to ask for a 3-judge court. A one-year delay of coverage under the title was provided. Exemptions included alien workers outside the U.S., religious and educational groups, hiring where religion, sex or national origin were bona fide occupational qualifications. Union seniority was upheld in the title.

Title VIII (Statistics) —Directed the Census Bureau to compile registration and voting statistics based on race, color and national origin wherever recommended by the Civil Rights Commission. Persons could not be questioned about party affiliation or past votes.

Title IX (Intervention) —Permitted the Attorney General to intervene in private suits where persons alleged denial of equal protection of the laws under the 14th Amendment and where he found the case to be of "general public importance." Permitted higher federal court review of the action of federal district

courts in remanding a civil rights case to state courts.
Title X (Community Relations Service)—Provided for a
Community Relations Service in the Commerce Department
to help communities resolve discrimination disputes.

Title XI (Miscellaneous)—Guaranteed jury trials for criminal contempt cases under any part of the act but *Title I*, with
a limit on the sentences of 6 months in prison and a $1,000
fine. (The *Title I* or voting rights cases were covered by the
1957 jury-trial provision that a judge may try a case without
a jury but that in such cases sentences were limited to $300
fine and 45 days in prison; in voting rights cases tried by
jury, sentences were limited to 6 months and $1,000.) Barred
both criminal prosecution and criminal contempt proceeding
against any one person for the same cause under the act.
Barred conviction for criminal contempt under the act unless
the action was proved to be intentional. Stated that it was not
the intent of the act to preempt or invalidate state laws unless
they were inconsistent with any of the purposes of the act.

New Law Brings Changes—& Litigation

Attitudes of Southern leaders toward the new law ranged
from outright defiance to assertions that even unpopular laws
must be obeyed by law-abiding people. Gov. Paul B. Johnson
Jr. of Mississippi was reported to have advocated noncompliance by businessmen until the law was tested in the courts.
Gov. George C. Wallace of Alabama July 2 also advocated a
court testing. Wallace had told newsmen in Raleigh, N.C. June
19: "It is not my responsibility to enforce the civil rights bill.
My attitude will be to leave it alone. It will take a police state
to enforce it." An appeal for "calm and reason" and not
"violence and emotion" was made by Sen. Allen J. Ellender
(D., La.), a foe of the rights bill in Congress. In a broadcast
July 4 recorded for Louisiana radio stations, Ellender said
any resistance to the new law "must be within the framework
of the orderly processes established by law." "Any other
course is foolhardy and indefensible," he said. "The doctrine
of civil disobedience has no more credence now than it did
before." Sen. Richard B. Russell (D., Ga.), who had been a
leader in the fight against enactment of the Civil Rights
Act, urged Georgians July 15 to accept the new law "for as
long as it is there." He warned that "violence and law violation will only compound our difficulties and increase our

troubles."

At least 10 Birmingham, Ala. restaurants desegregated July 3 in compliance with the new law. Morrison's, the largest cafeteria chain in the South (41 cafeterias in 7 Southern cities), announced that it would serve Negroes "rather than buck the federal government." Hotels, motels and restaurants in Jackson, Miss. were reported generally integrated, although Jackson's 3d largest hotel, the Robert E. Lee, closed July 6 rather than accept Negro guests. The Jackson Chamber of Commerce had appealed to businessmen July 3 to comply with the new law. But operators of restaurants and hotels in Beaumont, Tex., Selma, Ala., Valdosta, Ga., Atlanta and other Southern communities resisted integration.

A 3-judge federal court in Atlanta July 22 ordered the Pickrick Restaurant of Atlanta and the Heart of Atlanta Motel to admit Negroes within 20 days. This was the first court test of the Civil Rights Act of 1964, and it upheld the law's key section barring discrimination in public accommodations. Lester G. Maddox, Pickrick operator, had chased 3 Negro ministerial students away from his restaurant at gunpoint July 3, the day after Pres. Johnson had signed the rights act into law. The 3 Negroes sued Maddox, contending that the public accommodations clause of the act required him to serve them. Moreton Rolleston Jr., operator of the motel, had sued to stop the government from enforcing the act at his motel, maintaining that travelers ceased to be involved in interstate commerce once they entered his establishment. The court ruled that both the restaurant and motel were subject to the powers of Congress to regulate interstate commerce and thus bound to obey the public accommodations clause of the rights act. Maddox announced Aug. 13 that he was closing his restaurant "for good" to prevent Negroes from eating there.

U.S. District Judge Bryan Simpson Aug. 19 found 2 St. Augustine, Fla. men guilty of defying the key public accommodations section of the act. The Justice Department Sept. 2 filed suits accusing officials in Dallas County, Ala. and Selma, Ala. of depriving Negroes of their voting rights and 5 Selma restaurants of refusing to serve Negroes.

A 3-judge federal court ruled unanimously in Birmingham Sept. 17 that Ollie's Barbecue, a Birmingham restaurant, could not be compelled to serve Negroes under the public accommodations section of the 1964 Civil Rights Act. The judges held that the section was inapplicable to a restaurant not directly involved in interstate commerce. Ollie McClung and his son, Ollie McClung Jr., co-owners of the restaurant, had brought suit July 31 on the ground that the section forced them to serve Negroes and therefore required involuntary servitude in violation of the 13th Amendment. The decision, however, was reversed by the U.S. Supreme Court Dec. 14.

In its Dec. 14 ruling, the Supreme Court unanimously upheld the constitutionality of the act's public accommodations section. It also ruled, 5-4, that the accommodations section barred state prosecutions of demonstrators who had tried by peaceful means, even before the act was passed, to desegregate business places covered by the act. The court ruled that the Constitution's commerce clause gave Congress authority broad enough to ban racial discrimination that might affect interstate commerce. The court upheld the district court decision that had enjoined the Heart of Atlanta Motel in Atlanta from discriminating against Negroes.

Pres. Johnson Dec. 4 signed an order barring discrimination in any federal aid programs administered by the Interior, Agriculture, Labor and Health-Education-&-Welfare Departments or by the Housing & Home Finance Agency, General Services Administration or National Science Foundation. The order was the first implementation of Title VI of the 1964 Civil Rights Act. The President Dec. 10 named Vice Pres.-elect Hubert H. Humphrey to coordinate all federal civil rights programs and guide them "toward energetic pursuit of equal opportunity for all." (U.S. Education Commissioner Francis Keppel had warned at an annual conference of the National Urban League in Louisville, Ky. Aug. 3 that schools refusing to desegregate within a reasonable time would not receive federal funds under pending legislation providing $1.48 billion for aid-to-education programs for fiscal 1965. He said that the 1964 rights act clearly prohibited the use of federal funds "to perpetuate segregation.")

PRESIDENTIAL CAMPAIGN

A major subject debated during the 1964 Presidential campaign was the attitudes of the candidates—Pres. Lyndon B. Johnson, the successful Democratic candidate for re-election, and Sen. Barry Goldwater of Arizona, the unsuccessful Republican nominee—on the issue of civil rights. Pres. Johnson told a Florida audience Feb. 27 that "full participation in our society can no longer be reserved to men of one color." Speaking at a Democratic fund-raising dinner in Miami Beach, the President said: "The Constitution applies to every American, of every religion, of every region and of every race"; his Administration was committed "to protect the constitutional rights of every American" and would "press forward with legislation, with education, and with action, until we have eliminated the last barrier of intolerance."

Goldwater on Defensive

Goldwater was forced to defend himself frequently against charges that he opposed the Negro demand for equality. While campaigning in the New Hampshire Republican Presidential primary, Goldwater said in Keene Mar. 4 that he could "not condone or support" civil disobedience, boycotts and demonstrations by civil rights supporters. He held that such action "hardened" hearts and led to "more violence" and government intervention in private situations. Goldwater said in a speech in Madison Square Garden in N.Y. City May 12 that "you cannot pass a law that will make me like you or you like me; this is something that can only happen in our hearts. . . ."

Ex-Pres. Dwight D. Eisenhower, in a *N.Y. Herald Tribune* statement giving his view on the position the Republican Party should take in the campaign, said May 25 that civil rights was the nation's most critical domestic issue. He asserted that the U.S. was morally obligated to "strengthen our laws in a determined effort to see that each American enjoys the full benefits of citizenship." Eisenhower, referring specifically to Goldwater, told newsmen June 11 that he did not know how he could support any candidate maintaining that civil rights fell entirely within the province of the states.

Before voting June 19 against the Civil Rights Act of 1964, Goldwater went to Eisenhower's home in Gettysburg, Pa. June 18 to explain his action. Goldwater, who also had voted June 10 not to end the Southern filibuster against the bill, said he opposed the new law because its public accommodations and fair-employment provisions were unconstitutional and because the bill would foster the development of a "police state."

At the Republican National Convention in San Francisco, Goldwater backers defeated an attempt to strengthen the civil rights plank of the party's proposed platform. The strengthening amendment, which was rejected, called for "enforcement of the Civil Rights Act of 1964. The plank adopted demanded "full implementation and faithful execution" of the new law but did not use the word "enforcement." Goldwater, in a televised appearance before the Platform Committee July 10, had said he favored a platform calling for "a minimum of government" and for "equal opportunity to exercise our talents and fulfill our ambitions so long as we do not infringe the rights of others." (After winning the Republican nomination, Goldwater requested a meeting with Pres. Johnson to discuss civil rights and the campaign. After the meeting, which took place July 24, the White House issued a statement that said: "The President met with Sen. Goldwater and reviewed the steps he had taken to avoid the incitement of racial tensions. Sen. Goldwater expressed his position, which was that racial tensions should be avoided. Both agreed on this position.")

The Democratic platform, adopted by the Democratic National Convention in Atlantic City, N. J. Aug. 25, asserted that the 1964 Civil Rights Act "deserves and requires full observance by every American and fair, effective enforcement if there is any default."

In his first major civil rights speech of the campaign, Goldwater said in Chicago Oct. 16 that "forced integration is just as wrong as forced segregation." He held that the government "must ensure freedom of association" but that "it cannot and should not ensure association itself." At a Madison Square Garden rally in N.Y. City Oct. 26, Goldwater equated "the right to associate" with "the equally vital right not to associate." He said he favored "our system of neighborhood schools" and did not "want to see them destroyed or be sacrificed by a futile exercise in sociology" such as "forcibly busing your children . . . just to meet an arbitrary racial quota." "These are not matters of civil rights," he said. "They are matters of common sense, common concern and decency." "The Nazi and the Fascist types—the bigots—they're not going to vote for me," Goldwater declared, "because my grandfather was a Polish Jew."

In Cleveland Oct. 27, Goldwater attacked the Civil Rights Act of 1964 as treading "dangerously" in an area involving "the fundamental issue of our day . . . the issue of unfair intervention in the private affairs of men." He held that "civil rights" were a person's rights "in relation to his government, not in relation to his fellow man." "No person," he declared, "whether government official or private citizen, should violate the rights of some in order to further the rights of others." Again assailing the transportation of children to schools outside their neighborhoods to reverse racial imbalance, Goldwater warned: "If we extend the principle to its logical end, we are compelled to use racial quotas as a substitute for the principle of equal opportunity in every aspect of social life. Why not move families from one neighborhood to another so that quotas sent by some bureaucrat somewhere will be everywhere met? Or workers from one job to another? Or businessmen, or government officials, or any group of any description? Is this what we have in mind when we speak of freedom and equal opportunity? Of course not. Our aim . . . is neither to establish a segregated society nor to establish an integrated society. Our aim is to preserve a free society."

'White Backlash' Fails to Block LBJ Reelection

A predicted Northern "white backlash" vote against Pres. Johnson and his civil rights program apparently failed to develop. Mr. Johnson was reelected by an overwhelming vote. The only apparent backlash votes were reported among scattered voters of Polish, Slav and other Eastern European ethnic groups. Some of this backlash was reported in Baltimore, Md., in the Indiana steel area and in some sections of Pennsylvania, Ohio and Illinois. But the Democratic Party actually increased its Eastern European ethnic vote in New York, New Jersey, Connecticut, Michigan and Wisconsin. In areas such as Paterson and Jersey City, N.J. and Dixmoor, Ill., where Negroes had rioted during the summer, Democratic vote totals also showed an increase. One form of white backlash apparently emerged in California, where, by a margin of about 2-1, voters approved a constitutional amendment to guarantee a property owner the right to "decline to sell, lease, or rent residential real property to any person as he chooses." The vote had the effect of nullifying California's 1963 Rumford Act, which made it illegal to consider race, religion or national origin in selling, leasing or renting property. In Maryland, however, where Alabama Gov. George C. Wallace had gained considerable support from an apparent white backlash vote in the spring Democratic Presidential primary, voters defeated a proposal to repeal a new state law prohibiting discrimination in public accommodations.

The Negro vote went to the Democrats by massive margins

ranging from 85% to as high as 99½% in various states. The
total Negro vote for the Democrats was estimated at 90% compared with 40% in 1960. An intensive drive had resulted in an
estimated total of 6 million registered Negro voters, including
2 million in the South. It was estimated that more than 75% of
registered Negroes voted. Massachusetts Atty. Gen. Edward W.
Brooke, a Republican holding the highest state elective office
ever attained by a Negro, was reelected by more than 900,000
votes despite a record victory margin of more than a million
for Pres. Johnson. (Brooke had repudiated Goldwater.) Hundreds
of Negro school children boycotted classes in at least 7 Alabama cities and towns Nov. 2-3 in protest against the absence of
Mr. Johnson's name on the election ballot and in protest against
harsh voter registration rules that reportedly had been imposed
on Negroes. Anniston and Tuscaloosa reported especially heavy
pupil absenteeism. Negroes, most of them teen-agers, demonstrated outside the capitol in Montgomery Nov. 2 in an apparent
protest against alleged discrimination against Negro voters.

Negro leaders and the Democratic National Committee denounced as forgery leaflets, circulated late in the election campaign, that urged Negroes to cast write-in votes for the Rev. Dr.
Martin Luther King Jr. for President. The leaflets bore the
name of the non-existent "Committee for Negores in Government
of Louisville, Ky." as sponsor. King, other civil rights leaders
and Democratic spokesmen charged that Goldwater supporters
had distributed the leaflets in an effort to siphon away votes
from Pres. Johnson. New Jersey State Atty. Gen. Arthur J. Sills
said Nov. 2 that an official of the Atlantic City printing firm of
Brooks & Idler had reported that Clay Claiborne, identified as a
Republican National Committee field representative from the
committee's Washington headquarters, had ordered 1,400,000
copies of the leaflet. A GOP National Committee spokesman
said that the committee had no knowledge of the leaflets.

7 rights leaders Nov. 11 sent Pres. Johnson a letter congratulating him on his election and urging him to call a conference on methods by which they could help implement the
1964 Civil Rights Act and aid in programs to give Negroes
more economic opportunity. The leaders: Dr. King; NAACP
executive director Roy Wilkins; CORE director James Farmer;
SNCC Executive Secy. James Forman; Jack Greenberg of the
NAACP Legal Defense & Educational Fund; Mrs. Dorothy I.
Height, president of the National Council of Negro Women;
National Urban League director Whitney M. Young Jr.

SOUTHERN VIOLENCE

3 Rights Workers Slain in Mississippi

3 young civil rights workers disappeared in Mississippi June 21 after their release from a Philadelphia, Miss. jail in which they had been held for 5 hours by Deputy Sheriff Cecil Ray Price, 26, on a speeding charge. The 3 missing men were Michael Henry Schwerner, 24, of Brooklyn, N.Y., a white member of the Congress of Racial Equality (CORE); Andrew Goodman, 20, a white Queens College student from New York, and James Earl Chaney, 21, of Meridian, Miss., a Negro plasterer and CORE member. They were part of a group of 175 rights workers who had gone to Mississippi to help in the COFO (Council of Federated Organizations) summer campaign to register Negro voters.

Atty. Gen. Robert F. Kennedy ordered a fullscale FBI investigation June 22. Pres. Johnson June 25 authorized the use of 200 unarmed Navy men from the naval air station at Meridian to help search for the missing men. Gov. Paul B. Johnson Jr. of Mississippi asked residents June 26 to search their farms for them. FBI director J. Edgar Hoover visited Mississippi July 10-11, at Pres. Johnson's request, to investigate the disappearances. (Hoover, speaking at a news conference following the opening July 10 of an FBI field headquarters in Jackson, Miss., disclosed that the FBI force in the state had been increased to 153 agents —10 times the normal number— to protect civil rights workers.)

The bodies of the 3 rights workers were found by FBI agents Aug. 4 in a recently-built earth dam 5 miles southwest of Philadelphia, Miss. Autopsies showed that Chaney had been subjected to an "inhuman beating" before 3 bullets were fired into his body and that Schwerner and Goodman had been shot to death. But a Neshoba County coroner's jury in Philadelphia reported Aug. 25 that it had been unable to determine the cause of death of any of the 3 men.

FBI agents Dec. 4 arrested 19 men on federal conspiracy charges in connection with the murders. Those arrested included Neshoba County Sheriff Lawrence Andrew Rainey, 41; Deputy Sheriff Price, 26; Otha Neal Burkes, 71, a former Philadelphia, Miss. policeman; the Rev. Edgar Ray Killen, 39, a fundamentalist Baptist minister, and several leaders of the White Knights of the Ku Klux Klan of Mississippi. (Rainey,

Price and Burkes had been free on bond on an Oct. 3 federal conspiracy indictment charging them with beating Negro prisoners.) 2 others were arrested on charges of refusing to answer questions about their roles in the case. The FBI charged that Price and 9 others of the 19 had participated in the murders of the 3 rights workers. The remaining 9 (including Rainey, Burkes and Killen) were charged with taking part in the murder conspiracy.

FBI Director Hoover, who announced the arrests in Washington, declared: "In narrowing the massive field of possible suspects in the 5½-month investigation, the FBI directed its primary attention upon known members and sympathizers of the Ku Klux Klan—which group includes most of those arrested today." 153 FBI agents had worked on the case, and about 60 FBI agents were reported to have infiltrated the Ku Klux Klan in Mississippi in the previous few months to obtain the evidence. 1,000 residents of Mississippi, including 480 Klan members, were reportedly questioned by the FBI in its investigation.

Those accused of actually participating in the murders: Price; Jimmy K. Arledge, 27, a Meridian truck driver; Horace Doyle Barnette, 25, a salesman; Travis Maryn Barnette, 36, part owner and operator of the B&S Garage in Meridian; James Edward Jordan, 38, a Gulfport, Miss. construction worker, formerly of Meridian; Billy Wayne Posey, 28, a Williamsville, Miss. service station operator; Alton Wayne Roberts, 26, a Meridian salesman; Jimmy Snowden, 31, a Meridian truck driver; Jerry McGrew Sharpe, 21, manager of a Philadelphia pulpwood supply company; Jimmy Lee Townsend, 17, a Williamsville service station attendant. Those charged with conspiracy but not with actually participating in the murders: Rainey; Burkes; Killen; Olin Lovell Burrag, 34, owner of a small trucking firm and of the farm where the bodies were buried; Herman Tucker, 36, a Philadelphia contractor who had built the pond where the bodies were found; Bernard Lee Akin, 50, owner of Akin Mobile Homes in Meridian; James Thomas Harris, 30, a Meridian truck driver; Frank J. Herndon, 46, operator of a Meridian drive-in restaurant; Oliver Richard Warner Jr., 54, a Meridian drive-in grocery-store owner. Those charged with refusing to give information: Earl B. Akin, 32, of Meridian, a mobile-homes salesman; Tommy A. Horne, 28, owner of a Bonita, Miss. plumbing company.

U.S. Commissioner Esther Carter in Meridian, Miss. Dec. 12 dismissed the charges against 17 of the 19 men arrested on conspiracy charges and against the 2 arrested on charges of refusing to give information. She dismissed, as incompetent testimony and as hearsay evidence, a statement by FBI agent Henry Rask, 39, of Atlanta that the FBI had obtained a signed confession from Horace Doyle Barnette, one of the 10 men charged with actually participating in the slaying. Charges against Barnette and the remaining suspects subsequently were dismissed. Miss Carter, who acted at a preliminary hearing, ruled that no real evidence had been presented to hold them for federal grand jury action. A spokesman for the Justice Department said in Washington: "In the experience of the department, the refusal by a U.S. Commissioner to accept a law enforcement officer's report of a signed confession in a preliminary hearing is totally without precedent." The Justice Department decided not to reveal any more of its evidence in the case and instead to present the case to a federal grand jury and attempt to win direct indictments without the usual preliminaries.

U.S. Commissioner Verta Lee Swetman in Biloxi, Miss. Dec. 11, on the request of the Justice Department, dismissed the federal conspiracy charge against a 20th suspect, James Edward Jordan, 38, a construction worker accused of participating in the slaying.

The charge against Barnette was dropped by the Justice Department in Shreveport, La. Dec. 14. (Barnette had moved from Meridian to Shreveport.)

(The Rev. Dr. Martin Luther King Jr. reacted to the dismissals by calling Dec. 10 for a massive Northern economic boycott of goods produced in Mississippi. NAACP executive director Roy Wilkins appealed Dec. 13 to N.Y. City financial houses "to decline to participate" in bidding on 3 Mississippi bond issues totaling $32,650,000; 3 groups of investment bankers withdrew from the bidding Dec. 15 but said they had acted for business reasons, not because Wilkins had urged such action.)

(2 lower halves of bodies had been found in Mississippi River backwaters near Tallulah, La. July 12 and 13. The mutilated corpses, both of Negroes, were tentatively identified as those of Charles E. Moore, 20, and Henry Dee, 19, both of Meadville, Miss. Civil rights leaders said that 5 other Negroes had been killed under mysterious circumstances in the area in 1964 and that the slayers were still apparently at liberty.)

Negro Educator Murdered in Georgia

Lemuel Augustus Penn, 49, a Negro assistant superintendent of Washington, D.C. public schools, was killed July 11 by a shotgun blast as he was driving about 12 miles northeast of Colbert, Ga. The shot was fired from a passing car. Penn, an Army Reserve lieutenant colonel, was returning to Washington after 2 weeks of Reserve training at Ft. Benning, Ga. His 2 passengers were uninjured.

The FBI arrested 4 Ku Klux Klan members Aug. 6 in connection with the murder. A Madison County grand jury indicted 3 of them Aug. 25, but an all-white Madison County jury acquitted 2 of them Sept. 4.

U.S. District Judge W. A. Bootle in Macon, Ga. Dec. 29 dismissed federal indictments charging 6 white men, all allegedly active in the Ku Klux Klan, with conspiring to injure and oppress Penn. 2 of the 6, Joseph Howard Sims and Cecil William Myers, were the men acquitted of murder charges Sept. 4. Bootle insisted "that this court [must] not usurp jurisdiction where it has none."

Beckwith Juries Disagree

The Jackson, Miss. trial of Byron de la Beckwith, accused of the slaying of Negro leader Medgar W. Evers in 1963, ended in a hung jury Feb. 7. A 2d trial was declared a mistrial Apr. 17 when an all-white jury deadlocked, reportedly 8-4 for acquittal.

Violence in McComb

6 Negroes and 2 whites went to McComb, Miss. July 5 to open a 2-month rights-protection and voter-registration campaign in southwest Mississippi. Robert P. Moses, director of the project and a field secretary for the Student Nonviolent Coordinating Committee, said July 5 that there had been "5 or 6 unsolved murders, numerous cross-burnings and beatings" in the McComb area in recent months.

A Negro church and the home of Mrs. Aylene Quin, a Negro civil rights worker, were bombed in McComb Sept. 20. The bombings touched off a riot in which about 2,000 Negroes gathered and threw bricks and bottles at a police patrol car. The disorders resulted in the arrest of 24 Negroes under a state "criminal syndicalism" law banning any activity that could lead to political or social change in the state. The police called the bombings a hoax, and McComb Sheriff R.R. Warren charged Sept. 24 that the latest 4 explosions had been "staged" by Negroes to try to induce the federal government to intervene. Mrs. Quin, Mrs. Matti Lean Dillon and Mrs. Ora Bryant met with Pres. Johnson Sept. 24 and told him of alleged racial terrorism in McComb. The President ordered the Justice Department to recommend possible federal action.

Dynamite sticks had been exploded in McComb Sept. 23 outside the homes of 2 Negroes, one a former policeman. The attack raised to 16 the number of reported house bombings in the McComb area since April. 4 churches had been bombed. Gov. Paul B. Johnson Sept. 30 ordered a state investigation of the McComb bombings. He reported indications that some of the bombings "were plants set by COFO [the integrationist Council of Federated Organizations] people" and "some were bombings by white people." Johnson and FBI Director J. Edgar Hoover announced the arrests of 3 whites Oct. 5 on charges of illegal use of explosives in connection with the bombings. Arms and ammunition as well as explosives were seized when the arrests were made.

Other Instances of Violence

Rabbi Arthur J. Lelyveld of Cleveland and 2 other white civil rights workers were beaten with metal weapons by 2 unidentified segregationists in Hattiesburg, Miss. July 10. Lelyveld, 51, was hospitalized.

The number of Negro churches burned in Mississippi during the summer reached 24 Sept. 17 when 2 churches used in a Negro voter registration drive were burned in rural sections of Madison County.

The Rev. Snead Baldwin, pastor of 4 congregations in Adams County in the Natchez, Miss. area, charged July 15 that at least 4 Negro churches and one Negro meeting hall in the area had been destroyed by fires in rural Adams County in the past year. These included 2 churches leveled by arsonists July 12. The home of Natchez Mayor John Nosser, a white racial peacemaker, was bombed Sept. 25. This was the 3d explosion in 2 weeks on property he owned. About 15 blocks away, the home of Willie Washington, a Negro contractor, was bombed Sept. 25 for the 2d time in 3 months.

A bomb went off in Jackson, Miss. Sept. 27 at the home of
I. S. Sanders, Negro businessman active in the civil rights
movement. NAACP field secretary Charles Evers promptly
telegraphed Pres. Johnson an appeal for federal intervention
to halt "this mounting reign of terror." "I cannot and will not
be responsible for the action which the Negroes may take upon
themselves," the telegram warned.

2 persons were injured in a dynamite explosion Oct. 4 at
the Baptist Academy church in Vicksburg, Miss. The church
served as a freedom school operated by COFO.

An all-white federal jury in Jacksonville, Fla. acquitted
4 Ku Klux Klansmen Nov. 25 of conspiring to violate the civil
rights of a Negro boy, Donald Godfrey, 6, because he had been
admitted under court order to the all-white Lackawanna school.
The men were accused of dynamiting his home Feb. 16. 3 of
the 4 Klansmen also were acquitted of charges of conspiring
to obstruct the court order for the school's integration. A
previous federal jury had not been able to reach a verdict on
the 4, and a mistrial had been declared July 5. A 5th defendant
had been acquitted then, but a 6th, William Sterling Rosecrans
Jr., 30, had pleaded guilty to the bombing and was sentenced to
7 years in prison.

SOUTHERN DEMONSTRATIONS & RIOTS

Sit-In Convictions Voided

The Supreme Court June 22 reversed the trespass convictions of 42 sit-in demonstrators in 5 cases from Maryland,
South Carolina and Florida. By 6-3 rulings the court upset:
(a) the 1960 convictions of 12 student demonstrators at a
Baltimore restaurant; (b) the 1960 convictions of 2 Negro
students refused service at a lunch counter in Columbia,
S.C.; (c) the convictions of 5 Negroes arrested at a Maryland
amusement park. In 2 other cases, the court acted unanimously:
(1) 5 Columbia, S.C. convictions were reversed for lack of
evidence; (2) a Florida conviction was reversed because of
evidence that the state encouraged segregation at a restaurant
involved in the case. The court Apr. 6 had reversed breach-of-
peace convictions of 65 Negro students arrested in 1960 civil
rights demonstrations in Rock Hill, S.C. The court had ruled
against the convictions Oct. 14, 1963, but the South Carolina
Supreme Court, after reconsidering the case on the high court's

orders, had reaffirmed the convictions.

Turmoil Continues Throughout the South

Among other developments involving demonstrations and riots in Southern states:

Alabama—The Rev. Dr. Martin Luther King Jr. and his aide, the Rev. Fred Shuttlesworth, asserted at a news conference Mar. 4 that the city of Birmingham had failed to abide by its desegregation pledges, made after mass protests 6 months earlier, and that demonstrations would therefore be renewed. Negroes resumed anti-segregation demonstrations in Birmingham Mar. 19. 12 persons, including 8 children, were arrested for violating a city picketing ordinance during a demonstration against 2 downtown stores.

3 Negro pickets were wounded in Tuscaloosa June 5 during a demonstration in protest against segregation. 2 white men were arrested June 5 after oil of mustard had been thrown on Tuscaloosa demonstrators June 3-4. 94 Negro demonstrators planning a protest march were arrested June 9 at a Negro church in the city. Police again surrounded the church June 11 and arrested demonstration leaders. About 300 whites threw bottles and stones at an integrated movie theater in Tuscaloosa July 8. Police dispersed the crowd with tear gas and fire hoses. The outburst occurred after a rumor had spread that actor Jack Palance had escorted a Negro woman into the theater. The Tuscaloosa City Commission July 10 enacted an ordinance banning everyone under 21 years of age from the streets between 8 p.m. and 5 a.m. unless they were University of Alabama students or youths going to or from work.

Florida—283 persons were arrested in St. Augustine rights demonstrations Mar. 28-Apr. 1. Among those jailed was Mrs. Malcolm Peabody, 72, mother of Massachusetts Governor Endicott Peabody. She was arrested Mar. 31 with a biracial group in a segregated dining room. She spent 2 days in jail on state charges of trespassing, being an undesirable guest and conspiracy. She was released in $450 bond Apr. 2. Also arrested during the demonstrations were Mrs. Donald J. Campbell, wife of the dean of the Episcopal Theological Seminary at Cambridge, Mass.; Prof. J. Lawrence Burholder of Harvard Divinity School; the Rev. William Sloane Coffin Jr., 39, Yale University chaplain; the Rev. Arthur Brandenburg, 33, Methodist chaplain at Yale.

The Rev. Dr. Martin Luther King Jr. appealed May 28 to "men of conscience" throughout the U.S. to participate in demonstrations in St. Augustine as part of his Southern Christian Leadership Conference's "long hot summer" campaign for civil rights.

Federal District Judge Bryan Simpson ruled in Jacksonville June 9 that Negroes in St. Augustine could demonstrate "at any hour in the nighttime" (as well as during the day). He issued an injunction voiding orders by St. Augustine Police Chief Virgil Stuart and St. Johns County Sheriff L. O. Davis Jr., who had barred racial demonstrations at night. Simpson had told Davis that there was "danger . . . when you have members of the Klan and allied organizations in your organization as deputies." One of the "special deputies" was Holstead Richard (Hoss) Manucy, 45, an ex-bootlegger, leader of a group of segregationist toughs known locally as "Manucy's Raiders" and head of the Ancient City Hunting Club, which provided bail for segregationists arrested in racial disturbances.

King and 17 other integrationists were arrested June 11 when they refused to leave the Monson Motor Lodge restaurant in St. Augustine. Those arrested included the Rev. William England, white chaplain at Boston College. King was then released June 13 in $900 bail. 41 persons, including 16 rabbis, were arrested at the Monson Lodge June 18 after some had been pushed away from the segregated restaurant and 7 others had dived into the motel's pool. The rabbis, who had been attending the annual convention of the Central Conference of American Rabbis in Atlantic City, had gone to St. Augustine June 17, when King had telegraphed the convention for help. Other mass arrests were made during this period at restaurants and churches where Negroes had sought to pray with whites.

Gov. Farris Bryant June 20 prohibited night demonstrations on public property in St. Augustine. Simpson June 22 ordered Bryant to show cause why he should not be held in contempt of court for banning nighttime demonstrations despite the court order specifically authorizing them.

A white mob of about 800 attacked part of an integrationist parade of several hundred Negroes near the old St. Augustine slave market June 25. Most of the whites were said to have come from a rally conducted by the Rev. Connie Lynch of California, a white evangelist who had been preaching nightly for action against integrationists. About 30 Negroes were hospitalized, many other Negroes suffered minor injuries, and 3 whites were hospitalized. The white mob forced the police to free 4 whites who had been arrested. In another June 25 incident, segregationists forcibly prevented about 50 Negroes from swimming at the St. Augustine beach. But state troopers intervened, clashing with segregationists at the beach and arresting 12 who were trying to stop the "swim-in."

Manucy, leader of the white groups that had been attacking integrationists, warned June 25: "Violence will continue as long as Negroes continue to invade the public beach which has been used only by whites for hundreds of years. The violence won't stop until all Negroes and white outsiders leave St. Augustine."

Gov. Bryant June 30 appointed an emergency committee of 2 whites and 2 Negroes to "restore communications" between whites and Negroes in St. Augustine. King said the governor had shown "good faith," and he agreed to halt rights demonstrations temporarily. But he pledged he would not leave the city until "a meaningful resolution" had been achieved. Manucy agreed to halt his group's activities temporarily but expressed doubt that the emergency committee could accomplish anything.

About 80 hotel, motel and restaurant owners in St. Augustine June 30 announced their intention of complying with the public accommodations section of the 1964 Civil Rights Act and allowing Negroes to use their premises.

(King disclosed June 30 that he and 3 of the city's Negro leaders had been charged with contributing to the delinquency of minors by allowing youths who were wards of Juvenile Court to participate in racial demonstrations. King and 2 of the 3 leaders, Dr. Robert B. Haylong, a dentist, and James S. Jackson, were arrested and then released. Police could not find the 3d leader, the Rev. John Gibson.)

Black nationalist leader Malcolm X offered in a telegram to King July 2 to send armed Negroes to St. Augustine to protect demonstrators. He asserted that his followers "are ready to give the Ku Klux Klan a taste of its own medicine" in St. Augustine and Mississippi.

Racial rioting had erupted in Jacksonville Mar. 23 after 2 weeks of unsuccessful restaurant and hotel "sit-ins." The violence began when police tried to disperse Negroes meeting in a park. During the outbreak, a Negro housewife was killed by gunfire from a passing car. Students and bystanders hurled stones at police, firemen, school officials and newsmen at a Negro high school. At least 265 adults and 200 juveniles were arrested during 2 days of violence Mar. 23-24. The turmoil subsided after a biracial committee was formed at Mayor Haydon Burns' request and announced that it would seek "voluntary desegregation" of public accommodations.

Maryland—State police in Princess Anne used police dogs Feb. 22-24 in efforts to halt anti-segregation demonstrations aimed mainly at segregated restaurants. The demonstrators were Negro students from Maryland State College. Another demonstration by the students Feb. 26, countered by police with dogs and by firemen with hoses, led to disorders resulting in injuries to 62 Negroes, 14 with dog-bite wounds. 28 persons were arrested, and a nighttime curfew was imposed by the town council. Gov. J. Millard Tawes promised a delegation of Princess Anne protest leaders Mar. 4 that state troopers would not use dogs against rights demonstrators again "unless there is a riot." (16 members of the Princess Anne delegation were arrested in a demonstration at a segregated Annapolis restaurant near the state capitol Mar. 2 after an earlier meeting with Tawes.)

15 Negroes were arrested in Cambridge, Md. Feb. 25 while picketing a welfare office and an employment security office. National Guard troops made the arrests under a 1963 ruling banning demonstrations.

400-500 Negroes, demonstrating in Cambridge May 11 against the appearance of Alabama Gov. George C. Wallace, were dispersed by National Guardsmen using tear gas. 13 of the demonstrators, including Mrs. Gloria H. Richardson, leader of the Cambridge Nonviolent Action Committee, were arrested. Demonstrators May 12-13 were dispersed without gas.

A year of militia rule in Cambridge ended July 7 when Gov. Tawes ordered the National Guard to return civil authority to the city.

(Osvrey C. Pritchett, 62, a candidate of the anti-integration Dorchester Business & Citizens Association, was elected mayor of Cambridge July 14. He defeated S. Charles Walls Jr., 42, who ran with the backing of the Nonviolent Action Committee.)

North Carolina— 300 whites and Negroes clashed for 3 hours July 12 after a group of Negroes sought service at the Motor Freight restaurant near Henderson, N.C. 17 persons, including 12 Negroes, were jailed on charges of inciting a riot and refusing to obey police officers. 5 Negroes were injured.

Tennessee—A series of anti-segregation demonstrations were renewed in Nashville Apr. 27 and continued until May 4. Negro teen-agers picketed segregated restaurants and conducted street sit-downs that tied up traffic. More than 100 persons, including John Lewis, chairman of the Student Nonviolent Coordinating Committee, were arrested during the protests. Small groups of Negroes attended some white churches, and several whites attended Negro churches after religious leaders called for interracial worship services May 3.

NORTHERN UNREST

N.Y. World's Fair Demonstrations

Civil rights pickets demonstrated inside and outside the N.Y. World's Fair on its opening day Apr. 22. Demonstrations inside the fair were led by CORE National Director James Farmer, one of 294 persons arrested.

A threatened 2,000-car stall-in designed to block traffic to the fair failed to materialize when only 12 cars participated. N.Y. City Apr. 13 had announced a new traffic regulation setting a maximum penalty of a $50 fine and 30 days in jail for a motorist who ran out of gas on a major city highway. N.Y. Supreme Court Justice Joseph M. Conroy Apr. 20 had signed an injunction prohibiting the stall-in.

The protests were not designed as complaints about the fair but rather to dramatize the Negroes' plight in N.Y. City. Farmer warned when he was released from prison Apr. 24 that the U.S. faced "a longer and hotter summer than this country has ever seen." "Now is the time for anger," he declared.

N.Y. City Riots

Racial violence broke out in the Harlem section of N.Y. City July 18 and continued through July 21 despite stern police anti-riot action, including the firing of thousands of warning shots into the air. Negro mobs smashed store windows and hurled debris at police. The estimated 4-day toll: one Negro shot to death; 5 Negroes shot and wounded, none seriously; 81 civilians and 35 policemen injured; 112 stores and business establishments damaged; 185 persons arrested. The violence was attributed to racial tensions, heightened by an incident in which a 15-year-old Negro school boy (James Powell) was shot to death by an off-duty white police officer (Thomas Gilligan) in the Yorkville section July 16 after the boy reportedly had menaced the officer with a knife. (A N.Y. County grand jury refused Sept. 1 to indict the officer on a charge of criminal negligence.)

Immediately after the shooting of young Powell about 300 teen-agers, mostly Negroes, gathered at the scene and threw bottles and cans at policemen, injuring one of them. 200 Negro teen-agers staged another demonstration in Yorkville July 17 to protest the shooting.

The rioting began after a CORE rally, held in Harlem the evening of July 18, at which several Negro leaders charged New York police with brutality and demanded the dismissal of Lt. Gilligan. The rally's final speakers, drawn from the crowd after CORE representatives had turned the platform over to them, denounced the police, city officials and whites in strong language; one of them, the Rev. Nelson C. Dukes, a Harlem minister, declared that it was time for Harlem's Negroes to stop talking and to act. At Dukes' urging, the crowd, which had grown, marched to a nearby police station to present its protests and demands for Gilligan's ouster. The police barred the marchers from the precinct house, but the Negroes refused to leave the scene until their demands had been satisfied. The first scuffles ensued when police attempted to set up barricades between the demonstrators and the police station. The scuffle became a riot which spread to nearby streets and then throughout much of central Harlem.

For the next several hours Negroes on rooftops threw a stream of bottles and debris at hundreds of policemen sent to the area to maintain order. Groups of Negroes broke store windows and pillaged goods, and crowds of hundreds gathered on street corners. The police rushed the crowds with nightsticks and fired volley after volley of bullets into the air. Thousands of rounds of .38-caliber ammunition were fired. Jay Jenkins, 41, was shot and killed when he refused to stop throwing bricks at police from a rooftop. Police Commissioner Michael J. Murphy issued general orders to police to try to control the crowds peacefully but to resort to force when necessary.

Jesse Gray, leader of a recent Harlem rent strike, called July 19 for "100 skilled black revolutionaries who are ready to die" to correct "the police brutality situation in Harlem." Gray urged guerrilla warfare tactics and was applauded by an audience of about 500. James Farmer, CORE national director, was booed as he started to address the rally.

Rioting in Harlem took place again on a reduced scale the night of July 20. Police broke up a march by about 1,000 Negroes. The rioting continued the night of July 21, when a 12-year-old Negro boy reportedly was shot by a policeman.

Violence broke out in the predominantly Negro Bedford-Stuyvesant section of Brooklyn July 20-23. Policemen each night fired warning shots to disperse crowds of Negroes. A total of 10 civilians and 12 policemen were injured, 276 persons were arrested and 556 incidents of property damage were reported (mostly involving looting of shops and business establishments).

A N.Y. County grand jury Aug. 5 indicted William Epton, 32, chairman of the Progressive Labor Movement in Harlem, on charges of advocating the overthrow of the N.Y. State government by force and violence and of calling for the killing of police officers and judges. He was accused of advocating criminal anarchy. Epton was quoted as having said at a July 18 Harlem street meeting, just before the riots started, that "we're going to have to kill cops and judges." Witnesses testified that Epton, leader of the Harlem Defense Council, had advised that policemen be lured into side streets where they could be subjected to a barrage of bottles and missiles.

Racial clashes between Negroes and Puerto Ricans broke out on the Lower East Side of Manhattan in N.Y. City the nights of Aug. 29 and 30 after a Negro reportedly had shot a Puerto Rican to death. Several hundred persons participated. Molotov cocktails, bottles, stones and bricks were hurled from rooftops at firemen and policemen Aug. 30. The police responded by firing shots into the air. 30 persons were arrested.

(Police Commissioner Murphy appointed Capt. Lloyd Sealy Aug. 14 as commander of Harlem's largest police precinct, the 28th. Sealy was the first Negro to command a police precinct in Harlem. Negro leaders had demanded that more Negro policemen be stationed in Harlem and that Negro police officers be given command posts. Mayor Robert F. Wagner had agreed Aug. 6 on a program to recruit more Negro policemen and to develop a master plan to improve general conditions for New York Negroes.)

Outbreak in Rochester

Racial unrest flared in Rochester, N.Y. July 24-26 as Negroes, whites and police clashed in the streets and angry mobs smashed and looted white-owned stores. The toll: one white man killed; about 350 persons, 22 of them policemen, injured; at least 400 persons arrested; property damage estimated at several million dollars. The violence ended after N.Y. National Guard units and state police were sent to the city July 26 to aid local police in restoring order. (Rochester had a population of 320,000, of whom 40,000 were Negroes. The city's Negro community had charged police with brutality; whites were said to have become apprehensive at increased Black Muslim activity, and white and Negro parents had been battling in the courts over racial imbalance in the city's schools.)

The rioting started shortly before midnight July 24 in the city's Negro North Side section. The immediate cause was said to have been an incident in which a policeman reportedly tried to arrest a Negro man who was disturbing a Mother's Improvement Committee street dance. The man reportedly struck the policeman and in turn was attacked by the policeman's dog. Word spread among the dancers that policemen had clubbed and kicked the Negro; they began throwing beer cans and bottles at police, and reinforcements were sent to the area. The crowd quickly grew to 2,000 persons, among them many Negro youths, who were reported to have brawled with a band of white youths. During the next 10 hours, fighting between Negroes, whites and police occurred throughout the North Side. Police fired tear gas grenades at the rioters, and youths picked them up and threw them back. Mrs. Mildred Johnson of the Rochester NAACP chapter was booed when she pleaded with a street-corner crowd to present their demands to the city.

200 state troopers were sent to Rochester early July 25 at the request of City Public Safety Commissioner Donald Corbett and the Monroe County sheriff. By dawn July 25 most of the rioting had stopped. Deputy Police Chief Clarence DePrez reported July 25 that the mobs of looters had bypassed Negro-owned stores; he called the disturbances "well organized."

City Manager Porter W. Homer July 25 ordered an 8 p.m. curfew for the entire city. But violence erupted again that evening in Rochester's southwest section, about 1½ miles

from the scene of the previous night's riots. Hundreds of
Negroes remained on the streets after the curfew went into
effect, and state troopers attempted to enforce the order.
They were showered with bricks hurled from 2d-story porches
and roofs. One white man was killed, and a Negro man was
wounded by shots fired by a white civilian.

The rioting resumed in the North Side and continued in the
southwest section during the day July 26. Negro youths pelted
police with stones and bottles, and looters broke through the
plywood shop fronts that had been put up to replace shattered
windows. In the midst of the unrest, a civil defense helicopter
circling the southwest area crashed into a house, killing the
pilot and 2 occupants of the house.

Gov. Nelson A. Rockefeller mobilized 1,000 National
Guardsmen from Rochester, Binghamton and Auburn July 26
and ordered them to immediate emergency duty in Rochester.
The Guard units arrived in Rochester late July 26. An estimated 300 of the Guardsmen rode through the riot-affected
sections of the city in open trucks; they displayed steel hel-
mets and bayoneted rifles, but their officers reported that
none of the men had been issued ammunition. The Guardsmen
made camp in an armory and in 2 city parks. They were under
explicit orders not to intervene in any disturbances until
summoned by city authorities.

The rioting ebbed soon after the arrival of the Guard units.
Earlier July 26, Negro crowds had thrown rocks, bottles and
Molotov cocktails at police, and a city fire engine had been
the target of rifle fire as it ran through the emergency area.
But police were able to disperse the crowds and restore order
with warning shots, tear gas, and streams of water from high-
pressure hoses.

Robert Morrison, president of the Rochester chapter of the
NAACP, urged city officials July 26 to stop their emphasis on
"police force to put down the disturbances" and instead to
concentrate on long-range efforts to meet Negro demands. He
asked for "an immediate plan to provide jobs for the semi-
skilled and unskilled who are migrating to Rochester in large
numbers." (N.Y. State NAACP officials July 25 had banned the
group's 61 chapters from demonstrating.)

Victor Turyn, Buffalo FBI agent who worked with the
Rochester police, said July 26 that the riots were "spontaneous
as the result of the arrest of the youth [at the dance July 24]."
"We have no information that Communists or other subversive

groups were involved in the riots," he added.

North Philadelphia Riots

Racial rioting erupted the night of Aug. 28 in a 4-square-mile "ghetto" area of North Philadelphia in which 200,000 Negroes lived. The rioting continued on a smaller scale the nights of Aug. 29 and 30. The 3-day toll: 248 persons injured (including 66 policemen and 2 firemen), 312 persons arrested and hundreds of stores damaged and looted.

The trouble started Aug. 28 when a crowd gathered and menaced 2 policemen—one white and one Negro—who had pulled a recalcitrant Negro woman out of a stalled car that had blocked an intersection in the Negro district. A rumor spread that one of the policemen had killed the woman, and police reinforcements were rushed to the scene as rocks and bottles were hurled. Widespread violence and looting began 90 minutes later. The police tried to repulse the crowds with nightsticks. But, despite their efforts, store windows were smashed, shops were looted, police cars were battered, and the district's streets were littered with debris thrown from windows and roofs.

Acting under emergency powers conferred on him by an 1850 law, Philadelphia Mayor James H. J. Tate quarantined the 125 blocks of the Negro section Aug. 29. He ordered residents "to disperse themselves and peaceably depart to their habitations." 1,500 policemen were sent to the riot area. Some policemen were pelted with stones, but violence the night of Aug. 29 was sporadic and was controlled by the anti-riot forces. Tate had said at a news conference Aug. 29 that the rioting had "nothing to do with civil rights or any proper or fair grievance" and that he was not aware of any outside influences that could have instigated such rioting. But Terry Chisholm, executive director of the city's Commission on Human Relations, insisted there had been adequate warnings from other riot-torn northern cities that "blood brothers" would start riots in Philadelphia.

Police Commissioner Howard R. Leary lauded Negro leaders, especially Philadelphia NAACP Chapter Pres. Cecil B. Moore, who had toured the Negro section Aug. 29, appealing to its residents to avoid further violence and remain at home. Moore lauded the police Aug. 30 for having exercised "a remarkable degree of restraint" during the rioting. Rep. Robert N. C. Nix (D., Pa.), a Philadelphia Negro, said of the police: "I think they handled themselves admirably. I have higher respect for them now than I ever had before."

A squad of 100 patrolmen Aug. 31 raided the North Philadelphia headquarters of Shaykh Muhammad Harsan (formerly
Abyssinia Hayes), 33, Philadelphia leader of a separatist
Black Muslim group known as the National Muslim Improvement Association of America, and found a pistol, 2 bayonets,
2 assembled fire bombs (Molotov cocktails) and the materials
for 10 more. Muhammad was arrested on a charge of possessing
bombs and explosives. Muhammad was rearrested Sept. 14 with
a follower, Raymond Hall, 26, also known as Yusseff Abdulla.
They were arraigned Sept. 15 on charges of inciting the Aug.
28-30 riots in North Philadelphia. They were accused of
spreading a rumor that police had beaten a pregnant woman to
death and of encouraging looters. Florence Mobley, 23, a typist,
was arrested in Philadelphia Sept. 17 on the same charge. An
all-white jury Nov. 10 convicted Muhammad of complicity in
inciting the riots.

Riots in Other Northern Cities

Negroes fought police in Jersey City, N.J. Aug. 2-4
following a rumor of police brutality against an arrested
Negro. Looting and clashes between Negroes and police were
reported. At least 56 persons, including 22 policemen, were
injured. 36 persons were arrested. 68 stores were damaged
and 18 looted. Negro spokesmen stressed alleged police brutality as their major grievance.

Racial violence swept the New Jersey cities of Paterson
and Elizabeth Aug. 11-13. At least 22 persons were arrested
and 4 injured in Paterson, and 18 persons were arrested in
Elizabeth. Little looting was reported. The Paterson flare-up
began when Negro youths leaving a city-sponsored dance threw
rocks at police cars the night of Aug. 11.

Rioting broke out in the integrated Chicago suburb of
Dixmoor, Ill. Aug. 16 after a rumor spread that a white man
had attacked a Negro woman. The white man, a liquor store
owner, had accused her of shop-lifting a bottle of gin. About
1,000 Negroes clashed with 225 state troopers and other policemen, who fired shots into the air. 31 Negroes were arrested
and at least 50 persons, mostly white, injured. The liquor
store in which the trouble had started was looted Aug. 16 and
set afire the next day. 2 other houses were also set afire Aug.
17, and 50 autos (including police cars) were damaged.

President Orders Inquiry

Pres. Johnson July 21 ordered the FBI to investigate the N.Y. City riots for possible violations of federal laws and for the possible presence of Communist or subversive influence in the rioting. "It must be made clear, once and for all, that violence and lawlessness cannot, must not and will not be tolerated," he emphasized. Mr. Johnson asserted at his July 24 news conference that "extremist elements" had been involved in the New York disorders. This was "the impression I gain from reading" preliminary FBI reports on the recent racial disturbances, the President said.

Mr. Johnson declared at his July 30 news conference that he "would not argue with anyone who chose to pursue a policy of registration [to vote] in lieu of demonstration," but "it is understandable that those who are aggrieved will take the streets."

Speaking at the 87th annual meeting of the American Bar Association in New York Aug. 12 the President pledged that "we will not permit any part of America to become a jungle where the weak are the prey of the strong and the many." He condemned both the recent murders of civil rights workers in the South and the Negro riots in Northern cities. Mr. Johnson said at his Sept. 9 news conference: "I am asking the FBI to give me a compilation of their reports on the various problems that we have encountered in cities and in states that could involve a violation of federal laws, and do involve disturbances such as riots and disturbances of the peace. . . . I will review those [reports] and try to compile them if I find any pattern that is common to all of them, and ask that further study be made."

The FBI reported to the President Sept. 26 that the summer riots in Northern cities apparently had been spontaneous and were not "race riots in the accepted meaning of the phrase," although "racial tensions were a contributing factor." The FBI report said there was "no systematic planning or organization" behind the riots. They were described as not "riots of Negroes against whites or whites against Negroes" but rather "senseless attack[s] on all constituted authority without purpose or object." The report attributed the riots to youths "variously characterized by responsible people as 'school dropouts,' 'young punks,' 'common hoodlums' and 'drunken kids.'" It said that "rioting by these young people reflects an increasing breakdown across the nation in respect for the law and the rights of other people to be secure in their person and their property." 6 of the 7 major city riots began as "an escalation from a minor incident, normal in character," the FBI reported. It said that "the Communist Party U.S.A. does not appear to have officially instigated these riots, though its members were observed taking part" in some.

The report held that "where there is an outside civilian [police] review board the restraint of the police was so great that effective action against the rioters appeared to be impossible. . . . The police were so careful to avoid accusation of improper conduct that they were virtually paralyzed." (The Rev. William H. Gray Jr., executive secretary of Philadelphia's police review board, declared Sept. 27 that "it's oversimplifying the situation to say that the board has an effect on the rioting or the police behavior." Ross J. Guglielmino, executive director of the Rochester police review board, said that "if restraint weren't used, a more violent reaction might result that might bring permanent harm to the community.") The report asserted that "the arrival of large numbers of reporters and television cameras at the riots provided an opportunity for self-seeking individuals to publicize wild charges. . . . These circumstances provided additional incitement to the rioters and served to attract others to the scene."

Pres. Johnson Sept. 26 announced these actions to prevent a repetition of the riots: (a) His orders to the FBI to "make riot training available to all police departments" in the U.S. (b) His directions that the Army's riot control techniques be made "a larger part of the training of the National Guard of the various states" and "available to local police forces as well." (c) His instructions that Health-Education-Welfare Secy. Anthony J. Celebrezze study Washington, D.C.'s program to cope with school dropouts and determine "what further steps might be taken by the federal government to assist in meeting this important problem." (d) His decision to call, at an "appropriate time," a conference of state and city officials to discuss how the federal government could help solve local problems that tended to lead to riots.

Moratorium on Demonstrations Urged

4 Negro leaders July 29 signed a statement calling on Negroes to observe a "broad curtailment, if not total morato-

rium," on mass demonstrations until after the Nov. 3 Presidential election. The statement declared: "Our own estimate of the present situation is that it presents such a serious threat to the implementation of the Civil Rights Act . . . that we recommend a voluntary, temporary alteration in strategy and procedure." The 4 leaders charged that harmful "racism has been injected into the campaign by the Goldwater forces." The 4 signers were Roy Wilkins of the NAACP, the Rev. Dr. Martin Luther King Jr. of the Southern Christian Leadership Conference, Whitney M. Young Jr. of the National Urban League and A. Philip Randolph of the Negro American Labor Council. John Lewis of the Student Nonviolent Coordinating Committee and James Farmer of CORE refused to sign. Farmer explained July 31: "People must be allowed to protest, must be allowed to demonstrate."

SCHOOL INTEGRATION

Southern Public-Schoool Developments

Civil rights workers continued during 1964 to press for the integration of Southern schools. Despite several court victories and some voluntary integration, reports indicated that only token school desegregation had been achieved in the South. U.S. Education Commissioner Francis Keppel said at an annual conference of the National Urban League in Louisville, Ky. Aug. 3 that schools refusing to desegregate within a reasonable time would not receive federal funds under legislation providing $1.48 billion for aid-to-education programs for fiscal 1965.

Tuskegee (Ala.) High School was closed by the Macon County school board Jan. 31 under orders of Gov. George C. Wallace and the Alabama Board of Education. All white students had been withdrawn after the school's desegregation in Sept. 1963, and only 12 Negro students were attending. The Alabama Board of Education, acting Feb. 18 under a State Supreme Court advisory opinion, repealed its order closing Tuskegee High School and its authorization that the county board make state-aid tuition grants available to white pupils attending a private, segregated school. A temporary restraining order issued Feb. 3 by U.S. District Judge Frank M. Johnson Jr. had barred further state interference with public school desegregation in Tuskegee County. Under Johnson's orders, 6 of the 12 Negro students were transferred to Notasulga High School and the other 6 to Shorter High School; both schools were then boycotted by all white students, who transferred to a newly established private school, Macon Academy, which the state accredited Feb. 14. The Notasulga school was destroyed by fire Apr. 18. A 3-judge federal court in Montgomery, Ala. ordered Gov. Wallace and the Alabama Board of Education July 13 not to interfere with court orders barring school segregation. The court ordered the board to "promote and encourage the elimination of racial discrimination" in the schools.

Negroes enrolled in 4 of the 9 white high schools in Birmingham Sept. 3, and 2 Negroes started their 2d year at a previously all-white elementary school. About 100 white segregationists jeered the Negro pupils. 8 Negroes enrolled at 3 white schools in Montgomery Sept. 8, and 20 Negroes enrolled at 3 white schools in Gadsden. 7 Negro pupils entered 3 formerly white public schools in Mobile Sept. 10 in the 2d year of school desegregation.

The Little Rock (Ark.) Board of Education Mar. 24 adopted a plan to desegregate all 12 grades of its schools by the 1964-65 school year. But Negroes protested that integration was "painfully slow" and that only 118 of the city's 7,000 Negro pupils had been assigned to formerly all-white schools. Negro leaders announced a boycott of Little Rock public schools for Apr. 6 but called it off Apr. 3 when the school board reversed itself and agreed to appoint a biracial committee to look into the situation.

The U.S. Supreme Court May 25 unanimously held unconstitutional the closing of public schools (to avoid desegregation) in Prince Edward County, Va. while public schools remained open in other counties of Virginia. The court ruled, 7-2, that federal courts could order Prince Edward County to levy taxes and raise funds to reopen the schools. Federal District Judge Oren R. Lewis ruled in Richmond June 17 that Prince Edward County officials would have to levy new taxes to provide funds for the resumption of public education after a 5-year lapse. The County Board of Supervisors June 23 voted, 4-2, to appropriate $189,000 by taxation for school board use "in reopening, operating and maintaining public schools without racial discrimination." Federal Appeals Court Judge J. Spencer Bell in Charlotte, N.C. July 2 barred the Prince Edward County Board of Supervisors from making retroactive payments to parents of white children for tuition expenses incurred when they attended segregated private schools. He held that payment of retroactive school tuition grants, designed to circumvent a previous federal court injunction, would inflict "irreparable injury" on the rights of Negro parents. The Board of Supervisors Aug. 5 began disbursing tuition payments ($145 per elementary school child, $155 per high school pupil for a semester) to parents of white children planning to attend the private, segregated school of the Prince Edward School Foundation in September. 7 white children and 1,400 Negroes attended public schools in Prince Edward County Sept. 8 as public education resumed there after a 5-year lapse. 1,200 whites remained in private schools.

Federal District Judge John D. Butzner Jr. ruled in Richmond June 19 that public tax money could no longer be used for students attending private schools in Surry County, Va., which had closed its only white school in 1963 after all 431 students enrolled in the hastily-organized private segregated Surry Academy. The county had payed the white parents tuition grants of up to $275 a year, and Surry Academy had charged $380. Butzner enjoined the county from "failing to operate Surry school or any other school under its jurisdiction and control while any other school . . . in Virginia is operated."

Public schools in Amelia County, Va. were desegregated without incident Aug. 31.

Federal District Judge Sidney C. Mize in Jackson, Miss. July 7 ordered that public schools in Jackson, Biloxi and Leake County, Miss. be desegregated a grade at a time starting in September. Mize asserted that his order was "contrary to the facts and the law applicable thereto" but explained that he had no choice because of previous higher court rulings. (Mize cited evidence that he claimed was "conclusive to the effect that the cranial capacity and brain size of the average Negro is approximately 10% less than that of the average white person of similar age and size, and that brain size is correlated with intelligence.") The 3 affected school districts submitted desegregation plans July 15. 17 Negro pupils registered for the first grade in 4 previously all-white schools in Biloxi Aug. 14 and started school without incident Aug. 31; they were the first Negroes ever accepted in any Mississippi public school below college level. No Negroes applied Aug. 28 when 4 Leake County schools opened their rolls to Negroes. 8 Negro pupils authorized under Mize's order to enter Leake

County's white rural Carthage schools abandoned the idea Sept. 1. Their lawyer said white community leaders had brought pressure against the children's parents. But one Negro girl enrolled in the first grade under federal and local police protection. 24 Negroes, including Ben Chaney, brother of slain civil rights worker James Chaney, were turned down Sept. 4 when they sought to enroll at 5 white elementary schools in Meridian, Miss. 13 Negroes were denied admittance to the Canton, Miss. all-white high school Sept. 8. 39 Negroes attended first grade at 8 white elementary schools in Jackson without incident Sept. 14.

A study made public by the Civil Rights Commission in Washington July 25 reported that North Carolina had "made little progress in desegregating its public schools in 1962-63." The study, prepared by Prof. Richard E. Day of the University of North Carolina Law School, said that 155 of the state's 173 school districts remained totally segregated and that only one out of every 400 Negro students in the state attended school with white children.

2 Negro boys and a Negro girl attended a previously all-white St. Helena Parish high school in Greensburg, La. Aug. 17. This was the first desegregation of a school in rural Louisiana.

Kirkwood Elementary School in Atlanta and high schools in Monroe and Covington, Ga. refused to enroll Negroes Aug. 28, but 3 Negroes entered the formerly all-white high school in Americus, Ga. Aug. 31, and 16 Negroes entered 3 Macon, Ga. high schools under a court-approved plan Sept. 1. Negroes also attended public schools without incident in Augusta and Marietta, Ga. Aug. 31. 21 Negro first and 2d graders were admitted to 5 white schools in Albany, Ga. Sept. 8.

Formerly white Orangeburg, S.C. schools enrolled 19 Negroes Aug. 28, and 4 Negroes entered white schools in Ocone County, S.C. Public schools were desegregated without incident in Richland and Beaufort counties, S.C. Aug. 31. 49 Negroes entered 15 previously white schools in Greenville, S.C. Sept. 1; 13 enrolled in white schools in Darlington and Hartsville, S.C., and 7 entered Rock Hill (S.C.) High School. 84 Negroes attended integrated classes in Charleston, S.C. Sept. 2 at the start of the 2d year of court-ordered school desegregation.

Integrated classes began Sept. 8 in Mount Sterling, Ky., where the city's Negro school had been burned down Aug. 31.

More Negroes in 'White' Southern Universities

Auburn (Ala.) University enrolled its first Negro student for the graduate school's winter term Jan. 4 without incident. The admittance of the Negro, Harold Alonzo Franklin, 31, had been ordered by U.S. District Judge Frank M. Johnson Jr. Nov. 5, 1963. Auburn enrolled its 2d Negro, in a federally-financed graduate-school program, June 11.

2 Negro teachers were enrolled for the summer session at the University of Alabama June 8. This brought the total number of Negroes enrolled at the university to 3. Vivian Malone, the first of the 3, who had been attending regular classes, returned to the campus June 8 for the summer session.

A Negro was enrolled in pre-law courses at Louisiana State University June 8 and became the first Negro under-graduate admitted there. U.S. District Judge E. Gordon West ordered LSU later June 8 to enroll 7 other Negro under-graduates. Northeast Louisiana State College in Monroe, La. enrolled its first 3 Negroes June 10-11.

Southern Parochial Schools Integrate

The Most Rev. Thomas J. Toolen, archbishop of the Mobile-Birmingham Roman Catholic diocese, Apr. 26 ordered the desegregation in September of Catholic parochial schools in Alabama and in 11 counties of northwest Florida. The order affected about 25,000 pupils (5,000 Negroes) in Alabama, where there had been no integration.

The Most Rev. Richard O. Gerow, bishop of the Natchez-Jackson diocese, announced in a pastoral letter read at Roman Catholic church services throughout Mississippi Aug. 9 that all Catholic elementary schools in the state would admit Catholic pupils to the first grade in September "without regard to race."

Northern School Developments

Agitation to eliminate *de facto* segregation in Northern schools was continued at an accelerated rate during 1964. Among developments of the Northern school campaigns:

Boston—A school boycott was staged in Boston Feb. 26 in protest against alleged *de facto* segregation. Absences totaled 20,500, about twice the daily norm (12,000-14,000 Negro pupils were in the system). That night about 1,000 integrationists, mostly students, staged a silent march to city hall, where their leaders met with Mayor John F. Collins.

Chester, Pa.—Demonstrations against alleged *de facto* school segregation led to clashes between police and demonstrators in Chester, Pa. Mar. 28 and to the arrest Apr. 1 of 10[7] demonstrators, including 50 juveniles, who sat down in the street in front of police headquarters. Public schools in Chester were closed Apr. 22 following fighting between police and demonstrators. The demonstrations had been resumed after a 3-day truce and mediation by the State Human Relations Commission had yielded no results. 219 persons were arrested Apr. 22, and state police were called in 3 times during the following week. Gov. William W. Scranton called both sides to a meeting with him in Philadelphia Apr. 26 and ordered the Human Relations Commission to reenter the dispute. Schools then reopened without incident Apr. 17-28.

Chicago—172,350 pupils were absent in an anti-segregation boycott of Chicago public schools Feb. 25. (Normal absenteeism was 40,000.) The boycott was backed by local chapters of CORE and the Student Nonviolent Coordinating Committee and by Negro comedian Dick Gregory and gospel singer Mahalia Jackson. It was opposed by Mayor Richard J. Daley and Negro Congressman William L. Dawson (D.), and it lacked the participation of the local NAACP and Catholic and Presbyterian Interracial Councils, which had participated in an Oct. 1963 boycott.

Cincinnati—26,400 Cincinnati pupils were absent Feb. 11. About 19,000 of them were considered participants in a boycott called by CORE and the NAACP in protest against alleged *de facto* school segregation.

Cleveland—Integrationists picketed public schools in Cleveland, O. Jan. 29-Feb. 3 in protest against the segregation of Negro pupils in formerly all-white schools. The Negroes were being transported from predominantly Negro schools. Pickets demanding full integration appeared Jan. 29 at several of the schools and were attacked by some whites. The tension was eased when the Board of Education, which had planned to integrate the transported classes in September, agreed Feb. 4 to integrate immediately.

The Rev. Bruce William Klunder, 26, a white Presbyterian minister and local CORE official, was accidentally run over and killed by a bulldozer while participating in a civil rights demonstration at a school construction site in Cleveland Apr. 7. Rights groups had charged that construction of schools on disputed sites—in Negro neighborhoods—would perpetuate *de facto* segregation.

75,603 (86%) of Cleveland's 150,000 Negro public school pupils boycotted their schools Apr. 20 in protest against the building of schools on 3 sites in Negro neighborhoods instead of on sites that would promote integration. A 5-year-old Negro girl was accidentally killed by a bus while leaving one of the "freedom schools" set up during the boycott. The demonstration was sponsored by the United Freedom Movement, which had also called for a Negro boycott of downtown stores.

Gary, Ind.—Public schools were boycotted by Gary, Ind. Negroes Apr. 17 in protest against alleged *de facto* segregation. 19,182 pupils were absent out of an enrollment of 47,376; 16,103 of the absences were attributed to the boycott.

The U.S. Supreme Court May 4 declined to review a Circuit Court of Appeals ruling upholding Gary's neighborhood school policy. The NAACP, which had backed the suit, had argued that it was unconstitutional for the school board to "acquiesce" in alleged de facto segregation resulting from the neighborhood policy.

Kansas City—Public schools were boycotted by Negroes in Kansas City, Mo. Apr. 20 in protest against alleged *de facto* segregation. Attendance at schools with predominantly Negro enrollment was cut 50%.

N.Y. City—Negro, Puerto Rican and some white pupils boycotted N.Y. City public schools for one day Feb. 3 in protest against alleged *de facto* segregation. 464,362 (44.8%) of the school system's 1,037,757 pupils were absent (usual absentee rate: 10%), and 8.04% of the 43,974 teachers were also out (usual rate: 3%). Some teachers were among the 2,600 pickets marching at 300 of the city's 860 public schools. The generally peaceful boycott and demonstrations were directed by Bayard Rustin and were sponsored by the Citywide Committee for Integrated Schools, a coalition of 4 civil rights groups—the NAACP, CORE, the Harlem Parents Committee and the Parents' Workshop for Equality. (The Urban League of Greater New York, the National Association for Puerto Rican Civil Rights and several other groups joined later.) The Rev. Milton A. Galamison was committee chairman. The N.Y. City Board of Education Jan. 29 had attempted to forestall the boycott by presenting a 3-year school "pairing" plan. The board's plan provided for desegregating 20 of the 134 elementary schools and 10 of the 31 junior high schools with more than 85-90% Negro and/or Puerto Rican enrollment. But the plan did not satisfy the demands of integration leaders.

About 2,500 Puerto Ricans led by Gilberto Gerena-Valentin demonstrated Mar. 1 in a demand for better schools and integration of Puerto Rican students. They marched from City Hall in Manhattan over the Brooklyn Bridge to Board of Education headquarters in Brooklyn.

About 15,000 persons, most of them whites, demonstrated at City Hall Mar. 12 in favor of the current neighborhood school system and against the plan to pair schools.

A 2d school boycott took place Mar. 16 in protest against alleged *de facto* segregation, but the pupil absentee rate this time was only 26% (267,459 children), and teacher attendance was normal (1,933 absences). More than 2,000 demonstrators marched on Board of Education headquarters in Brooklyn, where James B. Donovan, board president, said: "We are encouraged that the boycott method of expressing a point of view is regarded with markedly diminishing favor." Galamison, however, called the boycott "a success," despite the fact that the national leadership of the NAACP, CORE, Urban League and other rights organizations refused to support it.

State Education Commissioner James E. Allen Jr. May 12 recommended a plan to eliminate racial imbalance in the N.Y. City school system and provide better education. City School Superintendent Calvin E. Gross May 28 announced a plan that was substantially the same as Allen's. Gross called for: (a) transferring 4,511 9th-graders from 10 junior high schools, 9 of which were predominantly Negro and Puerto Rican, to 36 integrated high schools; transferring 5,804 6th-graders from 44 elementary schools to the vacancies created in the 10 junior high schools; (b) pairing 4 predominantly Negro and Puerto Rican elementary schools with 4 schools that were predominantly white; (c) rezoning 8 junior high schools to reduce racial imbalance at 3 largely Negro schools; (d) establishing pre-kindergarten classes and expanding kindergarten programs; (e) increasing some children's instruction hours. Many white parents promptly opposed the plan on the ground that their children would have to be bused to schools outside their immediate neighborhoods; many integration leaders also opposed it at first as not going far enough. A series of subse-

quent court decisions generally favored the pairing and rezoning program.

When the new school year opened in N.Y. City, the Parents
& Taxpayers Coordinating Council and the Joint Council for
Better Education sponsored a public school boycott Sept. 14-
15 in protest against pairing and rezoning steps. Absentee rates
were reported at 27% the first day and 23% the 2d. About 2,000
white mothers picketed public schools. The boycotters insisted
that they did not oppose school integration and were acting not
because of prejudice but because the school plans adopted imposed undue hardships on their children. Leaders of groups
supporting the disputed plans rejected this explanation and
accused the boycotters of anti-Negro bias.

N.Y. State—An order to end *de facto* segregation in the
Manhasset, N.Y. elementary school grades was issued Jan. 24
by U.S. District Judge Joseph C. Zavatt. The suit was instituted
by the NAACP on behalf of Negro parents who charged that
their children were being discriminated against by being required to attend a predominantly Negro school although the
district had 2 all-white schools. Zavatt called the separation
of the children "state-imposed segregation." He said the plaintiffs "have the civil right not to be segregated, not to be compelled to attend a school in which all of the Negro children are
educated separate and apart from over 99% of their white con-
temporaries."

The Appellate Division of the N.Y. State Supreme Court
July 22 unanimously upheld a 1963 order by State Education
Commissioner Allen directing the Malverne public school district to reassign Negro pupils at an elementary school with a
75% Negro enrollment to schools with predominantly white
enrollments.

VOTING RIGHTS

Increased Registration Reported

The Southern Regional Council announced in Atlanta Feb.
12 that its voter education project, conducted in the South Apr.
1, 1962-Dec. 31, 1963 at a cost of $505,640, had resulted in the
registration of 327,588 persons. About 265,000 were Negroes,
about 60,590 (in Texas) white Latin Americans. The NAACP,
CORE, Southern Christian Leadership Conference, Student
Nonviolent Coordinating Committee and National Urban League

participated in the drive. By Apr. 1, the end of the 2-year period, 500,000 Southern Negroes had been added as registered voters, according to an Aug. 2 council announcement. This brought the total of registered Negro voters in 11 Southern states to almost 2 million. White registration was estimated at 13,600,000.

Courts Act on Bias Complaints

The Supreme Court Jan. 13 invalidated a Louisiana law requiring that the race of a political candidate be printed on the ballot. The court ruled that "race is the factor upon which the statute operates, and its involvement promotes the ultimate discrimination which is sufficient to make it invalid." The decision reversed a 2-1 ruling by a 3-judge federal district court that any discrimination involved was in the voter reaction to the label and not to the labeling itself, which was applied equally to all candidates. The suit had been instituted on behalf of Deputy H. Anderson and Acie J. Belton, unsuccessful Negro candidates for election to the East Baton Rouge school board in 1962.

U.S. District Judge J. Robert Elliott in Americus, Ga. Jan. 27 issued a permanent injunction ordering Terrell County, Dawson City and Sasser town officials and 8 Sasser residents to cease intimidation, threats and coercion against participants in a Georgia Negro voter registration drive.

A 3-judge federal court in Jackson, Miss. Mar. 6 dismissed, by a 2-1 decision, a Justice Department suit charging that Mississippi's voting laws were designed to bar Negroes from voting and were therefore unconstitutional. The suit had challenged provisions requiring voters to be of good moral character and able to read, write and interpret the U.S. Constitution. The court said that the state requirement "does discriminate—but in a way that is nowise unconstitutional" since it tended to "improve the quality of the electorate though . . . [it] might curtail its numbers." The majority consisted of District Judge Harold Cox and Appeals Court Judge Ben Cameron. Appeals Court Judge John R. Brown dissented.

The Justice Department Nov. 6 filed a suit asking the U.S. District Court in Birmingham, Ala. to bar the Board of Registrars of Jefferson County (which included Birmingham) from using a new voter registration questionnaire testing the ability of voter applicants to answer questions about the government and the Constitution. The suit charged that the new questionnaire was designed to discriminate against Negro applicants. U.S. District Judge Frank M. Johnson Jr. in Montgomery, Ala. Dec. 17 invalidated a Montgomery County voter registration questionnaire that also had required new applicants to answer a series of questions about the federal government and Constitution.

A 3-judge federal court in Alexandria, Va. Nov. 12 upheld the constitutionality of the $1.50-a-year Virginia poll tax imposed as a voting qualification in state and local elections. The court ruled against 6 Negroes who maintained they had been denied, "solely on account of [their] poverty, the privilege to vote."

Negroes Win Tuskegee (Ala.) Run-off

The Rev. K. L. Buford, a civil rights leader, and Dr. Stanley Hugh Smith, a sociology professor at Tuskegee Institute, both Negroes, defeated white incumbents in the Sept. 15 Tuskegee (Ala.) City Council run-off election. They were the first Negroes elected to public office against white opponents in Alabama in the 20th century.

ACCOMMODATIONS & FACILITIES

Widespread Desegregation Action

Efforts to end racial discrimination in public accommodations were continued in most areas of the country during 1964. Among developments reported:

Albany, Ga.—Recorders Court Judge Adie N. Durden July 9 sentenced 10 Negro civil rights workers to 30 days in a road gang or fines of $102 each for trying to enter the segregated Tift Park pool in Albany July 5. They were charged with violation of a city vagrancy ordinance. The judge called the defendants "agitators from New York," and told them: "Go back and clean up your own state."

Atlanta—Mayor Ivan Allen Jr. urged the Atlanta Board of Aldermen Jan. 6 to accept the "challenge to complete the elimination of discrimination from all public accommodations." He simultaneously noted a 93% increase in Negro employment in city jobs and abandonment of the "double register" in municipal employment. The following day John Lewis, national chairman of the Student Nonviolent Coordinating Committee, led more than 150 Negro high school students in an anti-segregation demonstration at Allen's office.

14 of Atlanta's major hotels and motels agreed Jan. 11 to accept reservations regardless of race. Some already had been under the "Dallas plan" of accepting Negroes as convention participants. The Negro Leadership Conference, a unified movement of 85 civil rights groups in Atlanta, decided later Jan. 11 on a "direct action" campaign against the city's remaining segregated hotels and restaurants. The plan was devised by Wyatt Tee Walker. A planned demonstration by Negroes at a hamburger restaurant led to a clash with police and the arrest of 78 persons Jan. 18. The demonstrators remained outside while robed and hooded Ku Klux Klan members filled the seats inside the restaurant. After the Klansmen left a scuffle broke out between police and demonstrators attempting to get into the restaurant. Similar confrontations between Negro demonstrators and Klansmen took place Jan. 25-27 at Leb's, a segregated midtown restaurant. More than 150 Negroes were arrested in 3 separate demonstrations Jan. 27; they included comedian Dick Gregory and James Forman, executive secretary of the Student Nonviolent Coordinating Committee.

Mayor Allen met Jan. 29 with more than 200 white and Negro leaders, appealed for a truce in demonstrations and warned that the city would be tougher toward future demonstrators. But tensions were eased Jan. 30 with the release of all but 43 of 154 demonstrators still in jail. 11 of them were fined $33 each and given 30-day suspended sentences. The Negro Leadership Conference agreed Jan. 31 to a 30-day truce if (a) charges against arrested demonstrators were dropped, (b) hotel, motel and restaurant operators were called together to devise voluntary desegregation plans, (c) open policies were adopted in the city's public hospital and in all federal housing facilities and (d) the city agreed to promote equal employment opportunities. Allen rejected the terms Feb. 1.

Gadsden—U.S. District Judge H. Hobart Grooms in Birmingham, Ala. Apr. 22 directed that all public facilities in Gadsden, Ala. be desegregated. He issued a permanent injunction to bar discriminatory acts by city officials against Negroes.

Jackson—The U.S. Supreme Court Feb. 17 rejected an appeal by the city of Jackson, Miss. against a 1963 U.S. Court of Appeals decision ordering the desegregation of all transportation in Jackson and the state of Mississippi. U.S. District

Judge Sidney C. Mize, under Supreme Court order to require integrated transportation service, had held segregation laws invalid but had refused to issue compliance orders against the carriers involved. The case had been brought by 3 Jackson Negroes, Samuel Bailey, Joseph Broadwater and Burnett L. Jacobs.

Following the passage of the Civil Rights Act of 1964, Mayor Allen C. Thompson joined the Jackson Chamber of Commerce in urging compliance with the act. Thompson, a White Citizens Council member, declared July 12 that although the law was "repugnant" it "must be obeyed until changed." Thompson and the city commissioners ordered a city park closed July 15 after almost 600 white residents of the area had protested that unruly groups of Negro youths had taken over the park and made it unsafe.

Kansas City–A Kansas City, Mo. ordinance barring discrimination in public accommodations was approved in a referendum Apr. 7 by 45,850-to-44,030 vote. It extended the city's 1962 ban on bias in hotels, motels, and restaurants to taverns, transportation facilities, retail stores, trade schools, amusement parks, hospitals and other places serving the public.

Kentucky–10,000 persons participated in an orderly march to the state capitol in Frankfort Mar. 5 to demonstrate support of passage of a state public accommodations law. The Rev. Dr. Martin Luther King Jr. addressed the participants and then conferred with Gov. Edward T. Breathitt. The rally was followed by a sit-in and fast by about 25 persons in the state House of Representatives Mar. 16-17. But the House Mar. 19 rejected a last effort to bring an accommodations law before the current General Assembly session. The House, however, approved by 72-0 vote a resolution favoring voluntary integration of public facilities. Breathitt Mar. 12 had rescinded the 1963 executive order of ex-Gov. Bert T. Combs barring discrimination in places of public accommodation.

Louisiana–The U.S. Supreme Court Jan. 6 upheld a lower court decision upsetting a Louisiana law requiring segregation at sports events and entertainments open to the public.

Maryland–The Maryland General Assembly Mar. 14 enacted a statewide Public Accommodations Law barring discrimination against Negroes in hotels, motels and restaurants that did not sell liquor. Gov. J. Millard Tawes' last-minute support enabled the bill's backers to repulse rural efforts to obtain local options or exemptions for certain counties. The law went into effect June 1.

McComb—10 Negro men and 10 Negro women led by NAACP field secretary Charles Evers ate in previously all-white restaurants in McComb, Miss. Nov. 18 without incident. By Nov. 17 more than 650 white citizens in the McComb area had signed a statement, drafted by 20 business and civic leaders, urging equal treatment for Negroes and an end to the area's racial violence.

Oklahoma City— The Oklahoma City Council June 2 adopted an ordinance barring public businesses from refusing services or facilities to persons because of race, religion, color, creed, ancestry or national origin. This was Oklahoma's first public accommodations ordinance. Hundreds of Negroes from several cities in Oklahoma marched around the state capitol in Oklahoma City June 6 demanding that the State Legislature adopt a state-wide public accommodations law in 1965.

Seattle—Seattle voters Mar. 10 rejected an "open housing" ordinance by a margin of more than 2-1.

Virginia—The Community Relations Service (CRS) established under the 1964 Civil Rights Act reported in a letter to U.S. District Judge John D. Butzner Jr. in Richmond, Va. Nov. 25 that it had "exhausted all of its means" but had failed to win "immediate and voluntary compliance" by the Lee House Diner, a Petersburg, Va. restaurant that refused to serve Negroes. Butzner had referred the dispute to the CRS Sept. 26. The CRS in Washington Nov. 25 called the Petersburg matter "our first clear failure." It also was the first case ever referred by a court to the CRS. (Among cases processed by the CRS so far, 8 were "resolved and cleared." 17 were referred to other agencies, and 45 were still being assessed or mediated.)

Hospitals—The U.S. Supreme Court Mar. 2 upheld, by refusing to review, a 1963 U.S. 4th Circuit Court of Appeals decision that hospitals built with federal aid may not segregate patients or staff.

EMPLOYMENT OPPORTUNITY

Discrimination in Unions Attacked

The N.Y. State Commission for Human Rights ruled Mar. 4 that Local 28 of the Sheet Metal Workers International Association had "automatically excluded" Negroes from membership throughout the union's 76-year history. The commission, declaring such discrimination contrary to state law, announced Mar. 23 that it had ordered the union to discard its apprenticeship list and take other measures to end its exclusion of Negroes.

White union plumbers on the N.Y. City Terminal Market construction project walked out Apr. 30 when 4 non-union men—3 Puerto Ricans and a Negro—reported for work. Plumbers Local 2, the union involved, contended that the sole issue was that of union membership and that racial bias was not involved. The union's position was supported by AFL-CIO Pres. George Meany, who had started his labor career as a Local 2 member. But plumbers who had walked off the job had made it clear that their motive was racial. CORE pickets blocked access to the plumber union's offices starting May 11 but withdrew May 15 when Mayor Robert F. Wagner announced that the union had agreed to give entrance tests to the 4 new men and they would be allowed to start work if they passed. 3 of the 4 took the union test for journeyman plumbers and failed May 18. The white plumbers then resumed work.

The National Labor Relations Board July 2 ruled, 3-2, that the Taft-Hartley Act banned racial discrimination by a labor union as an unfair labor practice. The board stripped Local 1 of the Independent Metal Workers Union of its certification as bargaining agent for employes of the Hughes Tool Co. of Houston, Tex. because the all-white local had refused to process a grievance filed by Ivory Davis, a Negro and member of the all-Negro Local 2 of the same union. Davis had protested his elimination from a list of employes who had applied for apprenticeship openings.

N.Y. State Supreme Court Justice Jacob J. Markowitz ruled Aug. 24 that the law and "the realities of today's society" demanded that unions drop any apprentice-selection plan that "could be used directly or indirectly, to discriminate against any person on the basis of race, color, creed or national origin." The ruling was handed down as an order that Local 28 of the Sheet Metal Workers International Association implement its agreement to end its practice of giving preference, in selecting apprentices, to the sons and sons-in-law of current or deceased members.

N.Y. State regulations aimed at ending anti-Negro discrimination by ending preference to relatives in some union apprentice programs went into effect Sept. 1.

San Francisco Hotel Pact

Negotiators for minority groups and the Hotel Employers Association, representing San Francisco's 33 largest hotels, signed an agreement in San Francisco Mar. 7 calling for an end to anti-bias demonstrations and for a "good faith effort" by member hotels to have 15%-20% of their staffs composed of minority groups by July 20. Charges against more than 100 demonstrators who had been arrested were dismissed. The agreement, signed in Mayor John F. Shelley's office, was reached after a night-long demonstration by about 1,200 pickets at all entrances and in the lobby of the Sheraton-Palace Hotel. 135 of the demonstrators were arrested, but the agreement provided for the dismissal of charges against them and against others arrested in recent demonstrations.

Auto Industry Bias Assailed by NAACP

San Francisco car dealers yielded Apr. 18 to NAACP demands that more Negro salesmen and mechanics be hired. 2,500 demonstrators, 75% of them white, had picketed 6 auto agencies since Apr. 11.

About 500 demonstrators picketed General Motors Corp. headquarters in Detroit May 4 in protest against what NAACP labor secretary Herbert Hill called "the deep pattern of Negro discrimination" at GM and throughout the auto industry. NAACP demonstrators previously had picketed GM offices in Grand Rapids, Mich. and New York.

Unions to Use 'Pressure'

AFL-CIO Pres. George Meany urged 90 union leaders at a Washington conference June 8 to apply "economic pressure" on employers who refused to provide equal job opportunities for Negroes. The idea was to implement the pledge signed by most unions in Nov. 1962 to strive for equal opportunity. The conference was sponsored by the Labor Advisory Council to the President's Committee on Equal Employment Opportunity. (The President's committee had started a program against discrimination in construction industry employment. The committee had trained 40 men, largely from federal agencies, to explain and enforce executive orders barring discrimination by construction contractors receiving any federal aid.)

Situation of Negro Found Precarious

A. Philip Randolph, president of the Negro American Labor Council and the AFL-CIO's only Negro vice president, warned at a Harlem job crisis conference in New York June 13 that "unskilled jobs are being liquidated by the amazingly high number of 2 million a year" and that "the gap between Negro education and training and the requirements of the labor market is widening." "Black workers face a virtually unsolvable problem," Randolph declared.

Pres. Johnson had sent to Congress Mar. 9 a report on unemployment. The report disclosed that: (a) Only 43% of non-white workers with vocational training were using their training; by comparison, 60% of all workers with such training were using their training. (b) Only 70% of Negro male college graduates (compared with 80% of white male college graduates) held professional, technical or managerial jobs. (c) The proportion of persons working in professional and technical occupations was 12% for the entire male population, 8% for men of Puerto Rican parentage who were born in the U.S. (compared with less than 3% for Puerto Ricans who were born in Puerto Rico), 4% for Negroes. (d) There was an increasing tendency for Negroes to withdraw from the work force and from job-hunting.

A July 7 report of the President's Committee on Equal Employment Opportunity showed that in 4,610 companies responding to committee questionnaires, Negro white-collar employment had increased by 17.4% from 1962 to 1963. But the increased Negro white-collar employment reported by the companies amounted to only 1.3% of their total white-collar employment.

An advisory committee reported to the U.S. Commission on Civil Rights July 14 that most Negroes still were restricted to low-echelon jobs in the federal government. It said: "The real test of equal opportunity in the years ahead will lie in the extent to which the government can overcome the restrictions which keep Negroes in the lower positions."

The White House Dec. 20 released a report showing that 299,430 Negroes were employed by the federal government in June 1964. The number of Negroes listed showed increases ranging from 6.8% to 19.5% (over June 1963) in the various federal pay categories. Pres. Johnson said "this progress" was due to "persistent efforts" of the government.

LEADERSHIP & NEGRO RIGHTS

Religious Groups Support Rights Efforts

The 2d national meeting of the National Conference on Religion & Race, a 3-faith conference organized in Chicago in Jan. 1963 to give effective religious support to the rights movement, was held in St. Louis Apr. 13-15. About 100 delegates attended from 18 states. A resolution adopted Apr. 15 opposed arrangements to close the organization's national headquarters in New York and to have its functions absorbed by the 3 organizing groups—the National Council of Churches, the National Catholic Welfare Council and the Synagogue Council of America—on an annually rotating basis. (Local conferences on race and religion had been set up in 56 cities since the national group was formed.)

More than 6,000 clerical and lay representatives of Protestantism, Roman Catholicism and Judaism met Apr. 28 for a National Interreligious Convocation on Civil Rights at Georgetown University in Washington. The convocation, a "witness to social justice," was sponsored by the National Council of Churches, the National Catholic Welfare Conference and the Synagogue Council of America. Pres. Johnson said in an address to the participants Apr. 29: "It is your job—as men of God—to reawaken the conscience of America . . . to direct the immense power of religion in shaping the conduct and thoughts of men toward their brothers in a manner consistent with compassion and love." The leaders of the convocation included the Most Rev. Patrick A. O'Boyle, Catholic archbishop of Washington; the Rev. Dr. Eugene Carson Blake, stated clerk of the United Presbyterian Church; Bishop B. Julian Smith (a Negro) of the Christian Methodist Episcopal Church; Rabbi Uri Miller of Baltimore, president of the Synagogue Council of America.

The General Assembly of the 937,000-member Southern Presbyterian Church, meeting in Montreat, N.C. Apr. 23-28, adopted Apr. 25 a pastoral letter supporting Negro demonstrations. The assembly Apr. 27 ordered the 4,000-church denomination, more than 99% white in membership, to integrate all of its 80 presbyteries in the 16-state Southern area it covered. The assembly Apr. 27 adopted a rule—subject to approval in 1965—that nobody could be excluded from "participation in public worship in the Lord's house on the basis of race, color or class."

The General Assembly of the 3,200,000-member 1,100-church United Presbyterian Church of the U.S.A., the largest U.S. Presbyterian body, urged Presbyterians May 27 to dedicate themselves to the struggle for racial justice. The assembly acted at its annual meeting, held in Oklahoma City May 21-27. The Rev. Edler G. Hawkins, 55, of New York was elected May 21 as the denomination's first Negro moderator.

The general conference of the 10 million-member Methodist Church, meeting in Pittsburgh Apr. 26-May 9, adopted May 4 a resolution in support of orderly civil rights demonstrations. It urged that the Methodist Church be opened to all and that "all Methodist organizations and individual church members . . . secure fair employment practices and non-segregated services in the companies and concerns with which they do business." The conference voted May 7 to provide financial aid to Methodists assailed or economically deprived because of their efforts to remove barriers. The conference also proposed negotiations to unify with Negro Methodist groups.

About 1,200 New Yorkers marched in Washington June 15 to dramatize demands that the civil rights bill be enacted without "crippling amendments" and fully enforced. They were led by the Rev. Edward T. Dugan of Resurrection Roman Catholic Church, Rabbi Alfred L. Friedman of the Union Temple and the Rev. Eugene Houston of Rendall Memorial Presbyterians Church, co-chairman of the Committee on Race & Religion of N.Y. City's Committee of Religious Leaders. Members of the group visited Congress members and joined theological students in a silent civil rights vigil at the Lincoln Memorial.

Martin Luther King Wins Nobel Prize

The Rev. Dr. Martin Luther King Jr., 35, was named by the Nobel Prize Committee in Oslo, Norway Oct. 14 as winner of the Nobel Peace Prize for 1964. King, an Alabama clergyman and president of the Southern Christian Leadership Conference, was the youngest recipient of the prize and the 12th American (the 2d U.S. Negro) to be so honored. King received the announcement in an Atlanta hospital, where he was undergoing a physical check-up. He said "every penny" (about $54,000) would be given to the civil rights movement.

King Oct. 1 had called for an expansion of nonviolent demonstrations to broad political action as the best means of coping with Negro social and economic problems. "Demonstrations can call attention to evil, arouse the conscience of the community, but such demonstrations are not a program for removing evil itself," King told the 8th annual convention of the Southern Christian Leadership Conference in Savannah, Ga. Oct. 1. He said: "We must add our political power to that of other groups, the religious communities, Catholic, Protestant and Jewish, to labor, to the liberals and intellectuals, in order to create a broad and strong political force to insure positive action." (A similar recommendation had been made by Norman Hill, who had resigned as national program director of CORE Sept. 3 and joined the AFL-CIO office in Washington. Hill had criticized CORE for depending too much on demonstrations. He proposed, instead, "a political alliance" with "the progressive sections of the labor movement, and of the churches, liberals, democratic radicals and intellectuals.")

FBI Director J. Edgar Hoover, at a private meeting with Washington newspaperwomen Nov. 18, assailed King as "the most notorious liar in the country." He denounced King for reportedly advising civil rights workers not to report rights violations to FBI agents in Albany, Ga. because the agents were Southerners and would not take any action. Hoover declared: "The truth is that 70% of the agents in the South were born in the North, and 4 out of 5 agents in Albany, Ga. are Northerners." King charged Nov. 19 that Hoover was pursuing the "path of appeasement" with Southern white leaders; he added, however, that Hoover's remarks were excusable because of the heavy burden of his work. King acknowledged in a separate telegram to Hoover Nov. 19 that he had challenged the effectiveness of the FBI in handling Southern racial violence, "particularly where bombings and brutality against Negroes are at issue." King conferred with Hoover at the Justice Department for more than an hour Dec. 1. King, who had requested the discussion, told reporters later that it had been "quite amicable." He said that "a nonviolent leader must seek to maintain communications" with law enforcement officials.

Negro Militants Form 'Act'

The formation of a new Negro group called Act was announced in Washington Apr. 18 by a dozen Negro leaders dissatisfied with current U.S. Negro leadership. Nahaz Rogers of the Negro American Labor Council said: "Act will not function in a manner that is acceptable to white people." Act contended that the 1964 civil rights bill was "not needed" and would be of little help to Northern, urban Negroes. Prominent Act members included: Mrs. Gloria H. Richardson of Cambridge, Md.; Stanley Branch, Chester, Pa.; A. A. Rayner, Chicago, of the Student Nonviolent Coordinating Committee; John Wilson, Princess Anne, Md.; CORE officials Julius W. Hobson, southeastern regional director, and Isiah Brunson, Herbert Callender and Vicki Morris, all of New York. Rep. Adam Clayton Powell Jr. (D., N.Y.) attended the meeting and said he was "a consultant" to Act.

NAACP Convention

The National Association for the Advancement of Colored People held its national convention in Washington June 22-27. Executive Director Roy Wilkins said June 22 that the NAACP would support for reelection all members of Congress who had voted for the 1964 Civil Rights Act. The conference June 27 adopted a resolution deploring Sen. Barry M. Goldwater's "ill-advised stand" against the rights bill and urging Republican National Convention delegates to deny him the Presidential nomination. This was the first time the association had gone on record for or against a Presidential candidate. The NAACP June 27 adopted a resolution urging Pres. Johnson to assume the administration of Mississippi on the ground that the state had failed to maintain the republican form of government guaranteed by Article IV, Section 4 of the Constitution. The resolution appealed to the federal government to intervene to "restore law and order and protect the life and liberties of all citizens in Mississippi." (The Supreme Court had ruled unanimously June 1 that the NAACP was entitled to operate in Alabama. A series of state court rulings had barred it from Alabama since 1956.)

Malcolm X Forms Black Nationalist Party

Malcolm X, who had been suspended as a Black Muslim leader in Nov. 1963, announced in New York Mar. 8 that he was forming a "black nationalist party" that would cooperate with non-Muslim Negro groups. He said the new movement would emphasize "black nationalism as a political concept and form of social action against the oppressors." He warned that "there can be no revolution without bloodshed" and said his group would encourage active self-defense by Negroes instead of nonviolence against white supremacists.

Malcolm X said in New York Mar. 12: "There will be more [racial] violence than ever this year. . . . It is criminal to teach a man not to defend himself when he is the constant victim of brutal attacks. It is legal and lawful to own a shotgun or a rifle." Negroes should form rifle clubs for "self-defence," and the Negro should "fight back whenever and wherever he is being unjustly and unlawfully attacked." "When our people are being bitten by dogs, they are within their rights to kill those dogs." He (Malcolm X) was forming an independent Muslim Mosque, Inc. in which non-Muslim Neroes could participate to achieve political, economic and social goals.

Humphrey to Coordinate Federal Programs

Pres. Johnson announced Dec. 10 that Vice Pres.-elect Hubert H. Humphrey would coordinate all federal civil rights programs and guide them "toward energetic pursuit of equal opportunity for all." In an address to an anti-poverty workshop sponsored by the National Urban League, Mr. Johnson said: "It is our task to carry forward nothing less than the full assimilation of more than 20 million Negroes into American life." He was "not going to be satisfied" until "every qualified person, regardless of the house where he worships or the state where he resides or the way he spells his name, or the color of his skin . . . has the right unquestioned and unrestrained to go in and cast his ballot in every precinct in this country." "Great social change tends to come rapidly, in periods of intense activity and progress. . . . I believe we are in the midst of such a period of change."

1965

On Pres. Johnson's request, Congress enacted a law to end 'illegal barriers' to Negroes' voting rights. A voting-rights campaign in Selma, Ala. was marked by demonstrations, mass arrests and a wave of sympathy from all parts of the U.S. Integrationists flocked to Selma to participate in a march to Montgomery, Ala., the state capital. After the march ended, a white participant, Mrs. Viola Gregg Liuzzo of Detroit, was murdered by white segregationists, and the Ku Klux Klansmen accused of the crime were acquitted. Rioting erupted in Watts, a Negro section of Los Angeles, and brought death to 34 people. Malcolm X, the black nationalist leader, was assassinated at a rally in New York. Slow progress was reported in most civil rights areas—school desegregation, voting registration, employment. Major protests took place in New York, Chicago and other Northern cities.

VOTING RIGHTS ACT OF 1965

Congress Joins President in Attack on Voting Bias

Congress in 1965 passed a controversial Administration-sponsored law to eliminate what Pres. Johnson had described as "illegal barriers" to the right of Negroes to vote. This Voting Rights Act of 1965 became law after an expected Southern filibuster was cut off by a Senate vote of cloture. The new law suspended the use of literacy or other voter qualification tests, authorized the appointment of federal voting examiners for Negro registration in areas not meeting certain voter-participation requirements and provided for federal initiation of court suits to bar discriminatory poll taxes.

The President had requested the new law Mar. 15 in a televised address before a rare evening joint session of Congress. His speech climaxed an explosive week of nationwide civil rights activity that focused on a violence-marked voting drive in Selma, Ala. "The efforts of American Negroes to secure for themselves the full blessings of American life . . . must be our cause," Mr. Johnson said. "Because . . . all of us . . . must overcome the crippling legacy of bigotry and injustice and we shall overcome." The final 3 words, the title of the song that had become the theme of the rights movement, were repeated by the President in identifying the nation's "enemies" as "not our fellow man, not our neighbor," but "poverty, ignorance, disease." "And these enemies too . . . we shall overcome," he pledged. The President stressed that the problem was not just a Negro problem nor a Southern problem but "an American problem." He said: "Rarely in any time does an issue lay bare the secret heart of America itself. Rarely are we met with a challenge . . . to the values and the purposes and the meaning of our beloved nation. The issue of equal rights for American Negroes is such an issue. And should we defeat every enemy, and should we double our wealth and conquer the stars, and still be unequal to this issue, then we will have failed as a people and as a nation." "The real hero of this struggle is the American Negro. His actions and protests, his courage to risk safety, and even to risk his life, have awakened the conscience of this nation. His demonstrations have been designed to call attention to injustice, designed to provoke change; designed to stir reform. He has called upon us to make good the promise of America. And who among us can say that we

would have made the same progress were it not for his persistent bravery and his faith in American democracy? For at the
real heart of the battle for equality is a deep-seated belief in
the democratic process. Equality depends, not on the force
of arms or tear gas, but depends upon the force of moral
right—not on recourse to violence, but on respect for law and
order." "We must preserve the right to free assembly. But
free assembly does not carry with it the right to block public
thoroughfares to traffic. We do have a right to protest. And a
right to march under conditions that do not infringe the constitutional rights of our neighbors. And I intend to protect all
those rights. . . ."

Referring to his voting-rights bill, the President said: "Many
of the issues of civil rights are very complex and most difficult. But about this there can and should be no argument: every
American citizen must have an equal right to vote." "To those
who seek to avoid action by their national government in their
home communities, who want to and who seek to maintain
purely local control over elections, the answer is simple:
Open your polling places to all your people." The issue had no
constitutional, moral, states' rights or national rights obstacles.
"There is only the struggle for human rights." "From the
window where I sit with the problems of our country, I recognize that from outside this chamber is the outraged conscience of a nation, the grave concern of many nations and the
harsh judgment of history on our acts."

Pres. Johnson sent his draft version of the voting rights
bill to Congress Mar. 17. It had been drawn up with the par-
ticipation of Atty. Gen. Nicholas deB. Katzenbach, Justice
Department aides and Congressional leaders of both parties.
One of the principal drafters was Senate minority leader
Everett M. Dirksen (R., Ill.). The bill was introduced in the
House Mar. 17 by Chrmn. Emanuel Celler (D., N.Y.) of the
Judiciary Committee. It was sponsored in the Senate Mar. 18
by 66 Senators.

Atty. Gen. Katzenbach was the first witness at the House
hearings Mar. 18. He said: Some states had "perverted [voter-
qualification literacy and other tests] to test not literacy, not
ability, not understanding—but race"; the coincidence of such
tests and low registration "is usually the result of racial
discrimination"; the Civil Rights Acts of 1957, 1960 and 1964 had
had only "minimal effect" in removing voter discrimination; in adopting the Administration bill, Congress

would be exercising not an "inherent" but an "express" power.

Versions of the bill broader than the original Administration request were approved Apr. 9 by the Senate Judiciary Committee and a House Judiciary subcommittee. Among provisions not requested by the Administration was an outright ban on state and local poll taxes as a voting requirement; the revised Administration bill would merely have permitted court suspension of such taxes if they were used to abridge voting rights. The poll-tax ban was opposed by Dirksen and Senate Democratic leader Mike Mansfield (Minn.) as unconstitutional and hence a risk to the bill's legality. A substitute bill eliminating this ban was introduced by Mansfield Apr. 30 with Dirksen's joint sponsorship. Sen. Edward M. Kennedy (D., Mass.), backed by 38 cosponsors, sought May 6 to restore the poll-tax ban as an amendment to the Mansfield-Dirksen bill, but the Senate rejected the amendment May 11 by 49-45 vote. Debate, however, continued to focus on the poll-tax issue until the Senate resolved the problem May 19 by approving, 69-20, an amendment, worked out by the bipartisan leadership, stating that "Congress declares" that poll taxes were being used "in certain states" to deny or abridge the right to vote.

The Senate May 20 accepted by 48-19 vote an amendment, sponsored by Sens. Robert F. Kennedy (D., N.Y.) and Jacob K. Javits (R., N.Y.), to give the right to vote to those who were unable to read or write in English but could demonstrate that they had an 8th-grade education in a school under the American flag that was conducted in a language other than English. The amendment was primarily for the benefit of the estimated 300,000-330,000 Puerto Rican citizens of New York who were eligible to vote but unregistered.

As debate dragged on and blocked a vote on the bill, Mansfield failed 3 times in appeals for unanimous consent to limit debate. He finally joined with Dirksen May 21 in filing a cloture petition, and cloture was invoked May 25, on the 24th day of debate on the bill, by a vote of 70-30 (47 D. & 23 R. vs. 21 D. & 9 R.). The bill was then passed by the Senate May 26 by 77-19 vote (47 D. & 30 R. vs. 17 D. & 2 R.).

House debate on the bill began July 6, and a House version of the measure was passed July 9 by 333-85 vote (221 D. & 112 R. vs. 61 D. & 24 R.). The House bill contained essentially the same provisions as the Senate version. The House measure, however, included a flat ban on poll taxes and did not carry the provision extending voting rights to Puerto Ricans unable to read or write English.

The final compromise version of the bill was worked out July 29 by Senate-House conferees after a 3-week impasse over 2 items: (1) the House ban on poll taxes, which was eventually deleted; and (2) the Senate provision, which was retained, enabling Spanish-speaking Puerto Ricans in New York to be registered without meeting the state requirement of literacy in English. Although the poll-tax ban was dropped, the conferees adopted a provision declaring that poll taxes denied or abridged the right to vote and directing initiation "forthwith" of federal court action against discriminatory poll taxes.

The bill was then passed by 328-74 House vote (217 D. & 111 R. vs. 54 Southern Democrats & 20 R.) Aug. 3 and by 79-18 Senate vote (49 D. & 30 R. vs. Strom Thurmond [R., S.C.] & 17 D.) Aug. 4.

Before signing the bill Aug. 6, Pres. Johnson went to the rotunda of the Capitol, before a statue of Abraham Lincoln, and, in a nationally televised ceremony, said: "Today the Negro story and the American story fuse and blend." "This good Congress acted swiftly in passing this act. I intend to act with equal dispatch in enforcing it." "If any county any-where in this nation does not want federal intervention, it need only open its polling places to all of its people." "Let me now say to every Negro in this country: You must register. You must vote. You must learn, so your choice advances your interest and the interest of our beloved nation." Negro leaders should respond to the act's "great challenge" not "simply by protests and demonstrations" but by working "around the clock to teach people their responsibilities." After his address, Mr. Johnson went to the "President's Room" in the Senate and signed the bill. This was the room where 104 years previously Lincoln had signed a law freeing slaves conscripted into military service by the Confederacy.

Administration Enforces New Vote Law

Within 25 hours after the bill was signed, the Justice Department filed suit in Jackson, Miss. Aug. 7 to have Mississippi's $2 poll tax abolished as discriminatory. Justice Department suits to abolish the poll tax as a prerequisite to voting in Texas, Alabama and Virginia, the only 3 states besides Mississippi levying poll taxes, were filed Aug. 10 in

U.S. district courts in Austin, Tex., Montgomery, Ala. and Richmond, Va.

The Census Bureau certified in the *Federal Register* Aug. 7 that the act's suspension of literacy and other voter qualification tests applied to 7 states—Alabama, Alaska, Georgia, Louisiana, Mississippi, South Carolina and Virginia—and to 26 counties in North Carolina and one (Apache) in Arizona.

9 counties in Alabama, Mississippi and Louisiana were designated by Atty. Gen. Nicholas deB. Katzenbach Aug. 9 as voting areas where federal examiners—2 to each county—were being sent to initiate registering of eligible Negroes. (The counties: Alabama—Dallas, Hale, Lowndes, Marengo. Louisiana—East Carroll, East Feliciana and Plaquemines Parishes. Mississippi—Leflore, Madison.) Federal registration offices in the 9 counties, in which only 1,764 Negroes were registered as voters, were opened Aug. 10, and 1,144 more Negroes were registered the first day. Other counties that had been scheduled to get examiners were exempted because of recent registration of Negroes or pledges by local officials to register Negroes; these counties included Sumter County, Ga., where 3 Negroes were appointed Aug. 6 as deputy registrars.

10 additional counties were designated Aug. 18 and Sept. 24 as counties to which examiners would be sent. The counties listed Aug. 18: Perry and Wilcox in Alabama; Jefferson Davis and Jones in Mississippi; Ouachita Parish in Louisiana. Those designated Sept. 24: Benton, Bolivar, Clay, Coahoma and Humphrey, all in Mississippi. Montgomery County, Ala. was added to the list Oct. 1. Atty. Gen. Katzenbach Dec. 20 ordered federal voting examiners into 4 additional Mississippi counties: Carroll, Newton, Simpson and Warren. This action brought to 36 the number of Southern counties (19 in Mississippi) to which federal registrars had been sent. Katzenbach's announcement indicated that the 4 counties had permitted some Negroes to register but had continued the use of literacy tests.

Regulations published by the Civil Service Commission Aug. 7 governing the duty of examiners specified that if an applicant were unable to complete registration forms "because of lack of literacy," the examiner could "orally examine" the applicant and assist in completion of the form. The regulation stated that the applicant could "sign his name or make his mark theron" to complete the process. Katzenbach said on the ABC-

TV "Issues & Answers" program Aug. 8 that the Southern states with literacy tests "have been registering white illiterates" and "it is not unfair to say . . . 'Now you have got to apply that same standard to Negroes.'" Asked if he meant "that you are going to register all Negroes, Negroes who can't read or write?" Katzenbach replied: "Yes, absolutely." The problem, he said, was not literacy but: "Don't keep Negroes from voting because they are Negroes."

(A state constitutional amendment liberalizing voter registration requirements was overwhelmingly approved by Mississippi voters Aug. 17. A voter applicant under the new legislation was required to tell no more than name, address and whether convicted of certain crimes and to take an oath verifying the truth of the statements.)

Courts Test Law's Provisions

A 3-judge federal court in Washington ruled in a 2-1 decision Nov. 15 that a provision of the 1965 Voting Rights Act enabling Spanish-speaking citizens to vote on the basis of a 6th-grade education in any school under the American flag was unconstitutional. Pointing out that "expediency, desirability and policy of legislation are not the concern of the judiciary," the majority opinion stated that the provision was an infringement of the right of states to establish voting standards. (The suit had been filed in August by 2 N.Y. City residents, John P. and Christine Morgan.)

But a 3-judge federal court in New York Dec. 8 unanimously upheld the provision giving the vote to Spanish-speaking citizens with a 6th-grade education in a school under the American flag.

The suit had been brought by the Justice Department after Mrs. Maria Lopez, 21, a Puerto Rican with a 9th-grade education in Spanish, had been refused registration by the Monroe County Board of Elections. The decision had the effect of permanently enjoining N.Y. State from refusing to register Puerto Ricans who qualified under Section 4(e) of the Voting Rights Act; it thus voided a provision of the state constitution that required voters to be literate in English. The court's opinion, written by Judge Irving R. Kaufman, cited Congress' establishment of a public school system in Puerto Rico in which Spanish was the medium of instruction. It said that "Congress acted well within its Constitutional limits

York State from prohibiting or, at the very least, substantially impeding the integration of Puerto Rican emigrants into its political life through the imposition of an English-language requirement for voter registration."

A 3-judge federal court in Montgomery, Ala. Nov. 23 invalidated injunctions issued by Alabama state courts against placing Negroes registered by federal voting examiners on the voting rolls. The federal court held that state courts lacked the authority to issue injunctions under the 1965 Voting Rights Act, which limited its injunctive provisions to the U.S. District Court for the District of Columbia and to U.S. Appeals Courts. The suit had been filed by 6 Alabama probate judges (the state's chief election officers), whom state courts had enjoined from enrolling Negroes registered by federal examiners. The probate judges said they faced state contempt charges if they disobeyed the injunctions but faced federal prosecution if they obeyed them. Asst. Atty. Gen. John Doar, in charge of the Justice Department's Civil Rights Division, appeared in court on behalf of Atty. Gen. Nicholas deB. Katzenbach, who had been named as a defendant in the suit. Alabama Gov. George C. Wallace had intervened in the case to ask that the court hold the Voting Rights Act unconstitutional and order federal voting examiners to leave the state.

VOTE CAMPAIGN IN SELMA (ALA.)

Martin Luther King Opens Campaign

A new Alabama-wide drive to register Negro voters was announced at a Negro rally in Selma, Ala. Jan. 2 by the Rev. Dr. Martin Luther King Jr., president of the Southern Christian Leadership Conference. King had chosen Selma as the starting place of the drive because the town was considered a symbol of the Deep South's resistance to the civil rights movement. He said an appeal to Gov. George C. Wallace and the state Legislature for equal registration practices was planned. If this failed, "we will seek to arouse the federal government by marching by the thousands to the places of registration," he said. "We are not asking, we are demanding the ballot."

The Selma drive opened Jan. 18. King and 11 other Negroes registered at the Hotel Albert and became the first Negroes accepted by a formerly "white" hotel in Selma; Negroes also were served at 7 "white" restaurants. But King was punched and kicked while registering. (His assailant, a Birmingham member of the National States Rights Party, was arrested, was fined $100 Jan. 19 and was given a 60-day jail sentence.)

Arrests of Negro demonstrators began Jan. 19 when 62 were detained on charges of unlawful assembly and 5 were arrested on charges of criminal provocation. The arrests were made when Negroes, attempting to register at the Dallas County courthouse, disobeyed Dallas County Sheriff James G. Clark's order to enter the courthouse through an alley door and not the front door. 156 more arrests were made Jan. 20. 105 Negro teachers appeared at the courthouse Jan. 22, but Clark and 5 deputies chased them away with nightsticks. A 226-pound Negro motel clerk, Annie Lee Cooper, 53, stepped out of the registration line Jan. 25 and punched Clark. She was wrestled to the ground by 3 deputies, clubbed by Clark and arrested. (King said: the sheriff "is determined to trample over Negroes with iron feet of brutality and oppression.") 34 more persons, including Chrmn. John Lewis of the Student Nonviolent Coordinating Committee (SNCC, or "Snick"), were arrested Jan. 26, and 24 more were arrested Jan. 27. Policemen, deputy sheriffs, posse men with cattle prods, state troopers, FBI agents and U.S. marshals were deployed throughout the area to keep order.

Mass marches and mass arrests began Feb. 1, when King and 263 other Negroes were arrested for parading without a permit. About 500 Negro school students picketing the courthouse were also arrested. 120 Negro adults and about 400 Negro high school pupils were arrested Feb. 2; more than 300 school children were arrested Feb. 3, more than 500 adults Feb. 5 and 50 more Feb. 8.

U.S. District Judge Daniel Thomas, ruling on cases arising from the Selma situation, barred Clark and other officials Jan. 23 from intimidating Negro voter applicants; Thomas also limited the registration line to 100. Thomas Jan. 30 barred arrests of rights workers as long as they were "peaceful and orderly." He ruled Feb. 4 that the Dallas County Board of Registrars "has deprived Negroes of the right to vote," and he ordered the board (a) to stop using a difficult literacy test initiated by the Alabama Supreme Court, (b) to process at least 100 applications each day it was in session and (c) not to reject voter registration applicants on technicalities.

Pres. Johnson declared at his news conference Feb. 4 that "all of us should be concerned with the efforts of our fellow Americans to register to vote in Alabama." "I intend to see," he said, that the right to vote "is secured for all of our citizens."

King, who had initially refused to pay his $200 bail and therefore remained temporarily in jail, agreed to be released on bail Feb. 5, and he conferred with Mr. Johnson, Vice Pres. Humphrey and Atty. Gen. Katzenbach in Washington Feb. 9 on Negro voting rights. He said afterwards that the President had told him voting-rights legislation was being drafted and a message on the subject would be sent to Congress "very soon." (Pres. Johnson made his request to Congress for the legislation Mar. 15, but Congress did not complete action on the bill until Aug. 4.) King said: "The President made it very clear to me that he was determined during his Administration to see all remaining obstacles removed to the right of Negroes to vote."

Alabama Gov. George Wallace announced Feb. 20 that he had ordered state troopers to help local officials "stop nighttime demonstrations [in Selma and nearby Marion]." Wallace conceded that "no one can contest" the right of peaceful assembly or the right of Negroes to register and vote if "qualified under the laws of this state." But he said that "mass demonstrations in the nighttime led by career and professional agitators with pro-Communist affiliations" were "not in the interest of any citizen of this state, black or white." King retorted at a Selma rally Feb. 22 that Wallace "said nothing about the problems that brought about the demonstrations." He called the ban on nighttime demonstrations "clearly unconstitutional." He also said: "We are going to have a motorcade to Montgomery in the next few days. We hope to have our forces mobilized to have carloads of people from all over the state to march on the capital. . . . We will be going there to tell Gov. Wallace we aren't going to take it any more."

(Demonstrations had taken place in Marion almost daily since Feb. 3 when about 700 Negro schoolchildren were arrested at the Perry County courthouse in Marion on charges of unlawful assembly or disobeying an officer. Violence erupted in Marion Feb. 18 after James Orange, a member of the Southern Christian Leadership Conference, was arrested on a charge of contributing to the delinquency of a minor. A crowd of 400 Negroes marched on the jail in protest. 50 state troopers led by Col. Al Lingo, Alabama public safety director, charged into the crowd. They pursued some of the Negroes into a cafe and others across house porches. Jimmy Lee Jackson,

26, reportedly was shot by a trooper in the cafe; the trooper allegedly acted after Jackson had come to the assistance of his mother, Mrs. Viola Jackson, who was being clubbed by a trooper. At least 10 Negroes were injured by troopers' nightsticks, and a trooper reportedly sustained a head injury from a missile thrown by a Negro. White onlookers attacked newsmen and smashed their cameras during the clash. Jackson died in a Selma hospital Feb. 26.)

March on Montgomery (Ala.) Blocked

Selma remained a focal point of national interest during early March as law enforcement officers twice broke up attempts by Negroes and white integrationists to march from Selma to the state capitol in Montgomery.

Shortly after the first of the 2 marches was started Mar. 7, the vanguard of about 525 marchers was attacked by 200 state troopers and sheriff's deputies, some on horses, using tear gas, nightsticks and whips. Some Negroes retaliated by hurling bricks and bottles as they were forced back from the white section of Selma to the Negro section. Many Negroes were injured. 17, including John Lewis, were hospitalized. Pres. Johnson Mar. 9 issued a statement deploring the "brutality" against the Negroes. He urged both Negro demonstrators and state officials to respect the law.

King led 1,500 Negroes and whites from Selma Mar. 9 in another unsuccessful effort to march to Montgomery. Participants included many white clergymen and other whites from throughout the U.S. But state troopers, shoulder-to-shoulder, formed a barricade on the outskirts of Selma, and the marchers turned back after one mile. Plans for the token march—and retreat at the first sign of resistance—had been worked out with King by LeRoy Collins, head of the Community Relations Service, who acted as Pres. Johnson's representative. A federal court order against the march was in effect at the time. King declared at the end of the march: "We had the greatest demonstration for freedom today that we've ever had in the South."

Rev. Reeb Slain, Suspects Acquitted

3 white Unitarian ministers who had participated in the march were beaten by a group of whites on a Selma street

corner Mar. 9. One of the 3, the Rev. James J. Reeb, 38, of
Boston, was beaten unconscious with a club. Reeb died in a
Birmingham hospital Mar. 11. Pres. Johnson, who had sent
yellow roses to the hospital, phoned Reeb's widow and sent a
jet plane for her return trip to Boston. 4 men arrested after
the assault—Namon O'Neal Hoggle, his brother, William
Stanley Hoggle, Elmer L. Cook and R. B. Kelly—were re-
arrested Mar. 11, charged with murder and released under
bond of $25,000 each. A grand jury indicted the 2 Hoggles
and Cook on murder charges Apr. 13 but did not indict Kelly.
The 3 defendants were acquitted Dec. 10 by an all-white
county jury in Selma.

Demonstrations Go on Daily Basis

Daily demonstrations were started in Selma Mar. 10 after
police barred a march on the courthouse and established a line
beyond which the Negroes were forbidden to pass. Eventually, a
rope was strung between police and demonstrators, who made
up a song about "The Berlin Wall" in Selma. The rope was cut
by authorities Mar. 12, but about 1,000 demonstrators, including nuns and other members of the clergy, threatened to
break through the line Mar. 13.

An agreement to allow a march as part of a memorial serv-
ice for Reeb was arranged Mar. 15 by Federal Judge Daniel
Thomas and Community Relations Service representatives.
More than 2,000 persons, including many whites, marched to the
courthouse, where King delivered the eulogy. Among those
attending: United Automobile Workers Pres. Walter Reuther;
Archbishop Iakovos, primate of the Greek Orthodox Church for
North & South America; Reps. Edward P. Boland (D., Mass.)
and Silvio O. Conte (R., Mass.), representing the Massachusetts
Congressional delegation; the Right Rev. William F. Creighton,
bishop of the Episcopal Church of Washington; Bishop John D.
Bright of the African Methodist Episcopal Church in Phila-
delphia; Rabbi Eugene Lippman of Washington, representing the
Union of American Hebrew Congregations; Methodist Bishops
Charles F. Golden of Nashville and Richard C. Raines of
Indianapolis; about 150 Roman Catholic priests and nuns.

2 attempted marches on the courthouse were stopped by
police Mar. 16, but a march by about 600 demonstrators took
place Mar. 17 after another agreement worked out with the
help of Judge Thomas. Most of the Mar. 17 marchers were

whites.

Demonstrations in support of the Selma rights campaign were held in cities throughout the U.S., and the protests gained in intensity after the death of the Rev. Reeb. Michigan Gov. George Romney and Detroit Mayor Jerome P. Cavanagh led 10,000 persons in a Detroit march Mar. 9. 800 clergymen, college students, professional men and civil rights workers marched along 5th Avenue in New York. Almost 1,000 persons demonstrated at the White House. Demonstrations also took place in Boston, Chicago, Los Angeles, Berkeley, Calif., Hartford, Conn., Syracuse, N.Y., Springfield, O. and Beloit, Wis. Almost 1,000 Negro students from Tuskegee Institute and several white ministers held a peaceful sit-down in front of the state capitol in Montgomery, Ala. Mar. 10 to protest the Mar. 7 "brutality" of the state troopers in Selma. 14 youths staged a 7-hour sit-down in the White House Mar. 11 after entering with tourists and then demanding federal intervention in Selma. Special security arrangements were tightened at the White House Mar. 12, and the President let it be known that no more sit-ins would be tolerated there. But pickets marched outside the White House Mar. 9-15 and again Mar. 17, when about 300 college students (the number eventually dwindled to about 125) began a 4-hour sit-down in the snow.

Thousands of clergymen from throughout the nation met in Washington Mar. 12 for a rally at which the President was denounced for "unbelievable lack of action" in the Selma crisis. A delegation from the rally, sponsored by the Commission on Religion & Race of the National Council of Churches, was received by Mr. Johnson, who said he had alerted 700 federal troops early Mar. 9 to intervene in Selma should there be any lapse in an understanding between state troopers and the rights demonstrators. The troops were still on alert. Mr. Johnson received a 2d ministerial delegation of Washington rights leaders and a group of Negro publishers Mar. 12 and held a briefing on the subject for 60 Congress members.

Other demonstrations in sympathy for the Selma rights campaigners took place in Los Angeles (where 6,000 persons participated Mar. 13), in New York (where 15,000 persons marched silently in Harlem Mar. 14), at the Liberty Bell in Philadelphia (where 8,000 persons met Mar. 15 to mourn for Reeb), in Boston, in Casper, Wyo. (Reeb's birthplace) and at the University of Toronto. A Freedom Run was started

Mar. 14 in New York and completed Mar. 16 in Washington, where an unlit torch was accepted at a White House gate by Clifford Alexander, a Negro and deputy special assistant to the President. Reeb's widow and son, John, 13, attended a memorial service Mar. 16 at All Souls Unitarian Church in Washington, where Reeb had served before moving to Boston in 1964; Vice Pres. Hubert H. Humphrey and Sen. Edward M. Kennedy attended a service. Francis Cardinal Spellman of New York announced Mar. 12 a $10,000 donation to the Good Samaritan Hospital of Selma as a memorial to Reeb. The American Friends Service Committee announced Mar. 12 that it was establishing, in association with the Unitarian-Universalist Association and the Southern Christian Leader-ship Conference, a fund "to lessen the hardship of those who have suffered as a result of the civil rights campaign to which James Reeb was so deeply committed."

Johnson-Wallace Confrontation

Pres. Johnson Mar. 12 received a wire from Gov. Wallace asking for a meeting on the Selma situation. The President replied that he would be "available . . . any time," and the 2 met at the White House in Washington for more than 3 hours Mar. 13.

Afterwards, with Wallace behind him at a televised news conference Mar. 13, the President said: "What happened in Selma was an American tragedy." "I told the governor that the brutality in Selma last Sunday must not be repeated" and that, "whether the governor agrees or not, that law and order would prevail in Alabama." The "full power of the federal government" was poised to strike against "lawlessness." He had asked Wallace to do 3 things—to "publicly declare his support for universal suffrage in Alabama," to assure "the right of peaceful assembly" and to call a biracial meeting. Wallace had expressed concern that the demonstrations were "a threat" to the peace and security of the people of Alabama. "I expressed my own concern about the need for remedying those grievances which led to the demonstrations by the people who feel their rights have been denied. . . . And I understand their concern."

Wallace presented his views Mar. 14 in 2 televised inter-views. He said he would not allow a civil rights march from Selma to Montgomery unless a federal court order requiring

him to permit the march were upheld on appeal. He also said
he would not receive representatives who came to see him "at
the head of a . . . demonstration." He contended that demonstrations would continue regardless of "anything we do in
Alabama" and that there had been "more" demonstrations
since the 1964 Civil Rights Act was enacted "than we ever
had before."

Court Authorizes March to Montgomery

U.S. District Judge Frank M. Johnson Jr. in Montgomery
Mar. 17 upheld the right of rights demonstrators to stage
an orderly march from Selma to Montgomery. Johnson enjoined Gov. Wallace and other state and county officials from
"harassing or threatening" the marchers and ordered them to
provide police protection during the march. Johnson said: He
realized that the march "reaches . . . the outer limits of what
is constitutionally allowed," but "the wrongs and injustice inflicted upon these plaintiffs . . . have clearly exceeded—and
continue to exceed—the outer limits of what is constitutionally
permissible."

The U.S. Justice Department, entering the case as a friend
of the court, had supported the efforts of the NAACP Legal
Defense & Educational Fund on behalf of the Negro plaintiffs.
Judge Johnson held that Sheriff James Clark and his aides, in
countering the Selma demonstrations, had exhibited "an almost
continuous pattern . . . of harassment, intimidation, coercion,
threatening conduct and, sometimes, brutal mistreatment."
He asserted that Clark and his men had not been "enforcing
any valid law of . . . Alabama or furthering any legitimate
policy of the state."

(About 600 civil rights marchers were attacked and routed
in Montgomery Mar. 16 by mounted state and county police
wielding ropes, nightsticks and electric prod poles. 8 persons
were reported injured. A public apology for the attack was made
later Mar. 16 by Montgomery County Circuit Solicitor David H.
Crozland, who said the attack stemmed from "a misunderstanding of orders." The mounted police were directed to
disperse only a small group of demonstrators considered unruly, Crozland explained. A 2d march, of about 1,000 persons,
was held under city police protection later Mar. 16. A meeting
to protest the violence was held that night at a Negro church.
At the meeting, Dr. King called for a mass protest march the

next day on the county courthouse. A permit was obtained, and the march was held Mar. 17, with city police protection. The 1,600 demonstrators who participated were led by King, James Forman, executive secretary of the Student Nonviolent Coordinating Committee [SNCC], and SNCC Chrmn. John Lewis. They marched a mile to the courthouse, where the leaders conferred for almost 4 hours with Sheriff Mac Sim Butler and John Doar, head of the Civil Rights Division of the U.S. Justice Department. King emerged from the meeting to tell the 700 persons outside that progress was being made toward an agreement to end police harassment of orderly demonstrations. Then he announced the just-released court decision upholding the demonstrators' right to march from Selma to Montgomery.)

Wallace went Mar. 18 before a joint session of the state Legislature to denounce the court order upholding the Negroes' right to undertake the march. He assailed Judge Johnson as a man who "prostitutes our law in favor of . . . mob rule." He denounced the marchers, called "many of them Communist-trained" but asked Alabamans for restraint.

Pres. Johnson summoned reporters to his office later Mar. 18 and read a telegram he had received from Wallace that evening. In the telegram Wallace said it would require 6,171 men, 489 vehicles and 15 buses to furnish adequate security for the march. The state had only 300 troopers and about 150 other officers available, Wallace said, and he "respectfully" requested that the federal government "provide sufficient federal civil authorities" to protect the marchers and citizens in and along the march route. The President then said that federal "civilian personnel approaching the figure" given by Wallace was unavailable but that more than 10,000 Alabama National Guardsmen were at Wallace's disposal. "If he is unable or unwilling to call up the Guard and to maintain law and order in Alabama," the President said, "I will call the Guard up and give them all the support that may be required."

In another telegram, Wallace told Pres. Johnson Mar. 19 that Alabama was "financially unable to bear the burden" of mobilizing the Guard to police the march. The governor quoted from a resolution, passed by the state Legislature Mar. 19, which said that since the march had been "sanctioned by a federal court, the financial resources of the federal government should be used to pay the cost of the mobilization."

Pres. Johnson Mar. 20 signed a proclamation noting the danger of "domestic violence" in Alabama. He then signed an executive order federalizing the Alabama National Guard and authorizing the use of whatever federal troops the Defense Secretary "may deem necessary" in the situation. At a televised news conference Mr. Johnson announced his action and said: "It is not a welcome duty for the federal government to ever assume a state government's own responsibility for assuring the protection of citizens in the exercise of their constitutional rights. It has been rare in our history for the governor and the legislature of a sovereign state to decline to exercise their responsibility and to request that duty be assumed by the federal government. . . . I have responded, both to their request, and to what I believe is the sure and the certain duty of the federal government in the protection of constitutional rights of all American citizens."

Integrationists March from Selma to Montgomery

The 54-mile march to Montgomery began at Browns Chapel Methodist Church in Selma at 12:47 p.m. Mar. 21. It ended in front of the state capitol shortly after noon Mar. 25.

Before leaving the church Mar. 21, Dr. King told the marchers: "You will be the people that will light a new chapter in the history books of our nation. Those of us who are Negroes don't have much. . . . Because of the system, we don't have much education. . . . But thank God we have our bodies, our feet and our souls. Walk together, children, . . . and it will lead us to the promised land. And Alabama will be a new Alabama, and America will be a new America."

The 3,200 persons who then began the march were led by King, Dr. Ralph J. Bunche (UN Undersecretary for special political affairs), the Right Rev. Richard Millard (suffragan bishop of the Episcopal Diocese of California), SNCC Chrmn. John Lewis, Deaconess Phyllis Edwards of the Episcopal Diocese of California, Rabbi Abraham Heschel of the Jewish Theological Seminary in New York, the Rev. Ralph D. Abernathy (King's top aide) and the Rev. Frederick D. Reese (a Selma Negro and president of the Dallas County Voters League). Among others who started the march: N.Y. City Council Pres. Paul R. Screvane; Mrs. Constance Baker Motley, president of the Borough of Manhattan (N.Y. City), holder of the highest elective office ever held by a Negro woman; Benjamin R. Epstein, national director of the Anti-Defamation League of B'nai B'rith.

The lead car carried Maj. John Cloud of the Alabama state police, who had been in charge of troopers who had routed Negro marchers with tear gas 2 weeks earlier. Federalized National Guardsmen lined the streets leading out of town, and federally manned helicopters flew over the procession. Federal agents included John Doar, chief of the Justice Department's Civil Rights Division, who walked near the head of the march, and Maj. Gen. Carl C. Turner, provost marshal general of the U.S. Army; they reported by radio to the Justice Department and Pentagon in Washington. Military policemen guarded every crossroad. Army trucks loaded with armed troops were in evidence nearby. Brig. Gen. Henry V. Graham directed the security operation along the route. Graham, of Birmingham, a National Guard officer and assistant divisional commander of the 31st Division, had been named by Pres. Johnson as field commander of all troops in the operation.

Equipment, supplies and personnel included: a mobile hospital lent by the AFL-CIO International Ladies Garment Workers Union; a "healthmobile" lent by the National Council of Churches; 13 ambulances, each manned by a physician; hot breakfasts and suppers and cold snacks and lunches prepared at a Negro church in Selma and trucked to the marchers; a tent gang to pitch 2 small and 2 large tents at the nightly campsites; a garbage truck to clear the route and campsites of litter; trucks with portable latrines and washing facilities.

The marchers covered 7.3 miles the first day, then camped. To conform with the federal court order on the march, about 2,750 of the marchers returned to Selma the evening of the first day on the Western Railway of Alabama; the trip was arranged by the Justice Department officials (fare: 75¢) because enough buses could not be found. 150 more marchers returned Mar. 22 to abide by the court-ordered 300-marcher limit where U.S. Highway 80, the march route, had only 2 lanes. Most of the celebrities left the march after the first day. The marchers walked 16 miles through Lowndes County Mar. 22 and covered 32.3 miles in all by Mar. 23 despite a torrential rain. They stopped Mar. 24 for the night 1.7 miles inside Montgomery at the City of St. Jude, a Roman Catholic hospital and school used predominantly by Negroes. (Previous campsites had been on land owned by Negroes.) About 1,500 more marchers joined the procession where Route 80 widened to 4 lanes outside Montgomery.

King left the march Mar. 23 to keep a speaking engagement

in Cleveland, then rejoined it Mar. 24 with his wife, Coretta, to lead it into Montgomery. On this last night of the march the demonstrators were entertained by many show-world celebrities assembled by singer Harry Belafonte at King's request.

There were no serious incidents reported during the march. The marchers encountered some heckling from whites along the route, and a small plane Mar. 22 dropped leaflets urging the firing of Negro employes; the leaflets were signed by White Citizens Actions, Inc. of Tuscaloosa.

By the time the marchers reached the capitol in Montgomery Mar. 25 their numbers had risen to about 25,000; their ranks had been swelled for the final 3½-mile walk from the outskirts of Montgomery. UN Undersecy. Bunche was again in the lead with King. Army troops and federalized Alabama National Guardsmen lined the final miles of the march route and stood guard on roofs. At the capitol, state property was guarded by state troopers.

King said to the throng at the capitol: "We are on the move now . . . and no wave of racism can stop us." Selma had become "a shining moment in the conscience of man. If the worst in American life lurked in the dark streets, the best of American instincts arose passionately from across the nation to overcome it."

The marchers carried with them a petition to Gov. Wallace that said: "We have come not only 5 days and 50 miles but we have come from 3 centuries of suffering and hardship. We have come . . . to declare that we must have our freedom NOW. We must have the right to vote; we must have equal protection of the law and an end to police brutality."

The governor sent word to the marchers that he would receive a delegation after the rally, but 2 attempts of a delegation to see him were rebuffed. (Wallace, however, met Mar. 30 with a delegation bearing the petition. This group was led by the Rev. Joseph E. Lowery of Birmingham, who said afterwards that they had been "cordially" received and that Wallace had "promised to give careful consideration" to the petition. The delegation included one white, the Rev. Joseph W. Ellwanger, a Lutheran minister from Birmingham.)

Mrs. Liuzzo Slain Following March

A white civil rights worker, Mrs. Viola Gregg Liuzzo, 39, of Detroit, a mother of 5 children, was shot to death on U.S.

Highway 80 in Alabama Mar. 25 while she was driving a car to Montgomery to bring civil rights marchers back to Selma. Pres. Johnson made a dramatic TV appearance Mar. 26 to deplore "the horrible crime," to announce the arrest of 4 Ku Klux Klansmen in connection with it and to request a Congressional investigation of the Klan, which he described as "a hooded society of bigots."

Mrs. Liuzzo, wife of Anthony J. Liuzzo, 51, a business agent for the International Bro'hood of Teamsters in Detroit, was murdered while returning to Montgomery after having driven marchers to Selma. Leroy Moton, 19, a Selma Negro helping with the transportation of marchers, was the only other occupant of the car. He reported later that a car had pulled alongside their auto as it sped along a lonely stretch of road and that a volley of shots was fired, killing Mrs. Liuzzo but missing Moton.

Mrs. Liuzzo's funeral was held in Detroit Mar. 30. Among those attending were Dr. King, NAACP Executive Director Roy Wilkins, CORE National Director James Farmer, SNCC Chrmn. John Lewis, UAW Pres. Walter P. Reuther, Teamsters Bro'hood Pres. James R. Hoffa, Michigan Lt. Gov. William Milliken and U.S. Atty. Lawrence Gubow, who represented Pres. Johnson. Mr. Johnson had phoned Liuzzo Mar. 26 to express his sorrow, and Vice. Pres. Humphrey visited Liuzzo and his children in Detroit Mar. 28 to convey the President's message that the "whole country was with them" in their grief. Michigan Gov. George Romney visited the Liuzzo family Mar. 27 and set Mar. 29-30 as official days of mourning for Mrs. Liuzzo.

Pres. Johnson said in a TV address Mar. 26 that Mrs. Liuzzo had gone to Alabama to "serve the struggle for justice" and had been "murdered by the enemies of justice who for decades had used the rope and the gun and the tar and feathers to terrorize their neighbors." He announced that the FBI had arrested 4 Ku Klux Klan members in connection with the murder. Mr. Johnson warned Klansmen "to get out of the Ku Klux Klan now and return to a decent society before it is too late." He pledged to submit legislation to bring the Klan "under effective control of law" and suggested that Congress investigate the Klan. (The House Un-American Activities Committee voted unanimously Mar. 30 to undertake a full investigation of the KKK.)

The 4 Klansmen identified by the President were charged with the federal crime of conspiring to deprive Mrs. Liuzzo of her civil rights (murder was not a federal crime unless committed on federal property). The accused men: Eugene Thomas, 43, and William Orville Eaton, 41, both of Bessemer, Ala.; Gary Thomas Rowe Jr., 31, of Birmingham; Collie LeRoy Wilkins Jr., 21, of Fairfield, Ala. The accused were described as members of the United Klan of America, Knights of the Ku Klux Klan, Inc., reportedly the largest of several Klan groups, but it was revealed later that Rowe actually was an FBI informant rather than a bona fide Klan member.

Wilkins was acquitted of Mrs. Liuzzo's murder after 2 trials. The first took place May 3-6 and ended in a mistrial May 7 when an all-white Lowndes County jury voted 10-2 to convict Wilkins of first-degree manslaughter; a mistrial was then declared because unanimity was required for either conviction or acquittal. Wilkins had been charged with first-degree murder in both trials, but Circuit Judge T. Werth Thagard had informed the jurors that they could convict Wilkins on a lesser charge. The prosecution in the 2d trial was handled by Alabama Atty. Gen. Richmond M. Flowers, who supplanted the county prosecutor on his own initiative and fought hard for a conviction. Rowe testified at both trials that he had been in the murder car and had seen Wilkins and Eaton shoot at Mrs. Liuzzo. But an all-white jury acquitted Wilkins Oct. 22. The trials of Eaton and Thomas had been postponed to await the outcome of Wilkins' trial.

Wilkins, Eaton and Thomas were convicted by an all-white federal jury in Montgomery, Ala. Dec. 3 of charges filed under an 1870 law outlawing conspiracy to deprive citizens of their civil rights. U.S. District Judge Frank M. Johnson Jr. sentenced them to 10-year prison terms, and they were released Dec. 4 on $10,000 appeal bonds. (Wilkins was sentenced in Birmingham Dec. 20 to a year and a day in prison for violating parole. He had been put on probation Nov. 16, 1964 for violation of a federal firearms statute and had been ordered not to leave the district of Northern Alabama U.S. District Court. Wilkins acknowledged having gone out of the district on 3 occasions.)

King Urges Boycott of Alabama

Dr. Martin Luther King called Mar. 28 for a national boycott of Alabama products, and he proposed that the federal government discontinue its support of all Alabama activities.

The purpose of his proposal, he said, was "to withdraw support from a society that has refused to protect life and the right to vote." Despite criticism of the boycott plan by Johnson Administration officials and some Negro leaders, who felt that a boycott would hit hardest at Alabama's Negroes, King Mar. 30 repeated his determination to press for a boycott of Alabama. The critics of the boycott proposal included Whitney M. Young Jr., executive director of the National Urban League, who said Mar. 29 that he had "reservations about a total boycott that makes no distinction between the good guys and the bad guys." (The 308 delegates to the biennial convention of the International Longshoremen's & Warehousemen's Union voted unanimously in Vancouver, B.C. Apr. 9 for a boycott by its 65,000 members of any products made in Alabama.)

RIOT IN WATTS

Violence Batters Los Angeles Area

34 persons were killed and a major section of Los Angeles was terrorized Aug. 11-16 in the U.S.' most destructive outbreak of racial violence in decades.

The loss due to looting, fire and other willful destruction was tentatively estimated as in excess of $40 million. Civic, church and civil rights leaders suggested that in terms of human relations, the riots were responsible for even greater damage. This damage, which might take years to repair, was the revival or creation of mutual hate and fear between Negroes and whites.

A minor incident in Los Angeles' 95%-Negro district of Watts erupted into 6 days of rioting, looting of stores, arson, rockthrowing and sniping by an estimated 7,000 to 10,000 Negroes. Weapons used by rioters included firearms and Molotov cocktails. The disorders devastated a 150-block area of southwestern Los Angeles. The National Guard was called out Aug. 13 to help municipal and county police restore order. The authorities finally announced Aug. 15-16 that the violence had been brought under control. 3,952 persons, most of them Negroes, were arrested during the disorders.

In addition to the 34 deaths, the riot toll included 1,032 persons injured. 28 of those slain were Negroes. Whites among the dead included a sheriff's deputy and a fireman killed by a falling wall as he fought a riot-caused fire.

The incident that led to the riot was the arrest of a Negro

driver in Watts. A white state highway patrolman, Lee Minikus, stopped a car at 7:45 p.m. Aug. 11 on suspicion that its driver, Marquette Frye, 21, a Negro, was drunk. As Minikus was giving Frye a sobriety test, which Frye failed, about 25 Negroes gathered at the scene. Frye's mother, Mrs. Rena Frye, 49, also appeared and began scolding her son. Frye then turned angrily on the officer, and Mrs. Frye sprang at Minikus when he tried to force Frye into his patrol car. As the Fryes scuffled with Minikus and a 2d white officer, the crowd grew to about 200, and people in the crowd began shouting threats and throwing rocks. The 2 officers called for help at 8:20 p.m. Other officers arrived with riot guns and forced the crowd to move. But within 2 hours the moving mob had tripled in size. Members of the crowd began stoning cars and buses at random, some began to smash store windows and to loot, and more policemen were rushed into the area.

As badly outnumbered Los Angeles police officers and sheriff's deputies fought the rioters Aug. 11, Lt. Gov. Glenn M. Anderson flew to the riot-torn city. At 5:05 p.m. he signed a proclamation ordering California National Guard units to the scene. Anderson was serving as acting governor in the absence of vacationing Gov. Edmund G. Brown, who revealed later that he had instructed Anderson by phone to use the Guard. Los Angeles Mayor Samuel W. Yorty and Police Chief William H. Parker 3d, who had appealed for National Guard help at 10:30 a.m., joined other city officials in criticizing Anderson for not moving sooner.

Elements of the National Guard began anti-riot patrols late Aug. 13, and the Guard force was increased to about 10,000 by Aug. 14. Roderick Hill, adjutant of the California National Guard, announced Aug. 14 that "we're committing all our National Guard resources in the state." The National Guard troops, armed with machineguns, rifles, bayonets and tear gas, went on patrol with police, set up road-blocks and rode fire engines to protect firemen. Los Angeles Police Department figures showed 12,364 Guardsmen, 1,430 city policemen, 1,017 county sheriff's deputies and 68 state highway patrolmen on riot duty in Los angeles by Aug. 16. As rioting continued and spread, Anderson Aug. 14 proclaimed the riot-stricken city a disaster area and announced an 8 p.m.-to-dawn curfew. Leaders of the anti-riot force, which was patrolling some 46 square miles centering on the Watts district, finally reported Aug. 15 that, although some violence continued, they had achieved control of the situation.

The first night's rioting had reached its peak at about 1:30 a.m. Aug. 12 as 1,000 or more Negroes, most of them teen-agers or in their 20s, smashed windows, fought police and stoned cars. The police reported gaining the upper hand by about 3 a.m., when the mobs began to disperse.

Police Chief Parker, 63, long a target of charges that he was unfair to Negroes, said the rioters were "young hoodlums who have no respect for the law." But he indirectly placed at least some of the blame on civil rights leaders. "When you keep telling people they are unfairly treated and teach them disrespect for the law," he said, "you must expect this kind of thing sooner or later."

After a nervous day of relative calm in Los Angeles, the disorders were resumed during the evening of Aug. 12, when an estimated 7,000 young Negroes, including many women, rioted again. Prime targets of the mob were gun shops, sporting-goods stores and pawnshops, where looters stole firearms and ammunition. Rioters used the weapons to shoot at police, at cars, at whites and even at aircraft. Wandering bands of Negroes began late Aug. 12 to engage in gunfights with the police. These groups and others continued to smash store windows, loot the stores and then set them afire to cries of "Burn, baby, burn." Many whites unwittingly entering the area in autos were dragged from their cars and beaten, and their autos were smashed and burned. Several cases were reported, however, of individual Negroes defying rioters to save whites. Ambulances sent to aid people injured in the rioting were often attacked. Fire engines sent to fight the many fires started by rioters were showered with rocks and occasional Molotov cocktails.

Robert Richardson, a Negro employed as a *Los Angeles Times* advertising salesman, wrote Aug. 13, after watching the rioting for 8 hours: "It's a wonder anyone with white skin got out of there alive. . . . Every time a car with whites in it entered the area the word spread like lightning down the street: 'Here comes Whitey—get him!' The older people would stand in the background egging on the teen-agers and the people in their 20s. . . . One white couple in their 60s . . . [was] beaten up and kicked until their faces, hands and clothing were bloody. . . . Those not hitting and kicking the couple were standing there shouting 'Kill! Kill!' . . . As some areas were blockaded [by police] . . . the mobs would move outside looking for more cars with whites. When there were no whites, they started throwing rocks and bottles at Negro cars. . . . Everybody got in the looting—children, grownups, old men and women. . . . Then everybody started drinking—even little kids 8 and 9 years old. That's when the cry started, 'Let's go where Whitey lives!' That's when I began to see guns. . . ."

Most of the stores in Watts were owned by whites, and these largely were the ones destroyed. Many stores owned by Negroes were also looted and burned. But amid the destruction were several untouched stores that apparently had been protected by signs bearing some variation of the announcements "Negro Owned," "Brother" or "Blood."

(As disorder was slowly being checked in Watts, scattered Negro outbreaks, all quickly subdued, were reported from surrounding areas. 110 Negroes were arrested Aug. 14 in the independent municipality of Compton, 5 miles south of Watts, after a mob smashed windows, looted stores and threw Molotov cocktails. A policeman was killed and a 2d policeman injured in Long Beach, Calif. Aug. 15 as they and other officers fought 50 Negro youths who had been stoning cars. National Guardsmen were sent to Long Beach, and a 10 p.m. to 4 a.m. curfew was imposed. Incidents of Negro rockthrowing, arson, use of Molotov cocktails, sniping or other riot-type activity were also reported in San Bernardino, Hollywood, San Diego, Pasadena, Van Nuys and other communities in the vicinity.)

Gov. Brown, who had arrived in Los Angeles late Aug. 14, asserted Aug. 16 that the rioting had been "ended" and that the remaining violence was no more than "guerrilla fighting with gangsters." But he continued the curfew and announced that the National Guard "will remain here in force until the streets of Los Angeles are safe." (Brown suspended the curfew Aug. 17.)

At the height of the rioting Pres. Johnson Aug. 14 "urge[d] every person in a position of leadership to make every effort to restore order in Los Angeles." The President reiterated his deep commitment "to the fulfillment of every American's Constitutional right" but held that "rights will not be won through violence." Mr. Johnson announced that he was sending Commerce Undersecy. LeRoy Collins and White House aide Lee C. White to New York to meet Gov. Brown on the latter's arrival that afternoon, from his vacation in Greece, "to discuss the situation and to inform him of our desire to be of any possible assistance." In a statement issued Aug. 15, Mr. Johnson again assailed "resort to terror and violence" but asserted that "it is not enought simply to decry disorder" without attacking the cause. The riot-torn district was treated much as a disaster area as the violence subsided. State and municipal officials and volunteer organizations arranged for the distribution of food to residents whose usual food stores had been destroyed or closed. Arrangements were made to restore transportation and other services that had been suspended during the disorders.

In an open letter to Pres. Johnson Aug. 21, 29 leading Soviet scientists and artists expressed their shock at "the monstrous massacre of the population of the Negro ghetto in Los Angeles." The letter, published in *Pravda* and distributed by Tass, linked "the events in Los Angeles . . . with the barbarous actions of the American soldiers in Vietnam and the Dominican Republic." "In the faces of the manhandled and mutilated Negroes," the letter said, "we see the same pain and suffering as in the eyes of the Vietnamese children burned by napalm." Signers of the letter included Pres. Mstislav V. Keldysh of the Soviet Academy of Sciences, Pres. Nikolai N. Blokhin of the Soviet Academy of Medical Sciences, composer Dmitri Shostakovich, writer Aleksandr Korneichuk, nuclear physicist Peter Kapitsa and Nobel Prize winners Nikolai N. Semenov, Igor E. Tamm, Nikolai G. Basov and Aleksandr M. Prokhorov.

Causes of Disorders Studied

The apparently unorganized rioting was ascribed by various political, church, civil rights and other observers to the heat wave then prevailing in the area, to charges of police brutality and unfairness to Negroes, to resentments, frustrations and hopelessness caused by such conditions as poverty, unemployment and *de facto* school segregation, to the nationwide civil rights movement, to the high percentage of broken families among Negroes, to the presence of a large criminal element in the area and to other sociological, psychological and physical causes. Many observers pointed out that the thousands of rioters represented only a fraction of the nearly 90,000 Negroes who lived in Watts and who were the chief sufferers from the disorders. The riots, it was said, were opposed bitterly by a large, frightened majority of Negroes who had as much cause for protest as the rioters had.

Gov. Brown met in Los Angeles Aug. 15 with a group of

Negro leaders, who charged the Los Angeles police with bias against their race. They reportedly urged Brown to create means of communication between the police and the Negro community. Brown Aug. 16 announced his intention to appoint a commission to "probe both underlying and immediate causes [of the riots] and recommend means to prevent recurrences." Brown Aug. 17 asked Pres. Johnson to assign Commerce Undersecy. LeRoy Collins as a consultant to the commission, and the White House immediately announced that the President was directing Collins to aid California officials concerned with the riots.

The Rev. Dr. Martin Luther King Jr. said in Miami, Fla. Aug. 15 that he would meet with the Negro leadership in Los Angeles "and try to see what can be done to restore order and instill a nonviolent approach." King, whose visit to Los Angeles was opposed by Brown, asserted that it was "also urgent that I meet with the political leadership in Los Angeles . . . [to work out] the program necessary to give the Negro people hope—to restore their faith in a democratic future." King said he had visited Watts 6 weeks previously, had predicted trouble and had "proposed a civil rights march, just for the purpose of distilling frustration." "When there is a march, they don't riot," he said. "But the white leadership encouraged the Negro leaders not to march." King Aug. 14 had indorsed the "use of the full force of the police power to quell the situation in Los Angeles." But "police power can only bring a temporary halt," he added, and a full program of aid to Negroes was needed. King arrived in Los Angeles Aug. 17.

NAACP Executive Secy. Roy Wilkins in New York Aug. 15 had also indorsed the use of "whatever force is required" to end the rioting and had called for the appointment of "a bi-racial, non-partisan, uninfluenced commission" to probe the riot's causes. Wilkins said that "the Negro community as well as the white community must assume adult responsibility in facing the revelations of such a study."

Community Relations Service officials in Washington said Aug. 16 that CRS workers had warned Mayor Yorty in the spring that a bad racial situation was brewing in Los Angeles but that he had rejected their offer of conciliation services. Yorty Aug. 16 denied receiving any such warning.

Yorty charged Aug. 17 that "one of the riot-inciting factors was the deliberate and well-publicized cutting off of poverty funds to this city." He said the funds had been frozen "pending our efforts to reorganize the [Los Angeles] Youth Opportunities Board to meet the chameleonic OEO [Office of Economic Opportunity] criteria." Yorty accused the OEO of "a reckless effort to incite the poor for political purposes." OEO Director Sargent Shriver replied that Yorty's charges were "unfounded and untrue," that "there have been no changes in the OEO criteria since the original grant to Los Angeles, which Mayor Yorty accepted." Referring to Police Chief Parker's Aug. 16 statement that "we are on top and they [the rioters] are on the bottom," Shriver charged that "that mentality and attitude is what's causing the riots. . . . It's that 'we-and-they' attitude on the part of the city officials that has caused the outbursts."

Commerce Undersecy. Collins, who had arrived in Los Angeles Aug. 18, announced Aug. 23 that city and federal officials had negotiated a compromise in the dispute that had led to a hold-up of some $20 million in federal anti-poverty funds for Los Angeles. The compromise, approved by Mayor Yorty, OEO Director Shriver and other officials, provided for the creation of a local Economic & Youth Opportunities Agency, which would provide the minority-group representation demanded by federal officials.

Gov. Brown Aug. 19 appointed an 8-member commission headed by ex-Central Intelligence Agency Director John A. McCone to investigate the riots. 2 of the panel's members were Negroes: the Rev. James E. Jones, pastor of the Westminister Presbyterian Church, and Judge Earl C. Broady of Los Angeles Superior Court, who had served as a Los Angeles policeman for 16 years.

The McCone commission submitted its report to Brown Dec. 6. The report, entitled "The Need for Leadership," described the migration of Southern Negroes to communities such as Los Angeles and the frustrations suffered by the migrants. It cited 3 "aggravating events" of the year preceding the riots: (1) "the angry exhortations" of civil rights leaders "and the resulting disobedience for law in many parts of our nation," (2) the repeal of California's Fair Housing Act in Nov. 1964 and (3) the publicity given federal anti-poverty programs that "did not live up to their press notices" in Los Angeles. The commission found "no reliable evidence of outside leadership or pre-established plans for the rioting," but it asserted that organized gangs had spread the violence once the disturbance had started. The violence was described as "not a race riot in the usual sense" because "what happened was an explosion—a formless, quite senseless, all but hopeless violent protest—engaged in by a few but bringing great distress to all."

OTHER RACIAL DISORDERS

Several hundred Negroes, most of them teen-agers or in their 20s, rioted in the largely-Negro Lawndale (West Garfield Park) district of Chicago's West Side the nights of Aug. 12-13 and 13-14. Some minor disturbances were reported the night of Aug. 14-15, but the area was considered under effective control by then. About 80 persons were injured and 140 arrested in the incidents. The disorders broke out after a freak accident Aug. 12 in which a Negro woman was killed by a fire engine from an all-white fire station that had been a target of Negro demands for integration. Negroes gathered near the fire house the evening of Aug. 13 to hear embittered speeches by Lawrence Landry and other leaders of a militant civil rights group called ACT. Rioting followed. Negroes beat whites, fought policemen and attacked cars and stores with rocks, bottles and several Molotov cocktails. Nearly 1,000 persons were involved. 60 persons, including 18 policemen, were injured and 122 more persons were arrested before the violence was ended. The Fire Department Aug. 13 transferred a fire company of 17 Negroes and one white into the controversial fire station.

A series of demonstrations against alleged police brutality in Springfield, Mass. led to the burning of 2 white-owned stores by young Negroes late Aug. 13 and the arrest of 72 civil rights demonstrators, most of them Negroes, by Aug. 16. The immediate brutality charge arose from the arrest of 17 Negro men and a white woman in a disturbance at a Negro bar July 17.

William Epton, 33, vice chairman of the Harlem (N.Y. City) branch of the leftist Progressive Labor Movement (PLM), was convicted in New York Dec. 20 of conspiring to riot, of advocating the forceable overthrow of the N.Y. State government ("criminal anarchy") and of conspiring to overthrow that government. Epton, a Negro, had been arrested Aug. 5, 1964, following the Harlem rioting of July 18-21, 1964. Asst. District Atty. Joseph Phillips charged that Epton had tried to use the Harlem riots to further a "national strategic plan" involving the assassination of policemen and judges. Epton testified

Dec. 13 that he had been a Communist Party member from 1958 to 1962, when he had left the party to join the PLM.

SOUTHERN PROTESTS

Integrationists continued demonstrations in Southern states throughout 1965 in efforts to end discrimination in voting, in schools and in other areas.

Alabama Demonstrations

Police used smoke bombs Mar. 31 to turn back about 120 Negro youngsters as they entered the city of Camden, Ala. during a school boycott backing a Negro voter registration drive. The march had originated in a Negro church 2½ miles away. More than 100 Negro demonstrators marching toward the Wilcox County courthouse in Camden Apr. 1 were turned back by Mayor E. R. (Reg) Albritton, 42, city police officers and deputies. Albritton told the members of the group to return Apr. 5 if they were interested in registering to vote. About 65 Negroes, mostly children, demonstrated near the courthouse Apr. 2 by singing and sprawling in the street. They objected to the fact that Negroes had to go to Camden's old jail building to register to vote whereas whites could register at the courthouse. About 150 Negroes staged 5 civil rights marches in Camden Apr. 5. 11 of the leaders were arrested, and the demonstrations were broken up with smoke and tear-gas bombs.

Policemen in the western Alabama town of Demopolis (population: 7,500) broke up a Negro demonstration Apr. 22 by using tear gas and smoke bombs. But the demonstrators, who had marched without permits Apr. 20 and 21, received a permit for another march, and it was conducted by 328 demonstrators the same day without any trouble. More than 350 Negroes marched again in Demopolis Apr. 23. The demonstrations were in protest against allegedly discriminatory voter registration practices and job bias. But Mayor Edward D. Bailey said Apr. 22: "I don't know why they are protesting. We've integrated all the restaurants, cafes, public parks, theaters and given them anything they wanted. When I asked them what they wanted, all they could answer was 'Freedom.'" The Demopolis demonstrations were part of a Southern Christian Leadership Conference campaign led by the Rev. Samuel B. Wills of Albany, Ga.

Negroes on a civil rights march in Demopolis Apr. 26 refused to heed police orders to disperse and instead sat or lay down in the street. Policemen then hurled tear gas at them, and some demonstrators were injured when other demonstrators ran over them in panic. 9 Negroes were arrested. About 250 Negro youths, boycotting school since Apr. 16, held a brief protest march in Demopolis Apr. 27 but dispersed under police orders.

A voter registration campaign was initiated by Greensboro, Ala. Negroes July 6 with an uneventful march by about 450 persons to the Hale County courthouse. But a gathering of about 75 Negroes July 16 was broken up by white persons wielding sticks, hammers and rubber hoses. 17 Negroes were taken to the hospital as a result of the attack. 2 Negro churches in the area burned to the ground the following night. Negroes planned a protest march past the courthouse to the site of one of the churches, but a parade permit routed the march away from the courthouse. The Negroes insisted on the courthouse route, however, and gathered there daily. The police used tear gas July 26 to disperse about 400 demonstrators, but as the gatherings continued, state troopers were sent into Greensboro, and mass arrests were begun July 28. The voter registration board announced July 19, after a talk with Justice Department Atty. John Nixon, that it was ending the use of a state literacy test that had been outlawed by federal court orders in at least 5 counties. An easier test and accelerated procedures were used Aug. 2, but the board said Aug. 3 that only 39 of 93 Negroes who had taken the new test had passed it.

Bogalusa (La.) Campaign

Bogalusa, La., a lumber and paper-mill town of some 22,000 inhabitants, 35% of them Negroes, was the target of an intensive civil rights campaign—punctuated by occasional minor violence—starting in early April.

The all-Negro Bogalusa Civic & Voters League Apr. 8 presented Bogalusa Mayor Jesse H. Cutrer Jr. with demands for equal economic and educational opportunity, desegregation of all public accommodations, extension of basic improvements to the entire community, inclusion of Negroes on city and county boards, elimination of discriminatory city laws and employment of Negro policemen. CORE National Director James Farmer said at a mass rally that night that he would sponsor a boycott against the city's largest employer, the Crown-Zellerbach Corp. paper and chemical products firm, unless the company ended racial discrimination in its plants and agreed to hire Negro women.

Negroes protected by police marched toward the Bogalusa city hall Apr. 9 but turned back after a series of incidents in which (a) white men attacked a news photographer and demonstrators, (b) a car driven by the city's assistant police chief, L. C. Terrell, hit and injured a white man, (c) angry whites denounced the police for protecting the Negroes. 400 Negroes and some CORE workers marched again later Apr. 9. There were no incidents this time, and Mayor Cutrer promised the marchers at city hall that the city would try to help solve the racial problems.

Negro pickets, protected by police, marched in front of Bogalusa stores Apr. 14-20 in a demand for equal job opportunities. White counter-pickets tried to offset the demonstrations with a "buy-in"—an effort to encourage sales at picketed stores. 400 Negroes marched on city hall Apr. 19 to present a petition demanding the discharge of 3 white policemen "for improper conduct" in failing to protect Negro pickets. Farmer led another march of 600 integrationists to city hall Apr. 20 and accused Cutrer of not being willing to negotiate in good faith. Negroes picketed city hall Apr. 21.

Vice Pres. Hubert H. Humphrey intervened after being informed by Louisiana Gov. John J. McKeithen Apr. 22 that Negroes and whites were arming themselves in the area's paper-mill towns. Humphrey was said to have persuaded Farmer and his associates that mediation rather than demonstrations was the only feasible solution. Farmer left Bogalusa Apr. 23 to ease the tension, and 3 mediators were tentatively accepted by town and Negro leaders Apr. 22-23.

The Justice Department filed suit Apr. 20 in U.S. District Court in New Orleans against 6 Bogalusa restaurants charged with violating the public accommodations section of the 1964 Civil Rights Act by refusing to serve Negroes.

Cutrer vowed in a local radio talk May 23 that he would fight for the repeal of all Bogalusa segregation ordinances and for the hiring of Negroes by the police force and possibly by other city government departments. He stressed that his statement was endorsed by Bogalusa's community affairs committee, composed of 24 business, labor, professional, civic and religious leaders.

Street fights between whites and Negroes broke out in Bogalusa May 29 and 31 as Negroes picketed downtown stores. City and state police helped quell the clashes, which were intensified May 31 after police had been decoyed from the scene by firecrackers exploded elsewhere. About 600 white men were milling around in a 2-block trouble area at one time May 31. 47 whites and Negroes were arrested during the 2 days.

O'Neal Moore, 34, a Negro deputy sheriff of Washington Parish, La., was killed late June 2, while on car-patrol near Bogalusa, by shots fired from a pick-up truck. Creed Rodgers, a Negro deputy riding in the car, was wounded in the shooting but gave a radio alarm that led to the arrest of Ernest Ray McElveen, 41, a white resident of Bogalusa, who was charged with murder. The Negro deputies were the first Negroes to serve in such posts in the parish.

The Negro rights campaign was resumed July 7 with a march to the city hall by about 350 persons, including a few white nonresidents, for presentation of desegregation demands to the mayor. State and local police stood guard. Another march took place July 8. As it broke up, a white man, Alton D. Crowe Jr., 25, attacked 2 Negroes—Henry Austin, 21, and Milton Johnson, 26—and was shot and seriously wounded. Austin (who reportedly fired the shots) and Johnson were immediately arrested. Further rights marches were canceled July 9-10 because of increased local tension. Several street fights between whites and Negroes were reported July 10.

U.S. District Judge Herbert W. Christenberry July 10 refused an appeal from Bogalusa officials for an order to temporarily halt the demonstrations. Ruling July 10 on a Negro appeal, Christenberry enjoined Bogalusa authorities from using violence or threats to prevent Negroes from exercising their civil rights and ordered that they be protected from harassment by white townspeople.

More than 600 Negroes and white sympathizers staged a silent march behind Farmer July 11 as about 400 police, some armed with submachineguns, enforced tight security along the route. Similar marches were held July 12-14.

A counter-protest march by segregationists took place in Bogalusa July 11, with more than 500 whites participating. The segregationists were led by J. B. Stoner of Atlanta and Connie Lynch of Riverside, Calif. Stoner and Lynch also had staged rallies in the Bogalusa area under the sponsorship of the National States Rights Party.

Gov. McKeithen intervened July 12. McKeithen conferred in Baton Rouge with A. Z. Young and Robert Hicks, president and vice president, respectively, of the Voters League, and appealed to them for a 30-day cooling-off period. Young and Hicks, flown to and from the meeting in the governor's private plane, returned to Bogalusa to present his proposal to the League. The McKeithen appeal for a moratorium was opposed by the league at a meeting held later July 12. Young then phoned McKeithen that his proposal would be rejected unless concessions were made to the Negro group. McKeithen flew to Bogalusa July 13 and met with the Negro leaders at the city airport, but he failed to reverse their rejection of his plan. Negro leaders said the demonstrations would be continued.

The 2 sides—Mayor Cutrer and the city council opposed by the CORE-backed Bogalusa Civic & Voters League—appealed to Pres. Johnson July 14 for help in settling the city's racial troubles.

Asst. Atty. Gen. John Doar was dispatched to Bogalusa by Pres. Johnson as his mediator in response to the appeals. Mr. Johnson also designated one of his counsels, Lee C. White, as his special adviser on Bogalusa developments. Doar met with Gov. McKeithen, with Mayor Cutrer and the council and with rights leaders July 15-16.

Doar July 19 filed separate criminal and civil contempt actions against both Bogalusa Public Safety Commissioner Arnold Spiers and Police Chief Claxton Knight. The suits were filed on the basis of their allegedly "willfull disobedience" of the July 10 federal court order requiring protection of demonstrators. In addition to the contempt suits, Doar also filed Justice Department suits against: (1) the Original Knights of the Ku Klux Klan, its leader and 20 members and 15 other persons in the Bogalusa area for allegedly following "a violent design to prevent Negro efforts to achieve equal rights"; (2) Washington Parish Deputy Sheriff Walter Vertrees Adams on counts of police brutality against Negroes; (3) 3 restaurants in Bogalusa on grounds of violation of the public accommodations clause of the 1964 Civil Rights Act. (A suit for the desegregation of 2 movie theaters in Bogalusa had been filed by the Justice Department July 13.)

After the court action was initiated, Knight and Spiers broadcast over radio and TV a warning that persons attempting to harass rights workers in the future would face arrest "on the spot." A rights march was staged without incident in

Bogalusa later July 19 as policemen kept crowds from forming. Radio appeals for law and order were continued July 20-21 by police officials and civic leaders. Marches and tests of compliance with the public accommodations provision continued.

The U.S. 5th Circuit Court of Appeals in New Orleans Dec. 1 issued an injunction ordering the Ku Klux Klan to cease "acts of terror and intimidation" against Negroes in Bogalusa. The defendants in the suit, brought by the Justice Department, were the Original Knights of the Ku Klux Klan, "its dummy front, the Anti-Communist Christian Association," and 38 individuals. They were forbidden to interfere with Negroes' rights to use public accommodations, to register and vote and to seek employment. The court found that "the Klan relies on systematic economic coercion, varieties of intimidation and physical violence in attempting to frustrate the national policy expressed in civil rights legislation."

Natchez (Miss.) Demonstrations

544 Negroes were arrested in Natchez, Miss. Oct. 1-7 on charges of violating an injunction forbidding demonstrations. The injunction had been issued Sept. 30 by the Chancery Court to halt street protests against segregated public facilities and other allegedly discriminatory practices. Marches had begun Sept. 7 with the withdrawal of 650 National Guardsmen. The Guardsmen had been sent into the city by Gov. Paul B. Johnson Jr. after the Aug. 27 bombing of the car of local NAACP Pres. George Metcalfe, who had been critically injured by the blast. 265 of those arrested, including NAACP Field Secy. Charles Evers, the campaign leader, were sent by bus to the state prison at Parchman, 200 miles from Natchez. After spending up to 5 days in prison, the demonstrators arranged for their release on bond of $200 each.

Demonstrations were suspended Oct. 7 to give city officials a chance to consider a revised list of NAACP demands. A boycott of most downtown stores by Negroes continued, and Mayor John Nosser said Oct. 12 that business was down 25-50%.

Negro leaders met with city officials Oct. 13, but disagreement broke out as to what the meeting had accomplished. Charles Evers said at a Negro rally Oct. 13 that the city had agreed to hire Negro policemen, appoint a Negro school board member, establish a biracial housing commission, integrate the local hospital and instruct city employees to address adult

Negroes by the courtesy titles "Mr.," "Miss" or "Mrs." Nosser Oct. 14 issued a statement denying that the city had promised to put a Negro on the school board, desegregate the hospital or use courtesy titles in addressing Negroes. A march of 600 Negroes through the business district took place Oct. 16 in protest against alleged "reneging on agreements"; Evers then announced that mass marches would be suspended but the boycott continued.

The Natchez boycott was suspended Dec. 3 after the city administration agreed to meet Negro demands, but Evers Dec. 23 announced the resumption of the boycott because of alleged police brutality in quelling a fight Dec. 22 between a white man and one of 7 Negroes picketing a store that had refused to hire Negroes.

(In Fayette, Miss., 23 miles from Natchez, Negro leaders had called a "black Christmas" boycott after receiving unsatisfactory answers to a list of 19 demands submitted to city officials Dec. 15. The demands included the hiring of Negro policemen and government employes, desegregation of public facilities, the use of courtesy titles and the improvement of conditions in Negro residential sections. The city had agreed only to the hiring of one Negro policeman and of Negro school guards.)

Other Mississippi Protests

Negroes and white integrationists staged a 2-day 14-mile march from Fannin to Brandon, Miss. May 28-29 in protest against vote discrimination, church burnings and the seating in Congress of Mississippi's 5 Representatives. (5 Negro churches had been burned in the area's Rankin County in the past year.) The march, which took place without incident, was sponsored by CORE and the Mississippi Freedom Democratic Party. About 135 persons began the march, and about 278 persons were in the group when it ended in Brandon at the county courthouse. The marchers were met there by the city and county officials, including Mayor C. J. Harvey. Negroes were guided into the registrar's office to begin voter registration, and other marchers were offered seats in the courtroom. State police, under instructions from Gov. Paul B. Johnson Jr., had escorted the marchers. CORE National Director James Farmer joined the group May 29.

Demonstrations June 14-18 at the Mississippi state capitol in Jackson, where the state Legislature had convened in special session June 14, resulted in the arrests of 856 integrationists. Gov. Johnson had called the special session to rewrite state voting and registration laws that conflicted with federal court rulings and the pending federal voting rights bill. The demonstrations were sponsored by the Freedom Democratic Party, which contended that officials elected by the overwhelmingly white electorate held office illegally and that the special session, therefore, was invalid. (About 100 college students, recruited from across the nation by the SNCC, went to Washington June 14 to demonstrate against the Mississippi delegation in the House of Representatives. They picketed near the Justice Department June 15. 12 Mississippi Negroes were arrested June 19 for refusing to leave the office of the House clerk, where they were seeking action on 800 depositions obtained by the National Lawyers Guild. The depositions, alleging vote discrimination, had been filed with the clerk May 17 to be printed and referred to the House Elections Subcommittee, which has jurisdiction over election challenges.) About 100 of those arrested in Jackson were juveniles who were later released. The remainder were confined in compounds at the state fairgrounds. Among those arrested were John Lewis, chairman of the SNCC, and Charles Evers, the state NAACP field secretary. Most of the arrests were made under city ordinances barring parades without permits and the distribution of handbills without authorization from the city council.

Charges of brutality by police against those arrested in Jackson were made June 22 by 3 members of the Commission on Religion & Race of the National Council of Churches and by Dr. David M. French of the Medical Committee on Human Rights. Rights lawyers reported that 60 of those arrested had signed statements charging police brutality. A Jackson medical center reported treating 4 demonstrators with visible injuries. All but about 225 of those arrested had been released by June 24 under bail raised by the Lawyers Constitutional Defense Committee. (Those remaining in jail had refused bail.) 70 demonstrators were arrested June 24 on breach-of-peace and resisting-arrest charges after protesting against alleged police brutality. (4 Negroes and 12 whites were arrested on disorderly-conduct charges June 23 in a New York demonstration against the Jackson jailings. The demonstrators, including 10 teen-agers, had chained themselves together and to entrances to the federal courthouse in Foley

Square. The incident was staged by the New York unit of the SNCC.)

A temporary restraining order barring Jackson officials from arresting voting-rights demonstrators under the city's parade and handbill ordinances was issued by a 3-judge federal court in New Orleans June 30. 3 days of peaceful protest marches were begun by rights leaders in Jackson July 1 under the protection afforded by the court order. The marchers were watched closely by local and federal officers as they followed procedures specified in the court order: demonstrators were to march 2 abreast and obey all traffic rules and other regulations. The marchers followed a 2-hour route that took them past the state capitol, the governor's mansion and through the downtown section of Jackson. No marchers were arrested during the 3 days, but police seized a white man July 3 when he attacked a Negro minister leading that day's march.

Americus (Ga.) Turmoil

Almost continuous civil rights demonstrations were held in Americus, Ga. following the arrest July 20 of 4 Negro women for refusing to move from a voting line marked "white women only." One of those arrested was Mrs. Mary Kate Bell, a candidate for justice of the peace in the election. The 4 women were jailed, and bail was set at $1,000 each.

At a joint news conference in Atlanta July 26, John Lewis of the SNCC and Hosea L. Williams of the Southern Christian Leadership Conference (SCLC) pledged a "massive united invasion upon segregation" in Americus until (1) the 4 women were freed without bail, (2) the election, which they claimed was illegal because of segregated voting procedures, was voided and rescheduled (Mrs. Bell was defeated in it), (3) demonstrators were protected, (4) at least one Negro voter-registration clerk was appointed and registration periods lengthened and (5) a biracial committee was set up.

Negroes conducted a "token" march to the county courthouse in Americus July 26 and held vigils at the jail until U.S. District Judge W. A. Bootle July 30 ordered the women released. Bootle also barred county and city officials from holding segregated elections. On their release, the women joined a vigil at the courthouse. (A suit for their release and for a ban on segregated elections had been filed by the Justice Department in Macon July 27.)

Picketing of white merchants was begun July 28, and 5 Negro pickets were attacked July 31 by white segregationists. 2 demonstrators, one of them white, were assaulted by white men Aug. 2 while police watched. 23 demonstrators were arrested for trespassing; 2 whites who attacked demonstrators were not arrested.

2 small integrated groups were rebuffed in attempts to enter the First Baptist Church and the First Methodist Church Aug. 1. A Baptist deacon told the group that "if you come down here looking for violence, you're going to get it." At the Methodist church, 12 white men stood at the top of the church steps with a line of youths behind them to bar the way.

A white, Andrew Whatley, 21, was killed July 28, 3 blocks from a demonstration at the jail, when stones were thrown by a group of whites at a passing car driven by a Negro and shots allegedly were fired from the car. Whatley, a bystander, was wounded fatally. 2 Negroes in the car—Charlie Lee Hopkins and Will Lamar—were arrested. They were indicted on first-degree murder charges by a county grand jury Aug. 3.

Attempts to form a biracial committee were started after a recommendation for such a body had been made by the Americus Merchants Association July 22. White business leaders had offered simultaneously to post the $4,000 total bond for the 4 women arrested in the voting line, but the women had refused the offer because of their stand that they should be released without bail. About 25 white businessmen attended a civil-rights rally July 23 in the interests of harmony. They were supported by the city's Junior Chamber of Commerce. White housewives and community leaders Aug. 3 appealed for peace negotiations between the Negro and white communities. They also backed County Atty. Warren Candler Fortson in the effort to create a biracial committee after a petition for his removal had been circulated and signed by more than 1,000 persons. Fortson called an informal biracial committee to a meeting Aug. 4, but Mayor T. Griffin Walker announced that he and other city and county officials did not support the committee. Representatives of the SCLC and SNCC and the Rev. J. R. Campbell, president of the Sumter County Movement, attended the meeting, and Gov. Carl E. Sanders appealed Aug. 4 for mediation.

The surprise appointment of 3 Negro voting clerks was announced Aug. 6 by county officials. Rights leaders, with the help of Negro comedian Dick Gregory, who arrived Aug. 6, rounded up Negro vote registrants. 647 Negroes had been registered by Aug. 9, when total Negro registration reached about 1,700, compared with about 7,000 white registered voters.

A Ku Klux Klan rally took place in Americus Aug. 8, and about 700 persons participated in a silent KKK march and memorial service for the white youth killed July 28. Later, about 300 integrationists marched to the courthouse through a white residential area.

22 whites and Negroes, including SNCC Chrmn. John Lewis, were arrested Aug. 8 in another unsuccessful attempt to enter the First Baptist and First Methodist churches.

Lincolnton (Ga.) Marchers Attacked

A Lincolnton, Ga. rights campaign, sponsored by the Southern Christian Leadership Conference (SCLC), was marked by violence Oct. 22, when about 30 white segregationists, shouting "Kill the niggers," attacked 95 Negro marchers. Several demonstrators were beaten, and the march was halted.

A protest march the following day was called off after 117 demonstrators were turned back by 52 state troopers and the march leaders asked the advice of SCLC headquarters in Atlanta. Highway Patrol Information Officer William Foster told reporters, "We've got word that the town [population 1,450] is laying in wait for them [the marchers] and with more than their fists." A few minutes later 7 civil rights workers were injured (one suffered a brain concussion) when their car overturned. SCLC Field Secy. Richard Smith charged that local whites had been "harassing and chasing" the car. Marches were suspended until Oct. 27.

About 50 local Negroes, most of them pulp mill workers, turned back an Oct. 28 march of 30 young Negroes led by Willie Bolden, 26, the Rev. Charley Brown and Edward Bedford, all of the SCLC. Sylvester Glaze, speaking for the group that confronted the demonstrators, said: "You can't change anything. . . . And after you leave here we'll be left alone to catch the devil. . . . Our children are too scared to go to school because of all this mess."

Bolden led a march of about 65 demonstrators escorted by about 40 state policemen Oct. 29 without interference. Speaking at a rally in front of the courthouse following the march, he accused local Negro laborers of "selling their souls to feed their families." Daily marches continued without incident through Oct. 31, and more than 20 Negroes lined up at the Lincoln County courthouse Nov. 1 and registered to vote.

Plymouth (N.C.) Trouble

Negro voting-rights demonstrations, started in Plymouth, N.C. in early August, were marked by outbursts of violence Aug. 26 and 31. The first incident involved a reported attack and beating of 27 Negro and white rights workers after a Ku Klux Klan rally downtown. The 2d incident occurred when a crowd of whites reportedly "closed in" on a small group of Negroes after a planned Negro march had been cancelled. One of the Negroes allegedly fired a pistol and wounded a white. Another white was stabbed in the ensuing melee. Albien Arrington, 33, a Negro accused of firing the pistol, was later arrested and charged with assault.

100 state highway patrolmen were dispatched to Plymouth by Gov. Dan Moore Aug. 31 on the strength of reports of a movement of Klansmen into the area. 2 white men were arrested Sept. 1 on charges of "going dangerously armed," and 11 more were arrested Sept. 2 at roadblocks set up for weapons checking. The governor met in Raleigh Sept. 2 with Robert Jones, "grand dragon" of the Ku Klux Klan in North Carolina. Jones said afterwards that he had ordered Klan members to stay out of Plymouth unless they lived there. Moore had sent to Plymouth his administrative assistant and a civil rights aide. The latter was instrumental in the formation by county and city officials Sept. 1 of a biracial committee composed of 9 Negro and 10 white members. Plans for further rights demonstrations were suspended Sept. 3 after reports that progress was being made by the committee.

Sharecropper Evictions Barred

U.S. District Judge E. Gordon West in Baton Rouge, La. Dec. 23 issued a temporary restraining order forbidding white landowners to evict Negro tenant farmers who had registered to vote. The order did not cover the cancellation of sharecropper or farming agreements. West ruled after the Justice Department had filed suit Dec. 17 under the 1965 Voting Rights Act charging intimidation of Negroes who had registered in West Feliciana Parish. One of the landowners involved was

Fletcher Harvey, registrar of the parish.

The American Civil Liberties Union's Southern regional office in Atlanta had announced Dec. 21 that it was submitting 11 complaints of intimidation to Atty. Gen. Nicholas deB. Katzenbach from Negro sharecroppers who had registered to vote in Wilcox County, Ala. According to ACLU regional director Charles Morgan Jr., the Negroes had either already been evicted from their land or had been told they must leave early in 1966. Other Negroes complained that they had lost their jobs or their credit after registering to vote, and 4 other sharecroppers said they had been evicted after taking part in civil rights demonstrations. Federal voting examiners had been ordered into Wilcox County Aug. 18.

Other Incidents

At least 15 state policemen used clubs Mar. 19 to force 25 Negro and white demonstrators away from the state capitol cafeteria in Little Rock, Ark. The demonstrators were also attacked with oil of mustard gas from an undisclosed source. It was their 3d futile effort to integrate the Arkansas state-house cafeteria, which had been operated as a private club since the passage of the 1964 Civil Rights Act.

59 Negroes were registered as voters in Allendale, S.C. Aug. 2, but a demonstration after the registration books were closed led to the arrest of 38 persons, including 9 whites. The Rev. C. A. Webster Jr., a white Baptist minister who was a part-time consultant to the federal Community Relations Service (CRS), signed a guarantee for a total of $3,732 in bonds for the release of the demonstrators (14 declined release), but a CRS official in Washington later affirmed that "it's not the policy, practice or the intent" of the service to post bonds, and Webster was recalled to Washington Aug. 5. Marches were held Aug. 4-5 in protest against the one-day-a-month regis-tration schedule.

54 persons, including 18 college students (11 from N.Y. City), were arrested in Orangeburg, S.C. Aug. 3 in a sit-in at the county courthouse in protest against an alleged voter registration slowdown. 590 Negroes were registered Aug. 2-3; this raised the total since June to 850. The students were members of SCOPE (Southern Community Operation in Political Education), organized by the Southern Christian Leadership Conference.

The U.S. Supreme Court Jan. 18 had reversed the convictions of the Rev. B. Elton Cox, a CORE field secretary, on breach of the peace and illegal demonstrating charges. He had been arrested in Baton Rouge, La. in 1961 after leading more than 1,500 students in a rights demonstration.

U.S. District Judge Bryan Simpson in Jacksonville, Fla. Dec. 1 dismissed about 1,000 charges against more than 400 persons who had participated in civil rights demonstrations in St. Augustine in 1964. The Rev. Dr. Martin Luther King Jr. and Mrs. Malcolm Peabody, mother of former Massachusetts Governor Endicott Peabody, were among those against whom charges had been pending. Simpson's ruling was based on a U.S. Supreme Court decision that the 1964 Civil Rights Act had the effect of stopping state prosecution of sit-in cases regardless of whether arrests had been made before or after passage of the act. Later decisions had extended the ruling to include forms of protest other than sit-ins, Simpson said.

Southern Whites Urge Peace & Fairness

The Mississippi Economic Council (Chamber of Commerce) appealed Feb. 3 for racial peace and obedience to the 1964 Civil Rights Act. The council's 100-member board of directors said in a statement issued in Jackson: "We recognize that the Civil Rights Act of 1964 has been enacted . . . as law. It . . . should not be unlawfully defied." The board urged "positive action" toward promoting "justice" and "harmony" in Mississippi. The board proposed this 4-point program: (1) "Order and respect for the law must be maintained. Lawless activities in the state by individuals and organizations cannot be tolerated." (2) "Communications must be maintained between the races within the state." (3) "Registration and voting laws should be fairly and impartially administered for all." (4) "Support of public education must be maintained and strengthened."

22 influential Alabama business groups called Apr. 15 for equal treatment of Negroes. Their appeal appeared in full-page advertisements in the *Birmingham* (Ala.) *Post-Herald* and *Wall Street Journal*. The groups were the Alabama Chamber of Commerce, the Alabama Bankers Association, the Alabama Textile Manufacturers Association, Associated Industries of Alabama, the Association of Huntsville Area Contractors and the Chambers of Commerce of 17 town and cities in Alabama.

The advertisement declared: "The vast majority of the people of Alabama, like other responsible citizens throughout our nation, believe in law and order, and in the fair and just treatment of all their fellow citizens. They believe in obedience to the law regardless of their personal feelings about its specific merits. They believe in the basic human dignity of all people of all races. . . . First, we believe in the full protection and opportunity under the law of all our citizens, both Negro and white. . . . We believe . . . in the right of every eligible citizen to register and to cast his ballot. . . . We call on business leaders all over the state to provide leadership in [non-discrimination in employment]. . . ."

Selma, Ala. government and business leaders appealed Aug. 25 for equal rights for Negroes. Their plea was made in advertisements in several Alabama newspapers and later in the *Wall Street Journal* and *Newsweek* magazine. The sponsors were the Selma City Council, Court of County Revenues, the Selma-Dallas County Chamber of Commerce and the Selma-Dallas County Committee of 100-Plus. The ad called for full opportunity under law for all citizens, guarantee of the right of every eligible citizen to vote, adherence to the 1964 Civil Rights Act and communication between white and Negro leaders.

SCHOOL DESEGREGATION

First School Suits Under '64 Act

The Justice Department Jan. 4 filed suits against school segregation in 2 counties in Louisiana and Tennessee. They were the first federal school desegregation suits to be filed under the 1964 Civil Rights Act. In one suit, filed in Shreveport, the department sought the right to intervene in support of Negro parents of Louisiana's Bossier Parish (county), who had filed suit Dec. 2 to restrain the parish Board of Education from continuing to segregate their children in parish schools. In the Tennessee suit, filed in Knoxville, the department sought the nullification of an Aug. 20, 1964 decision of the Campbell County Board of Education that denied applications of Negro children to attend elementary and high schools in Jellico, Tenn.; the 1964 decision forced them to attend schools outside of Jellico.

The Justice Department filed suit in Baton Rouge, La. Apr. 8 for an injunction to desegregate all 28 state-operated trade schools in Louisiana. The suit cited a letter to the department in which William J. Dodd, state superintendent of public instruction, had expressed his "opinion that these schools will continue operating on a segregated basis until either a federal court or the Louisiana Legislature changes their mode of operation."

(The department moved in U.S. District Court in Birmingham, Ala. June 16 to intervene in a private school desegregation suit filed by a group of Negroes May 24 against Bessemer school officials. The Bessemer Board of Education had refused to submit a school desegregation plan required under the 1964 law for schools seeking federal aid.)

Southern Compliance Starts

The South Carolina Board of Education agreed Jan. 15 to sign a pledge to comply with federal school desegregation policies. It thereby became eligible to receive $11,800,000 in federal aid. The penalty for noncompliance by any public school district: Federal funds would be cut off under Title VI of the 1964 Civil Rights Act.

The Georgia Board of Education agreed Jan. 20 to sign a school desegregation pledge. The state's school systems were receiving $55 million in federal aid.

The Mississippi Board of Education agreed Feb. 24 to comply with the federal requirements and thus keep from losing more than $23 million a year in federal aid funds for Mississippi schools. The Greenville (Miss.) Board of Education had agreed Jan. 15 to draft school desegregation plans to be sure of retaining $272,000 in federal aid. The first desegregation of Mississippi public schools without a court order was achieved in Greenville May 28 when 22 Negro children were registered without incident in the 2d grade of previously all-white schools. Greenville's plan called for integration of the first 2 grades in 1965, the next 3 grades in the next 3 years and the 6th grade in the 5th year.

A 3-judge federal court in Alexandria, Va. Mar. 10 enjoined Virginia from paying tuition grants to 10 private segregated schools that had been established in several sections of the state to avoid school integration.

The U.S. Office of Education had announced Jan. 22 that 199 Southern colleges, including the Universities of Mississippi and Alabama, had pledged to comply with the 1964 Civil Rights Act.

Colleges had to promise to end discrimination in order to qualify for federal aid under the National Defense Education Act (which provided loans for college students), the new higher education bill (providing aid for building classrooms and other facilities) and other federal programs.

The Justice Department June 14 sought to accelerate the pace of desegregation in 4 Mississippi school districts—Canton, Meridian, Biloxi and Leake counties—by filing suits of intervention in privately initiated suits that had resulted in court orders specifying desegregation. The action reportedly was aimed at protection of job security for Negro teachers. U.S. Education Commissioner Francis Keppel had said June 10 that "a school district cannot avoid the requirement that it desegregate its faculty by discriminatorily dismissing or releasing its Negro teachers." His statement followed receipt of complaints that hundreds of Negro teachers in the South might lose their jobs because of the transfer of Negro students to formerly all-white schools.

The department Oct. 1 filed motions to intervene under the 1964 Civil Rights Act in 3 cases originally filed by individual Negro citizens: (1) In Columbia, S.C., the department sought to bar school officials of the state and of Orangeburg, Sumter and Charleston counties from paying tuition grants to white students attending private schools. (2) In Jackson, Miss., it sought to bar enforcement of a 1965 state law requiring payment of tuition for public education by children whose parents were out of state. (3) In Mobile, Ala., it sought an end to segregation in the Dallas County courthouse.

Deadline Set, Aid Loss Threatened

U.S. Education Commissioner Francis Keppel announced Apr. 29 that the nation's 27,000 school districts would be required to desegregate all public schools completely by Sept. 1967. The school districts also would be required to demonstrate a "good-faith substantial start" toward desegregation by Sept. 1966 (at least 4 of a school's 12 grades integrated by then), Keppel said. The Office of Education notified 181 school districts, in a letter sent out Aug. 18, that pledges of desegregation would have to be made by Aug. 31 or steps would be instituted to eliminate federal school funds.

Forrest County (Miss.) school officials sued Atty. Gen. Nicholas deB. Katzenbach and Health, Education & Welfare

(HEW) Secy. John W. Gardner Oct. 8 for the release of educational funds withheld by the federal government. In a counter-claim filed Dec. 13, the Justice Department charged that the county board of education maintained total segregation of schools, teaching and administrative staffs and school buses in violation of HEW regulations. The department asked for a court injunction forbidding the county to operate a segregated school system.

Southern Integration Hailed

Pres. Johnson Aug. 31 issued a statement hailing as "deeply encouraging" the Southern compliance with the 1964 Civil Rights Act in desegregating public schools. Of more than 5,000 school districts in 17 Southern and border states, 4,463 (88%) were proceeding with compliance, the President said. He said "much patience and dedicated effort" were needed "if plans are to be translated into performance." Mr. Johnson Aug. 23 had expressed pleasure at an Office of Education report that all but about 180 of the nation's 25,000 school districts had indicated willingness to comply with desegregation regulations necessary to receive federal funds. Acceptable compliance pledges had been received from all state boards of education.

The Office of Education reported Sept. 30 that 217,000 Negro students, or 7½% of the Negro pupil population of the Deep South, had been enrolled with white pupils in the fall term. The total was about triple the 2.6% of the year before. In a report on the same situation, also issued Sept. 30, Chrmn. John Lewis of the Student Nonviolent Coordinating Committee sharply criticized the Office of Education's handling of the program under the 1964 Civil Rights Act. Lewis said the 7½% figure, while accurate, was "pitifully low." His report charged that the federal office had been "totally unprepared" to review compliance plans submitted by "conniving, scheming, evasive or downright dishonest" school officials and that a "false image" of progress had been reported to Pres. Johnson and relayed by him to the public.

A report criticizing Administration policy in enforcing school desegregation under the 1964 rights act's provisions was presented to Health, Education & Welfare Secy. John W. Gardner Nov. 15 by the NAACP Legal Defense & Education Fund, Inc. and was made public by the fund at a news conference Nov. 16. The American Friends Service Committee joined in submitting the report. Referring to Southern Regional Council findings that only 5.2% of Negro students in 11 Southern states were attending integrated schools, the report charged that "HEW must accept the blame for flagrant noncompliance, the resulting tokenism and the despair in the hearts of Negro children."

Taliaferro County (Ga.) School System Bankrupt

A 3-judge federal court in Augusta, Ga. Oct. 14 declared the Taliaferro County school system bankrupt and named state Schools Supt. Claude Purcell to take control of the system as receiver. The ruling was handed down in a suit brought by the Southern Christian Leadership Conference (SCLC) and the NAACP Legal Defense & Educational Fund after all 165 white students in the county had transferred to schools in adjoining counties rather than attend school with 72 Negroes who had registered in the county's only white school, in Crawfordville. The school was later closed.

The court directed Purcell to reopen the county white school, to allow Negroes to transfer to the other counties or to "come up with some other solution acceptable to the court." In compliance with the ruling, 42 Negro students accompanied white students Nov. 17 on school buses to schools in adjoining Warren, Greene and Wilkes counties.

The SCLC had led demonstrations in Crawfordville since Sept. 27, and Negro children each day had attempted unsuccessfully to board buses used to transport white students to neighboring counties. 200-300 of the county's 585 Negro students had boycotted the Negro schools and attended a freedom school. Frequent street marches had been held, but the Rev. Dr. Martin Luther King Jr. announced after the Oct. 14 court ruling that demonstrations would be halted.

Incidents accompanying the Negroes' demonstrations had included an attack on a teen-age demonstrator Oct. 4 by Georgia Ku Klux Klan grand dragon Calvin Craig. Craig twisted the demonstrator's arm and threw him against a car while onlooking crowds shouted "Kill him!" Craig was arrested on an assault charge and released on $100 bond.

SCLC photographer Brigido Cabe, 23, was attacked Oct. 12 by Cecil Myers, 26, a member of the Black Knights of the Ku Klux Klan; a fellow Klansman, Joseph Howard Sims, 43, was restrained by state troopers from joining in the assault. Myers was charged with assault and released on $100 bond; Sims was released after questioning. (Myers and Sims had been acquitted in 1964 of the shotgun murder of Negro educator Lemuel Penn.) Myers, Sims and 5 other Black Knights members were arrested Oct. 17 in Crawfordville on charges of forcing George Turner, a Negro farmer, off the road in his car and pointing guns at him after attempting to beat him. The 7 were released on bond of $250 each; 7 shotguns, 8 pistols and several clubs were taken from them by Sheriff M. B. Moore.

SCLC official Hosea Williams reported that methods used by segregationists to fight the Negro integration drive included beatings, jailings, the dismissal of 2 Negro teachers and a Negro principal from Negro schools, the dismissal of 3 Negro bus drivers, 2 school cooks and 2 school custodians, the dismissal from various jobs of 22 other Negroes whose children participated in the demonstrations, the evictions of 6 families from their homes and 4 foreclosures on homes and cars.

In nearby Washington, Ga., Negro students protesting alleged inferior school conditions demonstrated Oct. 18-20 under SCLC sponsorship. An injunction prohibiting interference with classes, issued Oct. 19 by Superior Court Judge Robert Stephens, was defied Oct. 20 as 300 teen-agers overturned desks and chairs in the Negro school. 200 students who then staged a sit-in in front of the white school were arrested en masse on disorderly conduct charges; most were given suspended sentences and released later in the day, but SCLC workers were sentenced to $30 fines or 30 days in jail.

Southern Universities

Vivian Malone, 22, received a Bachelor of Science degree from the University of Alabama in graduation ceremonies in Tuscaloosa May 30 and thus became the first Negro graduate in the school's 134-year history. Miss Malone, who had maintained a B-plus average, graduated with 1,725 white students.

Harvey B. Gantt, 22, graduated from Clemson University in South Carolina May 29. He was the first Negro in modern times to have attended a previously all-white state-supported school in South Carolina.

Richard Holmes, 21, a transfer student from Wiley College in Texas, was enrolled voluntarily and without incident in State College, Miss. July 19 as the first Negro student of Mississippi State University.

The U.S. 5th Circuit Court of Appeals in New Orleans May 5 had dismissed, in a 4-3 ruling, criminal and civil contempt charges it had initiated against ex-Mississippi Gov. Ross R. Barnett and his successor, Gov. Paul B. Johnson Jr. The court had charged Barnett, then governor, and Johnson, then lieutenant governor, with defying its orders in Sept. 1962 to allow James H. Meredith to enroll as the first Negro at the University of Mississippi.

Negro Teachers Lose Jobs

A joint study sponsored by the National Education Association and the Office of Education and released in Washington Dec. 21 documented 452 cases of Negro teachers in 17 Southern and border states who had been discharged or demoted as a result of school integration. The report cited an unwillingness of school officials to place Negro teachers in predominantly white schools and "an aura of fear," created by the possibility of job losses, that had been used by school administrators "to intimidate Negro teachers and to inhibit their personal and professional activities." The report was prepared by a 45-member group, headed by Robert L. Cousins of the Southern Education Foundation. It recommended the use of federal funds to improve the skills of displaced Negro teachers.

Northern Developments

The U.S. Supreme Court Mar. 1 upheld by refusing to review a 1964 ruling of the 10th U.S. Circuit Court of Appeals in Denver that, in effect, had held that *de facto* school segregation did not violate the Constitution. The appeals court, in a case involving the Kansas City, Kan. school system, had ruled that although the Constitution barred the segregation of public school pupils by race, it did not require integration.

Dr. Calvin E. Gross was ousted by the N.Y. City Board of Education Mar. 4 as superintendent of schools and placed on a 3-month leave of absence with pay. Dr. Bernard E. Donovan, 53, executive deputy superintendent, was named acting superintendent. The board had asked Gross confidentially Feb. 24 to resign, but he had refused to do so. Gross finally resigned June 14 (effective Aug. 31), and the board retained him as a special consultant. The board had made public Mar. 7 a racial integration plan for the city's school system. The plan had been prepared by Gross, although his name was omitted from it. The board reportedly had felt that Gross had delayed too long in devising the plan. Gross's plan recommended: (a) the conversion of regular academic and vocational high schools into 4-year comprehensive secondary schools by 1972-73; (b) a movement "in the direction of a new middle or junior high school" by creating new middle schools as grade 6-7-8 junior high schools, by trying "at least one" 4-4 organization (a school for the first 4 grades followed by a school for the 2d 4) and by building new junior high schools for Negro and Puerto Rican pupils outside their immediate areas.

The Central Zoning Unit of the N.Y. City school system reported Mar. 29 that the number of predominantly Negro and Puerto Rican public schools in the city had risen greatly in the past 4 years although more Negro pupils attended formerly all-white schools. In 1960-61, 40½% of the city's Negro and Puerto Rican pupils attended predominantly Negro and Puerto Rican public schools, 3.7% attended virtually all-white schools, and 55.8% attended integrated schools. In 1964-65, 48.9% of Negro and Puerto Rican pupils attended predominantly Negro-Puerto Rican schools, 3.3% predominantly white schools and 47.8% integrated schools.

The U.S. Supreme Court Nov. 8 declined to hear an appeal of a N.Y. State Court of Appeals decision that had upheld "school pairing" plans effected by the N.Y. City Board of Education in Sept. 1964. The appeal had been filed by 11 white parents from N.Y. City's borough of Queens. The plaintiffs had protested a Board of Education order "pairing" predominantly white Public School 149 in Jackson Heights with predominantly Negro P.S. 92 in Corona. The parents contended that the plan violated the Supreme Court's 1954 school desegregation decisions by requiring children to travel out of their former school districts for racial reasons.

The N.Y. State Court of Appeals, in a 5-2 decision Mar. 18, had upheld a 1964 ruling that affirmed the legality of State Education Commissioner James E. Allen Jr.'s June 17, 1963 directive requiring racial balance in Malverne elementary schools. Allen's order required that Negro pupils be shifted from predominantly Negro schools to predominantly white schools. 255 white students stayed away from 2 predominantly white elementary schools with a total enrollment of 779 in

Malverne Oct. 28 in protest against the projected implementation of the plan. The boycott had been preceded by a mass meeting the previous night. The protest came in reaction to an Oct. 11 Supreme Court rejection of an appeal of 3 white parents from a decision upholding Dr. Allen. The Supreme Court action had been followed Oct. 21 by a meeting in Albany of Malverne school board members and State Education Department officials at which it was agreed that the integration plan would be implemented in Jan. 1966.

The Mt. Vernon (N.Y.) Board of Education was picketed Nov. 4 by more than 200 civil rights demonstrators in a protest sponsored by the NAACP. Led by Floyd King Jr., president of the NAACP's Mt. Vernon chapter, the demonstrators included members of CORE and 12 other groups. At a press conference called in N.Y. City Nov. 3 by Fred Jones, NAACP state education commission chairman, the NAACP had announced that Mt. Vernon would be the organization's first of several N.Y. State "target" cities in which it would lead protests against school segregation. (The Mt. Vernon Board of Education had allowed Negro students to transfer to under-utilized white schools since 1963 but had not paid for transportation. The board had decided in Sept. 1965 to provide transportation for students living more than 1½ mile from their schools but had revoked the decision in October by 5-4 vote.)

Dr. Allen ordered the Mt. Vernon education board Dec. 21 to submit a plan for ending racial imbalance in its schools by Mar. 15, 1966, to take effect with the fall term. Allen acted after Negro parents had protested the board's adoption of a voluntary transfer plan rather than plans submitted by an advisory panel on racial imbalance and by Dr. Dan W. Dodson of the NYU Center for Human Relations.

Commissioner Allen ordered the school board of Roosevelt, N.Y. Nov. 24 to submit by Mar. 1966 a plan to end racial imbalance in the public schools. The plan was to be effective in Sept. 1966. The school board had anticipated the ruling by making public Nov. 23 a plan to end *de facto* segregation in 2 years by creating an educational park. The NAACP had picketed local merchants in a campaign to persuade them to put pressure on the school board.

Allen Dec. 22 ordered the Amityville, N.Y. school district to submit by Mar. 15, 1966 a plan to eliminate racial imbalance in its schools, effective Sept. 1966. Allen objected to the fact that one Amityville elementary school had 96.8% Negro attendance while another was 96% white.

The Massachusetts Board of Education's Advisory Committee on Racial Imbalance & Education had reported Apr. 14 that racial inequalities existed in Massachusetts public schools to a degree harmful to both white and Negro pupils. Of the state's 55 public schools with more than 10% non-white students 45 were listed as being in Boston. The report cited a Mar. 1964 census that "showed clearly that most Negro children in Massachusetts attend predominantly Negro schools while the overwhelming majority of white children attend schools that are either all white or have fewer than 5 non-white children enrolled."

43 persons were arrested by June 9 in 3 weeks of rights demonstrations against the Milwaukee schools. Most of the arrests were of demonstrators blocking school buses. The protests were against keeping Negro classes intact when they were moved to other schools during remodeling of their own overcrowded schools. Demonstrators included clergymen (5 of whom were arrested June 4) and nuns. CORE conducted almost daily sit-ins at the office of the school superintendent.

Milwaukee school children, most of them Negroes, stayed away from public and parochial schools in numbers ranging from 9,000 to 12,000 Oct. 18-21. (Total enrollment: more than 122,495.) The boycott, in protest against *de facto* school segregation, was sponsored by the Milwaukee United School Integration Committee (MUSIC), whose chairman, Assemblyman Lloyd A. Barbee (D.), was the only Negro in the state Legislature. The absentees attended 22 freedom schools and took part in marches Oct. 19 on the home of Mayor Henry Maier (D.) and Oct. 20 on the home of Schools Supt. Harold S. Vincent. Maier called the demonstrations "Ku Klux Klanism in reverse." The boycott ended Oct. 21 with a demonstration led by comedian Dick Gregory in front of school administration headquarters. Barbee said Oct. 21 that individual schools would be boycotted "soon and often." The boycott had raised the issue of civil rights participation by Roman Catholic clergy. Auxiliary Bishop Roman R. Atkielski Oct. 17 prohibited the use of pastoral facilities for freedom schools and warned priests of the danger of prosecution if they took part in the boycott. 3 priests announced that they were withdrawing their facilities from use by MUSIC, but they did so with "every protest short of direct disobedience." A newly formed group called Catholics for

Social Responsibility picketed the chancery office of the Milwaukee Archdiocese. 2 priests active in the boycott and demonstrations, the Rev. James E. Groppi, 34, and the Rev. William J. Whelan, were specifically ordered by Atkielski Oct. 19 and 20 to end their participation.

11 persons were arrested in Milwaukee Dec. 6 as they and 11 others picketed a school construction site in a MUSIC-sponsored demonstration. Among those arrested were Groppi and 4 other clergymen. The demonstrators argued that selection of the site, in a Negro area of the city, would continue *de facto* school segregation. Demonstrations continued at the school site Dec. 8 and Dec. 10 and resulted in the arrest of 4 pickets each day. CORE national director James Farmer joined the picket line Dec. 8 but was not among those arrested. One of those arrested Dec. 10 was Marilyn Morehauser, a former Roman Catholic nun, who was given a 30-day jail term for disorderly conduct after refusing to promise not to take part in future demonstrations.

656 persons were arrested in Chicago June 10-July 8 in demonstrations by anti-segregationists protesting the rehiring of Schools Supt. Benjamin C. Willis. Willis had been rehired May 27 until his 65th birthday, Dec. 23, 1966, at a $48,500 annual salary. A united front of civil rights groups, dissatisfied with what they termed the slow pace of school desegregation, announced May 28 that a public school boycott would be held in protest against Willis' rehiring. A state court injunction against the boycott was obtained June 8 by the school board, but it failed to halt the protests. Mass demonstrations, marches to city hall and the school board and street sit-downs began June 10. No arrests were made the first day although traffic was tied up for 4 hours in the business district. A similar demonstration took place June 11, and 225 persons were arrested, including CORE national director Farmer, Negro comedian Dick Gregory and 9 clergymen. The demonstrations continued, and arrests were made when demonstrators disobeyed orders to remain on the sidewalk, 2 abreast. Among the 441 persons arrested by June 12 were 14 Protestant ministers, 3 Roman Catholic priests and 6 nuns. After a demonstration June 15 resulted in 89 arrests, an accord was reached with the intervention of 4 clergymen, who met with Mayor Richard J. Daley. Daley agreed to permit a march on city hall on 2 traffic lanes and to negotiate with rights leaders. About 150 persons marched without incident June 16

to city hall. 80 more arrests occurred June 28, however, when demonstrators lay down in a midtown street in protest against Daley's repeated refusal to oust Willis.

U.S. Education Commissioner Francis Keppel notified the Illinois State Board of Education Oct. 1 that federal funds totaling $34 million were being withheld from the Chicago public school system as a result of a complaint filed July 4 under the 1964 Civil Rights Act by the Coordinating Council of Community Organizations (CCCO), a group representing 75 civil rights organizations. The CCCO had charged the Chicago Board of Education with deliberately perpetuating school segregation. Chicago Board of Education Pres. Frank M. Whiston announced Oct. 5 that the release of the funds had been secured, effective Oct. 6, at a meeting earlier that day with Health, Education & Welfare Undersecy. Wilbur J. Cohen. Under the agreement releasing the funds, the Board of Education would discontinue training at a segregated trade school and would create a committee to review such problems as school boundaries.

The New Jersey Supreme Court June 28 had canceled the Plainfield school board plan for reducing racial imbalance. The plan called for converting a school with 96% Negro enrollment into a 6th-grade school for the entire city. The court rejected the plan because it ignored 5 other schools with 57%-69% Negro enrollments.

New Jersey Education Commissioner Frederick M. Raubinger Nov. 29 approved a Teaneck school board plan to alleviate racial imbalance by converting a predominantly Negro school into a 6th grade school for the entire town. White parents protested against the cost ($47,946 in the fall of 1966) of busing students under the plan.

Educational Conferences

Pres. Johnson and top Administration leaders participated in the 2d White House Conference on Education July 20-21. About 700 educators, governors, labor leaders, businessmen and government officials attended. The President told the group July 21 he had asked its leaders to establish a task force on education to "provide a continuing flow of ideas from universities and private groups." Vice Pres. Hubert H. Humphrey, speaking July 21, warned that "unless we stop the erosion and the corrosion of urban centers, then all the power and wealth of the nation will be for naught." A preliminary report on the conference's work, presented to the President orally July 21, said that vigorous federal leadership was needed to accelerate school desegregation; pre-school education should be continued on a regular basis for the underprivileged; youth must be presented with more employment opportunities; the decline of city education must be resisted with more funds from local, state and federal governments.

More than 2,000 white and Negro Southern educators attended a Southern Regional Conference on Education in Richmond, Va. Dec. 2-3. Described as a follow-up meeting to the White House Conference on Education, the conference was held under the joint auspices of the White House and the Southern Association of Colleges & Schools. Vice Pres. Humphrey, giving the opening address Dec. 2, was applauded when he said: "If it is good enough for the American Republic to be defended in Vietnam by all citizens of all races, then it is good enough for this country to open up the opportunities of a full education to all citizens of all races."

The National Education Association (NEA) convention, held in New York, was addressed by Pres. Johnson July 2. The major points of the President's address were his announcement of proposals for a Teacher Corps and for aid to teachers displaced by school integration. Mr. Johnson hailed the NEA's announcement June 27 of a drive to raise $1 million to provide displaced Negro teachers with legal, job-placement and training services. An NEA panel had reported about 200 documented cases of Negro-teacher firings in the South since Apr. 29. An NAACP estimate put the number of such firings at nearly 1,000.

OTHER ADMINISTRATION ACTIVITY

Military Vs. Segregation

Deputy Defense Secy. Cyrus R. Vance warned in a Feb. 12 directive that beginning in the 1966-67 school year, the Defense Department would withdraw Reserve Officers Training Corps (ROTC) units from any school or college that practiced racial segregation.

Maj. Gen. Winston P. Wilson, chief of the U.S. National Guard Bureau, issued orders (made public Mar. 30) providing for the withdrawal of federal recognition from any National

Guard unit refusing to admit Negroes. The orders were issued
to the Army National Guard Feb. 15 and the Air National Guard
Mar. 23.

Farm Aid Bias Fought

The U.S. Civil Rights Commission charged in a report Feb.
28 that Southern Negro farmers suffered discrimination from
Agriculture Department agencies that administered federal
farm programs on the state and local levels. The report
said: "The 1.5 million Negroes in farm families and the 3.2
million rural nonfarm Negroes of the South comprise a major
element in the arc of poverty which sweeps from Maryland
to Texas—the largest geographic and social concentration of
the poor." "Few of the economic problems now burdening the
rural South can be solved until basic changes are made in the
federal programs designed to bring about solutions. These
changes must include the elimination of the segregated structur-
ing of services, the removal of racial limitations on opportunity,
and the inclusion in the decision-making process of broad
sections of the population previously denied participation. . . ."
In a letter made public at the same time as the report, Pres.
Johnson asked Agriculture Secy. Orville L. Freeman to report
within 30 days on the commission's recommendations. Freeman,
acknowledging discrimination, said that "a massive effort" was
being undertaken by his department to end discrimination. Freeman Apr. 2 announced his appointment of 3 Negro farmers to
their states' committees administering federal farm programs
in Arkansas, Mississippi and Maryland. They were the first
Negroes ever to serve on such committees in these states.
Freeman also named a citizens advisory committee to help him
implement the provisions of the 1964 Civil Rights Act that
applied to his department.

President Stresses Achievement of Ability

Speaking at commencement ceremonies at Howard University in Washington, D.C. June 4, Pres. Johnson declared that
the Negro battle for civil rights was entering a new stage—
one in which "achievement" rather than legal equality would
guarantee Negroes a full place in American society. The
President pledged that he would make this new aim "a chief
goal" of his Administration.

The President said that "American Negroes have been another nation, deprived of freedom, crippled by hatred." They had acted, he said, with "impressive restraint" in peaceful protests, "demanding a justice that has long been denied." Mr. Johnson called it "a tribute to America that, once aroused, the courts and the Congress, the President and most of the people, have been the allies of progress." But, he said, borrowing a phrase of the late Winston Churchill, enactment of the voting-rights bill was not the end nor even the "beginning of the end." It was, he said, "perhaps the end of the beginning" and "that beginning is freedom"—"freedom . . . to share . . . fully and equally in American society."

"It is not enough just to open the gates of opportunity," Mr. Johnson asserted. "All our citizens must have the ability to walk through those gates, and this is the next and the more profound stage of the battle for civil rights. We seek not just freedom but opportunity. We seek not just legal equity but human ability. . . ."

"The great majority of Negro Americans, the poor, the unemployed, the uprooted and the dispossessed," he said, were "another nation" that was "losing ground every day" in "the battle for true equality." The President cited 2 basic reasons for this defeat: Negroes were "trapped" in "inherited gateless poverty" and were victims of "the devastating heritage of long years of slavery and a century of oppression and hatred and injustice."

"Negro poverty," Mr. Johnson declared, "is not white poverty" and the differences between the 2 races "are not racial differences." One of the differences, he said, was the fact that more than 73% of American Negroes lived in urban areas, most of them in slums and most of them together, making of them "a separated people." The other major differences cited by the President: (a) unemployment, which "strikes most swiftly and broadly at the Negro"; (b) "the lacerating hurt of early collision with white hatred or prejudice"; (c) "the breakdown of the Negro family structure."

As for solutions to these problems, Mr. Johnson said, "there is no single easy answer," but jobs, welfare and social programs and care for the sick were parts of the answer, and "an understanding heart by all Americans is another big part of the answer." The Negro, he said, "will have to rely mostly on his own efforts, but he just cannot do it alone." The special differences displayed by Negro poverty "must be faced, and they must be dealt with, and they must be overcome," he said, "if we are ever to reach the time when the only difference between Negroes and whites is the color of their skins."

Rights Act Compliance Reported

A report released July 11 by Pres. Johnson on the effect of the first year of the 1964 Civil Rights Act said that the letter of the law had been complied with "perhaps faster than the drafters dared hope" but that "the next step is to achieve compliance in spirit." "It is not enough for a Negro . . . to win admittance to a previously segregated restaurant; he must be welcomed." The report continued: "Curiously, reluctance to make him feel welcome is now being expressed increasingly in the North—perhaps in reaction to pressures for open occupancy in housing. It is this dimension of the problem— the psychologically imprisoning aspects of prejudice—that needs to be attacked next, and on a massive scale."

The report said: The 1964 rights act (one year old July 2) was "well on its way toward accomplishment" of its principal aim—in Pres. Johnson's words: "to end divisions" in American society. Voluntary compliance with the act's accommodations provisions had been "substantial," and compliance with its health, education, welfare and vocational rehabilitation provisions had been "encouraging." Some desegregation of public facilities had taken place "in every major city where segregation . . . had formerly been required." "Improved police-community relations" was "one of the most crucial" civil rights needs as well as "perhaps the greatest hope for reducing tensions in the big cities." "Private organizations and private citizens of good will" were "a reservoir of voluntary manpower that we have only begun to tap" for civil rights problems.

Among data contained in the report: (a) During the act's first year, the U.S. had instituted 14 new voting discrimination suits, 19 public accommodations suits and 10 school desegregation suits; the Community Relations Service had acted in 141 conciliation cases and had established offices in 9 Northern cities (New York; Philadelphia; Oakland, Calif; Detroit; Cleveland; Boston; Newark, N.J.; Rochester, N.Y.; Garry, Ind.). (b) 404 recipients of Area Redevelopment Administration loans had complied since February with requests for signed pledges of compliance with the act. (c) 60% of Southern and border state school districts had submitted satisfactory compliance plans, another 30% had plans under review.

Employment Discrimination Attacked

After the 1964 rights act's Title VII went into effect July 2, hundreds of complaints of job discrimination were filed under it with the Equal Employment Opportunity Commission (EEOC). 374 of them were filed by the NAACP by Sept. 15. In filing 96 complaints Aug. 18, the NAACP listed building trades unions in Cincinnati, Pittsburgh, N.Y. City and Memphis and state employment services of Alabama, North Carolina and Mississippi. More complaints were filed by the NAACP July 15 against 10 companies and 5 unions in New Orleans, Memphis, Birmingham and in East St. Louis, Ill. The commission announced Aug. 18 that designation of a racial qualification in help-wanted advertisements would be considered a violation of Title VII and that mention of religion or national origin would also have to be excluded except in rare cases.

EEOC Chrmn. Franklin D. Roosevelt Jr., in a report to Pres. Johnson made public Nov. 4, revealed that 1,383 complaints of employment discrimination had been filed with the commission in its first 100 days of operation. The commission's probable jurisdiction had been established in 966 of these cases; 70% of them came from 11 Southern states. States with the greatest number of complaints (in which the commission had jurisdiction): Alabama 135, North Carolina 131, Louisiana 76, Mississippi 68, Texas 62, Iowa 53, Tennessee 52, South Carolina 51, Virginia 45, New York 43. 73% of the complaints charged discrimination by race, 16% discrimination by sex and 1% discrimination by national origin. 87% of the complaints were directed against employers, 20% against unions and 3% against state employment agencies. 530 complaints charged discrimination in hiring and promotion; 150 charged discrimination in seniority practices and 107 charged discrimination through the use of wage differentials. 14 complaints of discrimination by sex were filed by women and 7 by men.

The EEOC Dec. 12 filed job discrimination complaints against 11 employers and one union. The companies and the union were located in California, Louisiana, Missouri, Tennessee, Texas and Virginia; the commission said that names of the defendants could not be revealed under 1964 Civil Rights Act provisions. The complaints were the first to be filed by the commission, which had been empowered by the Rights

Act to take the initiative in filing complaints in cases where a pattern of discrimination existed or where individual complainants appeared to be in danger of suffering reprisals. Roosevelt announced at a New Orleans press conference Dec. 18 that the Crown Zellerbach Corp. and the Papermakers & Paperworkers Union had agreed to commission proposals for ending job discrimination in the firm's paper mill at Bogalusa. The agreement provided for the meshing of segregated promotion lines and the elimination of racially-linked wage scales in compliance with Title VII.

NAACP Labor Secy. Herbert Hill filed 29 employment discrimination complaints with the EEOC Dec. 28. The complaints included one against the *N.Y. Times* and Prentice-Hall International, Inc. of New York objecting to a classified advertisement placed in the *Times* by the latter publisher for a sales representative in South Africa. The complaint was filed on behalf of a Negro applicant who had been told that a Negro could not be considered for the post because of the *apartheid* policies of the South African government. Hill charged that the incident demonstrated "that major American corporations are acquiescing in South Africa's *apartheid* policies." He contended that "responsible newspapers have the duty to determine that advertisements accepted for publication are not based upon institutionalized discriminatory employment practices." *N.Y. Times* Executive Vice Pres. Harding F. Bancroft said Dec. 28 that the paper "will not knowingly accept any advertisement which discriminates on religious or racial grounds."

Vice Pres. Hubert H. Humphrey, chairman of the President's Committee on Equal Employment Opportunity, had appealed in Washington Jan. 26, at a conference of 500 leading executives and personnel officers of major corporations, for a "wartime effort" to reduce the "massive unemployment among non-white workers in our citites." He deplored the fact that while Negroes formed only 10% of the labor force, they represented 30% of the long-term unemployed. He said Labor Department studies showed that "at least half of the non-white labor force was unemployed at some time during the past year."

U.S. Civil Service Commissioner John W. Macy Jr. reported Nov. 2 that employment of Negroes by the federal government had increased by 9,511 in 1964 out of a total increase in federal employment of 18,420. The highest increase came in upper-level jobs (federal grades GS-12 through GS-18), in which Negro employment increased by 20.6% (481 jobs), while the total increase was 4½%. About 13% of the federal work force was said to be made up of Negroes although Negroes comprised only about 11% of the total population.

Federal Roles Realigned

A reorganization of federal civil rights activities was ordered by Pres. Johnson Sept. 24 on the recommendation of Vice Pres. Humphrey.

Under the realignment, (a) the President's Committee on Equal Employment Opportunity and the President's Council on Equal Opportunities were abolished, (b) the Civil Service Commission got the job of overseeing employment equality practices in all federal departments, (c) the Labor Secretary was made responsible for reviewing complaints of bias in federal employment and for requiring compliance by government contractors, (d) the Equal Employment Opportunity Commission created by the 1964 Civil Rights Act took responsibility for complaints of discrimination in private businesses that had no federal contracts, (e) the Plans for Progress program continued in private employment on a voluntary basis, (f) the Community Relations Service (CRS) would be shifted from the Commerce Department to the Justice Department (under a reorganization proposal to be submitted to Congress) and (g) the CRS' clearing house and data-gathering activities were transferred to the Civil Rights Commission. Wiley H. Branton, the Vice President's assistant in civil rights affairs, was named a special assistant to the Attorney General to handle voter registration under the new Voting Rights Act.

(The President's Committee on Equal Employment Opportunity had said Aug. 26 that jobs had been found for more than 100,000 Negroes and other non-whites in the past 2 years under the Plans for Progress program. Currently, 313 companies were participating in the program.)

Rights Commission Urges Action

The U.S. Civil Rights Commission submitted to Pres. Johnson and Congress Nov. 13 a 188-page report recommending broadened Justice Department activity in the civil rights field and new rights legislation. The document was drafted after field investigations in a number of states in 1964 and a formal hearing in Jackson, Miss. in Feb. 1965. The commission's members were: John A. Hannah (chairman), Eugen Patterson (vice chairman), Frankie M. Freedman, Erwin N. Griswold, the Rev. Theodore M. Hesburgh and Robert S. Rankin, with William L. Taylor as staff director.

The commission cited Southern communities in which "wrongs have been committed with the active or passive support of local officials and [which] will not readily yield to self-reform." Noting that "severe self-limitations have been imposed on the scope of federal protective action," the report recommended that "federal law enforcement officers be stationed at the scene of likely violence, that [more] . . . federal officials be assigned to communities where violence has occurred, that more extensive investigation and surveillance activities be undertaken by these officials and that federal law enforcement officers . . . make on-the-scene arrests for violations of federal law." It suggested that federal officials "place under surveillance persons and groups suspected of violence and . . . attempt to protect persons who are likely to be endangered."

The commission recommended enactment of a 2-part criminal law. One part would be based on Congress' power to regulate interstate commerce and would make harming or intimidating a person engaged in "certain protected activities" a felony if either the perpetrator or his victim were using an interstate commerce facility. (The "protected activities would include exercising a right protected by federal civil rights legislation or an activity covered by the First Amendment "when undertaken for the purpose of obtaining equality for individuals of a particular race or color.") The 2d part would hinge on the equal protection clause of the 14th Amendment and would allow violations of state laws to be prosecuted in federal courts "when local officials fail to act, or the nature of their action constitutes a denial of equal protection, or where it is determined that justice is administered in the community involved in a manner so as to deny equal protection of the laws." A 3-judge federal court would decide which cases should be transferred from state courts to federal courts.

The commission also recommended that the Attorney General appoint more Negroes to law enforcement agencies and courthouse staffs and that state and municipal governments be given a greater incentive to prevent police brutality by being made liable to suit by persons found to be victims of police misconduct.

Federal Funds to Be Denied if Bias Is Found

In a letter to the heads of 21 federal agencies, Atty. Gen. Nicholas deB. Katzenbach Dec. 27 issued guidelines covering the cutting off of funds to federally aided programs in which racial discrimination was found. Such cut-offs were authorized by Title VI of the 1964 Civil Rights Act. The guidelines gave each federal agency the responsibility of determining when programs were being administered in a discriminatory manner. They required the agencies to seek "voluntary compliance at the outset in every noncompliance situation and . . . through each stage of enforcement action." Funds could not be withheld until a hearing had considered evidence of discrimination. Agency heads were encouraged (a) to check on compliance through periodic inspections and (b) to achieve nondiscrimination through court suits as well as fund cut-offs. It was announced that funds were being withheld in 55 cases (most of them involving Southern school systems) while hearings were being conducted. (A withholding of funds Oct. 1 from the Chicago school system had been rescinded Oct. 5 after protests from a number of public officials, who denied that Chicago schools discriminated.)

At a Washington news conference Dec. 16, spokesmen for the NAACP Legal Defense & Educational Fund, the Medical Committee for Human Rights and the National Medical Association had charged that the Health, Education & Welfare Department had failed, in most cases, to fulfill Title VI requirements that it cut off federal funds from Southern hospitals practicing discrimination. The group declared that the Medicare program would serve as a "golden opportunity to wipe out discrimination in Southern hospitals," and it asked that Medicare funds be given only to integrated hospitals. A delegation from the 3 organizations, led by Dr. John L. S. Holloman Jr., Negro president of the Medical Committee for Human Rights, had met Dec. 15 with Asst. HEW Secy. James M. Quigley. Holloman Dec. 16 criticized HEW Secy. John W. Gardner for not receiving the delegation personally; he released the text of a telegram to Gardner in which he had said that his committee and the 2 associated organizations wondered "if your failure to meet with us has racial implications and may be symptomatic of the reluctance of your department to come to grips with the discriminatory practices in health care." (HEW officials insisted that nondiscrimination provisions would be enforced.)

MEETINGS & RIGHTS ORGANIZATIONS

Negro Objectives

45 national Negro leaders declared in a statement issued Jan. 31, after a 2-day program of discussions and workshops in N.Y. City: "The conference recognized that the Civil Rights Act of 1964 and the Economic Opportunity Act make possible a new climate in which the first responsibility of civil rights groups to consolidate the political consciousness of Negro Americans gained through the effective use of their vote in the 1964 Presidential campaign. Of equal importance is their responsibility for undertaking an intensive educational campaign to acquaint Negroes with their rights and expanded opportunities under the new legislation."

The meetings had been called by A. Philip Randolph, president of the Bro'hood of Sleeping Car Porters. Among those who attended: James Forman, executive secretary of the Student Nonviolent Coordinating Committee; Roy Wilkins, NAACP executive director; Whitney M. Young Jr., executive director of the National Urban League; the Rev. Andrew Young of the Southern Christian Leadership Conference; George Wiley, associate national director of CORE; Lawrence Guyot of the Mississippi Freedom Democratic Party; Bayard Rustin, organizer of the 1963 March on Washington; L. Joseph Overton of the Negro American Labor Council; Norman Hill, consultant to the AFL-CIO; the Rev. Dr. Gardner C. Taylor of the Concord Baptist Church; Dorothy I. Height, president of the National Council of Negro Women; Mrs. Anna A. Hedgeman of the United Church of Christ; Ossie Davis and Ruby Dee of Actors' Equity; Dr. Kenneth B. Clark of CCNY; Arthur Rice of the Catholic Interracial Council; Theodore Brown of the American Negro Leadership Conference on Africa.

A call for an "alliance of the Negro and labor and the black poor and white poor" was issued May 28 by Randolph in a keynote speech opening a convention of the Negro American Labor Council in Yonkers, N.Y. Randolph, president of the group, said that such an alliance would be "a new weapon against the problem of unemployment. It was needed, he said, because the civil rights revolution, "though indispensable to endow Negroes with full, first-class citizenship and with political potentiality to help shape and direct the course of the American government, is wholly inadequate successfully to grapple with the basic economic and social problems of black Americans." Randolph warned against the tendency of the civil rights movement "to lapse into a state of relaxation." Randolph also called for massive federal investment in public works. "The black and white poor are not jobless solely because of the lack of education," he said. "They are unemployed because there just are no jobs."

NAACP Activity

Plans to institute a nationwide program of "citizenship clinics" for Negroes were announced by the NAACP (National Association for the Advancement of Colored People) Jan. 4. NAACP Executive Director Roy Wilkins explained that the program's "broad goal will be the assumption of full citizenship responsibilities along with utilization of full citizenship rights."

Delivering the keynote address at the 56th annual convention of the NAACP, held in Denver June 28-July 3, Wilkins said that implementation of the 1964 Civil Rights Act was the NAACP's "principal task" for the immediate future. Speaking at the same session, Herbert Hill, NAACP director for labor affairs, expressed dissatisfaction with Negro gains in the labor field, which he described as largely a "symbolic breakthrough," and with the war on poverty, which he called "only a BB shot against poverty" and "an extension of white paternalism." Dr. Buell G. Gallagher, president of the College of the City of New York and a member of the NAACP board of directors, warned the convention June 29 that the organization's rights campaign would have to be conducted in such manner as not to leave any "permanent residue of undying bitterness."

The NAACP during 1965 filed almost 500 complaints of job discrimination with the newly created Equal Employment Opportunity Commission.

Southern Christian Leadership Conference

The SCLC's major drive during 1965 was aimed at securing voting rights for Alabama Negroes and was climaxed Mar. 21-25 by the dramatic Selma-to-Montgomery march.

Plans for an economic boycott of Alabama and for a new Negro voter registration drive in the South were announced by the Rev. Dr. Martin Luther King Jr., SCLC president, during an

SCLC conference in Baltimore Apr. 1-2. King said that a "program of escalated economic withdrawal" would be waged against Alabama in protest against the state's racial conditions. The 3 phases of the program would be: (1) to discourage business expansion or location in the state and to urge the withholding of federal funds in states where discrimination was practiced; (2) to seek withdrawal of federal tax funds deposited in Alabama banks and to ask private groups to ascertain that their investments in the state were not used to support "racism and brutality"; (3) to boycott consumer goods produced in Alabama. (Pres. Johnson, questioned about King's proposal, said at his news conference Apr. 1 that "we must be very careful to see that we do not punish the innocents.")

The SCLC's planned voter registration drive was to be waged in 120 "black belt" counties (in Virginia, North and South Carolina, Georgia, Florida, Alabama and Louisiana) having 724,710 potential Negro voters, of which only 150,924 were registered. (Of 627,764 potential white voters, 536,369 were registered.) The SCLC also approved increased rights demonstrations in Northern cities and called for the appointment of a Negro to the Supreme Court and of more Negroes to the federal judiciary.

An estimated 50,000 persons marched in Boston Apr. 23 from the Negro Roxbury section to the Common in a protest against racial inequality in the North. King warned in a speech at the Common that Americans "must not become a nation of onlookers" in the fight for equal rights and integration.

King and the SCLC conducted a rights campaign in Chicago July 24-26. The drive culminated in the largest rights demonstration in Chicago's history—a march to city hall July 26 by 10,000 (police estimate) to 20,000 (King's estimate) demonstrators. It was the 42d march to city hall in 47 days. King had announced the drive, the first large-scale civil rights campaign by his group in a major Northern city, after a meeting July 7 with Chicago rights leaders. The march July 26 was under the protection of hundreds of police. Demonstrators filled 7 blocks of the downtown "loop" section at the rally ending the demonstration.

At the invitation of Rep. Adam Clayton Powell Jr. (D., N.Y.), pastor of the Abyssinian Baptist Church in N.Y. City's Harlem, King preached a sermon Nov. 14 at 2 Sunday services at the church. The audiences totaled about 11,000. King urged Negroes to "get involved in the peace movement," which, he said, "can't

be separated now" from the civil rights movement, because
"we've got to have a negotiated settlement" in Vietnam. At a
press conference held between the 2 services, Powell called
reports of a feud between him and King "an unfounded lie."
Powell said King's SCLC should "go national, . . . expand into
the vacuums of leadership" in such places as Newark, N.J.,
which "is 50% Negro and . . . has no leadership." (After the
Harlem riots of July 1964, Powell had criticized King for con-
sulting with N.Y. City officials but not with Negro leaders;
after a meeting of the 2 men in July 1965, Powell said he had
told King that "we've got leadership in Harlem," a reference
to King's plan to visit Northern cities where Negro leadership
was weak. King announced that he had suspended the planned
expansion of the SCLC into the North in order to "grapple with
the maladministration of justice in the South."

Powell Urges Blacks to Seek Power

Rep. Powell urged American Negroes May 28 to aspire to
"audacious power" and become "mayors, United States Senators, presidents of companies and members of stock ex-
changes." Addressing an Ebenezer Missionary Baptist Church
meeting in Chicago's McCormick Place convention hall, Powell
said: "As the Negro revolt was our Sunday of protests, so the
black revolution must become our week of production." "This
can only be done," he said, "by black people seeking power—
audacious power." Powell said that Negro organizations should
be led by Negroes, that Negroes should refuse to accept anything less than a "proportionate percentage of the political
spoils," and that no Negroes over 21 should be permitted to
participate in civil rights protests unless they were registered
voters.

CORE Convention

Delegates to the 21st annual convention of the Congress of
Racial Equality (CORE), held in Durham, N.C. July 1-5,
approved plans for a civil rights drive in Bogalusa, La. and
first approved, then shelved, a resolution calling for the withdrawal of U.S. troops from Vietnam and the Dominican Republic.
CORE National Director James Farmer said the Bogalusa
project was "a new direction" for CORE in that "indigenous
leaders" would be supported in a "community organizational

program." The troop-withdrawal resolution was voted July 5 but was shelved after Farmer led a successful drive for CORE to remain apart from the peace movement and to concentrate solely on civil rights. The convention also (a) urged the creation of civilian police review boards throughout the nation; (b) refused to endorse the formation of self-defense groups such as the Deacons for Defense in Louisiana; (c) reelected Floyd B. McKissick, 44, to a 3d term as CORE national chairman.

(CORE Dec. 25 acknowledged the resignation of Farmer, 45, effective Mar. 1, 1966. Farmer was to become president of the Center for Community-Action Education, Inc., a new private agency to be based in Washington. The center, to be financed by an Office of Economic Opportunity grant and contributions from labor and industry sources, was to oversee a nationwide literacy and job-training program for Negroes and other minority-group members. A $50 million program was contemplated.)

Urban League Meets

Vice Pres. Hubert H. Humphrey, addressing the 55th annual conference of the National Urban League in Miami Beach, Fla. Aug. 3, asserted that the best way to deal with the Negro's "problems of spirit" in America was through the Administration's anti-poverty program. "Progress towards full citizenship," he said, "will come not only with liberation from discrimination in housing, education and jobs, but also with liberation of the spirit." The conference was held Aug. 1-4. Speakers included ex-Florida Gov. LeRoy Collins, who urged Negroes "who have made it" into "the mainstream of America" to become involved in the over-all Negro drive for equality. League Executive Director Whitney M. Young Jr., in a keynote address Aug. 1, urged the creation of a national work corps and of a national health insurance plan. He called for the retraining of workers made jobless by automation, for increasing the national hourly minimum wage to $1.50 and for "a major effort to break the color line in child adoptions."

White House Meeting Planned

About 250 delegates, including major civil rights leaders, met in Washington Nov. 17-18 at a planning session for a White House Conference on Civil Rights scheduled for spring

1966. At a White House reception Nov. 16, Pres. Johnson told
the delegates that he had instructed Atty. Gen. Nicholas deB.
Katzenbach to draft legislation that would attack "injustice to
Negroes at the hands of all-white juries." Calling the jury
"the cornerstone of our system of justice," Mr. Johnson said
that "if its composition is a sham, its judgment is a shame."
He announced that he would instruct the Civil Rights Commission
(CRC) to investigate school segregation "in all parts of the
country" and "to develop a firm foundation of facts on which
local and state governments can build a school system that is
colorblind." (It was reported Nov. 17 that the President had
sent a letter to CRC Chrmn. John A. Hannah, president of
Michigan State University, ordering the commission to prepare a report on discrimination in education "as rapidly as
possible." The letter referred to "racial isolation" in both
Northern and Southern schools and said that "it has become apparent that such isolation presents serious barriers to quality
education." Such education was called "the key to equality"
for Negroes. The White House Nov. 20 made public a reply in
which Dr. Hannah said that school segregation caused "serious
harm to all children" and that "the problem of securing equal
educational opportunity for American citizens . . . faces the
entire nation.")

In his keynote address Nov. 17, A. Philip Randolph, head of
the Bro'hood of Sleeping Car Porters and the conference's
honorary chairman, called for the federal government to spend
$100 billion on a "freedom budget" to wipe out slums. (The
$100 billion estimate had been made previously by Bayard
Rustin of New York, a participant in the Washington sessions.
Rustin said in Washington Nov. 18 that the U.S. was "produc-
tive enough to adopt the principle that all unemployable people
have a right to a decent annual income.") Randolph pointed to
the "increasingly explosive socio-racial dynamite in the black
ghettos" and said the cost of "the abolition of ghetto jungles"
would be "vastly less than the chance of another unhappy Watts
of Los Angeles."

Morris B. Abram, U.S. representative on the UN Human
Rights Commission and a conference co-chairman, called
Nov. 17 for "the discarding of some accepted and cherished
beliefs" to find "the means of matching opportunity with
achievement before hope turns to despair." (In a speech in
Philadelphia Nov. 20 before the National Executive Board
of the American Jewish Committee, Abram held that the

U.S. was divided "not by the institution of slavery but by its aftermath." He warned that the nation "can expect continued and inevitable tension on an increasing scale unless the country is united by economic and social justice—and soon." Dr. James M. Nabrit Jr., deputy U.S. representative to the UN, said at the same meeting that he was dissatisfied "with the progress to date in insuring that civil rights for Negroes has meaning and substance.")

Delegates to the Washington civil rights meeting heard recommendations Nov. 18 from 8 panels (their proposals were to be submitted to the President):

▲The panel on the administration of justice, headed by William T. Coleman Jr., a conference co-chairman, presented a resolution urging immediate implementation by Pres. Johnson of a CRC recommendation that more federal law-enforcement officials be sent to Southern trouble spots and that they be given power to make on-the-spot arrests. The resolution asked Mr. Johnson to "direct an immediate speed-up in the lagging enforcement" of the 1964 Civil Rights Act and the 1965 Voting Rights Act. An attempt by Washington NAACP director Clarence Mitchell, a panel member, to have the resolution adopted by the entire conference was ruled out of order by Chrmn. Randolph.

▲The resolution of the panel on education asked the President to order the Office of Education to accelerate enforcement of Title VI of the 1964 Civil Rights Act (this provision permitted the withholding of federal funds from federally assisted programs that discriminate).

Democratic Party

The Democratic National Committee Jan. 19 established a committee to help state party organizations eliminate racial bias in participation in party business. The creation of such a group had been ordered by the 1964 Democratic National Convention. The national committee Jan. 19 also adopted a report calling for the reform of registration and election laws. It proposed roving registrars and year-round registration except for short periods prior to elections.

At a meeting of the predominantly Negro Alabama Democratic Conference in Mobile Nov. 7, attorney Charles Morgan Jr. proposed the creation of a "National Democratic Party" aligned with the Democratic Party nationally and serving as a

forum for Alabama Negroes and white moderates. Alabama
Atty. Gen. Richmond M. Flowers told the conferees he would
"not mind a bit" being a candidate of such a party if it were
recognized by the Democratic National Committee. The conference did not endorse the 3d-party proposal but adopted a
resolution requesting a progress report from the Democratic
Party on a requirement established at the 1964 Democratic
National Convention that the party in Alabama allow full
participation by Negroes.

VIOLENCE

Malcolm X Assassinated

Malcolm X (originally Malcolm Little), 39, bearded Negro
founder and leader of an extremist black nationalist movement,
was shot to death at the Audubon Ballroom in New York Feb. 21
as he was about to speak at a rally of about 400 followers. A
Negro identified as Talmadge Hayer (alias Thomas Hagan and
Hayes), 22, of Paterson, N.J. was seen firing a sawed-off
shotgun at Malcolm and was himself shot in the thigh, apparently by Malcolm's personal bodyguard, Reuben Francis,
33. In the mêlée that ensued, 2 other Negroes were wounded
by gunshots. Hayer was kicked and beaten by members of
the crowd, and his leg was broken.

Police rescued Hayer from the crowd and arrested him at
the scene of the assassination. Francis was arrested on charges
of assault and possession of a pistol. Norman 3X (Norman
Butler), 26, a member of a paramilitary Black Muslim guard
group known as the Fruit of Islam, was arrested at his home
in the Bronx (N.Y. City) Feb. 26 on charges of participating
in the slaying. A 3d Negro suspect, Thomas 15X (Thomas Johnson), 29, of the Bronx, was arrested Mar. 3.

It was generally assumed that the assassination was
motivated by the split between the Black Muslims (known officially as the Nation of Islam) and Malcolm's nationalist
group (which he had named the Organization of Afro-American
Unity). Malcolm had quit the Black Muslims in Mar. 1964 and
had formed his Muslim Mosque, Inc. The house in which he
had been living in East Elmhurst, Queens (N.Y. City) had been
wrecked by a fire set off by firebombs Feb. 13, one week
before the assassination, but Malcolm, his wife and his 4
daughters had escaped uninjured. The house had been bought

by the Black Muslims for Malcolm's use while Malcolm headed the New York branch of the organization. After he left the group, the Black Muslims began legal action to evict him. Malcolm accused the Black Muslims of setting the fire and said frequently that they planned to murder him. (After breaking with the Black Muslims, Malcolm X had made a pilgrimage to Mecca and had acquired the new name Alhaji [signifying a Moslem who had made the Mecca pilgrimage] Malik Shabazz; Black Muslim doctrine holds that American Negroes are decendents of a tribe named Shabazz that originated in Asia.)

Police Feb. 22 set up elaborate security precautions to prevent retaliatory murders threatened by Malcolm's followers. Heavy police guards were placed in Chicago around Elijah Muhammad (originally Elijah Poole), 67, leader of the Black Muslims, and around Cassius Clay, world heavyweight boxing champion. Clay, who had taken the name Muhammad Ali, had been converted to the Black Muslim faith by Malcolm but had broken with him to back Muhammad. Black Muslim headquarters in Harlem (N.Y. City) and San Francisco were burned Feb. 23.

At the annual meeting of the Black Muslims at the Coliseum in Chicago Feb. 26 Muhammad asserted that Malcolm X was a "hypocrite" who "got just what he preached." 2 of Malcolm X's brothers, Philbert X of Lansing, Mich. and Wilfred X of Detroit, denounced their late brother at the Chicago meeting and reaffirmed their allegiance to Muhammad. Muhammad's son, Wallace Delaney Muhammad, who had defected in July and had accused his father of betraying Allah's teachings, announced at the Feb. 26 meeting that his faith in Muhammad was restored. (Muhammad was said to have been taught personally by Allah.)

2 Muslims Jailed for Philadelphia Riot

Judge Charles L. Guerin in Philadelphia, Pa. Jan. 8 sentenced Raymond Hall, 25, a member of the National Muslim Improvement Association of America, to 3 to 9 months in prison for helping to incite the North Philadelphia race riots and looting in Aug. 1964. Shaykh Muhammad Hassan (Abyssinia Hayes), 33, who described himself as the association's Philadelphia leader, was sentenced Jan. 11 to 18 months to 3 years in prison and fined $1,000 for inciting the riots. (Florence Mobley, 23, had received a suspended sentence Dec. 16, 1964 for helping to incite the riots.)

Los Angeles Muslims & Police Clash

59 persons were arrested and 4 hospitalized in Los Angeles Aug. 18 as a result of a clash between police and Black Muslims at Muhammad's Mosque, a Black Muslim headquarters headed by John Shabazz, leader of the movement in the city. The clash took place when police rushed to the mosque to investigate a report that men were carrying rifles into the building. As the police surrounded the mosque, a single shot was fired from it. The police answered with a hail of fire and then entered. They found 2 Molotov cocktails, 2 small fires presumably set in an effort to destroy records, no firearms but apparent evidence that some people had slipped out of the building.

Mississippi Suspects Indicted, Most Charges Dismissed

A federal grand jury in Jackson, Miss. Jan. 15 indicted 18 men in connection with the June 21, 1964 murder of civil rights workers Michael H. Schwerner, Andrew Goodman and James E. Chaney near Philadelphia, Miss.

A one-count felony indictment charged the 18 with violating a federal civil rights statute by conspiring to deprive the 3 murdered youths of their civil rights, and a 1-count misdemeanor indictment charged them with violating another federal rights statute by participating in a conspiracy in which law enforcement officials inflicted "summary punishments" on the 3 youths "without due process of law." There was no question of the jury indicting the defendants on murder charges since the crime of murder in this case was under state, not federal, jurisdiction.

10 of the 18 defendants, including Neshoba County Deputy Sheriff Cecil Price, were accused of participating in the lynch mob that killed the 3 youths. The other 8, including Neshoba County Sheriff Lawrence Andrew Rainey, were accused of participating in the conspiracy.

The indictment charged that: (a) Price had detained the 3 rights workers in the Philadelphia jail from shortly after sundown to about 10:30 p.m. June 21, 1964; (b) Price then released them so that they could be intercepted by the waiting lynch mob when they tried to drive back to their headquarters in Meridian; (c) Price shortly afterwards halted their car 9 miles south of Philadelphia, put them into a Neshoba County sheriff's car and drove them along a lonely side road to the spot where they were

murdered by a 10-man lynch mob, including Price; (d) Billy
Wayne Posey, 28, a member of the lynch mob, took the bodies
to a dam 5 miles southwest of Philadelphia, where a bulldozer
was used to cover the bodies with red clay soil.

According to the indictment, the lynch mob was made up of
Price, Posey, Horace Doyle Barnette, 25, James Edward
Jordan, 38, Jimmy Lee Townsend, 17, Jerry McGrew Sharpe,
21, Jimmy Snowden, 31, Jimmy Arledge, 27, Alton W. Roberts,
26, and Travis Maryn Barnette, 36. Those indicted as participating in the conspiracy but not named as members of the lynch
mob: Rainey, Richard A. Willis, 40, Edgar Killen, 39, Bernard
Lee Akin, Olin L. Burrag, 34, James T. Harris, 30, Frank J.
Herndon, 46, and Herman Tucker, 36.

The felony indictment against 17 of the defendants was
dismissed Feb. 25 by U.S. District Judge W. Harold Cox, who
ruled that the indictment specified a "heinous crime against
the state of Mississippi but not a crime against the United
States." (The 18th defendant, James Edward Jordan, had been
transferred to the jurisdiction of the U.S. District Court in
Atlanta.)

Cox Feb. 26 upheld one count of the misdemeanor indictment. He dismissed the 3 other misdemeanor counts, which
charged 14 of the 17 with actual violation of the law. The other
3, all law enforcement officials, remained charged with 3 counts
of acting under color of law against the murdered youths. The 3
officials were Rainey, Price and Willis, a Philadelphia policeman.

Negro Slain in Mississippi Jail

Allie W. Shelby, 18, a Flora, Miss. Negro, was shot to death
in the Hinds County Jailhouse in Jackson, Miss. Jan. 22 after
having been arrested, convicted and sentenced to 6 months in
jail on charges of making indecent gestures at a white woman in
Jackson earlier Jan. 22. Authorities said that Shelby had
attacked 2 Jackson policemen as he was being led into the jail.
According to the authorities, O. E. Sanderford, a deputy sheriff,
then fired one harmless warning shot and finally shot Shelby
in the head when he kept resisting. A coroner's jury later Jan.
22 ruled the death justifiable homicide.

4 state judges Jan. 28 barred a Negro protest demonstration planned for Jan. 29 at the Hinds County Courthouse in
Jackson, and Negro leaders called it off on the advice of

NAACP lawyers.

Charles Evers, Mississippi NAACP field secretary, telegraphed Jan. 29 to LeRoy Collins, federal Community Relations Service director, to ask Collins to come to Jackson
to investigate Shelby's death. "We have no authority to make
investigations leading to criminal court action," Collins
telegraphed back, but he added that agency representatives
would come to Jackson "to confer with various persons."

Seminarian Slain in Alabama

Jonathan Myrick Daniels, 26, a white seminary student on
leave from the Episcopal Theological School in Cambridge,
Mass., was slain, and a white Roman Catholic priest from
Chicago, Richard F. Morrisroe, 26, was seriously wounded
in Hayneville, Ala. Aug. 20 by shotgun blasts fired by a
special deputy sheriff.

The deputy, Tom L. Coleman, 52, a member of one of
Lowndes County's most prominent families and an engineer
for the Alabama Highway Department, was acquitted of manslaughter charges and freed Sept. 30.

Daniels and Morrisroe had been arrested with 27 other
demonstrators in Fort Deposit Aug. 14 after picketing for
equal job opportunities. The demonstrators were jailed in
Hayneville and released on recognizance bonds Aug. 20. Shortly
afterwards, the 2 men were shot as they approached a small
grocery store with 2 Negro girls. Daniels, of Keene, N.H.,
working for the Episcopal Society for Cultural & Racial Unity,
had been helping in the Negro voter drive in Lowndes County
after participating in other rights activity in nearby Selma.

Coleman was indicted by a county grand jury Sept. 15 on a
charge of first-degree manslaughter. State Atty. Gen. Richmond
Flowers, saying he was "shocked and amazed that the grand jury
did not see fit to return a first-degree murder indictment"
against Coleman, took over the prosecution. Flowers Sept. 27
requested postponement of the trial, mainly on the ground that
his key witness, Morrisroe, was still hospitalized and too ill
to testify. The request for postponement was denied by Circuit
Judge T. Werth Thagard. As the trial opened Sept. 28, Asst.
Atty. Gen. Joe Breck Gantt said the state could not proceed
with the prosecution unless Morrisroe were a witness. Thagard
then removed the attorney general's office as prosecutor in
the case and directed that the prosecution be taken over by

state attorneys who had presented the case to the grand jury.

During the trial Sept. 29, witnesses testified that Daniels had been armed with a knife and Morrisroe with a pistol. The defense contended that Coleman had shot in self-defense. 5 Negroes, however, testified that Daniels and Morrisroe had been unarmed. In a statement from his hospital in Chicago, Morrisroe said that neither he nor Daniels were armed. "The only thing I had in my hand," he said, "was a dime" for a soft drink he had intended to buy at the store.

The jury deliberated 1 hour 43 minutes before acquitting Coleman Sept. 30.

U.S. Atty. Gen. Nicholas deB. Katzenbach, commenting on the verdict, said Sept. 30: "It is difficult to get convictions in some areas. This is the price you have to pay for the jury system, but I don't think it is too high a price to pay."

White Slayer Convicted in Alabama

An all-white jury in Anniston, Ala. Dec. 2 convicted Hubert Damon Strange, 23, of 2d-degree murder in the shooting of Willie Brewster, 38, a Negro, on a highway near Anniston July 15. The jury imposed a 10-year sentence, the minimum for 2d-degree murder. The jury foreman reported that the 2d-degree verdict had been arrived at after the jury had deadlocked on a first-degree murder charge. 2 other white men under indictment in the slaying—Johnny Ira DeFries, 25, and Lewis Blevins, 26—were to be tried in 1966. (According to data compiled by the Southern Regional Council, only one previous conviction had been obtained in the estimated 34 Southern "civil rights murders" committed since 1960.)

The prosecution had based its case largely on the testimony of Jimmy Knight, 28, a white Alabaman, who said that 2 hours before the shooting he and Strange had attended a National States Rights Party rally at which the killing of Negroes had been encouraged by the Rev. Connie Lynch. That evening, Knight testified, the 3 defendants had boasted to him of having shot a Negro and had shown him a shotgun and 2 spent shells.

House Probes Ku Klux Klan

The House Committee on Un-American Activities opened a public investigation of the Ku Klux Klan Oct. 19. The hearings into alleged Klan violence were conducted in Washington by a 5-

man panel of the committee, headed by Chrmn. Edwin E. Willis (D., La.) and assisted by the committee's chief investigator, Donald T. Appell.

The first Klan official called to testify was Robert M. Shelton Jr., 36, imperial wizard" of the largest Klan group in the country, the United Klan of America, Inc., Knights of the Ku Klux Klan. Shelton invoked the First, 4th, 5th and 14th Amendments to the U.S. Constitution in refusing to answer 73 questions at the Oct. 19 session and 85 questions at the Oct. 20 session. He also refused to produce subpoenaed records. James R. Jones, who was "grand dragon" of Shelton's North Carolina group, invoked constitutional privilege in refusing to answer 60 questions Oct. 20. (The inquiry was denounced Oct. 20 by the American Civil Liberties Union, which said it "appear[ed] to be resulting in nothing less than 'trial by publicity'" and an invasion of the right of freedom of speech.)

During the first session, Appell reported that there were 381 local Klan units in the South and that 260 of them were part of the Shelton organization. Appell said that "a very real fear of the Klan" existed in certain areas of the South and that there had been "some infiltration of law enforcement agencies" by the Klan. The committee also released a list of prominent Klansmen; Daniel Burros, 28, whose name appeared on the list, was identified as a Klan leader in New York and as a person who had been active in the neo-Nazi National Renaissance Party. (Burros shot and killed himself in Reading, Pa. Oct. 31 after an article in the *N.Y. Times* that day had disclosed that he had been born and raised a Jew. McCandlish Phillips, author of the article, wrote that he had confronted Burros Oct. 29 with the information on his Jewish background and that Burros had told him: "If you publish that . . . I'll kill you. . . . I'll be ruined.")

According to data disclosed at the Oct. 19 inquiry, Shelton's Tuscaloosa headquarters operated under a "front" known as the Alabama Rescue Service. Investigators said Oct. 20 that checks drawn on the Service account had been used for automobile payments, for cash at supermarkets and filling stations and for a $469.97 payment to a diamond store. Appell said Oct. 20 that Jones had bought 3,757 yards of satin at a 64¢-a-yard average cost and that Klan robes, using 5 yards, sold for $15 apiece. He said Shelton had failed to report on his federal income tax a $4,000 fee from an Alabama engineering company for help in obtaining a state highway contract. (Shelton was said to have reported a corporate income of about $18,000 for fiscal 1965.)

Jones Oct. 21 refused to reply to questions. In questioning him, however, Appell brought out allegations that (a) Jones' income had increased several times after he became grand dragon, (b) Jones had falsified the 1965 corporate income of the Klan in reporting to the Klansmen, (c) Jones had made a "good profit" from a widows' benefit plan, (d) Jones had "coerced" Klansmen into buying him a $4,000 Cadillac, (e) Jones traveled through North Carolina with a pistol, a carbine, a rifle and "lots of ammunition."

In confronting grand dragon Marshal Robert Kornegay of Virginia, who also declined to testify, Appell said Kornegay was paid $150 a week as a Klan organizer and had received at least $3,562 in insurance commissions on KKK business for about 4 months. Appell said Kornegay had moved to Virginia from North Carolina because North Carolina Klansmen had objected to his "conduct," which reportedly included retaining premiums from cancelled Klan insurance.

The first cooperative Klan witness, Joseph D. DuBois, 40, testified Oct. 22 and unexpectedly resigned from the Klan on the witness stand. He turned over his records as klabee (treasurer) of his Goldsboro, N.C. klavern, which had the "front" name of the Wayne County Improvement Association.

Another cooperative witness, the Rev. Roy Woodle, 41, said he had joined the Klan 8 or 10 months previously, had been appointed grand kludd (chaplain) of the Klan's Realm of North Carolina but had resigned because the Klan, while preaching "good things—segregation and Christianity"—did nothing about them. Instead, he said, it practiced intimidation and enriched its leaders with diamond rings, "Cadillacs, ribeye steaks . . . and first-class motel rooms."

New Hanover County (N.C.) Sheriff Marion W. Mills, 49, told the subcommittee Oct. 26 that he would cooperate and then testified that he and 6 of his 19 deputies had joined the Klan in 1963 to "observe and see if anything happened as far as disorder was concerned." After "rumors got out that we were part of this organization," he said, he told the deputies to resign from the Klan, and he also quit. He said he had not learned for several months afterwards that one of the deputies (Charles B. Goodwin) had been elected grand klaliff of the North Carolina Klan.

The Rev. George Franklin Dorsett, 48, of Greensboro, N.C. invoked the 5th Amendment Oct. 27 in refusing to answer questions. Appell identified Dorsett, a house painter, as the imperial kludd (chaplain) of the Invisible Empire of the United Klans of America and quoted Dorsett as saying at Klan rallies that the "message of Christian love is a tool in Communist hands." Another uncooperative witness, Charles Elwood, was identified by the subcommittee as grand klabee of the South Carolina Rescue Service, which was operated by the Klan as a front organization.

Committee investigator Philip Manuel Oct. 28 questioned grand dragons Calvin F. Craig of Georgia and Robert E. Scoggin of South Carolina, both of whom declined to answer substantive questions. Manuel questioned Craig about instruction courses in violence allegedly held with Craig's "full knowledge and approval" near Macon, Ga. in Oct. 1961 and in Henry County Oct. 17, 1964. Manuel said Nov. 1 that a Klan offshoot called Nacirema, Inc. ("American" spelled backwards) had been organized in Atlanta in 1961 for Klansmen wanting "more violent action"; the 1961 instruction course in violence had been attended by Craig, Shelton and other Klansmen.

Manuel said that James Douglas Newberry, 55, grand klabee of the Klan's Georgia realm, had drawn $1,000 from the Klan's bank account Apr. 1 and had deposited it to his own account. Witness Wesley Guy Bailey 3d, 38, refused Nov. 2, on constitutional grounds, to answer questions as Manuel sought to identify him as a klekard (lecturer) of the Clayton County Klavern No. 52, United Klans of America, incorporated as the Clayton County Civic Club, and as having "agreed acts of violence were necessary to prevent integration." Manuel said Klavern 52 had sponsored the Oct. 1964 instruction course in violence. The subcommittee Nov. 4 questioned exalted cyclops (president) Robert L. Bing, 39, J. W. (Jimmy) Wells and Walter Parr of Clayton County Klavern 52, who refused to answer substantive questions on constitutional grounds.

Committee Chrmn. Willis announced Nov. 9 that the Klan investigation was being suspended until 1966, on the request of Atty. Gen. Nicholas deB. Katzenbach, for fear that public questioning of 2 Georgia Klan members allegedly involved in the 1964 murder of Lemuel A. Penn might prejudice litigation in the case, currently before the Supreme Court.

Wilmington (Del.) radio station WAMS reported Nov. 13 that grand dragon Ralph Pryor, 33, of the Delaware KKK had planned to resign from the Klan and testify at the hearings but had changed his mind after a meeting with Appell in Wilmington

Nov. 9. Pryor was quoted as saying: "The government can't protect me. . . . If I testify, some day they are going to find me in Selma, Ala., with 30 bullet holes in me, and that killer is going to get off scot free."

(Charles Baker [Rip] Riddlehoover, Florida grand dragon of the United Knights of the Ku Klux Klan, Inc., was arrested in Miami Oct. 29 on charges of possession of firearms [illegal for a convicted felon].)

Arson & Bombings

A Freedom School and library with 2,000 volumes in Indianola, Miss. was destroyed by fire Mar. 5. Police later Mar. 5 arrested 8 civil rights workers on charges of interfering with an investigation of possible arson suspects. (A Freedom House in Laurel, Miss. had been set afire a few days previously.)

A dynamite bomb exploded in an alley of a Negro neighborhood in north Birmingham, Ala. Apr. 1. Weymouth Crowell, 13, a Negro, suffered minor injuries when cut by glass from a bedroom window shattered by the blast. 2 unexpected time bombs were found shortly afterwards outside the homes of Birmingham Mayor Albert Boutwell and City Councilwoman Nina Miglionico, both considered moderates.

2 adjacent homes being built for Negroes in a predominantly white section of Lakewood, N.J. were burned Oct. 10 in an apparent case of arson. Members of the Township Council established a fund to help restore the property. Gov. Richard J. Hughes ordered state police to assist in searching for the presumed arsonists.

Dr. Beverly Holland White, a white Daytona Beach, Fla. physician, was charged Nov. 10 with the burning of an abandoned Negro church and an abandoned house in Jones County, Ga. and with the burning of another Negro church in neighboring Twiggs County. The buildings had been burned Nov. 8.

The home of Robert Lewis Jr. of Ferriday, La., Negro president of the Ferriday Freedom Movement, was damaged by what appeared to be a gasoline bomb Nov. 21. Lewis, his wife and 5 children were unhurt. Police arriving on the scene arrested Lewis, who had been standing with a shotgun in front of his house, on a charge of aggravated battery.

The Charlotte, N.C. homes of 4 Negroes active in civil rights were bombed in the early morning of Nov. 22. Damage was extensive, but nobody was hurt. The 4 men were Kelly

Alexander, NAACP state president; Fred D. Alexander, his brother and the first Negro since Reconstruction to be elected (in May 1965) to Charlotte's City Council; Julius L. Chambers, 29, a civil rights attorney whose car had been bombed in New Bern, N.C. in January; Dr. Reginald A. Hawkins, a dentist.

A bomb exploded early Nov. 29 in a car parked near a Negro grocery in Vicksburg, Miss., where local Negro leaders were reported to have been planning an economic boycott of certain white merchants. The explosion caused heavy damage to the store, injured at least 3 persons and demolished the car. Windows in several adjoining homes and stores were shattered and a passing taxi was overturned.

OTHER DEVELOPMENTS

Union & Job Bias Under Attack

The AFL-CIO's Civil Rights Department opened a special office in Atlanta Jan. 4 in its program to end anti-Negro bias in unions. The office was to be used in efforts to persuade unions in the Deep South not to practice discrimination in employment and to guide union leaders and members in complying with civil rights laws. Elmer T. Kehrer, Southern director for the International Ladies Garment Workers, headed the office.

The N.Y. State Human Rights Commission charged Nov. 17 that the International Bro'hood of Locomotive Engineers followed a policy of excluding Negroes from membership. The action resulted from a complaint filed by Donald Hendricks, 23, a Negro employed as a motor switchman. Francis J. Quilty, leader of the brotherhood's Division 497, denied the charge and said Hendricks had been accepted into the union Nov. 11. (Perry S. Heath, the brotherhood's grand chief engineer, reported that the brotherhood had granted membership in September to 2 Negroes employed by the Central of Georgia Railway.

The NNACP Legal Defense & Educational Fund filed 3 suits in federal district courts Nov. 19 charging employers with discrimination against Negro workers through discriminatory promotion and training practices and segregated facilities. Defendants in the suits were the Newport News Shipbuilding & Drydock Co. (the largest private employer in Virginia), Phillip Morris Co. of Richmond and Mead Corp. of Atlanta.

At a Detroit news conference Dec. 16 spokesmen for Protestant, Catholic, Eastern Orthodox and Jewish organizations announced that they were committing their "multimillion dollar purchasing power" to the elimination of job discrimination on the part of their suppliers. They said prospective suppliers would be required to demonstrate that they offered equal employment opportunities to Negroes. Archbishop Joseph T. McGucken of San Francisco announced Dec. 20 that the 2,500 suppliers serving the San Francisco archdiocese would be required to furnish racial and ethnic breakdowns of their employes and to promote without bias.

Police Review Boards Urged

Incidents involving the slaying of 2 Negroes by policemen in N.Y. City and Newark, N.J. brought renewed demands from civil rights groups for civilian police review boards.

In New York, Nelson Erby, 28, a Negro who had a criminal record of 12 arrests and 2 felonious assault convictions, was fatally shot by Patrolman Sheldon Liebowitz, 24, in the Bedford-Stuyvesant section of Brooklyn July 15 during an altercation witnessed by more than 100 persons.

Police said: Liebowitz, on the force one year and on relief for the regular neighborhood policemen, had accosted Erby for "acting strangely and in a loud and boisterous manner"; Erby then attacked Liebowitz with a stiletto and shot Liebowitz in the arm with Liebowitz' gun, which he had lost in the struggle; a passing truck driver came to the policeman's aid, clubbing Erby; Liebowitz regained his pistol and shot Erby, who died on the way to the hospital.

Some witnesses, backed by CORE, said, however, that Liebowitz had shot himself accidentally, that Erby did not have a stiletto and that 2 white men had helped subdue Erby while Liebowitz shot him.

Demands for an investigation were immediately made by CORE and the NAACP. The NAACP and the National Urban League also renewed their demands for an independent civilian board to review charges of police brutality.

Kings County District Atty. Aaron E. Koota July 15, the very day of the incident, announced the convening of a grand jury to investigage. After hearing testimony from 37 persons, the grand jury July 27 cleared Liebowitz, saying he had "acted in a lawful and justifiable manner in defense of himself."

CORE said the case "dramatizes the vastly inadequate system of police review adjudication in New York City."

5,000 off-duty policemen picketed city hall June 29 in protest against a proposal, being considered by the N.Y. City Council, to create a civilian-dominated board to review complaints against policemen. Reports that some of the pickets had made disparaging remarks at counter-picketing CORE demonstrators evoked a warning from Police Commissioner Vincent L. Broderick July 2, at a promotion ceremony for high-ranking officers, that "if you believe that a police officer is somehow superior to a citizen because the citizen is a Negro, or speaks Spanish . . ., you don't belong in the Police Department."

In Newark June 12, Patrolman Henry Martinez shot and killed Lester Long Jr., 22, a Negro, after Long allegedly slashed at Martinez' partner with a knife. Mayor Hugh Addonizio June 17 suspended Martinez with full pay pending a probe. His action led to picketing for the next 5 days by hundreds of off-duty policemen, some from surrounding communities, in protest against the suspension. The Newark Human Rights Commission reported that it had found that racial prejudice was not involved in the shooting, and an Essex County grand jury June 30 found no cause to indict Martinez. CORE sponsored a march by about 500 persons in the business district June 30 and said similar protests would be held every Wednesday until a civilian review board was established in Newark.

Exclusion from Juries Invalid

The Mississippi Supreme Court Jan. 25 reversed the conviction of William B. Harper, a Negro, and ordered a new trial because Negroes had been effectively excluded from juries that had indicted and convicted him for the attempted 1962 rape of a 16-year-old white girl near Forest, Miss. The court ruled that "token summoning of Negroes for jury service" was not sufficient.

Wisconsin Bars Housing Bias

The Wisconsin Assembly Nov. 2 adopted a Senate-passed bill outlawing discrimination in housing. It was estimated that the bill affected 25% of the state's 1,380,000 housing units, particularly in Milwaukee and other cities with large Negro populations.

1966

Dispute over a 'black-power' philosophy, espoused by alleged extremists among Negro leaders, enlarged a growing split in the civil rights movement. The controversy arose in Mississippi after rights leaders descended on the state to continue a march started by James H. Meredith but interrupted when Meredith was injured by shotgun blasts from ambush. Pres. Johnson proposed a 1966 civil rights act that would abolish discrimination in housing, jury selection and schools, but his bill was killed by a Senate filibuster. Major campaigns and demonstrations took place in 1966 in the big Northern cities as well as in the South as activists pressed efforts to secure voting rights for more Negroes and to end discrimination in education, housing, employment, accommodations and other areas. Racial disorders shook New York, Chicago, Cleveland, Los Angeles, San Francisco, Atlanta and other cities across the country.

1966 RIGHTS ACT DEFEATED

Johnson's Proposals Killed by Filibuster

In 1966 Congress rejected Presidential proposals for leg-islation to end discrimination in housing, the composition of juries and the racial make-up of public school classes. The proposed legislation, and particularly its "open-housing" pro-visions, was battered from the outset by a wave of opposition. Much of the resistance originated in a "white backlash" based on charges that the civil rights movement had started to make unjustified demands and was beginning to resort to violence. The bill was killed by a Southern filibuster in the Senate.

Pres. Johnson had sent to Congress Apr. 28 a civil rights message proposing federal legislation to prevent discrimi-nation in the selection of juries and in "the sale, rental and financing" of all housing. He asked for broadened legislation to protect civil rights workers, to empower federal author-ities to sue for the desegregation of schools and public facil-ities and to provide enforcement powers for the Equal Employ-ment Opportunity Commission.

The President proposed that the provisions against dis-crimination in housing be enforceable through civil suits brought by private individuals or, if a pattern of discrimination pre-vailed, by the Justice Department. State and local fair housing laws would remain in effect under Mr. Johnson's housing plan. The President's jury-selection proposal applied to grand or petit juries. It would have provided that challenges to bias could be instituted either by individuals or by the federal gov-ernment. A new criminal statute recommended by Mr. Johnson would have barred interference in the exercise of fundamental rights by threats or force by any person, acting individually or in a group, privately or officially. Maximum penalties pro-posed under the criminal statute: one year in prison, $1,000 fine if no bodily harm were done; 10 years, $10,000 fine if there were bodily injury; life imprisonment if death resulted from the crime.

A special headquarters was opened by the Leadership Conference on Civil Rights in Washington July 25 to coordi-nate lobbying efforts in support of a strong civil rights bill. 3 civil rights leaders—Roy Wilkins, executive director of the NAACP and chairman of the conference, Whitney M. Young Jr., executive director of the National Urban League, and A. Philip Randolph, president of the AFL-CIO Bro'hood of Sleeping Car Porters—addressed a Leadership Conference rally July 26 with appeals for pressure on Congress to pass the rights bill. Civil rights groups, however, were not united on the 1966 bill. The Congress of Racial Equality and the Student Nonviolent Coordinating Committee did not support the measure. SNCC Chrmn. Stokely Carmichael, who called the bill "a sham," attended the July 26 rally but did not participate. He told a reporter that he did not back the bill, "but we are not going to oppose those people who want it." At a press conference held prior to the rally July 26, Wilkins warned that if it did not pass the Administration's open-housing proposal in some form, Congress would "side-step the plain fact that 20 million Americans are cooped up and robbed of their money and their manhood through ironclad, lily-white, profit-encrusted real estate practices," and the nation would be "in for some heartbreaking developments that could be ugly as well."

Lobbying against the bill was conducted by the National Association of Real Estate Boards (NAREB) and other groups. The real estate lobby's chief counsel in Washington, John C. Williamson, told newsmen July 26 that his group considered the bill "unacceptable on principle." A bulletin dated July 18 called on NAREB's 83,000 members to "generate an immediate wave of indignation" against the bill's open-housing section.

An amended version of the Administration's proposed Civil Rights Act of 1966 (HR14765) was passed by the House Aug. 9 and sent to the Senate. The House passed the measure by 259-157 vote (183 D. & 76 R. vs. 95 D. & 62 R.). The vote came after 12 days of debate, much of it centered on Title IV, the open-housing section.

As submitted by the Administration, Title IV would have banned discrimination in the sale or rental of all housing. But this version engendered so much controversy that the Administration, to avert defeat of the section, consented to its amendment. The amendment, prepared by Rep. Charles McC. Mathias (R., Md.), exempted from the section's provisions the sale of owner-occupied apartments with 4 units or less. It also exempted real estate agents for individual home owners if the home owners gave the agents written consent to discriminate. The amendment excluded 60% of the nation's housing from the bill's anti-discrimination provisions. It passed by one vote in a preliminary, tentative poll of the House Aug. 3. Rep. Richard

Bolling (D., Mo.), presiding at the time, cast the deciding vote to break a 179-179 tie. Another vote taken prior to passage of the bill Aug. 9, was 237-176 in favor of the Mathias amendment. By another tentative vote Aug. 5, the House defeated, 198-179, a motion to delete the entire housing section from the bill. The same motion, offered just prior to the final vote for passage of the bill Aug. 9, was offered by Rep. Arch A. Moore Jr. (R., W. Va.) and was rejected by 222-190.

House debate on the bill had begun July 25 after a 200-180 vote to by-pass the House Rules Committee under the 21-day rule adopted in 1965. This permitted a committee chairman to bring up a bill that had not been approved by the Rules committee if the rules unit had not acted within 21 days.

A 66-34 vote Aug. 2 had defeated a proposal to eliminate the bill's Title III, authorizing individuals or the Justice Department to seek a federal court injunction barring any person from engaging in an act that would deprive an individual of his constitutional rights because of race or national origin.

An anti-riot amendment was approved by House voice vote Aug. 8; offered by Rep. William C. Cramer (R., Fla.), an opponent of the bill, the amendment would have made it a federal crime for anyone using interstate commerce to incite or carry out a riot or other violent civil disturbance. The House Aug. 9 approved an amendment negating the effectiveness of Title VI, which would have provided the Attorney General with authority to initiate school desegregation suits without a request to do so from the district involved.

In a statement issued Aug. 10, Pres. Johnson expressed regret that the open-housing section had been weakened but hailed House passage of the bill as "an important new milestone" toward "racial justice." He said that the House had "practically . . . barred bigotry in all new housing and in apartment houses" and had "symbolically . . . declared to all Negro Americans that many of their fellow citizens believe it is wrong to deny anyone a decent place to live solely because of the color of his skin." "The House also has declared that the law should be an instrument of justice in this cause," he said.

CORE Aug. 10 derided the bill as "worthless in some sections, racist in others." CORE's associate national director, Lincoln Lynch, referring to the housing section, said: "In essence the black man is being told by Congress that he only has constitutional rights in 40% of the nation's housing; in the other 60% he is not equal."

Senate Democratic leader Mike Mansfield (Mont.) had said Aug. 11 that "the key" to killing the anticipated filibuster was Senate Republican leader Everett M. Dirksen (Ill.), who opposed the bill's open-housing section. "Without him," Mansfield said, "we cannot get cloture [limitation of debate]." Mansfield made this comment in announcing that an attempt would be made to bring the House-passed rights bill before the Senate without referral to the Judiciary Committee, which was headed by Sen. James O. Eastland (D., Miss.), a foe of civil rights legislation.

The bill was placed on the Senate calendar for debate Sept. 6 after Southern Senators decided not to fight the maneuver. (3 such attempts in the past to prevent the Senate from bypassing the Eastland committee had failed.) Debate did not begin until Sept. 8, however, because the Senate was unable to muster a quorum Sept. 6 and 7. A 3d failure to obtain a quorum interrupted debate on the bill Sept. 9.

Dirksen, reiterating his opposition to the open-housing provision, had said Sept. 6 that he saw no hope of compromise on the section. He said Sept. 9 that he also opposed the bill's provision for barring discrimination in the selection of juries and for the preservation of election records to aid in the enforcement of voting rights. Mansfield said Sept. 10 that Atty. Gen. Nicholas deB. Katzenbach had made clear the Administration's position that the bill was not acceptable without the open-housing provision. (The Leadership Conference on Civil Rights had taken a similar stand Sept. 8.) Pres. Johnson told newsmen Sept. 12 that he had urged Dirksen by phone to "find some way to give his support" to the bill. Mr. Johnson also had a futile 90-minute conversation with Dirksen at the White House Sept. 13, but Dirksen told the Senate Sept. 14 that he would not alter his stand. (The liberal Council of Republican Organizations, made up of 10 Republican groups, criticized Dirksen Sept. 18 for his refusal to support the bill.)

The bill was withdrawn from Senate consideration and thereby killed Sept. 19 after 2 attempts to impose cloture failed by 10-vote margins. In the 2 attempts, cloture was favored by votes of 54-42 (42 D. & 12 R. vs. 21 D. & 21 R.) Sept. 14 and of 52-41 (42 D. & 10 R. vs. 21 D. & 20 R.) Sept. 19. But imposition of cloture required a 2/3 majority vote of Senators present and voting. The cloture vote was necessary to shut off a Southern filibuster on a motion to consider the bill.

'BLACK-POWER' CONTROVERSY

The civil rights movement was splintered in 1966 by the emergence of a militant philosophy described by its advocates as a demand for "black power." The exact definition of the term remained a matter of dispute. Vague though its meaning was, however, the "black-power" rallying cry quickly widened a growing rift between more militant groups such as CORE (the Congress of Racial Equality) and SNCC (the Student Non-violent Coordinating Committee) and more traditional organizations epitomized by the NAACP (National Association for the Advancement of Colored People) and the National Urban League. The Rev. Dr. Martin Luther King Jr. and his Southern Christian Leadership Conference (SCLC) occupied a position approximately in the middle.

The "black-power" philosophy was injected into the national rights picture in June by its most prominent proponent, Stokely Carmichael, 25, who only the previous month had become SNCC's top leader. The "black-power" issue brought the rights movement face-to-face with several difficult questions, among them being: (1) Would whites continue to find a place in the rights movement, and, if they would, what would their place be? (2) Would the rights movement's tactical emphasis shift from nonviolence to self-defense and possibly to taking the initiative in violent confrontations with the movement's foes?

The "black-power" controversy erupted after several major changes in the leadership of the bigger rights organizations.

Rights Groups Pick New Leaders

Dr. Arthur B. Spingarn, 87, announced his resignation as NAACP president at the organization's annual dinner in New York Jan. 2. Spingarn had been NAACP president for 26 years and a member of the organization since its founding in 1909. (The office of NAACP president was largely ceremonial; day-to-day operations were supervised by the executive director, Roy Wilkins.) At its annual meeting Jan. 3, the 60-member NAACP board of directors unanimously selected Kivie Kaplan, 61, Boston industrialist and philanthropist, to succeed Spingarn. (Both Spingarn and Kaplan were white.) The directors elected Spingarn honorary president for life.

CORE announced in New York Jan. 3 that its 25-member National Action Council had selected Floyd Bixler McKissick, 43, to succeed James Farmer as national director. Farmer's resignation, effective Mar. 1, had been announced Dec. 25, 1965. McKissick, a Negro attorney practicing in Durham, N. C., had served as CORE's unsalaried national chairman since 1963. At a Jan. 3 news conference McKissick said that CORE planned to develop new techniques, such as community organization, to help disadvantaged Negroes living under "feudalism in 1966." McKissick was to be succeeded as national chairman by Wilfred T. Ussery, a San Francisco architectural designer. Other appointments announced by CORE Jan. 3: Herbert Callender, 32, former chairman of Bronx (N.Y. City) CORE and currently a field secretary in Baltimore, was named director of organization. Callender succeeded James McCain, who was appointed a special assistant to McKissick for political organization in the South.

Officials at SNCC headquarters in Atlanta confirmed May 16 that Stokely Carmichael had been elected May 14 to replace John Lewis, 26, as SNCC chairman. According to one report, delegates to the weekend meeting, held at a camp near Nashville, Tenn., had originally voted to reelect Lewis but had later rescinded this choice. SNCC Executive Secy. James Forman, 37, who resigned, was replaced by Mrs. Ruby Doris Smith Robinson, 23. Lewis and Forman were both elected to a 10-member policy-making central committee. The 2 new officers, particularly Carmichael, were considered to be considerably more militant than their predecessors. Carmichael, a New Yorker and graduate of Howard University, had been active, as SNCC's senior field secretary in Alabama, in organizing the Lowndes County Freedom Organization, an all-Negro political party using a black panther as its symbol. He had taken the position that "to ask Negroes to get in the Democratic Party is like asking Jews to join the Nazi Party." The SNCC also decided at its meeting to stop using integrated teams of field workers. Carmichael said after the meeting that SNCC would "not fire any of our white organizers, but if they want to organize, they can organize white people. Negroes will organize the Negroes." (Lewis disclosed in an AP interview in Atlanta June 30 that he had submitted his resignation from SNCC June 11, effective July 22. Lewis declined to take issue with SNCC's new "black-power" slogan or to comment on whether it had any bearing on his resignation.)

'Black-Power' Demand Issued on Meredith March

The "black-power" slogan was used publicly for the first time in June during a widely publicized march through Mississippi. James H. Meredith, 32, who had been the first Negro admitted to the University of Mississippi, had started the march June 5 as a voting-rights demonstration. Meredith was halted June 6 when he was injured by 3 shotgun blasts fired from ambush. Civil rights leaders and supporters then flocked to Mississippi to continue the march.

Carmichael and other SNCC leaders repeatedly called for "black power" during the march, and their cry was taken up by many marchers. Carmichael and his followers indicated a hostility toward white participants in the march, and they urged self-defense rather than nonviolence when attacked. This attitude contrasted with that of Martin Luther King Jr. and his SCLC, who also took part in the march. King and his group emphasized nonviolence and expressed gratitude for white participation in the march.

In a June 17 statement Carmichael insisted that "I'm not anti-white." He compared his political strategy for Negroes with the methods employed by other ethnic groups by saying that "we're going to elect sheriffs . . . where we're in a majority."

In a June 20 interview, King agreed that "it is absolutely necessary for the Negro to gain power" but said that such power should be shared with whites and that "the term 'black power' is unfortunate because it tends to give the impression of black nationalism."

CORE Associate Director Lincoln Lynch said June 21 that King's statement "shows a basic misunderstanding of what the Negro on the farm and on the streets is really asking for." He said "history has shown that if you're really depending on the vast majority of whites to help, you're really leaning on a very broken reed." CORE Director McKissick had explained June 11 that "we appreciate" support from white liberals but that "the situation is sort of like when you are sick and your neighbor comes in to help you; you need his assistance, but you don't want him to run your house or take your wife."

CORE Adopts 'Black-Power' Philosophy

At its national convention, held in Baltimore July 1-4, CORE indorsed the "black-power" concept. McKissick explained the policy July 4 by saying: "As long as the white man has all the power and money, nothing will happen, because we have nothing. The only way to achieve meaningful change is to take power."

The convention agreed July 4 that Negroes should adopt a policy of self-defense rather than nonviolence when attacked. McKissick had told reporters July 2 that the nonviolence policy was passe. "The right of self-defense is a constitutional right," he said, "and you can't expect black people to surrender that right while whites maintain it. . . . You can't have white people who practice violence and expect black people to remain passive."

At the convention's opening session July 1, Carmichael had delivered a speech denouncing "the establishment" and white liberals and warning: "We will define our own tactics whether they like it or not." Carmichael said integration had become irrelevant, and he said he would not discuss nonviolence with whites while "the United States continues to commit violence in Vietnam." Carmichael criticized Dr. King's approach.

King had been expected to speak at the convention, but he notified CORE July 1 that his "duties as a pastor in Atlanta" would keep him from Baltimore; shortly after King's cancellation it was announced that Carmichael would speak. King told reporters July 1 that he was "trying desperately to keep the movement nonviolent, but I can't keep it nonviolent by myself. Much of the responsibility is on the white power structure to give meaningful concessions to Negroes." He said he would refuse to appear at any civil rights function at which racial violence might be urged.

James Farmer, ex-national director of CORE, addressed the convention July 3 and said: "If I am against black power, I would be against myself." But he expressed "concern" that "the concept of black power has been misinterpreted in the press" and stressed that "this is not a racist organization."

CORE's identification with the more militant wing of the rights movement was reflected in the choice of other speakers. They included Mrs. Fannie Lou Hamer of the Mississippi Freedom Democratic Party (MFDP), Jesse Gray, N.Y. City rent strike organizer, and Lonnie X, a Black Muslim minister from New York. (Many Black Muslims attended the July 4 session at which Lonnie X spoke.)

Much of the criticism at the meeting was leveled at middle-class and educated Negroes who had received good jobs from "the establishment." White CORE members at the convention reportedly took pains not to make themselves conspicuous. The term "black man" rather than "Negro" was used increasingly at the convention.

(2 resolutions adopted July 4 dealt with the Vietnamese war. One called for the withdrawal of U.S. troops from Vietnam; the other attacked the draft as placing "a heavy discriminatory burden" on minority groups and the poor and supported persons refusing to serve in the armed forces because of their objection to the Vietnamese war. CORE's 1965 convention had adopted a troop-withdrawal resolution but had tabled it on the urging of then-Director Farmer. Some convention activities were linked with CORE's desegregation drive in Baltimore, which CORE had picked as its "target city" for the summer. Baltimore Mayor Theodore R. McKeldin appeared before the convention July 3 to present a key to the city and was applauded when he expressed shame at the fact that Baltimore's housing was segregated.)

Author Lillian Smith, 68, notified McKissick July 5 that she was resigning from CORE's advisory committee. She charged that "CORE has been infiltrated by adventurers and by nihilists, black nationalists and plain old-fashioned haters, who have finally taken over." She called her resignation a "protest" against "the dangerous and unwise position CORE has taken on the use of violence in effecting racial change."

NAACP Stresses Moderation

The NAACP, holding its annual convention in Los Angeles July 5-9, dissociated itself from the "black-power" doctrine. Its position was backed by Vice Pres. Hubert Humphrey July 6 after the Rev. James Jones, a Los Angeles school board member and a Negro, had received cheers at the convention by declaring that "the NAACP must accept the challenge of defining black power and making it honorable and a factual part of the total power spectrum in America."

Addressing the 1,500 convention delegates July 6, Humphrey declared: "We must reject calls for racism whether they come from a throat that is white or one that is black." He warned against embracing "the dogma of the oppressors—the notion that somehow a person's skin color determines his worthiness or unworthiness." He asserted that "integration must be recognized as an essential means to the ends we are seeking—the ends of freedom, justice and equal opportunity for all Americans." Humphrey praised the NAACP, of which he was a member, as having, "through the years, . . . played a role 2d to none in terms of dedication and determination, of sacrifice and courage." But he urged the civil rights movement to "broaden [its] base . . . to enlist new sources of energy and strength." He called on state and local governments for "new initiatives and responsibilities in civil rights matters" to supplement the work of the federal government.

(Humphrey's speech was attacked at a Harlem news conference July 7 by CORE National Director McKissick. McKissick accused Humphrey of a "purely racist reaction" to the concept of "black power." McKissick defended "black power" as "a movement dedicated to the exercise of American democracy in its highest tradition, . . . a drive to mobilize the black communities of this country in a monumental effort to remove the basic causes of alienation, frustration, despair, low self-esteem and hopelessness." "Black power is not hatred," McKissick declared. "It is a means to bring the black American into the covenant of brotherhood." He insisted that "black power is not black supremacy" and "does not mean the exclusion of white Americans from the Negro revolution." He labeled Pres. Johnson as "racist" for failing to take actions urged by rights leaders.)

Roy Wilkins, the NAACP's executive director, had made a vehement disavowal of "black power" in a keynote address at the convention's opening session July 5. Insisting that the term "means anti-white power" and "separatism," Wilkins called it "a reverse Mississippi, a reverse Hitler, a reverse Ku Klux Klan" that "can mean in the end only black death." "We of the NAACP will have none of this," he declared. "We seek . . . for the inclusion of Negro Americans in the nation's life, not their exclusion." Wilkins also attacked the position taken by the CORE convention in espousing self-defense for Negroes rather than nonviolence. "Proclaimed protective violence," he warned, "is as likely to encourage counter-violence as it is to discourage violent persecution." He held that it "entails the risk of a broader, more indiscriminate crackdown by law officers under the ready-made excuse of restoring law and order."

A contrasting view, however, was presented by William Booth, chairman of the N.Y. City Commission on Human Rights. Booth said: "I'm not preaching violence. . . . But if people can't get what's coming to them, we've got to go out and take it."

In a memo issued to convention delegates July 7, Wilkins launched an attack on CORE, on SNCC and on other groups that had led the "Meredith march" through Mississippi. He characterized "the refusal of the 'march' organizations to join in a strong nationwide effort to pass the civil rights bill" as "a civil rights tragedy" and scored a manifesto issued by march leaders June 8 as reflecting "the wishes of the leaders of SNCC and CORE, who wanted only to 'put Pres. Johnson on the spot.'" Detailing charges against CORE, SNCC and the Southern Christian Leadership Conference (SCLC), the memo enumerated instances dating back to 1964 in which the NAACP had been obliged to furnish funds in support of their activities or to settle lawsuits when SNCC allegedly failed to meet its obligations. It said that the NAACP had supplied food, housing and transportation for the Meredith march and had furnished $300 bail when SNCC Chrmn. Carmichael was arrested on the march. During the NAACP summer project in Mississippi, the memo said, "the Mississippi Freedom Democratic Party tried to undermine our work, invaded our office and disrupted it, sought to keep Negroes from joining the effort, and attempted to break up a public meeting addressed by Roy Wilkins." "The whole business showed the NAACP again," the memo concluded, "how difficult it is to have genuine cooperation . . . with groups that do not have the same commitments and which may very well be pursuing certain goals that have nothing to do with civil rights at all."

A resolution adopted by the convention July 8 called "for a re-examination by our National Board of Directors of our program, financial and cooperative relationships with all other national or regional civil rights organizations." The resolution established guidelines to determine whether the NAACP and its local branches should cooperate with other rights groups in particular campaigns; such cooperation was made contingent on establishing "that the identity, the purposes, the public image of the NAACP shall not be distorted and that the cooperating organization is financially and otherwise responsible." Any group seeking the cooperation of the NAACP was to be barred from soliciting contributions from sources giving financial support to the NAACP.

Other resolutions adopted: (1) called for the merging of city and suburban public school systems as a means of achieving integration and urged the development of quality education in Negro neighborhoods; (2) recommended the achievement of a guaranteed annual wage through such measures as "negative income tax"; (3) attacked the Mormon Church for having "refused to take an affirmative stand on the great moral issue of civil rights and equal treatment of Negroes and other minorities"; (4) condemned organized labor for giving "a less than token response to the demands of Negro protests" and for maintaining segregated seniority lines. (NAACP Labor Secy. Herbert Hill had said at a July 7 workshop that there was a "rigid pattern in exclusion of the Negro from skilled craft unions in Hollywood's movie and television industry," although the Screen Writers Guild and the Screen Actors Guild had given the NAACP "complete support" in its integration efforts.)

The convention was the first NAACP convention at which the NAACP Legal Defense & Educational Fund, Inc. was not represented. Jack Greenberg, the fund's director, said in New York July 6 that he had received a letter from the NAACP asking him not to attend the convention because "our presence there would interfere with their publicity." It was reported from the convention July 5 that delegates felt the reason for the exclusion was competition for contributions between the fund, a separate, tax-exempt organization, and the legal section of the NAACP itself.

Chicago Rally Discusses 'Black Power'

A rally marking the opening of an SCLC fair housing and voting rights campaign in Chicago was the occasion for statements on "black power" by 2 major civil rights leaders—Dr. King, organizer of the Chicago campaign, and McKissick. But both men warned of the tendency of the rights movement to split into moderate and militant elements.

King, who did not use the term "black power," said that "a doctrine of black supremacy is as evil as a doctrine of white supremacy." He rejected "black separatism." "The Negro," he added, "needs the white man to free him from his fears; the white man needs the Negro to free him from his guilt." King called for formation of "a nonviolent army that no violent force can halt and no political machine can resist."

McKissick insisted in his speech that "black power is not hatred" nor advocacy of violence. He explained that "black power" could be manifested in "the developing of a black consumer bloc nationwide able to strike at any concern." "Black power," McKissick said, "means black people getting together to have voting strength. It means gathering power with their money and votes." He expressed willingness to meet with King and other rights leaders in a "summit conference."

(King had suggested such a conference at a Chicago news conference July 8. The idea had been proposed July 7 in New York by A. Philip Randolph. In urging such a meeting, King had said that the rights movement was "very, very close" to splitting over the "black-power" issue.)

Urban League Debates Militancy

The annual convention of the National Urban League, held in Philadelphia July 31-Aug. 4, was the scene of an unsuccessful attempt by young militant delegates to move the social-service, tax-exempt organization into the field of direct action.

One of the chief spokesmen for the militant element was David Rusk, 25, son of State Secy. Dean Rusk and associate director of the Washington, D.C. Urban League. In a speech July 31 that met with a standing ovation, Rusk called on the league to "use power to break out of the black ghetto" and to "forget about traditions, stop worrying about our present supporters' attitudes, ignore our institutional limitations." He offered this prescription for attacking school segregation: "You organize your black masses. You picket; you boycott; you force resignations; you bring court actions; you bring in the feds; you force curriculum changes, pupil redistribution, reallocation of more funds and teachers to Negro slum schools." He acknowledged that direct action by the league "may build up a set of powerful enemies," but he held that "if you have no enemies, you probably aren't doing anything worthwhile."

National Urban League Executive Director Whitney M. Young Jr. warned in an address at the convention's annual dinner Aug. 2 that adoption of Rusk's proposals would cost the league its tax-exempt status and lead to loss of financing from foundations and government agencies. In his keynote address preceding Rusk's speech, Young July 31 had characterized the league's commitment as that of "providing services needed by the impoverished urban masses, ... whose frustrations threaten to explode like dynamite, or, worse, who have become apathetic and resigned to their fate." To this end, he added, "the Urban League must reach the unreachable." He reaffirmed the

league's policy of biracial cooperation, calling such cooperation an "absolute necessity . . . to the success of the movement." He deprecated the "black-power" slogan as meaning
"all things to all men," but he also criticized the mass media
for having gone "beserk" in its coverage of the theme. Referring to a 5-day trip to Vietnam he had made in July, Young observed that Negro soldiers in Vietnam "share foxholes with
their white buddies at the same time that a house in a suburb,
an apartment in a good neighborhood, is denied other Negro
Americans. This makes no sense."

(Young had reported on his Vietnam trip to Pres. Johnson
July 26. He told newsmen following the meeting that he had
told the President that Negro servicemen were concerned a-
bout the dearth of Negro officers and the possibility that whites
received favorable consideration in the awarding of promotions; he said Mr. Johnson had "agreed that a greater effort
should be made to identify and promote" Negro servicemen.
He also reported that the morale of Negro troops in Vietnam
was "extremely high." At a news conference in Saigon July 23,
Young had said he found Negro servicemen "more concerned
about black progress than black power"; he added that Negroes
in Vietnam "were familiar with the negative things in the
United States" such as "the riots in Chicago, black power," but
were not familiar with "positive things, like the defeat of Congressman [Howard W.] Smith.")

Young issued a statement on "black power" Aug. 3. He said
that the National Urban League had "carefully refrained from
becoming involved in the fruitless dispute over the value of a
slogan which has not even yet been clearly defined by its orig-
inators." He said it was the league's intention to "expand and
develop positive programs of action" concerned with jobs,
housing, education and voting, which he saw as "the things in
our American system which bring power to both black and
white citizens."

The convention was addressed Aug. 1 by Housing & Urban
Development Secy. Robert C. Weaver, who warned that many
inhabitants of Negro ghettos had broken "with the established
order." He said, "Many nonwhites, who have been repeatedly
denied meaningful participation in the dominant society, now
look to a substitute social order which will afford them a significant role and provide a sense of full participation." "I do
not ignore the angry words of the militants," he added, "for
their tone, their demand for reform, their challenge of domi-

nant values, their repudiation of middle-class behavior are real and basic." (Ford Foundation Pres. McGeorge Bundy, addressing the convention Aug. 2, pledged his foundation to play "its full part" in the Negro cause. He said that new projects would be launched in the fields of leadership, research, communications and the administration of justice. He called on government and business to shoulder the greatest responsibility for achieving equality for Negroes. As "a citizen and not as a foundation executive," Bundy concluded, "it seems to me that it is right and reasonable to suggest that the level of effort—financial and political and personal—which here is required is fully comparable to the effort we now make as a nation in Vietnam.")

The National Urban League's policy-making delegate assembly met Aug. 3, amid reports that resolutions favored by the more militant delegates had been rejected in the resolutions committee, which screened resolutions before they were submitted to the delegates. Young told reporters Aug. 2 that "if you think there is going to be a revolt at the delegate assembly or a move to throw out Whitney Young, you have misread the signs." Resolutions adopted Aug. 3 touched on the Vietnamese war without taking a position on U.S. policies. One resolution cited the "loyalty to America and continued service in its defense by Negro citizens" as "yet another moral claim on the nation to strive for a true equality of condition"; another deplored "the tendency . . . to use this war and its attendant expenses as an excuse for reducing imperative domestic programs to alleviate social ills." At a business session closing the convention Aug. 4, Young reported that the National Urban League had placed more than 8,000 Negroes in jobs during the past year and that an additional 10,000 were receiving job training through the league. Replying to those who favored a league policy of direct action activities, Young asserted that "direct action means putting a man in a job."

SNCC Document Urges 'Black Power'

The *N.Y. Times* Aug. 4 published excerpts of a position paper said to have been drafted the previous winter by dissident SNCC members. The document's authors were said to have used the paper as a means of persuading the SNCC staff at its May 14 meeting to adopt its current policy of excluding whites from policy-making and from organizing among Negroes.

Stokely Carmichael, who was elected SNCC chairman at the May 14 meeting, was said to have been instrumental in drafting the document, described as "still considered confidential." The position paper's published excerpts provided a theoretical base for an all-Negro organizational policy, but they did not mention the term "black power."

Among the excerpts: "Negroes in this country have never been allowed to organize themselves because of white interference. . . . Blacks, in fact, feel intimidated by the presence of whites, because of their knowledge of the power that whites have over their lives. . . . A climate has to be created whereby blacks can express themselves. The reason that whites must be excluded is not that one is anti-white, but because the efforts that one is trying to achieve cannot succeed because whites have an intimidating effect. . . . This is not to say that whites have not had an important role in the movement. In the case of Mississippi, their role was very key in that they helped give blacks the right to organize, but that role is now over. . . . If we are to proceed toward true liberation, we must cut ourselves off from white people. We must form our own institutions, credit unions, co-ops, political parties, write our own histories. . . . We propose that our organization [SNCC] should be black-staffed, black-controlled and black-financed. . . . If we continue to rely upon white financial support, we will find ourselves entwined in the tentacles of the white power complex that controls this country. . . . Liberal whites have not begun to address themselves to the real problem of black people in this country. . . . It is very ironic and curious how aware whites in this country can champion anticolonialism in other countries, . . . but when black people move toward similar goals of self-determination in this country, they are viewed as racists and anti-white by these same progressive whites. . . . Re-evaluation of the white and black roles must NOW take place so that whites no longer designate roles that black people play but rather black people define white people's roles."

SCLC Convention Focuses on Economic Issues

The annual convention of the Southern Christian Leadership Conference, held in Jackson, Miss. Aug. 8-11, was marked by an emphasis on economic reform as the means to give the Negro people full equality. In opening addresses Aug. 8, SCLC

Pres. Martin Luther King Jr. and Sen. Edward Kennedy (D., Mass.) called for massive federal spending to upgrade the economic level of the American Negro.

King called for a "guaranteed annual income" for all low income families. A convention resolution adopted Aug. 11 set the figure at $4,000 a year. King said that he would begin campaigning for the guaranteed income after Congress had completed pending rights legislation and that his SCLC was considering demonstrations in Chicago to "dramatize the need" for such legislation. He suggested that the government could provide the income either through "massive public works and job training programs" or through direct cash payments. (The Census Bureau reported Aug. 11 that 36% [1,700,000] of the nation's non-white families and 14.4% [6,300,000] of white families had earned $3,000 or less each in 1965 and thus fell into the poverty category.)

Kennedy called for a "massive commitment of national resources to the upgrading of Negro life in America" and said the scale of the commitment should be equal to the $2 billion a month spent by the government in Vietnam. He recommended a crash program for the 1966 summer and fall that would increase recreational and educational facilities in Negro areas. "If we can get this started," Kennedy said, "we will buy time for the long-run and more-important projects, which involve no less than a major upgrading of the schools, the cities, the housing opportunities and the job opportunities of the Negro Americans."

In his annual report to the convention Aug. 10, King said that the "most significant event" of the past year had been the spread of the civil rights movement into the North. He referred to Chicago as "the test case for SCLC and indeed the freedom movement in the North." "Just as Mississippi stands as the largest bastion of crippling *de jure* segregation in the South," he said, "Chicago holds equal status as the most hostile bastion of *de facto* segregation in the North." King spoke out against the "black-power" doctrine and called instead for an alliance of Negroes and whites in nonviolent protest. The results of violence, he said, were "Negro women and children lying dead in the streets, the few places of employment and enterprise in the ghetto destroyed in anger, the continued breeding of resentment and frustration."

Some 400 convention delegates called Aug. 11 for a raise in the federal minimum wage to $2 an hour and the extension of its provisions to "every worker in every category of work, bar none." In a resolution adopted Aug. 11 the convention urged Pres. Johnson and both political parties to "reverse the immoral vote of the House of Representatives in the 'open-housing' title of the Civil Rights Bill of 1966." A resolution adopted Aug. 11 scored U. S. involvement in the Vietnamese war, called on Pres. Johnson to de-escalate unilaterally to see if there would be a positive response from the Viet Cong and charged that the present draft system was "undemocratic." The resolution stated that "the war is corrupting society from within and degrading it from without." It contended that "Negroes suffer double the unemployment rate of whites, double the poverty and double the combat responsibility to fight for the society that inflicts this discrimination on them." The resolution was the SCLC's first against the war.

Negro Leaders Debate 'Black Power' & 'Nonviolence'

The "black-power" and "nonviolence" concepts were debated Aug. 21 on a 90-minute NBC program, "Meet the Press," by Martin Luther King Jr., Whitney Young, Roy Wilkins, James H. Meredith, Stokely Carmichael and Floyd B. McKissick. The debate seemed to reflect a clear division between (a) King, Young and Wilkins, who reiterated their adherence to nonviolence, and (b) McKissick, Meredith and Carmichael, who identified themselves with "black power."

King said: Despite the fact that many Negroes and whites thought demonstrations had already served their purpose, he would continue them because demonstrations bring "the issues out in the open."

McKissick said: "Nonviolence is something of the past. . . . Most people will not agree to be nonviolent, not agree to be hit and passively stand there and not return the blow."

Meredith said: "Nonviolence is incompatible with American ideas. This is a military-minded nation, and it always has been." In response to a question as to whether Meredith thought Negroes should organize vigilantes, take the law into their own hands and punish those who attack Negroes, Meredith replied: "That is exactly what I am saying, exactly."

Carmichael concurred with Meredith and added: "We [Negroes] are the only people who have to protect ourselves against our protection. We have to protect ourselves against state troopers, against police in Mississippi. And if we do not protect ourselves, . . . then who is going to protect us! And I agree 150% that black people have to move to the position where they organize themselves and they are in fact their protection for each other."

Meredith and Carmichael disagreed on the subject of the war in Vietnam. Carmichael described Negroes fighting in Vietnam as "black mercenaries." He said: "I would not fight in Vietnam, absolutely not. I would advise every black man not to fight in Vietnam." Meredith said: "I fully support the war effort, not the conduct of the war effort. I am a soldier. I personally think one of the best things happening to the Negro is the war in Vietnam."

During a panel discussion in Philadelphia Oct. 25 McKissick said: "The civil rights movement is dead as a doornail, and what we have now is a black revolution, for black people to take what they can for themselves"; "black power means only one thing to black people, that they have no power and must get it any way they can."

Expanding on those views, McKissick said Dec. 8 at a Senate hearing on urban problems: "Black power" was the successor to the civil rights movement, which had expired with the "glorious picnic" of the 1963 March on Washington. The rights movement had been concerned primarily with integrating the 10% of the U. S.' Negroes who were middle class and did not deal with the 90% who were poor. Black power was not a call for violence but "a rational militant call . . . to do what you have not been able to do—destroy racism in this country, create full employment in the American ghetto, revise the educational system to cope with the 20th century, and make the American ghetto a place in which it is possible to live with hope." "I believe black power will be accepted just like Irish power has been accepted." A person's reaction to the black-power slogan was a true test of whether or not he was a sincere liberal and backer of civil rights; a true believer in civil rights would support black power.

7 Negro Leaders Reject 'Black Power'

7 national Negro leaders Oct. 14 repudiated the concept of "black power" and issued a restatement of civil-rights principles. They announced their stand in a 3/4-page advertisement in the N.Y. Times and in an NAACP memo. The signers of the statement were: Mrs. Dorothy Height (president of the

National Council of Negro Women), A. Philip Randolph, Bayard Rustin, Roy Wilkins, Whitney Young, Amos T. Hall (executive secretary of the Conference of Grand Masters, Prince Hall Masons of America) and Hobson R. Reynolds (grand exalted ruler of the Improved Benevolent & Protective Order of Elks of the World).

The statement's 4 points, in part:

"1. We are committed to the attainment of racial justice by the democratic process. . . .

"2. We repudiate any strategies of violence, reprisal or vigilantism, and we condemn both rioting and the demagoguery that feeds it. . . .

"3. We are committed to integration, by which we mean an end to every barrier which segregation and other forms of discrimination have raised against the enjoyment by Negro Americans of their human and constitutional rights. . . .

"4. As we are committed to the goal of integration into every aspect of the national life, we are equally committed to the common responsibility of all Americans, both white and black, for bringing integration to pass."

Martin Luther King Jr. announced in Atlanta Oct. 14 that he endorsed the principles of the statement although he did not sign it. In clarifying his position Oct. 16, King said that while he supported the statement's 4 major tenets of "nonviolence, democratic process, integration and Negro-white collaboration," he did not want to be part of any repudiation efforts that could be construed by the press and the public as an attempt to "excommunicate" the SNCC and CORE from the civil-rights movement. King said "Negro unity and Negro-white unity, both of which are decisive, can only be harmed by a precipitated effort to excommunicate any group even if silencing or isolating some groups is unintended."

Ex-CORE national director James Farmer and Dr. John A. Morsell, assistant executive director of the NAACP, scored the "black-power" concept at a race relations debate at the Brooklyn Center of Long Island University Dec. 1. Farmer said: "Black power, whatever the coiners of this slogan mean, to me means shared power—otherwise it leads to an illusion." Morsell warned of the possibility that the black-power movement might turn into a "genuine separation" and withdrawal of Negroes from the mainstream of American life. He said: "There is nothing in blackness that insures virtue. We don't claim we are better; we're just equally good."

MEREDITH MARCH

Meredith Shot in Mississippi

James H. Meredith, the Negro student who had been the focus of racial violence at the University of Mississippi in 1962,
was shot from ambush June 6 just one day after he had set out
afoot on a voting-rights pilgrimage from Memphis, Tenn. to
Jackson, the Mississippi capital. Meredith, currently a soph-
omore student at the Columbia University Law School in New
York, was shot and wounded as he walked along U.S. Highway
51, 2 miles south of Hernando, Miss., on the 2d day of his
march.

Meredith had begun the pilgrimage with a few companions
June 5. In announcing his plans May 31, he had described the
march as a personal attempt to "encourage the 450,000 unregistered Negroes in Mississippi to go to the polls and register"
and also to "point up and to challenge the all-pervasive and
overriding fear that dominates the day-to-day life of the Negro
in the United States—especially in the South and particularly
in Mississippi."

Meredith was hit by 3 blasts fired from a 16-gauge shotgun.
Sherwood Ross, a New York and Washington radio announcer
serving as Meredith's press coordinator, said he had seen a
white man appear in the brush at the side of the highway and
shout "James Meredith" twice before firing. Meredith was
able to crawl to the shoulder of the road after being shot and
remained conscious; an ambulance arrived almost immediately
and took him to Memphis, where emergency surgery was performed. Hospital authorities in Memphis said Meredith had
suffered 60-70 superficial wounds in the head, back and legs
and was in satisfactory condition following surgery.

In addition to Meredith's 6 companions, 15 law officers, including 2 FBI agents, and a number of reporters and photographers had been in the vicinity of the shooting.

Aubrey James Norvell, 40, a white resident of Memphis,
was arrested at the scene of the shooting and taken to the Hernando jail; Sheriff Lee Meredith of DeSoto County said later
that Norvell had admitted the shooting. Ross reported that
Sheriff Meredith had "stood at the side of the woods but didn't
pursue the man who shot the gun. He could have stopped it."
Norvell, whose car was found to contain a shotgun and a quantity

of beer, was arraigned June 7 on a charge of "assault with a deadly weapon with intent to murder" and was held under $25,000 bail. 10 days later Norvell won his temporary freedom by posting the $25,000. A De Soto County grand jury indicted him Nov. 18 on charges of assault and battery with intent to kill Meredith and of pointing and firing a firearm at N. Z. Trout, a special investigator for the Mississippi Highway Patrol. Norvell pleaded guilty Nov. 21 and was given a 5-year prison sentence, with 3 years of the term suspended. Norvell had changed his plea from not guilty after his attorneys failed in an attempt to have the indictments dismissed on the grounds that Norvell had been denied his constitutional rights by the exclusion of women and inclusion of Negroes on the county juries. (Norvell remained free on his $25,000 bail until Dec. 2, then started serving his sentence.)

The first report of Meredith's shooting, an AP dispatch transmitted at 6:33 p.m. June 6, erroneously reported that Meredith had been killed. A correction of the report was issued by the AP at 7:08, after the erroneous bulletin had been broadcast by the 3 major TV networks.

In a statement issued June 6 from his Texas ranch, Pres. Johnson deplored the shooting as "an awful act of violence." The President said he had instructed the Justice Department "to spare no effort in bringing the guilty person or persons to justice." Atty. Gen Nicholas deB. Katzenbach said June 6 that the incident appeared to violate a section of the 1965 Voting Rights Act making it a federal crime to intimidate a person for encouraging others to vote. Katzenbach added, however, that the Justice Department had no immediate intentions of prosecuting Norvell because state authorities seemed prepared "to move expeditiously" under state law. (Meredith had told TV interviewers June 6, before the shooting, that he had asked for Justice Department protection and had been told that "Katzenbach said it was not important enough to do anything.")

Gov. Paul B. Johnson Jr. of Mississippi said June 6 that, although he thought the march was "a very, very foolish thing," the shooting of Meredith was "a tragedy" and the perpetrator would be "prosecute[d] to the hilt." He added that he was "particularly pleased that this was not a Mississippian."

Meredith told reporters at his Memphis hospital room June 7 that he would never again "knowingly expose" himself in Mississippi without being armed; he said he was "sorry I didn't have something to take care of that man."

Rights Leaders Take Up Meredith March

The attack on Meredith brought an immediate reaction from leaders of civil rights organizations throughout the U.S. A continuation of Meredith's march was announced at a Memphis news conference early June 7 by the Rev. Dr. Martin Luther King, president of the Southern Christian Leadership Conference (SCLC), Floyd B. McKissick, national director of CORE, and Stokely Carmichael, chairman of SNCC.

The 3 leaders and about 20 supporters began their march immediately and encountered hostility from Mississippi state troopers, who jostled them from the pavement to the side of U.S. Highway 51 near Hernando. The marchers resumed walking on the shoulder of the highway for about 2 hours and then announced that they would resume the march June 8 and would continue it to Jackson. Meanwhile, Negro comedian Dick Gregory and a few companions were marching from the site of Meredith's shooting back to Memphis, 26 miles away.

Mississippi Gov. Johnson called on his state's residents June 7 to stay away from "these agitators and radical politicians." He said he would provide police protection for the marchers "provided they behave themselves, commit no acts of violence nor take a position of provocative defiance."

A manifesto outlining the march's purpose was issued June 8 with the indorsement of King, McKissick, Carmichael and dozens of other civil rights activists who took up the march. The June 8 manifesto called for federal voting examiners to be sent to 600 Southern counties, proposed a "freedom budget" of "billions" to aid low-income Negroes and urged passage of pending civil rights legislation with broadening amendments. The document characterized the march as "a massive public indictment and protest of the failure of American society, the government of the United States and the state of Mississippi to 'fulfill these rights.'" Charles Evers, the NAACP's Mississippi field secretary, repudiated the manifesto June 10 as "too critical of Pres. Johnson" but joined the march June 16. He called the march a "good thing" because of voter-registration canvassing that took place while the march was in progress.

Violence & Voter Registration During March

The "Meredith March Against Fear," the name given the march after the rights organizations took over from the fallen

Meredith, covered 260 miles and did not end until June 26—3 full weeks after Meredith had started out. The march stimulated the registration of about 4,000 Mississippi Negroes and involved at least 10,000 Negroes as temporary participants. A detour from the original route along U.S. Highway 51 was decided on June 12 as a means of increasing the emphasis on voter canvassing, and canvassing teams left the other marchers periodically to concentrate on individual towns. The marching column usually comprised 150-300 persons, dropping to as few as 34 when voter-registration teams left to do their work and rising to as many as 3,500 in certain cities. Incidents of violence took place during some of the canvassing operations. The march inspired sympathy rallies in New York, Los Angeles, Washington, Baltimore and other cities June 12 and in Detroit June 19.

Newsmen covering the march discovered June 8 that most pay phones along the march route were inoperable because their wires had been cut. Armistead Phipps, 58, a Mississippi Negro who had joined the march near Como, collapsed June 9 and died of a heart attack. Dr. King said Phipps' "death means that he was probably underfed, overworked and underpaid." The marchers spent the night in tents for the first time June 10; they had returned to Memphis for the night June 8 and 9 while awaiting the arrival of 2 circus tents from Atlanta.

A dispute between march leaders and state highway patrolmen escorting the march broke out June 10 near Sardis over a patrol order banning cars driven by rights leaders, medical personnel or newsmen from parking within a mile of the marchers. The order was relaxed after a conference between the Rev. Ralph D. Abernathy of the SCLC and Charles Snodgrass of the highway patrol. Gov. Paul B. Johnson Jr. June 16 reduced the number of patrolmen escorting the march from 20 to 4; he said the state did not intend "to wet-nurse a bunch of showmen all over the country."

An argument was reported June 13 between marchers advocating nonviolence and supporters of the Deacons for Defense & Justice, a Negro self-defense organization. Ernest Thomas of the Deacons told newsmen that he and others had been guarding the marchers' campsites with "pistols, rifles and shotguns" but that "we don't take guns with us when the people are marching [because] the march is nonviolent." CORE National Director McKissick told reporters he had no knowledge of armed guards being present at campsites.

The first voter registration inspired by the march took place in Batesville June 11, when about 50 local Negroes, including one aged 106, were persuaded to register. Virtually all of Batesville's white restaurants had been closed in anticipation of the march. Canvassing teams left the march June 13 and went into Tallahatchie, Bolivar, Quitman and Sunflower Counties.

A major breakthrough in voter registrations took place in Grenada, where about 150 Negro residents registered June 14 and about 500 more registered June 15. Local officials agreed June 14 to appoint Negro registrars, and 6 were on the job June 15; registration hours were also extended into the evening. Marchers desegregated the courthouse rest rooms June 14 and placed an American flag on a Confederate monument without incident. It was reported June 25, however, that the Negro registrars had been dismissed after the marchers had left and that Negroes had been asked not to register for a 3-week period while clerks caught up on accumulated paperwork. It was also reported that about 20 rights workers had remained in Grenada following the departure of the march and had succeeded in organizing a Grenada County Movement, with 200 local Negroes attending an organizing meeting June 20.

Police in Greenwood June 16 arrested 3 march leaders on trespassing charges for attempting to erect tents on public school property without permission of the school board. Those arrested—but soon released on bail provided by the NAACP—were Carmichael, Robert Smith of SNCC, logistics chairman of the march, and Bruce Baines of CORE, transportation chairman.

After 2 days without incident, the marchers June 21 encountered violence as they held a memorial service at the Neshoba County courthouse in Philadelphia to commemorate the 1964 slaying of 3 civil rights workers near Philadelphia. As the marchers, including about 250 local Negroes, began walking back toward the Negro community, they were attacked by a crowd of about 300 whites using fists, stones, clubs, bottles and firecrackers. Local police made no move to intervene until a few Negroes began fighting back with fists. An outbreak of shooting took place in Philadelphia's Negro section that evening; Stanley Stuart, a white man, fired a shot into Freedom House, a civil rights headquarters, and suffered a minor neck wound from a shot fired in return. Sporadic shooting followed. (The Justice Department June 27 filed suit in U.S. District

Court in Jackson charging Philadelphia officials with taking no action June 21 to prevent harassment of the marchers. The department requested a court order directing local authorities to provide police protection without discrimination, to arrest those violating the law and to discipline police who failed to provide protection. The department had announced June 19 that it would bring to trial Sept. 26 16 white Mississippians on charges stemming from the 1964 triple slaying near Philadelphia.)

Dr. King announced June 21, after flying to Indianola for a rally, that a return march to Philadelphia would be held "to straighten the place out." King, McKissick and Carmichael June 22 sent a telegram to Pres. Johnson requesting that federal marshals be sent to Philadelphia to protect the 2d march. The President responded June 23 with a telegram to King conveying Gov. Johnson's assurances that additional state highway patrolmen were being sent to Philadelphia to maintain law and order. A U.S. District Court judge in Jackson June 23 rejected a June 22 request by the march leaders that he issue a temporary restraining order instructing local, county and state law enforcement officials to provide police protection for the return march.

The 2d Philadelphia march took place June 24; 300 marchers held a rally at the courthouse and were separated from a crowd of 1,500-2,000 whites by about 100 highway patrolmen and local police. Bottles, eggs and epithets were hurled at the demonstrators, however, and a speeding car drove into the marchers as they were returning to the Negro district; the occupants of the car were arrested.

2,500 demonstrators assembled June 23 on the grounds of a Negro public school in Canton, where they hoped to camp for the night. But they were routed by state highway patrolmen using tear gas and irritant gas. 25-50 demonstrators who remained on the school grounds despite the gas were dragged away. (Troopers explained that local officials had ruled that school grounds could be used only for school-sponsored activities.) 11 march participants had been arrested earlier June 23 while attempting to pitch tents at the school; they were released on bond later in the day. One of the 11, C.O. Chinn Sr., the local MFDP director, was also charged with shooting a white man the previous night. Chinn denied the charge. He said he had been lying in his car, ducking bottle-throwing whites, when he heard a shot. This took place after he had helped chase a carload of whites who had thrown a fire bomb at him and other marchers. The marchers spent the night of June 23-24 in the gymnasium of a Roman Catholic mission. A rally on the school grounds was authorized by local officials June 4, and King told the marchers at the rally that they would spend a 2d night at the mission. The announcement met with groans, boos and occasional chants of "We want the tent." (Atty. Gen. Katzenbach said in Washington June 24 that the marchers had been offered 3 other camp sites as alternatives to the school grounds but had turned them down.)

March Shows Rights Leadership Split

Meredith returned to the march June 24 amid indications of growing differences among the various leaders of the march. Meredith arrived in Canton but did not take part in the June 24 rally, which had been expected to serve as a welcoming celebration. He led a few marchers from Canton June 25 while the bulk of the marchers were arriving at Tougaloo Southern Christian College, a Negro institution 8 miles from Jackson, at which they were to assemble and spend the night before ending the march June 26 in Jackson. Meredith explained June 25 that he had promised friends to "do some walking with them"; Dr. King said a "breakdown in communications" was responsible for the separate marches. Since his return to his New York home from a Memphis hospital June 8, Meredith had occasionally expressed criticism of the way the march was run. In a June 15 interview he had said that "as an old military man" he felt the march required a "hierarchy and someone to head that hierarchy." There had been widespread speculation that Meredith might return to the march armed. But Meredith said June 25 that he was not armed "because the Mississippi highway patrol chief has accepted all responsibility for security."

The march ended June 26 with a rally in front of the state capitol in Jackson. The rally was attended by an estimated 15,000 persons, most of them Mississippi Negroes. More than 1,000 law officers, National Guardsmen and state troopers separated the demonstrators from 1,500 white Mississippians. There were no serious incidents.

Speakers at the rally included Meredith, King and Carmichael, who called on Negroes to "build a power base . . . so strong that we will bring them [whites] to their knees every time they mess with us." Others attending the rally included

United Auto Workers Pres. Walter P. Reuther and film stars Marlon Brando and Burt Lancaster.

Representation on the speakers' platform reflected the differences that had been recurrent throughout the march; at a June 25 meeting, march leaders had voted to exclude NAACP officials by limiting speakers to those who had agreed to endorse the June 8 manifesto. Organizations taking part in the march that voted to exclude the NAACP from the rally were SNCC, CORE, the Mississippi Freedom Democratic Party (MFDP) and the Delta Ministry of the National Council of Churches. Those voting against the NAACP's exclusion were King's SCLC and the Medical Committee for Human Rights. Whitney Young of the National Urban League, who had not been among the manifesto's original signers and who had expressed reservations about the march's militancy, was allowed to speak at the rally after he agreed to sign the manifesto.

DEMONSTRATIONS: NORTH & SOUTH

King Begins Chicago Fair-Housing Drive

At the conclusion of a 3-day meeting in Chicago with local civil rights leaders, the Rev. Dr. Martin Luther King Jr. announced at a press conference Jan. 7 that his SCLC would launch its "first sustained Northern movement" in Chicago in 1966. Chicago had been chosen, he explained, because its slums were "the prototype of those chiefly responsible for the Northern urban race problem" and because the SCLC had been invited to conduct such a program by Chicago's Coordinating Council of Community Organizations (CCCO), a coalition of 45 local civil rights groups. Albert Raby, CCCO's convener, pledged his group's "enthusiastic" support at the press conference. King said the SCLC project involved the formation of "slum unions," including a "union of the unemployed," which would bargain with slum landlords and city officials for better living conditions and more jobs for Negroes.

The drive to make Chicago an "open city" was launched at a rally July 10. King addressed a predominantly Negro crowd of 30,000 to 45,000 that met in 98° heat in Soldier's Field. The rally and King's campaign to "end slums" in Chicago were part of a new Freedom Movement co-sponsored by CCCO. King had taken an apartment in a North Lawndale slum area on the city's Negro West Side Jan. 26 but had delegated day-to-day supervision of the program to the Rev. James A. Bevel, 29, of Itta Bena, Miss. and had appeared infrequently in the city. The campaign was run from the Warren Ave. Congregational Church 1½ miles north in the East Garfield section. Concrete results of the campaign were reported to be few; but it organized a "union" of welfare recipients and used a boycott to force 4 dairy companies to hire a total of 178 Negroes.

In his July 10 speech, King announced a series of demands on the administration of Mayor Richard J. Daley. Following the rally, he entered an air-conditioned car and led a 3-mile march from the stadium to city hall, on the door of which he taped a list of the demands. The list called for city action to end discrimination in housing, schools and employment, for recognition of unions of welfare recipients, for the establishment of a civilian review board to consider charges of police brutality and for a $2-an-hour state minimum wage. One demand was that the Chicago Housing Authority build no more public housing on the South and West Sides, both Negro areas, until a substantial amount of public housing—occupied by Negroes and whites—had gone up in non-Negro areas. (The Rev. Dr. James H. Jackson of Chicago, head of the National [Negro] Baptist Convention, had announced July 6 that he would not support the July 10 rally. In making public a letter to King, Jackson criticized King's espousal of civil disobedience and said that King's drive in Chicago was "a faint imitation and no match for the massive slum-clearance program that this city has had for years.")

James Meredith told the rally crowd that "if Negroes don't clean up their communities and Negro hoodlums don't stop chasing our women through the streets, then we're never going to amount to nothing."

In a message read at the rally, Roman Catholic Archbishop John P. Cody of Chicago pledged his archdiocese, the nation's largest, to elimination of the last "vestige of discrimination." Cody's message called on real estate boards to "support open occupancy laws" and to work for the elimination of "the blight and disgrace of our slums"; it urged trade unions and employers to extend membership and employment to minority-group members; it reported that the Chicago archdiocese was including a fair-employment clause in all contracts between parishes and suppliers or builders. A letter from Cody supporting the rally had been read in Chicago's Catholic churches.

King and local rights leaders met July 11 with Mayor Daley

and other city officials. (The mayor Feb. 10 had launched a program of building-code enforcement and rodent control and had issued a report on the city program July 10. According to the report: $2 million of federal anti-poverty funds had been spent on rodent control; in the 18 months ended July 1, 9,226 buildings housing 102,847 families had complied with building codes, with landlords spending $34 million for repairs.) At a joint news conference following the closed meeting, King charged Daley with making no "specific" commitments on his demands, while Daley charged that King had "had no solutions" when asked for suggestions. (King had told newsmen before the July 10 rally that Northern rights campaigns were complicated by the response of Northern mayors in making "some token concessions to take the wind out of your movement.")

The greatest reaction to King's Chicago drive was produced by its attacks on segregated housing in lower- and middle-class neighborhoods in Chicago and its suburbs. Demonstrations began July 29 with a vigil by 40 demonstrators at a real estate office in a Southwest Side neighborhood, Gage Park. The participants were removed from the area in police vehicles after angry whites gathered at the scene. About 250 demonstrators, most of them Negroes, marched into the neighborhood July 30 under the leadership of the Rev. Bevel and the Rev. Jesse H. Jackson, SCLC officials, and Albert Raby of CCCO. They carried signs reading "End Apartheid in Real Estate." Jeering onlookers pelted the marchers with rocks and bottles before being driven away by police. 8 persons were arrested; 6 persons were injured. About 350 demonstrators led by Bevel staged a car caravan and march into Gage Park July 31 but fled from about 300 white hecklers. 5 of their cars, parked at a nearby park at the request of police, were overturned and burned; 2 cars were pushed into a lagoon, and the windows of 23 others were broken and their tires slashed. 12 whites were arrested.

In a statement issued Aug. 1 at SCLC headquarters in Atlanta, King scored the Chicago police for "failure to exercise full responsibility for full protection" of the marchers. In a reference to rioting July 12-15 on Chicago's West Side, King called such police laxity "especially appalling" in view of the fact that "huge masses of police and National Guardsmen were mobilized to put down the violence of a few hundred Negroes on the West Side."

Returning to Chicago, King was struck in the head by a rock

Aug. 5 as he began leading a march by 600 demonstrators through crowds of angry white residents of the Gage Park district. Hit just above the right ear, King stumbled but resumed marching; a knife thrown at King later in the march missed him and hit a white youth in the neck. A crowd had begun gathering at the marchers' staging area before they arrived; their arrival was greeted by a volley of stones, bottles, eggs and cherry bombs. A crowd of about 200 whites then began marching in front of King, carrying signs with such slogans as "King would look good with a knife in his back" and throwing rocks and bottles at cars carrying Negro passengers. Other residents shouted epithets from their front steps, and windows of cars driven by Negroes were smashed. As the marchers returned to the staging area to board buses chartered by police, whites in a crowd of about 2,500 hurled bottles, smashed bus windows and fought police attempting to disperse them. The disorders continued after the marchers had left, and about 5,000 whites participated in a near-riot. 960 policemen, including 160 members of a riot-control force, fought the disorder for 5 hours. 44 persons were arrested; local hospitals treated 28 persons for injuries and admitted 3.

Another target in the open-housing campaign was the white Belmont-Cragin district on Chicago's Northwest Side, where marches were staged Aug. 2, 3 and 7. During the Aug. 2 demonstration, in which about 250 persons, most of them Negroes, took part, 140 policemen warded off 1,000 jeering whites and arrested about 10. Helmeted police arrested about 20 whites Aug. 3, as about 3,000 taunted 350 demonstrators marching through the area and picketing real estate offices. The Aug. 7 march, by 700 demonstrators, required the protection of a force of 500 policemen, who fired their guns into the air and used their nightsticks to control 3,000-5,000 angry whites surrounding the marching column. The onlookers shouted "white power!" and threw rocks, bottles and firecrackers at the marchers, while members of the National States Rights Party and the American Nazi Party mingled among them, distributing leaflets and membership applications. 25 persons were arrested.

The Rev. Jackson announced at a rally Aug. 8 that marches would be conducted in the all-white Chicago neighborhood of Bogan and in all-white Cicero, a suburb west of Chicago, "by the weekend." As a result, the Illinois state police force was ordered on standby alert Aug. 9, and Cook County Sheriff

Richard B. Ogilvie said the same day that he would seek a court order blocking the march into Cicero if it were not canceled. Mayor Daley appealed to rights leaders Aug. 9 to negotiate rather than march, and Archbishop Cody asked demonstrators Aug. 10 to halt the marches to avert "serious injury to many persons and even the loss of life." Rights leaders agreed Aug. 10 to postpone the marches. But King and Raby announced in a telegram to Police Superintendent O. W. Wilson Aug. 11 that the planned Bogan march would be held Aug. 12.

Fair-housing demonstrators paraded in Bogan Aug. 12, in Bogan again Aug. 14 and also in the all-white Chicago neighborhoods of Gage Park and Jefferson Park Aug. 14.

A group estimated at 500-700 persons, half of them whites, marched into Bogan Aug. 12. 1,000 white spectators spat on the marchers, threw stones at them and shouted "Nigger, nigger, nigger" and "Hate, hate, hate." White youths carried signs reading "white power" and decorated with Nazi swastikas. A force of some 600 policemen protected the marchers as they moved down Pulaski Road and conducted silent vigils in front of 3 real estate offices. Several of the demonstrators were hit by small stones, but there were no serious injuries resulting from the demonstration. 9 persons were arrested for disorderly conduct.

The Aug. 14 marches into the Bogan and Gage Park areas of Southwest Chicago and the Jefferson Park neighborhood on the Northwest Side constituted the first simultaneous operation in which civil rights leaders conducted demonstrations in more than one neighborhood in a single day. The Bogan march was led by the Rev. Jackson, the Gage Park march by SCLC Executive Secy. Andrew Young and Albert Raby, and the Jefferson Park march by SCLC Program Director James Bevel. As the 675-1,000 marchers moved into the 3 neighborhoods, white hecklers shouted derisive slogans and threw eggs, tomatoes, bottles and cherry bombs. Many white youths carried American Nazi Party flags imprinted with the swastika and the words "symbol of white power." At least 10 injuries were reported, and police arrested 20 persons. Rep. Roman C. Pucinski (D., Ill.), whose constituency included Jefferson Park, said Aug. 14 that he hoped to have legislation drawn up within 2 days to permit courts to limit the number of marchers in a civil rights demonstration. Pucinski said that "I am now convinced that these people [civil rights leaders] are not looking for any social justice. . . . When they plan 3 simultaneous drives in one day, it is obvious they want to dilute police protection."

After the Aug. 14 marches had concluded, at about 7 p.m., police clashed with a crowd of 1,500-2,000 whites, most of them teen-agers, in the Marquette Park area on the Southwest Side. Most of the whites had attended an American Nazi Party rally at which John Patler, a Nazi Party captain, had urged a "white revolution" and had said that "if Negroes can march into white areas, we can march into Negro areas." Attendance at the Nazi rally was estimated at 2,000. After the rally broke up, white youths began throwing rocks, bottles and firecrackers at Negro motorists. 2 cars containing Negroes were damaged and a 3d burned. 30 policemen arrived and restored order temporarily, but later 50 reinforcements had to be called in. Police fired shots in the air and used their nightsticks to break up the renewed disorder. At least 2 policemen and several Negroes were injured and several whites were arrested.

Civil rights leaders stepped up demonstrations Aug. 16. Small numbers of pickets paraded in front of city hall, the Chicago Real Estate Board headquarters, a savings-and-loan building, Cook County Welfare Department and Chicago Housing Authority offices. That evening violence broke out briefly during picketing of 6 real estate firms in the Jefferson Park neighborhood. About 500 whites threw bricks and firecrackers at the pickets, but 500 policemen dispersed the crowd.

King led a march of 500 persons into the all-white South Deering neighborhood on Chicago's South Side Aug. 21. About 2,000 residents lined the march route. White teen-agers cursed the marchers and threw rocks, bricks, beer cans, apples and firecrackers. 400 policemen protected the marchers and arrested about 15 persons. Nobody was reported injured. Followers of King simultaneously led about 300 marchers into Chicago Heights, a suburb south of Chicago, and about 200 into the Evergreen Park suburb west of Chicago.

George Lincoln Rockwell, commander of the American Nazi Party, addressed 500-1,000 persons in southwest Chicago's Marquette Park Aug. 21. Rockwell urged the crowd to form an armed "white guard" to fight integration efforts in "Coon County" (a play on the name Cook County). Elsewhere in the park, police arrested the Rev. Connie Lynch of the National States Rights Party and Ku Klux Klansman Evan Lewis when they attempted to speak without permits.

Rights leaders and Chicago officials agreed Aug. 26 on a

program to end *de facto* housing discrimination in Chicago. The meeting at which the agreement was reached was moderated by Ben W. Heineman, chairman of the Chicago & North Western Railway. Persons participating in the meeting included Mayor Daley, King, Chicago Real Estate Board head Ross Beatty and Archbishop Cody. None of the 79 participants voted against the agreement, which had been worked out the previous day by a 20-member subcommittee. King, praising the accord, said that "never before have such far-reaching and creative commitments been made and programs adopted and pledged to achieve open housing in a community." But he cautioned that the agreement represented only "an important first step in a 1,000-mile journey."

The accord included:

(1) A statement by the Chicago Real Estate Board that, "in a significant departure from its traditional position," it would "withdraw all opposition to the philosophy of open occupancy legislation at the state level provided it is applicable to owners as well as brokers."

(2) A provision that licenses of real estate brokers could be suspended or revoked if the Chicago Commission on Human Relations found that they had failed to comply with the fair-housing ordinance.

(3) A pledge by the Chicago Housing Authority to begin "a leasing program which places families in their best available housing without regard to the racial character of the neighborhood."

(4) A statement by the Cook County Board of Commissioners that the County Department of Public Aid would place aid recipients in the best housing available, regardless of location, and that "the department will not be satisfied if recipients live in less satisfactory accommodations than would be available to them if they were of a different race, color or national origin."

(5) A promise by the Department of Urban Renewal to relocate families, regardless of color, in the best housing available, regardless of location.

(6) An affirmation by the Cook County Council of Insured Savings Associations and the Chicago Mortgage Bankers Association that it was their policy "to lend mortgage money to all qualified families, without regard to race, for the purchase of housing anywhere in the metropolitan area."

(7) A statement by the U.S. Justice Department that it would

consider whether service should be continued by the Federal Deposit Insurance Corp. and the Federal Savings & Loan Insurance Corp. to financial institutions found guilty of racial discrimination.

(8) Pledges from representatives of Chicago's major religious faiths to exercise their authority "in effecting equal access to housing in the metropolitan area for all people."

(9) Pledges from representatives of commercial, industrial, labor and banking concerns, including·the Chicago Federation of Labor & Industrial Union Council, to secure their membership's support of the fair housing program.

(10) A pledge by the Chicago Conference on Religion & Race to establish a continued organization to "accept responsibility for the education and action programs necessary to achieve fair housing."

Prior to the Chicago accord, King had announced that the open-housing campaign would be extended to Cicero (population: 70,000), reportedly one of the toughest and most segregationist of the Chicago suburbs. In response to King's statement Aug. 20 that 3,000 persons would march through Cicero Aug. 28, warnings were voiced by local and state officials that a violent reaction might be expected. Cook County Sheriff Ogilvie urged King Aug. 22 to call off the march; Gov. Otto Kerner announced Aug. 24 that he would mobilize the National Guard to help Cicero officials maintain order.

Once the housing accord was reached, King agreed to defer the march, and Kerner canceled plans to call up the Guard. Other rights leaders, however, refused to call off the demonstration. King's efforts succeeded only in postponing the march for a week.

250 civil rights activists marched and demonstrated in Cicero for 2 hours Sept. 4. Robert Lucas, 41, chairman of the Chicago branch of CORE and leader of the march, denounced the Chicago accord as failing to "achieve anything concrete enough." Members of 3 other rights groups—Black Power (a new group), the League of Labor & Education and Brothers for Afro-American Equality—participated. More than 2,000 National Guardsmen and 500 local, county and state policemen were on hand to protect the marchers, who drew an estimated 3,000 spectators. 15 persons were injured, including 6 white hecklers bayoneted by Guardsmen, and 39 persons were arrested.

As the demonstrators, about 200 of whom were Negro, moved down the 30-block march route from the edge of Chicago, onlookers pelted them with rocks, bottles, bricks, eggs and firecrackers. Some of the marchers answered the epithets with taunts of their own and displayed signs reading "black power." At one point in the march the demonstrators held a prayer vigil at West 25th St. and South Laramie Ave. for Jerome Huey, 17, a Negro who had been fatally beaten by 4 white youths in May while he was looking for summer employment in Cicero. 700 anti-integrationist whites massed behind police barricades during the vigil. Later, as the demonstrators were returning to Chicago and were only 50 yards from the city limits, white youths threw bottles and attempted to rush the marchers. Police and Guardsmen held back the crowd.

At least 2 other protest marches against the Chicago housing accord were planned—one by CORE and one by the American Nazi Party. The CORE march, planned for Sept. 11, was forestalled by the arrest of Robert Lucas one day earlier. The Nazi march, joined by 150 white teen-agers, was held in southwest Chicago Sept. 10 under heavy police escort. George Rockwell was arrested at the start of the march for having made a speech without a permit at his Aug. 28 rally in Marquette Park; he paid a $400 fine Sept. 20.

SCLC Leads Birmingham Voting Rights Marches

The SCLC Jan. 4 began a campaign of daily marches through downtown Birmingham in a demand for the registration of Negro voters at night and Saturdays. The drive was marked by violence when demonstrators sought Jan. 11 to recruit Negro students from the Parker High School. Police fired shotguns into the air after 3 policemen had been slightly injured by rock-throwing students. Following this incident, 2 marches of several hundred Negroes each were led into downtown Birmingham by Hosea Williams, SCLC program director. Additional marches were staged by SCLC-led high school students Jan. 12-13, and several marchers were injured in clashes with police.

A 3-judge federal court (Judges H. Hobart Grooms, Seybourne Lynne and Clarence Allgood) in Birmingham Jan. 13 issued a temporary injunction against the use of high school students in demonstrations. But high school students continued to participate in the marches in response to direct persuasion by rights activists. The Rev. Fred Shuttlesworth of the SCLC said that "some persons weren't aware of the injunction, but we are contacting them and telling them to obey it." The Jefferson County Board of Education charged in a suit filed in federal court in Birmingham Jan. 24 that the SCLC had disrupted the school system.

Atty. Gen. Katzenbach Jan. 20 ordered federal voting examiners into Birmingham and surrounding Jefferson County. Katzenbach said that the 74,230 unregistered Negroes in the county represented the largest group of unregistered Negroes in the 518 counties covered by the 1965 Voting Rights Act and that the county Board of Registrars had not taken steps necessary to register them before the May 3 Alabama primary. 400 Birmingham residents, most of them Negroes, were registered by federal examiners on their first day of operation Jan. 24. (Federal officers also registered 400 Negroes in nearby Bessemer and 340 at a federal registration office established at Fairfield.)

5 Negroes were wounded in Birmingham Feb. 21 when a white motorist fired 8 pistol shots into a crowd of 150 Negroes picketing the Liberty Supermarket. The demonstrators had been demanding that the supermarket hire more Negroes and had been protesting the alleged beating of a picket by the supermarket's security guard. Emory Warren McGowan, 23, surrendered to the police later Feb. 21 and admitted firing the shots. About 90 Negro ministers, representing the Birmingham Baptist Ministers Conference and the Interdenominational Ministers Alliance, marched to the supermarket Feb. 22 in protest against the shooting. The clergymen demanded "better police protection" and integration of the city's police force.

CORE Seeks Open Housing in Baltimore

A proposed open-occupancy ordinance for Baltimore was defeated by the City Council Jan. 17 by 13-8 vote. A campaign of picketing in a demand for an end to housing discrimination in Baltimore was started by CORE in April, and CORE National Director McKissick announced that Baltimore had been chosen as a "target city" for demonstrations during the spring and summer.

CORE announced May 22 that as a result of the picketing campaign, 6 members of the city's 12-member Downtown Apartment House Association had agreed to rent to Negroes. Baltimore Mayor Theodore R. McKeldin said May 23 that a

7th downtown apartment house had agreed to an open-occu-pancy policy. Picketing centered on the luxury-class Horizon House and met with counter-picketing beginning May 1 by members of the Ku Klux Klan. 25 CORE members were ar-rested during the demonstrations.

Bogalusa (La.) 'Deacons' Protect Demonstrators

About 500 Negroes staged a march on city hall in Bogalusa, La. Jan. 28 to mark the first anniversary of the city's deseg-regation campaign. The demonstration was led by James Far-mer, then national director of CORE, and by A. Z. Young, pres-ident of the Bogalusa Civic & Voters League. Addressing the crowd at city hall, Young referred to the fact that 4 crosses had been burned the night of Jan. 27 near the site of a meeting to plan the march. He warned that if Ku Klux Klansmen burned another cross in a Negro neighborhood, "we shall strike a match on you, baby." The marchers were protected by police and members of a Negro protective organization named Dea-cons for Defense & Justice.

A confrontation of armed whites and Negroes in front of Bogalusa Junior High School was broken up by police Sept. 12 without anybody getting hurt. The threatening situation devel-oped after about 50 white men and 12 women met outside the school a few hours after classes had started. It was reported that they had heard a rumor that James H. Meredith had been invited to speak at the school. About 20 members of the Bo-galusa Civic & Voters League and of the Deacons for Defense went to the school on hearing rumors of impending Ku Klux Klan action. The 2 groups displayed guns but were persuaded to disperse.

Georgia Negroes March for Better Schools

300 Cordele, Ga. Negroes marched on the county court-house Mar. 31 in a protest against allegedly inferior condi-tions in Negro schools. After the demonstrators had lowered the U. S. and Georgia flags from the courthouse flagpole and raised a banner reading "Freedom Now," several of them rip-ped the American flag. Georgia Gov. Carl E. Sanders ordered 9 state highway patrolmen into Cordele Apr. 1 to prevent fur-ther desecrations of the flag, and 500 Ku Klux Klansmen and their sympathizers staged a rally Apr. 3 in protest against the

flag-ripping.

Cordele police Apr. 4 arrested 71 Negroes, most of them school children, after they had marched from a church to a Negro school; 40 teen-agers were released on condition that they return to school, but the remaining 31 were held on disorderly conduct charges.

Demonstrators Seek Voting Rights in Grenada (Miss.)

The Mississippi town of Grenada, one of the points on the Meredith marchers' route, was the scene of demonstrations throughout the summer. Grenada officials had promised concessions to head off demonstrations by the Meredith marchers. As a result, several hundred Negroes had registered to vote in the previously segregated court house. The concessions, however, were progressively withdrawn after the march ended.

43 Negro demonstrators led by SCLC staff members were arrested July 7 after they sat down in the street—and refused to disperse—in protest against the withdrawal of the concessions. In a statement issued through the Atlanta office of SCLC, Dr. King accused Grenada officials of having "gone back on every promise made" when the march had passed through the town. King also charged that Grenada police had been "harassing, beating and jailing our staff, as well as the local Negroes." About 300 Negroes July 10 staged a "sympathy march" to the jail in which those arrested July 7 were being held. After the demonstrators ignored an order to disperse, 25 helmeted highway patrolmen scattered them with billy clubs and gun butts.

Earlier July 10, 2 whites had been arrested on charges of shooting the previous evening at 3 white men entering a Negro church. Those shot at (none was hit) were James L. Draper of the federal Community Relations Service, Henry Aaronson, an NAACP attorney, and Oliver Rosengart, an NYU law student. The 2 arrested men were identified as Bobby Todd of Grenada and B. C. Bennett of nearby Montgomery County. Both were acquited Aug. 2 of charges of pointing and aiming a deadly weapon, a misdemeanor.

Major disorders broke out when local and state police used tear gas to disperse a Negro voter-registration rally the evening of Aug. 8. The Negroes, estimated at from several hundred to 1,200 persons, had gathered in front of a recently opened federal voter-registration office for a rally addressed by Hosea

Williams, Southern field director of the SCLC. (Atty. Gen. Katzenbach had appointed federal voting examiners to Grenada County July 21.) Violence erupted the evening of Aug. 9 when about 300 Negroes marched in protest against the Aug. 8 use of tear gas. 150-175 whites threw bricks, rocks, bottles, and fire-crackers at the Negroes while local and state police reportedly stood by laughing. Negro protest marches Aug. 9 and 13 were protected by law-enforcement officers, but police Aug. 14 arrested 19 Negroes, including Leon Hall, director of the civil rights drive in Grenada, when they attempted to enter the all-white First Baptist Church during morning services.

Milwaukee Negroes Protest Eagles' Bias

Civil rights workers picketed the homes of 2 judges and a Congressman in suburban and metropolitan Milwaukee Aug. 19-29 and Aug. 31-Sept. 2 in protest against membership by public officials in organizations that barred Negroes. The demonstrators, members of the Youth Council of the Milwaukee chapter of the NAACP, were led by the Rev. James E. Groppi, a white Roman Catholic priest and assistant pastor of St. Boni-face parish in Milwaukee's Negro ghetto. The group objected to the membership of Circuit Judge Robert C. Cannon, County Judge Christ T. Seraphim and Rep. Clement J. Zablocki (D., Wis.) in the Fraternal Order of Eagles, a national fraternity that restricted its membership to Caucasians.

Demonstrators picketed Cannon's home in Wauwatosa, a Milwaukee suburb, for 11 consecutive nights Aug. 19-29. The demonstrations stirred up an angry response among white res-idents. Large crowds, including members of the Ku Klux Klan, jeered the pickets and threw rocks and firecrackers. About 400 National Guardsmen, mobilized by Gov. Warren P. Knowles Aug. 26, were rushed into the neighborhood to protect the pick-ets.

The situation eased Sept. 3 after the council agreed to halt all picketing temporarily in order to discuss the issue with Eagles officials.

Slaying by Police Stirs St. Louis Disorder

Demonstrations were staged in St. Louis Sept. 25-28 in pro-test against a detective's slaying Sept. 22 of a Negro robbery suspect. The demonstrations ended in rioting Sept. 28. 14 persons were injured, but no arrests were made. At a coroner's inquest Sept. 28 police officers testified that Detective William Finnegan had shot and killed Russell Hayes, 24, a Negro, when the youth drew a weapon (which turned out to be a tear-gas pistol) on Finnegan and 2 other officers in the car. Hayes' hands were handcuffed behind him at the time of the shooting, and he had been searched after his arrest. Finnegan did not testify. The coroner's jury returned a verdict of justifiable homicide.

About 40 CORE members demonstrated vociferously outside during the hearing; marchers carried signs reading "Police Murderers Must Go."

A militant CORE faction demanding Finnegan's dismissal held a protest rally in front of police headquarters that evening. As the meeting broke up, about 50 youths began smashing store and auto windows. Some Negroes stoned firemen answering false alarms and policemen seeking to control the mob. Others hurled a park bench into the path of a bus.

State Rep. Raymond Howard, president of St. Louis CORE, said Sept. 28 that the militant group's meeting and demands were "unauthorized."

The NAACP Sept. 29 sent the police board a telegram demanding "an extensive investigation" into the killing and suspension of Finnegan pending its outcome.

Carmichael Arrested in Selma Demonstrations

SNCC Chrmn. Stokely Carmichael was arrested with 2 Negroes in Selma, Ala. Nov. 5 on charges of inciting a riot at the City Hall. Carmichael and William S. House, 20, were convicted of the charge Nov. 29. The 3d defendant, Lorenzo Taylor of Philadelphia, had been convicted previously on a lesser charge. Carmichael was fined $100 and sentenced to 60 days in jail at hard labor. Taylor was given a choice of $60 fine or 74 days in jail. House was fined $100 and sentenced to 30 days.

Selma Mayor Joseph T. Smitherman had charged that the 3 men had arrived in town in a sound truck with loudspeakers blaring and had blocked traffic in a Negro section. He said that the defendants ignored police orders to move the truck and had resisted arrest.

Carmichael and House conducted their own defense after their attorney, Donald A. Jelinek, 32, of New York, was denied permission to represent them because he was not licensed to practice in Alabama. The defendants denied the charges. Carmichael said he had come to Selma to encourage Negroes to vote for independent candidates in the Nov. 8 elections. (Jelinek was an Alabama staff counsel for the Lawyers Constitutional Defense Committee, a group of predominantly Northern Lawyers representing civil rights defendants in the South. Jelinek was jailed in Demopolis, Ala. Nov. 16 for practicing law without an Alabama license. He was taken from the Marengo County Circuit Court, where he was appealing 2 convictions of Richard Reavis, a white civil rights worker.)

(The first 5 of more than 160 demonstrators who were arrested in connection with the Mar. 1965 Selma-to-Montgomery march were convicted in Montgomery Municipal Court Nov. 11 on charges of disorderly conduct. The 5, including ex-SNCC Executive Secy. James Forman, were fined $100 and given 30-day jail sentences that were suspended. According to police testimony at the trial, which had been delayed for 18 months while the defendants appealed to a federal court, the 5 civil rights workers had obstructed traffic and had refused to obey commands to move. The defendants represented themselves after Jelinek was denied permission to represent them. The U. S. 5th Circuit Court of Appeals in New Orleans Nov. 15 ordered a stay in prosecution of about 155 remaining cases.)

Boycotts Hit Washington & Other Cities

An agreement ending a Negro boycott of St. Louis buses was reached Mar. 3 by CORE and the Bi-State Transit System. CORE had begun the boycott in Dec. 1965 after Bi-State had bought the Consolidated Service Car Co. and had discontinued its service car operation, which had been in predominantly Negro districts. CORE had protested the loss of jobs by Negroes working for the car service and the fact that buses were more expensive than the service cars. Under the Mar. 3 agreement, Bi-State agreed to employ qualified former service car drivers and to assume outstanding mortgages on former service cars.

A 2d NAACP-sponsored boycott of white merchants in Natchez, Miss. was lifted Mar. 3. The boycott, a resumption of an earlier boycott settled Dec. 3, 1965, had been started Dec. 23 in protest over a police beating of a Negro. The NAACP won assurances that the 2 policemen involved had been discharged and that Negro store employes fired during the original boycott would be rehired.

A boycott of Washington, D. C. merchants who refused to support home rule for the district was started Mar. 5 by the Free D. C. Movement, a civil rights coalition. The boycott plan, originated by Marion Barry Jr., Washington director of the SNCC, called for Negroes to refuse to shop at stores not displaying "Free D. C." stickers. Merchants had been given stickers on condition that they sign a home-rule petition and support home rule by such means as telegraphing the President or picketing the Greater Washington Board of Trade, which opposed home rule. About 175 of the nearly 300 stores in the northeast Washington target area displayed the stickers Mar. 5. Washington's Interreligious Committee on Racial Relations Mar. 8 issued a statement saying that "a selective buying policy, directed by . . . fair-minded seekers after justice, focusing only on those who are actively opposing home rule, can be a legitimate tool of persuasion and expression." But the Washington branch of the NAACP, an original supporter of the home-rule campaign, said Mar. 11 that it approved of a voluntary program of sticker-distribution but not of a boycott. The Jewish Community Council of Greater Washington Mar. 11 attacked the boycott as "irrelevant and ineffective."

Charles Evers, Mississippi state NAACP field secretary, announced in Fayette, Miss. June 8 that a 6-month Negro boycott of white merchants had been ended following agreement by city officials to a list of Negro demands. Fayette Mayor R. J. Allen confirmed the settlement. The boycott had been called after rejection of the Negroes' demands by the city Dec. 15, 1965. Among concessions made by city officials and white businessmen: Parks, playgrounds and public buildings were desegregated; juries were to be integrated; Negroes were appointed as one of Fayette's 2 policemen and one of Jefferson County's 2 deputy sheriffs; 11 of the town's 13 stores hired Negroes.

SCHOOL DESEGRATION

Token Desegregation Found the Rule

The Southern Education Reporting Service reported Jan. 5 that 89% of the school districts in Southern and border states were technically desegregated but that only 16% of the Negro students in those states (657,789 out of a total of 3,572,810) were enrolled in integrated schools. Among Southern states, Texas had the highest percentage—17%—of its Negro pupils in integrated schools; Tennessee followed with 16%, and Virginia was 3d with 11%. The District of Columbia and all border states except Oklahoma had more than half of their Negro students in integrated schools.

In its annual report, released May 17, the NAACP Legal Defense & Educational Fund, Inc. asserted that only 5.2% of Negro children in the Deep South were attending school with white pupils. The report, which did not include border states, charged that many schools maintained "segregated classrooms, white-only extracurricular activities and separate school buses."

Differing statistics were reported Dec. 10 by the U.S. Office of Education. It said that the number of Negro pupils attending schools with whites in the Deep South had increased to 16.9% (about 489,000 Negro pupils) of the total Negro enrollment. Texas ranked highest with about 30% of Negro pupils in desegregated classes. Alabama, Mississippi and Louisiana were lowest with 2½-3%.

The Justice Department filed or entered 66 school desegregation cases under Title IV of the 1964 Civil Rights Act during 1966. The number represented nearly double the number of cases filed or entered during 1965.

Federal Integration Guidelines Imposed

U.S. Education Commissioner Harold Howe 2d, at a news conference in Washington Mar. 7, outlined guidelines adopted by the Office of Education (OE) for enforcing school desegregation during 1966 under the 1964 Civil Rights Act. The guidelines applied to Southern school districts; Howe indicated that the OE had no immediate plans for attacking racial imbalance in Northern schools. Among the guidelines: (1) a "significant start" in the integration of faculties (or "progress" in school districts that had begun faculty integration); (2) the closing down of "small, inadequate" Negro schools; (3) the use of "freedom of choice" plans only when their implementation produced significant desegregation. Howe said the OE planned "more emphasis on compliance reviews, field visits and investigations in order to determine actual performance" in achieving school integration.

(In a letter sent to Health, Education & Welfare Secy. John

W. Gardner Feb. 16, the SNCC had suggested that the guidelines require that at least 20% of Negro pupils attend integrated schools and that "freedom of choice" plans be accompanied by affadavits in which school officials and sheriffs pledged to prevent intimidation of Negro pupils and parents. A Justice Department complaint filed with the U. S. District Court in Raleigh, N. C. Jan. 11 had charged the Franklin County school board with publishing in a local newspaper the names of Negro students applying for transfer to white schools.)

The OE reported May 7 that 255 school districts in Southern and border states had failed to file pledges of compliance with the school desegregation guidelines by the May 6 deadline. The original deadline for filing pledges had been extended Apr. 15 because fewer than 25% of the school districts involved had been heard from. The OE's May 7 announcement said that 1,-498 districts in 17 Southern and border states had submitted compliance pledges and that an additional 140 had indicated their intention of pledging compliance.

HEW Secy. Gardner announced May 13 that he had found 12 school districts in 3 Southern states in violation of the desegregation guidelines and had ordered a cutoff of federal funds to them, effective in 30 days. This was the first termination of federal school aid under Title VI of the 1964 Civil Rights Act. The action had been recommended by hearing examiners, who had found that the districts were operating totally segregated school systems; a final decision had been delayed to permit appeals to the Education Commissioner and the HEW Secretary, but no appeals had been filed. (A total of 45 Southern school districts were stricken from federal school aid rolls by Dec. 5. However, 8 of them had been reinstated by Dec. 5 following compliance with the guidelines.)

A letter to Pres. Johnson from the Senators of 9 Southern states protesting school desegregation guidelines established for the 1966-67 school year was made public May 14. The letter, dated May 2, objected to "the abuse of power involved in the bureaucratic imposition of the guidelines" and sought the President's "personal intervention to right this wrong and have this order revoked." Sen. Richard B. Russell (D., Ga.) was reported to have drafted the appeal; the states whose Senators were signatories were Alabama, Arkansas, Florida, Georgia, Louisiana, Mississippi, North Carolina, South Carolina and Virginia.

Gardner announced Dec. 30 that guidelines for the 1967-68

school year would be virtually unchanged from those of the current school year.

Alabama Fights Guidelines

Gov. George C. Wallace of Alabama met with state educators June 3 and 6 to consolidate opposition to the school-desegregation guidelines. Wallace Apr. 6 had announced his intention of defying the guidelines. 18 Alabama college and university presidents met with Wallace in Montgomery June 3 and then issued a statement urging public officials to "use every method at their disposal within the law to fight against attempted encroachment on the basic right of the people of Alabama and the United States to operate their own public school systems." About 400 public school officials attending a meeting with Wallace in Montgomery June 6 were assured by the governor that he would make state funds available to compensate for any loss of federal aid resulting from refusal to comply with the guidelines. He also promised "plenty of legal aid" to school districts facing court action.

A conference on means of implementing the desegregation guidelines was held in Birmingham June 11 under the sponsorship of the Alabama Advisory Committee to the U.S. Civil Rights Commission. The approximately 1,100 persons attending were predominately Negro teachers and members of civic action groups but also included some local school officials and state Education Supt. Austin R. Meadows. U.S. Education Commissioner Howe also attended; he said at a press conference that he would continue to enforce the guidelines through the withholding of federal funds unless overruled by court order. He told the conferees that Alabama represented "a special problem which is apparent in no other state, North or South."

An Alabama law declaring the desegregation guidelines unconstitutional in the state was approved by the State Senate Aug. 30 and by the House of Representatives Sept. 2. The bill, drafted by Gov. Wallace, was signed by him Sept. 2. It declared the guidelines to be "null and void" and prohibited Alabama schools from compliance with them. It appropriated $3.8 million to partially replace the nearly $40 million in federal funds that would be withheld from local school districts that refused to sign compliance forms.

Wallace said Sept. 2 that no penalty would be imposed on schools that chose to desegregate. But at a press conference

Sept. 9 he announced that "any assignment of teachers or students based on the guidelines" would violate state policy.

Several schools integrated peacefully Sept. 6 despite the new law.

The NAACP Legal Defense & Educational Fund, Inc. filed a motion in the U. S. District Court in Montgomery Sept. 12 to stop state officials from enforcing the new law. The 3-judge court Sept. 17 granted the Justice Department the right to intervene in the litigation against the Alabama law. The department's suit, filed Nov. 17, asked the court to invalidate the law. It charged that the state law's purpose and effect were "to facilitate and perpetuate maintenance of dual school systems based upon race . . . and to impede and interfere with efforts of local school boards to transform dual structures based upon race into single non-racial school systems."

Federal Court Upholds Guidelines

The U. S. Court of Appeals for the 5th Circuit in New Orleans Dec. 29 upheld the legality of the Mar. 7 desegregation guidelines. It ordered 7 school boards in Louisiana and Alabama to desegregate all classes by the fall of 1967 and to achieve substantial faculty desegregation by the fall of 1968. The 2-1 ruling, on 7 cases heard in May, involved the school boards in the Louisiana parishes of Caddo, Bossier, Jackson and Claiborne, the Jefferson County (Ala.) Board of Education and boards in Bessemer and Fairfield, Ala. Judge John Minor Wisdom of New Orleans wrote the majority opinion. Judge Homer Thornberry concurred, and Judge William Harold Cox dissented.

The Dec. 29 decision was seen as the virtual ratification of the controversial guidelines for all states in the 5th Circuit—Georgia, Florida, Alabama, Mississippi, Louisiana and Texas. The majority opinion said: "In evaluating desegregation plans, district courts should make few exceptions to the guidelines and should carefully tailor those so as not to defeat the policies of HEW or the holding of this court."

Howe Attacks 'Gradualism'

Education Commissioner Howe June 18 accused American educators of having a "blind faith in gradualism" that had "accomplished very little so far" in achieving school integration. He called on them "to form a 3d front for racial equality in the United States" differing from both gradualism and activism. Howe made these remarks in an address to 350 educators and school administrators from 76 cities who were meeting in New York at a conference sponsored jointly by the National Urban League and the Columbia University Teachers College under a grant from the Office of Education. Pointing out that "the schools throughout the nation remain almost as segregated today as they were in 1954, when the Supreme Court decided that racially segregated education was illegal," Howe said that educators "should either stop pretending that we care about racial equality or . . . start something definite in the way of a program." He called on school administrators to "consider such means as redrawing school district boundaries and consolidating with neighboring districts for educational purposes, even though political boundaries may remain unchanged." "There is no such thing as the perfect way to achieve school desegregation," he said. "We must simply bore ahead with the tools we have, and it won't be pleasant, and it won't be quiet, and it would be much nicer if someone else would share this work."

Howe concluded, however, that unless educators were "willing to put our jobs . . . on the line, we should admit that . . . [we] are no longer prepared to be the prime movers in American education."

Howe July 1 released results of a study of comparative educational opportunities that found predominantly Negro schools to be inferior to those that were predominantly white; in predominantly Negro schools Negroes scored progressively lower than whites on achievement tests as they continued in school. The study, carried out under the direction of Prof. James S. Coleman, head of the Johns Hopkins Sociology Department, had been ordered by Congress in passing the 1964 Civil Rights Act. Among other findings of the survey: (1) Almost 80% of white first-grade pupils and more than 65% of Negro first-grade pupils attended schools at which 90-100% of the pupils were of the same race. (2) White children attended elementary schools in which the average class size was 29, whereas average class size for minority group members ranged from 30 to 33. (3) Negro pupils had fewer facilities such as laboratories and libraries and fewer curricular and extracurricular programs than white pupils. (4) "The average Negro pupil attends a school where a greater percentage of the teachers appears to be somewhat less able than those in schools attended by the average white student." (5) The dropout rate for Negroes aged 16 and 17 was 17%, compared with 9% for whites. (Disregarding race, students from blue-collar families had a drop-out rate 4 times that of students from white-collar families.) (6) 4.6% of all college students were Negroes, of whom over half attended Southern Negro institutions. (7) Achievement-test scores reflected regional as well as racial differences: "By grade 12, both white and Negro students in the South score below their counterparts . . . in the North. In addition, Southern Negroes score farther below Southern whites than Northern Negroes score below Northern whites."

Howe was denounced by Southern Congress members Sept. 30 at a House Rules Committee hearing on his school desegregation policies. Committee Chrmn. Howard W. Smith (D., Va.) told Howe that OE field representatives were "harassing and hammering school people, telling them they've got to get some Negro children in white schools." Howe denied having sought to "establish racial balance." He said his office's guidelines were designed "to eliminate dual school systems for whites and Negroes" being operated in violation of the 1954 Supreme Court desegregation decision. He said the guidelines "do not mention and do not require racial balance or the correction of racial imbalance." On the House floor Sept. 30 Howe was attacked by Rep. L. Mendel Rivers (D., S.C.) as an "idiot" and a man who "talks like a Communist." Rivers said "the President should fire" Howe. Rep. William F. Ryan (D., N.Y.), in defense of Howe, said he was "shocked" that a Congressman would describe as a "Communist" a public official attempting to carry out the mandate of Congress.

Grenada (Miss.) Mob Attacks Negro Children

In Grenada, Miss. Sept. 12-13 mobs of whites attacked Negro children seeking to attend the city's 2 all-white schools. At least 30 Negro children and parents were reported beaten. 13 persons were arrested. The disorders led to Justice Department action against city officials Sept. 13 to insure the protection of the Negro children.

The initial clash took place the morning of Sept. 12 when whites (variously reported at from 200 to 400) armed with ax handles, chains and pipes barred about 40 of 160 Negro students from entering John Rundle High School. At the Lizzie Horn elementary school, Negro children entered peacefully in the morning but were attacked by a mob on leaving in the afternoon. Receiving little or no protection from local police—who frequently watched without interfering as whites beat Negro children—Negro parents and children retreated to the school building until state troopers were summoned to escort them home. 2 boys were hospitalized with severe head injuries and bruises. A 3d was treated for a broken leg. The crowd beat 2 *Memphis Scimitar Press* photographers and a UPI reporter; a constable barred the UPI man from safety on school grounds.

Violence continued Sept. 13, and only 35 or 40 Negro children were able to reach school. Henry Aaronson, attorney for the NAACP Legal Defense & Educational Fund, Inc., was beaten by 8 white men while nearby police ignored his cries for help. He was released only when his assailants discovered that an NBC camera crew was filming their behavior. The mob then chased the TV personnel. The mobs Sept. 13 assaulted 2 carloads of Negro children. 35 other Negro children, who were marching to school in a group from the Bell Flowers Baptist Church, were turned back by the mob. Negro parents, who charged police with failing to protect the children, started a march to the school the afternoon of Sept. 13 but were stopped a block from the school by state highway patrolmen, who assured them the children would be escorted home safely.

The Justice Department filed suit in Oxford, Miss. Sept. 13 against the city of Grenada and its officials, charging them with "willful failure and refusal" to protect the Negro children. The suit asked the U.S. district court in Oxford to grant temporary and permanent injunctions ordering Grenada officials "to provide protection to the children in the future and to arrest and prosecute those who assault or threaten them." A temporary injunction was immediately issued by U.S. District Judge Claude F. Clayton.

About 90 Negro children attended class Sept. 14, escorted by 150 state troopers and FBI agents. Only a few white spectators stood nearby, but local police, acting under the court order, arrested 6 on charges of assault and carrying concealed weapons. Clayton Sept. 16 issued a permanent restraining order requiring police to protect Negro children.

Negro pupils at the newly-integrated Grenada schools began a boycott Oct. 21 in protest against alleged abusive treatment by their teachers, school officials and white pupils. 214 Negroes, most of them school children, were arrested Oct. 24 when they demonstrated near the desegregated schools. A majority of the Negro pupils in the county school system—from

1,700 to 2,200 of the total of 2,600—took part in the boycott before it was ended Nov. 2.

Harlem Parents Demand School Control

A threatened boycott by Negro parents and civil rights groups delayed the planned opening of a new school in East Harlem (N.Y. City) in September, but the demonstration failed to win for Negro groups a power of control or veto over schools in the city's ghetto. The protesting Negroes demanded the removal of the school's white principal and his replacement by a Negro. The Board of Education agreed to give the Negro community a strong voice in the school's operation and to appoint a Negro to the post. The white principal offered to leave to restore harmony, but the city's teacher and supervisory associations protested against his ouster on purely racial grounds. He retained his position, therefore, and opened the school for classes Sept. 21.

The dispute centered on the new $5 million, air-contitioned, windowless Intermediate School 201 (IS 201), which had a Negro-Puerto Rican student enrollment of 560 and an integrated teaching staff of 26 Negroes and 29 whites, all volunteers. The site of the school, in the heart of a large Negro-Puerto Rican community, made integration unlikely. In an attempt to recruit white students, however, the board had sent 10,000 "invitations" in June 1966 to urge white families in adjacent areas to send their children to the school. Only 10 families expressed interest.

Negro parents and Harlem community groups had opposed the school site since its selection in 1962. When the chances of integrating the school vanished, parents became more militant. Late in August they issued an ultimatum threatening a boycott if the Board of Education did not meet 1 of 2 demands: either bring in white pupils to integrate IS 201 or give "total control" of the school to the community. The Board of Education asserted Sept. 1 that it could neither bus white children "long distances" involuntarily nor turn over to the community the board's authority to run the school.

The Board of Education and Superintendent of Schools Bernard E. Donovan met with 40 parents and community representatives Sept. 6. Dr. Donovan proposed a representative community council that would "help plan the program and watch how it is being carried out." He said the council could help screen candidates for the school staff "but would not have the right of hiring and firing." The parents rejected the compromise and demanded "total community control," including the power to hire and fire teachers and supervisors, to set academic standards and to allot school funds. This demand was rejected by Board of Education Pres. Lloyd K. Garrison, 68.

60 parents picketed the school Sept. 12 with signs demanding courses in black culture and the appointment of a Negro to replace the white principal, Stanley Robert Lisser, 40. After continued negotiations, Mrs. E. Babette Edwards, chairman of the East Harlem Union for Equal Achievement in Schools, warned Sept. 18 that the school would be boycotted unless the board met the demand for a Negro principal.

Supt. Donovan had announced that the school would remain closed Sept. 12-13 "to alleviate community tension." The board ordered IS 201 students and teachers to meet for classes Sept. 19 at PS 103 (an abandoned school slated for demolition). IS 201 teachers, however, refused Sept. 18 to teach at PS 103 because of inadequate facilities and supplies. After meeting at the old building Sept. 19, the teachers went to IS 201 prepared to teach.

Lisser, who had remained at PS 103, announced later Sept. 19 that he had "voluntarily" asked to be reassigned and that IS 201 would open Sept. 20. The Board of Education immediately announced the appointment of Mrs. Beryl Banfield, a Negro and one of Lisser's 3 assistants, as temporary principal. But Mrs. Banfield rejected the appointment the same day in resentment at being chosen "on the basis of color, not competence." The teachers then threatened to boycott the new school in protest against the removal of Lisser.

Lisser's removal was also protested by the Council of Supervisory Associations, 35 Harlem school principals, the Elementary School Principals Association and the United Parents Association. Dr. Frederick McLaughlin, director of the Public Education Association, accused the board of yielding to racism.

Lisser was reinstated Sept. 20 after IS 201 had opened with only 2 of its 55 teachers present. The board announced that he had withdrawn his request to be reassigned.

Lisser was met by about 60 white and Negro pickets when he arrived at the school Sept. 21. 5 persons were arrested when they tried to bar his entry into the building. Among the pickets were representatives of militant Negro and other groups, including the SNCC, the Black Muslims, the Organization of Afro-American Unity, the Communist Progressive Labor Party, Harlem's newly-formed Black Panther party and the Harlem chapter of CORE. SNCC Chrmn. Stokely Carmichael and CORE National Director Floyd McKissick were among the demonstrators. Also present were CORE Harlem chapter leader Roy Innis and Haryou-Act Executive Director Livingston Wingate, who accused the board of "defrauding the Harlem community." Wingate said Harlem was "a resegregated colony" whose goal was "quality education, segregated style."

Despite the disturbances, Lisser opened the school Sept. 21 with 2/3 of the students and 53 of the 55 teachers present. Attendance rose Sept. 22 from 390 to 441, but demonstrations continued, and 3 persons were arrested on charges of attempting to prevent children from attending school. 11 Negro and white demonstrators protesting the reinstatement of Lisser were arrested Sept. 23. The 50 pickets who demonstrated in the morning were led by Mrs. Helen Testamark of the United Block Association, Ron Clark of the Harlem chapter of CORE and Jesse Gray, Harlem rent strike leader. Demonstrations began to peter out the week of Sept. 26. By Sept. 28 there were no demonstrators at the school.

A Harlem committee representing parents and community leaders then proposed a 9-member "operations board" with "exclusive responsibility for the educational activities" of IS 201 and 3 nearby primary schools. The board would be composed of 4 representatives from 2 or more metropolitan universities, 4 representatives from a parents' advisory board and one member selected by the other 8. The board's responsibilities would be "the setting of standards and criteria for educational excellence" and "the selection of all staff: teachers, principals, auxiliary aides, clerical staff and others." The principal author of the plan was Dr. Kenneth B. Clark, professor of psychology at City College and a member of the State Board of Regents. The Board of Education met with 30 Harlem parents and community representatives Oct. 17 and turned down the Harlem group's proposal on the ground that it could not legally delegate authority to any outside agency.

The Board of Education Oct. 19 announced the details of its own plan to resolve the months of controversy over IS 201 specifically and over the city's ghetto schools in general.

The board statement proposed a "201 Board" with functions similar "in substance" to those of the board proposed by Clark. Composed of "democratically chosen" parents, members of the community, teachers and supervisors, the 201 Board would have authority to advise the school superintendent and the Board of Education on educational techniques, objectives and materials. It would not have authority to select school personnel or to "direct the work of the schools." The board simultaneously proposed a citywide "Task Force to Advance Education in Disadvantaged Areas." The Board of Education plan was rejected by Negro groups, and the dispute remained unsettled throughout 1966. The members of the local school board with jurisdiction over IS 201 resigned Nov. 1 in protest against the Board of Education's failure to negotiate beyond Oct. 19.

30 white and Negro West Harlem parents marched into the office of District Supt. Murray Hart Dec. 2 to demand a voice in the selection of the principal for a combination of the existing PS 125 and the new PS 36, to be completed in the spring of 1967. They called for the resignation of the newly appointed principal, Mrs. Kate M. Tuchman, while the community worked out the criteria for choosing a principal. 30 Harlem parents confined Mrs. Tuchman to her office Dec. 7 and did not let her leave until she announced: "I do not wish to be principal of 36-125." Schools Supt. Donovan announced later the same day, however, that he had rejected Mrs. Tuchman's request for a transfer.

CORE Official Attacks Mt. Vernon Jews

During a tumultuous meeting of the Mt. Vernon, N.Y. school board Feb. 3, Clifford A. Brown, 32, the local CORE education chairman, created a furor by telling the audience, which included several Jews: "Hitler made one mistake when he didn't kill enough of you." Among the Jews in the 100-member audience, which was participating in a discussion of school integration, was Dr. Harvey Felton, president of the Mt. Vernon Parents & Taxpayers, which opposed CORE in the Mt. Vernon integration dispute. Brown apologized later during the meeting.

CORE National Director James Farmer Feb. 7 ordered an investigation of Brown's remark, which he called "intolerable" (he added that the school board's "delaying tactics" on integration were also "intolerable"). Farmer said Feb. 8 that his investigation "in no way excused Mr. Brown's remark, which we unequivocally disavow, but it does serve to help us understand its provocation." Brown resigned from CORE Feb. 8. Will Maslow, executive director of the American Jewish Congress and a member of CORE's 38-member national advisory committee, resigned from the CORE committee Feb. 8 in protest not against Brown's "horrifying" comment but against CORE's "tepid and ambiguous response to it." (CORE expelled Brown's chapter May 27.)

The school board, under state order to devise an integration plan by Mar. 15, voted 7-2 Feb. 24 to adopt a plan presented by Dr. John Henry Martin, Mt. Vernon's superintendent of schools. Martin proposed that Mt. Vernon create a "children's academy." All children in grades 1-6 would spend 2 hours of each 5-hour school day at the academy studying nature, the arts and literature; they would spend the remainder of the day in their neighborhood schools. (High-school students would attend integrated schools full-time.) The local NAACP chapter expressed general approval of the plan Feb. 24, but at a public school board meeting Mar. 3 other civil rights spokesmen rejected it as inadequate. Some white speakers at the Mar. 3 meeting attacked the plan as "far-fetched" and "unrealistically expensive." N.Y. State Education Commissioner James E. Allen Jr. approved the academy plan Apr. 29. He said it would "provide a new level of educational excellence . . . and assure that every child would have integrated experiences." He instructed Mt. Vernon's school officials to "proceed forthwith to implement the plan."

Malverne (N.Y.) Plans Unresolved

The Malverne, N.Y. school board voted Feb. 14 to implement a school-pairing integration plan effective Feb. 23. The decision came after a final parents' suit to prevent integration had been dismissed by a federal court in Brooklyn. State Education Commissioner Allen had ordered the Malverne school district desegregated in 1963. 9 white housewives were arrested on disorderly conduct charges in Lynbrook Feb. 21 as they attempted to obstruct trucks transferring school equipment in preparation for operations under the pairing plan. The plan was implemented despite a school boycott, but the school board voted Aug. 10 to accept a state-ordered desegregation program that would supercede the pairing system Nov. 1. In a further attempt to delay enforcement of the state plan, the board voted Oct. 19 to implement a "freedom-of-choice" plan effective Nov. 1. But the state intervened Oct. 28 to suspend the Oct. 19 plan pending further study.

Court Decisions on Virginia Schools

School-desegregation litigation dating from 1956 was resolved in Norfolk, Va. Mar. 17 when U.S. District Judge Walter E. Hoffman approved an integration plan unanimously adopted by the school board earlier that day. The plan, which provided for integration of faculties as well as schools, had been devised in negotiations conducted by the board with the NAACP and the Justice Department's Civil Rights Division. (School desegregation had been initiated in Norfolk in 1959, but the NAACP had continued litigation against the city's desegregation plans.)

The U.S. 4th Circuit Court of Appeals ruled 3-2 in Richmond, Va. June 20 that the Prince Edward County, Va. Board of Supervisors was in civil contempt for its distribution of $180,000 in tuition grants to white parents in Aug. 1964. Distribution of the payments had been voted in a hastily called meeting while the appeals court was considering an NAACP request for a permanent injunction banning future tuition-grant payments. The grants enabled white parents to send their children to an all-white private school established when public schools were closed in 1959 to avoid desegregation. The court ordered that the $180,000 be restored to the county treasury.

Plaquemines (La.) School Boycott

Efforts to integrate the Plaquemines Parish (county), La. schools were thwarted by white boycotts—the resignation of white teachers and the transfer of white students from the Woodlawn school to a new private school.

U.S. District Judge Herbert W. Christenberry in New Orleans Aug. 26 had ordered grades 1, 2, 7, 9, 10 and 12 in Plaquemines Parish schools to desegregate immediately. But ex-Judge Leander H. Perez Sr., 76, militant segregationist and president of the county commission, said Aug. 27 that compliance "would be impossible."

5 Negroes registered at the formerly all-white Woodlawn school Aug. 31 while whites picketed it. No white pupils showed up. At the Belle Chasse school, only 124 of 2,000 white students attended and 30 white parents marched in front of the school. Only 1,082 of the parish's approximately 6,000 students attended the first day of school, and the boycott spread Sept. 1. After the Woodlawn school's teachers and bus drivers had joined students in the boycott, the Justice Department asked Judge Christenberry Sept. 14 to order Plaquemines Parish school officials to provide teachers for the 30 Negroes assigned to Woodlawn. Only one member of the faculty, the white principal, remained at Woodlawn with the 30 Negroes. Christenberry ordered the school board Sept. 22 to reassign the Negroes to other schools.

The first school in a proposed $2 million private school system for whites opened Sept. 16 at the former home of Perez. About 250 pupils attended classes there.

Jacksonville Negroes Boycott Schools

Negro students walked out of Duval County (Jacksonville), Fla. public schools Oct. 24-25 in protest against allegedly segregated and unequal facilities. 19,716 of the 31,851 students registered at predominantly Negro schools were absent Oct. 24, and 21,117 were absent Oct. 25. Arrest warrants were issued Oct. 26 against boycott leaders Rutledge Pearson, state president of the NAACP, and Wendell Holmes, head of the Citizens Committee for Better Education. Pearson and Holmes surrendered and were released in their own custody.

Girard College Ordered to Desegregate

U.S. District Judge Joseph S. Lord 3d in Philadelphia Nov. 2 issued a permanent injunction prohibiting Girard College, an elementary and secondary boarding school for boys in North Philadelphia, from excluding Negroes. Lord, who had issued a temporary injunction Sept. 2, acted on a motion filed Dec. 16, 1965 by lawyers for 7 Negro boys who had been denied admission to the 118-year-old school.

The trustees of Girard College had contended that Negro boys could not be admitted under the will of the college's founder, Stephen Girard, a 19th-century merchant and banker. The will stipulated that admissions be limited to "poor white male orphans." Lord, in issuing the temporary injunction Sept. 2, cited provisions of the Pennsylvania Public Accommodations Act of 1939 that prohibited barring persons from public institutions or accommodations by reasons of race. Lord said his decision did not mean that a person "may not leave his property as he sees fit." "It does mean," he said, "disposition by will or trust must comply with applicable laws extant when the disposition was made and with laws which the legislature may later enact."

The school's trustees then voted unanimously Sept. 14 to contest the ruling on the grounds that the state supreme court, not a federal court, was the proper arbiter of the meaning of a state law. The next day the local NAACP chapter announced plans to resume picketing the college. (The NAACP had demonstrated at Girard from May 1965 to Dec. 16, 1965. During that time hundreds of policemen had been assigned to the area to keep down sporadic outbreaks of violence.) Although the school's trustees filed a petition in Common Pleas Court Oct. 3 to enjoin NAACP leaders from organizing the picketing, more than 1,800 persons demonstrated outside the school Oct. 8.

When Lord issued the permanent injunction Nov. 2, he granted a stay in his ruling to allow for appeals. However, he directed the school immediately to begin processing the applications of the 7 Negro boys. A federal court of appeals Nov. 18 stayed Lord's injunction pending action on the trustees' suit.

VOTING RIGHTS & POLL TAXES

Negro Voters Increase in South

The number of Negro voters in the Deep South continued to increase as a result of voter-registration drives and the implementation of the Voting Rights Act of 1965. The Southern Regional Council announced in Atlanta Feb. 17 the launching of a Voter Education Project aimed at reaching 2 million unregistered Negroes in 11 Southern states. The drive was being financed by grants from the Field, Taconic and Ford Foundations and was to be directed by Vernon E. Jordan Jr., 30, an attorney and former Georgia state director of the NAACP. The council was to provide funds for expanded voter-registration efforts by 5 civil rights organizations (the NAACP, CORE, SNCC, SCLC and National Urban League) and was also to work with unaffiliated local organizations. (During an earlier campaign sponsored by the council in 1962-64 about 700,000 Negroes had been registered.)

Justice Department estimates released Apr. 10 indicated that the number of registered Negro voters in 5 Deep South states was 1,003,000, an increase of 47.4% since the passage of the 1965 Voting Rights Act. The breakdown by states: Alabama 228,000 (an increase of 116,000 since Aug. 1965), Georgia 248,000 (an increase of 17,000), Mississippi 122,000 (an increase of 87,000), Louisiana 231,000 (an increase of 68,000), South Carolina 174,000 (an increase of 35,000). John Doar, head of the Justice Department's Civil Rights Division, reported Nov. 11 that 47.8% of eligible Negroes were registered in the Deep South; 28.6% had been registered in Aug. 1965.

Federal observers were stationed in 27 counties in 4 Southern states Nov. 8, election day, to guard against violations of the Voting Rights Act. 20 Justice Department lawyers were also on duty there. 14 of the counties were in Mississippi, 7 in Alabama, 5 in Louisiana and one in Georgia.

Federal & Court Action on Voting Rights

Atty. Gen. Katzenbach addressed a predominantly Negro group of 4,500 in Mobile, Ala. Jan. 2 at a meeting marking the 103d anniversary of the signing of the Emancipation Proclamation. He said that Southern registrars had an obligation to accommodate potential Negro voters "through extra registration days, extra registrars and precinct registration" and that the Justice Department planned to write "every one of the 518 Southern registrars affected by the Voting Rights Act, explaining in considerable detail our view of their responsibilities concerning access." Katzenbach warned: "I have a message for those noisy few who may entertain thoughts of trying to frighten or coerce a Negro citizen—or any citizen—from trying to register or vote: If you do, you will have the federal government to reckon with."

The U.S. Supreme Court Mar. 7 upheld 7 major provisions of the 1965 Voting Rights Act. The court had agreed to assume original jurisdiction in a case brought by South Carolina against the U.S. Attorney General; friend-of-the-court briefs in support of South Carolina had been filed by Alabama, Georgia, Louisiana, Mississippi and Virginia. The government's case had been presented by Atty. Gen. Katzenbach; 20 states had filed friend-of-the-court briefs supporting him. Oral arguments had been heard Jan. 17-18. The court's opinion, written by Chief Justice Earl Warren, held that the challenged provisions of the Voting Rights Act "are an appropriate means for carrying out Congress's constitutional responsibilities" under the 15th Amendment "and are consonant with all other provisions of the Constitution." In upholding the act's provision that literacy tests be suspended in certain states, the court cited discriminatory use of literacy tests as "the principal method used to bar Negroes from the polls." It held that the provision for appointment of federal voting registrars "was clearly an appropriate response to the problem."

Among voting-rights actions in lower courts during 1966:

The 1965 municipal elections of Sunflower, Miss. were invalidated Mar. 11 by a unanimous decision of the U.S. 5th Circuit Court of Appeals in New Orleans on the ground that Negroes had been denied the right to vote for "many, many years" in Sunflower County. The ruling came on an appeal by Sunflower County Negroes from a federal district court decision denying their request that the May 1965 Democratic primary be delayed so that Negroes could qualify to vote in them.

The Justice Department filed suit in U.S. District Court in Montgomery, Ala. Mar. 22 in a move to prevent elections from being postponed in Bullock County, Ala., where the number of Negro voters registered had caught up with white registration. The suit sought to invalidate a 1965 Alabama law extending from 4 years to 6 the staggered terms of members of the Bullock County Court of Commissioners; the law had the effect of delaying scheduled 1966 elections until 1968.

A 3-judge federal court in Montgomery, Ala. Mar. 31 dismissed a suit seeking to invalidate the election of officials of Lowndes County, Ala. and to require that all offices be put up for election in November. The Negro plaintiffs had maintained that the county's minority white population had "seized and retained all political power" and had prevented Negroes from voting. The court ruled that other remedies were available.

In a suit filed June 16 in U.S. District Court in Oxford, Miss., the Justice Department charged Leflore County officials with violating the rights of Negro voters in the June 7 primary. The department charged that Negroes waiting in line when polling places closed were not allowed to vote whereas whites were permitted to vote out of turn.

A 3-judge federal district court in Baton Rouge, La. Aug. 10 ordered 5 Louisiana parishes to add to their voter rolls 13,000 persons—mostly Negroes—who had been registered by federal examiners under the 1965 act. The Supreme Court upheld the order Aug. 12. The parishes were East Feliciana, West Feliciana, East Carroll, Plaquemines and Ouachita.

All Poll Taxes Barred

The Justice Department had filed or entered suits to outlaw poll taxes in Texas, Alabama, Virginia and Mississippi, the last 4 states with such voting prerequisites. All 4 poll-tax laws were invalidated by court decisions in 1966.

Ruling unanimously, a 3-judge federal court in Austin, Tex. Feb. 9 invalidated Texas' poll tax. The court rejected a Justice Department argument that the tax discriminated against Negroes and declined to rule on whether it discriminated against the poor. The judges held, however, that the tax violated "the concept of liberty as protected by the due process clause" of the 14th Amendment.

A 3-judge federal court in Montgomery, Ala. ruled 2-1 Mar. 3 that Alabama's poll tax was unconstitutional. The decision took effect immediately. Judge Richard T. Rives called the poll tax "one of the last great pillars of racial discrimination." He said that "from its inception" it had been "illegal and invalid as an attempt to subvert the 15th Amendment." In a concurring opinion, Judge Frank M. Johnson Jr. added that a poll tax, regardless of its effect on Negroes, was a violation of the 14th Amendment. Judge Walter P. Gewin, in his dissenting opinion, cited pending suits before the U.S. Supreme Court challenging Virginia's poll tax and contended that the court should have waited for a Supreme Court ruling.

The Virginia poll-tax law—requiring payment of a poll tax as a voting prerequisite in state elections—was voided Mar. 25 by a 6-3 Supreme Court decision. The court acted on suits brought by Mrs. Evelyn Butts, a Norfolk civil rights leader, and by a group of Negroes from Fairfax County; the Justice Department had entered the case as a friend of the court. The decision overruled a 1951 Supreme Court decision upholding Virginia's poll-tax law and a 1937 decision affirming the constitutionality of Georgia's poll tax. The majority opinion, written by Justice William O. Douglas, held: "A state violates the equal protection clause of the 14th Amendment whenever it makes the affluence of the voter or payment of any fee an election standard." A dissenting opinion by Justice John M. Harlan, joined by Justice Potter Stewart, argued that elimination of the poll tax should have been left "to the affected states or to the federal political process" and that it was "all wrong . . . for the court to adopt the political doctrines popularly accepted at a particular moment of our history and to declare all others to be irrational and invidious." A separate dissent by Justice Hugo L. Black cited the court's 2 previous decisions upholding the poll tax; Black held that in those decisions the court "had properly respected its power under the equal protection clause" but that in the current decision the court was "giving that clause a new meaning."

A 3-judge federal court in Jackson, Miss. Apr. 8 outlawed Mississippi's $2 poll tax as voting requirement for state and local elections.

RACIAL UNREST & RIOTING

3d 'Long, Hot Summer' of Disorders

In many of the racial ghettos across the country, the summer of 1966 resembled the previous 2 summers in being a season of rioting and public disorders. Most of the unrest stemmed from incidents in which policemen were alleged to have acted with brutality toward a Negro or Puerto Rican. The rioting and increased militancy among Negro groups was cited by many observers as a prime contributor to the growth of "white backlash."

At his press conference July 20, Pres. Johnson commented on the spreading racial unrest in the cities. He cautioned that "while there's a Negro minority of 10% in this country, there is a majority of 90% that are not Negroes." Although most of the majority "have come around to the viewpoint of

wanting to see equality and justice given their fellow citizens,"
he said, "they want to see it done under the law and . . . without violence." Asked whether he thought "professional agitators" were behind the riots, Mr. Johnson said he "would not
want to say that the protests and the demonstrations are inspired by foreign foes," although "people who do not approve
of our system" might be a contributing factor.

Speaking July 23 at an Indianapolis Athletic Club luncheon
of 450 business executives and labor officials, the President
warned that "riots in the streets do not bring about lasting
reforms" but rather "make reform more difficult by turning
away the very people who can and must support reform."
"We refuse to condone riots and disorders," he added, "not
only to protect the society at large," but also "to serve the
real interests of those for whose cause we struggle."

In a New Orleans speech July 18, Vice Pres. Hubert
Humphrey had warned that rioting was to be expected as long
as slum conditions continued unabated. Humphrey said that if
he were a ghetto inhabitant, he might "lead a mighty good
revolt" himself. His remarks were immediately attacked by
Republicans who said that such statements encouraged disrespect for law. Humphrey said in a clarifying statement
July 20 that "there is no room in this nation for violence,
riot and disorder. Such actions only add to the troubles."
To "solve the basic problems" leading to riots, his statement concluded, "people who believe in law and order and
social justice must redouble their efforts to provide every
American with equal opportunity and a decent place in which
to live, work and play."

Atty. Gen. Nicholas deB. Katzenbach testified before a
Senate subcommittee Aug. 17 that there was "no indication"
that recent riots in Cleveland and Los Angeles were fo-
mented by "Communists or black nationalists or terrorists."
The real causes, he held, were "disease and despair, job-
lessness and hopelessness, rat-infested housing and long-
impacted cynicism." Katzenbach blamed the riots on "gen-
erations of indifference by all the American people to the
rot and rust and mold which we have allowed to eat into the
core of our cities."

Pres. Johnson, speaking at the University of Rhode Island
in Kingston, declared Aug. 20 that Negroes and other disadvantaged citizens "have the right to protest the condition
of their lives" but that "violence and discord" made social

progress difficult. He said: Protesters must remember their responsibility not to "injure the person or property of others in making that protest." "The Negro American has made great gains in the past decade behind the banner of peaceful protest. . . . The vivid contrast between lawful assemblies and lawless mobs has stirred our conscience. . . . Yet, I warn you, they can succeed only in conditions of civil peace, and civil peace can exist only when all men . . . are as dedicated to satisfying their responsibilities as they are to securing their rights."

Watts Area Battered Again

The scene of 1965's most serious racial rioting, the predominantly Negro Watts district of Los Angeles, was shaken by a new disturbance Mar. 15. The disorders occurred in a 12-square-block area located about 3 miles from the center of the 1965 riots. Casualties were 2 dead and about 20 injured; 49 persons were arrested and 19 buildings were damaged.

The turmoil started as classes were being released from the Jordan High School. A band of students began to throw stones and bricks at cars, and a white driver was hit and slightly injured. When police arrested one Negro boy, a mob of about 200 gathered and began throwing things at the police. Sporadic looting and burning of cars and buildings followed, and about 600 persons took part. A Mexican-American truck driver, Larry Gomez, 35, was pulled from his truck and shot to death. The other person slain, also by gunfire, was described by police as "a Negro named Crawford." (Sam Henry Fulton, 18, a Negro, was sentenced to life imprisonment Aug. 29 for the shooting of Gomez.) The rioting was brought under control in about 4 hours, with 200 policemen patrolling the area (the normal force was 24) and roadblocks set up at major streets.

The Watts area was tense again following the fatal shooting May 7 of Leonard Deadwyler, 25, a Negro, by Patrolman Jerold M. Bova, 23. A coroner's jury investigation of the incident, attended by up to 1,000 Negroes, found May 31 that the shooting had been accidental. Mrs. Barbara Deadwyler, 25, pregnant widow of the victim, testified May 24 that her husband had been speeding to get her to a hospital because she was suffering apparent labor pains; according to her testimony, Patrolman Bova had fired a shot without provocation after her husband had requested a police escort to the hospital. Bova, however, testified May 25 that his service revolver had discharged accidentally when the car had suddenly lurched forward while he was leaning through the right front window, his gun drawn, attempting to gain Deadwyler's attention. Police conduct in Watts was attacked May 16 by 2 Negro ministers preaching at Deadwyler's funeral, attended by several hundred Negroes. A rally held May 17 in protest against the shooting resulted in violence when members of a crowd of 500, who had marched from the rally to the police station, looted a liquor store, fired shots and attacked 2 reporters.

(The California Advisory Committee to the U.S. Civil Rights Commission issued in Los Angeles Jan. 22 a statement criticizing the report on the 1965 Watts riot issued Dec. 6, 1965 by the McCone investigating commission. The statement charged that the report "prescribes aspirin where surgery is required." The 14-member advisory committee was headed by the Right Rev. James A. Pike, Episcopal bishop of San Francisco. It accused the McCone commission of having "whitewashed" Los Angeles Police Chief William H. Parker. The committee accused Parker and Los Angeles Mayor Samuel W. Yorty of "gross negligence" in not acting to avert a riot and in not being prepared to deal with one.)

Rioting Hits Chicago Twice

Racial disorders shook Chicago twice during the summer of 1966. Both outbreaks apparently were ignited by disputes between ghetto dwellers and the police.

3 days of rioting were touched off June 12 in a Puerto Rican neighborhood of northwest Chicago by an incident in which Patrolman Thomas Munyon shot Cruz Arcelis, 21, in the leg. Munyon said Arcelis had pointed a gun at him; neighborhood witnesses disputed Munyon's story. A crowd of about 1,000 persons—later swelling to 4,000—gathered. 4 police squad cars were set afire, and firemen attempting to extinguish the blazes were attacked. About 100 helmeted policemen and a number of police dogs were brought in, and the initial outburst was quelled after 49 persons were arrested.

Violence was resumed the afternoon of June 13 after a squad car hit by a rock swerved onto the sidewalk toward the rock-throwing youth and barely missed several Puerto Ricans.

A crowd of about 500 then gathered, and community leaders, identified by red, white and blue ribbons issued by police, attempted to restore order. That evening, at a rally attended by 1,200 persons, Puerto Rican leaders called for an end to the rioting. But after the rally a large crowd broke windows and stoned cars. 36 persons were arrested, and 7 Puerto Ricans were shot, one of them critically injured with a head wound. A number of other persons, including several policemen and 3 reporters, were injured by rocks and bricks.

Community leaders conferred for 3 hours June 14 with Mayor Richard J. Daley and other city officials. Police Supt. Orlando W. Wilson then announced that the use of police dogs in the riot area would be discontinued, that the police would hold regular meetings with Puerto Rican leaders, that more Latin-American patrolmen would be hired and that other policemen would be encouraged to study Spanish. (The disorder was widely reported to have been exacerbated by the inability of the police to communicate with the area's Spanish-speaking residents.)

Minor outbreaks of violence June 14 resulted in 31 arrests. Helmeted patrolmen were stationed at close intervals around the riot area, and Police Supt. Wilson ordered 100 neighborhood taverns to remain closed until further notice.

3 nights of more serious rioting swept Chicago's West Side Negro district July 12-15. The disorders started after police July 12 shut off a fire hydrant that had been opened illegally to give Negro children relief from the 98° heat. Order was restored with the aid of National Guardsmen July 15, but 2 Negroes were killed, scores of police and civilians were wounded or injured and 372 persons were arrested. Losses from property damage and looting, primarily suffered by white-owned stores, were reported to be extensive. (The 800-square-block West Side area had an estimated population of 300,000 Negroes. It was the traditional destination in Chicago of Negroes newly arrived from the South and appeared to be a greater magnet for disturbances than the more established and somewhat more prosperous South Side Negro ghetto. 2 days of rioting had occurred in the area in Aug. 1965.)

The first arrest, which helped ignite the rioting, was of a neighborhood resident who had reopened a fire hydrant after police had shut it. Onlookers, some of whom claimed that police had permitted Italian children to play in the water from open fire hydrants in an adjoining Italian section, shouted

"Police brutality!" Before long they were stoning police cars, breaking store windows and looting. Police reinforcements were brought in, and 24 other persons were arrested. 9 persons reportedly were injured, including 2 policemen.

Rioting flared again July 13 after police shut another hydrant. A group of at least 100 Negro youths reacted by throwing rocks, bottles and bricks at a police car. During the night of July 13-14, roving Negro mobs traded gunfire with police, looted stores, tossed Molotov cocktails into buildings and stoned firemen attempting to put out the resulting fires. About 300 policemen restored order early July 14. They arrested about 35 persons. 32 policemen were reported injured. 2 Negroes were hospitalized with gunshot wounds, and about 50 others were otherwise injured.

The night of July 14-15 saw 7 hours of rioting in which more than 1,000 police tried to cope with about 5,000 rampaging Negroes. 2 Negroes—identified as Rosalynd Howard, 14, and Raymond Williams, 28—were killed in crossfire between police and rioters, and 6 policemen were shot by snipers. 282 persons were arrested, and about 50 were injured by gunfire or flying objects. A number of firemen were injured as they rushed to fires set by Molotov cocktails (6 neighborhood fire stations were evacuated later July 15 to protect firemen and their equipment). The worst fire set during the night (300 firemen and 60 pieces of equipment fought it) was in a bottling plant and adjoining packing company. Bus and "el" service was halted in the area during the rioting.

During the night of July 14-15, police raided a basement meeting and arrested 12 Negroes, including Frederick Andrews, a leader of the militant ACT group. Plans to charge them with "conspiracy to commit treason" were dropped although the arrest slips bore the treason charge. A gun and pamphlets proposing civil disobedience were seized in the raid.

Daytime looting took place for the first time the afternoon of July 15, and Illinois Gov. Otto Kerner called out the National Guard at the request of Chicago Mayor Richard J. Daley. 4,000 Guardsmen reported to Chicago armories. Armed with rifles, bayonets, pistols, machineguns and tear-gas grenades, 1,500 of them then entered the riot area in troop trucks and jeeps. Gen. Francis Kane, their commander, said he had ordered his men "to shoot to kill" if they were shot at. Before the Guardsmen entered the area, police had sealed off several streets; they said they were unable to control looting from stores whose windows had been smashed. After the Guardsmen moved in, violence was reduced to isolated outbreaks. 51 persons were arrested the night of July 15-16.

An 80-minute meeting to discuss the rioting was held July 15 by Mayor Daley and the Rev. Dr. Martin Luther King Jr., whose SCLC had been active on the West Side since January. At a joint news conference following the meeting, King and Daley announced agreement by the city to a 4-point program designed to ease tensions in the riot area. The city agreed to: (1) install spray nozzles on fire hydrants on the West Side; (2) seek federal funds to build swimming pools and other recreational facilities on the West Side (there were 4 public pools in the vicinity of the West Side, but hostile whites reportedly had kept Negroes from using all but one); (3) appoint a citizens committee to study relations between the police department and minority groups; (4) assign 2 neighborhood residents as assistants to each precinct captain to work in the area to calm disorders.

Daley charged at the press conference that SCLC staff members working in Chicago had "no other purpose than to bring disorder to the streets" and had been "instructing people in how to conduct violence." King retorted that the charge was "absolutely untrue"; he had accused the mayor July 13 of "inviting social disaster" by rejecting his demands for neighborhood improvement.

King had tried during the riot, without visible success, to stem the disturbances. He had met July 14 with 100 clergymen and nuns; then the group had walked through the West Side, pleading for nonviolence. King and his chief aides again toured the area during the climax of the rioting July 14-15.

King's calls for nonviolence won tentative acceptance July 16, after King and other SCLC officials had held a 5-hour conference through the night with 15 leaders of West Side youth gangs. The Rev. Andrew J. Young, the SCLC's executive director, announced July 16 that the young men had pledged their gangs—the Cobras, Vice Lords and Roman Saints—to "try nonviolence." Young said that youth gangs members had been responsible for most of the rioting and that their leaders were "the only ones who can control them." He outlined a number of grievances presented by the youths, including the "desperate need for jobs" (unemployment in the area was estimated at 25%), the alleged subservience of local politicians to "the Daley machine" and alleged "police intimidation and harassment."

The National Guard patrol, which had comprised about 2,000 men during the night of July 16-17, was cut to 1,500 July 17 and was progressively disbanded as calm continued.

The first of 10 portable swimming pools newly purchased by the city was installed in a West Side playground July 17; sprinklers had been installed on about 25 fire hydrants in the neighborhood the previous day. The hours during which permanent pools were open were extended, and it was announced that all pools were open to Negroes.

July 4th Disorders in Omaha

Omaha's Near North Side, a Negro area, was rocked by 3 nights of rioting, rock-throwing and looting July 3-5. 122 persons were arrested by the time order was restored July 5, and most white-owned stores in the neighborhood's business district had their windows broken. (Negro-owned stores were spared.) All those arrested were released by July 7.

The outburst began in the early hours of July 3, when youths threw a firecracker and a bottle into a police car answering a report that firecrackers were being exploded at a supermarket parking lot. A crowd of about 200 gathered. Members of the mob smashed windows and looted several stores. Police leaves were canceled July 3 as the threat of renewed disorder grew. 500 National Guardsmen were called into Omaha July 4. There was renewed window-breaking and looting by a band of Negro youths the night of July 3-4; more than 50 were arrested, and one 15-year-old boy was shot in the leg by an off-duty patrolman. A 3d night of vandalism July 4-5 brought 128 Guardsmen into the area to disperse crowds; 47 arrests were made. No incidents were reported July 6, and the Guardsmen were released from duty.

Nebraska Gov. Frank B. Morrison, who was in Los Angeles attending the National Governors Conference, said July 4 that the riot area was "an environment unfit for human habitation." Omaha Mayor A. V. Sorensen said July 5 that the riot "was an expression of discontent."

The Near North Side underwent 3 more nights of disorders July 30-Aug. 2. The new outbreak was attributed to tensions arising from the fatal shooting of a Negro burglary suspect by a policeman July 25.

Youth Gangs Precipitate N. Y. City Violence

The worst racial violence in N.Y. City during 1966 took place in the Brooklyn neighborhood known as East New York. Conflict among Negroes, whites and Puerto Ricans erupted in fighting July 15, and renewed clashes occurred July 17-18 and 21-22. The disorders ended with a city-arranged truce July 23. Unlike the disturbances in Cleveland and Chicago, the New York riots did not appear to be directed against the police. Most of the participants were members of youth gangs with long-standing rivalries. Most of the street fighting was between Negroes and whites, with the whites "defending" a boundary line between their chiefly Italian neighborhood and the Negro section. 15 blocks to the west, the conflict was between Negroes and Puerto Ricans, occupying the same neighborhood but usually segregated building by building.

The initial clashes involved 3 separate fights the night of July 15-16. 11 white youths were arrested; 2 whites and one Negro were hospitalized. Violence erupted again the evenings of July 17 and 18. A Negro youth was shot in the back and 2 Puerto Ricans were knifed July 17, and a Negro woman was shot in the hip July 18. The 2d shooting touched off what police described as 2 "overflow" incidents; the first was a fist-fight between Italians and Negroes, the 2d a fight involving Italians, Negroes and Puerto Ricans. 6 persons were injured and 6 arrested. In a series of incidents the night of July 21, one person was killed, one was critically injured by gunfire, 10 policemen and 4 civilians were injured by flying objects and 8 persons were arrested. A Negro child, Russell Givens, 3, was injured by a shot in the stomach from a sniper's rifle early in the evening.

Eric Dean, an 11-year-old Negro boy, was shot to death July 21 in an exchange of gunfire between Negro and white youths. The slaying occurred while Mayor John V. Lindsay was visiting the area for talks with community leaders. Police reinforcements quelled an immediate renewal of the rioting. The police July 27 arrested Ernest Gallashaw, 17, a Negro, on charges of shooting Dean while firing a caliber .25 pistol at a policeman.

(Gallashaw was indicted for the slaying Aug. 10 but was acquitted by a Brooklyn State Supreme Court jury Oct. 13. 3 boys who testified for the prosecution during the trial—James Windley, 14, a student at a school for emotionally disturbed children, Billy Johnson, 11, ruled incompetent to testify under oath, and Bruce Duren, 12, a former mental patient—offered confused and contradictory testimony. In a *N.Y. Times* interview Windley and Johnson repuidated their testimony against Gallashaw, but they revised their stories again in court.)

The night of July 22-23 was marked by outbreaks of violence as 1,000 extra police patrolled the area. 25 arrests were made. 5 persons, including 3 policemen, were slightly injured, and 2 Puerto Ricans were wounded by Negroes firing from a passing car. Crowds of Negroes threw Molotov cocktails and shot at police, and police broke up a group of Negroes shouting "Get the whites!"

(A Brooklyn grand jury Sept. 7 "deplored" the conduct of the N.Y. City Youth Board in using alleged gangsters to help ease community tensions following the East New York racial violence. Brooklyn District Atty. Aaron E. Koota had called for the grand jury investigation after he was informed that Youth Board Director Frank Arricale 2d had enlisted the aid of Albert and Larry Gallo to ease tensions in the riot-torn area. The Gallo brothers—reputed leaders of a rising Brooklyn Cosa Nostra faction—currently were under investigation for criminal activities by another grand jury. Arricale had offered the Gallos letters of identification as members of a committee for racial harmony in East New York. The Gallos had promised to avert further clashes between Italian-American and Negro youths. Arricale Aug. 8 praised their effectiveness in preventing further bloodshed.)

(William Epton, Progressive Labor Movement official, was sentenced by State Supreme Court Justice Arthur Markewich in New York Jan. 27 to one year's imprisonment on each of 3 counts of conspiracy and criminal anarchy during Harlem's 1964 riots. Markewich ruled that the sentences be served concurrently.)

4 Die in Cleveland's Hough Area

The Cleveland Negro neighborhood of Hough was the scene of the year's most severe racial rioting July 18-23. 4 persons were killed and 50 injured. The disorders were marked by shooting, firebombing and looting. Property damage, much of it stemming from the setting of nearly 250 fires, was widespread. 164 persons were arrested, most of them on looting charges.

The incident setting off the riot occurred in a neighborhood bar. According to one version, the bar's white management had refused to serve water to Negroes; according to another, a woman soliciting funds for a friend's funeral had been ejected from the bar. As the disturbance grew, bands of Negroes began roaming the area, looting and throwing firebombs. Firemen who tried to put out fires were driven away by gunfire. During the night's rioting one Negro woman was killed and 2 Negro men were wounded in crossfire between snipers and police (300 policemen had been sent into the area).

After touring Hough June 19, Cleveland Mayor Ralph S. Locher requested that the National Guard be sent to the city "in the interests of public safety." Ohio Gov. James A. Rhodes later July 19 issued a proclamation declaring that "a state of tumult, riot and other emergency" existed in Cleveland and activating 1,600 National Guardsmen for riot duty. An additional 400 Guardsmen were called up July 20 at Locher's request.

Rioting resumed shortly before nightfall July 19 with a sniper attack on police. In the ensuing exchange of gunfire, a Negro identified as Percy Giles, 36, was killed and 2 other persons were wounded. During 4 hours of violence, almost 40 fires were started by Molotov cocktails. A number of persons, both police and civilians, were injured, and about 50 arrests were made.

A few hundred Guardsmen moved into Hough late July 19. Beginning July 20 they patrolled the area in 2 1,000-man units on 12-hour shifts.

Members of a Negro family driving in an area east of Hough were shot at by police July 21 after the driver, Henry Towns, 22, allegedly refused to get out of the car. Towns' wife, Diana, 16, and her 3-year-old son by a previous marriage were wounded critically; the couple's 7-month-old son and Mrs. Towns' half-brother, Ernest Williams, 12, were also wounded, but not seriously. Towns was arrested and was charged July 22 with assault with a deadly weapon (the auto). The family, reportedly frightened by a fire in a nearby building, had been driving to a relative's home outside the riot area. (A grand jury later refused to indict Towns on the assault charge.)

Scattered fire-bombing continued in the riot area July 22, and a Negro was killed as he walked to a bus stop about 2 miles from Hough. The victim, Sam Winchester, 54, told police before he died that he had been shot by whites in a passing car. Another Negro, Donoris Toney, 20, was mortally wounded by whites July 23 as he drove through a parking lot between Hough and the Italian neighborhood of Murray Hill. His attackers drove their car alongside his and fired shotgun blasts through the closed window. Toney died of head wounds after 3 hours of surgery. Police patrolling the parking lot apprehended 2 white men shortly after the incident. Patrols between white and Negro areas were reinforced July 23. (Warren R. Lariche, 28, and Patsy C. Sabetta, 21, said to be members of a white "vigilante" group, were charged July 25 with 2d-degree murder in the shooting of Toney. A 3d suspect, Michael Jacobucci, 17, faced Juvenile Court proceedings.)

Calm continued in the riot area July 24 and 25. The National Guard force was reduced in strength July 26 and was completely disbanded July 31.

The Cuyahoga County Grand Jury, headed by retired *Cleveland Press* editor Louis B. Seltzer, began an investigation of the riots July 26 and returned 8 indictments of Hough residents July 29 on charges ranging from larceny to carrying concealed weapons. The grand jury report, issued Aug. 9, charged that the rioting had been "organized and exploited" by a small group of "trained and disciplined professionals," who were aided by "misguided people, many of whom are avowed believers in violence and extremism, and some of whom also are either members or officers in the Communist Party." It specifically mentioned leaders of a privately operated community center in the Negro area of Cleveland known as the JFK House, named for Jomo (Freedom) Kenyatta (former Mau-Mau leader and currently the president of Kenya). The report said: "Irrefutable evidence was shown to the effect that [director of the center Lewis G.] Robinson pledged reciprocal support to and with the Communist Party of Ohio." (Robinson Aug. 10 denied any Communist ties and dismissed the report as "nothing but a lot of garbage.") The report also singled out the W. E. B. DuBois Club, asserting that its leaders, together with Communist youth leaders, had arrived in Cleveland only a few days before the violence erupted. (Keith Allen, 25, a newscaster who had joined the club for a short time to get a feature story, had told the grand jury Aug. 1 that "as early as November of last year the Marxist-oriented group had planned racial strife in the Hough area to further the aims of socialism." Hugh Fowler, executive secretary of the clubs' national organization, rejected Allen's testimony Aug. 6. Fowler admitted that members of the club had been in the riot area but claimed that "the only thing [they] tried to do was to keep people from getting hurt." He insisted that their purpose was peaceful.)

Negro leaders in Cleveland denounced the report Aug. 10 as a "camouflage" to cover the white community's responsibility for the riots. Bertram E. Gardner, Negro director of the Municipal Community Relations Board, said: "Actually, the living conditions were the things that caused the riots. . . . They [the rioters] didn't need any Communists to tell them they're suffering. . . . I think [the grand jury report] represents generally the average white man's emotional blindness against the real causes. . . ." (A biracial committee had been formed in Cleveland Aug. 1 to study means of solving social problems in the city's Negro areas. Ralph M. Bessee, president of the Cleveland Electric Illuminating Company, was named head of the committee.)

2 undercover agents for the Cleveland police force's antisubversive squad, Jessie Thomas and Fred L. Giardini, both 26, who had infiltrated allegedly subversive organizations, said Aug. 11 that they had "no personal knowledge of direct Communist involvement in the riots." They said, however, that there was a connection between the DuBois Club and JFK House.

States Rights Party Stirs Up Baltimore Troubles

A Negro district in East Baltimore was invaded July 28 by white teen-age gangs. The attack followed a National States Rights Party rally at which Charles Conley (Connie) Lynch, a minister from San Bernardino, Calif., had attacked Baltimore Mayor Theodore R. McKeldin as a "nigger-lover" and had told the audience of about 1,000 whites: "To hell with the niggers, and those who don't like it, they can get the hell out of here." As hundreds of white youths moved from the rally into the neighborhood, most Negroes fled into their homes, but some retaliated by throwing bricks and bottles. 10 persons were arrested, most of them white.

3 officials of the States Rights Party, Lynch, 53, Richard Norton, 31, and Joseph Carroll, 19, were indicted on charges of causing the riot. They were convicted and sentenced Nov. 21 to 2 years in prison.

Puerto Ricans in Perth Amboy (N.J.) Riot

Puerto Ricans clashed with police in Perth Amboy, N.J. for 4 nights July 30-Aug. 2. The incidents apparently developed in reaction to a city anti-loitering ordinance enacted in late July. (City authorities agreed Aug. 3 to rewrite the ordinance in consultation with a committee of Puerto Ricans. Community relations officials had advised that "loitering" Puerto Ricans in fact were gathering for after-dinner chats in the Latin tradition.)

The incidents began the night of July 30-31 when 200 Puerto Rican youths gathered at the corner of Hall Ave. and Charles St. in protest against the arrest of a Puerto Rican for loitering. There was some rock- and bottle-throwing, but no injuries or arrests were reported. Crowds varying in size from 100 to 600 persons gathered at the same intersection the nights of July 31-Aug. 2 and clashed with police; a total of 37 persons were injured by stones and bottles, and 41 persons were arrested.

A hastily-formed Puerto Rican Grievance Committee, headed by Santos Torres, 24, conferred with city officials Aug. 3 and won the agreement on easing of the ordinance.

Unrest in Michigan Cities

Scattered racial violence took place in Michigan during August as police clashed with Negroes and whites in Lansing Aug. 7-8, in Detroit Aug. 9-11, in Muskegon Aug. 12, in Ypsilanti early Aug. 13 and in Benton Harbor Aug. 28-31.

11 persons were injured and 31 arrested in the disorders that swept a section of Lansing's southwest side the nights of Aug. 7 and 8. Both Negroes and whites, mainly teen-agers, were involved in the incidents. The violence broke out when Negroes began throwing rocks, apparently in reaction to insults shouted by gangs of white youths.

58 persons were arrested in the disorders in Detroit Aug. 9-11. The violence apparently was touched off when police attempted to arrest 3 Negroes for loitering; one policeman, a Negro, was knifed during the arrest attempt. The rioting continued for 2 days.

Police clashed with about 1,500 persons, mostly Negroes, the night of Aug. 12 in a downtown section of Muskegon. The incident began when a crowd gathered outside a hotel, apparently after a rumored assault on 2 white men by Negroes.

Rock-throwing broke out early Aug. 13 in Ypsilanti, where Negro youths broke car windows and stoned cars. Police arrested 11 persons, all Negroes, aged 12-19, who admitted participating in the vandalism.

Racial violence rocked Benton Harbor Aug. 28-31. For 4 consecutive nights Negro youths in crowds varying in size from 50 to 400 persons threw stones and bottles at store windows, cars and policemen. Several persons were injured. The violence culminated Aug. 31 in the death of Cecil Hunt, 18, a Negro, who had been shot the previous night by 2 white men in a passing car.

Guardsmen Quell Dayton (O.) Disturbances

Rioting and looting by Negroes in Dayton, O. Sept. 1-2 was touched off by the fatal shooting of Lester Mitchell, 40, a Negro. Nearly 1,000 National Guardsmen were mobilized to restore order. About 30 persons were injured in the outbreak. More than 100 people were arrested.

Mitchell was hit in the head by a shotgun blast early Sept. 1 as he was sweeping his sidewalk. The shot reportedly came from a passing car containing 3 white men. (Police later arrested 2 white men and held them for questioning until Sept. 5.) As news of the shooting circulated through the Westside Negro neighborhood Sept. 1, roving bands of Negroes began throwing rocks at pedestrians and vehicles, breaking windows and looting stores. The violence spread during the day to the downtown area; windows were broken and merchandise looted at about 50 stores.

Ohio Gov. James A. Rhodes mobilized the National Guard on Mayor Dave Hall's request. The Guardsmen and city police eventually cordoned off the entire Westside neighborhood. The violence was not renewed, and the Guardsmen were withdrawn by Sept. 6.

SNCC Role Charged in Atlanta Riots

2 nights of Negro rioting swept Atlanta Sept. 6-7 and 10-11. In each case the riot occurred after a Negro had been shot. Sporadic violence continued Sept. 11 and 12. More than 35 persons were injured in the incidents, and about 138 persons were arrested.

The rioting broke out Sept. 6 in the Negro neighborhood of Summerhill after an Atlanta detective had shot and wounded Louis Prather, 25, a Negro, when Prather allegedly resisted arrest for suspected car theft. Shortly after the shooting, SNCC Chrmn. Stokely Carmichael entered the area. He was quoted as telling a crowd of Negroes: "We're going to be back at 4 o'clock and tear this place up." Carmichael was seen later with 2 other SNCC members—William Ware and Bob Vance Walton, 20. The latter 2 then toured the area with a sound truck. According to a Negro police sergeant, D. J. Perry, they "were bringing different people into the area and they were saying . . . [Prather] was murdered by white police." Ware and Walton were arrested and charged with inciting to riot and creating a disturbance.

Shortly afterwards, about 1,000 Negroes, chanting "black power" and "police brutality," began throwing rocks, sticks and bottles at policemen, newsmen and white bystanders. At one point Mayor Ivan Allen Jr., 55, was toppled from the top of a car as he attempted to calm the crowd; he was not injured. About 750 city policemen used tear gas and fired shotguns and pistols in the air to disperse the crowd. 16 persons were injured and 73 were arrested. Sporadic violence was reported Sept. 7. Police arrested 10 Negroes in a disturbance allegedly begun by 2 SNCC members.

Some Negroes in Atlanta assailed the SNCC for allegedly causing violence. Negroes in the Vine City section Sept. 7 burned an outdoor stand containing SNCC literature; others allegedly threatened to "run Snick out" before it brought trouble to the neighborhood. But SNCC officials denied that the committee had been responsible for the rioting. Carmichael said Sept. 7 that SNCC "cannot start a rebellion just like that. . . . It is started by conditions of oppression."

Carmichael was arrested Sept. 8 and charged with inciting to riot and disorderly conduct. He was bound over to the Fulton County grand jury Sept. 9 and transferred to the county jail. (Indicted with 14 others Sept. 13, he was released on $1,000 bond 2 days later.)

The 2d night of rioting began Sept. 10 after a white man fatally shot Hubert (Dukie) Vorner, 16, a Negro, and wounded another Negro, Roy Milton Wright, 16. (Police Sept. 13 arrested William Haywood James, 42, and charged him with the murder.) The incident touched off rioting in the predominantly Negro Boulevard neighborhood near the center of

Atlanta. As policemen arrived to investigate the sho
crowd of about 400 Negroes gathered and began th
bottles and bricks in a wild outbreak that lasted only minutes.
Violence, including the use of firebombs, continued the nights
of Sept. 11 and 12.

Moderate Negro rights leaders held a public meeting Sept.
12 to form a community council to help restore order in the
Boulevard neighborhood. At one point, however, militants
disrupted the meeting. SNCC member Willie Ricks grabbed the
microphone and shouted, "We're going to put every cracker in
Atlanta on his knees. . . . Mayor Allen is the killer." The
audience answered with shouts of "black power."

(A 3-judge federal court in Atlanta Dec. 13 invalidated an
Atlanta disorderly conduct ordinance under which 70-90
Negroes, including Carmichael, were convicted following the
rioting. The court held the city ordinance too broad and in-
clusive, but it delayed the effective date of its decision in
order to allow the city to enact a new ordinance and to press
new charges.)

Shooting Sparks San Francisco Outbreak

Racial violence swept Negro sections of San Francisco Sept.
27-28 after a white policeman shot and killed a Negro youth.
The rioting started in 95° heat during the hottest day of the
year. 3,600 National Guardsmen were called in, and a curfew
was imposed. Minor violence did not end until Sept. 30. 349
persons were arrested, and at least 80 persons were reported
injured.

The disturbances erupted in the Hunter's Point section
Sept. 27 after a white policeman, Alvin Johnson, 51, fatally
shot Matthew Johnson, 16, a Negro. The policeman said he had
fired warning shots as the youth fled from a car that later
was reported stolen. San Francisco Mayor John F. Shelley immediately ordered Johnson suspended from duty pending
investigation.

During the rioting, hundreds of Negro youths roved the
streets, smashing windows, looting stores, hurling bricks and
firebombs at police and overturning autos. They lured fire
trucks into the area by setting false alarms and then attacked the trucks and firemen. By midnight disorder had
spread to the Fillmore district 2 miles away. (The Fillmore
area had been the scene of rioting July 16-17 after a Negro

suspected of robbery was wounded by a policeman.) Mayor
Shelley imposed an 8 p.m.-to-6 a.m. curfew and sent aug-
mented police forces into the areas with orders "not to
shoot," except in self-defense.

More extensive rioting broke out late in the afternoon
of Sept. 28. 2,000 National Guardsmen, ordered out by Gov.
Edmund G. Brown, entered the area to clear the streets
and quell the rioting. They were commanded by Maj. Gen.
Paul Teihl, a veteran of the 1965 Watts riots in Los Angeles.
Police and Guardsmen exchanged gunfire with rioters, and
100 Guardsmen rode fire trucks to defend them from mob
attacks. In the Fillmore district there was a major fire,
and sniping at policemen and whites was reported. Negro
groups opposing the riots equipped themselves with bull-
horns to spread "the word" that "rioting isn't the way." The
rioting ended later that day.

Shelley Sept. 28 sent a telegram to Pres. Johnson to appeal
for emergency funds to remedy the "critical unemployment
situation." He asked Cyril Magnin, president of the Greater
San Francisco Chamber of Commerce, to meet with business
leaders and ask them "to search their employment records
and practices and see what could be done to help Negro
youths." He called on labor unions to end restrictions on
Negro membership and appealed to all citizens to end racial
discrimination.

Oakland (Calif.) Riot Spreads to Schools

Sporadic outbreaks of racial violence in Oakland, Calif.
Oct. 18-20 coincided with a 3-day boycott of the city's schools.
More than 50 persons were arrested, and 13 were reported
injured. The rioting started Oct. 18 after a Negro woman's
car was involved in a traffic accident. Gangs of teen-age
Negroes formed in East Oakland and rioted in the downtown
business area. 5 whites were beaten, and 47 business establishments were reported damaged.

The Ad Hoc Committee for Quality Education, a group
formed by Oakland Negroes, launched a 3-day boycott of
predominantly Negro public schools Oct. 19 in protest against
alleged *de facto* segregation. About 250 Negroes, many of
them nonstudents, rioted for 2 hours Oct. 19 at Oakland's
Castlemont High School. The disturbance forced the predominantly Negro 2,700-student school to close early. The

youths smashed windows and school equipment, threw gasoline bombs, rang false alarms and looted a nearby food market.

Oakland Mayor John H. Reading and City Manager Jerome Keithly Oct. 20 issued statements absolving the Ad Hoc Committee of charges of instigating the disorders. School officials had blamed the committee for the riots.

Disorders in North Philadelphia

White persons demonstrated Oct. 2-5 in front of the home of the first Negro family to move into the Kensington section of North Philadelphia. During the disorders, 42 persons were arrested and 7 persons were reportedly injured. The demonstrations began when Mr. and Mrs. Leon Wright and their 3 children moved into a rented house Oct. 2. A small crowd gathered. Some members of the crowd jeered and hurled eggs at the house. The following night about 500 persons gathered, and some threw bottles and firecrackers at the home. Police estimated that more than 1,000 persons demonstrated Oct. 4 in defiance of a preliminary injunction issued on a motion filed by the NAACP. 15 adults and 5 juveniles were arrested Oct. 4 and 22 Oct. 5. Order was restored late in the evening Oct. 6 after 400 policemen were called in.

KILLINGS & TERRORISM

Tuskegee (Ala.) Rights Worker Slain

Samuel L. Younge Jr., 21, a Negro active in the civil rights movement and a student at Tuskegee Institute, was shot and killed Jan. 3 in Tuskegee, Ala. Marvin Segrest, 67, a white service station attendent, was arrested Jan. 4 and charged with the slaying. Macon County Sheriff Harvey Sadler said Jan. 6 that Segrest had admitted the shooting.

The slaying resulted in a series of demonstrations by the institute's students and faculty members. Marches were held in downtown Tuskegee Jan. 4-8, and students presented the city council with a series of demands, among them the hiring of more Negroes for city jobs, the establishment of a civilian review board to investigate charges against the police, the discharging of Public Safety Commissioner Alton B. Taylor, the adoption of an ordinance desegregating public accommodations and the increased use of federal voting examiners and of federal troops to safeguard Negroes. The city council Jan. 25 adopted an ordinance that met one of the demands—the barring of discrimination in places of public accommodation.

Segrest was acquitted Dec. 8 by an all-white jury in Lee County, Ala. of charges of 2d-degree murder. Segrest had testified that he shot Younge in self-defense. 700 students rioted in Tuskegee on learning of the verdict.

Firebomb Kills Hattiesburg (Miss.) NAACP Official

Vernon Dahmer, 58, a Negro and civil rights leader, died in Hattiesburg, Miss. late Jan. 10 of burns received when Molotov cocktails were thrown into his house and adjoining store early that morning. Dahmer's wife, Ellie, 41, and his daughter, Betty, 10, were hospitalized for burns. The house, store and family car were destroyed in the explosion and fire that followed. The attack took place one day after Dahmer, a past president of the local NAACP chapter, had announced over Hattiesburg radio that he would collect poll taxes from local Negro voters and deliver the money to the sheriff's office.

Atty. Gen. Nicholas deB. Katzenbach said in Washington Jan. 10 that Dahmer had been "engaged in the highest kind of citizenship—helping to secure basic rights for his fellow citizens." Katzenbach announced in Washington Mar. 28 that FBI agents earlier that day had arrested 13 members of the White Knights of the Ku Klux Klan in connection with the slaying. A search was under way for a 14th man, Sam Holloway Bowers Jr., 41, the White Knights' imperial wizard. The 13 arrested were released Mar. 28 and Mar. 29 on $10,000 to $15,000 bond. Bowers surrendered to the FBI in Hattiesburg Mar. 31 in the company of his 2 attorneys. He was released on $25,000 bond.

2 Klan Members Guilty in Penn Slaying

2 Ku Klux Klan members were sentenced by U.S. District Judge William A. Bootle in Athens, Ga. July 9 to 10 years' imprisonment for conspiracy to violate the right to interstate travel of Lemuel A. Penn, a Washington, D.C. educator murdered on a Georgia highway July 11, 1964. The 2, Joseph

Howard Sims, 43, and Cecil William Myers, 28, were among 6 Klansmen tried for the charge in 2 separate trials. The trial of Sims, Myers and George Hampton Turner, 32, had taken place June 27–July 2; the jury's July 2 verdict had been sealed until the completion of the trial of the 3 other defendants, James S. Lackey, 30, Herbert Guest, 40, and Denver Willis Phillips, 24. The 2d trial began July 5. The verdicts in both trials were announced July 8. All defendants other than Sims and Myers were acquitted.

Sims and Myers had been acquitted in a state court in Sept. 1964 of charges of murdering Penn; Lackey had also been charged with murder but had never been brought to trial. Federal charges against all 6 men under an 1870 conspiracy statute had been dismissed by Judge Bootle in Dec. 1964 on the ground that murder was not covered by the Reconstruction-Era law. The U.S. Supreme Court had reversed the dismissal of charges Mar. 28, 1966; it ruled that federal prosecutions could be brought against violations of the constitutional right to interstate travel.

The prosecution in both trials, conducted by U.S. Atty. Floyd M. Buford, had sought to establish a pattern of conspiracy by the defendants to "injure, intimidate or oppress" Negroes seeking to exercise their rights. The slaying of Penn was presented as only one instance of conspiracy; the prosecution's case included testimony June 29 by 2 Negro brothers of a beating they had received in Oct. 1965 from Sims, Myers and 5 other Klansmen. The prosecution also introduced in evidence a cache of weapons seized from the defendants' car following the beating. Sims and Myers had been linked to Penn's murder by the testimony June 30 of Thomas Stevens (then a member of the Klan's Athens Klavern), who reported that in a conversation following the slaying, Sims and Myers had told him that "the timing was off on the shooting." Thomas also told of a conversation with Guest, the morning of the murder, in which Guest had said that Sims, Myers and Lackey had left his auto repair garage "chasing a nigger car with D.C. tags on it."

The major prosecution evidence presented at the 2d trial consisted of confessions by Lackey and Guest. Lackey's statement said that on the day of the murder he had been driving a car also occupied by Sims and Myers, that Sims had told him to follow Penn's car, saying "I'm going to kill me a nigger," and that Sims and Myers had both fired shotgun blasts as he pulled alongside Penn's car. Guest's confession said that Sims, Myers and Lackey had driven away from his garage at about the time of Penn's murder and had returned late that afternoon.

(Sims was sentenced Aug. 13 to an additional 10 years in prison on his plea of guilty to a charge of assault with intent to kill in the shooting of his wife, Betty, in May.)

Ku Klux Klan Inquiry

The investigation of the Ku Klux Klan by a 5-member House Un-American Activities subcommittee was resumed Jan. 4, and subcommittee hearings continued through Feb. 24. The hearings had begun Oct. 19, 1965. In a closing statement Feb. 24, Rep. Joe Pool (D., Tex.), the committee's acting chairman, said the 35 days of hearings had revealed the Klan's record to be "a record of the activities of sneaky, cowardly men" and "a record of floggings, beatings, killings for no other reason than the color of their [victims'] skin or the fact they disapprove of the policies and activities of the Klan."

The committee reported Oct. 21 that "on the basis of the latest available information, it is estimated that the total Klan membership is now about 15,000 persons." Discussing its hearings on the Klan, the committee said: "More than a dozen different Klan groups are presently active in at least 15 states," and "the largest of the Klan organizations now has units operating in at least 15 states." "Secrecy is the cornerstone of the structure of Klanism. Members must take an oath, 'forever' to keep 'sacredly secret' within the Klan, and not to divulge to 'any person in the whole world,' all Klan 'matters and knowledge' and to 'die rather than divulge same.' Information about treason, rape, and malicious murder only is excepted from the oath. This oath is considered by Klansmen to be superior to any other oath, in court or elsewhere. . . . In order to conceal the existence of units within the Klans as well as bank accounts and other matters, innocent-sounding cover names are used to create the impression that they are civic, improvement, sporting, or even rescue organizations. The largest existing Klan organization operates under the cover name 'Alabama Rescue Service.' . . . Klans engage in threats, cross-burnings, the firing of churches and schools, bombings, beatings, maimings, mur-

ders, and other acts of violence to further their goal of
white supremacy as well as other objectives. These acts,
however, are not always racially motivated and sometimes are
directed against citizens who are not racially oriented but who
are conducting themselves to the dislike of the Klans, which
take the law into their hands as vigilantes. . . . Klansmen frequently carry pistols, rifles, shotguns, and bombs. . . .
Radios and telephones are frequently used by Klans in their
terroristic activities. Some Klan members have been issued federal licenses as gun dealers and have sold guns
to members in wholesale lots. Secret Klan schools instruct
in the fabrication of bobby traps, bombs, and Molotov cocktails and teach the use of bombs, firearms, judo, and karate.
Evidence was received of the misuse and embezzlement by
Klan officials of dues money, insurance premiums, and other
Klan funds. . . ."

Robert M. Shelton Jr., 37, imperial wizard of the United
Klans of America, Inc., was convicted of contempt of Congress by a federal jury in Washington, D.C. Sept. 14. Shelton
had refused to produce Klan records on membership and fi-
nances subpoenaed by the committee during hearings in Oct.
1965. He was sentenced by U.S. District Judge John J. Sirica
Oct. 14 to a year in prison and was fined $1,000, and he was
then freed on $500 bond pending appeal.

Among developments at the subcommittee hearings:

Jan. 4—Committee Chrmn. Edwin E. Willis (D., La.) and
subcommittee member Charles L. Weltner (D., Ga.) said Klan
activity had slackened as a result of the hearings.

John D. Swenson, 55, of Boss City, La., identified by the
subcommittee as the "modern-day father of the Klan" in
Louisiana, invoked the 4th and 5th Amendments in refusing to
answer most of the subcommittee's questions. He said he was
unable to produce records of the "Original Knights of the
Ku Klux Klan" because he had burned them in 1964 to keep
them from falling "into the hands of the enemy—the Communists." Weltner introduced testimony to indicate that the
record burning could have been motivated by charges that
Swenson had enriched himself from the sale of Klan robes.

Murray H. Martin, 41, of Winnsboro, La., identified as the
current imperial dragon of the Original Knights, also invoked
constitutional protection in refusing to answer questions.

During the questioning of Martin, chief committee investigator Donald T. Appell said that Martin and other Klan leaders had met in Montgomery, Ala. May 25, 1965 and had agreed "not to participate in castration, but if it was necessary to liquidate someone to prove the Klan was not kidding, this would be done." Appell said that one of the participants at the meeting was James R. Venable, 61, of Atlanta, who served as counsel to Swenson and Martin at the hearing and who himself was an imperial dragon. Venable headed the National Knights of the Ku Klux Klan, based in Atlanta, and the National Association of Ku Klux Klans.

Jan. 12–Appell said Klansmen attending a meeting near Raleigh, Miss. Jan. 7, 1964 had been told: "You have a right to kill" civil rights workers.

Jan. 13–Louis A. DiSalvo, 38, of Waveland, Miss. invoked the 5th Amendment in refusing to answer questions as Appell confronted him with sworn testimony that DiSalvo had tried in Sept. 1964 to recruit other Klansmen for a plan, later dropped, to dynamite a campaign train carrying the President's wife, Mrs. Lyndon B. Johnson, through southern Mississippi. Appell identified DiSalvo as exalted cyclops of the Hancock County Klavern. He said DiSalvo had handed out firearms and ammunition to klavern members, had taught them to murder with snakes and had tried to form a firing squad.

The subcommittee made public a document, dated May 3, 1964, said to have been read to members of the White Knights in reference to the expected influx of civil rights workers into Mississippi. The document said: "When the black wave hits our communities we must attack the individual leaders at night. . . ."

Jan. 14–Subcommittee investigators questioned Charles M. Edwards, 33, of Meadville, Miss. and James Ford Seale, 30, both of whom invoked their constitutional rights in declining to answer questions about their Nov. 1964 arrest on murder charges that were later dropped by local authorities. Appell produced a statement allegedly made by Edwards Nov. 6, 1964 to a Mississippi Highway Patrol the day of his arrest. In the statement Edwards allegedly confessed his own participation and implicated Seale in the abduction and whipping of 2 Negroes, last seen alive May 2, 1964; the bodies of the 2 Negroes–Charles Moore and Henry Dee, both 20–were found in a river July 14, 1964. Appell said all members of the group that committed the crime were members of the White Knights.

Jan. 18—Billy Wilson, 23, testified that he had joined Klavern 700 of the United Klans of America, Inc. in McComb, Miss. July 7, 1964 and had participated in 3 Klan-planned bombings in McComb of the homes of civil rights workers. Wilson said that his first klavern was headed by Ray Smith. He testified that its membership swelled so greatly that he and other members were told to transfer to a new klavern known as the South Pike Marksmanship Association, headed by Paul Wilson.

Jan. 28—George L. Williams, 45, of Greenville, N.C. testified that while he had been a member of the United Klans (he had joined July 28, 1965 and had resigned in Nov. 1965): Members were told to buy guns where permits were not required; he had been ordered by Charles Edwards, a Grimesland, N.C. policeman and Klan official, to go to Plymouth, N.C. during Aug. 1965 to help "stop" Negro demonstrations; the Klan had paid medical expenses for a superficial wound he had incurred in Plymouth while lunging at a Negro who had pulled a gun on some heckling whites. Williams said he resigned after the KKK's North Carolina grand dragon James R. Jones had said publicly that Klansmen had not been in Plymouth during the racial trouble. Williams said he had seen about 1,000 Klansmen in Plymouth.

Feb. 1—Sam H. Bowers Jr. of Laurel, Miss., imperial wizard of the White Knights of the Ku Klux Klan, invoked the 5th Amendment in refusing to tell Appell whether he (Bowers) had ordered the "extermination" of "the Goatee" and whether "the Goatee" was Michael Schwerner, one of 3 civil rights workers murdered in Mississippi in 1964.

Feb. 3—Henry Allen Lee, 37, of McComb, Miss. and Ernest Parker, 35, of Morgantown, Miss. refused to answer questions about: (a) a letter Appell said Lee had written (in the letter Lee allegedly had boasted of making bombs used in McComb by the Klan); (b) the possible use of Parker's barge to get rid of the bodies of 2 Negroes (Charles Moore and Henry Dee) found in 1964 near property owned by Parker.

Feb. 4—Appell asked Robert S. Thomas, 37, identified by Appell as "one of the most influential members of the United Klans of America in Alabama," whether he had ordered the accused slayers of Mrs. Viola Gregg Liuzzo to go to Selma Mar. 25, 1965 on a "night-rider mission." Thomas, identified as great titan of one of the United Klans' Alabama "provinces," invoked the 5th Amendment.

Feb. 10–Testimony that Ohio Klansmen had plotted to blow up buildings and sewer lines in Columbus to incite a race riot was given by Sgt. Donald W. Schwartz of the Columbus Police Department and by Bobby J. Stephens, 28, identified by Schwartz as an undercover police agent in the Ohio Klan. Schwartz said the police had found in caches near Columbus dynamite that had been transported from Stone Mountain, Ga., headquarters of the National Knights of the Ku Klux Klan. Stephens said James Venable had started organizing klaverns in Ohio in 1964.

Other Slayings & Violence

Donald Sims, 29, a Negro Army captain, was shot and injured in Bogalusa, La. early Mar. 11 as he was using a public phone in a service station. 4 caliber-.22 bullets were fired through the service station's front window; one hit Sims in the shoulder and neck. Sims drove to a hospital and was reported in good condition. Bogalusa Public Safety Commissioner Arnold Spiers announced Mar. 12 that Thomas Bennett, 43, a white native of Bogalusa, had been arrested and charged with attempted murder in the shooting.

A white Fayette, Miss. resident, K. D. Dennis, 50, was arrested May 26 following the shotgun wounding of Charles Knight, 16, a Negro, in front of Dennis' house. Dennis was charged with shooting with intent to kill and freed on $5,000 bail. Charles Evers, state NAACP field secretary, addressed 350 Negroes May 27 at a protest rally in a Negro church and then led his audience in a march to the county courthouse.

The body of Ben Chester White, 65, a Negro, was found June 12 in a creek near Natchez, Miss. He had been shot 16 times with a rifle, and his head had been partly blown away by a shotgun blast. Sheriff Odell Anders, in announcing June 14 the arrest of 3 white men in connection with the slaying, said White had been killed June 10. Those arrested, all identified as members of the Ku Klux Klan, were James Lloyd Jones, 56, Claude Fuller, 46, and Ernest Avants, 35. All were employes of the International Paper Co. at Natchez. Jones turned state's witness and testified at a preliminary hearing June 17 that he had watched Fuller and Avants shoot White and dump his body in the creek.

The Rev. Melvin DeWitt Bullock, 38, a Negro, was found beaten to death Sept. 17 in his house in New Rochelle, N.Y.

Bullock, ex-president of the New Rochelle NAACP chapter, had been active in recent drives to end *de facto* segregation in New Rochelle public schools.

A Negro minister's newly-purchased but as yet unoccupied home in the all-white Westlake suburb of Cleveland, O. was swept by fire Sept. 24. The Rev. John R. Compton, recently appointed executive director of the Cleveland Metropolitan Commission of the Ohio Society of Christian Churches, had bought the $23,250 home with the assistance of Fair Housing, Inc. Westlake Mayor Roman R. Alexander said Sept. 26 that Compton and his wife should have warned local officials they were moving into the neighborhood.

An assault and battery indictment against Thomas L. Coleman, 56, was dismissed by Circuit Judge Werth Thagard in Hayneville, Ala. Sept. 26. Coleman had been accused of shooting the Rev. Richard Morrisroe of Chicago, a civil rights worker, Aug. 20, 1965. State Atty. Gen. Richmond M. Flowers had fought unsuccessfully Sept. 13 in an attempt to have Coleman indicted on a charge of assault with intent to murder. Flowers then had sought to have the indictment dismissed for want of prosecution—in order to allow a later grand jury to return a different indictment. But the judge dismissed the charge "with prejudice" and thereby precluded any further indictment of Coleman.

Eugene Thomas, 43, a member of the Ku Klux Klan, was acquitted Sept. 27 of the murder of Mrs. Viola Gregg Liuzzo. He was found not guilty by a jury of 8 Negroes and 4 whites in Hayneville, Ala. Mrs. Liuzzo had been killed Mar. 25, 1965 after a rights march from Selma to Montgomery. In the 4 trials arising from the killing, this was the first jury to include Negroes. Atty. Gen. Richmond M. Flowers, state prosecuter, called the verdict "a complete breakdown of justice and law and order."

Malcolm X's Slayers Convicted

Talmadge Hayer (alias Thomas Hagan), 24, Norman 3X Butler, 27, and Thomas 15X Johnson, 30, were convicted by a state Supreme Court jury in New York Mar. 10 of first-degree murder in the assassination Feb. 21, 1965 of black nationalist leader Malcolm X. They were sentenced Apr. 14 to life imprisonment.

During the 8-week trial Butler and Johnson had acknowledged

being members of the Fruit of Islam, the paramilitary arm of
the dominant Black Muslim organization, with which Malcolm X
had been in competition. Hayer had denied being a Black
Muslim; but after testifying to his innocence Feb. 23, he had
repudiated this testimony Feb. 28 and admitted shooting a
pistol at Malcolm "about 4 times." Hayer said that he and
3 accomplices had been hired to carry out the shooting; he
refused to identify his accomplices or the person who had
ordered the murder. He insisted that the Black Muslims were
not involved in the assassination and that the other 2 defendants "had nothing to do with this."

Butler had testified Mar. 1 that he had been home in bed
with an infected leg the afternoon of the murder; his doctor
had testified that he had treated Butler that morning and ordered him to keep his leg elevated. Johnson had testified
Mar. 3 that he had spent the day of the shooting at home with
his family.

The prosecution had presented 26 witnesses, including 2
who refused to testify until the courtroom was cleared. 3
testified to having seen Hayer shoot Malcolm. 6 prosecution
witnesses identified Butler as having been in the ballroom,
and 4 similarly identified Johnson.

Asst. District Atty. Vincent J. Dermody, in summing up
Mar. 8, contended that Malcolm X had been assassinated
publicly as "an object lesson" to members of his Organization of Afro-American Unity (OAAU). But Dermody denied
that the prosecution had "said we'd prove that Elijah Muhammad [leader of the Black Muslims] ordered this death."

OTHER DEVELOPMENTS

Rifts Disrupt White House Conference

An Administration-sponsored White House Conference on
Civil Rights took place in Washington June 1-2 but immediately
ran into difficulty when important civil rights leaders rebelled
against plans of the Steering Council to issue a report in the
name of the entire conference without a formal vote. The
conference—which included 2,400 participants from the civil
rights movement, business, labor, government and the churches
—had as its formal aim the recommendation of measures to
assure the fulfillment of Negro rights and aspirations. The

conference initially had been proposed by the President in an address at Howard University June 4, 1965. Plans for the conference had been set at a preparatory meeting held in Washington Nov. 17-18, 1965.

A draft program for the conference had been worked out by a 29-member Steering Council headed by Chrmn. Ben W. Heineman of the Chicago & North Western Railway, who served as chairman of the full conference. Conference planners had provided for discussion of the draft in panel sessions but had not intended that delegates vote on the draft's contents, either in the panels or in the conference as a whole. Dissension over the lack of voting arrangements broke out May 31, when Floyd B. McKissick of CORE announced that he would introduce a motion to compel voting on resolutions. The Steering Council June 1 amended conference rules to permit votes to be taken in panel sessions but not in the conference as a whole.

McKissick June 2 introduced the Vietnam controversy into the conference with a resolution calling on the U.S. to "make equal opportunities for its minority citizens the No. 1 priority . . . and cease its involvement in Vietnam." The resolution was ruled out of order.

Other attacks on the conference's aims and organization had come from the SNCC and from a group of N.Y. City civil rights leaders. The SNCC announced May 23 that it would boycott the conference. The executive committee of the New York Pre-White House Conference Committee May 30 issued a statement calling the conference a "hoax."

Pres. Johnson appeared unexpectedly at the conference's evening session June 1. The President, who introduced Solicitor Gen. Thurgood Marshall, told the delegates: "We are moving. I came here today at the end of a long day to tell you that we shall not turn back."

Employment & Union Bias Fought

Edward C. Sylvester Jr., director of the Labor Department's Office of Federal Contract Compliance, asked the Justice Department Jan. 21 to take legal action against AFL-CIO building trades unions working in St. Louis, Mo. on a federally assisted project. Union members assigned to a visitors' center at St. Louis' Gateway Arch under a National Park Service contract had refused to work since Jan.

10, when 3 Negro plumbers had reported for work there. The AFL-CIO Building & Construction Trades Council of St. Louis had defended the refusal as based on the Negroes' membership in the Congress of Independent Unions, which was not an AFL-CIO affiliate. A Sept. 24, 1965 Presidential executive order against job discrimination in federally-assisted construction projects had authorized the Labor Department to initiate legal action through the Justice Department to obtain compliance. The Labor Department's Jan. 21 request was its first such action under the executive order. Atty. Gen. Katzenbach announced Feb. 4 that the Justice Department had filed suit that day in U.S. District Court in St. Louis. The suit, filed under the executive order and under Title VII of the 1964 Civil Rights Act, charged the Trades Council and 5 member locals with discrimination.

Chrmn. John W. Macy Jr. of the Civil Service Commission Feb. 24 issued new regulations governing job-discrimination grievances on the part of federal employes. Under a Sept. 1965 executive order abolishing the President's Committee on Equal Employment Opportunity and transferring its functions to the CSC, the commission was empowered to order federal agencies to correct instances of discrimination. Records (separate from other personnel records) were to be kept of the race or national origin of all federal employes.

Labor Secy. W. Willard Wirtz May 18 ordered that racial indentifications be made on employment records kept by programs operating under Labor Department jurisdiction. The directive, reversing a policy in effect since 1962, primarily affected the 2,000 offices of federal-state employment services, whose records encompassed an estimated 10 million job seekers. Wirtz explained that "at this point in the long, but now winning, battle for equal employment," racial identifications would provide a "statistical tool" for identifying "where the problems are, how we are doing and what we are doing." He said he was "sick and tired of the false piety of those who answer inquiries about racial aspects of their employment or membership practices with the bland, smug answer that 'we don't know because of course we don't keep records about that kind of thing.'"

The International Chemical Workers Union (ICWU) and 5 union members sued the Planters Manufacturing Co. of Clarksdale, Miss. in U.S. District Court in Clarksdale Mar. 9 on charges of discriminating against Negro employes in wages, vacations and seniority. The suit was the first filed by a union against an employer under the 1964 Civil Rights Act. Union spokesmen said Mar. 10 that the ICWU had won a bargaining election at the Planters factory in May 1965 but that the company had refused to grant its contract demands for a nondiscrimination clause and for equal pay and vacations for white and Negro workers. (The Equal Employment Opportunity Commission Aug. 30 upheld the union's complaint against Planters.)

The NAACP Legal Defense & Educational Fund, Inc. charged in a suit filed in U.S. District Court in Birmingham May 31 that the U.S. Steel Corp. was guilty of job discrimination at its nearby Fairfield, Ala. works. The company was charged with promoting white employes while bypassing equally qualified Negroes. The plaintiffs, 2 employes at the Fairfield works, had filed a complaint with the EEOC in 1965 but had been informed that while the EEOC had "reasonable cause" to believe that U.S. Steel's employment practices were discriminatory, its conciliation efforts had failed.

The EEOC and the Newport News (Va.) Shipbuilding & Drydock Co. Apr. 4 signed an agreement giving priority for supervisory positions to Negro employes with qualifications and seniority comparable to those of white employes who had received past promotions. Other Negro employes were to be given preference for training programs. The agreement, whose execution was to be supervised by an outside expert, followed the EEOC's receipt of 41 complaints charging Newport News with job discrimination. The EEOC had found the firm in violation of Title VI of the 1964 Civil Rights Act.

NAACP Labor Secy. Herbert Hill announced in Washington June 29 that he had filed charges of discrimination with the EEOC against the Bro'hood of Railway Clerks for maintaining segregated locals in Georgia and against the United Papermakers Union for similar practices in Virginia. His June 29 statement also accused the AFL-CIO of rejecting an EEOC suggestion for a meeting of union officials with rights leaders and EEOC representatives.

The Brotherhood of Locomotive Engineers announced in Cleveland, O. July 15 that it had dropped its constitution clause requiring prospective union members to be white males.

A National Industrial Conference Board (NICB) study of Negro employment, released June 12, found that gains were being made in the hiring of Negroes but that firms had difficulty finding qualified Negro applicants and that problems existed in promoting Negroes once they were hired. According to a study by the Labor Department's Bureau of Labor Statistics June 3, Negro employment had gained substantially since 1955 but the gains were endangered by Negroes' concentration in unskilled jobs. The NICB study, conducted under a $195,000 Ford Foundation grant and using information provided by 47 companies (out of 96 asked to participate), found that "few companies are doing as well with Negro employment as they want to do. And few are doing as well as their top executives think they are doing. Also, many top-level executives think the Negro is making more economic progress than he, in fact, is making." The study pointed to a 1964 unemployment rate among non-whites of 9.8% (the rate for whites: 4.6%) and to the fact that 60% of Negro families earned less than $4,000 yearly. The Labor Department report showed that non-white employment in the 1955-65 period had increased from 6,400,000 to 7,700,000, but less than 1/5 of employed non-whites held white-collar jobs.

The Roman Catholic bishops of 4 Michigan dioceses—Lansing, Grand Rapids, Marquette and Saginaw—announced in Lansing June 9 that firms from which they made purchases would be required to pledge nondiscriminatory employment practices and to make periodic reports on how many minority-group members were among their employes and on what positions they held. They described this move as "an affirmative use of the hiring and purchasing power of Catholic institutions to end employment discrimination." (A similar policy had been announced in Detroit Dec. 16, 1965 by spokesmen for all major religious groups.)

Medical Discrimination Attacked

U.S. Surgeon Gen. William H. Stewart Mar. 7 announced non-discrimination guidelines for hospitals receiving federal funds. The rules included a requirement that hospitals seeking Medicare funds submit by Mar. 15 a "medical facilities compliance report" to the Public Health Service (PHS); the report was to specify by race the number of patients occupying various hospital facilities. Dr. Stewart said the new regulations had been sent to 10,000 hospitals and that a compliance unit was being established in the PHS to supervise their enforcement.

HEW Secy. John W. Gardner reported May 7 that compliance questionnaires had been received from 6,923 (85%) of the 8,237 hospitals to which they had been sent. Of hospitals reporting, 5,023 (about 75%) had been certified to the Social Security Administration as in compliance with the non-discrimination guidelines.

The U.S. Civil Rights Commission Feb. 23 had released results of field investigations conducted in 40 communities in 12 Southern and border states to determine the extent of compliance with Title VI of the 1964 Civil Rights Act, which barred discrimination in federally aided programs. The study covered 4 medical programs administered by the HEW Department and Project Head Start, run by the OEO (Office of Economic Opportunity). The CRC report charged that the HEW Department had "failed to take the steps necessary to achieve compliance" with Title VI by hospitals and other health facilities. The study of the Head Start program found that "the majority of children . . . were enrolled in segregated projects located in segregated schools and taught by teachers of their race." It noted, however, that the OEO had investigated Title VI compliance and had revised its Head Start guidelines to prevent segregation. In reply to the CRC report, HEW Secy. Gardner said Feb. 23 that the department planned to carry out the commission's recommendation that compliance reviews be conducted. He said that 220 hospitals and 87 school districts had been ruled ineligible to receive federal assistance.

35 Negro physicians and dentists charged in Atlanta July 27 that the federal government had violated the 1964 rights act by granting Medicare funds to some hospitals that had not been fully integrated. The Negroes, including NMA (National Medical Association) Pres. Leonidas H. Berry and representatives of Negro dental and medical societies in North Carolina, Georgia and Mississippi, issued the statement during a meeting at which they formed a new organization—the Hospital Improvement Association—to press for tighter federal enforcement of non-discrimination in hospitals. Deputy Surgeon Gen. Leo J. Gehrig spoke at the meeting and said that, as of July 19, the government was withholding funds from 219 hospitals (more than 95% of them in the South) out of 6,681 that had applied under the Medicare bill.

The Justice Department filed suit in U.S. district court in Jackson, Miss. Sept. 1 on charges that the Marion County

General Hospital of Columbia, Miss. practiced racial discrimination. The suit sought temporary and permanent injunctions against segregation in the 82-bed hospital. This was the first Justice Department suit brought against a hospital under the 1964 rights act.

Alabama Gov. George C. Wallace Apr. 26 had ordered the re-segregation of Alabama's mental hospitals, which had been desegregated a week earlier. The decision to desegregate the hospitals had been made by the State Hospitals Board Dec. 16, 1965 and had been announced Mar. 14. The re-segregation was effected by a transfer of patients Apr. 27.

Dr. John L. S. Holloman Jr., new president of the largely-Negro NMA, charged in his inaugural address Aug. 9 that the Negro physician was doomed "to a career of medical mediocrity and his patients to inferior medical care" because of racial discrimination. He said that "the higher mortality rate for Negroes is, in reality, a statistical reflection of the discriminatory denial of good health because of race." He charged that Negro doctors were "cut off from the mainstream of modern medicine, and our patients must pay the penalty." Holloman, an AMA (American Medical Association) member, accused the AMA of a "pattern of discrimination in both theory and practice, which limits the advance of the Negro physician." (AMA Vice Pres. F. J. L. Blasingame retorted that Holloman "is thoroughly familiar with the AMA's strong stand against racial discrimination in all aspects of the practice of medicine, its efforts to recruit more qualified Negro applicants for medical schools, and the series of constructive meetings between NMA and AMA leaders during the last 2 years.")

Georgia House Bars Bond

The Georgia House of Representatives voted by 184-12 Jan. 10 not to seat State Rep.-elect Julian Bond, 25, because Bond had publicly opposed U.S. policy in Vietnam and had backed avoidance of the draft. Bond, communications director of SNCC, was one of 8 Negroes elected to the House in Nov. 1965 following court-ordered reapportionment. The other 7 Negroes were seated without challenge Jan. 10 and became the House's first Negro members in 58 years.

A 3-judge federal court ruled 2-1 in Atlanta Feb. 10 that the Georgia House had violated no "fundamental federal rights" in refusing to seat Bond. The court had ruled unanimously Jan. 28 that Bond had not been denied his House seat because he was a Negro. The Feb. 10 ruling was on the issue of whether the House action had been a violation of Bond's rights of free speech.

A special election was held Feb. 23 to fill the vacant House seat. Bond, running unopposed, won the election, but again was denied entry to the House. Bond won election to the House for the 3d time in November.

Ruling unanimously, the U.S. Supreme Court Dec. 5 accepted Bond's contention that the Georgia House had violated his constitutional rights. It reportedly was the first decision by any American court overruling a legislature's decision on the qualifications of an elected member. Chief Justice Earl Warren wrote the court's opinion. Holding that Bond had been denied his rights of free speech, Warren said that legislators needed "the widest latitude to express their views on issues of policy" and had "an obligation to take positions on controversial political questions so that their constituents can be fully informed by them and be better able to assess their qualifications for office." Warren said Georgia legislators had no right to question Bond's declaration that he would uphold his oath of office.

Kentucky Rights Law

The Kentucky General Assembly completed action Jan. 25 on a bill barring racial discrimination in employment and public accommodations. The bill's coverage was broader than that of the federal 1964 Civil Rights Act; its employment section applied to firms employing 8 or more persons (the federal law, by July 1967, was to cover firms employing 25 or more), and its public accommodations section applied to such businesses as bowling alleys and automatic laundries (not covered by the federal law). The legislation, to take effect July 1, was to be administered by the Kentucky Human Rights Commission and enforced by court action if conciliation efforts failed. Gov. Edward T. Breathitt signed the bill Jan. 27.

Housing Progress Reported

The results of a study of 27 "stable, integrated neighborhoods" were released July 5 by the National Opinion Research

Center, an affiliate of the University of Chicago. According to the study, progress toward integration in housing was "far larger than anyone had expected to find." The 3 cities studied, Washington, Atlanta and San Jose, Calif., were said to contain 82 integrated neighborhoods—51 in Washington (containing 29.6% of the city's white population), 7 in Atlanta (3.8% of the city's whites) and 24 in San Jose (34.2%). The conclusions were based on interviews with educators, businessmen and community leaders in 18 neighborhoods in Washington, 5 in Atlanta and 4 in San Jose. No difference was found in the value of housing in the integrated areas as compared with comparable nonintegrated neighborhoods. The theory that housing integration caused a decline in housing values was called "thoroughly debunked." "The degree of personal contact" between the races was described as "small," although "there may be more socializing between Negroes and whites in integrated neighborhoods than between different white ethnic groups in nonintegrated neighborhoods." A conclusion was drawn that "the higher the proportion of Negroes, the less certainty there would be that the area will remain stable."

Gov. Otto Kerner July 13 signed an executive order barring real estate agents in Illinois from discriminating on the basis of "race, color, creed, religion or national origin" in the sale or rental of housing. The order did not apply to a home sold by its owner. (The Democratic-controlled state House had passed 8 open-occupancy bills during the 1965 session, but all had been defeated by the Republican-controlled state Senate.)

Other Court Action

Judicial decisions of federal and state courts during 1966 touched on a wide range of civil rights matters, including jury selection, housing discrimination, miscegenation and public accommodations.

Juries & Legal Rights—U.S. District Judge Frank M. Johnson Jr. in Montgomery, Ala. Jan. 19 ordered the Macon County Jury Commission to compile within 30 days a new jury list that did not discriminate against Negroes. Johnson ruled in a suit filed in June 1964 by local Negroes who charged the Jury Commission with deliberate exclusion of Negroes from jury duty.

A 3-judge federal court in Montgomery Feb. 7 ordered

the jury rolls of Lowndes County immediately reconstituted because of discrimination and ruled that state laws excluding women from jury service "shall be of no effect on and after June 1, 1967."

The Mississippi Supreme Court, ruling in Jackson Feb. 7, reversed the conviction of Richard Bass, a Negro facing execution for rape, and ordered a new trial. The reversal was based on the exclusion of Negroes from the jury trying Bass and on errors occurring during his trial.

The U.S. 5th Circuit Court of Appeals in New Orleans Mar. 31 reversed the rape conviction of Andrew J. Scott, a Livingston Parish, La. Negro, because of "the systematic exclusion of members of the Negro race" from the jury list. The court ordered that Scott either be retried or released.

The U.S. 5th Circuit Court of Appeals ruled unanimously in New Orleans July 20 that federal juries within its 6-state Southern jurisdiction must be "broadly representative of the community." The decision nullified the so-called "key man" system of jury selection under which outstanding ("key") citizens made nominations for jury lists. The court found that the system had "resulted in Negroes being substantially underrepresented."

The New Jersey Supreme Court June 6 ruled 5-1 that a Negro convicted of manslaughter was entitled to a new trial because the judge at his trial had used the word "nigger."

U.S. District Judge Daniel H. Thomas in Mobile, Ala. Dec. 2 ordered Perry, Hale and Wilcox counties in Alabama "to clean house" within 30 days and select new juries without discrimination by race or color.

Rights of Assembly & Public Accommodations—In a 6-3 decision Jan. 17, the U.S. Supreme Court reversed a Georgia Supreme Court ruling and barred the city of Macon, Ga. from withdrawing as a trustee of Baconsfield Park as a means of permitting the park to exclude Negroes.

The New Jersey Supreme Court ruled unanimously Feb. 21 that a barber's refusal to cut Negroes' hair was a violation of state and federal anti-discrimination laws.

The U.S. Supreme Court, in a 5-4 decision Feb. 23, overturned breach-of-the-peace convictions of 5 Negro CORE members who had attempted to integrate a white public library in Clinton, La. in Mar. 1964. (The defendants had been refused service by the librarian and had remained quietly in the library until they were arrested.)

The U.S. 5th Circuit Court of Appeals, in decisions rendered in New Orleans Mar. 8 on appeals brought by the NAACP, (1) ordered the state of Mississippi to grant the NAACP a charter and (2) directed U.S. District Judge Harold Cox in Jackson, Miss. to issue an injunction against arrests of rights demonstrators designed to break up demonstrations. Mississippi Atty. Gen. Joe T. Patterson had refused to grant the NAACP a state charter on the ground that to do so would not be in "the best interests of the state of Mississippi."

In a 5-4 ruling Apr. 27 the Supreme Court refused to review a Georgia court decision holding the NAACP liable for damages arising out of a picketing campaign conducted in 1962 by its Savannah, Ga. branch.

The Mississippi Supreme Court ruled May 9 that Clarksdale's parade-permit ordinance was "clearly unconstitutional" because it gave unlimited discretion to the police chief in deciding whether a parade permit would be issued.

U.S. District Judge Edward S. Northrop ruled in Baltimore May 12 that a swimming pool and skating arena operated in Cambridge, Md. by a volunteer fire company were public accommodations and thus were required to admit Negroes under the 1964 Civil Rights Act.

A 3-judge panel of the U.S. Court of Appeals for the 5th Circuit in New Orleans Oct. 28 directed the U.S. District Court in Jackson, Miss. to order city officials to protect legal pickets from arrest in Jackson and to require the state to charter the NAACP.

The U.S. Supreme Court Nov. 14 upheld the Florida trespass convictions of 32 civil rights demonstrators. The 5-4 ruling was considered by many observers to run counter to a series of decisions upholding the right of demonstrators to assemble peacefully in public places to protest racial discrimination. The case stemmed from arrests made at a Sept. 16, 1963 rally of students from Florida A. & M. University in Tallahassee. About 200 students had gathered in front of the county jail to protest the arrest of demonstrators who had attempted to desegregate local movie theaters. In the majority opinion, Justice Hugo L. Black declared that the court's action did not contradict a 1963 ruling reversing breach of peace convictions of 187 peaceful demonstrators at the South Carolina State Capitol in Columbia. "Traditionally," Black said, "state capitol grounds are open to the public" and are appropriate places to assemble and petition a government.

"Jails, built for security purposes, are not."

Fair Housing—The California Supreme Court ruled 5-2 May 10 that a state constitutional amendment nullifying state fair-housing laws violated the federal Constitution. (The amendment, known as Proposition 14, placed on the ballot in Nov. 1964, had been approved by a 2-1 margin. It provided that no state or municipal agency could interfere with a real-estate owner's "absolute discretion" in the sale and rental of property.) Justice Paul Peek, author of the court's majority opinion, held it "beyond dispute that the 14th Amendment, through the equal protection clause, secures the right to acquire and possess property of every kind" without racial or religious discrimination. California Gov. Edmund G. Brown, who had announced in March that $200 million in federal urban-renewal funds had been withheld from the state because of Proposition 14, said May 10 that the decision would be appealed to the U.S. Supreme Court and that until then he would "continue to enforce" Proposition 14. State Atty. Gen. Thomas C. Lynch said, however, that he planned to begin enforcing the 1959 and 1963 open-occupancy laws wiped out by Proposition 14.

The California Supreme Court June 9 partially reversed its May 10 decision. The unanimous June 9 ruling, based on a reconsideration of one of 7 cases covered by the earlier decision, held that the owner of a single-family home not financed by federal funds was not covered by state open-occupancy legislation and thus could refuse to sell or lease his home to a Negro.

Other Decisions—The U.S. 4th Circuit Court of Appeals ruled in Richmond, Va. Jan. 20 that the functions of the North Carolina Dental Society "have the character of state action" and that consequently its all-white membership policy was unconstitutional. In a reversal of a federal district court decision, the circuit court ordered reconsideration of the membership application of Dr. Reginald A. Hawkins, a Negro dentist.

The New Jersey Supreme Court ruled unanimously in Trenton Jan. 24 that school children of Black Muslim families were within their rights in refusing to salute the American flag. The court found that Black Muslims were entitled to the exemption from the flag salute given to other religious groups. It rejected the contention of the Elizabeth (N.J.) Board of Education that "the religion of Islam" was based on political rather than religious beliefs. The school board had suspended a number of Black Muslim students in 1963 because of their refusal to salute the flag.

U.S. District Judge Seybourn H. Lynne in Birmingham, Ala. Feb. 8 dismissed libel suits brought against Time, Inc. by 5 Mississippi residents. The plaintiffs had each asked $1 million damages, citing an article printed in the Dec. 15, 1964 issue of *Life* dealing with the slaying of the 3 civil rights workers in Philadelphia, Miss. They claimed that the article had identified them as members of the Ku Klux Klan and had damaged their businesses.

Virginia's anti-miscegenation law was upheld unanimously Mar. 7 by the Virginia Supreme Court of Appeals. The court affirmed the 1959 conviction of Mr. and Mrs. Richard Perry Loving, who had married in Washington, D.C. in 1958 and had moved to Virginia in 1959. (Loving, 32, was white; his wife, 26, was part Negro, part Indian.)

The U.S. Supreme Court June 20 handed down 2 rulings on the right of arrested civil rights demonstrators to be tried in federal, rather than state, courts. The high court, by 5-4, reversed a 5th Circuit Court of Appeals decision and ruled that 29 demonstrators arrested in 1964 in Greenwood, Miss. were not entitled to trial in a federal court under a Reconstruction-Era law. Justice Potter Stewart said in the majority opinion that the law—which provided for the removal of cases from state to federal courts—applied only when a state prosecution would violate a right sanctioned by Congress. In a companion case, involving 20 demonstrators arrested for trespassing while conducting a restaurant sit-in in Atlanta in 1963, the court ruled unanimously in favor of the defendants and remanded the case to federal district court.

A 3-judge federal court in Montgomery, Ala. ruled Dec. 12 that Alabama's compulsory segregation in jails and prisons was unconstitutional and had to be eliminated on all levels within one year. The ruling was in a suit filed by 5 Negroes, including the Rev. Hosea L. Williams, and one white person in February. Williams then had been in jail in Birmingham on a traffic charge (he pleaded guilty). The court ordered the immediate desegregation of honor farms, educational programs, hospitals in prisons and youth centers. Minimum security penitentiaries and city and county jails were given 6 months to desegregate, and maximum security penitentiaries were given one year.

INDEX

72. Public accommodations—55, 79-80, 160-162, 238, 239, 273-274. Riots—445-447. Sit-in demonstrations—7, 12, 19-20. Voting rights—40, 142

ATLANTA Journal-Constitution (newspaper)—47

ATLANTIC Steel Co.—146

ATLANTIC White Tower Restaurants —56

AUBURN, N.Y.—258

AUBURN, University of—153, 267

AUGELLI, Judge Anthony T.—133, 135

AUGUSTA, Ga.—148, 157, 266

AUSTIN, Tex.—290

AUSTIN, Henry—317

AUTOMOBILE Industry—278

AVANTS, Ernest—456

AYCOCK, C.C.—46, 96

BAILEY, Edward D.—314

BAILEY, Samuel—275

BAILEY 3d, Wesley Guy—364

BAINES, Bruce—394

BAKER, Ella J.—15

BAKER, Horace & Sara—213

BALDWIN, Rev. Snead—248

BALTIMORE, Md.—56, 76-77, 107, 195-196, 242, 249, 378, 393, 406-407, 443

BANFIELD, Mrs. Beryl—421

BAPTISTS—170, 249, 398, 406

BARBEE, Lloyd A.—337

BARNETT, Ross R.—58, 110-111, 113-117, 121-124, 191, 194, 220, 334

BARNETTE, Horace Doyle—245, 246, 359

BARNETTE, Travis Maryn—245, 359

BARRETT, St. John—114

BARRY Jr., Marion S.—15, 412

BASOV, Nikolai G.—310

BASS, Richard—467

BATES, Mrs. Daisy—57

BATESVILLE, Miss.—394

BATON Rouge, La.—14, 69, 81, 82, 131-132, 142, 207, 219, 328-329

BEACHES—56-57, 106, 252

BEADLE, George Wells—151

BEATTY, Ross—403

BEAUMONT, Tex.—238

BECKWITH, Byron de la—192, 247

BEDFORD, Edward—324

BELAFONTE, Harry—303

BELL, David E.—164

BELL, Mrs. Mary Kate—322

BELL, Judge J. Spencer—264-65

BELL Telephone Laboratories—145

BELOIT, Wis.—297

BELTON, Acie J.—272

BENEDICT College (Columbia, S.C.) —12

BENNETT, B.C.—408

BENNETT, Thomas—456

BENNETT College (Greensboro, N.C.)—6

BENNINGTON (Vt.) College—8

BENTON Harbor, Mich.—444, 445

BERGMAN, Dr. Walter—60

BERKELEY, Calif.—132, 297

BERNHARD, Berl I.—101

BERRY, Leonidas H.—463

BESSEE, Ralph M.—443

BESSEMER, Ala.—406, 416

BEVEL, Mrs. Diane Nash—194

BEVEL, Rev. James A.—181, 398, 399, 401

BIBB Transit Co.—157

BIDA, Aliyn Y.—76

BIEMILLER, Andrew J.—138

BILLINGSLEA, Brig. Gen. Charles— 112

BILLUPS, Rev. Charles—206

BILOXI, Miss.—56-58, 265

BING, Robert L.—364

BINGHAMTON, N.Y.—258

BIRMINGHAM, Ala.: Boycotts—148. Demonstrations—182, 186, 188, 206, 250, 405-406. Education—186, 215-216, 264. Employment—148, 406. Freedom Rides—60, 61. Prisons—470. Public accomodations—106, 148, 159, 238-239. Violence—168, 179-189, 365. Voting rights—40, 272-273, 405-406

BIRMINGHAM Post-Herald (newspaper)—327-328

BI-State Transit System—411

BLACK, Justice Hugo L.—37, 55, 67, 114, 431, 468

BLACK Muslims (Nation of Islam)—58, 134, 167, 229-230, 252, 257, 260, 283, 356-358, 377, 422, 458, 469-470

BLACK Nationalist Party—283-284

BLACK Power—352, 369, 374-389, 404

BLAIK, Earl H.—188-189

N.Y.)—29, 102, 137-139, 288
JAWORSKI, Leon—122
JELINEK, Donald A.—410-411
JELLICO, Tenn.—328
JENKINS, Jay—255
JENKINS Jr., Judge W. A.—180
JENSEN, Herluf M.—8
JERSEY City, N.J.—151, 159, 242, 260
JEWEL, J. Thomas—46, 97
JEWS & Judaism—55, 155, 280, 281, 412, 423-424
JFK House (Cleveland O.)—442, 443
JHA, Chandra S.—78
JOB Discrimination—See LABOR
JOHNSON, Alvin—447
JOHNSON, Andrew—2
JOHNSON, Billy—440
JOHNSON Jr., Judge Frank M.—34-35, 64-65, 95, 140, 158, 215, 263-264, 267, 273, 299, 300, 305, 430, 466
JOHNSON, George M.—84
JOHNSON, Leroy R.—143
JOHNSON, Lyndon Baines—168, 231, 280, 283, 284, 341-343, 346, 379, 380. Demonstrations—295, 296, 298, 300-301, 318. Education—331, 339-340, 414. Employment & labor —98-99, 144-145, 209, 228, 279, 341, 344, 448. Legislation—22-25, 27-29, 137, 178, 232-234, 238, 239, 243, 285, 369-373, 387. March on Washington—172. Meredith March —391, 392, 395. 1964 Presidential campaign—239-243, 263. Riots & violence—244, 248, 249, 261-262, 304, 309-311, 431-433. Vietnamese war—383, 387. Voting rights—137, 286-289, 293-294, 297, 351. White House Conference on Civil Rights —354, 355, 458-459
JOHNSON, Mrs. Lyndon Baines (Claudia Alta Taylor) (Lady Bird)—454
JOHNSON, Matthew—447
JOHNSON, Mrs. Mildred—257
JOHNSON, Milton—317
JOHNSON Jr., Gov. Paul B. (D., Miss.)—110, 113, 115-116, 121, 237, 244, 248, 319, 320, 324, 334, 391, 393, 395
JOHNSON, Thomas 15X—457-458
JOHNSON City, Tenn.—93
JOHNSTON, Sen. Olin DeWitt (D., S.C.)—139

JOLIET, Ill.—132
JONES, Fred—336
JONES, Rev. James E.—312, 378
JONES, James Lloyd—456
JONES, James R.—362, 363, 455
JONES, Joseph Charles—6, 63, 155
JONES, Rev. Dr. Paul Tudor—160
JONES, Robert L.—150, 325
JONES, Judge Walter B.—34, 35, 105
JORDAN, Sen. B. Everett (D., N.C.) —29
JORDAN, James Edward—245, 246, 359
JORDAN Jr., Vernon E.—427
JURIES—237, 354, 368, 370, 373, 391, 412, 466-467
JUSTICE, Department of (U.S.)—29-33, 103, 346, 347. Demonstrations —19, 202, 206, 299, 391, 394-395. Education—32-33, 46, 87, 90, 91, 113-117, 120-122, 128, 131, 186, 215-217, 222, 232-233, 235, 328-331, 372, 413, 414, 416, 418, 419, 425, 426. Employment—236, 459, 460. Freedom Rides—61, 64-65, 68, 73. Housing—370, 403. Ku Klux Klan—318, 319. Legislation—175, 372. Police 'brutality'—104, 177, 318, 319. Public accommodations— 55-57, 156, 158, 159, 161, 235, 238, 316, 318, 319, 463-464. Violence—58, 180, 187, 246, 248, 391, 394-395. Voting rights—21, 25-27, 34-39, 95-97, 140-141, 153, 193, 207-208, 232, 235, 248, 272, 287, 289-292, 322, 325, 395, 428-431

KANE, Gen. Francis—436
KANSAS—79, 334
KANSAS City, Kan.—334
KANSAS City, Mo.—269, 275
KAPITSA, Peter—310
KAPLAN, Kivie—374
KATZENBACH, Nicholas deB(elleville)—120, 217, 326, 330, 348, 354, 361, 364, 373, 391, 396, 432, 450, 460. Voting rights—287-288, 290-292, 294, 326, 406, 409, 428, 429
KAUFMAN, Judge Irving R.—90-91, 291
KEARSE, Rev. Logan—76
KEATING, Sen. Kenneth B. (R., N.Y.)

—29, 102, 123, 137, 138
KEESLER Air Force Base—56
KEFAUVER, Estes—28
KEHRER, Elmer T.—366
KEITHLY, Jerome—449
KELDYSH, Mstislav—310
KELLEY Jr., Asa D.—74, 154
KELLY, R. B.—296
KENNEDY, Sen. Edward M(oore) (Ted) (D., Mass.)—233, 288, 298, 386
KENNEDY, John F(itzgerald)—19, 166. Administration—76, 104, 105, 142, 162-165, 191, 223-225; see other appropriate headings below. Birmingham—179, 180, 182, 184-186, 187, 188. Black Muslims—229-230. Education—78, 84, 110-111, 117-118, 123-124, 134, 168, 216-218. Freedom Rides—62, 63, 75. Housing—149-150. Labor—98, 144, 145. Legislation—27-28, 29, 101-103, 136, 152-153, 163-165, 173-179. March on Washington—169, 170, 171-172. Public accommodations—75, 108, 154, 156. Voting rights—139, 142

KENNEDY, Mrs. John F.—191
KENNEDY, Robert F(rancis)—19, 77, 152, 177, 197, 244. Birmingham—182, 183, 184. Education—116-118, 122, 128. Freedom Rides—61-63, 72, 75. Voting rights—137, 288

KENTUCKY—17, 208, 275, 465. Education—40, 91, 266. Public accommodations—79, 275, 465
KENYATTA, Jomo—442
KEPPEL, Francis—239, 263, 330, 339
KERNER, Gov. Otto (D., Ill.)—78, 163, 404, 436, 466
KILL (magazine)—134
KILLEN, Rev. Edgar Ray—244-245, 359
KIMBELL, Judge Daniel—201
KING, Rev. A. D. William—180, 184
KING Jr., Edward B.—70
KING Jr., Lloyd—336
KING Jr., Rev. Dr. Martin Luther—61, 153, 243, 246, 282, 304-306, 381-382, 386. Birmingham—179-188. Black-power controversy—374, 376, 377, 381-382, 386, 387, 389. Campaigns & demonstrations—214, 250, 263, 299-300, 327, 332,

350-351, 386, 408; see other appropriate headings in this section. Chicago—351, 381-382, 397-405, 437. Freedom Rides—62, 64-66, 73, 75. March on Washington—169, 171-173. Meredith march—376, 392, 393, 395-397. Nobel Prize—231, 281-282. Peace movement & Vietnam—351-352. Police 'brutality'—202. Public accommodations—154-155, 275. Riots—251-252, 311, 437. Selma campaign & Selma-to-Montgomery march—292-296, 301-303. Sit-in demonstrations—10, 15, 19-20. Voting rights—40, 97-98, 350-351, 381-382, 408
KING Jr., Mrs. Martin Luther—19
KINGSPORT, Tenn.—93
KIRKWOOD, Robert C.—17
KLUNDER, Rev. Bruce William—268
KNIGHT, Charles—456
KNIGHT, Claxton—318
KNIGHT, Jimmy—361
KNOWLES, Gov. Warren P. (R., Wis.)—409
KNOXVILLE, Tenn.—50, 93, 142, 222
KODAK Co., Eastman—145
KOOTA, Aaron E.—367-440
KORNEGAY, Marshal Robert—363
KORNEICHUK, Aleksandr—310
KRESGE, S. S.—80
KRESS & Co., S. H.—6-7, 9, 16, 17, 206
KU KLUX KLAN—11, 20, 64, 154, 274, 285, 304, 305, 318, 319, 324, 325, 402, 407-409. Congressional investigations—361-365, 452-456. Violence—11, 224-245, 247, 249, 251, 252, 332-333, 450-452, 456, 457, 470
KUNSTLER, William—202

LABOR—3, 4. Black Muslims—230. Demonstrations—147-148, 208-210, 360, 386. Employment bias—20, 29-33, 53, 98-103, 144-145, 147-148, 179, 183, 190-192, 197, 203, 223-225, 227, 233, 236, 273, 274, 278, 279, 316, 344-346, 350, 366-367, 383, 384, 387, 388, 397, 398, 406, 411, 412, 437-449, 459-462, 465. Farmers—325-326, 341. Legislation—174-176, 178, 213.

MARRIAGES—466, 470
MARSHALL, Tex.—13
MARSHALL, Burke—172, 182, 187
MARSHALL, Thurgood—16, 106, 459
MARSHALS, Federal—87, 110-112, 114-119, 124, 220, 293
MARTIN, Dr. John Henry—424
MARTIN, Murray H.—453-454
MARTIN Co.—144
MARTINEZ, Vincent L.—368
MARYLAND: Baltimore—See under 'B.' Campaigns & demonstrations —76, 195-198, 253, 378, 406-407. Education—40, 130, 197, 219. E-lections—242, 253. Farm programs —341. Housing—378, 406-407. National Guard—196-197, 253. Population—107. Public accommodations—56, 75-77, 79, 229, 253, 275-276, 468. Riots—443. Sit-in demonstrations—17, 249. Voting rights—393
MARYLAND State College (Princess Anne, Md.)—253
MASLOW, Will—424
MASON, Mrs. E. G.—179
MASON, Dr. Gilbert R.—56
MASONS of America—389
MASSACHUSETTS: Boston—See under 'B.' Demonstrations—213, 297, 313, 351. Education—213, 267-268, 337. Elections—143, 243. Freedom Rides—160. Population—107
MASSACHUSETTS Institute of Technology (Cambridge, Mass.)—8
MATHIAS, Rep. Charles McC(urdy) (R., Md.)—371-372
MAYWOOD, Ill.—132
MAZO, Sal—210
McCAIN, James—375
McCLELLAN, Sen. John L. (D.,Ark.) —27, 139, 164
McCLUNG, Ollie & Ollie Jr.—239
McCOLLUM, Mary—163
McCOMB, Miss.—68-69, 72, 247-248, 276, 455
McCOMB Enterprise-Journal—69
McCONE, John A.—312, 434
McCORMACK, Rep. John W. (D., Mass.)—172
McCRORY Corp. (including McCrory-McLellan Corp.)—16, 17, 80, 206
McCULLOCH, Rep. William M. (R., O.)—25, 177

McDANIEL, Thomas—199
McDONOUGH, Bishop Thomas—91
McDOWELL, Cleve—220-221
McELVEEN, Ernest Ray—317
McENTIRE, Prof. Davis—54-55
McFARLAND, John—41
McGLATHERY, Dave M.—217
McGOWAN, Emory Warren—406
McGUCKEN, Archbishop Joseph T.—367
McKEITHEN, Gov. John (D., La.)—316, 317
McKELDIN, Theodore R.—378, 406, 443
McKISSICK, Floyd Bixler—226, 353, 375, 378. Black-power controversy —376-379, 381-382, 387-388. Demonstrations—203, 422. Housing—406. March on Washington—172. Meredith March—392, 393, 395. Voting rights—381-382. White House conference—459
McLAUGHLIN, Dr. Frederick—421
McLAUGHLIN, Judge John R.—204
McNAIR, Prof. Everett W.—160
McNAIR, Landy—194
McNAMARA, Robert S(trange)—185, 228, 229
McSHANE, James J. P.—114, 115, 117-118
MEAD Corp.—366
MEADOWS, Austin R.—415
MEANY, George—54, 99-100, 145-147, 277, 278
MEDICAL Asociation, National—348, 463, 464
MEDICAL Committee for Human Rights—322, 348, 397
MEDICAL Sciences, Soviet Academy of—310
MEDICARE—348
MEDICINE & Health Services—223, 462-464, 469; see also HOSPITALS
MEHARRY Medical College (Nashville, Tenn.)—9
MELCHER, John C.—148
MEMPHIS, Tenn.: Education—93, 130. Employment—101. Meredith March —390, 392, 393. Population—107. Public accommodations—158-160, 222. Sit-in demonstrations—12-13. Voting rights—142
MEMPHIS (Tenn.) Naval Air Base—111
MEMPHIS Scimitar Press (newspa-

WISDOM, Judge John Minor—86, 141, 416
WISE, Sherwood—137
WOOD, Rev. Virgil A.—81
WOODLE, Rev. Roy—363
WOODSON, Rev. S. Howard—210
WOOLWORTH Co., F. W.—6-8, 12, 13, 16-17, 80, 189-190
WORKER Defense League—209
WORLD'S Fair, N.Y.—254
WRIGHT, Judge Caleb M.—92
WRIGHT, Judge J. Skelly—36, 41-44, 86, 127-129
WRIGHT, J. W.—148
WRIGHT, Mr. and Mrs. Leon—449
WRIGHT, Roy Milton—446
WRIGHT, Dr. Theo R.—186
WYCHE, Judge C. C.—129
WYCOFF, Elizabeth Porter—67
WYOMING: Demonstrations—297

X, Lonnie—377
X, Malcolm—See MALCOLM X
X, Wilbert—357
X, Wilfred—357
X, Philbert—357

YALE University (New Haven, Conn.) —7, 8

YARBOROUGH, George—113
YARBOROUGH, Sen. Ralph W. (D., Tex.)—179
YORTY, Samuel W.—307, 311-312, 434
YOUNG, A. Z.—318, 407
YOUNG, Rev. Andrew J.—349, 401, 437
YOUNG, Sen. Milton R. (R., N.D.)— 25, 103, 140
YOUNG Jr., Dr. Whitney M.—153, 171, 173, 227, 243, 263, 306, 349, 353, 370-371, 382-384, 387, 389, 397
YOUNGE Jr., Samuel L.—449-450
YOUNG Women's Christian Association (YWCA)—20
YPSILANTI, Mich.—444, 445
YUSSEFF Abdulla—See HALL, Raymond

ZABLOCKI, Rep. Clement J. (D., Wis.)—409
ZAVATT, Judge Joseph C.—271
ZELLNER, Robert—69
ZIMMERMAN, Charles S.—146
ZINN, Dr. Howard—156
ZIRPOLI, Judge Alfonso J.—136
ZUBER, Paul B.—133-134, 135-136

COM